The Irwin Series in Accounting

Consulting Editor

WILLARD J. GRAHAM, Ph.D., C.P.A.

University of North Carolina

BOOKS IN THE IRWIN SERIES IN ACCOUNTING

Fundamental Accounting Principles

Fundamental

Principles

FOURTH EDITION—1966

RICHARD D. IRWIN, INC.—HOMEWOOD, ILLINOIS

Accounting

WILLIAM W. PYLE
College of Business Administration
Arizona State University

JOHN ARCH WHITE
College of Business Administration
University of Texas

FOURTH EDITION
First Printing, March, 1966

Library of Congress Catalogue Card No. 66–11813

PRINTED IN THE UNITED STATES OF AMERICA

Preface

This fourth edition of *Fundamental Accounting Principles*, like the previous editions, is designed for use in a first-year accounting course at the college level. It presents a graded, accurate, and realistic approach to the study of accounting that is as nearly self-teaching as possible. It was written to meet the needs of those students who will make accountancy a career as well as those who will use accounting as a tool in some other field of specialization or in carrying on their personal affairs.

The purpose of this revision has been threefold: (1) to make the subject matter still easier to teach and grasp, (2) to increase the emphasis on theory, and (3) to expand the material dealing with uses and limitations of accounting data. To accomplish these objectives much of the material has been rewritten, the use of color as a teaching device has been expanded, the visual aids have been improved, and new material has been added.

The object of a first course in accounting is to convey an understanding of accounting, how its data are accumulated and reported, and the uses and limitations of the data. A sound first course should be neither too mechanical nor too slanted toward business policy making; a balance is desirable. Nevertheless, since the needs of students differ, the assignment flexibility of the previous editions has been kept. A minimum of time may be devoted to Chapters 6, 7, and 8; and beyond that point almost any chapter or chapter portion may be omitted or quickly covered without detriment to an understanding of the subject matter that follows.

Among the many users of the previous edition who offered valuable suggestions for its improvement, the authors owe a special debt of gratitude to Professor V. E. Breidenbaugh of Indiana State University, Professor Claude Shinn of the University of Oklahoma, Professor Robert L. Grinaker of the University of Houston, and Professors Virginia Huntington, Calvert Krueger, and A. R. Burton of Arizona State University.

March, 1966

WILLIAM W. PYLE
JOHN ARCH WHITE

Contents

Introduction
through
the Accounting
Equation

ACCOUNTING is the art of recording and summarizing business transactions and of interpreting their effects on the affairs and activities of an economic unit. A business transaction is an exchange of property or services; and the institution we call business is a never-ending cycle of these exchanges. The taxicab owner who exchanges money for a taxicab, gasoline, oil, and tires so that he may exchange transportation service to the public for money is said to be in business. For the taxicab owner, and others, accounting is the art used to record the many transactions of a business, to summarize them, and to interpret their effects upon the affairs and activities of the business.

Accounting has been called the language of business, and it has received its greatest development in this field; however, accounting is not limited to business but is applicable to every unit that makes up our economic society. These units include not only business units, where this text will place its emphasis, but also political units, such as school districts, cities, states, and the federal government; and social units, such as clubs, fraternities, and churches.

USE OF ACCOUNTING DATA

When the transactions of a business are recorded, accounting data are accumulated. These data when summarized and interpreted answer for the business owner or manager such questions as: What property is owned?

1

What debts are owed? Were there earnings? Are expenses too large in relation to sales? Is too little or too much merchandise being kept? Are amounts owed by customers being collected as rapidly as they become due? Will the business be able to meet its own debts when they mature? Should the plant be expanded? Should a new product be introduced? Should selling prices be increased?

Beyond the foregoing, grantors of credit such as banks, wholesale houses, and manufacturers use accounting data in answering such additional questions as: Are the customer's earning prospects good? What is his debt-paying ability? Has he paid his debts promptly in the past? Should he be granted additional credit?

Likewise, governmental units make use of accounting data in regulating businesses and in collecting taxes; labor organizations use accounting data in negotiating working conditions and wage agreements; and investors make wide use of accounting data in deciding where and in what to invest.

ACCOUNTING AND BOOKKEEPING

Many people confuse accounting and bookkeeping and look upon them as one and the same—in effect they identify the whole with one of its parts. Actually, bookkeeping is only part of accounting, the record-making part. A comparison of the work of a bookkeeper and an accountant illustrates this.

A bookkeeper records transactions. In a small concern he may record all transactions completed; but in a larger business he may spend his day recording only one kind of transaction, for instance, sales on credit. His work is often routine and primarily clerical in nature.

An accountant's work goes beyond that of a bookkeeper. An accountant must, among other things, be able to survey a business as to the number and kinds of its transactions, the uses to be made of its accounting records, its outlook for growth, and so on; and from his survey he must be able to design an accounting system to fit the particular needs of that business. After designing and installing the system, he must be able to supervise the bookkeepers of the business in recording its transactions; and finally, he must be able to take the results of the bookkeeper's work, check it for accuracy, and organize its information into reports from which management, investors, the government, and others can secure maximum benefits.

Although a bookkeeper is engaged primarily in recording transactions and the accountant may seldom record a transaction, it is hard to draw a line where a bookkeeper's work ends and the accountant's begins. The bookkeeper who records all the transactions of a business must be able to exercise judgment in their recording, he should have an understanding of the entire accounting system with which he works, and he should have some ability in organizing and reporting the information contained in his records.

ACCOUNTANCY AS A PROFESSION

Over the past half century accountancy as a profession has attained a stature comparable with that of law or medicine. All states license *certified public accountants* or C.P.A.'s just as they license doctors and lawyers, and for the same reason, to help insure a high standard of professional service. Only individuals who have passed a rigorous examination of their accounting and related knowledge, met other requirements, and have received a license may designate themselves as certified public accountants.

The requirements for the C.P.A. certificate or license vary with the states. In general an applicant must be a citizen of unquestioned moral character and at least a high school graduate; some states require that he be a college graduate with a major in accounting. He must have passed a rigorous three-day examination in accounting theory, accounting practice, auditing, and business law; and he must have had from one to five years' experience in the office of a certified public accountant or an acceptable equivalent. Some states permit an applicant to substitute collegiate level accounting education for one or more years of the experience requirement. The three-day examination is uniform in all states, although some states require an additional examination in, for example, economics. The examination is prepared by the American Institute of Certified Public Accountants and is given in all states on the same days twice each year. The American Institute of Certified Public Accountants is the accounting profession's equivalent of the American Medical Association or the American Bar Association.

Although all states license certified public accountants, many states do not restrict the practice of public accounting to such license holders. In some states, those in which the law does not expressively prohibit it, any person may designate himself a public accountant or P.A. and practice public accounting. In others both C.P.A.'s and P.A.'s are licensed and the practice of public accounting is limited to such license holders. Commonly, states licensing P.A.'s have granted such licenses to people who were practicing public accounting at the time laws providing for such licenses became effective and now grant such licenses only to applicants who have passed one or more sections of the certified public accounting examination and have met other requirements.

THE WORK OF AN ACCOUNTANT

Accountants are commonly employed in one or the other of three main fields: (1) in public accounting, (2) in private accounting, or (3) in government.

Public Accounting. A public accountant is one who offers his professional services and those of his employees to the public for a fee, in much the same manner as a lawyer or a consulting engineer.

Auditing. The principal service offered by a public accountant is auditing. Banks commonly require an audit of the accounting records of a company applying for a sizable loan, and usually the audit must be made by a certified public accountant. Also, companies whose securities are offered for sale on a major stock exchange must have such an audit before the securities may be sold, and thereafter additional audits must be made periodically if their sale is to continue.

The purpose of an audit is to enable the accountant making it to express the independent opinion that he believes the audited company's financial reports fairly reflect its financial position and operating results. Banks, investors, and others rely on information in a company's financial reports in making loans, granting credit, and in buying and selling securities; and they rely on the independent certified public accountant's opinion that the reports fairly reflect the company's position.

In making an audit, a certified public accountant carefully examines the audited company's financial reports and the accounting records from which they were prepared, making such tests and checks of their information as he deems necessary in order that he may risk his professional reputation on the accuracy of the opinion he expresses.

Management Advisory Services. In addition to auditing, accountants commonly offer management advisory services.

An accountant gains from an audit an intimate knowledge of the audited company's accounting procedures and its financial position; and thus, he is in an excellent position to offer constructive suggestions for improving the procedures and strengthening the position. Clients expect these suggestions as a useful audit by-product, and they also commonly engage certified public accountants to conduct additional surveys for the purpose of determining ways in which their operations may be improved. Such surveys and the suggestions growing from them are known as management advisory services.

Management advisory services include the design, installation, and improvement of a client's general accounting system and any system he may have for determining and controlling manufacturing and distribution costs. They also include the application of punched cards, electronics, and other modern machine methods to these systems, plus advice in financial planning, budgeting, forecasting, inventory control—in fact, in all phases of record keeping and related matters.

Tax Services. In this day of increasing complexity in income and other tax laws and continued high rates, few important business decisions are made without consideration being given to their tax effect. A certified public accountant, through his training and experience, is well qualified and does render important service in this area. The service includes not only the preparation and filing of tax returns but also advice as to how transactions may be completed so as to incur the smallest tax.

Private Accounting. When an accountant is employed by a single business enterprise, he is said to be in private accounting. A small business may employ only one accountant or it may depend upon the services of a public accountant and employ none. A large business, on the other hand, may have several hundred employees in its accounting department, working under the supervision of a chief accountant or controller who is often a C.P.A.

The one accountant of the small business and the accounting department of a large concern do a variety of work, including general accounting, cost accounting, budgeting, and internal auditing.

General Accounting. Although it is hard to draw a line of demarcation, general accounting has to do primarily with recording transactions and preparing financial and other reports for the use of management, owners, creditors, and governmental agencies. The private accountant may design or help the public accountant design the system used in recording the transactions, and he will supervise the bookkeeping staff in recording and preparing the reports.

Cost Accounting. The phase of accounting that has to do with collecting, determining, and controlling costs, particularly costs of producing a given product or service, is called cost accounting. Since a knowledge of costs and controlling costs are vital to good management, a large company may have a number of accountants engaged in this activity.

Budgeting. Planning business transactions before they occur is called budgeting. The objective of budgeting is to provide management with an intelligent plan for future operations, and after the plan has been put into effect, to provide summaries and reports comparing actual accomplishments with the plan. Many large companies have within their accounting departments a number of people who devote all their time to this phase of accounting.

Internal Auditing. In addition to an annual audit by a firm of certified public accountants, some companies maintain a staff of internal auditors who constantly check the records prepared and maintained in each department or company branch. It is the responsibility of these internal auditors to make sure that established accounting procedures and management directives are being followed throughout the company.

Governmental Accounting. Furnishing governmental services is a vast and complicated operation in which accounting is just as indispensable as in business. Elected and appointed officials must rely on data accumulated by means of accounting if they are to complete effectively their administrative duties. Accountants are responsible for the accumulation of these data. Accountants also check and audit the millions of income, payroll, and sales tax returns that accompany the taxes upon which governmental units depend. And finally, federal and state agencies, such as the Interstate Commerce Commission, Securities and Exchange Commission, Federal

Power Commission, Federal Communication Commission, and so on, use accountants in many capacities in their regulation of business.

BEGINNING THE STUDY OF ACCOUNTING

The study of accounting may be begun by learning how transactions are recorded and how the financial statements or reports of a business are prepared from the recorded transactions; or it may be begun by examining the financial statements. The authors of your text feel the former approach is the better because it is easier to understand financial statements after seeing how information upon which they are based is accumulated and how the statements are prepared. Therefore your text begins the study of accounting with transactions and their recording.

HOW TRANSACTIONS ARE RECORDED

A few years back all transactions were recorded with pen and ink; but today only small concerns use this method, concerns small enough that their bookkeeping may be done by one employee working as the book-keeper a part of his or her day. Larger, modern concerns use electric bookkeeping machines, punched paper tape, punched cards, and magnetic tape in recording transactions. Nevertheless, almost all students begin their study of accounting by learning how pen-and-ink records are kept. There are several reasons for this. First, it is the simplest and easiest system to learn, and there is little lost motion from its being learned since almost everything about pen-and-ink records is applicable to machine methods. Primarily, the machines replace pen and ink as the recording medium, taking the drudgery out of the recording. Second, few schools can afford to supply bookkeeping machines, punched card equipment, and electronic data processing equipment for use of their beginning accounting students. And last, for students who will start, own, or manage a small business, a business small enough to use a pen-and-ink system, the pen-and-ink methods apply just as they are taught.

THE COST PRINCIPLE IN RECORDING
TRANSACTIONS

When a business transaction is to be recorded, it is the transaction price that sets the accounting value for the property or service acquired. For example, when a building is purchased, the agreed price between the buyer and the seller measures the amount to be used in recording the transaction. If the agreed price is $100,000, then the building is valued at $100,000 in the accounting records of the purchaser. The seller may have acquired the building for $80,000; it may have been assessed for tax purposes at $50,000; it may have been appraised for sale as being worth $125,000; and the buyer may have received a $110,000 offer for it on the day he completed its purchase. However, although the $110,000 offer indicates a worth in excess of the purchase price, it is the $100,000 cost of the building that establishes the amount to be used in recording the purchase.

In accounting, as with the foregoing $100,000 building, all properties and services acquired are accounted for at cost. This is a fundamental accounting principle, the so-called *cost principle of accounting*. The need for such a principle is obvious; if amounts other than costs were used in recording transactions, for example, amounts established by estimates, judgments, and appraisals, then accounting records would lose much of their usefulness. When cost is the basis for recording a transaction, a buyer and a seller dealing at arms' length determine the amount to be used in recording the transaction. It is usually a fair measure of the goods or services acquired.

PROPERTY AND PROPERTY RIGHTS

Property is something of value that is owned. Every unit of property has value, is owned, and its ownership gives to its owner certain rights, called property rights, that have value. For example, if a building is purchased for $100,000, the buyer acquires the building and a bundle of rights. The rights include the rights of possession, use, and exchange. The new owner may possess the building, he may use the building, and he may exchange it for other property. Actually it is the rights that give the building its value, and the value of the building is equal to the value of the rights. This may be expressed in equation form as follows:

$$\text{Value of the Building, } \$100{,}000 \quad = \quad \text{Value of the Rights in the Building, } \$100{,}000$$

Since a business normally owns and uses many properties, the preceding equation may be expanded as follows to express the situation commonly found in a business:

$$\text{Value of the Properties of a Business} \quad = \quad \text{Value of the Rights in the Properties}$$

The idea in the foregoing equation is simple, but from it grows the fundamental accounting equation—the equation on which all double-entry accounting is based.

THE FUNDAMENTAL ACCOUNTING EQUATION

In accounting, the properties of a concern are known as *assets*, and rights in assets are called *equities*. Consequently, if in the last equation the word "assets" is substituted for the word "properties" and the word "equities" is substituted for "property rights," then the equation showing the relation between properties and property rights will read:

$$\text{Value of the Assets of a Business} = \text{Value of the Equities in the Assets}$$

or

$$\text{Assets} = \text{Equities}$$

When a business is owned by one man and there are no rights in its assets other than those of the owner, the equation showing the relation between assets and owner equity is:

$$\text{Value of the Assets of the Business} = \text{Value of the Owner's Equity in the Assets}$$

To illustrate a situation in which there are no claims against the assets of a business other than those of the owner, assume that George Nash owns a small business that is free of all debts and which has the following assets: cash, $1,000; merchandise, $5,000; and store fixtures, $2,000. Since the business has no debts, the equation that shows the relation between its assets and Nash's equity in the assets is:

Assets		=	Owner Equity	
Cash	$1,000		George Nash, capital	$8,000
Merchandise	5,000			
Store fixtures	2,000			
Total Assets	$8,000		Total Equity	$8,000

The equity of the owner in a business is commonly shown in accounting by giving his name, followed by the word "capital," and then the amount of the equity, as shown in the foregoing example.

Most businessmen find it to their advantage to use in their businesses more assets than they are able to provide with their own resources. They normally obtain these additional assets either (1) by borrowing money from others and using the money to buy assets, or (2) by buying the additional assets *on account* or *on credit*. Buying on account or buying on credit means buying with a promise to pay at a later date, and those from whom businessmen borrow or from whom they buy on account are known as *creditors*.

The creditors of a business have a claim against the assets or a right in the assets of the business. This right is the right to receive payment of the amounts owed them. Law recognizes the right of creditors to receive payment from the assets of their *debtor*. Furthermore, if the debtor does not pay, law gives the creditors the right to force the sale of the debtor's assets. If a debtor's assets are sold, money from the sale is used first to pay his creditor's claims, with any remainder going to the debtor. Obviously then, by law the claims of the creditors of a business take precedence over those of the owner. Creditor claims are called *liabilities*.

From the foregoing paragraphs it is evident that the assets of a business are commonly subject to two types of claims, the claims of the owner or owners and the claims of the creditors. Consequently, to show both types the original equation must be expanded and expressed as follows:

$$Assets \ = \ Liabilities \ + \ Owner \ Equity$$

Note that this equation still preserves the original hypothesis: *Value of the properties equals the value of the rights in the properties.*

To illustrate a situation in which both owner and creditor equities are involved, assume that Paul Becker buys a store building priced at $45,000. He pays $30,000 of his own cash and borrows the balance from Coast Mortgage Company by placing a $15,000 mortgage on the property. (A mortgage is a legal document that involves a promise to pay at a later date.) The equation that illustrates this situation is:

Assets	=	*Liabilities*	+	*Owner Equity*
Store Building, $45,000	=	*Coast Mortgage Co.,* $15,000	+	*Paul Becker, Capital,* $30,000

The accounting value of the store building, $45,000, is equal to the rights of both Coast Mortgage Company and Paul Becker. Paul Becker may possess and use the building, and his equity is measured at $30,000. This is $15,000 less than the $45,000 amount shown for the building because Becker must pay $15,000 to Coast Mortgage Company at a later date. Coast Mortgage Company's claim against the building is measured at $15,000. This claim is the right to receive $15,000. If Becker pays $15,000 to Coast Mortgage Company, the right of the company is ended. If Becker does not pay the amount when due, then Coast Mortgage Company has the additional right to force the sale of the building to secure its money.

The equation, *Assets = Liabilities + Owner Equity, is the fundamental equation upon which all double-entry accounting is based.* Its thorough understanding is necessary to the study of accounting.

Like any mathematical equation the elements may be transposed and the equation may be expressed:

$$Assets \ - \ Liabilities \ = \ Owner \ Equity$$

The equation in this form illustrates that owner equity is secondary to creditor claims. While the owner of assets has the right of possession and use, his right continues only if he pays the claims of his creditors. This has led to the following variation of the fundamental equation:

$$Assets \ - \ Liabilities \ = \ Net \ Worth$$

An individual's *net worth* is the amount remaining after subtracting from the sum of his assets the amount of any creditor claims against the assets. In other words, a man's net worth is the amount of his equity in his assets.

When a business is owned by one man, he is often called the *proprietor;*

and his equity in the business is referred to as his *proprietorship*. Consequently, for such a business the fundamental equation may be and commonly is expressed:

$$Assets \ = \ Liabilities \ + \ Proprietorship$$

From the foregoing it may be seen that the terms net worth, proprietorship, and owner equity are very nearly synonymous. Often they are so treated in accounting.

EFFECT OF TRANSACTIONS ON THE ACCOUNTING EQUATION

Business transactions affect the elements of an accounting equation. For example, on the first day of July, Larry Owen invested $5,000 in a real estate agency and began business as a real estate agent. After the investment, the one asset of the new business and the equity of Owen in the one asset is shown by the following equation:

$$Assets \ = \ Owner \ Equity$$
$$Cash, \$5,000 \ = \ Larry \ Owen, \ Capital, \$5,000$$

After its first transaction the Owen Real Estate Agency has one asset, cash, $5,000. It has no liabilities; therefore, the equity of Owen in this business is $5,000. The $5,000 equity in the real estate agency may not be all of Owen's assets. In addition to the equity in the new business, he may also own a farm, a service station, and many personal assets. However, the foregoing equation does not show these; it shows only the one asset of Owen Real Estate Agency, and it shows Owen's equity in the business.

The Business Entity Concept.   The discussion in the preceding paragraph is elementary; yet it emphasizes a fundamental accounting concept, the *business entity concept*. Because of this concept, in accounting and for accounting purposes, every business is treated as a separate entity, separate from all other businesses and separate from the person or persons who own it. This in turn results in a separate set of records for each business in which the assets are equal to the equities of its owner or owners and its creditors.

To continue the illustration, after investing $5,000 cash, (1) Owen used $300 of the business cash to pay the rent for three months in advance on an office, (2) $3,000 to buy an automobile that he planned to use only for business purposes, and (3) $1,000 to buy office furniture. The effects of these three transactions on the accounting equation are shown in Illustration 1. Observe that the equation remains in balance after each transaction.

The nature of the Owen Real Estate Agency assets was changed by the three transactions, the effects of which are shown in Illustration 1. After their completion only $700 of the concern's original $5,000 cash remains; however, in exchange for the cash the business acquired three new assets:

Illustration 1

	Cash	+	Prepaid Rent	+	Automobile	+	Office Equipment	=	Larry Owen, Capital
	$5,000								$5,000
(1)	−300		+$300						
	$4,700		$300						$5,000
(2)	−3,000				+$3,000				
	$1,700		$300		$3,000				$5,000
(3)	−1,000						+$1,000		
	$ 700	+	$300	+	$3,000	+	$1,000	=	$5,000

(column header above table labeled **Assets** = **Owner Equity**)

(1) the right to occupy office space for three months, (2) an automobile, and (3) office furniture.

Continuing the illustration, assume that Owen found it necessary to have some additional equipment in his office. He felt that he should conserve the business cash; consequently, he purchased on credit or on account from Standard Supply Company $350 of office furniture (transaction No. 4). The effects of this transaction on the agency assets and equities are shown in color in Illustration 2.

Illustration 2

	Cash	+	Pre- paid Rent	+	Automobile	+	Office Equipment	=	Standard Supply Co.	+	Larry Owen, Capital
	$5,000										$5,000
(1)	−300		+$300								
	$4,700		$300								$5,000
(2)	−3,000				+$3,000						
	$1,700		$300		$3,000						$5,000
(3)	−1,000						+$1,000				
	$ 700		$300		$3,000		$1,000				$5,000
(4)							+350		+$350		
	$ 700	+	$300	+	$3,000	+	$1,350	=	$350	+	$5,000

(column headers: **Assets** = **Liabilities** + **Owner Equity**)

The assets were increased by the purchase of the additional office equipment; however, the owner equity remained unchanged because Standard Supply Company acquired a claim against the assets equal to the asset increase.

The amount owed Standard Supply Company is known as an *account payable*. Accounts payable are debts that result from the purchase of goods or services on credit.

At this stage assume that Larry Owen realized he had one piece of office equipment for which he had no need. Assume further that he was able to sell the equipment to Dale Hall for the $150 it cost. Mr. Hall paid $100 in cash on delivery and promised to pay the $50 balance at a later date. The effects of this transaction (No. 5) on the accounting equation are shown in color in Illustration 3.

Illustration 3

	Assets					= Lia-bilities	+ Owner Equity
	Cash +	Dale Hall +	Pre-paid Rent +	Auto-mobile +	Office Equip-ment	= Standard Supply Co.	+ Larry Owen, Capital
	$5,000						$5,000
(1)	−300		+$300				
	$4,700		$300				$5,000
(2)	−3,000			+$3,000			
	$1,700		$300	$3,000			$5,000
(3)	−1,000				+$1,000		
	$ 700		$300	$3,000	$1,000		$5,000
(4)					+350	+$350	
	$ 700		$300	$3,000	$1,350	$350	$5,000
(5)	+100	+$50			−150		
	$ 800 +	$50 +	$300 +	$3,000 +	$1,200	= $350	+ $5,000

The sale of the unneeded office equipment was an exchange of office equipment for (1) cash, $100; and (2) a new asset, the right to collect $50 from Dale Hall at a future date. This last asset, the right to collect money from someone to whom goods or services have been sold on credit, is known as an *account receivable*.

A few days after the foregoing transaction, Dale Hall paid the amount owed (transaction No. 6) and upon receipt of the money Larry Owen in turn paid Standard Supply Company one half the amount owed to them (No. 7). The effect of these two transactions is shown in Illustration 4.

Illustration 4

	Assets					= Lia-bilities	+ Owner Equity
	Cash +	Dale Hall +	Pre-paid Rent +	Auto-mobile +	Office Equip-ment	= Standard Supply Co.	+ Larry Owen, Capital
	$5,000						$5,000
(1)	−300		+$300				
	$4,700		$300				$5,000
(2)	−3,000			+$3,000			
	$1,700		$300	$3,000			$5,000
(3)	−1,000				+$1,000		
	$ 700		$300	$3,000	$1,000		$5,000
(4)					+350	+$350	
	$ 700		$300	$3,000	$1,350	$350	$5,000
(5)	+100	+$50			−150		
	$ 800	$50	$300	$3,000	$1,200	$350	$5,000
(6)	+50	−50					
	$ 850	0	$300	$3,000	$1,200	$350	$5,000
(7)	−175					−175	
	$ 675 +	0 +	$300 +	$3,000 +	$1,200	= $175	+ $5,000

Observe that the first, the receipt of cash from Dale Hall, is an exchange of assets; the second results in equal decreases in both assets and liabilities.

Increasing Owner Equity. The primary objective of a business is to increase owner equity by earning a profit or a net income. The Owen Real Estate Agency will accomplish this objective by selling real estate on a commission basis for its clients. Of course the business will accomplish this objective only if the amounts received as commissions are greater than the expenses resulting from making the sales.

Commissions earned and expenses incurred affect the elements of an accounting equation. To illustrate their effect, assume that on July 12 Larry Owen sold a house for a client and collected an $850 commission for his services (No. 8). Also, on the same day he paid his office secretary a $100 salary for her work during the first two weeks in the month (No. 9). The effects of these two transactions are shown in Illustration 5.

Illustration 5

	Cash	+	Dale Hall	+	Pre-paid Rent	+	Auto-mobile	+	Office Equip-ment	=	Standard Supply Co.	+	Larry Owen, Capital
	$5,000												$5,000
(1)	−300				+$300								
	$4,700				$300								$5,000
(2)	−3,000						+$3,000						
	$1,700				$300		$3,000						$5,000
(3)	−1,000								+$1,000				
	$ 700				$300		$3,000		$1,000				$5,000
(4)									+350		+$350		
	$ 700				$300		$3,000		$1,350		$350		$5,000
(5)	+100		+$50						−150				
	$ 800		$50		$300		$3,000		$1,200		$350		$5,000
(6)	+50		−50										
	$ 850		0		$300		$3,000		$1,200		$350		$5,000
(7)	−175										−175		
	$ 675		0		$300		$3,000		$1,200		$175		$5,000
(8)	+850												+850
	$1,525		0		$300		$3,000		$1,200		$175		$5,850
(9)	−100												−100
	$1,425	+	0	+	$300	+	$3,000	+	$1,200	=	$175	+	$5,750

The $850 commission is an example of what is known in accounting as *revenue.* A revenue is an inflow of cash, accounts receivable, or other assets in exchange for goods or services. Rent and interest earned are also examples of revenues.

The handling of the $850 commission in Illustration 5 demonstrates the effects of revenue on the assets and owner equity. Revenue increases both assets and owner equity. Likewise, the secretary's salary shows the effects of an expense. Expenses decrease owner equity and either decrease assets or increase liabilities.

Whether or not the Owen Real Estate Agency actually earned a profit or a net income during the first two weeks of July depends upon the concern's expenses for this period in addition to the secretary's salary. If the expenses were less than $850, the amount of the revenue, there was a profit and a net increase in owner equity.

QUESTIONS FOR CLASS DISCUSSION

1. Define accounting.
2. Name several ways in which a businessman uses accounting data.
3. Differentiate between accounting and bookkeeping.
4. Differentiate between a public accountant and a certified public accountant.
5. What is the American Institute of Certified Public Accountants?
6. What is the purpose of an audit? What does a certified public accountant do when he makes an audit?
7. A public accountant may engage in management advisory services. Of what does this consist?
8. What do the tax services of a public accountant include beyond preparing and filing tax returns?
9. What is a private accountant? A public accountant?
10. What media are used in recording transactions?
11. What is the cost principle of accounting? Why is such a principle necessary?
12. What is the effect in accounting of the business entity concept?
13. Define (1) asset, (2) liability, (3) equity, and (4) owner equity.
14. Give a synonym for "owner equity."
15. Name five assets of a business with which you are familiar. Name two liabilities of the business.
16. What is the fundamental accounting equation? Why is an understanding of this equation essential to the student of accounting?
17. Is it possible for a transaction to affect one asset item without affecting any other asset, liability, or owner equity item? Is it possible for a transaction to increase or decrease a single liability without affecting any other asset, liability, or owner equity item?
18. Fred Smith owns cash in the bank, $650; a house, $17,500; a car, $1,200; and household furniture, $3,000. He owes a savings and loan association $5,000, the balance due on the mortgage on his house. What are the totals of Mr. Smith's (1) assets? (2) his liabilities? (3) his net worth?
19. Which of the following are business transactions and which are not?
    a) Gave $400 in payment of the October rent.
    b) Hired a salesclerk, agreeing to pay him $50 per week.
    c) Purchased merchandise for cash.
    d) Sold merchandise for cash.
    e) Sold merchandise on credit.
    f) Paid the clerk's salary.

    g) Asked the clerk to place a merchandise order with a traveling salesman.

    h) Transferred cash from the cash register to the office safe.

20. Give a transaction that will—

    a) Increase an asset and decrease an asset.

    b) Increase an asset and increase a liability.

    c) Decrease an asset and decrease a liability.

    d) Increase an asset and increase owner equity.

    e) Decrease an asset and decrease owner equity.

PROBLEMS

Problem 1–1

Tom Church began a real estate agency which he called Green Valley Realty Company. During a short period he completed the following transactions:

    a) Sold a personal investment in General Motors stock for $8,952, and deposited $8,500 of the proceeds in a bank account opened in the name of Green Valley Realty Company.

    b) Purchased for $12,000 a small building to be used as an office by paying $6,000 in cash and signing a mortgage contract promising to pay the balance over the succeeding ten years.

    c) Took his personal automobile, which had a fair market value of $3,000, for permanent and exclusive use in the business.

    d) Purchased $800 of office equipment for cash.

    e) Purchased a $300 typewriter from Royal Equipment Company on credit.

    f) Paid $25 for an announcement on the local TV station of the opening of the real estate agency.

    g) Sold at cost $150 of unneeded office equipment to George Green for $100 in cash and a promise to pay the balance within a few days.

    h) Collected a $1,150 commission for the sale of real estate.

    i) George Green dropped by the office and paid the $50 he owed.

    j) Paid Royal Equipment Company the amount owed to them.

    k) Paid the office clerk's wages, $75.

    l) Wrote a check on the bank account of the real estate agency for payment of personal living expenses, $125.

Required:

  1. Arrange the following asset, liability, and owner equity titles in an expanded accounting equation like that in Illustration 5: Cash; George Green; Office Equipment; Automobile; Building; Royal Equipment Company (a creditor); Mortgage Payable; and Tom Church, Capital.

  2. Show by additions and subtractions, as in Illustration 5, the effects of each transaction on the assets, liabilities, and owner equity of Green Valley Reality Company. Show new totals for all items after each transaction.

Problem 1–2

Craig Flake recently began a moving and storage business which he calls Valley Moving and Storage Company. Since starting the company he has completed the following transactions:

a) Sold a personal investment in United States savings bonds for $8,324, and deposited $7,500 of the proceeds in a checking account opened in the name of the new company.

b) Paid the rent for three months in advance on a building to be used as an office and warehouse, $450.

c) Purchased a new truck for cash, $4,350.

d) Purchased $500 of office equipment and $50 of office supplies from Office Supply Company on credit.

e) Took from home for permanent use in the business a filing cabinet having a fair market value of $50.

f) Sold John Lance at cost $100 of the office equipment not needed by the company for $50 in cash and a promise to pay the balance within ten days.

g) Collected $350 for moving the household effects of a customer.

h) Paid Office Supply Company one half of the amount owed them.

i) Collected the amount owed by John Lance.

j) Paid the truck driver's wages, $100.

k) Used $50 of company cash (wrote a check on the company bank account) to pay personal living expenses.

Required:

1. Arrange the following asset, liability, and owner equity items in an expanded accounting equation like in Illustration 5: Cash; John Lance; Prepaid Rent; Office Supplies; Office Equipment; Trucks; Office Supply Company (a creditor); and Craig Flake, Capital.

2. Show by additions and subtractions, as in Illustration 5, the effects of each transaction on the assets, liabilities, and owner equity of Valley Moving and Storage Company.

Problem 1–3

Ottis Clark is the owner of Package Delivery Company. At the beginning of the current month the company had the following assets: cash, $500; office supplies, $75; office equipment, $700; and delivery equipment, $5,500; and it owed Apex Garage, $110. During the month the company completed the following transactions:

a) Mr. Clark invested an additional $2,500 in the business.

b) Sold a motorcycle carried in the accounting records at $200 to Jay Melcher for $150. Mr. Melcher paid $50 in cash and promised to pay the remainder in ten days.

c) Mr. Clark took from home for permanent use in the business a typewriter having a fair market value of $75.

d) Purchased $25 of office supplies for cash.

e) Gave $2,000 in cash and an old delivery truck carried in the accounting records at $900 for a new truck costing $2,900.

f) Purchased on credit from Valley Equipment Company a $150 desk and chair.

g) Received $300 from stores for the delivery of packages.

h) Paid Apex Garage one half the amount owed.

i) Paid the employees' wages, $125.

j) Sold for $25 an old desk and chair carried in the accounting records at $50.

k) Collected the $100 owed by Jay Melcher.

l) Paid Honda Sales Company $60 for repairs to a motorcycle.

m) Mr. Clark issued a $200 check on the company bank account in payment of his personal living expenses.

Required:

1. Arrange the following asset, liability, and owner equity titles in an expanded accounting equation like that of Illustration 5: Cash; Jay Melcher; Office Supplies; Office Equipment; Delivery Equipment; Apex Garage (a creditor); Valley Equipment Company (a creditor); and Ottis Clark, Capital.

2. Enter the assets and liabilities of Package Delivery Company under the titles of the equation. Determine the equity of Ottis Clark in the company and enter it under the title, Ottis Clark, Capital.

3. Show by additions and subtractions, as in Illustration 5, the effects of the transaction on the elements of the equation. Show new totals after each transaction.

Problem 1–4

Dent Stark has owned and operated Cactus Cabinet Shop for the past year without keeping separate business and personal records. The following information about Mr. Stark's affairs is available:

a) Mr. Stark has two checking accounts. In one, which has a balance of $550, the revenues of the shop are deposited; and on this account checks carrying the shop name are written in payment of shop bills. The other account has a balance of $315 and is used in paying Mr. Stark's personal expenses. Mr. Stark signs his name, Dent Stark, on the checks written on both accounts.

b) There are tools and equipment having a fair market value of $1,235 in the shop. The tools and equipment are owned by Mr. Stark and are used in the business. However, among the tools and equipment is a jointer recently purchased from Tempe Hardware Company for $345, and which has not been paid for by Mr. Stark.

c) Mr. Stark's residence has a fair market value of $15,500; but First State Bank holds a mortgage on it upon which there is an unpaid balance of $12,200.

d) Shop supplies having a fair market value of $335 are on hand in the shop.

e) Of the shop supplies on hand, supplies costing $75 were received from Payless Lumber Company two days ago and have not been paid for as yet.

f) Mr. Stark has a personal automobile that has a fair market value of $1,350.

g) On the current date Mr. Stark owes Dr. T. T. Davis, a dentist, $35 for extracting a tooth for Mrs. Stark.

h) The furnishings in Mr. Stark's home have a fair market value of $2,900.

Required:

Construct two accounting equations: (2) In the first show the assets, liabilities, and Mr. Stark's equity in the cabinet shop. (2) In the second list his personal assets, liabilities, and net worth. (Be sure to list his equity in the shop among his personal assets.)

Problem 1–5

Charles David is a practicing attorney, and in addition he owns Vista Theater. On September 1 of the current year he had the following assets, liabilities, and net worth: cash in personal checking account, $850; residence, $22,000; household effects, $7,000; automobile, $4,200; equity in Vista Theater, $49,350; equity in law firm assets, $13,410; stocks and bonds, $9,500; mortgage payable on residence, $9,000; and net worth, $97,310.

The assets, liabilities, and owner equity of Vista Theater on September 1 were: cash in theater bank account, $300; theater supplies, $250; furniture and equipment, $7,700; land and building, $41,450; Lion Films (a liability), $350; and Charles David, capital, $49,350.

On September 1 the assets, liabilities, and owner equity of the law firm were: cash, $4,500; prepaid rent, $300; office supplies, $150; law library, $5,000; office equipment, $3,600; Legal Publishing Company (a liability), $140; and Charles David, capital, $13,410.

During September Mr. David completed the following transactions:

a) Used $600 of personal funds to buy a color TV set for his home.
b) Transferred $1,000 of law firm cash to his personal bank account.
c) Transferred $2,500 of law firm cash to the bank account of the theater.
d) Purchased new theater equipment for (theater) cash, $800.
e) Paid Legal Publishing Company $140 from law firm cash.
f) Purchased law books on credit from Legal Publishing Company, $300.
g) Used theater cash to pay Lion Films, $200.
h) Sold $4,000 of personally owned bonds for $5,000.
i) Earned and collected $1,500 of legal fees and incurred and paid $800 of law office expenses.
j) The theater collected $2,000 in admissions and incurred and paid $2,300 of expenses.

Required:

1. Prepare three accounting equations like that of Illustration 5. In the first enter the September 1 assets, liabilities, and owner equity of Vista Theater. In the second enter the assets, liabilities, and equity of Mr. David in the law firm as of September 1; and in the third enter the personal assets (include the equities in the theater and law firm), liabilities, and net worth of Mr. David as of that date.
2. After completing the equations, show therein by additions and subtractions (see Illustration 5) the effects of the foregoing transactions.

CLASS EXERCISE

Exercise 1–1

In the first of the following equations are shown the assets, liabilities, and Larry Wilson's equity in Varsity Theater. In the second equation are shown Mr. Wilson's personal assets, liabilities, and net worth. In both equations are shown the effects of several transactions, with each transaction identified with a letter. Note that several transactions simultaneously affected both equations. On a sheet of notebook paper describe the nature of each transaction.

	Cash	+	Theater Supplies	+	Equipment	+	Land and Building	=	Fox Film Company	+	Mortgage Payable	+	L. Wilson, Capital
	$ 250		$ 100		$6,400		$38,500		$ 150		$22,000		$23,100
b)	+2,000												+ 2,000
	$2,250		$ 100		$6,400		$38,500		$ 150		$22,000		$25,100
c)	−1,500				+1,500								
	$ 750		$ 100		$7,900		$38,500		$ 150		$22,000		$25,100
e)	− 100								− 100				
	$ 650		$ 100		$7,900		$38,500		$ 50		$22,000		$25,100
f)	+2,300												+ 2,300
	−2,500												− 2,500
	$ 450		$ 100		$7,900		$38,500		$ 50		$22,000		$24,900

	Cash	+	Residence	+	Furniture	+	Equity in Theater	+	Stocks and Bonds	=	Mortgage Payable	+	L. Wilson, Net Worth
	$ 875		$25,000		$5,400		$23,100		$8,500		$15,000		$47,875
a)	+4,500								−3,000				+ 1,500
	$5,375		$25,000		$5,400		$23,100		$5,500		$15,000		$49,375
b)	−2,000						+ 2,000						
	$3,375		$25,000		$5,400		$25,100		$5,500		$15,000		$49,375
d)	− 600				+ 600								
	$2,775		$25,000		$6,000		$25,100		$5,500		$15,000		$49,375
f)							− 200						− 200
	$2,775		$25,000		$6,000		$24,900		$5,500		$15,000		$49,175
g)	−1,000										− 1,000		
	$1,775		$25,000		$6,000		$24,900		$5,500		$14,000		$49,175

ALTERNATE PROBLEMS

Problem 1–3A

Dennis Fetty owns and operates a small plumbing shop he calls Service Plumbing Shop. At the beginning of this month the shop had the following assets: cash, $415; plumbing supplies, $1,240; tools, $965; and trucks, $2,780. At that time the concern owed Plumbing Supply Company $155. During the month the following transactions were completed by Service Plumbing Shop:

a) Purchased tools for cash, $15.

b) Purchased plumbing supplies from Plumbing Supply Company on credit, $175.

c) Received $335 from several customers for cash repair work done for them.

d) Completed $150 of repair work for George Thumb on credit.

e) Paid Plumbing Supply Company the amount owed to them on the first of the month.

f) Sold for $150 an old truck carried in the accounting records at $200 to James Funk for $100 in cash and a promise to pay the remaining $50 within a few days.

g) George Thumb paid $100 of the amount he owed.

h) Gave tools carried in the accounting records at $100 plus $150 in cash for new tools priced at $250.

i) Paid Redtop Service Station $35 for gas and oil placed in the truck during the month.

j) Traded plumbing supplies carried in the accounting records at $40 for tools.

k) Paid for advertising on the local radio station, $25.

l) Purchased plumbing supplies on credit from Plumbing Supply Company, $110.

m) Mr. Fetty wrote a $65 check on the bank account of the shop in payment of his own personal living expenses.

Required:

1. Arrange the following asset, liability, and owner equity items in an accounting equation like that of Illustration 5: Cash; George Thumb; James Funk; Plumbing Supplies; Tools; Trucks; Plumbing Supply Company; and Dennis Fetty, Capital.
2. Enter the beginning of the month assets and liability under the item names of the equation. Determine Mr. Fetty's beginning of the month equity in the plumbing shop and enter it under Dennis Fetty, Capital.
3. Show by additions and subtractions, as in Illustration 5, the effects of each transaction on the elements of the equation. Show new totals after each transaction.

Problem 1—4A

On June 1 Ralph Sims sold a personal investment in land for $55,000 and deposited $52,000 of the proceeds in a bank account opened in the name of Bowlero Lanes. On the same date he purchased the assets of an existing bowling alley, changing its name to Bowlero Lanes. The assets purchased and their costs were: land, $15,000; building, $35,250; and bowling equipment, $12,500. For these assets Mr. Sims gave $25,000 in cash and signed a mortgage contract promising to pay the remainder over a period of ten years.

During June Mr. Sims remodeled the building at a cost of $22,500 and purchased $14,400 of new bowling equipment. On July 3 he invested an additional $5,000 in the business to help cover the remodeling costs and the equipment purchased, but on July 31 he still owed $2,500 of remodeling costs and $3,000 on the new equipment. During most of the remodeling period the alley remained open and in active operation, and on July 31 its bank balance was $2,050.

Required:

1. Prepare an accounting equation showing the assets, liabilities, and owner equity of Bowlero Lanes at the close of business on June 1 and a second equation showing the assets, liabilities, and owner equity on July 31.
2. Calculate the amount of change in owner equity between June 1 and July 31 and give reasons for the change.

DECISION PROBLEM 1—QUICK
DELIVERY SERVICE

On September 1 of the current year, Bill Bond started a city delivery service with one truck worth $4,800 and $1,360 cash. On October 1, Jack Gray, owner of two small department stores, approached Mr. Bond about an expansion plan for the delivery service in which Mr. Gray would furnish the funds for the expansion. Since the department stores of Mr. Gray have used the delivery service for the past month, it appeared that it might be advantageous to both Mr. Gray and Mr. Bond to enter into the partnership agreement through which the expansion of the delivery service could be effected.

Mr. Bond has not kept a regular set of books during the first month of his operations, but is able to supply the following data in regard to the month's operation:

1. On September 1, he rented a small building and an adjacent parking lot, paying $600 cash as the rental for September and October.
2. He purchased an additional delivery truck for $4,500, paying $500 in cash and giving a note payable due in six months for the balance.
3. Revenue earned during the month: cash, $900; and on credit to the Gray Department Stores, $300.
4. Expenses for September totaling $600 were paid in cash.
5. Invoices for purchases during the month were as follows:
    a) Sinclair Oil Corporation, oil and gas, $80.
    b) City Office Supply Company: 1 desk, $110; 1 chair, $40.

Neither of these invoices had been paid on October 1. It may be assumed that for all practical purposes the gasoline and oil was consumed during September.

Mr. Gray agrees to invest sufficient cash to give him an interest in the Quick Delivery Service equal to Mr. Bond's equity. Mr. Gray requests a report showing how much he must invest.

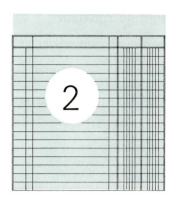

2

Recording
Transactions

IN THE previous chapter, accounting was described as the art of recording and summarizing transactions and of interpreting their effects on the affairs and activities of an economic unit. This chapter deals with some of the devices used in recording and summarizing transactions, the first of which is the *account.*

THE ACCOUNT

An account is a bookkeeping device used in recording and summarizing the increases and decreases in a single asset, liability, or owner equity item. In its most simple form an account looks like the letter "T," is called a "T-account," and appears as follows:

(Place for the Name of the Item Recorded in This Account)	
(Left side)	*(Right side)*

Note that the "T" gives the account a left side, a right side, and a place for the name of the asset, liability, or owner equity item the changes in which are recorded therein.

When a T-account is used in recording increases and decreases in an item, the increases are placed on one side of the account and the decreases on the other. For example, if the increases and decreases in the cash of

Owen Real Estate Agency of the previous chapter are recorded in a T-account, they appear as follows:

Cash

Investment	*5,000*	*Payment of rent*	*300*
Sale of equipment	*100*	*Purchase of automobile*	*3,000*
Collection from Hall	*50*	*Purchase of furniture*	*1,000*
Receipt of commission	*850*	*Payment of account*	*175*
		Payment of salary	*100*

The reason for putting the increases on one account side and the decreases on the other is that this makes it possible to summarize quickly all the transactions that have affected the account over a period of time and to learn their aggregate effect.

For example, the increases in Owen Real Estate Agency cash were:

Investment	*$5,000*
Sale of unneeded equipment to Dale Hall	*100*
Collection of balance owed by Dale Hall	*50*
Receipt of a commission	*850*
Sum of the increases	*$6,000*

And the decreases were:

Payment of office rent	*$ 300*
Purchase of automobile	*3,000*
Purchase of furniture for cash	*1,000*
Payment of account payable	*175*
Payment of secretary's salary	*100*
Sum of the decreases	*$4,575*

Therefore, the aggregate effect of the increases and decreases may be learned by subtracting the decreases from the increases, as follows:

Sum of the increases	*$6,000*
Sum of the decreases	*4,575*
Balance of cash remaining	*$1,425*

The subtraction indicates that the gross effect of Owen Real Estate Agency's cash transactions was a net reduction in its cash from $5,000 (the investment) to $1,425.

When accounting terminology is used to express the foregoing, it is said that after transactions are recorded in a T-account, they may be summarized and their net effect determined by adding (called "footing") the items on the increases side, adding ("footing") the items on the decreases side, and subtracting the sum of the decreases from the sum of the increases. This is called securing the *balance* of an account. The balance of an account is the difference between its increases and its decreases.

THE LEDGER

When transactions are recorded by a business, a separate account is required for each asset, liability, and owner equity item for which an individual record is desired. Consequently, a large number of accounts, often several hundred, is needed by even a small business. Each account is placed on a separate page in a bound or a loose-leaf book, or on a separate card in a tray of cards.

A group of accounts used by a business in recording its transactions is called a *ledger*. If the accounts are kept in a book, the book is also known as a ledger; and if the accounts are kept on cards in a file tray, the tray of cards is a ledger.

ACCOUNTS COMMONLY USED

The specific accounts used by a business in recording its transactions vary from one concern to another. In any business, the accounts used depend upon the assets owned, the debts owed, and the information to be secured from the accounting records. Nevertheless, although the specific accounts vary, the following are common.

Asset Accounts. If useful records of a concern's assets are to be kept, an individual account is needed for recording the increases and decreases in each kind of asset owned. Some of the more common assets for which accounts are maintained are as follows:

Cash. Increases and decreases in cash are recorded in an account called "Cash." The cash of a business consists of money or any media of exchange that a bank will accept at face value for deposit. Cash usually includes coins, currency, checks, postal and express money orders, and money on deposit in a bank or banks. Increases and decreases in both the cash on hand in the store or office and that on deposit in the bank are recorded in a single Cash account.

Notes Receivable. A formal written promise to pay a definite sum of money at a fixed future date is called a promissory note. (Promissory notes are illustrated and discussed in detail in Chapter 9.) When amounts due from others are evidenced by promissory notes, the notes are known as *notes receivable* and are recorded in a Notes Receivable account.

Accounts Receivable. Goods and services are commonly sold to customers on the basis of oral or implied promises of future payment. Such sales are known as "sales on credit" or "sales on account"; and the oral or implied promises to pay are known as accounts receivable. Individual accounts receivable are increased by sales on credit and are decreased by the customer's payments. Since it is necessary to know the amount currently owed by each customer, a separate account must be kept for each. Each account carries the name of the customer whose purchases and payments are recorded therein.

Prepaid Insurance. Fire, liability, and other types of insurance protection are normally paid for in advance. The amount paid is called a "premium" and may give protection from loss for from one to five years. As a result, a large portion of each premium is an asset for a considerable time after payment. When insurance premiums are paid, the asset "prepaid insurance" is increased by the amount paid; and the increase is normally recorded in an account called "Prepaid Insurance." Day by day, insurance premiums expire. Consequently, at intervals the insurance policies are examined; the insurance that has expired is calculated; and the balance of the Prepaid Insurance account is reduced accordingly.

Office Supplies. Stamps, stationery, paper, pencils, and like items are known as office supplies. They are assets when purchased, and continue to be assets until consumed. As they are consumed, the amounts consumed become expenses. Increases and decreases in the asset "office supplies" are commonly recorded in an account called "Office Supplies."

Store Supplies. Wrapping paper, cartons, sacks, string, and similar items used by a store are known as store supplies. Increases and decreases in store supplies are usually recorded in an account of that name.

Other Prepaid Expenses. Prepaid expenses are items that are assets at the time of purchase but become expenses as they are consumed or used. Prepaid insurance, office supplies, and store supplies are examples. Other examples are prepaid rent, prepaid taxes, and prepaid wages. Each type of prepaid expense is normally accounted for in a separate account which carries the name of the item, the increases and decreases of which are recorded therein.

Equipment Accounts. Increases and decreases in such things as typewriters, desks, chairs, and other office equipment having long lives are commonly recorded in an account called "Office Equipment." Likewise, changes in the amount of counters, showcases, shelves, cash registers, and like items used by a store are recorded in an account called "Store Equipment." And a company that owns and uses such things as lathes, drill presses, and the like records the increases and decreases in these items in an account called "Machinery and Equipment."

Buildings. A building used by a business in carrying on its operations may be a store, garage, warehouse, or factory; but regardless of the use, an account called "Buildings" is commonly employed in recording the increases and decreases in the buildings owned by a business and used in carrying on its operations.

Land. An account called "Land" is commonly used in recording increases and decreases in the land owned by a business. Although land and the buildings placed upon it are inseparable in physical fact, it is usually desirable to account for land and its buildings in separate accounts, because buildings depreciate or wear out, but land does not.

Liability Accounts.   Most companies do not have as many liability accounts as asset accounts; however, the following are common.

Notes Payable.   Increases and decreases in amounts owed because of promissory notes given to creditors are accounted for in an account called "Notes Payable."

Accounts Payable.   An account payable is an amount owed to a creditor which resulted from an oral or implied promise to pay. Most accounts payable result from the purchase on credit of merchandise, supplies, equipment, and services. Since it is necessary to know the amount owed each creditor, an account bearing the name of each must be kept.

Other Short-Term Payables.   Wages payable, taxes payable, and interest payable are illustrations of other short-term liabilities for which individual accounts must be kept.

Mortgage Payable.   A mortgage payable is a long-term debt for which the creditor has a secured prior claim against some one or more of the debtor's assets. The mortgage gives its holder, the creditor, the right to force the sale of the mortgaged assets through a foreclosure if the mortgage debt is not paid when due. An account called "Mortgage Payable" is commonly used in recording the increases and decreases in the amount owed on a mortgage.

Owner Equity Accounts.   Many transactions affect the owner's equity in a business, either increasing it or decreasing it. These transactions include the owner's investment, his withdrawals of cash and other assets for personal use, revenues earned, and expenses incurred. Of these, the more numerous and, from a managerial viewpoint, the more important are the revenue and expense transactions.

In the previous chapter, where the effects of transactions on the elements of the accounting equation were shown, all increases and decreases in owner equity, including revenues and expenses, were placed in a single column under the name of the owner. The single column helped to simplify the material, but it did not readily provide information as to each kind of increase and decrease. A single owner equity account would have the same disadvantage; it too would summarize transactions but would not readily supply information as to each kind of increase and decrease recorded therein. Consequently, in order that information as to the various kinds of increases and decreases in owner equity can readily be secured, numerous owner equity accounts are used, a different one for each kind of increase or decrease. Among these accounts are the following:

Capital Account.   When a person invests in a business of his own, his investment is recorded in an account carrying his name and the word "Capital." For example, an account called "Larry Owen, Capital" is used in recording the investment of Larry Owen in his real estate agency. In addition to providing a place for recording the original investment, the Capital account is also used in recording any permanent increases or decreases in owner equity.

Withdrawals Account. Usually a man invests in a business to earn profits or a net income. Normally, he expects the income to be large enough to pay his personal living expenses. Often, before income is earned or before it is known that income has been earned, a businessman finds it necessary to withdraw from his business money or other assets for his personal living expenses. These withdrawals reduce in like amounts both the assets and the owner's equity. However, since at the time of the withdrawals it is expected that sufficient income will be earned to make good the withdrawals, such withdrawals are called "withdrawals in anticipation of income" and are commonly recorded in an account carrying the name of the proprietor and the word "Withdrawals." For example, an account called "Larry Owen, Withdrawals" is used to record Owen's withdrawals in anticipation of income. The Withdrawals account is also known as the "Personal" account or the "Drawing" account.

Revenue and Expense Accounts. Revenues increase and expenses decrease owner equity. Actually, over a period of time, owner equity is increased or decreased by the difference between revenues earned and expenses incurred. It is increased when revenues exceed expenses, and decreased when expenses exceed revenues. When revenues exceed expenses, a profit or a net income is earned; and when expenses exceed revenues, a loss or a net loss is incurred.

Earning a net income and avoiding a loss is the primary objective of a business; and if a business is to earn income and avoid a loss, the owner or manager must normally have rather detailed information as to each kind of revenue earned and each kind of expense incurred. This information is secured by providing in the ledger a separate account for each revenue and expense and then, as transactions are completed, by recording in the separate accounts the amount of each kind of revenue earned and each kind of expense incurred.

Recording revenues and expenses in separate accounts requires a number of accounts in any business. In addition, all concerns do not have the same revenues and expenses; and consequently, it is impossible to list all revenue and expense accounts to be encountered. However, Revenue from Repairs, Commissions Earned, Fees Earned, Rent Earned, and Interest Earned are common examples of revenue accounts; and Advertising Expense, Store Supplies Used, Depreciation of Store Equipment, Office Salaries, Office Supplies Used, Rent Expense, Heating and Lighting Expense, Utilities Expense, and Insurance Expense are common examples of expense accounts. It should be noted that the kind of revenue or expense recorded in each above-mentioned account is evident from its title. This is generally true of such accounts.

DEBIT AND CREDIT

In bookkeeping, the left side of any account is called the *debit* side, abbreviated "Dr."; and the right side is called the *credit* side, abbreviated "Cr." Furthermore, when amounts are entered on the left side, they are called *debits*, and the account is said *to be debited*; and when amounts are entered on the right side of an account, they are called *credits*, and the account is said *to be credited*. Likewise, the difference between the total debits and the total credits recorded in an account is the account *balance*; and this balance may be a *debit balance* or a *credit balance*. An account has a debit balance when the sum of its debits exceeds the sum of its credits. Also, an account has a credit balance when its credits exceed its debits, and it is said to be *in balance* when its debits and credits are equal.

The terms "to debit" and "to credit" should not be confused with "to increase" and "to decrease." To debit means simply to enter an amount on the left side of an account, to credit means to enter an amount on the right side, and either may be an increase or a decrease. This may readily be seen by examining the way in which the investment of Larry Owen is recorded in his Cash and Capital accounts which follow:

Cash			*Larry Owen, Capital*	
Investment 5,000			*Investment* 5,000

When Owen invested $5,000 in his real estate business, both the business cash and Owen's equity were increased. Observe in the foregoing accounts that one increase, the increase in cash, is recorded on the left or debit side of the Cash account; while the other increase, the increase in owner equity, is recorded on the right or credit side. The transaction is recorded in this manner because of the mechanics of *double-entry bookkeeping*.

MECHANICS OF DOUBLE-ENTRY BOOKKEEPING

The mechanics of double-entry bookkeeping are such that every transaction affects and is recorded in two or more accounts with equal debits and credits. Transactions are so recorded because equal debits and credits offer a means of proving the recording accuracy. The proof is, if every transaction is recorded with equal debits and credits, then the sum of the debits in the ledger must equal the sum of the credits.

The person who first devised double-entry bookkeeping based the system on the fundamental accounting equation, $A = L + OE$, and he assigned the recording of increases in assets to the debit sides of asset accounts. He then recognized that the goal of equal debits and credits was possible only if increases in liabilities and owner equity were recorded on the opposite or credit sides of liability and owner equity accounts, or he recognized that, if increases in assets were to be recorded as debits, then increases and decreases in all accounts would have to be recorded as follows:

Assets		$=$	*Liabilities*		$+$	*Owner Equity*	
Debit for Increases	*Credit for Decreases*		*Debit for Decreases*	*Credit for Increases*		*Debit for Decreases*	*Credit for Increases*

From the foregoing T-accounts it is possible to formulate rules for recording transactions under a double-entry system. The rules are:

1. Increases in assets are debited to asset accounts; consequently, decreases must be credited.
2. Increases in liability and owner equity items are credited to liability and owner equity accounts; consequently, decreases must be debited.

At this stage, the beginning student will find it helpful to memorize these rules.

THE TRIAL BALANCE

When a business uses a double-entry system, the equality of the debits and credits in its ledger is periodically tested by preparing a *trial balance*. If, when the trial balance is prepared, debits equal credits, it is assumed that errors have not been made. (The trial balance and its preparation are discussed in more detail later in this chapter.)

TRANSACTIONS ILLUSTRATING THE RULES OF DEBIT AND CREDIT

The following Owen Real Estate Agency transactions are used to illustrate the application of the debit and credit rules and to show how transactions are recorded in the accounts. The number preceding each transaction is used throughout the illustration to identify the transaction as it appears in the accounts. Note that ten of the first eleven transactions are the same transactions that were used in Chapter 1 to illustrate the effect of transactions on the accounting equation.

1. Larry Owen invested $5,000 in a real estate agency.
2. He paid three months' office rent in advance, $300.

3. Paid $3,000 for a business automobile.
4. Purchased office equipment for cash, $1,000.
5. Purchased office equipment on credit, $350.
6. Purchased office supplies on credit from A. B. Gordon Company, $60.
7. Sold unneeded office equipment to Dale Hall, $100 cash and $50 to be paid at a later date.
8. Collected $50 from Dale Hall.
9. Paid Standard Supply Company, $175.
10. Sold a house and collected a commission, $850.
11. Paid the secretary's salary for first two weeks of the month, $100.
12. Sold a building lot and collected a commission, $75.
13. Paid the secretary's salary for second two weeks of the month, $100.
14. Larry Owen withdrew $200 for his personal use.
15. Paid telephone and utilities, $20.
16. Paid for gas and oil used in the agency car, $25.
17. Paid for newspaper advertising that had appeared, $60.

Before a transaction can be recorded, it must be analyzed into its debit and credit elements. The analysis consists of (1) determining what asset, liability, or owner equity items are increased or decreased by the transaction; and then (2) applying the rules of debit and credit to determine the debit and credit effect of the increases or decreases. An analysis of each of the following transactions is given in order to demonstrate the process.
1. On July 1 of the current year, Larry Owen invested $5,000 in a real estate agency.

Analysis of the transaction: The transaction increased the Owen Real Estate Agency cash, and at the same time, it increased the equity of Owen in the assets of the company. Increases in assets are debited, and increases in owner equity are credited. Consequently, Cash should be debited and Larry Owen, Capital should be credited for $5,000.

Cash		Larry Owen, Capital	
(1) 5,000		*(1)* 5,000	

2. Paid the office rent for three months in advance, $300.

Cash	
(1) 5,000	*(2)* 300

Prepaid Rent	
(2) 300	

Analysis of the transaction: The asset, prepaid rent, the right to occupy the office for three months, is increased, and cash is decreased. Increases in assets are debited, and decreases in assets are credited. Therefore, debit Prepaid Rent and credit Cash for $300.

3. Paid $3,000 for an automobile to be used for business purposes only.

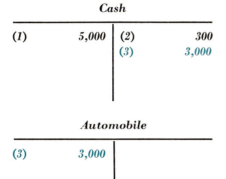

Cash		
(1) 5,000	(2) 300	
	(3) 3,000	

Analysis of the transaction: The asset, automobile, is increased, and the asset, cash, is decreased. Debit Automobile and credit Cash for $3,000.

Automobile	
(3) 3,000	

4. Purchased office equipment for cash, $1,000.

Cash	
(1) 5,000	(2) 300
	(3) 3,000
	(4) 1,000

Analysis of the transaction: The asset, office equipment, is increased, and the asset, cash, is decreased. Debit Office Equipment and credit Cash for $1,000.

Office Equipment	
(4) 1,000	

5. Purchased office equipment from Standard Supply Company on credit, $350.

Analysis of the transaction: This transaction increased the asset, office equipment; but also increased the liabilities by granting Standard Supply Company a claim against the assets. Increases in assets are debited, and increases in liabilities are credited. Consequently, Office Equipment is debited and an account carrying the name, Standard Supply Company, is credited for $350.

Office Equipment		*Standard Supply Company*	
(4) 1,000			(5) 350
(5) 350			

6. Purchased office supplies on credit from A. B. Gordon Company, $60.

Analysis of the transaction: In this transaction there is an increase in assets and an increase in liabilities. Debit Office Supplies and credit A. B. Gordon Company.

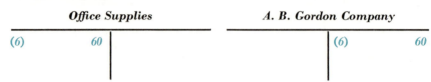

Office Supplies			*A. B. Gordon Company*	
(6)	*60*		*(6)*	*60*

7. Sold unneeded office equipment to Dale Hall at its $150 cost, $100 in cash and $50 to be paid at a later date.

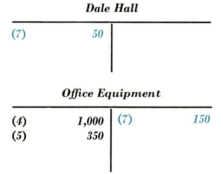

Cash

(1)	*5,000*	*(2)*	*300*
(7)	*100*	*(3)*	*3,000*
		(4)	*1,000*

Analysis of the transaction: The assets, cash and Dale Hall, increased, and the asset, office equipment, decreased. Debit Cash and Dale Hall for the increases and credit Office Equipment for the decrease.

Dale Hall

(7)	*50*	

Office Equipment

(4)	*1,000*	*(7)*	*150*
(5)	*350*		

8. Collected $50 from Dale Hall.

Cash

(1)	*5,000*	*(2)*	*300*
(7)	*100*	*(3)*	*3,000*
(8)	*50*	*(4)*	*1,000*

Analysis of the transaction: One asset was increased and the other decreased. Debit Cash for $50 to record the increase in cash, and credit Dale Hall $50 to record the decrease in the account receivable.

Dale Hall

(7)	*50*	*(8)*	*50*

9. Paid Standard Supply Company $175 of the amount owed.

Analysis of the transaction: Payments to creditors decrease in like amounts both assets and liabilities. Decreases in liabilities are debited, and decreases in assets are credited. Debit Standard Supply Company and credit Cash.

Cash				Standard Supply Company		
(1)	5,000	(2)	300	(9)	175	(5)	350
(7)	100	(3)	3,000				
(8)	50	(4)	1,000				
		(9)	175				

10. Sold a house and collected a commission, $850.

Analysis of the transaction: The transaction increased both assets and owner equity. Increases in assets are debits, and increases in owner equity are credits. Therefore, Cash is debited; and in order to show the nature of the increase in owner equity, the owner equity account, Commissions Earned, is credited.

Cash				Commissions Earned	
(1)	5,000	(2)	300	(10)	850
(7)	100	(3)	3,000		
(8)	50	(4)	1,000		
(10)	850	(9)	175		

11. Paid the secretary's salary for the first two weeks in the month, $100.

Analysis of the transaction: This transaction decreased both assets and owner equity. Debit the account, Office Salaries, to show the decrease and the nature of the decrease in owner equity; and credit Cash to show the decrease in the asset.

Cash				Office Salaries	
(1)	5,000	(2)	300	(11)	100
(7)	100	(3)	3,000		
(8)	50	(4)	1,000		
(10)	850	(9)	175		
		(11)	100		

12. Sold a building lot and collected a $75 commission.

Analysis of the transaction: Assets and owner equity increased. Debit Cash and credit Commissions Earned.

		Cash				Commissions Earned	
(1)	5,000	(2)	300			(10)	850
(7)	100	(3)	3,000			(12)	75
(8)	50	(4)	1,000				
(10)	850	(9)	175				
(12)	75	(11)	100				

13. Paid the secretary's salary for the second two weeks of the month, $100.

Analysis of the transaction: Assets and owner equity decreased. Debit Office Salaries and credit Cash.

		Cash			Office Salaries	
(1)	5,000	(2)	300	(11)	100	
(7)	100	(3)	3,000	(13)	100	
(8)	50	(4)	1,000			
(10)	850	(9)	175			
(12)	75	(11)	100			
		(13)	100			

14. Larry Owen withdrew $200 for his personal use.

Analysis of the transaction: This transaction reduced in equal amounts both assets and owner equity. However, since the withdrawal is a withdrawal in anticipation of income, it is debited to the Withdrawals account rather than the Capital account. Consequently, debit Larry Owen, Withdrawals and credit Cash.

		Cash			Larry Owen, Withdrawals	
(1)	5,000	(2)	300	(14)	200	
(7)	100	(3)	3,000			
(8)	50	(4)	1,000			
(10)	850	(9)	175			
(12)	75	(11)	100			
		(13)	100			
		(14)	200			

15. Paid the telephone and utilities, $20.
16. Paid for gas and oil used in the agency car, $25.
17. Paid for newspaper advertising that had appeared, $60.

Analysis of the transactions: The foregoing transactions are alike in that each decreased cash; they differ in each case as to the kind of expense involved. Consequently, in recording them, Cash is credited and a different expense account, one showing the nature of the expense in each case, is debited.

Cash				Telephone and Utilities	
(1)	5,000	(2)	300	(15)	20
(7)	100	(3)	3,000		
(8)	50	(4)	1,000		
(10)	850	(9)	175		
(12)	75	(11)	100	**Gas, Oil, and Repairs**	
		(13)	100		
		(14)	200	(16)	25
		(15)	20		
		(16)	25		
		(17)	60		
				Advertising Expense	
				(17)	60

THE ACCOUNTS AND THE EQUATION

In Illustration 6 the foregoing transactions of Larry Owen are shown in the accounts, with the accounts brought together and classified under the elements of an accounting equation.

Illustration 6

Assets	=	Liabilities	+	Owner Equity

Cash

(1) 5,000	(2) 300		
(7) 100	(3) 3,000		
(8) 50	(4) 1,000		
(10) 850	(9) 175		
(12) 75	(11) 100		
	(13) 100		
	(14) 200		
	(15) 20		
	(16) 25		
	(17) 60		

A. B. Gordon Company

	(6) 60

Standard Supply Company

(9) 175	(5) 350

Larry Owen, Capital

	(1) 5,000

Larry Owen, Withdrawals

(14) 200	

Dale Hall

(7) 50	(8) 50

Prepaid Rent

(2) 300	

Office Supplies

(6) 60	

Automobile

(3) 3,000	

Office Equipment

(4) 1,000	(7) 150
(5) 350	

Commissions Earned

	(10) 850
	(12) 75

Office Salaries Expense

(11) 100	
(13) 100	

Telephone and Utilities

(15) 20	

Gas, Oil, and Repairs

(16) 25	

Advertising Expense

(17) 60	

PREPARING A TRIAL BALANCE

As previously stated, in a double-entry bookkeeping system every transaction is recorded with equal debits and credits so that the equality of the debits and credits may be tested as a proof of recording accuracy; and this equality is tested at intervals by preparing a trial balance.

A trial balance is prepared by (1) determining the balance of each account in the ledger, (2) listing in their ledger order the accounts having balances, with the debit balances in one column and the credit balances in another (as in Illustration 7), (3) adding the debit balances, (4) adding

Illustration 7

OWEN REAL ESTATE AGENCY
Trial Balance, July 31, 19--

Cash.	$1,095	
Prepaid rent.	300	
Office supplies	60	
Automobile.	3,000	
Office equipment.	1,200	
A. B. Gordon Company.		$ 60
Standard Supply Co.		175
Larry Owen, capital		5,000
Larry Owen, withdrawals	200	
Commissions earned.		925
Office salaries expense	200	
Telephone and utilities	20	
Gas, oil, and repairs	25	
Advertising expense	60	
	$6,160	$6,160

the credit balances, and then (5) comparing the sum of the debit balances with the sum of the credit balances.

Illustration 7 shows a trial balance of the Owen Real Estate Agency ledger. It was prepared from the accounts in Illustration 6. Note that its column totals are equal, or in other words, the trial balance is in balance.

THE PROOF OFFERED BY A TRIAL BALANCE

If when a trial balance is prepared it does not balance—the two columns are not equal—errors have been made either in recording transactions, in securing the account balances, in copying the balances on the trial balance, or in adding the trial balance columns. On the other hand, if a trial balance balances, it is assumed that no errors have been made. However, a trial balance that balances is not absolute proof of accuracy. Errors may have been made that did not affect the equality of the trial balance. For example, an error in which a correct debit amount is debited to the wrong account or a correct credit amount is credited to the wrong account will not cause a trial balance to be out of balance. Likewise, an error in which a wrong amount is both debited and credited to the right accounts will not cause a trial balance to be out of balance. Consequently, a trial balance in balance is considered only presumptive proof of recording accuracy.

A STANDARD ACCOUNT FORM

T-accounts like the ones just described are commonly used in teaching and are also commonly used by accountants in solving problems. In either case details are eliminated by their use and the student or accountant can

Illustration 8

DATE	EXPLANATION	FO-LIO	DEBIT	DATE	EXPLANATION	FO-LIO	CREDIT
1966 July 1		1	500 00	1966 July 1		1	30 00
				3		1	300 00
				3		1	100 00

Cash — ACCOUNT NO. 1

concentrate on ideas. However, such accounts are not used in business for recording transactions. In business, accounts like the one of Illustration 8 are sometimes used.

An examination of the Illustration 8 account will reveal that this account is like a T-account in that it has two sides and a place for the name of the item recorded therein. However, it differs in that each side is divided into columns for recording specific additional information, as indicated by the column headings.

When accounts like Illustration 8 are used, each account is placed on a separate page in a loose-leaf ledger or a separate card in a tray of cards; and twenty to a hundred or more accounts, each on a separate page or card, are required in recording a company's transactions.

NEED FOR A JOURNAL

It is possible to record transactions by entering debits and credits directly in the accounts, as was done earlier in this chapter. However, when this is done and an error is made, the error is difficult to locate. It is difficult to locate because, even with a transaction having only one debit and one credit, the debit is entered on one ledger page or card and the credit on another, and there is nothing to link the two together.

Consequently, to overcome this objection and to provide in one place a complete record of each transaction, it is the universal practice in pen-and-ink systems to record all transactions in a *journal* and then to copy the debit and credit information about each transaction from the journal to the ledger accounts.

Each transaction recorded in a journal is recorded with a separate *journal entry*, and the process of recording transactions in a journal is called *journalizing transactions*. Also, since transactions are recorded in a journal as the first or original step in their recording, and their debit and credit information is copied from the journal to the ledger as a second or last step, a journal is called *a book of original entry* and a ledger *a book of final entry*.

THE GENERAL JOURNAL

The simplest and most flexible type of journal is a *General Journal*. A General Journal provides for each transaction places for recording (1) the transaction date, (2) the names of the accounts involved, (3) an explanation of the transaction, (4) the account numbers of the accounts to which the transaction's debit and credit information is copied, and (5) the transaction's debit and credit effect on the accounts named. A standard ruling for a general journal page with two of the transactions of Owen Real Estate Agency recorded therein is shown in Illustration 9.

Illustration. 9

GENERAL JOURNAL   PAGE *1*

DATE	ACCOUNT TITLES AND EXPLANATION	FO-LIO	DEBIT	CREDIT
1966				
July 9	Cash		100 00	
	Dale Hall		50 00	
	Office Equipment			150 00
	Sold unneeded office			
	equipment at cost.			
11	Cash		50 00	
	Dale Hall			50 00
	In full of amount owed.			

RECORDING TRANSACTIONS IN A GENERAL JOURNAL

To record transactions in a General Journal:

1. The year is written in small figures at the top of the first column.
2. The month is written on the first line in the first column. The year and the month are not repeated except at the top of a new page or at the beginning of a new month or year.

3. The day of each transaction is written in the second column on the first line of the transaction.
4. The names of the accounts to be debited and credited and an explanation of the transaction are written in the Account Titles and Explanation column. The name of the account debited is written first, beginning at the left margin of the column. The name of the account credited is written on the following line, indented about one inch. The explanation is placed on the next line, indented about a half inch from the left margin. The explanation should be short but sufficient to explain the transaction and set it apart from every other transaction.
5. The debit amount is written in the Debit column opposite the name of the account to be debited. The credit amount is written in the Credit column opposite the account to be credited.
6. A single line is skipped between each journal entry to set the entries apart.

At the time transactions are recorded in the General Journal, nothing is entered in the Folio column. However, when the debits and credits are copied from the journal to the ledger, the account numbers of the ledger accounts to which the debits and credits are copied are entered in the Folio column. The use of the Folio column is discussed in more detail later in this chapter.

COMPOUND JOURNAL ENTRIES

The first entry in Illustration 9 records the sale of unneeded office equipment by Owen Real Estate Agency, and three accounts are involved. When a transaction involves three or more accounts and is recorded with a general journal entry, a compound entry is required. A compound entry is one involving three or more accounts.

POSTING TRANSACTION INFORMATION

The process of copying journal entry information and transferring it from the journal to the ledger is called *posting*. Normally, near the end of a day all transactions recorded in the journal that day are posted to the ledger. In the posting procedure, journal debits are copied and become ledger account debits and journal credits are copied and become ledger account credits.

The posting procedure for a journal entry is shown in Illustration 10, and it may be described as follows. To post a journal entry:

1. Find in the ledger the account named in the debit of the entry to be posted.
2. Enter on the debit side of this account (*a*) the transaction date as recorded in the entry, (*b*) the page number of the journal from which the entry is being posted, and (*c*) the debit amount.
3. Enter in the Folio column of the journal the account number of the account to which the amount was posted.

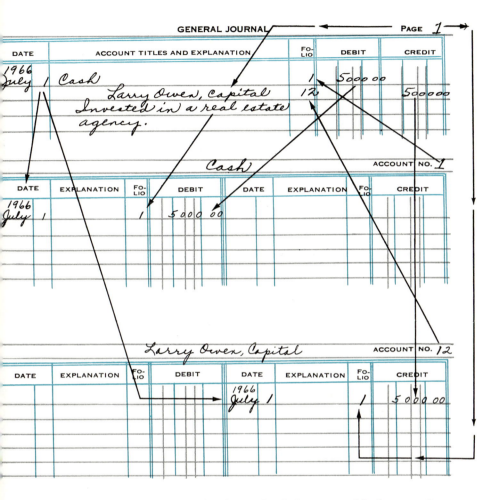

4. Repeat the foregoing steps for the credit of the entry, with the exception that the transaction date, journal page number, and credit amount are entered on the credit side of the account.

Observe that the last step (Step 3) in the posting procedure for either the debit or the credit of an entry is the insertion of the account number in the Folio column of the journal. Inserting the account number in the journal Folio column serves two purposes: (1) The account number in the journal and the journal page number in the account act as a cross-reference when it is desired to trace an amount from one record to the other. And, (2) writing the account number in the journal as a last step in posting indicates that posting is completed. If posting is interrupted, the book-keeper, by examining the journal Folio column, can easily see where posting stopped.

Account numbers and journal page numbers are often called *posting reference numbers*. The reason they are called this is obvious.

BOOKKEEPING TECHNIQUES

Periods and Commas in Dollar Amounts.   When amounts are entered in a journal or a ledger, commas to indicate thousands of dollars and periods to separate dollars and cents are not necessary because the ruled lines accomplish this purpose. However, when statements are prepared on unruled paper, the periods and commas are necessary.

Dollar Signs.   Dollar signs are not used in journals or ledgers, but they are required on the financial reports prepared on unruled paper. On the reports, a dollar sign is placed (1) before the first amount in each column of figures, and (2) before the first amount appearing after a ruled line that indicates an addition or a subtraction. Examine Illustration 11 on page 54 for examples of the use of dollar signs on a financial report.

Omission of Zeros in the Cents Columns.   When an amount to be entered in a ledger or a journal is an amount of dollars and no cents, some bookkeepers will use a dash in the cents column in the place of two zeros to indicate that there are no cents. They feel that the dash is easier and more quickly made than the two zeros. This is a matter of choice in journal and ledger entries. However, on financial reports the two zeros are preferred because they are neater in appearance.

Often in this text, where space is limited, exact dollar amounts are used in order to save space. Obviously, in such cases, neither zeros nor dashes are used to show that there are no cents involved.

QUESTIONS FOR CLASS DISCUSSION

1. What is an account? What is a ledger?
2. What determines the number of accounts a business will use?
3. What are the meanings of the following words and terms: (1) debit, (2) to debit, (3) credit, and (4) to credit.
4. If increases in assets were recorded as credits rather than as debits, how would increases in liabilities and owner equity be recorded? Why?
5. Does debit always mean increase and credit always mean decrease?
6. A transaction is to be entered in the accounts. How do you determine the accounts in which amounts are to be entered? How do you determine whether a particular account is to be debited or credited?
7. Why is a double-entry bookkeeping system so called?
8. An accounting student in his first lessons confused the words "debit" and "credit." He consistently recorded debits on the right side of accounts and credits on the left side. What difficulty, if any, did he experience in recording transactions and making a trial balance? Would you recommend that he change his procedure? Why?

9. Give the rules of debit and credit for (1) asset accounts, and (2) liability and owner equity accounts.

10. Why is the rule of debit and credit the same for both liability and owner equity and accounts?

11. List the steps in the preparation of a trial balance.

12. What is the reason for preparing a trial balance?

13. Why is the trial balance considered to be only presumptive proof of recording accuracy? What types of errors are not revealed by a trial balance?

14. Is it possible to record transactions directly in the ledger accounts? What is gained by first recording transactions in a journal and then posting to the accounts?

15. In recording transactions in a journal, which is written first, the debit or the credit? How far is the name of the account credited indented? How far is the explanation indented?

16. What is a compound entry?

17. Are dollar signs used in journal entries? In the accounts?

18. If a period is not used in a journal debit to separate dollars from cents, what accomplishes this purpose?

19. Define or describe each of the following:

   a) Journal.
   b) Ledger.
   c) Book of original entry.
   d) Book of final entry.

   e) Folio column.
   f) Posting.
   g) Footing.
   h) Posting reference numbers.

20. Entering in the Folio column of the journal the account number to which an amount was posted is the last step in posting the amount. What is gained by making this the last step?

PROBLEMS

Problem 2–1

a) Barry Nash opened an air-conditioning service and repair shop and began business by investing $1,000 in cash and the following additional assets at their fair market values: office equipment, $350; tools, $500; and truck, $1,200. He called his business Coolair Service Company, and during a short period completed the following transactions:

b) Paid the rent for three months in advance on the shop space, $300.

c) Purchased $150 of repair supplies on credit from Tri-City Supply Company.

d) Traded a typewriter carried in the accounting records at $50 for additional tools.

e) Purchased for cash a new typewriter to replace the one traded, $160.

f) Paid for radio advertising announcing the opening of the shop, $35.

g) Completed repair work for George Thomas and received $60 in full payment therefor.

h) Completed repair work for Ralph Sims, $175. Accepted $100 in cash and a promise to pay the balance within a short period.

i) Completed repair work for Walter Rice on credit, $85.
j) Ralph Sims paid the amount owed from transaction (*h*).
k) Paid Tri-City Supply Company one half the amount owed to them.
l) Paid the utility bills, $15.
m) Mr. Nash withdrew $100 from the cash of the business to be used for personal living expenses.

Required:

1. Set up the following T-accounts: Cash; Ralph Sims; Walter Rice; Repair Supplies; Prepaid Rent; Office Equipment; Tools; Truck; Tri-City Supply Company; Barry Nash, Capital; Barry Nash, Withdrawals; Revenue from Repairs; Advertising Expense; and Utilities Expense.
2. Record the transactions by entering debits and credits directly in the T-accounts. Use the transaction letters to identify each debit and credit amount.
3. Prepare a trial balance using the current date.

Problem 2–2

Kent Sims has just begun the operation of a cleaning and pressing business. During the past few days he completed the following transactions:

Oct.   1   Sold 100 shares of personally owned General Electric Company stock for $9,500 and deposited $9,000 of the proceeds in a checking account opened in the name of his company, Ideal Cleaners.

   2   Paid the rent for three months in advance on the cleaning plant building, $600.

   2   Purchased $7,500 of cleaning equipment, giving $5,000 in cash and a $2,500 promissory note.

   3   Purchased $150 of cleaning supplies and $650 of additional cleaning equipment from Cortez Supply Company on credit.

   4   Delivered cleaning to customers and collected cash in full payment therefor, $110.

   4   Delivered cleaning to Modern Motel on credit, $50.

   5   Paid the wages of the employees, $200.

   5   Paid Cortez Supply Company $500 of the amount owed to it.

   6   Modern Motel paid the $50 it owed.

Required:

1. Open the following accounts: Cash; Modern Motel; Cleaning Supplies; Prepaid Rent; Cleaning Equipment; Notes Payable; Cortez Supply Company; Kent Sims, Capital; Revenue from Cleaning; and Wages Expense.
2. Prepare general journal entries to record the transactions; post to the accounts; and prepare a trial balance as of October 6.

Problem 2–3

Thomas Howe owns and operates Cactus Realty Company, and on September 1, 19—, a trial balance of the concern's ledger appeared as follows:

CACTUS REALTY COMPANY
Trial Balance, September 1, 19—

Cash..	$ 1,170	
Walter Haig......................................	70	
Office supplies....................................	145	
Office equipment.................................	2,465	
Automobile......................................	2,700	
Land..	5,000	
Building...	12,000	
Valley Supply Company...........................		$ 50
Mortgage payable................................		10,000
Thomas Howe, capital............................		13,500
	$23,550	$23,550

During September Mr. Howe completed the following transactions:

a) Purchased $55 of office supplies and $150 of office equipment from Valley Supply Company on credit.

b) Sold a house and collected a $1,250 commission from the sale.

c) Paid Valley Supply Company $50 of the amount owed to them.

d) Sent the local newspaper a $75 check in payment for advertising that had appeared.

e) Walter Haig paid the $70 he owed.

f) Purchased a typewriter from Valley Supply Company on credit, $225.

g) Mr. Howe took the old company typewriter, carried in the accounting records at $65, home for permanent use of his high school children as a practice typewriter.

h) Sold a house and collected a $950 commission from the sale.

i) Billed Walter Haig $70 and George Ruston $50 for property management services.

j) Mr. Howe withdrew $450 from the company bank account to pay personal living expenses.

k) Received a $50 check from George Ruston in payment for the services billed in transaction (*i*).

l) Paid the salary of the office clerk, $250.

m) Gave $1,000 in cash and the old company car for a new company car.

n) Sent a $45 check to the local newspaper for advertising that had appeared.

o) Paid the telephone and other utilities, $35.

Required:

1. Open the following T-accounts: Cash; Walter Haig; George Ruston; Office Supplies; Office Equipment; Automobile; Land; Building; Valley Supply Company; Mortgage Payable; Thomas Howe, Capital; Thomas Howe, Withdrawals; Commissions Earned; Property Management Fees; Advertising Expense; Salaries Expense; and Telephone and Utilities.

2. Enter the September 1 trial balance amounts in the accounts. Identify each amount by writing the abbreviation "Bal." before it.

3. Record the transactions by entering debits and credits directly in the T-accounts. Use the transaction letters to identify each debit and credit amount.
4. Prepare a trial balance.

Problem 2–4

Neal Able, a young lawyer, completed the following transaction during October of the current year:

Oct.   1   Began the practice of law by investing $1,200 in cash and a law library having a fair market value of $800.

     1   Paid two months' rent in advance on suitable office space, $200.

     2   Purchased $1,200 of office equipment, paying $200 in cash and giving a promissory note payable for the balance.

     3   Purchased $45 of office supplies and $175 of office equipment from Office Supply Company on credit.

     6   Completed legal work for James Mohr and collected $50 in full payment therefor.

     10   Paid insurance premiums totaling $95 on several policies taken out in the name of the firm.

     15   Billed First State Bank $300 for legal work completed for it.

     15   Paid the semimonthly salary of the legal secretary, $150.

     18   Paid Office Supply Company for the items purchased from it on October 3.

     25   Received a $300 check from First State Bank for the legal work completed on October 15.

     28   Neal Able withdrew $200 from the bank account of the law practice to be used for personal expenses.

     30   Billed First State Bank for additional legal work completed, $150.

     31   Paid the legal secretary's salary, $150.

     31   Paid $5 interest expense and a $100 installment due on the note payable.

     31   Paid the monthly utility bills, $25.

Required:

1. Open the following accounts: Cash; First State Bank; Prepaid Rent; Office Supplies; Prepaid Insurance; Office Equipment; Legal Library; Note Payable; Office Supply Company; Neal Able, Capital; Neal Able, Withdrawals; Revenue from Law Practice; Salaries Expense; Utilities Expense; and Interest Expense.
2. Prepare general journal entries to record the transactions, post to the accounts, and prepare a trial balance under the name of Neal Able, Attorney.

Problem 2–5

On October 1 George Hunter began a business he called Modern Cabinet Shop, and he completed the following transactions during the month:

Oct.   1   Cashed three mature United States savings bonds and deposited the $3,000 proceeds in a checking account of the shop.

Oct. 2   Paid $180 for three months' rent in advance on the shop building.
      3   Purchased $2,500 of shop machinery, giving $1,000 in cash and a promissory note payable for the balance.
      5   Purchased $1,500 of shop supplies from Northside Planing Mill on credit.
      9   Collected cash on delivery of $350 of cabinet work to Ralph Watson.
     13   Billed David McKeen for $400 of cabinet work delivered today.
     15   Paid the wages of the shop workmen, $325.
     15   Paid Red Ball Delivery Service $35 for delivery services rendered during the first half of the month.
     18   Paid Northside Planing Mill $750 of the amount owed to it.
     20   George Hunter took $40 of shop supplies home for use in repairing his carport.
     23   Received a $400 check from David McKeen for the cabinet work delivered on October 13.
     25   George Hunter withdrew $150 from the business to be used for his personal living expenses.
     28   Collected cash on the delivery of $450 of cabinet work.
     31   Paid Red Ball Delivery Service $25 for cabinet work delivered by the company during the last half of the month.
     31   Paid the wages of the shop workmen, $300.
     31   Paid the light and power bill, $40.

Required:
1. Open the following accounts: Cash; David McKeen; Prepaid Rent; Shop Supplies; Shop Machinery; Notes Payable; Northside Planing Mill; George Hunter, Capital; George Hunter, Withdrawals; Revenue from Cabinet Work; Delivery Expense; Wages Expense; and Light and Power Expense. Number the accounts beginning with 1.
2. Prepare general journal entries to record the transactions, post to the accounts, and prepare a trial balance.

CLASS EXERCISE

Exercise 2–1

During a short period an inexperienced bookkeeper made the following errors:
   a) A $7.92 item for office supplies purchased was debited to the Office Supplies account as though it were $9.72.
   b) A customer paid his account. The customer was debited and Cash was credited for the $15 paid.
   c) A $7.50 credit to Office Supplies was debited to Office Equipment.
   d) A $12 credit to Office Equipment was recorded as a credit to Office Supplies.
   e) The debit side of a creditor's account totaled $34, and the credit side totaled $56. The bookkeeper added the two sides and entered the $90 total as the debit balance of the account.

Required:

1. Tell the effect of each error on the trial balance.
2. The debit side of the trial balance prepared after the foregoing errors were made, totaled $13,574.80 and the credit side totaled $13,446. Determine the correct totals.

ALTERNATE PROBLEMS

Problem 2–1A

a) Barry Nash opened a television repair shop and began business by investing $1,200 in cash and the following assets at their fair market values: repair supplies, $450; tools, $300; and truck, $200. He called his business Ready TV Service, and during a short period completed the following transactions:

b) Paid $25 for newspaper advertising announcing the opening of the shop.

c) Paid the rent for two months in advance on the shop space, $200.

d) Purchased a desk, chair, and filing cabinet from Tri-City Supply Company on credit, $175.

e) Traded the old truck for additional tools.

f) Purchased for cash a secondhand truck to replace the one traded, $750.

g) Completed repair work for Walter Ruston and received $50 in full payment therefor.

h) Completed repair work for Walter Rice on credit, $75.

i) Completed repair work for Ralph Sims, $125. Accepted $80 in cash and a promise to pay the balance in few days.

j) Paid Tri-City Supply Company $100 of the amount owed to them.

k) Ralph Sims paid the amount he owed.

l) Paid the utility bills, $20.

m) Mr. Nash wrote a $65 check on the bank account of the business in payment of his personal living expenses.

Required:

1. Set up the following T-accounts: Cash; Ralph Sims; Walter Rice; Repair Supplies; Prepaid Rent; Office Equipment; Tools; Truck; Tri-City Supply Company; Barry Nash, Capital; Barry Nash, Withdrawals; Revenue from Repairs; Advertising Expense; and Utilities Expense.
2. Record the transactions by entering debits and credits directly in the T-accounts. Use the transactions letters to identify each debit and credit amount.
3. Prepare a trial balance using the current date.

Problem 2–2A

Kent Sims has just begun operating a cleaning and pressing plant he calls De Luxe Cleaners. During the first week in operation he completed the following transactions:

Sept. 21   Sold 100 personally owned shares of General Motors stock for $9,750 and deposited $8,500 of the proceeds in a checking account opened in the company name.

21   Purchased $8,000 of cleaning equipment, giving $6,000 in cash and a $2,000 promissory note payable.

Sept. 21   Paid the rent for two months in advance on the cleaning plant building, $300.

       22   Purchased $350 of additional cleaning equipment and $200 of cleaning supplies from Cortez Supply Company on credit.

       23   Delivered $175 of cleaning to customers for cash.

       24   Delivered $25 of cleaning to Modern Motel on credit.

       26   Collected the $25 owed by Modern Motel.

       26   Paid Cortez Supply Company $300 of the amount owed to them.

       27   Paid the wages of the employees, $150.

Required:

1. Open the following accounts: Cash; Modern Motel; Cleaning Supplies; Prepaid Rent; Cleaning Equipment; Notes Payable; Cortez Supply Company; Kent Sims, Capital; Revenue from Cleaning; and Wages Expense.
2. Prepare general journal entries to record the transactions; post to the accounts; and prepare a trial balance as of September 27.

Problem 2–3A

Thomas Howe began a real estate agency called Apex Realty Company, and during a short period completed the following transactions:

a) Began business by investing $10,000.

b) Purchased the small office building and office equipment of Cactus Realty Company, consisting of office equipment, $2,00; building, $12,000; and land, $4,000. Gave $8,000 in cash and signed a mortgage contract agreeing to pay the balance over a period of years.

c) Took his personal automobile, which had a fair market value of $2,500, for permanent and exclusive use in the business.

d) Earned and collected a $1,300 commission from the sale of a house.

e) Purchased $75 of office supplies and $250 additional office equipment from Valley Supply Company on credit.

f) Paid the salary of the office clerk, $110.

g) Billed Walter Haig $75 and George Ruston $60 for property management services performed.

h) Paid Valley Supply Company the amount owed to them.

i) Received a $60 check from George Ruston in payment for the services billed in transaction (*g*).

j) Purchased $65 of office supplies from Valley Supply Company on credit.

k) Earned and collected a $750 commission from the sale of property.

l) Paid the salary of the office clerk, $110.

m) Paid for newspaper advertising that had appeared, $85.

n) Paid the telephone and utilities bills, $25.

o) Mr. Howe wrote a check on the bank account of the realty company in payment of his personal living expenses, $250.

Required:

1. Open the following T-accounts: Cash; Walter Haig; George Ruston; Office Supplies; Office Equipment; Automobile; Land; Building; Valley Supply Company; Mortgage Payable; Thomas Howe, Capital; Thomas Howe, Withdrawals; Commissions Earned; Property Management Fees; Advertising Expense, Salaries Expense; and Telephone and Utilities.

2. Record the transactions by entering debits and credits directly in the T-accounts. Use the transaction letters to identify each debit and credit amount.
3. Prepare a trial balance.

Problem 2–4A

Neal Able began the practice of law and completed the following transactions during September of the current year:

Sept. 1 Began the practice of law by investing the legal library acquired during his college years. The library had a fair market value of $500.

2 Sold 30 shares of Republic Steel stock for $1,350 and deposited $1,250 of the proceeds in a bank account opened in the name of the law firm, Neal Able, Attorney.

2 Rented office space, paying $300, the first three months' rent in advance.

2 Purchased $1,500 of office equipment, paying $300 in cash and signing a promissory note payable for the balance.

3 Paid the premiums on several insurance policies taken out in the name of the law practice, $85.

5 Purchased $55 of office supplies and $115 of office equipment from Office Supply Company on credit.

8 Completed legal work for John Morehead and collected $150 in full payment therefor.

12 Billed First State Bank $250 for legal work completed for it.

15 Paid the semimonthly salary of the legal secretary, $120.

15 Paid Office Supply Company for the items purchased on September 5.

22 Received a $250 check from First State Bank in payment for the legal work billed on September 12.

27 Neal Able wrote a $150 check on the bank account of the law practice in payment of the rent on his apartment.

30 Billed First State Bank for additional legal work completed, $100.

30 Paid $5 interest and a $150 installment due on the note payable of the third September 2 transaction.

30 Paid the legal secretary's salary, $120.

30 Paid the utility bills of the month, $20.

Required:

1. Open the following accounts: Cash; First State Bank; Prepaid Rent; Office Supplies; Prepaid Insurance; Office Equipment; Legal Library; Note Payable; Office Supply Company; Neal Able, Capital; Neal Able, Withdrawals; Revenue from Law Practice; Salaries Expense; Utilities Expense; and Interest Expense.
2. Prepare general journal entries to record the transactions, post to the accounts, and prepare a trial balance in the name of Neal Able, Attorney.

Problem 2–5A

During October George Hunter began a small business that he called A-1 Cabinet Shop, and during the month he completed the following transactions:

Oct.   1   Withdrew $4,000 from his personal savings account and deposited it in a checking account opened in the name of A-1 Cabinet Shop.

      1   Paid $1,200 in cash for new shop machinery.

      2   Rented a shop building, paying three months' rent in advance, $195.

      3   Purchased $800 of shop supplies from Northside Planing Mill on credit.

      5   Bought $1,500 of additional shop machinery, giving $750 in cash and a promissory note payable for the balance.

      8   Delivered $350 of cabinet work to a customer and collected cash on delivery.

    10   Mr. Hunter took $50 of shop supplies home for use in repairing his carport.

    13   Billed David McKeen $450 for cabinet work delivered today.

    15   Paid the employees' wages for the first half of the month, $340.

    18   Sent Northside Planing Mill a check in full payment for the supplies purchased on October 3.

    23   Received a $200 check in partial payment for the cabinet work delivered to David McKeen on October 13.

    25   Collected $400 for cabinet work delivered to Robert Shell today.

    28   Mr. Hunter withdrew $150 from the business to be used to pay certain of his personal living expenses.

    31   Paid Motor Delivery Service $45 for delivery services rendered during October.

    31   Paid the light and power bill, $50.

    31   Paid the wages of the employees for the last half of the month, $350.

Required:

1. Open the following accounts, numbering them beginning with 1: Cash; David McKeen; Prepaid Rent; Shop Supplies; Shop Machinery; Notes Payable; Northside Planing Mill; George Hunter, Capital; George Hunter, Withdrawals; Revenue from Cabinet Work; Delivery Expense; Wages Expense; and Light and Power Expense.

2. Prepare general journal entries to record the transactions, post to the accounts, and prepare a trial balance.

DECISION PROBLEM 2—CITY MEAT MARKET

Walter Koch has operated City Meat Market for several months but has failed to keep a regular set of books. During the night of November 3 of the current year his market burned and he is now faced with the problem of supplying his insurance company with some proof of his loss.

Mr. Koch always took the day's cash receipts home at night and deposited all cash except that needed as a change fund the next morning. The morning following the fire he had $214 cash from the market at home. All other assets of the market (other than the land) were completely destroyed by the fire.

Mr. Koch's wife customarily paid the bills of the market. At the time of the fire she had the following unpaid invoices and bills at home:

Mercer Packing Company for meat and meat prod-
ucts..*$567*
Ace Supply Company for printing and supplies...... *42*
City Utility Department, water and lights........... *21*

All canceled checks and bank statements were destroyed in the fire, but Mrs. Koch had the checkbook at home and from its stubs and from other sources the following data were obtained:

1. Balance on deposit per checkbook on November 3, $897.
2. Mr. Koch originally invested the land, value $10,000, and the building, value $20,000, in which the business was operated.
3. Checks issued to date were for market equipment, $1,800; meat and meat products, $1,650; salaries, $900; other expenses, $370.
4. Bank deposits in summary were: $1,000 original investment of Mr. Koch; from daily receipts of the market, $4,617 (does not include the $214 of the last day's receipts).
5. The insurance adjuster agrees that nine days' supply of meat and meat products were on hand at date of the fire, amount $460.

Prepare a report to Mr. Koch including (1) a list of the assets, liabilities, and owner equity as of the date of the fire and (2) the amount of the loss caused by the fire.

Adjusting the Accounts

and

Preparing the Statements

ALTHOUGH a business has earnings whenever its revenues exceed its expenses, it is impossible to determine the exact earnings until after the business has completed its last transaction and all of its assets have been converted into cash. This is because it is impossible over a short period of time to measure precisely some items that enter into the calculation of earnings, for example, depreciation. Nevertheless, although earnings cannot be exactly measured over a short period, it is impractical to wait until the life of a business ends to learn its exact earnings. It is impractical because successful companies continue in business for many years, because income tax regulations require the payment each year of taxes on earnings, and because of management's need for information. Consequently, it has become universal practice to divide the life of a business into accounting periods of equal length, a year being the most common length, and to measure, as accurately as possible, the earnings of each period.

It has also become common practice at the end of each accounting period to prepare at least two financial reports or statements for a business. The first is called an *income statement*, and reports, as nearly as it can be measured, the gain or the loss incurred by the business during the accounting period. The second is called a *balance sheet*, and reports the end-of-the-period assets owned, liabilities owed, and the equity of the owner or owners. Both statements are prepared primarily from information contained in the accounts.

THE INCOME STATEMENT

The income statement is perhaps the more important of the two reports, because it shows how the business accomplished or failed to accomplish its primary objective, earning a "profit," or, as an accountant would say, earning a net income. As is demonstrated in Illustration 11, an income

---

Illustration 11

SNOWHITE LAUNDRY

Income Statement for Year Ended December 31, 19--

Revenue:
Laundry receipts $22,807

Operating expenses:
Laundry expenses:
Laundry wages. $8,400
Laundry supplies used.   960
Water and electricity.   384
Rent expense   1,200
Depreciation of laundry equipment   360
Total laundry expenses $11,304

Delivery expenses:
Delivery wages $4,200
Gas, oil, and repairs.   720
Depreciation of delivery equipment   480
Total delivery expenses.   5,400
Total operating expenses . . .   16,704
Net Income . . . . $ 6,103

---

statement shows how a net income was earned or a loss incurred by (1) listing the revenue earned, (2) listing with their totals the expenses incurred, and (3) showing, by subtracting the expenses from the revenue, the net income or net loss.

The Committee on Terminology of the American Institute of Certified Public Accountants recommends that when revenues exceed expenses, the excess be listed on the income statement as "net income."[1] This excess also sometimes appears as "net profit." However, since it is difficult to measure profit or loss exactly over a short period, many accountants prefer to use the term "net income" when revenues exceed expenses and "net loss" when expenses exceed revenues. These accountants reserve the word "profit" for describing the gain on a particular transaction, for instance, the sale of an asset.[2]

---

[1] *Accounting Terminology Bulletin No. 2*, "Proceeds, Revenue, Income, Profit, and Earnings" (New York: American Institute of Certified Public Accountants, 1955), pp. 3 and 4.

[2] *Ibid.*, pp. 3 and 4.

HEADING OF THE INCOME STATEMENT

An income statement is always prepared for a specific business and covers a specific period of time, and both the business name and period covered are always given in the statement's heading. Normally the heading is written on two lines, with the business name on the first and the name of the statement and the period covered on the second.

The time covered by an income statement is of extreme significance, because the items on the statement have no importance except when interpreted in connection with a period of time. For example, the item "Laundry receipts, $22,807," on the income statement of Illustration 11 has little significance until it is known that the amount represents one year's receipts and not the receipts of a week, a month, or six months.

CLASSIFICATION OF INCOME STATEMENT ITEMS

Selling a service or product normally requires the performance of several functions. For example, Snowhite Laundry of Illustration 11 performs at least two main functions: (1) laundering, and (2) delivering the finished laundry. Notice in Illustration 11 how the expenses are classified as either laundry expenses or delivery expenses. An income statement on which expenses are classified by functions is known as a *classified income statement.* Such a statement is more useful than an unclassified statement because it sets out the cost of each function and enables management to observe the variations in function costs when income statements of successive accounting periods are compared.

THE BALANCE SHEET

A balance sheet is a statement prepared to show financial position. It does this by listing the amounts of the various assets of the business for which it is prepared and the claims against these assets. In addition to showing assets and claims, a balance sheet, by classification and arrangement, also attempts to show the probability of an adequate supply of funds being available to meet each claim as it becomes due.

A balance sheet is closely related to the fundamental accounting equation. Actually, it is an elaboration of the equation in which the assets, liabilities, and owner equity are listed, and the sum of the assets is shown to be equal to the sum of the liabilities and owner equity. This may be seen by examining Illustration 12, where the sum of the assets, $41,259, equals the sum of the liabilities and owner equity, $41,259.

HEADING OF THE BALANCE SHEET

A balance sheet is prepared to show the financial position of a specific business on a specific date, and the business name and date are always

Illustration 12—A Report Form Balance Sheet

VALLEY HARDWARE STORE
Balance Sheet, December 31, 1966

ASSETS

Current Assets:
Cash		$ 1,050	
Notes receivable		300	
Accounts receivable.		3,961	
Merchandise inventory.		10,248	
Prepaid insurance.		109	
Office supplies.		46	
Stores supplies.		145	
Total Current Assets			$15,859

Fixed Assets:
Office equipment	$ 1,500		
Less: Accumulated depreciation	300	$ 1,200	
Store equipment.	$ 3,200		
Less: Accumulated depreciation	800	2,400	
Buildings.	$25,000		
Less: Accumulated depreciation	7,400	17,600	
Land		4,200	
Total Fixed Assets			25,400
Total Assets			$41,259

LIABILITIES

Current Liabilities:
Notes payable.		$ 3,000	
Accounts payable		2,715	
Accrued wages payable.		112	
Total Current Liabilities.		$ 5,827	

Long-Term Liabilities:
First-mortgage payable, secured by a mort-			
gage on land and buildings		10,000	
Total Liabilities.			$15,827

OWNER EQUITY

Samuel Jackson, capital, January 1, 1966 . . .		$23,721	
Net income for the year ended December 31,			
1966	$ 7,711		
Less: Withdrawals.	6,000		
Excess of income over withdrawals.		1,711	
Samuel Jackson, capital, December 31, 1966 . .			25,432
Total Liabilities and Owner Equity .			$41,259

shown in its heading. Since transactions change balance sheet amounts, the heading must give the exact date on which the statement is prepared. The date indicates that the balance sheet shows assets, liabilities, and owner equity at the close of business on that day.

CLASSIFICATION OF BALANCE SHEET ITEMS

A balance sheet showing a number of items becomes more useful when the items are classified into significant groups of assets and liabilities. This is because the reader of a *classified balance sheet* can thereby better judge the adequacy of the different kinds of assets used in the business, and he can also better estimate the probable availability of funds to meet the various liabilities as they become due.

Accountants are not in full agreement as to the best way in which to classify balance sheet items. Consequently, they are classified in several ways. One common way classifies assets into (1) current assets, (2) long-term investments, (3) fixed assets, (4) intangible assets, and (5) deferred charges. It classifies liabilities into (1) current liabilities, and (2) long-term or fixed liabilities.

Of the five asset classifications just listed, only two, current assets and fixed assets, appear on the balance sheet of Valley Hardware Store, Illustration 12, because the store is small and does not have long-term investments, intangible assets, or deferred charges. For a balance sheet showing all five classifications, examine Illustration 121 in Chapter 19.

CURRENT ASSETS

When a balance sheet is prepared, the assets listed under the current asset caption are primarily those to which the current creditors (current liabilities) may look for payment. As presently defined, current assets consist of (1) cash and assets that will be realized in cash within a short time, usually one year; and (2) prepaid expenses. The American Institute of Certified Public Accountants through its Committee on Accounting Procedure has defined current assets as "cash and other assets or resources commonly identified as those which are reasonably expected to be realized in cash or sold or consumed during the normal operating cycle of the business."[3] The words "or consumed" place prepaid expenses in the current asset classification. The Committee classifies prepaid expenses as current assets because, as it says: "Prepaid expenses are not current assets in the sense that they will be converted into cash but in the sense that, if not paid in advance, they would require the use of current assets during the operating cycle."

Notice in Illustration 12 that the sum of Valley Hardware Store's accounts receivable is shown in one amount, "Accounts receivable, $3,961." Retail companies selling on credit normally have from several dozen to several thousand accounts receivable, one for each credit customer, and it is the usual practice to show only the sum of their balances on the balance sheet. The same practice is also followed with accounts payable; and since the sum of all prepaid expenses is often not material in amount when compared with other current assets, the practice of showing only their total is also common.

---

[3] *Accounting Research Bulletin No. 43*, "Restatement and Revision of Accounting Research Bulletins" (New York: American Institute of Certified Public Accountants, 1953), p. 20.

LONG-TERM INVESTMENTS

The second balance sheet classification is long-term investments. Several items are placed under this caption. Among them are items that will be realized in cash but not within a year; and also items that will be realized in cash but, when realized, the cash will not be available to meet current debts. A more complete discussion of long-term investments is not needed at this time and is deferred until a later chapter.

FIXED ASSETS

Fixed assets are relatively long-lived assets that are held for use in the production or sale of other assets or services, for example, items of office equipment, store equipment, buildings, and land. The order in which fixed assets are listed within the balance sheet classification is not uniform; however, it is often from the ones of least permanent nature to those of most permanent nature.

INTANGIBLE ASSETS

Intangible assets are assets having no physical nature, their value being derived from the rights conferred upon their owner by their possession. Goodwill, patents, and trademarks are examples.

DEFERRED CHARGES

Long-term prepaid expenses are known as "deferred charges." They are the last asset classification. A full discussion of deferred charges is also unnecessary at this point, and it is delayed until a future chapter.

LIABILITY CLASSIFICATIONS

Most companies do not have as many liability items on their balance sheets as asset items. The two most common liability classifications are: (1) current liabilities, and (2) long-term liabilities.

Current Liabilities. Current liabilities are obligations that will become due within a short period, usually one year, and will normally be paid, when due, from current assets. The order of their listing is not uniform. Often notes payable are listed as the first current liability because notes receivable are listed first after cash in the current asset section. Common current liabilities are notes payable, accounts payable, wages payable, taxes payable, interest payable, and unearned revenues.

Unearned revenues, normally the last items in the current liability section, commonly grow out of transactions in which money is received for goods or services to be delivered at a future date. Subscriptions received in advance by a publisher, rent received in advance by a landlord, and payments received for future delivery of merchandise are examples. Each is a liability, an obligation to deliver goods or services at a future date. Each is classified as a current liability because current assets will normally be required in its liquidation. For example, payments for future delivery of merchandise will be earned and the obligation for delivery will be liquidated by delivering merchandise, a current asset.

Long-Term Liabilities. The second main liability classification is long-term liabilities. Liabilities that are not due and payable for a comparatively long period, usually more than one year, are listed under this classification. Common long-term liability items are mortgages payable and bonds payable.

OWNER EQUITY ON THE BALANCE SHEET

Owner equity, proprietorship, net worth, and capital are used synonymously in accounting. All four indicate the equity, in the assets, of the owner or owners of a business. Of the four terms, owner equity, proprietorship, and capital are considered the better. This is because the phrase "net worth" seems to indicate that the amount shown as the owner's equity is the net or exact "worth" of his equity, while, actually, the amount shown may or may not be the equity's "worth" on the balance sheet date. This is because when assets are purchased, they are recorded at cost; and in most cases until sold or consumed in the business operations, cost remains the basis upon which they are accounted for even though their "worth" may change. Thus, if a building lot is bought for $20,000, its purchase is recorded at $20,000 and the lot remains on the records at that amount even though a year later it may be sold for $30,000. The lot remains on the records at $20,000 until sold; and the change in its "worth" along with the resulting change in its owner's "net worth" is not recorded until a sale is completed.

The manner of reporting owner equity on a balance sheet depends upon the type of business for which the balance sheet is prepared. A business may be a single proprietorship, a partnership, or a corporation.

Single Proprietorship. When a business is owned by one person, it is called a single proprietorship and the owner's equity may be reported on the balance sheet as follows:

```
                        OWNER EQUITY

James Gibbs, capital, January 1, 1966                      $13,152
   Net income for year ended December 31, 1966. . . $3,753
   Withdrawals. . . . . . . . . . . . . . . . . . .  4,800
   Excess of withdrawals over earnings. . . . . . .            1,047
James Gibbs, capital, December 31, 1966. . . . . .         $12,105
```

The just illustrated manner of presenting owner equity shows the increase and decrease resulting from earnings and withdrawals. Some accountants prefer to put these details on a supplementary schedule attached to the balance sheet and called a statement of owner equity. When such a statement is prepared, owner equity is shown on the balance sheet as follows:

OWNER EQUITY

James Gibbs, capital (see schedule attached) . . . $12,105

Partnership. When two or more people own a business as partners, changes in their equities resulting from earnings and withdrawals are normally shown on a supplementary statement attached to the balance sheet and only the amount of each partner's equity and the total equities are shown on the balance sheet itself, as follows:

PARTNERS' EQUITIES

James Smith, capital $16,534
Robert Burns, capital. 18,506
   Total Partners' Equities $35,040

Corporation. Corporations are created under and are regulated by state and federal laws, and these laws require that a distinction be made between the amount invested in the corporation by its owners (its original stockholders) and the increase or decrease in that investment due to losses and gains. As a result, the equity of the owners or stockholders in a corporation's assets is commonly shown on its balance sheet as follows:

STOCKHOLDERS' EQUITY

Capital stock. $500,000
Retained earnings.   63,450
   Total Stockholders' Equity $563,450

The amount shown after "Capital stock" represents the orginal stockholder investment in the corporation, and the amount shown after "Retained earnings" is the increase in the equity resulting from retaining earnings in the business.

Partnerships and corporations are discussed in more detail later in this text.

NEED FOR ADJUSTMENTS BEFORE THE STATEMENTS ARE PREPARED

An income statement prepared at the end of an accounting period should reflect as nearly as it can be measured the revenue earned during the period and the amount of each expense incurred in earning the revenue. Likewise, a balance sheet prepared at that time should show as accurately as possible the amounts of the various assets, liabilities, and the owner's equity.

Occasionally, at the end of a period, statements reflecting proper amounts may be prepared directly from the accounts just as soon as all transactions are recorded. However, this is unusual. Normally, several account balances as they appear on the end-of-the-period trial balance do not show proper statement amounts. This is because some account balances become inaccurate for statement purposes simply through the expiration of costs brought about by the passage of time. For example, the second item on the

---

Illustration 13

OWEN REAL ESTATE AGENCY
Trial Balance, July 31, 19--

Cash.	$1,095	
Prepaid rent.	300	
Office supplies	60	
Automobile.	3,000	
Office equipment.	1,200	
A. B. Gordon Company.		$ 60
Standard Supply Co.		175
Larry Owen, capital		5,000
Larry Owen, withdrawals	200	
Commissions earned.		925
Office salaries expense	200	
Telephone and utilities	20	
Gas, oil, and repairs	25	
Advertising expense	60	
	$6,160	$6,160

---

trial balance of Owen Real Estate Agency, as prepared first in Chapter 2 and reproduced again as Illustration 13, is "Prepaid rent, $300." This $300 represents the rent for three months paid in advance on July 1. On July 31 $300 is not the correct amount for this asset because one month's rent, or $100, has expired and only $200 remains as an asset. Likewise, a portion of the office supplies as represented by the $60 debit balance in the Office Supplies account has been used; and the automobile and office equipment have begun to wear out and depreciate. Obviously, then, the end-of-the-period balances of the Prepaid Rent, Office Supplies, Automobile, and Office Equipment accounts, as they appear on the trial balance, simply do not reflect the proper amounts for preparing the July 31 statements. The balance of each and the balance of the Office Salaries Expense account must be *adjusted* before they will show proper amounts for the July 31 statements.

ADJUSTING THE ACCOUNTS

Prepaid Expenses. As the name implies, a prepaid expense is an expense that has been paid for in advance of its use. At the time of payment an asset is acquired that will be used or consumed and, as it is used or consumed, it will become an expense. For example:

On July 1 Owen Real Estate Agency paid three months' rent in advance. This payment gave the right to occupy a rented office for the following three months. On July 1 this right was an asset valued at its $300 cost; but day by day the agency occupied the office; and each day a portion of the prepaid rent expired and became an expense. On July 31 one month's rent, valued at one third of $300, or $100, had expired. Consequently, if the agency's July 31 accounts are to reflect proper asset and expense amounts, the following adjusting entry is required:

July	31	Rent Expense.............................	100.00	
		Prepaid Rent.........................		100.00
		To record the expired rent.		

Posting the adjusting entry has the following effect on the accounts:

Prepaid Rent				*Rent Expense*	
July 1	300	July 31	100	July 31	100

After the entry is posted, both the Prepaid Rent and the Rent Expense accounts show proper statement amounts.

To continue, early in July, Owen Real Estate Agency purchased some office supplies and placed them in the office for use; and each day the secretary used a portion. The amount used or consumed each day was an expense that daily reduced the assets and Owen's equity. However, the daily reductions were not recognized in the accounts because day-by-day information as to amounts used and remaining was not needed and because bookkeeping labor could be saved if only a single amount, the total used during the entire month, was recorded.

Consequently, if on July 31 the accounts are to reflect proper statement amounts, it is necessary to record the office supplies used during the month. To do this, it is first necessary to learn the amount used; and to learn the amount used, it is necessary to count or inventory the unused supplies remaining, and to deduct the amount remaining from the amount purchased. If, for example, $45 of unused supplies remain on hand in the office, then $15 ($60 − $45 = $15) of supplies have been used, and the following entry is required to record the supplies used:

July	31	*Office Supplies Used*........................	15.00	
		Office Supplies........................		15.00
		To record the supplies used.		

The effect of the foregoing adjusting entry on the accounts is:

Office Supplies		*Office Supplies Used*	
July 5 60	July 31 15	July 31 15	

Often, unlike in the two previous examples, items that are prepaid expenses at the time of purchase are both bought and fully consumed within the period between the beginning and end of a single accounting period. For example, a company that operates with annual accounting periods pays its rent in advance on the first day of each month. Each month the amount paid results in a prepaid expense that is entirely consumed before the month's end and before the end of the accounting period. In such cases, it is best to ignore the fact that an asset results from each prepayment. In such cases bookkeeping labor, an end-of-the-accounting-period adjustment, can be saved if each amount paid is recorded as an expense at the time of payment.

Other prepaid expenses that are handled in the same manner as prepaid rent and office supplies are prepaid insurance, store supplies, and factory supplies.

Depreciation. When a business buys a fixed asset, it in effect buys a "fund of usefulness"; and day by day, as the asset is used in carrying on the business operations, a portion of this "fund of usefulness" is consumed or expires. In accounting, this expiration of a fixed asset's "fund of usefulness" is known as *depreciation.*

Depreciation is an expense just like the expiration of prepaid rent is an expense. For example, if a company purchases and installs a machine at a total cost of $1,200, and the machine is expected to be worn-out and valueless at the end of ten years, the company has purchased a $1,200 fund of usefulness that, on a straight-line basis, expires and becomes an expense at the rate of $120 per year ($1,200 × $\frac{1}{10}$ = $120). Actually, the primary difference between depreciation and the expiration of a prepaid expense like rent or insurance is that, since it is often impossible to determine in advance just how long a fixed asset will last, the amount it depreciates each accounting period is commonly only an estimate.

Estimating and apportioning depreciation can be simple, as in the foregoing example, or it can become complex. A discussion of more complex situations is not necessary at this point and is deferred to Chapter 11. However, to illustrate the recording of depreciation, assume that—

On July 31 Owen Real Estate Agency estimated its automobile's depreciation for the month at $35 and the depreciation of its office equipment at $10. In both cases the depreciation reduced the assets and increased expenses. To record the depreciation the following adjusting entries are required:

July	31	*Depreciation Expense, Automobile*.....................	*35.00*	
		Accumulated Depreciation, Automobile..........		*35.00*
		To record the July depreciation.		
	31	*Depreciation Expense, Office Equipment*...............	*10.00*	
		Accumulated Depreciation, Office Equipment....		*10.00*
		To record the July depreciation.		

The effect of the entries on the accounts is:

Automobile		*Depreciation Expense, Automobile*	
July 3 *3,000*		*July 31* *35*	

Accumulated Depreciation, Automobile	
	July 31 *35*

Office Equipment		*Depreciation Expense, Office Equipment*	
July 3 *1,000*	*July 9* *150*	*July 31* *10*	
5 *350*			

Accumulated Depreciation, Office Equipment	
	July 31 *10*

Two important points should be observed in regard to the entries just given: (1) note that separate expense accounts are used in recording depreciation on each kind of fixed asset; and (2) that estimated depreciation is not credited directly to the fixed asset accounts.

Separate depreciation expense accounts are used because they make it possible on the income statement to classify the various depreciation expenses according to functions performed in carrying on the business operations. For example, a firm that owns and uses store equipment, office equipment, and delivery equipment should provide a Depreciation Expense, Store Equipment account; a Depreciation Expense, Office Equipment account; and a Depreciation Expense, Delivery Equipment account. The balance of the Depreciation Expense, Store Equipment account can then be placed on the income statement in the selling expense section, the office equipment depreciation expense can be placed in the administrative expense section, and the delivery equipment depreciation expense can be placed in the delivery expense section.

Depreciation is recorded at the end of each accounting period in a fixed asset's life. For example, in this illustration, at the end of the fourth month in the life of Owen Real Estate Agency's automobile the Automobile account and its related accumulated depreciation account will appear as follows:

Automobile		*Accumulated Depreciation, Automobile*	
July 3 *3,000*		*July 31* 35	
		Aug. 31 35	
		Sept. 30 35	
		Oct. 31 35	

And the automobile's cost and four months' accumulated depreciation will be shown on the agency's October 31 balance sheet as follows:

```
Automobile. . . . . . . . . . . . . . . . . . . $3,000
     Less:  Accumulated depreciation . . . . . .    140    $2,860
```

Normally, a decrease in an asset is recorded as a direct credit to the asset account. However, as the Automobile account and its related accumulated depreciation account show, this procedure is not followed in recording depreciation. Depreciation, as in the examples just given, is normally recorded in a *contra account* such as "Accumulated Depreciation, Automobile." (A contra account is an account the balance of which is subtracted from the balance of a second account to show a more proper amount for the items recorded in the second account.) There are good reasons for using contra accounts in recording depreciation. First, at its best, depreciation is only an estimate; and, second, the use of a contra account better preserves the facts of an asset's life. In this case the asset account, Automobile, preserves the auto's historical cost, and the Accumulated Depreciation, Automobile account shows its accumulated depreciation to date.

Accumulated depreciation accounts are commonly found in ledgers and on statements under titles such as "Allowance for Depreciation, Store Equipment" or "Reserve for Depreciation, Office Equipment." However, newer terminology is "Accumulated Depreciation, Store Equipment" and "Accumulated Depreciation, Office Equipment." The newer terminology is better because it is more descriptive.

Accrued Expenses. Most expenses are recorded during an accounting period at the time they are paid. However, when a period ends there are most always a few expenses that have been incurred but have not been paid and recorded because payment is not yet due. These unpaid and unrecorded expenses for which payment is not due are called *accrued expenses.* Earned but unpaid salaries and wages are a common example. To illustrate:

Owen Real Estate Agency has a secretary who is paid $10 per day or $50 per week for a five-day week that begins on Monday and ends on Friday. Her wages are due and payable every two weeks on Friday night; and during July were paid on the 12th and 26th and recorded as follows:

Cash			*Office Salaries Expense*		
July 12	*100*		*July 12*	*100*	
26	*100*		*26*	*100*	

If the calendar for July appears as illustrated and the secretary worked on Monday, Tuesday, and Wednesday, July 29, 30, and 31, then, at the close of business on Wednesday, July 31, she has earned three days' wages that are not paid and recorded because they are not yet due. However, this $30 of earned but unpaid wages is just as much a part of the July expenses as the $200 of wages that have been paid. Furthermore, on July 31, the unpaid wages are a liability. Consequently, if the agency's accounts are to show the correct amount of secretary's wages for July and all liabilities owed on July 31, then an adjusting entry like the following must be made:

JULY						
S	M	T	W	T	F	S
	1	2	3	4	5	6
7	8	9	10	11	12	13
14	15	16	17	18	19	20
21	22	23	24	25	26	27
28	29	30	31			

July	*31*	*Office Salaries Expense*...................... *30.00*		
		Salaries Payable.......................		*30.00*
		To record the earned but unpaid wages.		

The effect of the entry on the accounts is:

Office Salaries Expense		*Salaries Payable*	
July 12	*100*		
26	*100*	*July 31*	*30*
31	*30*		

THE ADJUSTED TRIAL BALANCE

A trial balance prepared before adjustments is known as an *unadjusted trial balance,* or simply as a trial balance. One prepared after adjusting entries are recorded and posted is known as an *adjusted trial balance.* If, after the adjustments are posted, an adjusted trial balance of the Owen Real Estate Agency ledger is prepared, it will appear as in Illustration 14.

Illustration 14

OWEN REAL ESTATE AGENCY
Adjusted Trial Balance, July 31, 19--

Cash.	$1,095	
Prepaid rent.	200	
Office supplies	45	
Automobile.	3,000	
Accumulated depreciation, automobile.		$　35
Office equipment.	1,200	
Accumulated depreciation, office equipment.		10
A. B. Gordon Company.		60
Standard Supply Co.		175
Salaries payable.		30
Larry Owen, capital		5,000
Larry Owen, withdrawals	200	
Commissions earned.		925
Office salaries expense	230	
Telephone and utilities	20	
Gas, oil, and repairs	25	
Advertising expense	60	
Rent expense.	100	
Office supplies used.	15	
Depreciation expense, automobile.	35	
Depreciation expense, office equipment.	10	
	$6,235	$6,235

PREPARING THE STATEMENTS FROM THE ADJUSTED TRIAL BALANCE

At the end of an accounting period the items on an adjusted trial balance show proper balance sheet and income statement amounts; and, consequently, the adjusted trial balance may be used in preparing the statements. To prepare statements from an adjusted trial balance is an easy task. All that is required is a rearrangement of the revenue and expense items into the income statement and a rearrangement of the asset, liability, and owner equity items into the balance sheet. To demonstrate the ease with which this may be accomplished, the revenue and expense items from the adjusted trial balance of Owen Real Estate Agency are rearranged into an income statement in Illustration 15 on page 69; and the asset, liability, and owner equity items are rearranged into a balance sheet in Illustration 16 on page 70.

When the statements are prepared from an adjusted trial balance, the income statement is normally prepared first because the net income, as calculated on the income statement, is needed in completing the balance sheet's owner equity section. Observe in Illustration 16 how the net income from the income statement is combined with the withdrawals, and the excess of income over withdrawals, $230, is added to Owen's July 1 capital to show his July 31 capital.

ARRANGEMENT OF THE ACCOUNTS IN THE LEDGER

Early in this chapter it was pointed out that asset, liability, owner equity, revenue, and expense amounts are classified and arranged on the statements in such a manner as to make the statements more useful. Likewise, accounts are classified and logically arranged in the ledger. A logical ledger arrangement has two purposes: (1) it aids in locating any account, and (2) it aids in preparing the statements. Obviously, statements can be prepared with the least difficulty if accounts are arranged in the ledger in the order of their statement appearance. This arrangement causes the accounts to appear on the adjusted trial balance in their statement order, which in turn aids in rearranging the adjusted trial balance items into a balance sheet and an income statement. Consequently, the balance sheet accounts beginning with the first current asset, cash, and ending with the owner equity accounts appear first in the ledger. These are followed by the revenue and expense accounts in the order of their income statement appearance.

QUESTIONS FOR CLASS DISCUSSION

1. Is the item "net income" as reported on an income statement the exact amount of income earned? Why?

Illustration 15

OWEN REAL ESTATE AGENCY
Adjusted Trial Balance, July 31, 19--

Cash.	$1,095	
Prepaid rent.	200	
Office supplies	45	
Automobile.	3,000	
Accumulated depreciation, automobile.		$ 35
Office equipment.	1,200	
Accumulated depreciation, office equipment		10
A. B. Gordon Company.		60
Standard Supply Co.		175
Salaries payable.		30
Larry Owen, capital		5,000
Larry Owen, withdrawals	200	
Commissions earned.		925
Office salaries expense	230	
Telephone and utilities	20	
Gas, oil, and repairs	25	
Advertising expense	60	
Rent expense.	100	
Office supplies used.	15	
Depreciation expense, automobile.	35	
Depreciation expense, office equipment.	10	
	$6,235	$6,235

PREPARING THE INCOME STATEMENT FROM THE ADJUSTED TRIAL BALANCE

OWEN REAL ESTATE AGENCY
Income Statement for Month Ended July 31, 19--

Revenue:		
Commissions earned.		$925
Operating expenses:		
Office salaries expense	$230	
Telephone and utilities	20	
Gas, oil, and repairs	25	
Advertising expense	60	
Rent expense.	100	
Office supplies used.	15	
Depreciation expense, automobile.	35	
Depreciation expense, office equipment.	10	
Total operating expenses.		495
Net Income.		$430

Illustration 16

OWEN REAL ESTATE AGENCY
Adjusted Trial Balance, July 31, 19--

Cash.	$1,095	
Prepaid rent.	200	
Office supplies	45	
Automobile.	3,000	
Accumulated depreciation, automobile. . .		$ 35
Office equipment.	1,200	
Accumulated depreciation, office equipment.		10
A. B. Gordon Company.		60
Standard Supply Co.		175
Salaries payable.		30
Larry Owen, capital.		5,000
Larry Owen, withdrawals	200	
Commissions earned.		925
Office salaries expense	230	
Telephone and utilities	20	
Gas, oil, and repairs	25	
Advertising expense	60	
Rent expense.	100	
Office supplies used.	15	
Depreciation expense, automobile.	35	
Depreciation expense, office equipment. .	10	
	$6,235	$6,235

OWEN REAL ESTATE AGENCY
Balance Sheet, July 31, 19--

ASSETS

Current Assets:
Cash.		$1,095	
Prepaid rent.		200	
Office supplies		45	
Total Current Assets.			$1,340
Fixed Assets:			
Automobile.	$3,000		
Less: Accumulated depreciation . .	35	$2,965	
Office equipment.	$1,200		
Less: Accumulated depreciation . .	10	1,190	
Total Fixed Assets			4,155
Total Assets.			$5,495

LIABILITIES

Current Liabilities:
A. B. Gordon Company.	$ 60	
Standard Supply Co.	175	
Salaries payable.	30	
Total Liabilities.		$ 265

OWNER EQUITY

Larry Owen, capital, July 1, 19-- . .			$5,000
July net income.	$ 430		
Less: Withdrawals.	200		
Net increase in capital		230	
Larry Owen, capital, July 31, 19--. .			5,230
Total Liab. and Owner Equity. . . .			$5,495

July net income
from the July
income statement

2. Why is the period of time covered by an income statement of extreme significance?

3. What is a classified income statement?

4. What are the characteristics of a current asset? A fixed asset?

5. If a current asset is an item that will be realized in cash or consumed within one year, how would you classify a note receivable that the owner intends to hold to its maturity which is three years hence?

6. Why are prepaid expenses classified as current assets?

7. Would it be possible to keep accounting records in such a manner that end-of-the-period adjustments of the accounts were unnecessary? Explain.

8. Why are adjustments usually necessary before statements can be prepared at the end of an accounting period?

9. If at the end of an accounting period an asset account called "Postage" has a $235 debit balance and there is $45 worth of postage stamps on hand, what adjustment is required?

10. What is a contra account?

11. If a firm's sales employees are paid a total of $500 per weekly pay period beginning on Monday and ending on Friday, what adjustment is required if the accounting period ends on Tuesday? On Thursday?

12. Under what situation might it be wise to record the payment of a prepaid expense as an expense? Why?

13. On September 1 a company debited Prepaid Insurance for $180, the premium on a three-year policy paid that day. What adjustment is required when the accounting period ends on December 31? What are the effects on the balance sheet and income statement prepared on December 31 if the adjustment is not made?

14. On January 1 of the current year the balance of the Advertising Supplies account was $84. During the year $312 of advertising supplies were purchased. On December 31 an inventory showed $124 of supplies on hand. What adjustment is required? What are the effects on the balance sheet and income statement if the adjustment is not made?

PROBLEMS

Problem 3–1

On December 31, at the end of a yearly accounting period, the following information for adjustments was available:

a) The Prepaid Insurance account carried the following items:

Prepaid Insurance

Jan. 1	Balance	110
Mar. 1		180
Dec. 1		132

The January 1 balance represented the unexpired premium on a one-year policy purchased on December 1 of the previous year. The March 1 debit resulted from paying the premium on a three-year policy and the December 1 debit represented the cost of a one-year policy.

b) The Office Supplies account had an $85.50 balance at the beginning of the year, $321.15 of office supplies were purchased during the year, and an inventory of unused office supplies on hand at the year-end totaled $106.40.

c) The three office employees earn $12 per day, $15 per day, and $18 per day, respectively. They are paid each Friday for a weekly pay period that begins on Monday. This week they have worked on Monday and Tuesday, December 30 and 31.

d) The company owns and occupies a building that was completed and occupied for the first time on May 1 of the current year. Previously the company had occupied rented quarters. The building cost $96,000, had an estimated 40-year useful life, and was not expected to have any salvage value at the end of that time.

Required:

(1) Give the adjusting entry required by each of the foregoing units of information, and (2) in each case tell the effect on the balance sheet and income statement of failing to make the adjustment.

Problem 3–2

Pinetop Realty Company operates with annual accounting periods that end each December 31. At the end of the current year, after all transactions were recorded, a trial balance of the concern's ledger appeared as follows:

PINETOP REALTY COMPANY
Trial Balance December 31, 19—

Cash...	$ 3,120	
Prepaid insurance................................	195	
Office supplies..................................	335	
Office equipment................................	2,975	
Accumulated depreciation, office equipment.....		$ 615
Automobile......................................	3,645	
Accumulated depreciation, automobile...........		1,150
Scottsdale Evening News.........................		90
Wayne Norling, capital..........................		6,085
Wayne Norling, withdrawals.....................	8,600	
Commissions earned.............................		16,370
Salaries expense................................	3,530	
Advertising expense.............................	565	
Rent expense....................................	1,200	
Telephone expense..............................	145	
	$24,310	$24,310

Required:

1. Open the accounts of the trial balance plus these additional ones: Expired Insurance; Office Supplies Used; Depreciation of Office Equipment; Depreciation of Automobile; and Salaries Payable. Enter the trial balance amounts in the accounts.

2. Use the following information to prepare and post adjusting entries:
    a) Insurance expired during the year, $130.
    b) An inventory of office supplies showed $105 of supplies on hand.
    c) Estimated depreciation of office equipment, $265; and of automobile, $575.
    d) Four days' of accrued wages at $15 per day had been earned by the office clerk but were unpaid on December 31.
3. Prepare an adjusted trial balance, income statement, and classified balance sheet.

Problem 3–3

Rapid Delivery Service operates with annual accounting periods that end each December 31. On that date of the current year a trial balance of its ledger carried the following balances:

RAPID DELIVERY SERVICE
Trial Balance, December 31, 19—

Cash	$ 1,175	
Hertz Department Store	165	
Fair Discount Store	210	
Prepaid insurance	380	
Office supplies	245	
Office equipment	1,965	
Accumulated depreciation, office equipment		$ 790
Delivery equipment	11,960	
Accumulated depreciation, delivery equipment		3,425
Notes payable (due in five months)		1,200
Service Garage		115
Walter Knott, capital		6,685
Walter Knott, withdrawals	5,400	
Revenue from delivery service		32,235
Office rent expense	550	
Office salaries expense	3,475	
Telephone and utilities expense	215	
Truck drivers' wages	15,990	
Gas, oil, and repairs	1,895	
Garage rent expense	825	
	$44,450	$44,450

Required:
1. Open the accounts of the trial balance plus these additional ones: Rent Payable; Salaries and Wages Payable; Depreciation of Office Equipment; Insurance Expense, Office Equipment; Office Supplies Used; Depreciation of Delivery Equipment; and Insurance Expense, Delivery Equipment. Enter the trial balance amounts in the accounts.
2. Prepare and post adjusting journal entries, using the following information:
    a) Expired insurance on office equipment, $45; and on delivery equipment, $185.
    b) Office supplies used during the year, $175.

c) Estimated depreciation of office equipment, $135; and of delivery equipment, $1,110.

d) Accrued office salaries payable, $45; and accrued truck drivers' wages, $220.

e) Rapid Delivery Service rents a small building for $125 per month, $50 of which it charges to Office Rent Expense and $75 of which it charges to Garage Rent Expense. Rent for the month of December had not been paid on the trial balance date. (Treat as an accrued expense.)

3. After posting the adjusting entries, prepare an adjusted trial balance, a classified income statement, and a classified balance sheet. On the income statement classify expenses as either office expenses or delivery expenses.

Problem 3–4

In the first two money columns below is the December 31 trial balance of U-Bowl, and in the third and fourth columns is its adjusted trial balance of the same date:

U-BOWL
Trial Balance and Adjusted Trial Balance, December 31, 19—

Cash..............................	$ 3,235	$	$ 3,235	$ .....
Bowling supplies...................	1,175	.....	325	.....
Prepaid insurance..................	865	.....	355	.....
Bowling equipment.................	32,550	.....	32,550	.....
Accumulated depreciation, bowling equipment......................	.....	8,140	.....	11,395
Building.........................	92,600	.....	92,600	.....
Accumulated depreciation, building	.....	8,560	.....	10,400
Land............................	12,500	.....	12,500	.....
Brunswick Corporation.............	.....	585	.....	585
Salaries payable...................	.....	.....	.....	215
Property taxes payable.............	.....	.....	.....	325
Interest payable...................	.....	.....	.....	255
Mortgage payable..................	.....	76,000	.....	76,000
Gary Lipscomb, capital.............	.....	38,115	.....	38,115
Gary Lipscomb, withdrawals........	6,000	.....	6,000	.....
Bowling revenue...................	.....	31,980	.....	31,980
Salaries expense...................	12,440	.....	12,655	.....
Advertising expense................	675	.....	675	.....
Heat, lights, and power.............	1,340	.....	1,340	.....
Bowling supplies used..............	.....	.....	850	.....
Insurance expense, bowling equipment.........................	.....	.....	135	.....
Insurance expense, building.........	.....	.....	375	.....
Depreciation of bowling equipment.	.....	.....	3,255	.....
Depreciation of building............	.....	.....	1,840	.....
Property taxes expense.............	.....	.....	325	.....
Interest expense...................	.....	.....	255	.....
	$163,380	$163,380	$169,270	$169,270

Required:

Analyze the two trial balances and prepare in general journal form the adjusting entries that were made by U-Bowl.

Problem 3–5

At the close of business on the last day of its annual accounting period the following trial balance was taken from the ledger of Valet Cleaners:

VALET CLEANERS
Trial Balance, December 31, 19—

Cash..	$ 1,057	
Cleaning and pressing supplies..................	569	
Prepaid insurance.............................	352	
Prepaid rent..................................	600	
Cleaning and pressing equipment...............	15,154	
Accumulated depreciation, cleaning and pressing		
equipment...................................		$ 3,352
Delivery equipment...........................	5,534	
Accumulated depreciation, delivery equipment...		1,845
Walter Robbins, capital.......................		13,394
Walter Robbins, withdrawals...................	7,200	
Cleaning and pressing revenue.................		32,234
Cleaning plant wages..........................	10,678	
Rent expense.................................	1,050	
Heat, lights, and power.......................	886	
Truck drivers' wages..........................	7,184	
Gas, oil, and repairs..........................	561	
	$50,825	$50,825

The following information for adjusting entries was available:

a) The inventory of unused cleaning and pressing supplies totaled $135.

b) Examination of insurance policies showed: expired insurance cleaning and pressing equipment, $107; and delivery equipment, $152.

c) On January 1, at the beginning of the year, four months' rent was prepaid on the building occupied by the cleaning plant. Rent for the months of May through November was paid on the first day of each of these months and was debited on payment to the Rent Expense account. Rent for December was unpaid on the trial balance date.

d) Depreciation of cleaning and pressing equipment, $1,170; and depreciation of delivery trucks, $847.

e) There were accrued cleaning plant wages of $87 and accrued truck drivers wages of $38 on the trial balance date.

f) On the trial balance date there were unpaid and unrecorded personal property taxes accrued on the cleaning and pressing equipment amounting to $167. The taxes were applicable to year ended that date.

Required:

1. Open the accounts of the trial balance plus any additional accounts needed, and enter the trial balance amounts in the accounts.

2. Prepare and post adjusting entries.
3. Prepare an adjusted trial balance, classified income statement, and classified balance sheet.

CLASS EXERCISE

Exercise 3–1

Early in January of this year Walter Nash began a new business, called Quick Delivery Service, with a motorcycle having a fair market value of $500 and $100 in cash. He has kept no accounting records and now, at the year-end, has engaged you to determine the amount of his net income or loss for the year. You find that the year-end bank balance of Quick Delivery Service is $775, and there is $15 in the office cashbox. The company still has the motorcycle, but it has depreciated $100 during the year. In addition it has a new delivery truck that cost $3,000, which has depreciated $150 since its purchase, and on which the concern still owes the finance company $1,700. When the truck was purchased, Mr. Nash borrowed, free of interest, $1,000 from his father-in-law to be used as the down payment. The loan has not been repaid. Finally, Mr. Nash has withdrawn from the business $100 per week (52 weeks) to be used for personal living expense.

Required:
Determine the income or loss of the business for the year.

ALTERNATE PROBLEMS

Problem 3–1A

Prepare a neat calculation for each of the following:
1. Calculate the number of dollars of store supplies consumed during the accounting period when (*a*) the balance of the store supplies account at the beginning of the period was $217; (*b*) $356 of store supplies were purchased during the accounting period; and (*c*) there were $187 of unused store supplies on hand at the end of the period.
2. Determine the balance of the Office Supplies account after adjusting entries were posted when (*a*) the account balance at the beginning of the accounting period was $246; (*b*) $457 of office supplies were purchased during the period; and (*c*) $513 of supplies were used during the period.
3. Determine the number of dollars of office supplies bought during the accounting period when (*a*) the balance of the Office Supplies account at the beginning of the period was $239; (*b*) the balance of the account at the end of the period was $197; and (*c*) $317 of office supplies were used during the period.
4. Calculate the beginning-of-the-period balance of a company's store supplies account when the company (*a*) purchased $523 of store supplies during the accounting period; (*b*) its income statement for the period

showed an expense item of $493 for store supplies used; and (c) its end-of-the-period balance sheet showed an asset item, "Store supplies, $247."

Problem 3–2A

Mesa Realty Company operates with annual accounting periods that end each December 31. At the end of the current year, after all transactions were recorded, a trial balance of the concern's ledger appeared as follows:

MESA REALTY COMPANY
Trial Balance, December 31, 19—

Cash..	$ 3,120	
Prepaid insurance..............................	195	
Office supplies................................	335	
Office equipment..............................	2,975	
Accumulated depreciation, office equipment.....		$ 615
Automobile....................................	3,645	
Accumulated depreciation, automobile...........		1,150
Scottsdale Evening News........................		90
Wayne Norling, capital.........................		6,085
Wayne Norling, withdrawals.....................	8,600	
Commissions earned............................		16,370
Salaries expense...............................	3,530	
Advertising expense............................	565	
Rent expense..................................	1,200	
Telephone expense.............................	145	
	$24,310	$24,310

Required:

1. Open the accounts of the trial balance plus these additional ones: Expired Insurance; Office Supplies Used; Depreciation of Office Equipment; Depreciation of Automobile; and Salaries Payable. Enter the trial balance amounts in the accounts.
2. Use the following information to prepare and post adjusting entries:
   a) Insurance expired during the year, $155.
   b) An inventory of office supplies showed $145 of supplies on hand.
   c) Estimated depreciation of office equipment, $280; and of automobile, $610.
   d) Two days' wages at $15 per day had been earned by the office clerk but were unpaid on December 31 because they were not due.
3. Prepare an adjusted trial balance, income statement, and classified balance sheet.

Problem 3–3A

On December 31 of the current year, at the end of its annual accounting period, the following trial balance was taken from the ledger of Snowhite Laundry:

SNOWHITE LAUNDRY
Trial Balance, December 31, 19—

Cash	$ 1,235	
Valley Hotel	110	
Prepaid insurance	330	
Laundry supplies	465	
Laundry equipment	10,140	
Accumulated depreciation, laundry equipment		$ 2,885
Delivery equipment	5,960	
Accumulated depreciation, delivery equipment		2,455
Building	21,975	
Accumulated depreciation, building		6,250
Land	4,500	
Eager Service Station		115
Mortgage payable		10,000
Warren McGraw, capital		16,535
Warren McGraw, withdrawals	6,000	
Laundry revenue		24,240
Laundry plant wages	7,220	
Heat, lights, and power	485	
Delivery wages	3,540	
Gas, oil, and repairs	520	
	$62,480	$62,480

Required:

1. Open the accounts of the trial balance plus these additional ones: Expired Insurance, Laundry Plant; Expired Insurance, Delivery Equipment; Laundry Supplies Used; Depreciation Expense, Laundry Equipment; Depreciation Expense, Delivery Equipment; Depreciation Expense, Building; and Wages Payable. Enter the trial balance amounts in the accounts.

2. Use the following information to prepare and post adjusting journal entries:

   a) An examination of insurance policies showed expired insurance, laundry plant, $145; and expired insurance, delivery equipment, $130.

   b) An inventory of laundry supplies showed $115 of unused laundry supplies on hand.

   c) Estimated depreciation of laundry equipment, $755; of delivery equipment, $640; and of building, $390.

   d) There were accrued laundry plant wages of $105 and delivery wages of $50.

   e) Through an oversight, a delivery truck driver had failed to turn in charge tickets for gas and oil placed in a delivery truck during the week ended December 31 by Eager Service Station; consequently, these tickets totaling $10 were unrecorded when the trial balance above was prepared.

3. After posting the adjusting entries, prepare an adjusted trial balance, a classified income statement, and a classified balance sheet.

Problem 3—4A

An inexperienced bookkeeper prepared the first of the following two income statements, but he forgot to adjust the ledger accounts before its preparation. However, the oversight was discovered and the second correct statement was prepared. Analyze the two statements and prepare the adjusting journal entries that were made between the construction of the statements.

DESERT REALTY COMPANY
Income Statement for Year Ended December 31, 19—

Revenue:		
Commissions earned		*$22,345.50*
Operating expenses:		
Office salaries	*$7,115.23*	
Entertainment expense	*942.47*	
Rent expense	*1,375.00*	
Advertising expense	*1,116.74*	
Utilities expense	*356.87*	
Telephone expense	*291.43*	
Gas, oil, and repairs	*379.78*	
Total operating expenses		*11,577.52*
Net Income		*$10,767.98*

DESERT REALTY COMPANY
Income Statement for Year Ended December 31, 19—

Revenue:		
Commissions earned		*$22,345.50*
Operating expenses:		
Office salaries	*$7,204.31*	
Entertainment expense	*942.47*	
Rent expense	*1,500.00*	
Advertising expense	*1,116.74*	
Utilities expense	*356.87*	
Telephone expense	*302.51*	
Gas, oil, and repairs	*379.78*	
Office supplies used	*143.25*	
Expired insurance	*123.15*	
Depreciation of office equipment	*156.50*	
Depreciation of automobile	*610.00*	
Total operating expenses		*12,835.58*
Net Income		*$ 9,509.92*

DECISION PROBLEM 3—RICHEY LOCKSMITH

Morton Richey operates a small locksmith business, being assisted by his son, Dan, and one employee. He pays the employee $60 per week. His son is unmarried and lives with his parents. The father and son had agreed to share the profits equally. At the end of the first year Mr. Richey states that he "figures" the shop made a profit of $8,000. He and Dan agree, however, that the business has little money to evidence this profit. They ask you to investigate and report to them on the reality of their profitability estimate and to make recommendations for more precise accounting.

Upon investigation you discover the following facts:

1. No regular set of books has been maintained. They have retained all canceled checks and bank statements. They have two unpaid invoices for key blanks and other supplies, totaling $420.

2. Both Mr. Richey and Dan by mutual agreement drew cash from daily receipts to meet living costs and personal expenses. No record was kept of these drawings. Both agree that Mr. Richey withdrew several times as much as Dan, since he needed to pay the cost of maintaining the home.

3. The initial capital of $2,000 cash was invested by Mr. Richey. Dan invested nothing in the business, but it was agreed that Dan would leave at least half of his share of profits in the business until his capital equaled that of his father.

4. The building in which the shop is located is rented for $180 per month. Assets and liabilities of the locksmiths are:

Cash...$ *280*
Machinery and tools......................... *1,910*
Furniture, workbenches, etc.................. *1,260*
Key blanks and supplies......................   *328*
Accounts payable............................   *420*
Notes payable............................... *1,600*

In the report present (*a*) a statement of the present equities of the shop owners; (*b*) comments on Mr. Richey's estimate of the profit for the year; (*c*) an explanation of the probable causes for change in owner equities; and (*d*) recommendations for improvements in accounting for the shop.

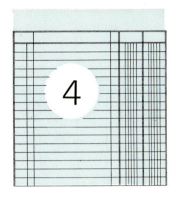

4

Balance Column Accounts, the Work Sheet, and Clearing the Accounts

SINCE THEY have definite debit and credit sides, accounts like the ones in the previous two chapters help a beginning student learn debits and credits. However, when such accounts are used and it becomes necessary to know the balance of an account, the balance must be calculated; and this is at times inconvenient. Consequently, since a student should by now have some understanding of debits and credits, it is time to introduce a more convenient and more commonly used kind of account, the *balance column account*.

BALANCE COLUMN ACCOUNT

Illustration 17 shows a balance column account. Such an account differs from the accounts in the previous chapters in that its debit and credit columns are placed side by side and a third or Balance column is provided for the account's current balance. In this Balance column the account's new balance is entered each time the account is debited or credited. For example, in Illustration 17 the account was debited to record the purchase of office equipment on July 3, and with this entry its balance became $1,000. On July 5 the account was debited again and its new $1,350 balance entered; and on July 9 it was credited for $150 and its balance reduced to $1,200.

From the foregoing illustration the convenience of a Balance column in

Illustration 17

DATE	EXPLANATION	FO-LIO	DEBIT	CREDIT	BALANCE
1966					
July 3		1	1 000 00		1 000 00
5		1	350 00		1 350 00
9		1		150 00	1 200 00

Office Equipment   ACCOUNT NO. 7

an account is obvious, at any time it shows at a glance the current balance of the account.

When a balance column account like that of Illustration 17 is used, the heading of the Balance column does not tell whether the balance is a debit balance as, for example, it would normally be for an asset account or a credit balance as it would normally be for a liability. However, this does not create a problem because an account is always assumed to have its normal kind of balance, unless the contrary is indicated in the account.

The Normal Balance of an Account. Since its column headings do not tell the nature of an account's balance and the balance is always assumed to be the normal kind for that account, unless otherwise indicated, it follows that an accountant must know the normal balance of any account. Fortunately this is not difficult because the balance of an account normally results from recording in it a larger sum of increases than decreases. Consequently, if increases are recorded as debits, the account normally has a debit balance; and if increases are recorded as credits, the account normally has a credit balance. Or, increases are recorded in an account in each of the following classes as shown and its normal balance is:

Type of Account	Increases Are Recorded as—	And the Normal Balance Is—
Asset	Debits	Debit
Contra asset	Credits	Credit
Liability	Credits	Credit
Owner equity:		
Capital	Credits	Credit
Withdrawals	Debits	Debit
Revenue	Credits	Credit
Expense	Debits	Debit

An Account with a Different from Normal Balance. When an unusual transaction causes an account to have a balance different from its normal kind, this different from normal balance is indicated in the account by entering it in red or by entering it in black and encircling the amount as in the customer account shown in Illustration 18.

The account of Illustration 18 is an account receivable, and when it has

Illustration 18

Z. M. Pope
1114 First Avenue, Portland, Oregon   ACCOUNT NO.

DATE	EXPLANATION	FO-LIO	DEBIT	CREDIT	BALANCE
1966					
May 4		16	123 00		123 00
14	Overpaid account	17		132 00	(9 00)

a balance, the balance is normally a debit. However, in this instance the customer made an error and overpaid his account, changing its normal debit balance to a $9 credit balance. Notice how this is shown by encircling the $9 amount.

An Account Without a Balance. When a posting to a balance column account causes the account to have no balance, some bookkeepers place a –0–, in the Balance column on the line of the posting. Others and bookkeeping machines write 0.00 in the Balance column to indicate the account does not have a balance.

NEED FOR A WORK SHEET

In the accounting procedures described in the previous chapter, at the end of an accounting period, as soon as all transactions were recorded, (1) adjusting entries were entered in the journal and posted to the accounts and, (2) an adjusted trial balance was prepared and used in making an income statement and balance sheet. For a small business these are satisfactory procedures.

However, if a company has more than a very few accounts and adjustments, errors in adjusting the accounts and constructing the statements are less apt to be made if an additional step is inserted in the procedures. The additional step is the preparation of a *work sheet*. When a work sheet is prepared, it is prepared before the statements are constructed and before the adjusting entries are entered in the journal and posted. Actually, the work sheet is a tool for bringing together in an orderly manner the information used in preparing the statements, adjusting entries, and clearing entries. (Clearing entries are discussed in more detail later in this chapter.)

A work sheet differs from a balance sheet or an income statement in that it is normally prepared with a pencil. A work sheet is a tool of the accountant upon which he (1) achieves the effect of adjusting the accounts before entering the adjustments in the accounts, (2) sorts the adjusted account balances into columns according to whether they are used in preparing the income statement or balance sheet, and (3) calculates and proves the mathematical accuracy of the net income. It is not for publication or management's use, and preparing it with a pencil makes changes and corrections easy as its preparation progresses.

PREPARING A WORK SHEET

Owen Real Estate Agency of the previous chapters does not have sufficient accounts or adjustments to warrant use of a work sheet. However, since its transactions and adjustments are familiar, they may be used to illustrate the preparation of a work sheet.

During July, Owen Real Estate Agency completed a number of transactions; and on July 31, after these transactions were recorded, but BEFORE ANY ADJUSTING ENTRIES WERE PREPARED AND POSTED, a trial balance of its ledger appeared as in Illustration 19.

Illustration 19

OWEN REAL ESTATE AGENCY
Trial Balance, July 31, 19--

Cash.	$1,095	
Prepaid rent.	300	
Office supplies	60	
Automobile.	3,000	
Office equipment.	1,200	
A. B. Gordon Company.		$ 60
Standard Supply Co.		175
Larry Owen, capital		5,000
Larry Owen, withdrawals	200	
Commissions earned.		925
Office salaries expense	200	
Telephone and utilities	20	
Gas, oil, and repairs	25	
Advertising expense	60	
	$6,160	$6,160

Notice that the illustrated trial balance is an UNADJUSTED TRIAL BALANCE. The accounts have not been adjusted for expired rent, supplies consumed, depreciation, and accrued wages. Nevertheless, this unadjusted trial balance is the starting point in preparing a work sheet, and it is copied in the first two money columns of the work sheet form.

THE WORK SHEET ILLUSTRATED

Note that the work sheet shown in Illustration 20 has five pairs of money columns, and that the first pair is labeled "Trial Balance." In this first pair of columns is copied the unadjusted trial balance of Owen Real Estate Agency. Often when a work sheet is prepared, the trial balance is prepared for the first time in its first two money columns.

Illustration 20

Owen Real Estate Agency
Work Sheet for Month Ended July 31, 19--

ACCOUNT TITLES	TRIAL BALANCE		ADJUSTMENTS		ADJUSTED TRIAL BALANCE		INCOME STATEMENT		BALANCE SHEET	
	DR.	CR.	DR.	CR.	DR.	CR.	DR.	CR.	DR.	CR.
Cash	1,095.00				1,095.00				1,095.00	
Prepaid rent	300.00			(a) 100.00	200.00				200.00	
Office supplies	60.00			(b) 15.00	45.00				45.00	
Automobile	3,000.00				3,000.00				3,000.00	
Office equipment	1,200.00				1,200.00				1,200.00	
A.B. Rollins Company		60.00				60.00				60.00
Standard Supply Co.		175.00				175.00				175.00
Larry Owen, Capital		5,000.00				5,000.00				5,000.00
Larry Owen, Withdrawals	200.00				200.00				200.00	
Commissions earned		925.00				925.00		925.00		
Office salaries expense	200.00		(e) 30.00		230.00		230.00			
Telephone and utilities	20.00				20.00		20.00			
Gas, oil, and repairs	25.00				25.00		25.00			
Advertising expense	60.00				60.00		60.00			
	6,160.00	6,160.00								
Rent expense			(a) 100.00		100.00		100.00			
Office supplies used			(b) 15.00		15.00		15.00			
Depr. expense, automobile			(c) 35.00		35.00		35.00			
Accum. depr., automobile				(c) 35.00		35.00				35.00
Depr. expense, office equip.			(d) 10.00		10.00		10.00			
Accum. depr., office equip.				(d) 10.00		10.00				10.00
Salaries payable				(e) 30.00		30.00				30.00
			190.00	190.00	6,235.00	6,235.00	495.00	925.00	5,740.00	5,310.00
Net Income							430.00			430.00
							925.00	925.00	5,740.00	5,740.00

The second pair of work sheet columns is labeled "Adjustments," and the adjustments are entered in these columns. In the work sheet shown in Illustration 20, the adjustments are the same as those for which adjusting journal entries were prepared and posted in the previous chapter, prior to the construction of the statements. Note that the adjustments on the illustrated work sheet are keyed together with letters. When a work sheet is prepared, after it and the statements are completed, the adjusting entries still have to be entered in the journal and posted to the ledger. At that time the key letters help identify each adjustment's related debits and credits. Explanations of the adjustments on the illustrated work sheet are:

Adjustment (*a*): To adjust for the rent expired.
Adjustment (*b*): To adjust for the office supplies consumed.
Adjustment (*c*): To adjust for depreciation of the automobile.
Adjustment (*d*): To adjust for depreciation of the office equipment.
Adjustment (*e*): To adjust for the accrued secretary's wages.

Each adjustment on the Owen Real Estate Agency work sheet required that one or two additional account names be written in below the original trial balance. These accounts did not have balances when the trial balance was prepared, and, consequently, were not listed in the trial balance. Often, when a work sheet is prepared, the effects of the adjustments are anticipated; and any additional accounts required are provided, without amounts, in the body of the trial balance.

When a work sheet is prepared, after the adjustments are entered in the Adjustments columns, the columns are totaled to prove the equality of the adjustments.

The third set of work sheet columns is labeled "Adjusted Trial Balance." In constructing a work sheet each individual amount in the Trial Balance columns is combined with its adjustment in the Adjustments columns, if there is an adjustment, and is entered in the Adjusted Trial Balance columns. For example, in Illustration 20, the Prepaid Rent account has a $300 debit balance in the Trial Balance columns. This $300 debit is combined with the $100 credit in the Adjustments columns to give the Prepaid Rent account a $200 debit balance in the Adjusted Trial Balance columns. Rent Expense has no balance in the Trial Balance columns, but it has a $100 debit in the Adjustments columns. Therefore, no balance combined with a $100 debit gives Rent Expense a $100 debit in the Adjusted Trial Balance columns. Cash, Standard Supply Company, and several other accounts have trial balance amounts but no adjustments. As a result, their trial balance amounts are carried unchanged into the Adjusted Trial Balance columns. Notice that the result of combining the amounts in the Trial Balance columns with the amounts in the Adjustments columns is an adjusted trial balance in the Adjusted Trial Balance columns.

After the amounts in the Trial Balance columns are combined with the amounts in the Adjustments columns and carried to the Adjusted Trial Balance columns, the Adjusted Trial Balance columns are added to prove their equality. Then, after equality is proved, the amounts in these columns are sorted to the proper Balance Sheet or Income Statement columns according to the statement on which they will appear. The asset amounts are carried to the Balance Sheet debit column. The liability amounts and the balance of the Capital account go to the Balance Sheet credit column. The balances of the accumulated depreciation accounts represent subtractions from assets; consequently, their amounts are placed in the Balance Sheet credit column. Likewise, the balance of the Withdrawals account represents a subtraction from owner equity and is placed in the Balance Sheet debit column. The revenue amounts go to the Income Statement credit column and the expense amounts to the Income Statement debit column.

After the amounts are sorted to the proper columns, the columns are totaled; and at this point, the difference between the debit total and the credit total of the Income Statement columns is the net income or loss. The difference is the net income or loss because revenues are entered in the credit column and expenses in the debit column. If the credit column total exceeds the debit column total, the difference is a net income; and if the debit column total exceeds the credit column total, the difference is a net loss. In the illustrated work sheet, the credit column total exceeds the debit column total, and the result is a $430 net income.

On the Owen Real Estate Agency's work sheet, after the net income is determined in the Income Statement columns, it is added to the total of the Balance Sheet credit column. The reason for this is that, with the exception of the balance of the Capital account, the amounts appearing in the Balance Sheet columns are "end-of-the-period" amounts. Therefore, it is necessary to add the net income to the Balance Sheet credit column total to make the Balance Sheet columns equal. Adding the income to this column has the effect of adding it to the Capital account.

Had there been a loss, it would have been necessary to add the loss to the debit column. This is because losses decrease owner equity, and adding the loss to the debit column has the effect of subtracting it from the Capital account.

Balancing the Balance Sheet columns by adding the net income or loss is a proof of the accuracy with which the work sheet has been prepared. If the income or loss, when added in the Balance Sheet columns, makes these columns equal, it is assumed that no errors have been made. However, if the income or loss does not make the columns equal, it is proof that an error or errors have been made. The error or errors may have been either mathematical, or an amount may have been sorted to a wrong column.

Although balancing the Balance Sheet columns with the net income or loss is a proof of the accuracy with which a work sheet has been prepared, it is not an absolute proof. These columns will balance even when errors have been made if the errors are of a certain type. For example, an expense carried into the Balance Sheet debit column or an asset carried into the debit column of the income statement section will cause both of these columns to have incorrect totals. Likewise, the net income will be incorrect. However, when such an error is made, the Balance Sheet columns will still balance, but with the incorrect amount of income. Because of this, when a work sheet is prepared, care must be exercised in sorting the adjusted trial balance amounts into the correct Income Statement or Balance Sheet columns.

WORK SHEET AND THE FINANCIAL STATEMENTS

As previously stated, the work sheet is a tool of the accountant and is not for management's use or publication. However, as soon as it is completed, the accountant uses it in preparing a formal income statement and balance sheet. To do this he rearranges the items in the work sheet's Income Statement columns into a formal income statement, and he rearranges the items in the Balance Sheet columns into a formal balance sheet.

WORK SHEET AND ADJUSTING ENTRIES

When a work sheet is used in preparing the statements, both the work sheet and statements are prepared before the accounts are adjusted. As a result, after the work sheet and statements are completed, it is still necessary to prepare and post adjusting journal entries. Fortunately this is an easy task because the adjusting entries may be taken directly from the work sheet's Adjustments columns. When adjusting entries are taken from these columns, a journal entry is made for each adjustment appearing in the columns. Furthermore, to make preparation of the entries still easier, at the time the work sheet is prepared each adjustment's debits and credits are keyed together with a letter.

WORK SHEET AND CLEARING ENTRIES

In addition to being an information source for adjusting entries, the work sheet, as is explained later, is also a source of information for clearing entries, the entries that clear and close the revenue and expense accounts.

NEED FOR CLEARING ENTRIES

At the end of an accounting period clearing entries clear the revenue and expense accounts of their balances. These accounts are cleared because:

- *a*) An income statement reports the revenues and expenses of a single accounting period, and is prepared from the amounts recorded in the revenue and expense accounts.
- *b*) Consequently, these accounts must begin each new accounting period with zero balances if their end-of-the-period balances are to reflect only a single period's transactions.

Clearing entries that are posted to the revenue and expense accounts at the end of an accounting period cause the revenue and expense accounts to begin the new period with zero balances.

In addition to providing zero balances, clearing entries also summarize a period's revenues and expenses and transfer the difference, the net income or loss, from the revenue and expense accounts to the owner's Capital account. This too is necessary because—

- *a*) Revenues increase owner equity and expenses decrease it.
- *b*) But throughout an accounting period these increases and decreases are recorded in revenue and expense accounts rather than in the owner's Capital account.
- *c*) Consequently, clearing entries are necessary at the end of a period to transfer the net effect of the revenue and expense increases and decreases to the owner's Capital account.

CLEARING ENTRIES ILLUSTRATED

At the end of July, after its work sheet and statements were prepared and its adjusting entries posted, but before its accounts were cleared, the owner equity accounts of Owen Real Estate Agency had balances as shown in Illustration 21. (An account's Balance column heading, as a rule, does not tell the nature of an account's balance. However, in Illustration 21 and in the illustrations immediately following the nature of each account's balance is shown by means of a color overprint. The authors feel the student needs this extra help until such time as he becomes more familiar with the normal balances of different accounts.)

Observe in Illustration 21 that Owen's Capital account shows only its $5,000 July 1 balance. This is not the amount of Owen's equity on July 31; clearing entries are required to make this account show the July 31 equity.

Note also the third account in Illustration 21, the Income Summary account. This account is used only at the end of the accounting period in summarizing and clearing the revenue and expense accounts.

Clearing Revenue Accounts.   Before clearing entries are posted, revenue accounts have credit balances; consequently, to clear a revenue

Illustration 21

Larry Owen, Capital

Date	Explanation	Debit	Credit	Balance
July 1			5,000	5,000

Gas, Oil, and Repairs

Date	Explanation	Debit	Credit	Balance
July 31		25		25

Larry Owen, Withdrawals

Date	Explanation	Debit	Credit	Balance
July 26		200		200

Advertising Expense

Date	Explanation	Debit	Credit	Balance
July 31		60		60

Income Summary

Date	Explanation	Debit	Credit	Balance

Rent Expense

Date	Explanation	Debit	Credit	Balance
July 31		100		100

Commissions Earned

Date	Explanation	Debit	Credit	Balance
July 12			850	850
18			75	925

Office Supplies Used

Date	Explanation	Debit	Credit	Balance
July 31		15		15

Office Salaries Expense

Date	Explanation	Debit	Credit	Balance
July 12		100		100
26		100		200
31		30		230

Depreciation Expense, Automobile

Date	Explanation	Debit	Credit	Balance
July 31		35		35

Telephone and Utilities

Date	Explanation	Debit	Credit	Balance
July 31		20		20

Depreciation Expense, Office Equipment

Date	Explanation	Debit	Credit	Balance
July 31		10		10

account of its balance, an entry debiting the account and crediting Income Summary is required. Owen Real Estate Agency has only one revenue account, and the entry to clear it is:

July 31	Commissions Earned........................		925.00	
	Income Summary......................			925.00
	To clear the Commissions Earned account.			

Posting this entry has the following effect on the accounts:

Commissions Earned

Date	Explanation	Debit	Credit	Balance
July 12			850	850
18			75	925
31		925		–0–

Income Summary

Date	Explanation	Debit	Credit	Balance
July 31			925	925

Note that the entry that clears the Commissions Earned account has a dual effect: (1) it clears the account of its balance and (2) transfers the account balance to the credit side of the Income Summary account.

Clearing the Expense Accounts. Before clearing entries are posted, expense accounts have debit balances; consequently, to clear a concern's expense accounts a compound entry debiting the Income Summary account and crediting each individual expense account is required. Owen Real Estate Agency has eight expense accounts, and the compound entry to clear them is:

July	31	Income Summary.....................................	495.00	
		Office Salaries Expense........................		230.00
		Telephone and Utilities.......................		20.00
		Gas, Oil, and Repairs.........................		25.00
		Advertising Expense...........................		60.00
		Rent Expense..................................		100.00
		Office Supplies Used..........................		15.00
		Depreciation Expense, Automobile.............		35.00
		Depreciation Expense, Office Equipment........		10.00
		To clear the expense accounts.		

Posting this entry has the effect shown in Illustration 22. Note again that the effect is a dual one: (1) it clears the expense accounts of their balances and (2) transfers the account balances in a total to the debit side of the Income Summary account.

Clearing the Income Summary Account. After a concern's revenue and expense accounts are cleared and their balances transferred to the Income Summary account, the balance of the Income Summary account is equal to the net income or loss. When revenues exceed expenses, there is a net income and the Income Summary account has a credit balance. On the other hand, when expenses exceed revenues, there is a loss and the account

Illustration 22

Office Salaries Expense

Date		Explanation	Debit	Credit	Balance
July	12		100		100
	26		100		200
	31		30		230
	31			230	–0–

Telephone and Utilities

Date		Explanation	Debit	Credit	Balance
July	31		20		20
	31			20	–0–

Gas, Oil, and Repairs

Date		Explanation	Debit	Credit	Balance
July	31		25		25
	31			25	–0–

Income Summary

Date		Explanation	Debit	Credit	Balance
July	31			925	925
	31		495		430

Advertising Expense

Date		Explanation	Debit	Credit	Balance
July	31		60		60
	31			60	–0–

Rent Expense

Date		Explanation	Debit	Credit	Balance
July	31		100		100
	31			100	–0–

$230
20
25
60
100
15
35
10
$495

Office Supplies Used

Date		Explanation	Debit	Credit	Balance
July	31		15		15
	31			15	–0–

Depreciation Expense, Automobile

Date		Explanation	Debit	Credit	Balance
July	31		35		35
	31			35	–0–

Depreciation Expense, Office Equipment

Date		Explanation	Debit	Credit	Balance
July	31		10		10
	31			10	–0–

has a debit balance. But, regardless of the nature of its balance, the Income Summary account is cleared and its balance, the amount of the net income or loss, is transferred to the Withdrawals account.

Owen Real Estate Agency earned $430 during July; consequently, after its revenue and expense accounts are cleared, its Income Summary account has a $430 credit balance, and the account is cleared and this balance is transferred to the Larry Owen, Withdrawals account with an entry like this:

> July 31 *Income Summary*........................ 430.00
>   *Larry Owen, Withdrawals*..............   430.00
>   *To clear the Income Summary account.*

Posting this entry has the following effect on the accounts:

Income Summary

Date	Explanation	Debit	Credit	Balance
July 31			925	925
31		495		430
31		430		–0–

Larry Owen, Withdrawals

Date	Explanation	Debit	Credit	Balance
July 26		200		200
31			430	(230)

Observe again that the clearing entry serves a dual purpose: (1) it clears the Income Summary account and (2) transfers the balance of the account, the amount of the net income in this case, to the Withdrawals account. Note also that crediting the net income to the Withdrawals account caused the Withdrawals account, in this case, to have a credit balance, a different from normal balance, which is indicated by encircling the $230 amount.

Clearing the Withdrawals Account. Withdrawals of cash or other assets by a business owner for his personal use are called "withdrawals in anticipation of income" and are debited to his Withdrawals account. Consequently, after the Income Summary account is cleared and its balance transferred to the Withdrawals account, the balance of the Withdrawals account shows the excess or deficiency of income over withdrawals.

If there is an excess of income over withdrawals, the excess may be left in the Withdrawals account on the assumption the business owner will withdraw the amount for personal use during the next accounting period. However, if the owner does not desire to withdraw the excess income but plans to leave it permanently invested in the business, the balance of the

Withdrawals account is transferred to the Capital account with an entry like this:

July	31	Larry Owen, Withdrawals..................	230.00	
		Larry Owen, Capital...................		230.00
		To clear the Withdrawals account.		

Posting the entry has this effect on the accounts:

Larry Owen, Withdrawals

Date	Explanation	Debit	Credit	Balance
July 26		200		200
31			430	
31		230		–0–

Larry Owen, Capital

Date	Explanation	Debit	Credit	Balance
July 1			5,000	5,000
31			230	5,230

Observe that after the entry clearing the Withdrawals account is posted, the two reasons for making clearing entries are accomplished: (1) all the revenue and expense accounts have zero balances; and (2) the net effect of the period's revenues, expenses, and withdrawals on the owner's equity is shown in his Capital account.

SOURCES OF CLEARING ENTRY INFORMATION

After adjusting entries have been posted, information for the clearing entries may be taken from the individual revenue and expense accounts; however, the work sheet provides this information in a more convenient form. For example, if the Owen Real Estate Agency work sheet on page 85 is examined, it will be seen that every account having a balance extended into the Income Statement debit column has a debit balance in the ledger and must be credited in clearing. Now compare the amounts in this column with the compound clearing entry on page 91, and observe how the column amounts and their account titles are a source of information for the entry. Observe also that if the work sheet is used as an information source for the entry, it is not even necessary to add the entry's individual credit amounts in order to learn the amount of the debit, the debit amount can be taken from the work sheet column total.

The Owen Real Estate Agency work sheet has only one account the balance of which is extended into the Income Statement credit column. However, if there were more than one, they would normally be cleared with a compound entry, and the work sheet would be a convenient information source for this entry.

THE ACCOUNTS AFTER CLEARING

At this stage, after both adjusting and clearing entries have been posted, the Owen Real Estate Agency accounts appear as in Illustration 23 on this and the next several pages. Observe in the illustration that the asset, liability, and the owner's Capital accounts show their end-of-the-period balances. Observe also that the revenue and expense accounts are clear of balances and are ready for recording the new accounting period's revenues and expenses.

Illustration 23

Cash   ACCOUNT NO. 1

DATE	EXPLANATION	FO-LIO	DEBIT	CREDIT	BALANCE
1966					
July 1		1	500000		500000
1		1		30000	470000
3		1		300000	170000
3		1		100000	70000
9		1	10000		80000
11		1	5000		85000
11		1		17500	67500
12		2	85000		152500
12		2		10000	142500
18		2	7500		150000
26		2		10000	140000
26		2		20000	120000
31		2		2000	118000
31		2		2500	115500
31		2		6000	109500

Dale Hall   ACCOUNT NO. 2

DATE	EXPLANATION	FO-LIO	DEBIT	CREDIT	BALANCE
1966					
July 9		1	5000		5000
11		1		5000	—0—

Prepaid Rent   ACCOUNT NO. 3

DATE	EXPLANATION	FO-LIO	DEBIT	CREDIT	BALANCE
1966					
July 1		1	30000		30000
31		3		10000	20000

Illustration 23—Continued

Office Supplies — ACCOUNT NO. 4

DATE	EXPLANATION	FO-LIO	DEBIT	CREDIT	BALANCE
1966					
July 5		1	60 00		60 00
31		3		15 00	45 00

Automobile — ACCOUNT NO. 5

DATE	EXPLANATION	FO-LIO	DEBIT	CREDIT	BALANCE
1966					
July 3		1	3000 00		3000 00

Accumulated Depreciation Automobile — ACCOUNT NO. 6

DATE	EXPLANATION	FO-LIO	DEBIT	CREDIT	BALANCE
1966					
July 31		3		35 00	35 00

Office Equipment — ACCOUNT NO. 7

DATE	EXPLANATION	FO-LIO	DEBIT	CREDIT	BALANCE
1966					
July 3		1	1000 00		1000 00
5		1	350 00		1350 00
9		1		150 00	1200 00

Accumulated Depreciation - Office Equipment — ACCOUNT NO. 8

DATE	EXPLANATION	FO-LIO	DEBIT	CREDIT	BALANCE
1966					
July 31		3		10 00	10 00

A. B. Gordon Company — ACCOUNT NO. 9

DATE	EXPLANATION	FO-LIO	DEBIT	CREDIT	BALANCE
1966					
July 5		1		60 00	60 00

Illustration 23—Continued

Standard Supply Co.   ACCOUNT NO. *10*

DATE	EXPLANATION	FO-LIO	DEBIT	CREDIT	BALANCE
1966					
July 5		1		350 00	350 00
11		1	175 00		175 00

Salaries Payable   ACCOUNT NO. *11*

DATE	EXPLANATION	FO-LIO	DEBIT	CREDIT	BALANCE
1966					
July 31		3		30 00	30 00

Larry Owen, Capital   ACCOUNT NO. *12*

DATE	EXPLANATION	FO-LIO	DEBIT	CREDIT	BALANCE
1966					
July 1		1		5000 00	5000 00
31		3		230 00	5230 00

Larry Owen, Withdrawals   ACCOUNT NO. *13*

DATE	EXPLANATION	FO-LIO	DEBIT	CREDIT	BALANCE
1966					
July 26		2	200 00		200 00
31		3		430 00	(230 00)
31		3	230 00		—0—

Income Summary   ACCOUNT NO. *14*

DATE	EXPLANATION	FO-LIO	DEBIT	CREDIT	BALANCE
1966					
July 31		3		925 00	925 00
31		3	495 00		430 00
31		3	430 00		—0—

Commissions Earned   ACCOUNT NO. *15*

DATE	EXPLANATION	FO-LIO	DEBIT	CREDIT	BALANCE
1966					
July 12		2		850 00	850 00
18		2		75 00	925 00
31		3	925 00		—0—

Illustration 23—Continued

Office Salaries Expense ACCOUNT NO. 16

DATE	EXPLANATION	FO-LIO	DEBIT	CREDIT	BALANCE
1966					
July 12		2	100 00		100 00
26		2	100 00		200 00
31		3	30 00		230 00
31		3		230 00	—0—

Telephone and Utilities ACCOUNT NO. 17

DATE	EXPLANATION	FO-LIO	DEBIT	CREDIT	BALANCE
1966					
July 31		2	20 00		20 00
31		3		20 00	—0—

Gas, Oil, and Repairs ACCOUNT NO. 18

DATE	EXPLANATION	FO-LIO	DEBIT	CREDIT	BALANCE
1966					
July 31		2	25 00		25 00
31		3		25 00	—0—

Advertising Expense ACCOUNT NO. 19

DATE	EXPLANATION	FO-LIO	DEBIT	CREDIT	BALANCE
1966					
July 31		2	60 00		60 00
31		3		60 00	—0—

Rent Expense ACCOUNT NO. 20

DATE	EXPLANATION	FO-LIO	DEBIT	CREDIT	BALANCE
1966					
July 31		3	100 00		100 00
31		3		100 00	—0—

Illustration 23—Continued

Office Supplies Used   ACCOUNT NO. 21

DATE	EXPLANATION	FO-LIO	DEBIT	CREDIT	BALANCE
1966					
July 31		3	1 5 00		1 5 00
31		3		1 5 00	0

Depreciation Expense, Automobile   ACCOUNT NO. 22

DATE	EXPLANATION	FO-LIO	DEBIT	CREDIT	BALANCE
1966					
July 31		3	3 5 00		3 5 00
31		3		3 5 00	0 —

Depreciation Expense, Office Equipment   ACCOUNT NO. 23

DATE	EXPLANATION	FO-LIO	DEBIT	CREDIT	BALANCE
1966					
July 31		3	1 0 00		1 0 00
31		3		1 0 00	0 —

THE POST-CLEARING TRIAL BALANCE

It is easy to make errors in adjusting and clearing the accounts. Consequently, after all adjusting and clearing entries are posted, a new trial balance is prepared to retest the equality of the accounts. This new, after-clearing trial balance is called a *post-clearing trial balance*; and for Owen Real Estate Agency appears as in Illustration 24.

Compare Illustration 24 with the accounts having balances in Illustration 23. Note that only asset, liability, and the owner's Capital account have balances in Illustration 23, and that these are the only accounts that appear on the post-clearing trial balance of Illustration 24. The revenue and expense accounts have been cleared and have zero balances at this point.

MATTERS OF TERMINOLOGY

Clearing Entries, Closing Entries. Clearing entries are also called closing entries. They are so-called because after the revenue and expense accounts are cleared, they are also closed and have no balances. Thus far these entries have been called clearing entries because this title is a little more descriptive of what the entries do. However, from this point on the phrases closing entries and clearing entries, closed account and cleared

Illustration 24

OWEN REAL ESTATE AGENCY
Post-Clearing Trial Balance, July 31, 19--

Cash.	$1,095	
Prepaid rent.	200	
Office supplies	45	
Automobile.	3,000	
Accumulated depreciation, automobile.		$ 35
Office equipment.	1,200	
Accumulated depreciation, office equipment.		10
A. B. Gordon Company.		60
Standard Supply Co.		175
Salaries payable.		30
Larry Owen, capital		5,230
	$5,540	$5,540

account, and post-closing trial balance and post-clearing trial balance will be used interchangeably.

Temporary Proprietorship Accounts. Revenue and expense accounts plus the Income Summary and Withdrawals accounts are called *temporary proprietorship accounts.* A moment's thought will reveal the reason for this is that, in a sense, the items recorded in these accounts are only temporarily recorded therein. At the end of each accounting period the items, through the account balances, are, in a sense, transferred out and on to the owner or proprietor's Capital account.

Real and Nominal Accounts. Balance sheet accounts are commonly called *real accounts,* presumably because the items recorded in these accounts exist in objective form. Likewise, income statement accounts are called *nominal accounts* because the items recorded in these accounts exist in name only.

Working Papers. As an aid in their work, accountants prepare numerous memoranda, analyses, notes, and informal papers that serve as a basis for the more formal reports given to management or to their clients. These analyses, notes, and memoranda are called "working papers" and are invaluable tools of the accountant. The work sheet of this chapter is a so-called working paper. Others will be discussed from time to time.

THE ACCOUNTING CYCLE

The life of a business is divided into accounting periods; and each period is a recurring accounting cycle, beginning with transactions recorded in a journal and ending with a post-closing trial balance. All the steps in the cycle have now been discussed, and a knowledge of accounting requires that each step be understood and its relation to the others seen. The steps in the accounting cycle in the order of their occurrence are:

1. *Journalizing* . . . . Analyzing and recording transactions in a journal.
2. *Posting* . . . . Copying the debits and credits of journal entries in the ledger accounts.
3. *Preparing a trial balance* . . Summarizing the ledger accounts and testing the recording accuracy.
4. *Constructing a work sheet* . . . . Affecting the adjustments without making entries in the accounts. Then sorting the account balances into balance sheet and income statement accounts and finally determining the income or loss.
5. *Preparing the statements* . . . . Rearranging the work sheet information into a balance sheet and an income statement.
6. *Adjusting the ledger accounts* . . . . Preparing adjusting journal entries from information in the Adjustments columns of the work sheet and posting the entries in order to bring the account balances up to date.
7. *Closing the temporary proprietorship accounts* . . Preparing and posting entries to close the temporary proprietorship accounts and transfer the net income or loss to the Capital account.
8. *Preparing a post-closing trial balance* . . . . Proving the accuracy of the adjusting and closing procedure.

ACCOUNTING PERIODS; THE NATURAL
BUSINESS YEAR

In order to shorten the material presented, textbooks commonly use problems and illustrations in which businesses operate with accounting periods one month in length. In actual practice monthly accounting periods are seldom if ever used. An occasional business will close its books every three or every six months; however, most operate with annual accounting periods or accounting periods one year in length.

Any accounting period of twelve consecutive months is known as a *fiscal year*. A fiscal year or annual accounting period may coincide with the calendar year, or it may follow the *natural business year*. The natural business year of a company begins and ends when the company's business activity is at its lowest point. For example, in the automobile sales business the natural business year begins October 1, just before the new models are brought out, and ends the following September 30. When accounting periods follow the natural business year, the books are closed when inventories are at their lowest point and business activity is at its lowest ebb.

QUESTIONS FOR CLASS DISCUSSION

1. A balance column account is more convenient than the kind of account described in earlier chapters. Why?
2. A work sheet is a tool of the accountant upon which he accomplishes three tasks. What are these tasks?
3. Is it possible to complete the statements and adjust and clear the accounts without preparing a work sheet? What is gained by preparing a work sheet?
4. At what stage in the accounting process is a work sheet prepared?
5. From where are the amounts that are entered in the Trial Balance columns of a work sheet obtained?
6. Why are the adjustments in the Adjustments columns of a work sheet keyed together with letters?
7. What is the result of combining the amounts in the Trial Balance columns with the amounts in the Adjustments columns of a work sheet?
8. Why must care be exercised in sorting the items in the Adjusted Trial Balance columns to the proper Income Statement or Balance Sheet columns?
9. In extending the items in the Adjusted Trial Balance columns of a work sheet, what would be the result of extending: (a) an expense into the Balance Sheet debit column; (b) a liability into the Income Statement credit column; and (c) a revenue into the Balance Sheet debit column? Would each of these errors be automatically detected on the work sheet? Which would be automatically detected? Why?
10. Why are revenue and expense accounts called "temporary proprietorship accounts"?
11. What two purposes are accomplished by recording closing entries?
12. What accounts are affected by closing entries? What accounts are not affected?
13. Explain the difference between adjusting and closing entries.
14. What is the purpose of the Income Summary account?
15. Why is a post-closing trial balance prepared?
16. A bookkeeping student's post-closing trial balance listed "Depreciation expense, building, $672." What did this indicate?

PROBLEMS

Problem 4–1

On November 30 of the current year, at the end of the shop's annual accounting period, a trial balance of the ledger of TV Tom, a television repair shop owned by Thomas Hardy, carried the following amounts:

TV TOM
Trial Balance, November 30, 19—

Cash...$	975	
Prepaid insurance...............................	240	
Repair supplies..................................	1,425	
Repair equipment...............................	7,215	
Accumulated depreciation, repair equipment.....		$ 1,050
General Electronics, Inc.........................		260
Thomas Hardy, capital..........................		4,535
Thomas Hardy, withdrawals.....................	5,200	
Revenue from repairs............................		15,135
Wages expense..................................	4,760	
Rent expense...................................	900	
Advertising expense.............................	265	
	$20,980	$20,980

Required:

1. Enter the trial balance amounts in the Trial Balance columns of a work sheet and complete the work sheet using the following information:

   a) Expired insurance, $185.

   b) An inventory of repair supplies showed $310 of unused supplies on hand.

   c) Estimated depreciation of repair equipment, $725.

   d) Wages earned by the one employee but unpaid on the trial balance date, $80.

2. From the work sheet prepare an income statement and a balance sheet.

3. From the work sheet prepare adjusting journal entries and compound closing entries.

Problem 4–2

On November 1 of the current year John Howe opened Quick Service Repair Shop; and During the month he completed the following transactions:

Nov. 1 Withdrew $1,000 from his personal savings account and deposited it in the account of the shop.

 1 Paid the rent on the shop space for one month, $100.

 1 Paid the premium on a one-year insurance policy, $96.

 2 Signed a lease for the installation and use of shoe repair equipment. The lease called for a monthly rental of $40. Paid the first month's rent.

 4 Purchased on credit from Shop Equipment Company a showcase, chairs for the shop, and other shop furniture, $500.

 5 Purchased shop supplies on credit from Leather Supply Company, $90.

 8 Paid for advertising on the local radio station, $25.

 15 Cash shoe repair revenue for the first half of the month, $72.

 20 Paid Shop Equipment Company $100 on account.

 25 Paid Leather Supply Company in full.

 30 Cash shoe repair revenue for the last half of the month, $134.

Required work for November:

1. Open the following accounts: Cash; Prepaid Insurance; Shop Supplies; Shop Furniture; Accumulated Depreciation, Shop Furniture; Shop Equipment Company; Leather Supply Company; John Howe, Capital; John Howe, Withdrawals; Income Summary; Shoe Repair Revenue; Shop Rent; Equipment Rent; Advertising Expense; Expired Insurance; Shop Supplies Used; and Depreciation of Shop Furniture.
2. Prepare and post journal entries to record the November transactions.
3. Prepare a trial balance in the Trial Balance columns of a work sheet, and complete the work sheet using the following information:
   a) One month's insurance has expired.
   b) An inventory of shop supplies shows $40 of supplies on hand.
   c) Estimated depreciation of shop furniture, $10.
4. Prepare a November income statement and a balance sheet as of November 30.
5. Prepare and post adjusting and compound closing entries.
6. Prepare a post-closing trial balance.

During December John Howe completed the following additional transactions for Quick Service Repair Shop:

Dec. 1   Paid the rent on the shop space, $100.
     1   Paid the December rent on the shop equipment.
     4   Purchased on credit from Shop Equipment Company additional chairs for the shop, $125.
     8   Purchased shop supplies on credit from Leather Supply Company, $160.
     15   Cash shoe repair revenue for the first half of the month, $280.
     18   Paid for newspaper advertising that had appeared, $40.
     23   Paid Shop Equipment Company $400 on account.
     30   Withdrew $200 to be used for personal living expenses.
     30   Cash shoe repair revenue for the second half of the month, $305.

Required work for December:

1. Prepare and post journal entries to record the December transactions.
2. Prepare a trial balance in the Trial Balance columns of a work sheet, and complete the work sheet using the following information:
   a) One month's insurance has expired.
   b) An inventory of shop supplies shows $65 of supplies on hand.
   c) Estimated depreciation of shop furniture, $12.
3. Prepare a December income statement and a December 31 balance sheet.
4. Prepare and post adjusting and compound closing entries.
5. Prepare a post-closing trial balance.

Problem 4–3

The following trial balance was taken from the ledger of Sunshine Laundry at the end of its annual accounting period:

SUNSHINE LAUNDRY
Trial Balance, December 31, 19—

Cash...	$ 1,160	
Delux Hotel..	105	
Prepaid insurance...............................	145	
Laundry supplies.................................	415	
Laundry equipment.............................	9,280	
Accumulated depreciation, laundry equipment...		$ 1,990
Delivery equipment.............................	3,160	
Accumulated depreciation, delivery equipment...		1,085
Building...	22,340	
Accumulated depreciation, building..............		6,300
Land..	3,400	
Laundry Supply Company......................		175
Mortgage payable................................		9,500
Martin Keller, capital...........................		14,760
Martin Keller, withdrawals....................	4,800	
Laundry revenue.................................		22,235
Laundry plant wages............................	6,775	
Heat, light, and power..........................	410	
Delivery wages....................................	3,560	
Gas, oil, and repairs.............................	495	
	$56,045	$56,045

Required:
1. Open the accounts of the trial balance plus these additional accounts: Expired Insurance, Laundry Plant; Expired Insurance, Delivery Equipment; Laundry Supplies Used; Depreciation Expense, Laundry Equipment; Depreciation Expense, Delivery Equipment; Depreciation Expense, Building; and Wages Payable. Enter the trial balance amounts in the Balance columns of the accounts.
2. Enter the account balances in the Trial Balance columns of a work sheet and complete the work sheet using the following information:
   a) An examination of insurance policies showed expired insurance, laundry plant, $55; and expired insurance, delivery equipment, $70.
   b) An inventory of laundry supplies showed $110 of supplies on hand.
   c) Estimated depreciation of laundry equipment, $525; delivery equipment, $295; and of the building, $430.
   d) There were accrued wages owed the laundry plant workers of $85 and owed the delivery truck driver, $40.
3. Prepare a classified income statement and a classified balance sheet.
4. Prepare and post adjusting and compound closing entries.
5. Prepare a post-closing trial balance.

Problem 4–4
The following trial balance was taken from the ledger of At-Once Delivery Service at the end of its annual accounting period:

AT-ONCE DELIVERY SERVICE
Trial Balance, December 31, 19—

Cash..	$ 1,880	
The Fair Store...............................	215	
Alpha Department Store......................	175	
Prepaid insurance...........................	495	
Office supplies..............................	230	
Office equipment............................	2,460	
Accumulated depreciation, office equipment.....		$ 470
Delivery equipment..........................	10,790	
Accumulated depreciation, delivery equipment...		3,150
Notes payable (due in six months)..............		1,500
Sheldon's Service Station.....................		145
Harvey Jenkins, capital.......................		8,500
Harvey Jenkins, withdrawals...................	6,800	
Revenue from delivery service..................		32,585
Office rent expense..........................	600	
Office salaries expense........................	3,060	
Telephone and utilities expense.................	185	
Truck drivers' wages.........................	16,320	
Gas, oil, and repairs.........................	2,180	
Garage rent expense.........................	960	
	$46,350	$46,350

Required:

1. Open the accounts of the trial balance plus these additional ones: Salaries and Wages Payable; Depreciation of Office Equipment; Expired Insurance, Office Equipment; Office Supplies Used; Depreciation of Delivery Equipment; and Expired Insurance, Delivery Equipment. Enter the trial balance amounts in the Balance columns of the accounts.
2. Also enter the trial balance in the Trial Balance columns of a work sheet and complete the work sheet using the following information:
    a) Expired insurance office equipment, $55; and delivery equipment, $325.
    b) Office supplies used during the year, $145.
    c) Estimated depreciation of office equipment, $120, and of delivery equipment, $2,125.
    d) Accrued office salaries payable, $60; and accrued truck drivers' wages payable, $320.
3. From the work sheet prepare a classified income statement and a classified balance sheet.
4. From the work sheet prepare and post adjusting and closing entries.
5. Prepare a post-closing trial balance.

CLASS EXERCISE

Exercise 4–1
Following is a list of trial balance accounts and their balances. To save your time, the balances are in one and two digit numbers; however, to increase

your skill in sorting adjusted trial balance amounts to the proper work sheet columns, the accounts are listed in alphabetical order.

Trial Balance Accounts and Balances

Accounts payable............	$2	Perry Price, capital.........	$11
Accounts receivable..........	4	Perry Price, withdrawals....	2
Accumulated depreciation,		Prepaid insurance..........	3
shop equipment...........	3	Revenue from services......	21
Advertising expense..........	1	Shop equipment............	10
Cash......................	5	Supplies..................	4
Notes payable..............	2	Utilities expense...........	2
		Wages expense............	8

Required:
1. Prepare a work sheet form on ordinary notebook paper and enter the trial balance accounts and amounts on the work sheet in their alphabetical order.
2. Complete the work sheet using the following information:
    a) Estimated depreciation of shop equipment, $2.
    b) Expired insurance, $1.
    c) Unused shop supplies on hand per inventory, $1.
    d) Accrued wages, $1.

ALTERNATE PROBLEMS

Problem 4–1A

At the end of its annual accounting period a trial balance of Palms Theater's ledger carried the following amounts:

PALMS THEATER
Trial Balance, December 31, 19—

Cash...	$ 1,230	
Advertising supplies............................	670	
Prepaid insurance..............................	545	
Prepaid rent...................................	1,500	
Theater furniture..............................	12,450	
Accumulated depreciation, theater furniture.....		$ 6,130
Projection equipment...........................	10,470	
Accumulated depreciation, projection equipment.		5,960
Foxy Films....................................		230
Percy Casper, capital..........................		16,640
Percy Casper, withdrawals......................	6,000	
Revenue from admissions.......................		37,180
Popcorn concession rent........................		1,200
Salaries and wages.............................	13,130	
Film rentals...................................	12,315	
Advertising expense............................	2,820	
Heat, lights, and power........................	2,265	
Equipment repairs.............................	445	
Theater rent..................................	3,500	
	$67,340	$67,340

Required:

1. Enter the trial balance amounts in the Trial Balance columns of a work sheet and complete the work sheet using the following information:
   a) An advertising supplies inventory showed $125 of unused advertising supplies on hand.
   b) An examination of insurance policies showed $165 of insurance prepaid on the trial balance date.
   c) The theater building rents for $500 per month. On January 1, at the beginning of the year, three months' rent was prepaid. The rent for each of the months April through October was paid on the first day of each month and was debited to the expense account, Theater Rent. The rent for November and December was unpaid on the trial balance date.
   d) Estimated depreciation of theater furniture, $810; and (e) of projection equipment, $735.
   f) Salaries and wages of $135 have been earned by the employees but are unpaid on the trial balance date.
2. Prepare an income statement and balance sheet.
3. Prepare adjusting and closing entries.

Problem 4–3A

At the end of its annual accounting period a trial balance of the ledger of OK Janitorial Service appeared as follows:

OK JANITORIAL SERVICE
Trial Balance, October 31, 19—

Cash	$ 1,185	
American Bank Building	414	
Prepaid insurance	353	
Cleaning supplies	581	
Cleaning equipment	3,196	
Accumulated depreciation, cleaning equipment		$ 1,537
Trucks	5,969	
Accumulated depreciation, trucks		2,159
Building	13,500	
Accumulated depreciation, building		3,525
Land	3,000	
Janitorial Supply Company		134
Mortgage payable		5,000
Jeffro Jenkins, capital		14,161
Jeffro Jenkins, withdrawals	6,000	
Janitorial revenue		23,614
Wages expense	14,803	
Advertising expense	317	
Gas, oil, and repairs	812	
	$50,130	$50,130

Required:

1. Open the accounts of the trial balance plus any additional ones required. Enter the trial balance amounts in the accounts and enter the trial bal-

ance on a work sheet form. Complete the work sheet using the following information:

a) Expired insurance, $245.

b) The cleaning supplies inventory showed $172 of unused supplies. However, when this amount was subtracted from the balance of the Cleaning Supplies account, the amount remaining was not sufficiently large as to represent the amount of supplies used. (c) Consequently, the bookkeeper examined his records and found a $195 purchase of cleaning supplies that had been debited in error to the Cleaning Equipment account. (Make an adjustment to correct the error before making the adjustment to record the supplies used.)

d) Depreciation was estimated at $300 on the cleaning equipment; (e) $810 on the trucks; and (f) $270 on the building.

g) There were $115 of accrued wages on the trial balance date.

h) The $317 debit balance in the Advertising Expense account resulted from $205 of payments for newspaper advertising that had appeared and a $112 payment for advertising desk calendars that were to be distributed to customers and prospective customers beginning on December 15.

2. From the work sheet prepare an income statement and a balance sheet.
3. Prepare and post adjusting and closing entries.
4. Prepare a post-closing trial balance.

Problem 4–4A

At the end of its annual accounting period a trial balance of the ledger of U-Bowl Alleys appeared as follows:

U-BOWL ALLEYS
Trial Balance, December 31, 19—

Cash...	$ 1,945	
Office supplies...................................	280	
Bowling supplies.................................	2,340	
Prepaid insurance...............................	475	
Office equipment................................	2,695	
Accumulated depreciation, office equipment......		$ 515
Bowling equipment..............................	37,735	
Accumulated depreciation, bowling equipment...		8,855
Mortgage payable................................		10,000
Gary Rand, capital..............................		13,805
Gary Rand, withdrawals.........................	7,200	
Bowling revenue.................................		38,250
Salaries expense.................................	12,985	
Advertising expense..............................	665	
Equipment repairs...............................	325	
Rent expense....................................	3,600	
Utilities expense.................................	935	
Taxes expense...................................	245	
	$71,425	$71,425

Required:

1. Open the accounts of the trial balance plus these additional ones: Salaries Payable; Taxes Payable; Rent Payable; Income Summary; Office Supplies Used; Bowling Supplies Used; Expired Insurance; Depreciation of Office Equipment; and Depreciation of Bowling Equipment. Enter the trial balance amounts in the Balance columns of the accounts and enter the trial balance on a work sheet form. Complete the work sheet using the following information:

   a) Office supplies inventory, $110; and *(b)* bowling supplies inventory, $655.

   c) Expired insurance, $360.

   d) Estimated depreciation of office equipment, $265; and *(e)* of bowling equipment, $3,775.

   f) Salaries accrued but unpaid on the trial balance date, $230.

   g) The lease contract on the building called for an annual rental equal to 10 percent of the gross annual bowling revenue, with $300 payable in advance on the first day of each month. The $300 had been paid each month and debited to the Rent Expense account.

   h) On the trial balance date $125 of taxes on the bowling equipment had accrued but was unrecorded and unpaid.

2. Prepare an income statement and a classified balance sheet.

3. Prepare and post adjusting and closing entries.

4. Prepare a post-closing trial balance.

DECISION PROBLEM 4—FM MACHINE SHOP

F. M. "Dusty" Rhodes operates a machine shop and keeps his own books. After three years of operations Mr. Rhodes finds himself so completely engaged in the actual operations of the shop that he no longer has time to keep his own books. Consequently, he has employed Mary Boswell, an experienced bookkeeper, to take over all of his accounting duties.

Upon investigation Miss Boswell found that Mr. Rhodes has never made any adjusting entries for depreciation, accrued expenses, and prepaid expenses. His ledger reveals the following:

	1st Year	2d Year	3d Year
Net income per books	*$ 8,200*	*$ 8,800*	*$ 9,500*
Shop equipment at original			
cost	*20,400*	*30,000*	*32,000*
Truck for shop use	*3,600*	*3,600*	*3,600*

She proceeded to record depreciation for the past three years, setting up 10 percent of cost per annum on the shop equipment and 25 percent per annum on the truck. As the result of these adjustments for depreciation Miss Boswell reported to Mr. Rhodes that the adjusted profit figures for the last three years were $5,260, $4,900, and $5,400, respectively.

In addition she stated that adjustments should have been made for accrued machinists' wages, taxes, and utility expenses, and for unexpired insurance and unused shop supplies. (Insurance premiums on three-year policies and supplies purchased were charged to expenses when paid.) She has not attempted to prepare these adjustments for the first three years since she lacked precise information. She recommends that annual entries be made in the future, not only for depreciation, but for all accrued and prepaid expenses.

Mr. Rhodes is very unhappy with Miss Boswell's statement of his past earnings as well as with her recommendations for annual adjustments in the future. He argues that a recent offer to purchase his business at more than the original costs of its assets is proof that no depreciation expense should be taken into account in computing net income. He does admit that the truck will have to be replaced within the next few months. He also feels that there is little use "fooling" with adjustments for accrued and prepaid items, for everything "will be all right in the long run."

Miss Boswell is afraid that Mr. Rhodes has lost confidence in her ability and asks you to prepare a statement expressing opinions on (a) the necessity of adjustments of accounts prior to the preparation of financial statements; (b) the adjusted profit figures for the past three years; (c) Mr. Rhodes contention that the increase in the sales price of his business refutes the alleged need for depreciation adjustments; and (d) Mr. Rhodes feeling that little is gained by making periodic adjustments for accrued and prepaid expenses.

Accounting for a
Merchandising Business

A SERVICE-TYPE enterprise depends upon sales of services for its earnings; a merchandising business differs in that it depends upon sales of goods or merchandise. However, although the two differ in this respect, the accounting principles presented in previous chapters as applicable to a service-type concern apply to a merchandising business. The principles apply, but since a merchandising concern must account for the purchase, handling, and sale of a stock of merchandise, it does make use of accounts and methods not previously discussed.

MERCHANDISING ACCOUNTS

The accounts and methods used in recording transactions connected with purchasing, handling, and selling merchandise are as follows:

The Purchases Account. When merchandise is purchased for later resale, its cost is commonly debited to an account called *Purchases*, as follows:

Oct.	*2*	*Purchases*...............................	*850.00*	
		Eastlake Wholesale Company.........		*850.00*
		Purchased merchandise on credit.		

The Purchases account has as its sole purpose the accumulation and summarization of the cost of all merchandise purchased during an accounting period. The account does not at any time show whether the purchased merchandise is on hand or has been disposed of through sale or other means.

The Purchases Returns and Allowances Account. Merchandise received from suppliers sometimes and for a variety of reasons is not acceptable and must be returned or, if kept, is kept only because the supplier grants an allowance or reduction in its price. When merchandise is returned, the purchaser "gets his money back"; but from a managerial viewpoint more is involved. Buying merchandise, receiving and inspecting it, deciding that the merchandise is unsatisfactory, and returning it is a costly procedure that should be held to a minimum; and the first step in holding it to a minimum is to know the amount of returns and allowances.

When merchandise is purchased and returned, or an allowance on its cost is received, the situation is the opposite of a purchase and could be recorded by a credit to the Purchases account. However, if returns and allowances are recorded in this manner, the entries in the Purchases account must be analyzed in order to learn the amount of returns and allowances. Therefore, in order to make information as to returns and allowances readily available to management, returns and allowances on purchases are commonly recorded in an account called *Purchases Returns and Allowances* with entries similar to the following:

Oct.	*9*	*Eastgate Wholesale Company*.............. *54.00*	
		Purchases Returns and Allowances.......	*54.00*
		Returned merchandise previously pur-	
		chased on credit.	

The Freight-In Account. Sometimes a manufacturer or wholesaler pays freight, express, or other transportation costs on merchandise he sells, and the total cost of the goods to the purchaser is the amount paid the manufacturer or wholesaler. Other times the purchaser must pay transportation costs; and when he does so, such charges are a proper addition to the cost of the goods and may be recorded by a debit to the Purchases account. However, more complete information is obtained if such costs are debited to an account called *Freight-In*, as follows:

Dec.	*11*	*Freight-In*.................................. *24.50*	
		Cash.....................................	*24.50*
		Paid express charges on merchandise	
		purchased.	

When an income statement is prepared at the end of an accounting period, the balance of the Purchases Returns and Allowances account is subtracted from the balance of the Purchases account to show *net purchases*, and then the balance of the Freight-In account is added to show *net cost of purchases*, as follows:

Purchases	$49,400	
Less: Purchases returns and allow-		
ances	275	
Net purchases	$49,125	
Add: Freight-in	1,100	
Net cost of purchases		$50,225

The Sales Account. When merchandise is sold, the transaction is recorded in most stores simply by debiting an asset account and crediting the *Sales* account for the selling price of the goods. For example, a concern sold for $50 merchandise that cost $32. The company records the sale as follows:

Nov.	1	*Cash (if the sale is for cash)*	*50.00*	
		Sales		*50.00*
		Sold merchandise for cash.		
		or		
	1	*Frank Smith (if the sale is on credit)*	*50.00*	
		Sales		*50.00*
		Sold merchandise on credit.		

Each of the foregoing debits records an increase in an asset; the credits to Sales record the revenue from the merchandise sold.

The foregoing entries illustrate the method of recording sales when a *periodic inventory system* is in use. Observe that in neither entry is the cost of the goods sold recorded. This is a distinguishing characteristic of the periodic inventory system. When such a system is in use, cost of goods sold is not recorded at the time of a sale; rather, cost of goods sold is ignored in the accounts until the end of each accounting period when a physical inventory or count of the remaining unsold goods is made and the cost of all goods sold during the period is calculated. (Both physical inventories and the calculation of cost of goods sold are discussed in more detail later in this chapter.)

In passing it should be said that another accounting system for merchandising transactions called the *perpetual inventory system* is sometimes used by companies that sell a limited variety of items having rather high individual values. However, since the periodic inventory system is the more common, it is made the subject of this chapter, and a discussion of the perpetual inventory system is deferred until Chapter 10.

The Sales Returns and Allowances Account.   Since a merchandising company depends for earnings upon sales of merchandise, it is important that it watch carefully for signs of dissatisfaction among its customers with the merchandise they have purchased. Normally, a dissatisfied customer is permitted to return unsatisfactory goods and is either given a refund or credit on his account for the items returned. Sometimes a customer is permitted to keep the unsatisfactory merchandise and is granted a reduction in its sales price or an allowance on its sales price. Either a return or an allowance has the reverse effect of a sale and could be recorded with a debit in the Sales account. However, as in the case of purchases returns and allowances, it is important for managerial purposes that the amounts be accumulated in such a manner that their total is readily available. Consequently, returns and allowances are commonly recorded and accumulated in an account called *Sales Returns and Allowances,* with entries like the following:

Dec.	*15*	*Sales Returns and Allowances..............*	*35.00*	
		Frank Welch.........................		*35.00*
		Customer returned merchandise.		

When an income statement is prepared, sales returns and allowances are deducted on it from sales to show *net sales,* as follows:

```
                    NELSON HARDWARE COMPANY
          Income Statement for Year Ended December 31, 19--

Revenue:
   Gross sales . . . . . . . . . . . . . . . . .    $79,300
        Less: Sales returns and allowances. . . .        650
   Net sales . . . . . . . . . . . . . . . . . .   $78,650
```

The Merchandise Inventory Account.   To satisfy its customer's needs, a merchandising concern must keep a stock of goods on hand at all times. Consequently, it begins and ends an accounting period with merchandise on its shelves and in its stock room. The merchandise on hand at the beginning of a period is known as *the beginning inventory* and that on hand at the end is known as *the ending inventory.* Furthermore, since accounting periods follow one after another, the ending inventory of one period is always the beginning inventory of the next.

When a periodic inventory system is in use, no effort is made throughout an accounting period to keep a record of the goods on hand

Rather, periodically, at the end of each period, the cost of the merchandise on hand is determined by (1) physically counting the items on the shelves in the store and in the stock room, (2) multiplying the count for each item by its cost, and (3) adding the costs of the items. After the dollar amount of inventory is determined in this manner, it is used in calculating cost of goods sold and is entered in an account called *Merchandise Inventory*, where it remains as the record of the inventory at the end of the period ended and the beginning of the new period.

It should be emphasized at this point that entries are made in the Merchandise Inventory account only at the end of each accounting period; that during a period the account does not show the cost of goods on hand; and that, after a period begins, the account becomes a historical account, the balance of which shows only the cost of the merchandise that was on hand at the beginning of the period.

CALCULATING COST OF GOODS SOLD

As previously stated, a company using a periodic inventory system makes no effort to keep track of the cost of the goods it sells. Consequently, at the end of an accounting period, when such a company wishes to learn its net income, it must first calculate the cost of the goods it has sold during the period. To make this calculation, information must be available as to—

1. The cost of the beginning inventory.
2. The net cost of goods purchased.
3. The cost of the ending inventory.

At the end of an accounting period (1) the balance of the Merchandise Inventory account shows the cost of the beginning inventory; (2) the balances of the Purchases, Purchases Returns and Allowances, and Freight-In accounts carry information as to net cost of purchases; and (3) a physical inventory or count of the unsold merchandise on hand is made to learn the ending inventory.

At the end of a period, as soon as the ending inventory is completed, information as to the beginning inventory, net cost of purchases, and the ending inventory are combined as follows to compute the cost of goods sold during the period:

```
Cost of goods sold:
  Merchandise inventory, January 1, 19--. . .        $ 7,750
  Purchases . . . . . . . . . . . . . . . . . $49,400
    Less:  Purchases returns and allowances .     275
  Net purchases . . . . . . . . . . . . . . . $49,125
    Add: Freight-in . . . . . . . . . . . .     1,100
  Net cost of purchases . . . . . . . . . .          50,225
  Goods available for sale. . . . . . . . .         $57,975
  Merchandise inventory, December 31, 19--. .         8,950
        Cost of goods sold. . . . . . . . .                  $49,025
```

A merchandising business has available for sale and may sell during an accounting period the merchandise it had on hand at the beginning of the period plus any merchandise purchased during the period. If it sells all of these goods, then its cost of goods sold is equal to the cost of the goods that were available for sale. However, if any goods remain unsold at the end of the period, then cost of goods sold is equal to the cost of the goods available for sale less the cost of the ending inventory of unsold goods. Observe that this is the essence of the cost of goods sold calculation just illustrated.

INCOME STATEMENT OF A MERCHANDISING CONCERN

A classified income statement for a merchandising firm has three sections: (1) the revenue section, (2) the cost of goods sold section, and (3) the operating expenses section. Each section appears on the income statement of Nelson Hardware Company in Illustration 25 (next page).

Observe in Illustration 25 how cost of goods sold is subtracted from net sales to show "Gross profit from sales." For a better understanding of this item, "Gross profit from sales," recall what a merchant does. He buys an item for $0.60, marks it for sale at $1.00, and sells it. If he then constructs an income statement showing the effect of this one sale, the statement will show "Gross sales," $1.00; "Cost of goods sold," $0.60; and "Gross profit from sales," $0.40.

Gross profit or gross margin is the amount of "profit" before operating expenses are subtracted. If a net income is to be earned, gross profit must be sufficient to cover all operating expenses and leave something over for net income.

In the Nelson Hardware Company income statement, Illustration 25, note how the operating expenses are classified as either "Selling expenses" or "General and administrative expenses." Selling expenses include expenses of storing and preparing goods for sale, promoting sales, actually making sales, and, if there is not a delivery department separate from the selling departments, the expenses of delivering goods to customers. General and administrative expenses include the general office, accounting, personnel, and credits and collections expenses.

Sometimes an expenditure should be divided or prorated part to selling expenses and part to general and administrative expenses. Nelson Hardware Company divided the rent on its store building in this manner, as an examination of Illustration 25 will reveal. However, it did not prorate its insurance expense because the amount involved was so small the company felt the extra exactness did not warrant the extra work.

Illustration 25

NELSON HARDWARE COMPANY
Income Statement for Year Ended December 31, 19--

Revenue:
Gross sales			$79,300
Less: Sales returns and allowances. .			650
Net sales			$78,650

Cost of goods sold:
Merchandise inventory, January 1, 19--		$ 7,750	
Purchases	$49,400		
Less: Purchases returns and allowances	275		
Net purchases	$49,125		
Add: Freight-in	1,100		
Net cost of purchases		50,225	
Goods available for sale.		$57,975	
Merchandise inventory, December 31, 19--		8,950	
Cost of goods sold.			49,025
Gross profit from sales			$29,625

Operating expenses:
Selling expenses:
Sales salaries	$ 8,200		
Rent expense, selling space	4,800		
Advertising expense	900		
Freight-out and delivery expense. . .	1,350		
Store supplies used	425		
Depreciation expense, store equipment	775		
Total selling expenses.		$16,450	

General and administrative expenses:
Office salaries	$ 3,100		
Rent expense, office space.	600		
Expired insurance	65		
Office supplies used.	125		
Depreciation expense, office equipment	160		
Total general and administrative expenses.		4,050	
Total operating expenses.			20,500
Net Income.			$ 9,125

WORK SHEET OF A MERCHANDISING CONCERN

A concern selling merchandise, like a service-type company, uses a work sheet in bringing together the end-of-the-period information needed in preparing its income statement, balance sheet, and adjusting and clearing entries. Such a work sheet, that of Nelson Hardware Company, is shown in Illustration 26.

Note in Illustration 26 that the merchandising accounts are stressed by the use of color. This is done because the remainder of the accounts receive

Illustration 26

NELSON HARDWARE COMPANY
Work Sheet for Year Ended December 31, 19—

Account Titles	Trial Balance Dr.	Trial Balance Cr.	Adjustments Dr.	Adjustments Cr.	Adjusted Trial Balance Dr.	Adjusted Trial Balance Cr.	Income Statement Dr.	Income Statement Cr.	Balance Sheet Dr.	Balance Sheet Cr.
Cash	2,400				2,400				2,400	
Accounts receivable	3,300				3,300				3,300	
Merchandise inventory	7,750				7,750		7,750	8,950	8,950	
Prepaid insurance	195			(a) 65	130				130	
Store supplies	590			(b) 425	165				165	
Office supplies	185			(c) 125	60				60	
Store equipment	7,910				7,910				7,910	
Accumulated depreciation, store equipment		3,200		(d) 775		3,975				3,975
Office equipment	1,590				1,590				1,590	
Accumulated depreciation, office equipment		250		(e) 160		410				410
Accounts payable		1,700				1,700				1,700
George Nelson, capital		14,095				14,095				14,095
George Nelson, withdrawals	4,800				4,800				4,800	
Sales		79,300				79,300		79,300		
Sales returns and allowances	650				650		650			
Purchases	49,400				49,400		49,400			
Purchases returns and allowances		275				275		275		
Freight-in	1,100				1,100		1,100			
Sales salaries	8,200				8,200		8,200			
Rent expense, selling space	4,800				4,800		4,800			
Advertising expense	900				900		900			
Freight-out and delivery expense	1,350				1,350		1,350			
Office salaries	3,100				3,100		3,100			
Rent expense, office space	600				600		600			
	98,820	98,820								
Expired insurance			(a) 65		65		65			
Store supplies used			(b) 425		425		425			
Office supplies used			(c) 125		125		125			
Depreciation expense, store equipment			(d) 775		775		775			
Depreciation expense, office equipment			(e) 160		160		160			
			1,550	1,550	99,755	99,755	79,400	88,525	29,305	20,180
Net Income							9,125			9,125
							88,525	88,525	29,305	29,305

the same work sheet treatment as do the accounts of a service-type concern; and since this was fully discussed in Chapter 4, only the treatment of the merchandising accounts needs consideration here.

Trial Balance Columns.   The Trial Balance columns of the Nelson Hardware Company's work sheet, Illustration 26, show the balances of the company's accounts as of December 31, 19—. The account balances were taken from the company's ledger on that date and indicate that—

1. The January 1 beginning-of-the-year inventory was $7,750.
2. Sales totaling $79,300 were made during the year.
3. Customers returned $650 of the commodities they had purchased.
4. The year's purchases of merchandise amounted to $49,400.
5. Merchandise purchases totaling $275 were returned.
6. Freight, express, and postage amounting to $1,100 was paid on shipments of goods purchased.

Adjustments Columns and Adjusted Trial Balance Columns.   Generally none of the merchandising accounts require adjustments. Consequently, no adjustments appear opposite these accounts in the Adjustments columns and the unadjusted trial balance amounts are carried directly into the Adjusted Trial Balance columns.

Income Statement Columns.   In any company the income statement accounts are the ones the balances of which are carried into the Income Statement columns of the work sheet, and in a merchandising concern these are the (1) revenue, (2) cost of goods sold, and (3) operating expense accounts. (The work sheet treatment of the operating expense accounts was discussed in Chapter 4 and needs no further consideration here.)

Revenue Accounts.   The Sales account is the primary revenue account of a merchandising concern. It is credited throughout each accounting period for the selling price of goods sold, and always reaches the end of the period with a credit balance, which is carried into the work sheet's Income Statement credit column.

Sales returns and allowances are in effect negative sales; and the Sales Returns and Allowances account, although classified as a revenue account, is really a negative revenue account. Throughout each accounting period it is debited for returns and allowances, and at the period end its debit balance is carried into the Income Statement debit column, where in effect the returns are subtracted from the sales, when the debit column total is subtracted from the credit column total in arriving at net income.

Cost of Goods Sold Accounts.   When a work sheet is prepared for a company selling merchandise, (1) the debit balances of its Merchandise Inventory, Purchases, and Freight-In accounts are carried into the Income Statement debit column; (2) the credit balance of the Purchases Returns and Allowances account is carried into the Income Statement credit column; after which (3) the dollar amount of the ending inventory is entered directly in both the Income Statement credit column and Balance Sheet debit column.

It is easy to understand why the balances of the Merchandise Inventory, Purchases, and Freight-In accounts are carried into the Income Statement debit column—the balances are debit balances and they enter into the calculation of the net income. Likewise, it is easy to understand why the credit balance of the Purchases Returns and Allowances account is carried into the Income Statement credit column—it is in effect a subtraction from Purchases in the debit column. However, the reasons for the work sheet treatment of the ending inventory are not so apparent and require the following explanations:

First: Note that there are two inventories to be dealt with on the work sheet of a company selling merchandise—the beginning-of-the-period inventory and the end-of-the-period inventory.

Second: At the end of a period, before closing entries are posted, it is the beginning inventory amount that appears in the accounts as the debit balance of the Merchandise Inventory account, and it is this beginning inventory amount that is entered in the Trial Balance debit column opposite the account title, Merchandise Inventory, and is carried into the Adjusted Trial Balance and Income Statement debit columns.

Third: Before closing entries are posted, the dollar amount of the ending inventory does not appear in any account. As was explained earlier, the ending inventory is determined at the end of each period by counting the items of unsold merchandise on hand, multiplying the count for each kind by its cost, and adding the dollar amounts of the several kinds to determine the number of dollars of inventory.

Fourth: As soon as the number of dollars of ending inventory is determined, it is entered directly on the work sheet in both the Income Statement credit column and the Balance Sheet debit column. It is thus entered for three reasons: (1) After the other income statement items (including the operating expenses) have been carried into the Income Statement columns, it is necessary to enter the amount of the ending inventory, if the difference between the two columns is to equal the net income or loss. (2) Entering the ending inventory in the Income Statement credit column puts this amount on the work sheet in position to become part of one of the closing entries and thus be taken into the accounts as the historical record of the inventory on hand at the end of the period. (Closing entries for a company selling merchandise are discussed in more detail later.) And finally, (3) since the amount of the ending inventory is an end-of-the-period asset, entering it in the Balance Sheet debit column puts this item in position to be added to the other end-of-the-period assets and to appear on the balance sheet.

Completing the Work Sheet.   After the various income statement and balance sheet amounts of a company selling merchandise are sorted and entered in the proper columns of its work sheet, the columns are totaled and the work sheet is completed in the usual way.

PREPARING THE STATEMENTS; ADJUSTING ENTRIES

As in a service-type concern, the work sheet of a company selling merchandise is a tool for bringing together information needed in preparing the financial statements. The income statement is prepared from information in the Income Statement columns, the balance sheet from the Balance Sheet columns, and no essentially new techniques are required in the preparation of either.

Likewise, no new techniques are required in preparing and posting adjusting entries. Each adjustment in the work sheet's Adjustments columns requires an adjusting entry that is journalized and posted in the usual manner.

CLOSING ENTRIES

As in a service-type company, the Income Statement columns of its work sheet provide the information needed by a merchandising concern in making its closing entries. Furthermore, an examination of the following closing entries and the work sheet of Illustration 26, from which they were prepared, will show these closing entries are prepared in the same way as are those of a service-type company. In both types of companies the Income Summary account is debited for the work sheet's Income Statement debit column total and each account having an item in the column is

Dec.	31	Income Summary...............................	79,400.00	
		Merchandise Inventory....................		7,750.00
		Sales Returns and Allowances.............		650.00
		Purchases.................................		49,400.00
		Freight-In................................		1,100.00
		Sales Salaries............................		8,200.00
		Rent Expense, Selling Space..............		4,800.00
		Advertising Expense......................		900.00
		Freight-Out and Delivery Expense........		1,350.00
		Office Salaries...........................		3,100.00
		Rent Expense, Office Space...............		600.00
		Expired Insurance........................		65.00
		Store Supplies Used......................		425.00
		Office Supplies Used.....................		125.00
		Depreciation Expense, Store Equipment...		775.00
		Depreciation Expense, Office Equipment..		160.00
		To close the temporary proprietorship accounts having debit balances.		

Dec.	31	Merchandise Inventory............................	8,950.00	
		Sales..	79,300.00	
		Purchases Returns and Allowances..............	275.00	
		Income Summary............................		88,525.00
		To close the temporary proprietorship accounts having credit balances and to set up the ending inventory.		
	31	Income Summary..............................	9,125.00	
		George Nelson, Withdrawals..............		9,125.00
		To close the Income Summary account.		
	31	George Nelson, Withdrawals.................	4,325.00	
		George Nelson, Capital...................		4,325.00
		To close the Withdrawals account.		

credited. Then, each account having an item in the Income Statement credit column is debited and the Income Summary account is credited for the column total. And so on, as was explained in Chapter 4.

CLOSING ENTRIES AND THE INVENTORY ACCOUNT

Although there is nothing new about the closing entries of a merchandising concern, their effect on the Merchandise Inventory account should be observed.

Before closing entries were posted, the Merchandise Inventory account of Nelson Hardware Company showed in its $7,750 debit balance the amount of the company's beginning-of-the-period inventory,[1] as follows:

Merchandise Inventory   ACCOUNT NO. *114*

DATE	EXPLANATION	FO-LIO	DEBIT	CREDIT	BALANCE
196A Dec. 31		63	7 7 5 0 00		7 7 5 0 00

[1] The date of the beginning inventory, 196A, is intended to convey the idea that the $7,750 beginning inventory amount was posted to this account at the end of the preceding year.

Then, when the first closing entry was posted, its $7,750 credit to the Merchandise Inventory account had the effect of clearing the beginning inventory from the account, as follows:

Merchandise Inventory   ACCOUNT NO. 114

DATE	EXPLANATION	FO-LIO	DEBIT	CREDIT	BALANCE
196A Dec 31		63	7750 00		7750 00
196B Dec 31		77		7750 00	—0—

After this, when the second closing entry was posted, its $8,950 debit to Merchandise Inventory put back into the account the amount of the ending inventory, as follows, where the amount remains throughout the succeeding year as the debit balance of the account and as a historical record of the amount of inventory on hand at the end of 196B and the beginning of 196C.

Merchandise Inventory   ACCOUNT NO. 114

DATE	EXPLANATION	FO-LIO	DEBIT	CREDIT	BALANCE
196A Dec 31		63	7750 00		7750 00
196B Dec 31		77		7750 00	—0—
31		77	8950 00		8950 00

TAKING THE ENDING INVENTORY

Counting the unsold merchandise on hand at the end of an accounting period is often a difficult task; and unless great care is exercised, items may be omitted from the count or they may be counted more than once. Because of this, inventories are commonly taken at night, on holidays, and on weekends; or the store is closed for business in order to take the inventory.

A store's salesclerks who are familiar with the store and its merchandise are usually best equipped to make an inventory count. Before the count is started, the merchandise should be straightened and arranged in an orderly fashion on the shelves and in the showcases. Items are less apt to be counted twice or omitted if prenumbered inventory tickets like the one shown in Illustration 27 are used in making the count. At the start of the count, if inventory tickets are used, a sufficient number of tickets, at least one for each type of product on hand, is issued to each department in the store. When the inventory count is made, a clerk counts the quantity of

Illustration 27—An Inventory Ticket

○

INVENTORY TICKET

Ticket No. _____ *786* _____

Item _____

Quantity counted _____

Sales price _____

Cost price _____

Purchase date _____

Counted by _____

Checked by _____

each product and, from the count and the price tag attached to the merchandise, fills in the information on the inventory ticket. He then initials the ticket and attaches it to the counted items. A department head or other responsible person usually examines and recounts a sufficient proportion of the items to insure an accurate count. In each department, after the clerks complete the count, the department is examined for uncounted items. At this stage, inventory tickets are attached to all counted items. Consequently, any products without tickets attached are uncounted. After all items are counted and tickets attached, the tickets are removed and sent to the accounting department for completion of the inventory. To insure that no ticket is lost or left attached to merchandise, all the prenumbered tickets issued are accounted for when the tickets arrive in the accounting department.

In the accounting department, the information of the tickets is copied on inventory summary sheets, and the sheets are completed by multiplying the number of units of each product by its cost. This gives the dollar amount of each product on hand, and the total for all products is the amount of the inventory.

For many years it has been a common practice to price inventory items at *cost or market, whichever is lower.* "Cost" is the actual price that was paid for an item when it was purchased. "Market" is the price that would have to be paid if the item were being purchased on the inventory date. In other words, "market" is the replacement cost of the item. For example, on the inventory summary sheet of Illustration 28, the Ajax claw hammers are valued at cost because their $1.00 cost price is below their $1.25 market price. Likewise, the Sharp hand saws are valued at market because their $2.90 market price is below their $3.00 cost price.

ITEMS INCLUDED ON AN INVENTORY

A concern's inventory should include all goods owned by the business and held for sale, regardless of where the goods may be located at the time of the inventory. In the application of this rule, there are generally no problems with respect to most items. For most items all that is required is to see that they are counted, that nothing is omitted, and that nothing is counted more than once. However, goods in transit from a manufacturer or wholesaler, goods sold but not delivered, goods on consignment, and obsolete and damaged goods do require special attention.

Illustration 28

Inventory Summary Sheet

Item	Quantity on Hand	Date Purchased	Sales Price	Cost Price	Market Price	Inventory Value
Ajax claw hammers	4	12–12–66	1.50	1.00	1.25	4.00
Sharp hand saws	2	11–3–66	4.50	3.00	2.90	5.80
Danley 24-inch levels	2	9–14–66	5.50	3.50	3.50	7.00

When goods are in transit on the inventory date, the purchase should be recorded and the goods should appear on the purchaser's inventory if title has passed to the purchaser. The general rule as to the passing of title is: if the buyer is responsible for paying the freight charges, title passes as soon as the goods are loaded aboard the means of transportation; if the seller is to pay the freight charges, title passes when the goods arrive at their destination.

Goods on consignment are goods shipped by their owner (known as the consignor) to another person or firm (called the consignee) who is to sell the goods for the owner. Consigned goods belong to the consignor and should appear on his inventory.

Damaged goods and goods that have deteriorated or become obsolete should not be placed on the inventory if they are not salable. If such goods are salable but at a reduced price, they should be placed on the inventory at a conservative estimate of their realizable value (sale price less the cost of making the sale). This causes the accounting period in which the goods are damaged, deteriorated, or become obsolete to suffer the resultant loss.

DISPENSING WITH THE ADJUSTED TRIAL
BALANCE COLUMNS

Thus far, because the use of such columns makes the learning procedure easier, all illustrated work sheets have had Adjusted Trial Balance columns. However, the experienced accountant commonly omits these columns from his work sheet in order to reduce the time and effort required in its preparation. When he does so, after he has entered the adjustments in the Adjustments columns, he combines the adjustment amounts with the trial balance amounts and sorts the combined amounts directly into the Income Statement and Balance Sheet columns in a single operation. In other words, he simply eliminates the adjusted trial balance from his work sheet.

CODE NUMBERS AS A MEANS OF IDENTIFYING
ACCOUNTS

The account numbering scheme used in the chapters before this has been a simple one in which the accounts have been numbered consecutively. Such a scheme is satisfactory in a small business. However, in a larger more complicated accounting system, account numbers commonly become code numbers that not only identify accounts but also tell their statement classifications. For example, in one numbering system three-digit numbers with each digit having a significant meaning are used. In this system the first digit in each account number signifies the major balance sheet or income statement classification of the account to which it is assigned. For example, account numbers with first digits of 1, numbers 111 to 199, are assigned to asset accounts, and liability accounts are assigned numbers with the first digits of 2, numbers 211 to 299. When this system is used, main balance sheet and income statement account classifications are assigned the following numbers:

111 to 199 are assigned to asset accounts.
211 to 299 are assigned to liability accounts.
311 to 399 are assigned to owner equity accounts.
411 to 499 are assigned to sales or revenue accounts.
511 to 599 are assigned to cost of goods sold accounts.
611 to 699 are assigned to operating expense accounts.
711 to 799 are assigned to other revenue and expense accounts.

When accounts are assigned code numbers having several digits, all of the digits have a significant meaning. In the system under discussion where the first digit indicates the main balance sheet or income statement classification, the second and third digits further classify the account. For example, the second digits under each of the following main classifications indicate the subclassification shown:

111 to 199.   Asset accounts
    111 to 119.   Current asset accounts (second digits of 1)
    121 to 129.   Long-term investment accounts (second digits of 2)
    131 to 139.   Fixed asset accounts (second digits of 3)
    141 to 149.   Intangible asset accounts (second digits of 4)
    151 to 159.   Deferred charges (second digits of 5)

211 to 299.   Liability accounts
    211 to 219.   Current liability accounts (second digits of 1)
    221 to 229.   Long-term liability accounts (second digits of 2)

611 to 699.   Operating expense accounts
    611 to 629.   Selling expense accounts (second digits of 1 and 2)
    631 to 649.   Delivery expense accounts (second digits of 3 and 4)
    651 to 669.   General administrative expense accounts (second digits of 5 and 6)

The third digit in each number further classifies the account. For example, in the system under discussion, all selling expense accounts, which have account numbers with first digits of 6 and second digits of 1 and 2, are further classified as follows:

611 to 699.   Operating expense accounts
    611 to 629.   Selling expense accounts
        611.   Sales salaries (third digit of 1)
        612.   Advertising (third digit of 2)
        613.   Depreciation of store equipment (third digit of 3)

QUESTIONS FOR CLASS DISCUSSION

1. How and when is cost of goods sold determined in a store using a periodic inventory system?
2. May a store sell goods at a price above their cost and still suffer a loss? How?
3. Why should a concern be interested in the amount of its sales returns and allowances?
4. Since total sales returns and allowances is subtracted from the balance of the Sales account on the income statement, why not save the effort of this subtraction by debiting each return or allowance to the Sales account.
5. If a concern may return for full credit all unsatisfactory merchandise purchased, why should it be interested in the amount returned?
6. Which of the following are debited to the Purchases account of a grocery store: (a) the purchase of a cash register; (b) the purchase of a roll of wrapping paper; (c) the purchase of advertising space in a newspaper; and (d) the purchase of a case of tomato soup?
7. What is gross profit?

8. At the end of an accounting period which inventory, the beginning inventory or the ending, appears on the trial balance?

9. Why is the amount of the ending inventory entered in the work sheet's Income Statement credit column? Why is it entered in the Balance Sheet debit column?

10. What effect do closing entries have on the Merchandise Inventory account?

11. Why are inventory tickets used in taking a physical inventory?

12. When applied to an inventory item and used in the phrase, "cost or market, whichever is lower," what is the meaning of the words: (a) cost and (b) market?

13. During a year a company purchased merchandise costing $25,000. What was the company's cost of goods sold if there were:
    a) No beginning or ending inventories?
    b) A beginning inventory of $11,000 and no ending inventory?
    c) A beginning inventory of $8,000 and an ending inventory of $9,500?
    d) No beginning inventory and an ending inventory of $7,000?

14. In counting the merchandise on hand at the end of an accounting period, a clerk failed to count, and consequently omitted from the inventory, all the merchandise on one shelf. If the cost of the merchandise on the shelf was $100, what was the effect of the omission on (a) the balance sheet, and (b) the income statement?

15. Suppose that the omission of the $100 from the inventory (Question 14) was not discovered. What would be the effect on the balance sheet and income statement prepared at the end of the next accounting period?

16. Copy the following tabulation and fill in the missing amounts. Indicate a loss by placing a minus sign before the amount. Each horizontal row of figures is a separate problem situation.

Sales	Beginning Inventory	Purchases	Ending Inventory	Cost of Goods Sold	Gross Profit	Expenses	Net Income or Loss
85,000	50,000	40,000	?	55,000	?	20,000	?
90,000	35,000	?	45,000	50,000	?	25,000	20,000
125,000	50,000	?	40,000	?	55,000	35,000	20,000
?	40,000	70,000	35,000	?	40,000	35,000	?
100,000	40,000	65,000	?	60,000	?	25,000	?
70,000	30,000	?	35,000	40,000	?	?	10,000
?	40,000	50,000	30,000	?	40,000	?	−5,000
85,000	?	50,000	35,000	?	30,000	?	10,000

17. When a three-digit account numbering system like the one described in this chapter is in use, which digit of an account's number is the most significant?

PROBLEMS

Problem 5–1

Prepare general journal entries to record the following transactions:

Dec. 3 Sold merchandise to Robert Hill for cash, $165.
     5 Purchased merchandise on credit from Krueger Industries, $880.
     6 Purchased store supplies on credit from Store Supply Company, $130.
     7 Returned for credit $25 of the store supplies purchased on December 6.
     9 Purchased merchandise on credit from B. T. Sanders, Inc., $1,215.
     9 Paid Western Railroad $45 freight charges on the merchandise purchased from B. T. Sanders, Inc.
     9 Returned for credit $85 of the merchandise purchased from B. T. Sanders, Inc.
    11 Sold merchandise on credit to J. R. Murphy, $375.
    13 J. R. Murphy returned for credit $50 of the merchandise purchased on December 11.
    15 Purchased on credit from Store Supply Company a new cash register, $450.
    17 Sold for cash from the store office an old unneeded typewriter, $65.

Problem 5–2

The following condensed trial balance was taken from the ledger of The Campus Shop at the end of its annual accounting period:

THE CAMPUS SHOP
Trial Balance, December 31, 19—

Cash...	$ 1,800	
Merchandise inventory...........................	8,000	
Other assets....................................	12,000	
Liabilities.....................................		$ 4,400
V. R. Huntington, capital.......................		16,200
V. R. Huntington, withdrawals...................	6,000	
Sales..		52,300
Sales returns and allowances....................	500	
Purchases......................................	30,000	
Purchases returns and allowances................		600
Freight-in......................................	200	
Selling expenses................................	10,000	
General and administrative expenses.............	5,000	
	$73,500	$73,500

Required:

1. Copy the trial balance onto a work sheet form and complete the work sheet under the assumptions that there are no adjustments and the ending inventory is $9,000.

2. Prepare an income statement for The Campus Shop.
3. Prepare compound closing entries from the work sheet.

Problem 5–3

Jones Clothing Store

The following trial balance was taken from the ledger of ~~The Man's Shop~~ at the end of its annual accounting period:

Jones Clothing Store

~~THE MAN'S SHOP~~
Trial Balance, December 31, 19—

Cash..	$ 2,870	
Merchandise inventory............................	15,245	
Store supplies....................................	810	
Prepaid insurance................................	195	
Store equipment..................................	10,865	
Accumulated depreciation, store equipment.......		$ 3,340
Accounts payable................................		3,110
Douglas Murphy, capital..........................		16,120
Douglas Murphy, withdrawals.....................	6,000	
Sales..		75,225
Sales returns and allowances.....................	1,875	
Purchases.......................................	~~40,540~~ 41,510	
Purchases returns and allowances................		865
Freight-in.......................................	970	
Sales salaries....................................	11,890	
Rent expense....................................	6,000	
Advertising expense..............................	825	
Utilities expense.................................	575	
	$98,660	$98,660

Required:

1. Copy the trial balance into the Trial Balance columns of a work sheet and complete the work sheet using the following information *for adjustments:*
   a) Store supplies inventory, $185.
   b) Expired insurance, $115.
   c) Estimated depreciation of store equipment, $1,100.
   d) Accrued sales salaries payable, $135.
   e) Ending merchandise inventory, $16,730.
2. Prepare the trading section of an income statement for the store (an income statement complete through the calculation of gross profit from sales).
3. Prepare compound closing entries.
4. Open a Merchandise Inventory account and enter the beginning inventory as its balance. Then post those portions of the closing entries that affect the account.

Problem 5–4

At the end of its annual accounting period a trial balance of the Desert Haberdashery appeared as follows:

DESERT HABERDASHERY
Trial Balance, December 31, 19—

Cash..	$ 1,875	
Merchandise inventory.........................	18,190	
Store supplies.................................	1,120	
Office supplies................................	275	
Prepaid insurance.............................	315	
Office equipment..............................	2,850	
Accumulated depreciation, office equipment...		$ 795
Store equipment..............................	14,780	
Accumulated depreciation, store equipment....		4,135
Notes payable.................................		2,500
Accounts payable..............................		4,540
Harry Johnson, capital........................		21,465
Harry Johnson, withdrawals...................	7,200	
Sales...		85,785
Sales returns and allowances..................	1,560	
Purchases....................................	52,180	
Purchases returns and allowances.............		715
Freight-in....................................	570	
Sales salaries.................................	9,255	
Rent expense, selling space....................	4,320	
Advertising expense...........................	590	
Delivery expense..............................	235	
Heating and lighting expenses.................	585	
Office salaries................................	3,555	
Rent expense, office space....................	480	
	$119,935	$119,935

Required:
1. Enter the trial balance on a work sheet and complete the work sheet using the following information:
    a) Store supplies inventory, $335.
    b) Office supplies inventory, $120.
    c) Expired insurance, $245.
    d) Estimated depreciation of office equipment, $310; and (*e*) of store equipment, $1,260.
    f) Accrued sales salaries, $165; and accrued office salaries, $45.
    g) Ending merchandise inventory, $19,770.
2. From the work sheet prepare a classified balance sheet and a classified income statement.
3. From the work sheet prepare adjusting and closing entries.
4. Open a Merchandise Inventory account and enter the $18,190 beginning inventory as the debit balance of the account. Then post the portions of the closing entries that affect this account.

Problem 5–5
The following accounts are in the ledger of Pioneer Hardware Store:

Cash

Notes Receivable

Accounts Receivable

Merchandise Inventory

Prepaid Insurance

Store Supplies

Office Supplies

Store Equipment

Accumulated Depreciation, Store
  Equipment

Office Equipment

Accumulated Depreciation, Office
  Equipment

Notes Payable

Accounts Payable

Wages Payable

Mortgage Payable

Scott Moyer, Capital

Scott Moyer, Withdrawals

Sales

Sales Returns and Allowances

Purchases

Purchases Returns and Allowances

Freight-In

Sales Salaries

Advertising

Store Supplies Used

Depreciation, Store Equipment

Rent Expense, Selling Space

Taxes Expense, Selling

Office Salaries

Office Supplies Used

Expired Insurance

Depreciation, Office Equipment

Rent Expense, Office Space

Taxes Expense, Office

Required:

Design an account numbering system for Pioneer Hardward Store. List the foregoing accounts on a sheet of notebook paper, placing the account number you would assign to each account after the account name.

CLASS EXERCISE

Exercise 5–1

Following is a list of trial balance accounts and their balances. To simplify the problem and to save time, the balances are in numbers of not more than two digits. However, in order to increase your skill in sorting adjusted trial balance amounts to the proper columns, the accounts are listed in alphabetical order.

Trial Balance Accounts and Balances

Accounts payable..........$ 2	*Merchandise inventory*.....$ 4
Accounts receivable......... 3	*Prepaid insurance*.......... 3
Accumulated depreciation,	*Purchases*................... 10
store equipment.......... 2	*Purchases returns*.......... 1
Advertising expense....... 4	*Salaries expense*............ 5
Cash..................... 2	*Sales*....................... 30
Freight-in................. 1	*Sales returns*............... 2
Jack James, capital........ 13	*Store equipment*........... 9
Jack James, withdrawals... 2	*Store supplies*.............. 3

Required:

Prepare a work sheet form on ordinary notebook paper and copy the trial balance accounts and amounts on the work sheet without changing their alphabetical arrangement. Then complete the work sheet using the following information:

a) Estimated depreciation of store equipment, $1.
b) Ending merchandise inventory, $2.
c) Expired insurance, $2.
d) Accrued salaries payable, $3.
e) Ending inventory of store supplies, $1.

ALTERNATE PROBLEMS

Problem 5–1A

A new and inexperienced bookkeeper made the following errors during the last two weeks of December in recording the transactions of The College Store, a store owned by Walter Gursell.

Dec. 18 A purchase of store equipment costing $165 was debited to the Office Equipment account.

21 A $125 store check paying for a portable typewriter delivered to the proprietor's home for use of his college Freshman son was recorded with a debit to the Office Equipment account and a credit to Cash.

22 A $265 purchase of office equipment was debited in error to the Purchases account.

22 Office equipment costing $210 was returned as unsatisfactory on this date. The transaction was recorded with a debit to the creditor, Office Supply Company, and a credit to Purchases Returns and Allowances.

26 Sixty-five dollars received from a customer, Walter Bash, in payment of his account was credited to the account of William Basham.

31 An adjusting entry to record $45 of accrued sales salaries was not made at the end of the annual accounting period. The salaries were paid and recorded in the usual manner on January 4.

31 Merchandise costing $260 was counted twice in taking the year-end inventory.

Required:

1. Prepare entries to correct the foregoing errors under the assumption that they were discovered on December 31 before the accounts were closed for the year.

2. Prepare a second set of entries to correct the foregoing errors under the assumption they were discovered on January 18, after the accounts had been closed on the previous December 31.

Problem 5–2A

The following trial balance was taken from the ledger of The University Store at the end of its annual accounting period:

THE UNIVERSITY STORE
Trial Balance, December 31, 19—

Cash..	$ 1,595	
Accounts receivable.............................	1,045	
Merchandise inventory..........................	14,540	
Store supplies..................................	675	
Prepaid insurance..............................	220	
Store equipment................................	9,890	
Accumulated depreciation, store equipment......		$ 3,210
Accounts payable...............................		2,225
Earl Dashman, capital..........................		18,045
Earl Dashman, withdrawals......................	6,600	
Sales...		72,985
Sales returns and allowances....................	1,345	
Purchases......................................	41,320	
Purchases returns and allowances...............		635
Freight-in......................................	855	
Sales salaries..................................	11,435	
Rent expense...................................	6,000	
Advertising expense............................	815	
Heating and lighting expense...................	765	
	$97,100	$97,100

Required:

1. Enter the trial balance on a work sheet form and complete the work sheet using the following information:
    a) Store supplies inventory, $135.
    b) Expired insurance, $115.
    c) Estimated depreciation of store equipment, $920.
    d) Accrued sales salaries payable, $180.
    e) Ending merchandise inventory, $15,930.
2. Prepare an income statement complete through the calculation of gross profit from sales.
3. Prepare compound closing entries.

Problem 5–3A

The following trial balance was taken from the ledger of Sportswear Shop at the end of its annual accounting period:

SPORTSWEAR SHOP
Trial Balance, December 31, 19—

Cash	$ 1,190	
Merchandise inventory	12,655	
Store supplies	780	
Office supplies	145	
Prepaid insurance	235	
Store equipment	9,835	
Accumulated depreciation, store equipment		$ 1,370
Office equipment	1,775	
Accumulated depreciation, office equipment		235
Accounts payable		2,145
Larry Duncan, capital		18,045
Larry Duncan, withdrawals	5,400	
Sales		73,720
Sales returns and allowances	1,510	
Purchases	40,235	
Purchases returns and allowances		715
Freight-in	865	
Sales salaries	11,230	
Rent expense, selling space	4,950	
Advertising expense	830	
Office salaries	3,560	
Rent expense, office space	550	
Telephone and utilities	485	
	$96,230	$96,230

Required:

1. Enter the trial balance in the Trial Balance columns of a work sheet form and complete the work sheet using the following information:

    a) Store supplies inventory, $155.

    b) Office supplies inventory, $65.

    c) Expired insurance, $105.

    d) Estimated depreciation of store equipment, $1,030; and (*e*) of office equipment, $190.

    f) Accrued sales salaries, $175; and accrued office salaries, $40.

    g) Sportswear Shop allocates 10 percent of its rent to the office and the remainder to selling space. Rent for the month of December has not been paid or recorded.

    h) Ending merchandise inventory, $11,940.

2. Prepare a classified income statement.

3. Prepare compound closing entries.

4. Open a Merchandise Inventory account and enter the beginning inventory as its balance. Then post the portions of the closing entry that affect this account.

Problem 5–4A

The following trial balance was taken from the ledger of Phoenix Sales Company at the end of its annual accounting period.

PHOENIX SALES COMPANY
Trial Balance, December 31, 19—

Cash..	$ 1,945	
Accounts receivable............................	3,980	
Merchandise inventory..........................	17,760	
Prepaid insurance..............................	455	
Prepaid rent...................................	1,200	
Store supplies.................................	1,230	
Office supplies................................	295	
Store equipment...............................	17,115	
Accumulated depreciation, store equipment....		$ 8,230
Office equipment..............................	3,210	
Accumulated depreciation, office equipment...		1,560
Notes payable.................................		5,000
Accounts payable..............................		3,625
J. C. Jacks, capital...........................		32,650
J. C. Jacks, withdrawals.......................	4,800	
Sales...		81,710
Sales returns and allowances..................	1,240	
Purchases.....................................	55,120	
Purchases returns and allowances.............		860
Freight-in....................................	1,185	
Sales salaries................................	13,535	
Rent expense, selling space....................	4,860	
Advertising expense...........................	815	
Delivery expense..............................	630	
Office salaries................................	3,335	
Rent expense, office space.....................	540	
Telephone and utilities........................	385	
	$133,635	$133,635

Required:

1. Enter the trial balance on a work sheet form and complete the work sheet using the following information:
   a) Expired insurance, $325.
   b) Phoenix Sales Company prorates its rent expense, charging 10 percent to the office and the remainder as a selling expense. On January 1 of the trial balance year two months' rent was prepaid, as shown by the balance of the Prepaid Rent account. Rent for each of the months, March through November, was paid on the first day of the month and debited to the rent expense accounts. The December rent was unpaid and unrecorded at the year-end.
   c) Store supplies inventory, $285.
   d) Office supplies inventory, $120.

    e) Estimated depreciation of store equipment, $1,525; and (*f*) of office equipment, $315.

    g) Accrued sales salaries, $235; and accrued office salaries, $60.

    h) Ending merchandise inventory, $19,185.

2. Prepare a classified income statement and a classified balance sheet.
3. Prepare adjusting and closing entries.
4. Open a Merchandise Inventory account and enter the $17,760 beginning inventory as its balance. Then post those portions of the closing entries that affect this account.

DECISION PROBLEM 5—MORGAN GUY

Morgan Guy has operated the Quality Laundry for the past ten years. He has had no experience in a merchandising business. Last week he acquired the rights to distribute at wholesale two standard brands of frozen foods and a new line of milled products. To give him a more complete line, he has decided to add several brands of canned and packaged foods. He will employ a number of salesmen to offer his merchandise to retail stores.

Mr. Guy's bookkeeper at the laundry has had little or no experience in accounting for a trading business. You are requested to write a report to Mr. Guy outlining the major differences in accounting for the wholesale grocery firm from those now employed in the laundry. Please be fairly specific as to the problems of accounting for merchandising costs, inventory determination, and reporting of net income.

6

Controlling
Purchases and Sales
with Business Papers

Thus far in the discussion accounting has been presented primarily as a tool for recording and reporting the effects of transactions. This is one of its functions, but accounting has another important use. Accounting is also a tool of management for controlling business operations. For example, management uses accounting to control sales procedures so that every customer gets the goods he orders and every sale is recorded. It also uses accounting to control purchasing procedures so that only properly requisitioned goods are ordered and paid for.

NEED FOR BUSINESS PAPERS AND PROCEDURES

To insure that all transactions are properly completed and recorded, systematic business and accounting procedures are designed for handling transactions. These systematic procedures commonly require that business papers be prepared to record and report the steps of each transaction as they are completed. The transaction is then controlled, and recording is insured by providing within the procedure a systematic method for collecting and recording the papers prepared.

The procedures and business papers discussed in this chapter for handling purchases and sales are illustrative of those found in many companies. However, all companies do not use the same procedures and papers in completing identical transactions. Procedures and papers vary from company to company because both are designed to meet particular needs. Among companies of the same size, procedures and papers are similar. However, those of a large company often vary greatly from those of a small one. This is because the owner or manager of a small company is usually actively engaged in all phases of his company's operations, and his active participation helps to control the operations. In a large company, duties and responsibilities must be divided and delegated to various employees; and when duties and responsibilities are divided and delegated, there is greater need for business papers to coordinate and control the operations carried on by the business.

SALES PROCEDURES OF A SMALL BUSINESS

In a small retail store many sales are for cash, with the customers selecting, with the aid of salesclerks, the merchandise desired, and the clerks wrapping the merchandise and ringing up the sales on a cash register or registers. In such stores it is common practice to require a salesclerk to record each sale on a cash register before the merchandise is wrapped. This helps to insure that each sale is recorded; and by placing the cash register in such a position that the customer can see the amount "rung up," the customer will help insure that the proper amount is "rung up." At the end of each day, total sales as shown by the cash register or registers is recorded by a journal entry debiting Cash and crediting Sales.

A small retail firm makes use of sales tickets when goods are sold on credit, with each clerk being issued a book of prenumbered tickets. Then when goods are sold on credit, the credit customer selects the merchandise desired. The salesclerk fills out a sales ticket in duplicate, secures approval of the customer's credit standing from the store office, and wraps and gives the merchandise to the customer. One copy, the customer's copy, of the sales ticket is normally wrapped with the merchandise because, since the customer will usually check his copy, this helps to insure that the ticket is made out for the proper amount. The other copy is sent to the store office where it is used to make a journal entry debiting the customer and crediting Sales. Accounting for all sales ticket numbers helps insure that every credit sale is recorded.

PURCHASING PROCEDURE OF A SMALL BUSINESS AND SALES PROCEDURE OF A LARGE BUSINESS

A small retail business orders most of its merchandise from traveling sales representatives of wholesalers and manufacturers. These representatives call upon the retailer at set intervals to take orders. Some display samples; others sell from catalogues.

A small business owner or manager, from his close contact and familiarity with his business, usually knows the items of merchandise in need of restocking. Often he keeps an informal "want book." This is commonly an ordinary notebook in which he writes down, as they come to his attention, items in need of restocking. When the sales representative calls, orders are placed for the merchandise needed. The representative usually "writes up" the order in his order book, listing the items and quantities desired. The store owner or manager signs the order blank and is given a copy for his files, and the salesman transmits the original order copy to his home office.

Most wholesaling and manufacturing companies reserve the right to review and to either accept or reject orders obtained by their salesmen. Consequently, such companies do not consider the taking of an order to be a sale, and as a result, no formal debit and credit record of an order is made by either party.

Upon receipt of the order from its salesman, the wholesaler begins its processing. Normally, the wholesaler processes hundreds of orders daily; and to do so efficiently, he must divide the processing procedure into parts and assign each part to a specialized department, with the whole procedure controlled and coordinated in such a manner as to insure that the buyer receives the merchandise ordered and is charged for the sale. Coordination and control is often obtained by use of several copies of an *invoice*.

The Invoice. An invoice is an itemized statement of goods bought or sold. It is prepared by the seller who is often called the *vendor*. To the seller it is known as a *sales invoice*. A copy of the same invoice, when received by the buyer or *vendee*, is known to the buyer as a *purchase invoice*. In manufacturing and wholesaling, invoices are of the general type shown in Illustration 29 on page 142.

An invoice such as the one in Illustration 29 sets forth the quantity, description, and unit prices of the goods sold, plus the total amount charged. It also commonly shows to whom the goods were sold, terms of the sale, seller's invoice number, date of the invoice, purchase order number, manner in which the goods were shipped, number of packages, where the goods were shipped, and often other data.

Processing the Order. A large wholesaler begins the processing of an order by preparing several duplicate copies of the sales invoice. The copies are prepared from information contained in the order sent in by the traveling salesman or from a purchase order or a letter sent by the prospective buyer. All copies are produced in one operation with carbon paper, usually on different colors of paper to facilitate their identification.

Coordination and control of an order's processing is best explained by a chart, Illustration 30, showing the movement of the different copies of the invoice. An examination of the chart will disclose that—

Copies The sales department starts the processing procedure by sending
2 and 3 Copies 2 and 3 of the invoice to the credit department for approval of the buyer's credit standing. In manufacturing and wholesaling

Illustration 29—An Invoice

THE EUGENE MANUFACTURING COMPANY	Invoice No.
2590 Chula Vista Street	**3216**
Eugene, Oregon	

Sold to

_____   Date_____

_____   Purchase Order_____

_____   Shipped Via_____

Shipped to_____   Number of Packages_____

_____

_____

Terms_____

Quantity	Description	Unit Price	Amount

almost all sales are on credit; therefore, care must be exercised to see that goods are not sold to customers who cannot pay. In such concerns the duty of granting credit is normally assigned to a credit department rather than to the sales department, because the sales department might be swayed in its judgment of the customer's ability to pay by a desire to make a sale. The credit department approves or rejects the customer's credit standing and returns the sales department copy of the invoice with its decision shown thereon. Rejections are not too numerous, and in each case the sales department attempts to arrange a cash sale.

When the approval of the customer's credit standing is received from the credit department, the sales department distributes the remaining invoice copies.

Copies   Copies 4 and 5 are sent to the stock room where the merchandise is
4 and 5   assembled and sent to the shipping department with Copy 4, the

Illustration 30—Copies of the Invoice Used to Control the Procedure for Processing a Customer's Order

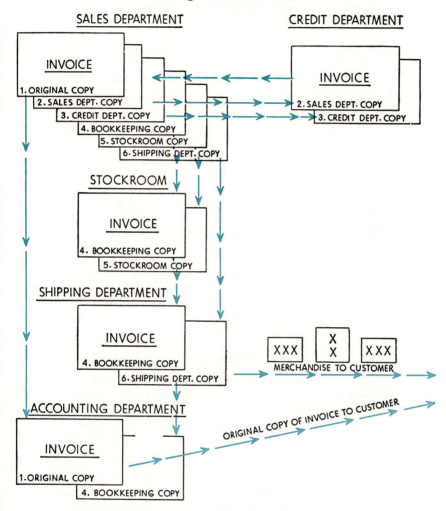

bookkeeping copy of the invoice. In the shipping department, the merchandise is packed for shipment and dispatched to the customer. After this, Copy 4, the bookkeeping copy, is sent to the accounting department as notification that the goods have been shipped.

Copy 6   Copy 6 is sent directly to the shipping department so that it may be used to check back, if the goods do not arrive in the shipping department. Copy 1 may be used by the accounting department to check back, if the bookkeeping copy does not arrive from the shipping department as notification that the shipment has been made.

Copy 1   Copy 1 is sent directly to the accounting department where it awaits the bookkeeping copy's arrival. Upon receipt of the bookkeeping copy notifying that the goods have been shipped, the accounting department mails Copy 1 of the invoice to the customer. It then uses the bookkeeping copy to record the sale by an entry debiting the customer and crediting Sales.

Receipt of the Invoice by the Buyer. Upon receipt of the invoice and merchandise, the buyer first examines the invoice for clerical errors. He then compares the invoice with the copy of the order left by the salesman or with a copy of his own letter or purchase order to see that all items were ordered. Next, the merchandise received is compared with the invoice to see that all items listed were received. If the invoice is correct and the goods were ordered and received in good condition, the invoice is then used by the buyer to make a journal entry recording the purchase.

PURCHASING PROCEDURE OF A LARGE BUSINESS

In a large business it is necessary to divide the responsibilities connected with purchasing merchandise and other assets and to coordinate and control these responsibilities with business papers. The papers commonly used are listed in Illustration 31. An explanation of each with its use will illustrate a large concern's purchasing procedure.

Illustration 31

Business Paper	Prepared by	Sent to
1. *Purchase requisition*	*Selling department manager desiring that merchandise be purchased*	*Purchasing department*
2. *Purchase order*	*Purchasing department*	*Vendor and the accounting department*
3. *Invoice*	*Company selling the merchandise*	*Accounting department*
4. *Receiving report*	*Receiving department*	*Purchasing, accounting, and requisitioning departments*
5. *Invoice approval form*	*Accounting department*	*Attached to invoice in the accounting department*

Purchase Requisition. A large merchandising company is normally divided into selling departments and service departments, with each department under the supervision of a manager. The selling departments sell different types of merchandise, and the service departments perform services for the selling departments. For example, the purchasing department is a service department responsible for buying for all departments.

In a large concern the purchasing department generally cannot know, first hand, the merchandise needs of all its selling departments; therefore, the responsibility for keeping an adequate supply of the right kinds of merchandise in each department is usually delegated to the department manager. However, the department managers cannot be permitted to purchase directly from supply sources because if each manager were permitted to deal directly with wholesalers and manufacturers, the amount of merchandise purchased and the resulting liabilities could not be controlled. Therefore, in order to secure control over purchases and resulting liabilities, department managers are commonly required to place all orders through the purchasing department. In such cases the function of the department managers in the purchasing procedure is to inform the purchasing department of their needs. Each manager performs this function by preparing in triplicate a purchase requisition, Illustration 32, listing the merchandise desired.

The original and a duplicate copy of the purchase requisition are sent to

Illustration 32—A Purchase Requisition

PURCHASE REQUISITION

Eugene Manufacturing Company

Requisition No. **2613**

Date_____ Department_____

Date Wanted_____

Quantity	Description

Requisitioned by_____ Approved by_____

Purchase Order No._____ Date Ordered_____

Ordered from_____

the purchasing department. The third copy is retained by the requisitioning department as a check on the purchasing department. All requisitions are prenumbered so that each may be accounted for. Requisitioning merchandise is not a transaction in the accounting sense of the term; therefore, no formal debit and credit record of a requisition is made.

Ordinarily, the purchasing department does not make purchases except upon requisition. However, it may call the attention of interested department managers to any attractively priced articles normally required by their departments.

Purchase Order. The purchase order is a business form used by the purchasing department in placing an order with a manufacturer or wholesaler. It authorizes the supplier to ship the merchandise ordered and takes the place of a typewritten letter placing the order. A sample purchase order is shown in Illustration 33.

On receipt of a purchase requisition from a selling department, the

Illustration 33—A Purchase Order

PURCHASE ORDER	Purchase Order No. **4238**

EUGENE MANUFACTURING COMPANY
2590 Chula Vista Street
Eugene, Oregon

Date_____

To_____

_____

_____

Please enter our order for the following:

Quantity	Description	Unit Price	Total

Do not enclose invoice with merchandise. Mark order number on all packages.

DELIVER NO MERCHANDISE WITHOUT A WRITTEN ORDER ON THIS FORM	EUGENE MANUFACTURING COMPANY By_____

purchasing department prepares five copies of the purchase order. More may be prepared if needed. The five copies are distributed as follows:

Copy 1   Copy 1, the original copy, is sent to the supplier as a request to purchase and as authority to ship the merchandise listed.

Copy 2   Copy 2 is sent to the accounting department where it will ultimately be used in approving the invoice of the purchase for payment.

Copy 3   Copy 3 is sent to the department issuing the requisition to acknowledge the requisition and as notification of the action taken.

Copy 4   Copy 4 is sent to the receiving department as authority to receive the merchandise. The receiving department is a service department responsible for receiving, unpacking, and checking all merchandise received. Usually the receiving department copy of the purchase order does not list the quantities ordered. This insures that the receiving department will make an independent count of the items received. The reason for the statement "Do not enclose invoice with merchandise," which is commonly printed on purchase order forms, is to avoid making available to the receiving department a list of the merchandise shipped.

Copy 5   Copy 5 of the purchase order is retained on file by the purchasing department.

When a purchase results from the call of the supplier's salesman, the original purchase order copy may be attached to the salesman's order blank for transmission to the supplier. The copy of the salesman's order left with the buyer is then attached to the copy of the purchase order retained on file in the purchasing department.

Invoice. As previously stated, the original copy of the purchase order is sent to the supplier. Upon its receipt, the manufacturer or wholesaler processes the order, shipping the merchandise and mailing the invoice covering the shipment. The goods are delivered to the buyer's receiving department, and the invoice is sent to his accounting department.

Receiving Report. Most large companies maintain a special department assigned the duty of receiving all merchandise purchased. As each shipment is received, counted, and checked, the receiving department prepares four copies of a receiving report. On this report is listed the quantity, description, and condition of the items received. The original copy is sent to the accounting department; the second copy to the department that requisitioned the merchandise; the third copy is sent to the purchasing department; and the fourth copy is retained on file in the receiving department. The copies sent to the purchasing and requisitioning departments act as notification of the arrival of the goods. An example of a receiving report is shown in Illustration 34.

Illustration 34—A Receiving Report

RECEIVING REPORT		No. **4383**
The Eugene Manufacturing Company		

Received from _____

_____

_____

_____

Date_____

Purchase Order No._____

Supplier's Invoice No._____

Received Via_____

Quantity	Description	Condition

Counted and Inspected by_____

Invoice Approval Form. When the receiving report arrives in the accounting department, the accounting department has in its possession copies of the—

1. Requisition listing the items requested by the requisitioning department.
2. Purchase order that lists the merchandise ordered.
3. Invoice showing quantity, description, unit price, and total of the goods shipped by the seller.
4. Receiving report that lists quantity and condition of the items received.

With the information on these papers, the accounting department is in position to approve the invoice for entry on the books and ultimate payment. In approving the invoice, the accounting department checks and compares the information on all the papers. To facilitate the checking and to insure that no step in the checking procedure is omitted, an invoice approval form (Illustration 35) is commonly used. The invoice approval form may be a separate business paper that is attached to the invoice, or the information shown on the illustrated form may be stamped directly on the invoice by means of a rubber stamp.

As each step in the checking procedure is completed, the clerk making

Illustration 35

INVOICE APPROVAL FORM

Purchase Order No._____

Requisition Check_____

Purchase Order Check_____

Receiving Report Check_____

Invoice Check
  Price Approval_____

  Calculations_____

  Terms_____

  Transportation_____

Accounting Distribution_____

_____

Final Approval_____

---

the check initials the invoice approval form. Initials in each space on the form indicate:

1. Requisition Check . . . .   The items on the invoice agree with the requisition and were requisitioned.

2. Purchase Order Check .   The items on the invoice agree with the purchase order and were ordered.

3. Receiving Report Check   The items on the invoice agree with the receiving report and were received.

4. Invoice Check:
    Price Approval . . . . . .   The invoice prices are the agreed prices.
    Calculations . . . .   The invoice has no mathematical errors.
    Terms . . . .   The terms are the agreed terms.
    Transportation . . . . .   The seller followed shipping instructions of the purchasing department. This is important because failure to follow instructions may result in additional transportation costs.

5. Accounting Distribution   Since the purchasing department is responsible for buying for all departments, an invoice may list items of supplies, equipment, or merchandise. Therefore, the account or accounts to be debited in recording the invoice must be indicated under accounting distribution.

Recording the Invoice. After the invoice is checked and approved, the purchase requisition, purchase order, receiving report, and invoice approval form, if a stamp is not used, are attached to the invoice. An entry to record the invoice is then made debiting Purchases, if merchandise was purchased, and crediting the creditor. After this the papers are filed.

DEBIT MEMORANDUM AND CREDIT MEMORANDUM

(1) Invoice errors, (2) goods received in damaged condition, (3) goods received that were not ordered, and (4) goods received short of the amount ordered and billed are points for adjustment between the buyer and seller. In some cases the buyer can make the adjustment, and in others adjustment is a subject for negotiation between the buyer and seller. When goods are received that were not ordered or when there are errors on the invoice, the buyer may make the adjustment. If he does, he must notify the seller of his action. The buyer commonly notifies the seller by sending a *debit memorandum* or a *credit memorandum*.

For instance, Salem Department Store, in checking an invoice for merchandise purchased from Acme Wholesale Company, discovers an invoice error that increases the dollar total of the invoice. This causes Salem Department Store to increase the amount credited to its account payable with Acme Wholesale Company. Salem Department Store notifies

Illustration 36

CREDIT MEMORANDUM

SALEM DEPARTMENT STORE
SALEM, OREGON

DATE December 3, 19__

To: Acme Wholesale Company
1234 N.W. First Avenue
Portland, Oregon

WE *CREDIT* YOUR ACCOUNT AS FOLLOWS:

Your invoice No. 72-245, dated 12-1-__, error in calculations. Invoice should total $135 not $125. $10.00

SALEM DEPARTMENT STORE

Frank Hatts
Manager, Purchasing Department

Acme Wholesale Company of the adjustment by sending a credit memorandum, Illustration 36, indicating that it is crediting and increasing its account payable. Salem Department Store in its checking procedure should discover an error such as this before the invoice is recorded. If it does, the Purchases account is debited and the Acme Company account payable is credited for the correct larger $135 amount. A copy of the memorandum is attached to the recorded invoice to indicate the adjustment. On receipt of the memorandum, Acme Wholesale Company will debit The Salem Department Store account receivable and credit its Sales account for an additional $10.

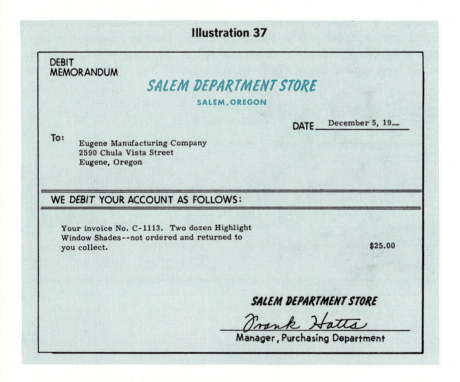

If in checking another invoice, Salem Department Store discovers an error that decreases the invoice amount, it notifies the seller with a debit memorandum. This debit memorandum, shown in Illustration 37, indicates that the store is debiting and decreasing its amount payable to Eugene Manufacturing Company. Salem Department Store records the invoice to which this debit memorandum applies by debiting Purchases and crediting Eugene Manufacturing Company for $25 less than the original invoice amount.

Some adjustments, such as merchandise received in damaged condition or merchandise not meeting specifications, normally require negotiations between the buyer and seller. In such cases the buyer may debit Purchases for the full invoice amount and enter into negotiations with the seller for a return or an adjustment. If the seller agrees to a return or adjustment, he notifies the buyer with a credit memorandum. This memorandum is a credit memorandum to the seller because the return or adjustment reduces the amount of his account receivable with the buyer. For example, Salem Department Store purchased a number of items from Novelty Supply Company, totaling $100. When the merchandise arrived, five ceramic figurines were found to have been improperly packed and were consequently damaged in transit. Salem Department Store recorded the full amount of the invoice by debiting Purchases and crediting Novelty Supply Company for $100. It then entered into negotiations for an adjustment equal to the value of the broken figurines. Novelty Supply Company agreed to the adjustment and notified Salem Department Store with the credit memorandum shown in Illustration 38.

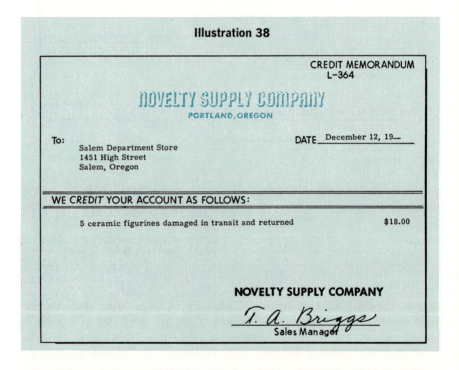

Illustration 38

CREDIT MEMORANDUM
L-364

NOVELTY SUPPLY COMPANY
PORTLAND, OREGON

To:
Salem Department Store
1451 High Street
Salem, Oregon

DATE December 12, 19—

WE *CREDIT* YOUR ACCOUNT AS FOLLOWS:

5 ceramic figurines damaged in transit and returned $18.00

NOVELTY SUPPLY COMPANY

T. A. Briggs
Sales Manager

Since Salem Department Store debited Purchases and credited Novelty Supply Company for the full amount of the original invoice, it records the credit memorandum by a debit to Novelty Supply Company and a credit to Purchases Returns and Allowances for $18.

A debit or credit memorandum may originate with either party to a transaction. The memorandum secures its name from the action of the party originating it. If the originator debits, he sends a debit memorandum. If the originator credits, he sends a credit memorandum.

Debit and credit memorandum forms are often very similar in physical appearance; and this similarity creates the possibility of errors because, for example, the clerk responsible for preparing the required form may use a debit memorandum form when a credit memorandum form is required. To reduce errors of this nature and to facilitate identification of the two forms, most companies print debit memoranda on one color of paper and credit memoranda on a different color.

CREDIT TERMS AND CASH DISCOUNTS

Most manufacturers and wholesalers find sales are increased by granting a period of time in which the buyer may make payment for merchandise purchased. Sales are increased because the buyer is enabled by the credit period to carry a larger stock of merchandise and thereby increase his own sales. The buyer is able to carry a larger stock because part of the merchandise in his store is placed there for a period of time without a cash investment on his part. In many cases the storekeeper is able to buy merchandise and sell it before payment must be made to the manufacturer or wholesaler.

In extending credit, business concerns make the terms of payment definite so that there will be no disagreement as to the amount and time of payment. The terms always appear on the invoice and are part of the sales agreement. Exact terms granted usually depend upon the custom of the trade. In some trades it is customary for invoices to become due and payable within ten days after the end of the month in which the sale took place. Invoices in these trades carry terms, "n/10 E.O.M." In other trades, it is customary for invoices to become due and payable 30 days after the invoice date. Invoices in these trades carry the terms "n/30." This means that the net amount of the invoice is due 30 days after the invoice date.

When credit periods are long, creditors usually grant discounts, called *cash discounts*, for early payments. This practice has two favorable results for the creditor. It reduces the amount invested in accounts receivable and decreases losses from uncollectible accounts. When discounts for early payment are granted, they are made part of the credit terms and appear on the invoice as, for example, "Terms: 2/10, n/60." Terms of 2/10, n/60 mean that the credit period is 60 days but that the debtor may deduct 2 percent from the invoice amount if payment is made within ten days after the invoice date.

Although cash discounts may be recorded at the time of a sale or purchase (discussed in Chapter 13), they are commonly recorded at the time payment is made and received. For example, on November 15, Valley Hardware Company received merchandise priced at $1,000 from Foster Wholesale Company. The invoice for this merchandise was dated November 12, and the terms were 2/10, n/60. The purchase was recorded by Valley Hardware Company with the following entry:

Nov.	15	Purchases................................	1,000.00	
		Foster Wholesale Company............		1,000.00
		Purchased merchandise, terms 2/10, n/60.		

Valley Hardware Company may pay the full amount of this invoice any time before November 22 by mailing a $980 check to Foster Wholesale Company. Or, if it wishes, it may wait until January 11 and pay the full $1,000. If the company choses to pay by November 22 and to take advantage of the cash discount, it records the payment with the following entry:

Nov.	22	Foster Wholesale Company.............	1,000.00	
		Purchases Discounts................		20.00
		Cash................................		980.00
		Paid the invoice of November 12 less the discount.		

Businesses find it advantageous to take cash discounts even if money must be borrowed to do so. For instance, in the above example the interest on $980 at 6 percent for 50 days is $8.17. This is less than half the discount.

The series of transactions previously illustrated between Valley Hardware Company and Foster Wholesale Company are a sale and a collection to Foster Wholesale Company. It records the transactions with entries like the following:

Nov.	12	Valley Hardware Company.............	1,000.00	
		Sales................................		1,000.00
		Sold merchandise, terms 2/10, n/60.		
	24	Cash................................	980.00	
		Sales Discounts.....................	20.00	
		Valley Hardware Company...........		1,000.00
		Received full payment of the invoice of November 12 less the discount.		

CASH DISCOUNTS ON THE INCOME STATEMENT

Until within the last few years cash discounts were commonly shown on the income statement as separate revenue and expense items. Today, the more common practice is to show purchases discounts as a deduction from the cost of goods purchased and sales discounts as a deduction from revenue from sales, as in Illustration 39.

Illustration 39

HASKIN LUMBER COMPANY
Income Statement for Year Ended February 28, 19--

```
Revenue:
  Gross sales . . . . . . . . . . . . . .                              $153,710
    Less: Sales returns . . . . . . . .        $ 2,450
          Sales discounts . . . . . .            2,510        4,960
  Net sales . . . . . . . . . . . . . .                      $148,750

Cost of goods sold:
  Merchandise inventory, March 1, 19--          $17,205
  Purchases . . . . . . . . . . . . .  $104,300
    Less: Purchases returns .  $2,250
          Purchases discounts  1,910             4,160
  Net purchases . . . . . . . . . . .  $100,140
```

TRADE DISCOUNTS

Cash discounts, just discussed, are granted for the prompt payment of an invoice. Trade discounts have no relation to payments. A trade discount is a deduction from a list or catalogue price and is used in determining the actual selling price of goods. Trade discounts are commonly used by manufacturers and wholesalers to avoid frequent republication of catalogues when selling prices change. If selling prices change, catalogue prices can be adjusted by merely issuing a new list of discounts to be applied to the catalogue prices.

Trade discounts may be stated as a single percentage or as a chain of percentages. For example, a single discount of 40 percent off the listed catalogue price may be granted or discounts of 20 percent, 10 percent, and 10 percent may be granted. If a single 40 percent discount is granted, the selling price of the goods is calculated:

> *List or catalogue price* *$1,000*
>   *Less: Trade discount of 40 percent* *400*
> *Selling price* . . . . *$ 600*

If a chain of discounts such as 20 percent, 10 percent, and 10 percent is given, the selling price is calculated:

```
List or catalogue price...........................$1,000
    Less: First 20 percent discount..................  200
Amount remaining...............................$  800
    Less: Second 10 percent discount...............   80
Amount remaining...............................$  720
    Less: Third 10 percent discount................   72
Selling price..................................$  648
```

Trade discounts are not entered in the accounts; only selling prices are used. For example, the sale of the chain discount calculation just given is recorded:

Dec.	10	*University Supply Company*....................	648.00	
		Sales.......................................		648.00
		Sold merchandise on account.		

TRANSPORTATION TERMS

The terms of an invoice commonly designate the party responsible for transportation charges. Terms are usually either "F.O.B. Shipping Point" or "F.O.B. Destination."

F.O.B. Shipping Point. The letters "F.O.B.'" are an abbreviation for the words "free on board." Terms "F.O.B. Shipping Point" mean that the seller will place the goods on board the means of transportation at the shipping point free of charges, and the buyer must pay transportation charges from there. For example, Maley Wholesale Company of St. Louis received a $1,000 invoice for merchandise from Trenton Manufacturing Company of Chicago, terms F.O.B. Chicago.

Freight Is Paid by Buyer upon Receipt of Goods. If freight is paid by the buyer upon receipt of the goods, Maley's entries, without explanations, for the purchase and freight payment are:

Nov.	3	*Purchases*....................................	1,000.00	
		Trenton Manufacturing Company..........		1,000.00
	3	*Freight-In*...................................	90.00	
		Cash.......................................		90.00

Freight Is Prepaid by Shipper. Sometimes the shipper prepays the freight on an F.O.B. factory shipment, either because the regulations require prepayment on that class of merchandise or because the customer has requested it. In this event the shipper adds on the amount of the prepaid freight to the invoice. If Trenton prepaid the freight on the above shipment in spite of the freight terms, Maley would record the invoice as follows:

Nov.	3	Purchases...	1,000.00	
		Freight-In..	90.00	
		Trenton Manufacturing Company..........		1,090.00

If a cash discount is allowed for early payment of the above invoice, the discount must be based on the price of the merchandise only. For example, if this invoice is paid in time to take a 2 percent cash discount, the discount is 2 percent of $1,000 and the entry for payment is:

Nov.	9	Trenton Manufacturing Company..............	1,090.00	
		Cash...		1,070.00
		Purchases Discounts......................		20.00

F.O.B. Destination. This means "free on board" means of transportation to destination of the shipment and that the seller agrees to pay the freight.

Freight Is Paid by Buyer upon Receipt of Goods. If the terms on the Trenton Manufacturing Company invoice are F.O.B. St. Louis, the shipper is responsible for the freight. Therefore, if the freight is not prepaid by the shipper, Maley should deduct its amount from the invoice before paying Trenton, and Maley's entries for the purchase and for freight payment are:

Nov.	3	Purchases...	1,000.00	
		Trenton Manufacturing Company...........		1,000.00
	3	Trenton Manufacturing Company (for freight)...	90.00	
		Cash...		90.00

Any cash discount allowed should be based on the cost of the merchandise (net of any returns or allowances, of course). Maley would record payment, less 2 percent discount in this case, as follows:

Nov.	9	*Trenton Manufacturing Company*..........	*910.00*	
		Cash...............................		*890.00*
		Purchases Discounts.................		*20.00*

Freight Is Prepaid by Shipper. Since the shipper is responsible for the freight under terms of F.O.B. destination, he should prepay it. Where this is done, the buyer needs only to record the amount of the purchase as a debit to Purchases and a credit to the creditor.

QUESTIONS FOR CLASS DISCUSSION

1. Explain why there is a greater need in a large business than in a small one for business papers to control transactions.
2. How does the requirement that clerks record each cash sale on a cash register before wrapping the merchandise help to insure that all cash sales are correctly recorded?
3. An order taken by a traveling salesman is usually not considered an accounting transaction. Why?
4. Why is the granting of credit usually assigned to a credit department rather than to the department responsible for sales?
5. How are the several copies of an invoice used to control the processing of an order by a large wholesaler?
6. In a large store, why are the department managers not permitted to deal directly with the sources of supply in purchasing merchandise?
7. What are the duties of the selling department managers in the purchasing procedure of a large company?
8. Why is the statement, "Do not include invoice with merchandise," printed on many purchase orders?
9. As the term is used in this chapter, what is a "service" department? Name several "service" departments found in large companies.
10. What is the difference between a debit memorandum and a credit memorandum? When a debit memorandum is issued, who debits, the one originating the memorandum or the one receiving it?
11. An invoice is dated November 15. What is the last day of the credit period if the terms are: (1) n/10 E.O.M.; (2) 2/10, n/30; and (3) 2/20, n/60?
12. Tell (1) who prepares, (2) who receives, and (3) the purpose of each of the following business papers:
    a) Purchase requisition.

    b) Purchase order.
    c) Invoice.
    d) Receiving report.
    e) Invoice approval form.

13. Robert Short purchased $2,000 of merchandise, terms 2/10, n/60. If Mr. Short borrowed sufficient money to pay this invoice on the last day of the discount period at 6 percent interest, how much did he save by borrowing to take advantage of the discount?

14. George Long purchased $400 of merchandise from Blue Company, terms 2/10, n/30. He paid for the purchase within the discount period. Give the general journal entries to record: (1) the purchase and payment on the books of Long; and (2) the sale and collection on the books of Blue Company.

15. Robert Short received from Blue Company an invoice totaling $54 and the merchandise covered by the invoice. In checking the invoice, Mr. Short found its correct total to be $64. Mr. Short sent Blue Company a memorandum pointing out the error.
    a) Was this a debit memorandum or a credit memorandum?
    b) Give the entry or entries made by Short to record the purchase.
    c) Give the entry made by Blue Company to record the memorandum.

16. Frank Brown purchased merchandise from Ajax Company, $500. Upon receipt and examination of the merchandise, Mr. Brown felt that $100 of it did not meet specifications. Nevertheless, he recorded the entire $500 purchase and entered into negotiations to return the unsatisfactory portion. He received permission from Ajax to make the return, and did so, receiving a memorandum showing that Ajax had entered the return in his account.
    a) Was this a debit memorandum or a credit memorandum?
    b) Give the journal entries to record the purchase and return on the books of Brown.
    c) Give the entries to record the sale and return on the Ajax books.

17. Can you give a logical reason for deducting sales discounts from gross sales and deducting purchases discounts from gross purchases?

18. Distinguish between a cash discount and a trade discount.

PROBLEMS

Problem 6–1

Western Sales Company received quotations from two different manufacturers on an item of merchandise. The quotations were:

From Western Manufacturing Co.:   List price $1,000, less 20 percent, 10 percent, and 10 percent, F.O.B. destination, 1/10, n/30.

From Southwest Products, Inc.:   List price $1,000, less 35 percent, F.O.B. destination, 2/10, n/30.

Western Sales Company accepted the best offer including the cash discount and completed the following transactions:

Nov.   3   Received the merchandise and an invoice dated November 1.
       3   Paid $84 of freight charges on the shipment which the vendor had failed to pay; charged the amount paid to the account of the vendor.
      10   Sent the vendor a check in full payment of the amount due, less the discount.

Required:
  1. General journal entries to record the foregoing transactions on the books of the vendee.
  2. General journal entries to record the foregoing transactions on the books of the vendor.

Problem 6–2

Green Products, Inc., sold Mesa Wholesale Company merchandise having a list price of $1,250, less a chain trade discount of 20 percent, 5 percent, and 5 percent, F.O.B. destination, terms 2/10, n/60. The invoice was paid within the discount period.

Required:
  1. Under the assumption that the vendor shipped the goods with the freight prepaid, give without dates (*a*) the entries to record the purchase and the payment of the invoice by Mesa Wholesale Company and (*b*) the entries to record the sale and collection by Green Products, Inc.
  2. Give (*a*) the entries to record the purchase and payment by Mesa Wholesale Company and (*b*) the entries to record the sale and collection by Green Products, Inc., under the assumption that the vendor shipped the goods freight collect, asking the vendee to pay the freight charges and to deduct their amount, $52.50, in remitting.

Problem 6–3

Old Town Suppliers purchased merchandise as follows:

Date of Invoice	List Price	Trade Discount	Freight Charges	Terms	Returns	Date of Payment
a) *Nov. 3*	*$3,000*	*20%, 10%, and 5%*	*$185*	*2/10, n/60, F.O.B. destination*	*$ 0*	*Nov. 13*
b) *Nov. 16*	*3,600*	*25% and 10%*	*150*	*n/10 E.O.M., F.O.B. destination*	*0*	*Dec. 10*
c) *Dec. 11*	*1,200*	*25%*	*100*	*2/10, n/60, F.O.B. factory*	*150*	*Dec. 21*
d) *Dec. 22*	*1,400*	*20% and 5%*	*125*	*2/10, 1/15, n/60, F.O.B. factory*	*0*	*Jan. 6*
e) *Jan. 7*	*1,200*	*35%*	*140*	*1/10, n/60, F.O.B. destination*	*0*	*Mar. 8*

The vendors paid the freight charges on the November 3, December 11, and January 7 invoices, adding the charges to the invoice in the case of the December 11 invoice. The vendee paid the freight charges on the remaining invoices upon receipt of the goods. The credit memorandum for the return was recorded on December 18, and the amount of the return was at the invoice price.

Required:

Prepare entries to record the foregoing transactions on the books of Old Town Suppliers. In recording each purchase use a date two days after the invoice date and use the account title "Accounts Payable" in the place of each creditor's name.

Problem 6–4

The following information was taken from the income statement of Golden Products, Inc., for the year ended last December 31.

Sales	$68,860	Purchases returns	$ 575
Sales returns	1,140	Purchases discounts	?
Sales discounts	1,230	Freight-in	580
Beginning inventory	13,875	Ending inventory	14,295
Purchases	42,435	Gross profit from sales	25,315

Required:

1. From the foregoing information determine the amount of the purchases discounts.
2. Prepare an income statement for the concern complete through the calculation of gross profit from sales.

Problem 6–5

The following trial balance was taken from the ledger of The Sports Shop at the end of its annual accounting period:

THE SPORTS SHOP
Trial Balance, December 31, 19—

Cash	$ 1,870	
Merchandise inventory	14,180	
Store supplies	840	
Prepaid insurance	355	
Store equipment	10,465	
Accumulated depreciation, store equipment		$ 3,125
Accounts payable		2,240
Dale Kope, capital		22,465
Dale Kope, withdrawals	7,330	
Sales		69,160
Sales returns and allowances	1,230	
Sales discounts	1,335	
Purchases	41,650	
Purchases returns and allowances		770
Purchases discounts		815
Freight-in	445	
Sales salaries	13,195	
Rent expense	4,200	
Advertising expense	585	
Heating and lighting expense	895	
	$98,575	$98,575

Required:
1. Copy the trial balance onto a work sheet form and complete the work sheet using the following information:
    a) Store supplies inventory, $195.
    b) Expired insurance, $220.
    c) Estimated depreciation of store equipment, $1,115.
    d) Accrued sales salaries, $85.
    e) Included in the debit balance of the Advertising Expense account is a $225 debit for 1,000 ball-point pens carrying advertising material on ` the store. The pens are in the store and will be given to customers and prospective customers beginning on January 15 of the new accounting period.
    f) Ending merchandise inventory, $13,675.
2. Prepare a partial income statement that is complete through the calculation of gross profit from sales.
3. Prepare compound closing entries.

CLASS EXERCISE

Exercise 6–1
Following are two of the closing entries made by Southwest Sales, Inc., at the end of its last annual accounting period:

Dec.	*31*	*Income Summary*	*120,780.00*	
		Merchandise Inventory		*21,345.00*
		Sales Returns and Allowances		*1,785.00*
		Sales Discounts		*1,520.00*
		Purchases		*64,795.00*
		Freight-In		*1,250.00*
		Sales Salaries		*19,215.00*
		Rent Expense		*7,200.00*
		Heating and Lighting Expense		*1,160.00*
		Telephone Expense		*185.00*
		Store Supplies Used		*755.00*
		Expired Insurance		*225.00*
		Depreciation of Store Equipment		*1,345.00*
	31	*Merchandise Inventory*	*20,760.00*	
		Sales	*93,235.00*	
		Purchases Returns and Allowances	*815.00*	
		Purchases Discounts	*1,070.00*	
		Income Summary		*115,880.00*

Required:
From the information in the closing entries prepare an income statement for Southwest Sales, Inc., that is complete through the calculation of gross profit from sales.

ALTERNATE PROBLEMS

Problem 6–1A

Drywall Company sent a purchase order to Gypsum Products, Inc., on November 3 for merchandise having a catalogue list price of $1,200, less a chain trade discount of 20 percent and 10 percent, F.O.B. factory, terms 2/10, n/60. Gypsum Products, Inc., shipped the entire order on November 6, prepaying the $82.40 freight charges and adding this amount to the invoice price of the goods.

Drywall Company received and inspected the goods on November 8, finding that one fourth did not meet specifications. Nevertheless, the company recorded the entire purchase and entered into negotiations to return the unsatisfactory portion. Gypsum Products, Inc., agreed to the return with the understanding it would pay the freight charges on the return shipment and grant full credit for the goods returned plus one fourth of the freight charges on the original shipment. The unsatisfactory goods were returned with freight charges of $22.35, C.O.D.

On November 16 Drywall Company received a credit memorandum giving credit for the return and the freight charges as agreed. On the same day it mailed a check in full for the remaining amount owed.

Required:

Prepare entries to record the foregoing transactions for Drywall Company.

Problem 6–2A

Uptown Sales Company completed the following transactions:

Oct. 3 Received merchandise and the invoice from Purple Manufacturing Company, terms 2/10, n/60, F.O.B. destination. The list price of the goods was $1,250 with a trade discount of 20 percent, 10 percent, and 5 percent. The invoice was dated October 1, and the vendor had prepaid the freight charges of $112.

7 Received merchandise and the invoice from Splendor Paint Company, terms 2/10, 1/15, n/60, F.O.B. factory. The list price of the merchandise was $1,680, and there was a 25 percent trade discount. Uptown Sales Company paid $87 freight charges on delivery. The invoice was dated October 5.

9 Received a $155 credit memorandum from Purple Manufacturing Company for goods received from them on October 3 and returned.

11 Mailed Purple Manufacturing Company a check in full payment of the Invoice of October 1, less the return and the discount.

13 Received merchandise and the invoice from Arizona Supply Company, terms n/10 E.O.M., F.O.B. destination. The goods had a list price of $1,500 less a chain trade discount of 20 percent and 5 percent. The vendor failed to pay the $150 freight charges; consequently, Uptown Sales Company gave the freight company a check for the freight and charged the amount to the account of the vendor. The invoice was dated October 11.

Oct. 15 Received merchandise and the invoice from Red Spot Paint Company, terms 1/10, n/30, F.O.B. factory. The goods had a $750 list price with a 20 percent trade discount. The vendor had prepaid the freight charges, adding the amount, $45, to the invoice. The invoice was dated October 13.

20 Mailed Splendor Paint Company a check in payment of its invoice of October 5, less the discount.

23 Mailed Red Spot Paint Company a check in payment of its invoice of October 13, less the discount.

Nov. 10 Mailed Arizona Supply Company a check in payment of the amount due on its invoice of October 11.

Required:
Prepare general journal entries to record the foregoing transactions.

Problem 6–4A

The following items appeared on the income statement prepared for Orange Products, Inc., for the year ended last December 31:

Sales.....................$63,110		*Purchases returns*.......$ 915	
Sales returns............ 1,370		*Purchases discounts*.... 745	
Sales discounts.......... 1,080		*Freight-in*.............. 795	
Beginning inventory.... ?		*Ending inventory*....... 14,960	
Purchases............... 41,390		*Gross profit from sales*.. 21,120	

Required:
1. Determine the amount of the beginning inventory.
2. Prepare an income statement for the concern that is complete through the calculation of gross profit from sales.

Problem 6–5A

The unadjusted trial balance at the end of an annual accounting period and a portion of the closing entries of Desert Sales Company follow:

DESERT SALES COMPANY
Trial Balance, December 31, 19—

Cash	$ 2,785	
Merchandise inventory	14,265	
Store supplies	780	
Prepaid insurance	210	
Store equipment	11,240	
Accumulated depreciation, store equipment		$ 6,795
Accounts payable		8,530
David Ryan, capital		18,740
David Ryan, withdrawals	4,800	
Sales		62,865
Sales returns and allowances	1,370	
Sales discounts	1,080	
Purchases	41,390	
Purchases returns and allowances		815
Purchases discounts		555
Freight-in	775	
Sales salaries	12,960	
Rent expense	5,500	
Heating and lighting expense	1,015	
Telephone expense	130	
	$98,300	$98,300

Dec.	*31*	*Income Summary*	80,880.00	
		Merchandise Inventory		14,265.00
		Sales Returns and Allowances		1,370.00
		Sales Discounts		1,080.00
		Purchases		41,390.00
		Freight-In		775.00
		Sales Salaries		13,190.00
		Rent Expense		6,000.00
		Heating and Lighting Expense		1,015.00
		Telephone Expense		130.00
		Store Supplies Used		545.00
		Expired Insurance		160.00
		Depreciation of Store Equipment		960.00
	31	*Merchandise Inventory*	15,180.00	
		Sales	62,865.00	
		Purchases Returns and Allowances	815.00	
		Purchases Discounts	555.00	
		Income Summary		79,415.00

Required:

1. From the information given prepare a work sheet for the concern.
2. From the work sheet prepare an income statement complete through the calculation of gross profit from sales.

DECISION PROBLEM 6—PRO-AM GOLF SHOP

Dick Kerr and Cy Young operate a golf shop at the Riverside Golf Club on a franchise basis. The franchise requires that 20 percent of the profit from the shop be paid to the club for use of facilities and for the exclusive right to operate the shop. The board of directors of the club asked the club's auditor to check the records and procedures of the golf shop, since it was felt the shop should be more profitable than the returns have indicated over the last three years.

The auditor discovered the following facts:

1. The inventory is too high in proportion to sales. The excess inventory consists largely of golf accessories, especially shirts, shoes, windbreakers, hats, and caps. Many of these have been written down 50 percent in an attempt to move items which have not proven popular.

2. Purchase procedures have not been carefully controlled. Purchases are made both from catalogue selections and mail orders and from salesmen who call at the shop. Most mail orders have been made on blanks furnished by suppliers, and no carbon copies have been retained. Salesmen leave copies of orders which they take at the shop, but these are referred to by Kerr and Young only to determine when certain items requested by customers will probably be received. Purchase invoices are checked against goods received. The partners feel that they can detect from memory any discrepancies between goods received and those ordered.

   Purchase orders have been placed by both Kerr and Young, and occasionally by John Davis, assistant pro, depending on who happened to be in charge of the shop when salesmen called.

3. A fairly good number of used golf clubs are on hand. These have been acquired by trade on the sale of new clubs. No record of the trade-in values is kept. The used clubs are sold at whatever price seems reasonable at the time of the sale. It is admitted that these sales prices are generally less than the trade-in allowances on the used clubs.

4. Most purchases, especially of golf clubs, bags, and balls, are subject to 2 percent discount for payment by the tenth of the month following the date of purchase. Yet actual purchases discount taken has averaged four tenths of 1 percent of purchases. Mr. Kerr explains that the books are kept in the club's offices and that neither he nor Mr. Young has felt able to see that payments are made within the discount period.

Prepare a report including the recommendations which you feel the auditor should make to the board of directors.

Special Journals
and Subsidiary Ledgers

A GENERAL JOURNAL like the one described in previous chapters is a flexible journal in which it is possible to record any transaction. However, since each debit and credit entered in a General Journal must be individually posted, its exclusive use in recording all transactions results in the expenditure of too much posting labor.

Several ways have been devised to avoid the heavy load of posting labor required by the exclusive use of a General Journal. One is to record transactions in a columnar journal or journals. In a small concern, one in which all the record keeping is done with pen and ink by one bookkeeper, a single columnar journal (discussed later in this chapter) called a Combination Journal is often used. Likewise, separate special journals that enable several people to work on the records at the same time may be used. In either case the journals are designed to save posting labor.

SEPARATE SPECIAL JOURNALS

When a concern uses separate special journals, it classifies its transactions into classes of like transactions and provides a special journal for each class having a sufficient number of transactions to warrant a separate journal. For example, if an average mercantile company's transactions are examined, it will be seen that the great majority fall into four distinct classes. If a special journal is provided for each, the classes and special journals provided are:

Classes of Transactions	Special Journals Provided
1. Sales on account.................	Sales Journal
2. Purchases on account............	Purchases Journal
3. Receipts of cash.................	Cash Receipts Journal
4. Payments of cash................	Cash Disbursements Journal

While the four journals listed are the more common, other special journals are often used. Also, most transactions of a business using special journals are recorded in one of its special journals. However, regardless of the special journals provided, there are always a few miscellaneous transactions plus adjusting, closing, and correcting entries which cannot be recorded in any of the special journals. For these, a General Journal must be provided.

HOW COLUMNAR JOURNALS SAVE POSTING LABOR

When columnar journals are used, posting labor is saved by taking advantage of the fact that in any one class of transactions either the debit or the credit is always to the same account. For example, when charge sales are recorded, each sale results in a credit to Sales; the customer accounts debited differ, but each sale results in a credit to Sales. If a Sales Journal is used in recording charge sales, the repetitive credits to Sales are taken advantage of and posting labor is saved by placing the amounts in a column and posting to the credit of the Sales account only the column total. This is graphically shown in Illustration 40.

Observe in Illustration 40 how (1) each charge sale is recorded on a single line, (2) the amount of each sale is individually debited to a customer's account, and (3) only the column total, the sum of all the sales, is credited to the Sales account. The Sales Journal of Illustration 40 has recorded therein only seven charge sales. If it is assumed that these seven sales represent seven hundred or seven thousand sales, the tremendous amount of posting labor saved by the single credit to Sales can better be visualized.

The single-column Sales Journal is one of the more simple columnar journals. It has been used to introduce columnar journals and to demonstrate the savings in posting labor that may be achieved by recording like transaction amounts in a column and posting the column total. However, before additional columnar journals are discussed, the subject of subdividing the ledger should be introduced.

Illustration 40

SALES JOURNAL

Date		Account Debited	Invoice No.	F	Amount
Oct.	1	James Henry...............................	307	✓	−200.00
	6	Albert Smith.............................	308	✓	−100.00
	12	John Wright..............................	309	✓	−150.00
	15	Paul Roth................................	310	✓	−225.00
	22	Sam Moore...............................	311	✓	−125.00
	25	Frank Booth..............................	312	✓	− 50.00
	28	Sam Moore...............................	313	✓	−175.00
	31	Total—Sales Credit...................			1,025.00

Individual amounts are posted daily.

Frank Booth

Date	Debit	Credit	Balance
Oct. 25	50.00		50.00

Paul Roth

Date	Debit	Credit	Balance
Oct. 15	225.00		225.00

James Henry

Date	Debit	Credit	Balance
Oct. 1	200.00		200.00

Albert Smith

Date	Debit	Credit	Balance
Oct. 6	100.00		100.00

Sam Moore

Date	Debit	Credit	Balance
Oct. 22	125.00		125.00
28	175.00		300.00

John Wright

Date	Debit	Credit	Balance
Oct. 12	150.00		150.00

Total is posted at the end of the month.

Sales

Date	Debit	Credit	Balance
Oct. 31		1,025.00	1,025.00

NEED FOR SUBDIVIDING THE LEDGER

If a company has a large number of accounts, placing them all in a single ledger has several disadvantages. These disadvantages are: A ledger with many accounts is large and awkward, a division of posting labor is difficult, the trial balance of such a ledger is long, and if errors are made, they are hard to find because they cannot be localized. To overcome these disadvantages, many companies subdivide their ledger.

BASIS FOR SUBDIVIDING THE LEDGER

When a ledger is subdivided, it is subdivided by removing from it any one or more large classes of like accounts. Each class removed is placed in a separate ledger called a *subsidiary ledger*. The original ledger is then called the *General Ledger*. When a ledger is subdivided by removing a class of like accounts, it is necessary to substitute in the original or General Ledger a summary account, the balance of which is equal to the sum of the balances of the accounts removed. This is necessary because the ledger will not balance with a portion of its accounts removed. The summary account, the balance of which takes the place of the account balances removed, is called a *controlling account* or a *control account*.

In most companies the two largest classes of like accounts are accounts receivable and accounts payable, and these are usually the first accounts removed from a ledger. When the accounts receivable are removed from the General Ledger, they are placed in a subsidiary ledger called the *Accounts Receivable Ledger* and a controlling account called *Accounts Receivable* is substituted in their place. Likewise, when the accounts payable are removed, they are placed in a subsidiary ledger called the *Accounts Payable Ledger* and a controlling account called *Accounts Payable* is substituted in their place.

Accounts receivable and accounts payable are the most common classes of accounts placed in subsidiary ledgers. However, it should be understood that any class of accounts may be removed from the General Ledger and placed in a subsidiary ledger. For example, companies with many operating expense accounts commonly place an Operating Expenses controlling account in their General Ledger and place the individual expense accounts in a subsidiary ledger.

ESTABLISHING A SUBSIDIARY LEDGER
ILLUSTRATED

Sloan Novelty Company, a firm that has previously kept all its accounts in one ledger, decides to subdivide the ledger by removing therefrom all customer accounts, which are to be placed in a subsidiary Accounts Receivable Ledger. Since the company's General Ledger, like that of most companies, is a loose-leaf ledger, this is a simple task. To accomplish the task, it is only necessary to—

1. Remove from the loose-leaf General Ledger all of the pages containing accounts with customers.

2. Place these customer account pages in a separate ledger binder.
3. Place in the General Ledger a summary controlling account, the balance of which equals the sum of the customer account balances removed.

In Illustration 41, on the left, is shown the trial balance of Sloan Novelty Company's ledger before the accounts receivable were removed; and on the right is shown the ledger's trial balance after the accounts were removed. In Illustration 41, there are only six accounts receivable; but if it

Illustration 41

SLOAN NOVELTY COMPANY		
Trial Balance		
December 31, 19—		
Cash..........................	$ 1,600	
Notes receivable..............	400	
A. B. Dean...................	75	
Frank Fish....................	125	
T. M. Johnson................	250	
W. C. Nagle...................	160	
John Roak....................	100	
Sam Warren..................	140	
Store supplies...............	125	
Prepaid insurance............	75	
Land.........................	1,000	
Building.....................	14,900	
Equipment...................	2,000	
Acme Mfg. Company.........		$ 450
Horn Supply Company.......		600
Mortgage payable............		5,000
C. Sloan, capital.............		14,900
	$20,950	$20,950

SLOAN NOVELTY COMPANY		
Trial Balance		
December 31, 19—		
Cash..........................	$ 1,600	
Notes receivable..............	400	
Accounts receivable..........	850	
Store supplies...............	125	
Prepaid insurance............	75	
Land.........................	1,000	
Building.....................	14,900	
Equipment...................	2,000	
Acme Mfg. Company.........		$ 450
Horn Supply Company.......		600
Mortgage payable............		5,000
C. Sloan, capital.............		14,900
	$20,950	$20,950

is assumed that these six accounts represent six hundred accounts, the tremendous reduction in the length of the trial balance may be appreciated.

A subsidiary Accounts Payable Ledger or a subsidiary Operating Expense Ledger would be established in the same way.

PREPARING SCHEDULES OF SUBSIDIARY LEDGERS

After a group of like accounts, such as the accounts receivable, are removed from the General Ledger, the equality of the accounts remaining is still tested by preparing a trial balance. Also, at the time the General Ledger is tested for equality, each subsidiary ledger is normally proved by preparing a list or a schedule of the account balances in each subsidiary ledger and seeing, for example, that the sum of the balances on the accounts receivable schedule is equal to the balance of the Accounts Receivable controlling account. A schedule of Sloan Novelty Company's

Accounts Receivable Ledger appears as in Illustration 42. Note that the schedule total, $850, is equal to the balance of the Accounts Receivable controlling account in the trial balance on the right in Illustration 41. Often a simple adding machine list rather than a formal schedule is used in proving a subsidiary ledger.

POSTING PRINCIPLE OF CONTROLLING ACCOUNTS AND SUBSIDIARY LEDGERS

As previously stated, any class of accounts taken from the General Ledger is removed to reduce the number of accounts in the ledger. And, since a General Ledger's trial balance will not balance with part of its account balances removed, a controlling account having a balance equal to the sum of the account balances removed is substituted in the General Ledger. Thereafter, the posting principle upon which the subsidiary ledger

Illustration 42

SLOAN NOVELTY COMPANY
Schedule of Accounts Receivable
December 31, 19--

A. B. Dean	$ 75
Frank Fish	125
T. M. Johnson.	250
W. C. Nagle.	160
John Roak.	100
Sam Warren	140
Total accounts receivable.	$850

and its controlling account operate requires that (1) the controlling account must be debited periodically for an amount or amounts equal to the sum of the debits to its subsidiary ledger accounts, and (2) the controlling account must be credited periodically for an amount or amounts equal to the sum of the credits to its subsidiary ledger accounts. Periodically debiting the controlling account for the sum of the debits to the subsidiary ledger and crediting the controlling account for the sum of the credits brings the balance of the controlling account up to date and, if no errors have been made, makes it equal to the sum of the balances of its subsidiary ledger.

ACCOUNTS RECEIVABLE LEDGER AND THE SALES JOURNAL

When an Accounts Receivable Ledger and controlling account are used, the individual sales recorded in the Sales Journal are posted daily as debits to the customer accounts in the Accounts Receivable Ledger. Consequently, periodically, in line with the posting principle under which controlling accounts and their subsidiary ledgers operate, the journal's column total must be credited to the Sales account and also debited to the Accounts Receivable account. Posting the column total to both the debit of Accounts Receivable and to the credit of Sales accomplishes two purposes: (1) Since the Sales and the Accounts Receivable accounts are both in the General Ledger, the posting keeps this ledger in balance. (2) The posting also provides a debit to the Accounts Receivable controlling account that is equal to the sum of the debits to the customer accounts in the subsidiary ledger. The posting of the Sales Journal when a subsidiary ledger is used is demonstrated in Illustration 43 on the next page.

Note the check marks in the Sales Journal's Folio column (Illustration 43). The Accounts Receivable Ledger is generally a loose-leaf ledger or a tray of ledger cards, and its accounts are arranged alphabetically to aid in locating any account. Furthermore, new accounts are placed in the ledger in their proper alphabetical position as required. Consequently, since the accounts are arranged alphabetically and new accounts are added in their proper alphabetical position, it is impractical to number the accounts. Therefore, when posting the individual amounts from the Sales Journal, a check mark, rather than an account number, is placed in the journal's Folio column to indicate that the amount has been posted. However, when the column total is posted, the posting is indicated by placing the Accounts Receivable and Sales account numbers in parentheses below the column total.

As previously stated, in posting the Sales Journal the debits to customer accounts are posted daily. These daily postings keep each customer's account up to date and make it possible to determine at any time the current amount owed by a customer. This information is important in granting credit because the total credit granted to any one customer is usually limited, and before a decision to grant further credit can be made, the person responsible for its granting must know the amount currently owed by the customer and his promptness in meeting past obligations. This information is obtained from the customer's account, and if all postings have not been made, the one responsible for granting further credit is deceived.

SALES TAXES

Many cities and states require retailers to collect sales taxes from their customers and periodically remit these taxes to the city or state treasurer. When a columnar Sales Journal is used, a record of taxes collected can be obtained by adding special columns as shown in Illustration 44.

In posting a journal like Illustration 44, the individual amounts in the Accounts Receivable column are posted daily to customer accounts in the Accounts Receivable Ledger and the column total is posted at the end of the month to the Accounts Receivable controlling account. The individual

Illustration 43
Posting the Sales Journal to the Accounts Receivable

SALES JOURNAL

Date		Account Debited	Invoice No.	F	Amount
Oct.	1	James Henry...............................	307	✓	◄200.00
	7	Albert Smith...............................	308	✓	◄100.00
	10	John Wright...............................	309	✓	◄150.00
	15	Paul Roth...............................	310	✓	◄225.00
	22	Sam Moore...............................	311	✓	◄125.00
	25	Frank Booth...............................	312	✓	◄ 50.00
	28	Sam Moore...............................	313	✓	◄175.00
	31	Total—Accts. Rec. Dr., Sales Cr..........			1,025.00
					(113/411)

Individual amounts are posted daily to the subsidiary ledger.

Total is posted at the end of the month to the general ledger accounts.

ACCOUNTS RECEIVABLE LEDGER

Frank Booth

Date	Debit	Credit	Balance
Oct. 25	50.00		50.00

James Henry

Date	Debit	Credit	Balance
Oct. 1	200.00		200.00

Sam Moore

Date	Debit	Credit	Balance
Oct. 22	125.00		125.00
28	175.00		300.00

Paul Roth

Date	Debit	Credit	Balance
Oct. 15	225.00		225.00

Albert Smith

Date	Debit	Credit	Balance
Oct. 7	100.00		100.00

John Wright

Date	Debit	Credit	Balance
Oct. 10	150.00		150.00

GENERAL LEDGER

Accounts Receivable   113

Date	Debit	Credit	Balance
Oct. 31	1,025.00		1,025.00

Sales   411

Date	Debit	Credit	Balance
Oct. 31		1,025.00	1,025.00

Illustration 44

SALES JOURNAL

Date	Account Debited	Inv. No.	F	Accounts Receivable Debit	Sales Taxes Payable Credit	Sales Credit
Dec. 1	D. R. Horn.......	7–1698		103.00	3.00	100.00

amounts in the Sales Taxes Payable and the Sales columns are not posted. However, at the end of the month the total of the Sales Taxes Payable column is credited to the Sales Taxes Payable account, and the total of the Sales column is credited to Sales.

A concern making cash sales upon which sales taxes are collected may add a special Sales Taxes Payable column in its Cash Receipts Journal.

SALES INVOICES AS A SALES JOURNAL

To save recording labor, many large companies do not enter charge sales in a Sales Journal. These companies post each sales invoice directly to the customer's account in a subsidiary Accounts Receivable Ledger. The invoices are then bound in numerical order in a binder; and at the end of the month, all the invoices of that month are totaled on an adding machine, and a general journal entry is made debiting the Accounts Receivable controlling account and crediting Sales for the total. In effect, the bound invoice copies act as a Sales Journal. Such a procedure eliminates the labor of entering each invoice in a Sales Journal and is known as direct posting of sales invoices.

CASH RECEIPTS JOURNAL

Thus far in this chapter two important accounting techniques have been presented: (1) a technique for reducing posting labor by placing, for example, the many repetitive credits to an account in a journal column and posting them in one amount, the column total; and (2) a technique for reducing the number of accounts in the General Ledger and on the trial balance by placing accounts in subsidiary ledgers.

Both techniques affect the design of a Cash Receipts Journal suitable for a mercantile concern, causing it to be a multicolumn journal such as that shown in Illustration 45. A multicolumn journal is necessary because although all cash receipts are alike in that they result in debits to Cash, cash receipts differ as to their sources and, consequently, as to the accounts credited when cash is received. If the average company's cash receipts are classified as to sources, they fall into three groups: (1) cash from custom-

Illustration 45

Posting the Cash Receipts Journal to the Accounts Receivable Ledger and to the General Ledger

CASH RECEIPTS JOURNAL

Date	Account Credited	Explanation	F	Sundry Accounts Credit	Acct. Rec. Credit	Sales Credit	Sales Dis. Debit	Cash Debit
Oct. 1	Sales...........	Cash sales........	✓			400.00		400.00
10	James Henry....	Invoice, 10/1.....	✓		200.00		4.00	196.00
13	Sales...........	Cash sales.......	✓			390.00		390.00
17	Albert Smith....	Invoice, 10/7.....	✓		100.00		2.00	98.00
18	Notes Payable....	Note to bank....	211	1,000.00				1,000.00
20	Sales...........	Cash sales.......	✓			450.00		450.00
20	John Wright.....	Invoice, 10/10....	✓		150.00		3.00	147.00
25	Paul Roth.......	Invoice, 10/15....	✓		225.00		4.50	220.50
27	Sales...........	Cash sales.......	✓			398.50		398.50
31	Totals......			1,000.00	675.00	1,638.50	13.50	3,300.00
				(✓)	(113)	(411)	(413)	(111)

Total is not posted.

Totals posted at the end of the month.

Individual amounts in the Sundry Accounts credit and Accounts Receivable credit columns are posted daily.

ACCOUNTS RECEIVABLE LEDGER

James Henry

Date	Debit	Credit	Balance
Oct. 1	200.00		200.00
10		200.00	–0–

Paul Roth

Date	Debit	Credit	Balance
Oct. 15	225.00		225.00
25		225.00	–0–

Albert Smith

Date	Debit	Credit	Balance
Oct. 7	100.00		100.00
17		100.00	–0–

John Wright

Date	Debit	Credit	Balance
Oct. 15	150.00		150.00
20		150.00	–0–

GENERAL LEDGER

Cash   111

Date	Debit	Credit	Balance
Oct. 31	3,300.00		3,300.00

Accounts Receivable   113

Date	Debit	Credit	Balance
Oct. 31	1,025.00		1,025.00
31		675.00	350.00

Notes Payable   211

Date	Debit	Credit	Balance
Oct. 18		1,000.00	1,000.00

Sales   411

Date	Debit	Credit	Balance
Oct. 31		1,025.00	1,025.00
31		1,638.50	2,663.50

Sales Discount   413

Date	Debit	Credit	Balance
Oct. 31	13.50		13.50

ers in payment of their accounts; (2) cash from cash sales; and (3) cash from miscellaneous sources. Note in Illustration 45 that a special column is provided for the credits resulting when cash is received from each of these sources.

Cash from Charge Customers. When a receipt from a charge customer in payment of his account is recorded in a columnar Cash Receipts Journal like Illustration 45, the customer's name is entered in the Account Credited column; the amount credited to his account is entered in the Accounts Receivable credit column; and the debits to Sales Discounts and Cash are entered in these last two columns.

Give close attention to the Accounts Receivable credit column in the journal of Illustration 45. Observe that (1) only credits to customer accounts are entered in this column; (2) the individual credits are posted daily to the customer accounts in the subsidiary Accounts Receivable Ledger; and (3) the column total is posted at the month end to the credit of the Accounts Receivable controlling account. This is the normal recording and posting procedure when controlling accounts and subsidiary ledgers are used. When controlling accounts and subsidiary ledgers are used, transactions are normally entered in a journal column, the individual amounts are posted to the subsidiary ledger accounts, and the column total is posted to the controlling account. Note that this recording and posting procedure keeps the controlling account balance equal to the sum of the balances in its subsidiary ledger.

Cash Sales. In the average company cash sale amounts are accumulated each day on one or more cash registers and their total is recorded by means of a journal entry at the end of the day. All of these entries are alike; all have repetitive debits to Cash and repetitive credits to Sales.

When cash sales are recorded in a Cash Receipts Journal like that of Illustration 45, the repetitive debits to Cash are entered in the Cash debit column and a special column headed "Sales credit" is provided for the repetitive credits to Sales. By entering each day's cash sales in the Sales column, the cash sales of a month may be posted at the month's end as a single amount, the column total. (Although cash sales are normally recorded daily from the cash register reading, the cash sales of Illustration 45 are recorded only once each week in order to shorten the illustration.)

At the time daily cash sales are recorded in the Cash Receipts Journal, many bookkeepers, as in Illustration 45, place a check mark in the Folio column to indicate that no amount is individually posted from that line of the journal.

Miscellaneous Receipts of Cash. The major share of an average company's cash receipts come from customer collections and cash sales. However, cash is occasionally received from other sources such as, for example, a cash sale of an unneeded fixed asset or a promissory note given a bank in order to borrow money. For transactions such as these the Sundry Accounts credit column is provided in the Cash Receipts Journal.

POSTING THE CASH RECEIPTS JOURNAL

The individual items in the Cash Receipts Journal's Accounts Receivable column are posted daily as credits to the customer accounts named in the Account Credited column. These items must be posted daily so that the accounts receivable ledger accounts show for each customer the current amount owed.

In the average company, the items in the Sundry Accounts credit column are few and are posted to a variety of general ledger accounts. Normally, postings are less apt to be omitted if these items are also posted daily. Furthermore, if the individual items in both the Sundry Accounts and the Accounts Receivable columns are posted daily, only the column totals remain to be posted at the end of the month.

The Accounts Receivable, Sales, Sales Discounts, and Cash column totals are posted at the end of the month. However, since the transactions recorded in any journal must result in equal debits and credits to general ledger accounts, the debit and credit equality in a columnar journal such as the Cash Receipts Journal is proved by *crossfooting* or cross adding the column totals before these totals are posted. In crossfooting, the debit column totals are added together, the credit column totals are added together, and the two sums are compared for equality. For example, if the debit column totals of the Cash Receipts Journal in Illustration 45 are added and the credit column totals are added, the two sums appear as follows:

Debit Columns		Credit Columns	
Sales discounts debit............$ 13.50		Sundry accounts credit...........$1,000.00	
Cash........................... 3,300.00		Accounts receivable credit......... 675.00	
		Sales credit...................... 1,638.50	
Total......................$3,313.50		Total.......................$3,313.50	

Since the sums are equal, the debits in the journal are assumed to equal the credits.

After the debit and credit equality is proved by crossfooting, the totals are posted. The Accounts Receivable column total is posted to the credit of the Accounts Receivable controlling account in the General Ledger; the Sales column total is posted to the credit of the Sales account; the Sales Discounts column total is posted to the debit of the Sales Discounts account; and the Cash column total is posted to the debit of the Cash account. Since any individual items in the Sundry Accounts column are posted daily, this column total is not posted. This posting procedure is demonstrated in Illustration 45.

Posting items daily from the Sundry Accounts column of the Cash Receipts Journal with a delayed posting of the offsetting totals causes the ledger to be out of balance throughout the month. However, this is of no consequence because the offsetting totals are posted before a trial balance is prepared.

The Cash Receipts Journal's Folio column is used only for daily postings from the Sundry Accounts and Accounts Receivable columns. The account numbers appearing in the Folio column indicate items posted to the General Ledger from the Sundry Accounts column; and the check marks indicate either that an item like a day's cash sales was not posted or that an item was posted to the subsidiary Accounts Receivable Ledger. The total of the Sundry Accounts column is not posted. Note in Illustration 45 the check mark below this column. The check mark indicates that when the journal was posted, this column total was not posted. The account numbers of the accounts to which the Accounts Receivable, Sales, Sales Discounts, and Cash column totals of Illustration 45 were posted are indicated in parentheses below each column.

MISCELLANEOUS CREDITS TO ACCOUNTS RECEIVABLE

Credits to accounts receivable occur when merchandise previously sold on credit is returned. A company having few such returns records them in a General Journal with an entry like the following:

Oct.	*17*	*Sales Returns and Allowances.............*	*412*	*17.50*		
		Accounts Receivable—Geo. Ball.....	*113/✓*		*17.50*	
		Returned defective merchandise.				

The debit of the foregoing entry is posted to the Sales Returns and Allowances account; and the credit is posted to both the Accounts Receivable controlling account and to the customer's account. Note the account number and the check, 113/✔, in the Folio column on the credit line. This indicates that both the Accounts Receivable controlling account in the General Ledger and the Geo. Ball account in the Accounts Receivable Ledger were credited for $17.50.

Companies having sufficient sales returns can save posting labor by recording them in a special Sales Returns and Allowances Journal like that of Illustration 46. Note that this is in keeping with the idea that a company can design and use a special journal for any class of like transactions in which there are within the class sufficient transactions to warrant the journal. When a Sales Returns and Allowances Journal is used to record returns, the individual amounts entered in the journal are posted daily to the credit of each affected customer account. At the end of the

Illustration 46
Posting the Sales Returns and Allowances Journal

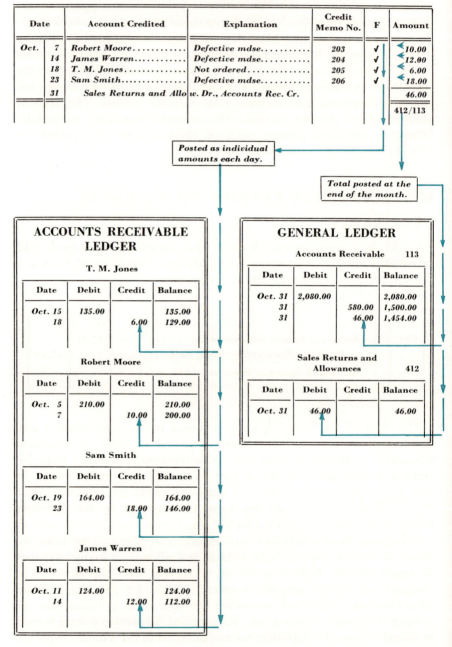

SALES RETURNS AND ALLOWANCES JOURNAL

Date		Account Credited	Explanation	Credit Memo No.	F	Amount
Oct.	7	Robert Moore............	Defective mdse..........	203	√	10.00
	14	James Warren............	Defective mdse..........	204	√	12.00
	18	T. M. Jones.............	Not ordered.............	205	√	6.00
	23	Sam Smith...............	Defective mdse..........	206	√	18.00
	31	Sales Returns and Allow. Dr., Accounts Rec. Cr.				46.00
						412/113

Posted as individual amounts each day.

Total posted at the end of the month.

ACCOUNTS RECEIVABLE LEDGER

T. M. Jones

Date	Debit	Credit	Balance
Oct. 15	135.00		135.00
18		6.00	129.00

Robert Moore

Date	Debit	Credit	Balance
Oct. 5	210.00		210.00
7		10.00	200.00

Sam Smith

Date	Debit	Credit	Balance
Oct. 19	164.00		164.00
23		18.00	146.00

James Warren

Date	Debit	Credit	Balance
Oct. 11	124.00		124.00
14		12.00	112.00

GENERAL LEDGER

Accounts Receivable   113

Date	Debit	Credit	Balance
Oct. 31	2,080.00		2,080.00
31		580.00	1,500.00
31		46.00	1,454.00

Sales Returns and Allowances   412

Date	Debit	Credit	Balance
Oct. 31	46.00		46.00

month, the journal total is posted to both the debit of the Sales Returns and Allowances account and the credit of the Accounts Receivable controlling account. A Sales Returns and Allowances Journal and its posting are shown in Illustration 46.

Occasionally a customer is unable to pay his account when due. In such cases, a promissory note is sometimes given by the customer to secure an extension of time on the amount due. The note does not pay the debt, but it does change its form from an informal promise to pay to a formal written promise to pay, and the change must be reflected in the accounting records because informal promises appear on the balance sheet as accounts receivable, while formal written promises appear as notes receivable. A general journal entry to record the receipt of a note to gain an extension on an account appears as follows:

Oct.	19	*Notes Receivable*............................	112	*239.50*	
		Accounts Receivable—D. A. Root	113/√		*239.50*
		Received a 60-day, 6 percent note			
		in settlement of the account.			

In some companies where the receipt of notes is common, a special Notes Receivable Journal is used. In others, if the receipt of notes is common, a special column is added to the General Journal, and all debits to Notes Receivable are entered in this column. This makes it possible to post the total debits to Notes Receivable in one amount, the column total. The use of a Notes Receivable Journal or the addition of a Notes Receivable debit column to the General Journal follow the principle that a special column may be added to a journal or a special journal may be added to the accounting system whenever like transactions warrant the addition.

ESTABLISHING A SUBSIDIARY ACCOUNTS PAYABLE LEDGER

The controlling account, subsidiary ledger, and columnar journal principles demonstrated thus far with accounts receivable apply equally well to accounts payable. For example, a firm wishing to establish a subsidiary Accounts Payable Ledger does so by following steps similar to those previously outlined for establishing an Accounts Receivable Ledger. Then, after establishing the ledger, it normally makes use of a Purchases Journal, a Cash Disbursements Journal, and perhaps a Purchases Returns and Allowances Journal in recording most of the transactions that affect the ledger. These journals operate in the same manner as the journals described thus far.

THE PURCHASES JOURNAL AND ITS POSTING

A one-column Purchases Journal is very similar to the Sales Journal previously described, and both journals operate in the same manner. The information recorded in the Purchases Journal usually includes the date of each entry, the creditor's name, the invoice date, terms, and the amount of the purchase. This information is recorded from approved purchase invoices; and its use, in the main, is apparent. The invoice date and the terms together indicate the date on which payment is due.

The one-column Purchases Journal is posted in the same manner as a Sales Journal: (1) The individual amounts in the Amount column are posted daily to the subsidiary Accounts Payable Ledger, and (2) the column total is debited at the end of the month to the Purchase account and credited to the Accounts Payable controlling account. This posting is demonstrated in Illustration 47.

THE CASH DISBURSEMENTS JOURNAL AND ITS POSTING

The Cash Disbursements Journal, like the Cash Receipts Journal, has columns that make it possible to post repetitive debits and credits in column totals. The repetitive debits and credits of cash payments are debits to the Accounts Payable controlling account and credits to both Purchases Discounts and Cash. In most companies the purchase of merchandise for cash is not common; therefore, a Purchases column is not needed, and a cash purchase is recorded as on line 3 of Illustration 48. However, although cash purchases are commonly treated as on line 3, it should be pointed out that any company having many such purchases would find it advantageous to place a Purchases column in its Cash Disbursements Journal.

In posting the Cash Disbursements Journal, the individual amounts in the Sundry Accounts column are posted daily to the debit of the general ledger accounts named in the Account Debited column; and the individual amounts in the Accounts Payable column are posted daily to the subsidiary Accounts Payable Ledger to the debit of the creditors named in the Account Debited column. At the end of the month, after the column totals are crossfooted to prove their equality, the Accounts Payable column total is posted to the debit of the Accounts Payable controlling account; the Purchases Discounts column total is posted to the credit of the Purchase Discounts account; and the Cash column total is posted to the credit of the Cash account. Since the items in the Sundry Accounts column are posted individually, this column total is not posted. Posting of the Cash Disbursements Journal is demonstrated in Illustration 48.

When several special journals are used, it is necessary to indicate in the

Illustration 47

Posting the Purchases Journal

PURCHASES JOURNAL

Date		Account Credited	Date of Invoice	Terms	F	Amount
Oct.	3	Horn Supply Co........................	10/2	n/30	✓	◄ 350.00
	5	Acme Mfg. Co.........................	10/5	2/10, n/30	✓	◄ 200.00
	13	Wycoff & Company....................	10/10	n/30	✓	◄ 150.00
	20	Smith and Company...................	10/19	2/10, n/30	✓	◄ 300.00
	25	Acme Mfg. Co.........................	10/24	2/10, n/30	✓	◄ 100.00
	27	A. Evans and Son.....................	10/27	1/10, n/30	✓	◄ 50.00
	29	H. A. Green Co........................	10/28	2/10, n/60	✓	◄ 175.00
	31	Total—Purchases Dr., Accounts Payable Cr.				1,325.00
						(511/212)

Individual amounts are posted daily.

Total is posted at the end of the month.

ACCOUNTS PAYABLE LEDGER

Acme Mfg. Co.

Date	Debit	Credit	Balance
Oct. 5		200.00	200.00
15	200.00		–0–
25		100.00	100.00

A. Evans and Son

Date	Debit	Credit	Balance
Oct. 27		50.00	50.00

H. A. Green Co.

Date	Debit	Credit	Balance
Oct. 29		175.00	175.00

Horn Supply Co.

Date	Debit	Credit	Balance
Oct. 3		350.00	350.00

Smith and Company

Date	Debit	Credit	Balance
Oct. 20		300.00	300.00

Wycoff & Company

Date	Debit	Credit	Balance
Oct. 13		150.00	150.00

GENERAL LEDGER

Accounts Payable   212

Date	Debit	Credit	Balance
Oct. 31		1,325.00	1,325.00

Purchases   511

Date	Debit	Credit	Balance
Oct. 12	25.00		25.00
31	1,325.00		1,350.00

Illustration 48

Posting the Cash Disbursements Journal

CASH DISBURSEMENTS JOURNAL

Date		Account Debited	Explanation	F	Sundry Accounts Debit	Accts. Pay. Debit	Pur. Dis. Credit	Cash Credit
Oct.	3	Freight-In........	Frt. on mdse......	514	◄ 4.50			4.50
	10	Misc. Gen. Exp....	Utilities..........	641	◄14.00			14.00
	12	Purchases........	Cash purchase....	511	◄25.00			25.00
	15	Acme Mfg. Co.....	Invoice, 10/5.....	✓	◄	200.00	4.00	196.00
	15	Salaries Expense..	Salaries..........	611	◄86.00			86.00
	20	Horn Supply Co...	Invoice, 10/3.....	✓	◄	75.00		75.00
	29	Smith and Co.....	Invoice, 10/9.....	✓	◄	300.00	6.00	294.00
	31	Totals..........			129.50	575.00	10.00	694.50
					(✓)	(212)	(513)	(111)

Individual amounts in the Sundry Accounts debit column and Accounts Payable debit column are posted daily.

Totals posted at the end of the month.

GENERAL LEDGER

Cash   111

Date	Debit	Credit	Balance
Oct. 31	3,300.00		3,300.00
31		694.50	2,605.50

ACCOUNTS PAYABLE LEDGER

Acme Mfg. Co.

Date	Debit	Credit	Balance
Oct. 5		200.00	200.00
15	200.00		-0-
25		100.00	100.00

Accounts Payable   212

Date	Debit	Credit	Balance
Oct. 31		1,325.00	1,325.00
31	575.00		750.00

Horn Supply Co.

Date	Debit	Credit	Balance
Oct. 3		350.00	350.00
20	75.00		275.00

Purchases   511

Date	Debit	Credit	Balance
Oct. 12	25.00		25.00
31	1,325.00		1,350.00

Smith and Company

Date	Debit	Credit	Balance
Oct. 20		300.00	300.00
29	300.00		-0-

Purchases Discounts   513

Date	Debit	Credit	Balance
Oct. 31		10.00	10.00

Freight-In   514

Date	Debit	Credit	Balance
Oct. 3	4.50		4.50

Miscellaneous General Expense   641

Date	Debit	Credit	Balance
Oct. 10	14.00		14.00

Salaries Expense   611

Date	Debit	Credit	Balance
Oct. 15	86.00		86.00

account Folio column before each posted amount the journal as well as the page number of the journal from which the amount was posted. The journal is indicated by using its initial or initials. Because of this, items posted from the Cash Disbursements Journal carry the initial "D" before their journal page number in the Folio columns. Likewise, items from the Sales Journal carry the initial "S," items from the Purchases Journal carry the initial "P," and so on.

MISCELLANEOUS DEBITS TO CREDITOR ACCOUNTS

A company having sufficient purchases returns and allowances may use a Purchases Returns and Allowances Journal like that shown in Illustration 49. If such a journal is used, the individual amounts entered in the journal

Illustration 49

PURCHASES RETURNS AND ALLOWANCES JOURNAL

Date		Account Debited	Explanation	F	Amount
Oct.	8	Medford Mfg. Co..............	Defective mdse................	✓	32.00
	12	Towne & Shell................	Below specifications...........	✓	10.00
	23	Sports Weavers...............	Defective mdse................	✓	23.00
	28	Short Novelty Co.............	Damaged in transit...........	✓	14.00
	31	Accts. Pay. Dr., Purchases Ret. and Allow. Cr.			179.00
					(212/512)

Individual amounts are posted daily to the Accounts Payable Ledger.

Total is posted at the end of the month to the General Ledger.

are posted daily as debits to creditor accounts in the Accounts Payable Ledger. At the end of the month the journal total is posted to both the debit of the Accounts Payable controlling account and to the credit of the Purchases Returns and Allowances account.

A company having but few purchases returns and allowances may record each with a general journal entry like the following:

Oct.	8	Accounts Payable—Medford Mfg. Co.....	212/✓	32.00	
		Purchases Returns and Allowances..	512		32.00
		Returned defective merchandise.			

Sometimes a note is issued in settlement of an account with a creditor. The note changes the form of the liability and is recorded with a general journal entry like the following:

Oct.	24	Accounts Payable—Springfield Co......	212/ ✓	500.00	
		Notes Payable.....................	211		500.00
		Gave a 30-day, 6 percent note.			

PURCHASE AND SALE OF ASSETS USED IN THE BUSINESS

When single-column purchases and sales journals are used, only purchases and sales of merchandise may be recorded in these journals. This is because the column total of the Purchases Journal is debited to the Purchases account; the column total of the Sales Journal is credited to the Sales account; and purchases and sales of assets other than merchandise do not affect either of these accounts. However, every company must purchase assets for use in the business; and when these assets are no longer needed, they may be sold. If the purchase or sale is for cash, the transaction is recorded in one of the cash journals. But if the purchase or sale is on credit, the transaction must be recorded in either the General Journal or, in cases where assets are purchased and such a journal is used, a multicolumn Purchases Journal similar to that shown in Illustration 50.

Illustration 50

PURCHASES JOURNAL

Date		Account Credited	F	Accts. Pay- able Credit	Pur- chases Debit	Store Sup- plies Debit	Office Sup- plies Debit
Oct.	2	Marsh Wholesale Co......		154.10	154.10		
	2	Office Supply Co.........		18.75			18.75

Some companies save posting labor by using a multicolumn Purchases Journal like Illustration 50. Note that the journal has one credit column and, in this case, three debit columns; more debit columns could be added. The credit column is used to record the amounts credited to each creditor;

and the items purchased are recorded in the debit columns. Such a journal is sometimes known as an "Accounts Payable Register."

In companies using an ordinary one-column Purchase Journal, rather than a multicolumn Purchases Journal, purchases of assets for use in the business are recorded in the General Journal with an entry like the following:

Oct.	*29*	*Office Supplies*..........................	*119*	*23.75*	
		Accounts Payable—Ace Supply Co...	*212/ √*		*23.75*
		Bought office supplies.			

THE COMBINATION JOURNAL

In a large concern it is usually necessary for several people to work on the accounting records at the same time, and separate journals make this possible. However, in a business small enough for one person to do all the bookkeeping, separate journals are both unnecessary and inconvenient. They are inconvenient because the bookkeeper must put aside one journal and pick up another each time a different kind of transaction is recorded. Therefore, in a small business it is common practice to combine the several columns of the journals described in this chapter into a single journal called a Combination Journal or Combined Cash Journal.

A Combination Journal is a combined sales, purchases, cash receipts, cash disbursements, and general journal. Transactions are entered in its columns and amounts and column totals are posted from it in the same way transactions are entered in and posted from the separate sales, purchases, cash receipts, cash disbursements, and general journals of this chapter.

QUESTIONS FOR CLASS DISCUSSION

1. How do special columnar journals save posting labor?
2. How do special journals take advantage of the fact that for any single class of transactions either the debit or the credit of each transaction is always to the same account?
3. A business uses a Cash Receipts, a Cash Disbursements, a single-column Sales, a single-column Purchases, and a General Journal. In which journal will it record each of the following transactions?
   a) Sale of merchandise on credit.
   b) Purchase of office supplies on credit.
   c) Purchase of merchandise on credit.
   d) Purchase of office equipment for cash.
   e) Sale of unneeded office equipment on credit.

f) Return of a charge sale.
g) Return of a cash sale.
h) Return of a credit purchase.
i) Payment of a creditor.
j) Correction of a posted error, wrong account.
k) Adjusting entries.
l) Closing entries.

4. What is gained by the use of subsidiary ledgers and controlling accounts?

5. A company has the following numbers of accounts with balances in its General Ledger:

> a) *Asset accounts (not including customer accounts)*... 25
> b) *Accounts with customers*..........................500
> c) *Liability accounts (not including creditor accounts)*.   5
> d) *Accounts with creditors*.......................... 50
> e) *Owner equity accounts (including income statement*
>   *accounts)*..................................... 20
>   *Total*.......................................600

How many items appear on the trial balance of this company? If the accounts with customers and creditors are removed from the General Ledger and placed in subsidiary ledgers, how many items will appear on the trial balance?

6. Why must an Accounts Receivable controlling account be substituted in the General Ledger in the place of the customer accounts when the customer accounts are removed and placed in a subsidiary ledger?

7. You have been asked to establish a subsidiary Accounts Receivable Ledger and an Accounts Receivable controlling account for a firm that has previously kept its customer accounts in its General Ledger. Explain how you propose to accomplish this.

8. How is the equality of a controlling account and its subsidiary ledger maintained?

9. Why is a schedule of accounts receivable prepared when the accounts receivable are kept in a subsidiary ledger?

10. Why are postings to customer accounts made daily?

11. After all posting is completed, the balance of the Accounts Receivable controlling account does not agree with the sum of the balances in the Accounts Receivable Ledger. If the trial balance is in balance, where is the error apt to be? Why?

12. How is a multiple-column journal crossfooted? Why is a multiple-column journal crossfooted?

13. How is it possible to tell from which journal a particular amount in a ledger account was posted?

14. When a general journal entry is used to record a returned charge sale, the credit of the entry must be posted twice. Does this cause the trial balance to be out of balance? Why or why not?

15. Both credits to customer accounts and credits to miscellaneous accounts are individually posted from a Cash Receipts Journal like that of Illustration 45. Why not place both kinds of credits in the same column and thus save journal space?

16. A company uses a Sales Journal, an Accounts Receivable controlling account, and a subsidiary Accounts Receivable Ledger similar to the ones described in this chapter. If it makes the following errors, when is each error apt to be first discovered?

   a) A $10 sale on account is recorded in the Sales Journal as a $100 sale.

   b) A $10 sale is correctly recorded in the Sales Journal but is posted to the customer's account as a $100 sale.

   c) An error is made in securing the balance of a customer's account.

   d) An error is made in totaling the Amount column in the Sales Journal.

PROBLEMS

Problem 7–1

The following sales, cash receipts, and miscellaneous transactions were completed by Ballard Automotive Supply during December of the current year:

Dec. 2 Sold merchandise on credit to Robert Nance, Invoice No. 878, $1,200. (Terms of all sales are 2/10, n/30.)

   4 William Ballard, the proprietor of Ballard Automotive Supply, invested an additional $1,500 in the business.

   6 Sold merchandise on credit to Scott Taylor, Invoice No. 879, $1,600.

   8 Robert Nance returned for credit $200 of merchandise purchased on December 2 because it did not meet specifications.

   10 Sold merchandise on credit to Carl Gordon, Invoice No. 880, $2,200.

   12 Received a check from Robert Nance in full payment of Invoice No. 878, less the return and the discount.

   13 Sold merchandise on credit to Carl Gordon, Invoice No. 881, $900.

   13 Sold at cost $250 of unneeded office equipment to Scott Taylor on credit.

   15 Cash sales for the first half of the month were $2,350. (Cash sales are commonly recorded daily from the cash register reading. They are recorded only twice in this problem in order to shorten the problem.)

   15 *Make the individual postings from the journals. Normally, items that are posted as individual amounts from the journals are posted daily; but since such items in this problem are few, you are asked to post them on only two occasions.*

   16 Gave the First National Bank a 60-day, 6 percent promissory note in order to borrow $2,000.

   18 Sold merchandise on credit to Robert Nance, Invoice No. 882, $1,300.

   20 Received a check from Carl Gordon in full payment of Invoice No. 880, less the discount.

Dec. 22   Sold merchandise on credit to Carl Gordon, Invoice No. 883, $1,700.

22   23   Received a check from Carl Gordon in full payment of Invoice No. 881, less the discount.

25   Received a check from Scott Taylor in full payment of Invoice No. 879.

28   Received a check from Robert Nance in full payment of Invoice No. 882, less the discount.

31   Cash sales for the last half of the month were $2,675.

31   *Make the individual postings from the journals.*

31   *Make the month-end postings from the journals.*

Required:

1. Open the following general ledger accounts: Cash; Accounts Receivable; Office Equipment; Notes Payable; William Ballard, Capital; Sales; Sales Returns and Allowances; and Sales Discounts.
2. Open the following accounts receivable ledger accounts: Carl Gordon; Robert Nance; and Scott Taylor.
3. Prepare a Sales Journal similar to Illustration 43, a Cash Receipts Journal similar to Illustration 45, and a General Journal. Enter the transactions in the journals and post at the points where you are instructed to do so.
4. Prepare a trial balance and a schedule of accounts receivable. (An asset account will have a credit balance in the trial balance because you have not been asked to record all of the transactions of the business.)

Problem 7–2

The following purchases, cash disbursements, and miscellaneous transactions were completed by Central Sales during December of the current year:

Dec. 3   Received merchandise and an invoice dated November 30, terms 2/10, n/60, from Bigbee Manufacturing Company, $2,800.

5   Paid advertising expense, $210.

6   Received merchandise and an invoice dated December 4, terms 2/10, n/60, from Robert McBroom, Inc., $1,800.

8   Received merchandise and an invoice dated December 6, terms 2/10, n/60, from Joslin and Kerns, $2,300.

10   Sent Bigbee Manufacturing Company a check in payment of the invoice of November 30, less the discount.

13   Sent Robert McBroom, Inc., a check in payment of the invoice of December 4, less the discount.

13   Purchased $400 of store equipment from West Equipment Sales, terms n/10 E.O.M.

16   Paid the sales salaries for the first half of the month, $750.

16   Sent Joslin and Kerns a check in payment of the invoice of December 6, less the discount.

16   *Make the individual postings from the journals. Normally, items that are posted as individual amounts from the journals are posted daily; but since such items in this problem are few, you are asked to post them on only two occasions.*

18   Purchased $50 of store supplies for cash.

Dec. 19   Received merchandise and an invoice dated December 18, terms 2/10, n/60, from Robert McBroom, Inc., $1,700.

22   Received a credit memorandum from Robert McBroom, Inc., for defective merchandise received on December 19 and returned for credit, $300.

25   Received merchandise and an invoice dated December 23, terms 2/10, n/60, from Joslin and Kerns, $600.

27   Sent a check to Robert McBroom in payment of the invoice of December 18, less the return and the discount.

31   Paid the sales salaries for the last half of the month, $750.

31   Gary Bolton, the owner of Central Sales withdrew $500 for his personal use.

31   *Make the individual postings from the journals.*

31   *Make the month-end postings from the journals.*

Required:

1. Open the following general ledger accounts: Cash; Store Supplies; Store Equipment; Accounts Payable; Gary Bolton, Withdrawals; Purchases; Purchases Returns and Allowances; Purchases Discounts; Advertising Expense; and Sales Salaries.

2. Open the following accounts payable ledger accounts: Bigbee Manufacturing Company; Joslin and Kerns; Robert McBroom, Inc.; and West Equipment Sales.

3. Prepare a Purchases Journal similar to Illustration 47, a Cash Disbursements Journal similar to Illustration 48, and a General Journal. Enter the transactions in the journals and post at the points where you are instructed to do so.

4. Prepare a trial balance and a schedule of accounts payable. (The Cash account will have a credit balance.)

Problem 7–3

Munzel Sales Company completed the following transactions during February of the current year:

Feb. 2   Sold merchandise on credit to Tyler and Vance, $1,250. (Terms of all sales are 2/10, n/30. Number sales invoices beginning with 758.)

2   Sold merchandise on credit to Bruce Sawyer, Inc., $1,500.

3   Received merchandise and an invoice dated January 31, terms 2/10, n/60, from Globe Manufacturing Company, $2,800.

4   Paid advertising expense, $185.

5   Sold unneeded store equipment at cost for cash, $140.

7   Cash sales for first week of February, $1,200.

7   *Make the individual postings from the journals. Normally items that are posted as individual amounts are posted daily. You are asked to post such items only once each week in this problem in order to shorten the problem.*

8   Issued a credit memorandum to Bruce Sawyer, Inc., for defective merchandise purchased on February 2 and returned for credit, $400.

Feb. 10   Sold merchandise on credit to Rice and Son, $800.

10   Received merchandise and an invoice dated February 6, terms 1/10, n/60, from Western Supply Company, $1,850.

10   Sent a check to Globe Manufacturing Company in full of the invoice of January 31, less the discount.

12   Received a check from Tyler and Vance in full payment of the sale of February 2, less the discount.

12   Received a check from Bruce Sawyer, Inc., in full payment of the sale of February 2, less the return and the discount.

14   Cash sales for the week ended February 13, $1,450.

14   *Make the individual postings from the journals.*

15   Sold merchandise on credit to Rice and Son, $900.

15   Paid the sales salaries for the first half of the month, $600.

17   Issued a credit memorandum to Rice and Son for defective merchandise purchased on February 15 and returned, $150.

18   Sold merchandise to Bruce Sawyer, Inc., $1,300.

18   Received merchandise and an invoice dated February 15, terms 2/10, n/30, from F. M. Pope, Inc., $3,500.

19   Received store equipment and an invoice dated February 18, terms n/10 E.O.M., from Ryan Equipment Company, $650.

20   Received a check from Rice and Son in full of the sale of February 10, less the discount.

20   Cash sales for the week ended February 20, $1,550.

21   *Make the individual postings from the journals.*

22   Received merchandise and an invoice dated February 18, terms 1/10, n/60, from Western Supply Company, $1,250.

22   Received merchandise and an invoice dated February 18, terms 2/10, n/60, from Globe Manufacturing Company, $2,650.

23   Received a credit memorandum from F. M. Pope, Inc., $350. The merchandise covered by the memorandum did not meet specifications and had been returned.

24   Received a check from Rice and Son in full of the invoice of February 15, less the return and the discount.

24   Sent F. M. Pope, Inc., a check in full of the invoice of February 15, less the return and the discount.

25   Sold merchandise on credit to Tyler and Vance, $1,175.

27   Borrowed $5,000 from the United States National Bank by giving a 60-day, 6 percent note payable.

28   Sent Globe Manufacturing Company a check in full of the invoice of February 18, less the discount.

28   Paid the sales salaries for the last half of the month, $600.

28   Cash sales for week ended February 28, $1,225.

28   *Make the individual postings from the journals.*

28   *Crossfoot and make the month-end postings.*

Required:

1. Open the following general ledger accounts: Cash; Accounts Receivable; Store Equipment; Notes Payable; Accounts Payable; Sales; Sales Re-

turns and Allowances; Sales Discounts; Purchases; Purchases Returns and Allowances; Purchases Discounts; Advertising Expense; and Sales Salaries.

2. Open the following subsidiary accounts receivable ledger accounts: Bruce Sawyer, Inc.; Rice and Son; and Tyler and Vance.
3. Open the following subsidiary accounts payable ledger accounts: Globe Manufacturing Company; F. M. Pope, Inc.; Ryan Equipment Company; and Western Supply Company.
4. Prepare a Sales Journal similar to Illustration 43, a Sales Return and Allowances Journal similar to Illustration 46, a Purchases Journal similar to Illustration 47, a Cash Receipts Journal similar to Illustration 45, a Cash Disbursements Journal similar to Illustration 48, and a General Journal.
5. Enter the transactions in the journals and post when instructed to do so.
6. Prepare a trial balance and schedules of accounts receivable and accounts payable.

Problem 7–4 *If the working papers that accompany this text are not being used, omit this problem.*

Assume that Small Sales Company operates with monthly accounting periods, that it is the last week of February of the current year, and that you have just been hired as bookkeeper. The company's previous bookkeeper has journalized the transactions of the first three weeks of the month, and has posted those portions that would be posted as individual amounts. An examination of the journals and ledgers of the problem as they appear in the booklet of working papers will reveal this. It will also show that, for sake of brevity, the January postings are omitted from the accounts and only the January 31 balances are shown.

During the last week of February the following transactions were completed:

Feb. 23 Received merchandise and an invoice dated February 20, terms 2/10, n/60, from Arizona Supply Company, $650.

23 Sold merchandise on credit to Albert Getty, Invoice No. 716, $700. *The terms of all sales are 2/10, n/60.*

24 Douglas Murphy, the proprietor, withdrew $250 for personal living expenses.

25 Received a check from Albert Getty in full of the sale of February 16, less the normal 2 percent discount.

26 Purchased on credit from Store Supply Company a new cash register and several other small items of store equipment, terms n/10 E.O.M., $400.

27 Paid the Southwest Wholesale Company invoice of February 17, less the discount.

28 Paid the sales salaries for the last two weeks of the month, $320.

28 Paid the utility bills, $108.

28 Cash sales for the last half of the month, $685. (Cash sales are usually recorded daily, but are recorded only twice each month in this problem to reduce the repetitive transactions.)

Required for February:
1. Record the transactions for the last week of February:
2. Make the individual postings from the journals for the last week of February. (Individual transaction amounts posted from the journals are normally posted each day, but they are posted only twice each month in this problem in order to simplify the problem.)
3. Make the month-end postings from the journals.
4. Prepare a trial balance in the Trial Balance columns of a work sheet form and complete the work sheet using the following information: (*a*) store supplies inventory, $197; (*b*) expired insurance, $48; (*c*) estimated depreciation of store equipment; $110; and (*d*) February 28 merchandise inventory, $15,998.
5. Complete the work sheet and prepare an income statement, a balance sheet, and schedules of accounts receivable and accounts payable.
6. Prepare and post adjusting and closing entries.
7. Prepare a post-closing trial balance.
8. Double rule the date and amount columns of the columnar journals so that they may be used for recording the March transactions.

Small Sales Company completed the following transactions during March:

Mar. 2 Paid the March rent, $250.
  2 Mailed a check to Arizona Supply Company in full of their invoice of February 20, less the discount.
  3 Received a check from Robert Johnson in full of the sale of February 21, less the discount.
  5 Received a check from Albert Getty in full of the sale of February 23, less the discount.
  6 Sold merchandise to George Mohr, Invoice No. 717, $650.
  7 Purchased merchandise from Western Manufacturing Company, invoice dated March 4, terms 2/10, n/60, $450.
  9 Sold the local Y.M.C.A. a roll of wrapping paper (store supplies) at cost for cash, $18.
  10 Paid Store Supply Company for the items purchased on February 26.
  11 Received merchandise and an invoice dated March 9 from Southwest Wholesale Company, terms 2/10, n/60, $750.
  12 Sold merchandise to Robert Johnson, Invoice No. 718, $950.
  14 Mailed Western Manufacturing Company a check in payment of their invoice of March 4, less the discount.
  14 Paid the biweekly sales salaries, $320.
  14 Cash sales for the first half of the month, $765.
  14 *Make the individual postings from the journals.*
  16 Received a check from George Mohr in full of the sale of March 6, less the discount.
  19 Mailed a check to Southwest Wholesale Company in full of their invoice of March 9, less the discount.
  21 Received a check from Robert Johnson in full of the sale of March 12, less the discount.
  23 Sold merchandise to James Scott, Invoice No. 719, $865.

Mar. 24   Sold merchandise to George Mohr, Invoice No. 720, $985.
26   Received merchandise and an invoice dated March 23, terms 2/10, n/60, from Western Manufacturing Company, $915.
28   Paid the biweekly sales salaries, $320.
29   Received a credit memorandum from Western Manufacturing Company for defective merchandise received on March 26 and returned, $111.
31   Paid the utility bills, $112.
31   Cash sales for the last half of the month, $820.
31   *Make the individual postings from the journals.*
31   *Make the month-end postings from the journals.*

Required for March:

1. Record the transactions in the journals and post at the points indicated.
2. Prepare a March 31 trial balance in the Trial Balance columns of a work sheet form and complete the work sheet using the following information: (*a*) store supplies inventory, $113; (*b*) expired insurance, $48; (*c*) depreciation of store equipment, $110; (*d*) accrued sales salaries, $106; and (*e*) March 31 merchandise inventory, $14,885.
3. Prepare an income statement, balance sheet, and schedules of accounts receivable and accounts payable.
4. Prepare and post adjusting and closing entries and prepare a post-closing trial balance.

Problem 7–5

Valley Sales Company completed the following credit transactions:

Dec. 3   Purchased $935 of merchandise from Mesa Wholesale Company.
5   Purchased $75 of office supplies from Store and Office Suppliers.
9   Purchased $1,245 of merchandise from Boswell and Boswell.
11   Purchased $120 of store supplies and $650 of merchandise from Phoenix Wholesale Company.
15   Purchased a desk and chair for the office from Store and Office Suppliers, $225.
19   Purchased $985 of merchandise from Phoenix Wholesale Company.
23   Purchased $110 of store supplies and $65 of office supplies from Store and Office Suppliers.
26   Purchased $450 of merchandise from Boswell and Boswell.
28   Purchased $735 of merchandise from Mesa Wholesale Company.

Required:

1. Prepare a General Journal and a multicolumn Purchases Journal similar to Illustration 50. Enter the foregoing transactions in the journals.
2. Open the required general ledger and accounts payable ledger accounts and post the journals.

CLASS EXERCISE

Exercise 7–1

Following are the condensed journals of a merchandising concern. The journal column headings are incomplete in that they do not indicate whether the columns are debit or credit columns.

Required:

1. Prepare T-accounts on a sheet of ordinary notebook paper for the following general ledger and subsidiary ledger accounts. Separate the accounts of each ledger group.

General Ledger Accounts	*Accounts Receivable Ledger Accounts*
Cash	A. Able
Accounts Receivable	B. Best
Prepaid Insurance	C. Call
Store Equipment	
Notes Payable	
Accounts Payable	
Sales	*Accounts Payable Ledger Accounts*
Sales Returns	Company One
Sales Discounts	Company Two
Purchases	Company Three
Purchases Returns	
Purchases Discounts	

2. Without referring to illustrations showing complete column headings for the journals, post the following journals to the proper T-accounts.

SALES JOURNAL		SALES RETURNS AND ALLOWANCES JOURNAL		PURCHASES JOURNAL	
Account	**Amount**	**Account**	**Amount**	**Account**	**Amount**
A. Able..........	1,000	B. Best..........	300	Company One....	1,200
B. Best..........	1,500	C. Call..........	200	Company Two...	1,400
C. Call..........	2,000		500	Company Three..	1,600
	4,500				4,200

GENERAL JOURNAL

....	..	*Accounts Payable—Company Three........*	*300.00*	
		Purchases Returns..................		*300.00*

CASH RECEIPTS JOURNAL

Account	Sundry Accounts	Accounts Receivable	Sales	Sales Discounts	Cash
A. Able..........................	......	1,000	....	20	980
Cash Sales......................	......	......	1,450	......	1,450
Notes Payable..................	2,000	......	......	......	2,000
Cash Sales......................	......	......	1,650	......	1,650
C. Call..........................	......	1,500	......	30	1,470
Store Equipment..............	150	......	......	......	150
	2,150	2,500	3,100	50	7,700

CASH DISBURSEMENTS JOURNAL

Account	Sundry Accounts	Accounts Payable	Purchases Discounts	Cash
Prepaid Insurance.....................	100	......	......	100
Company Two.........................	......	1,400	28	1,372
Company Three.......................	......	1,300	26	1,274
Store Equipment.....................	500	......	......	500
	600	2,700	54	3,246

ALTERNATE PROBLEMS

Problem 7–3A

Webster Supply Company completed the following transactions during February of the current year:

Feb. 2   Received merchandise and an invoice dated January 30, terms 2/10, n/30, from Globe Manufacturing Company, $1,535.

3   Purchased store equipment from Ryan Equipment Company, n/10 E.O.M., $585.

3   Sold merchandise on credit to Rice and Son, $950. (Terms of all credit sales are 2/10, n/60. Number sales invoices beginning with 617.)

4   Sold merchandise on account to Tyler and Vance, $1,265.

5   Received merchandise and an invoice dated February 3, terms 1/10, n/60, from F. M. Pope, Inc., $1,690.

6   Received a credit memorandum from Globe Manufacturing Company for unsatisfactory merchandise received from them on February 2 and returned, $135.

7   Received a credit memorandum from Ryan Equipment Company for store equipment received on February 3 and returned, $60.

7   Cash sales for the first week of February, $1,445.

7   *Make the individual postings from the journals. (Normally such items are posted daily; but to shorten the problem you are asked to post them only once each week.)*

9   Issued a credit memorandum to Tyler and Vance for defective merchandise sold on February 4 and returned, $115.

Feb. 9   Sent Globe Manufacturing Company a check in payment of their invoice of January 30, less the return and discount.

11   Sold merchandise to Bruce Sawyer, Inc., $1,595.

12   Received a check from Rice and Son in payment of the sale of February 3, less the discount.

13   Received a check from Tyler and Vance in payment of the sale of February 4, less the return and discount.

14   Received merchandise and an invoice dated February 11, terms 2/10, n/60, from Western Supply Company, $1,850.

14   Paid the sales salaries for the first half of the month, $815.

14   Cash sales for the week ended February 14, $1,395.

14   *Make the individual postings from the journals.*

16   Issued a credit memorandum to Bruce Sawyer, Inc., for defective merchandise sold on February 11 and returned, $45.

17   Received merchandise and an invoice dated February 14, terms 2/10, n/60, from Western Supply Company, $1,450.

18   Received merchandise and an invoice dated February 16, terms 1/10, n/60, from F. M. Pope, Inc., $435.

18   Sold merchandise to Rice and Son on credit, $650.

21   Received a check from Bruce Sawyer, Inc., in payment of the sale of February 11, less the return and discount.

21   Sent Western Supply Company a check in payment of their invoice of February 11, less the discount.

21   Cash sales for the week ended February 21, $1,425.

21   *Make the individual postings from the journals.*

24   Sent Western Supply Company a check in payment of their invoice of February 14, less the discount.

25   Borrowed $4,000 by giving Valley National Bank a 60-day, 6 percent promissory note payable.

26   Sold merchandise to Bruce Sawyer, Inc., on credit, $915.

27   Sold merchandise to Tyler and Vance on credit, $1,085.

28   Paid advertising expense, $375.

28   Paid the sales salaries for the last half of the month, $815.

28   Received a check from Rice and Son in payment of the sale of February 18, less the discount.

28   Cash sales for the last week of the month, $1,345.

28   *Make the individual postings from the journals.*

28   *Make the month-end postings from the journals.*

Required:

1. Open the following general ledger accounts: Cash; Accounts Receivable; Store Equipment; Notes Payable; Accounts Payable; Sales; Sales Returns and Allowances; Sales Discounts; Purchases; Purchases Returns and Allowances; Purchases Discounts; Advertising Expense; and Sales Salaries.

2. Open the following accounts receivable ledger accounts: Bruce Sawyer, Inc.; Rice and Son; and Tyler and Vance.

3. Open the following accounts payable ledger accounts: Globe Manufacturing Company; F. M. Pope, Inc.; Ryan Equipment Company; and Western Supply Company.

4. Prepare a one-column Sales Journal, a one-column Purchases Journal, a Sales Returns and Allowances Journal, a Cash Receipts Journal, a Cash Disbursements Journal, and a General Journal similar to the ones illustrated in this chapter.
5. Enter the foregoing transactions in the journals and post when instructed to do so.
6. Prepare a trial balance and schedules of the accounts receivable and accounts payable.

Problem 7—4A *If the working papers that accompany this text are not being used, omit this problem.*

Assume that Small Sales Company operates with annual accounting periods that end each January 31, that it is now the last week of February of the current year, and you have just been hired as the company's bookkeeper. The previous bookkeeper has journalized the transactions for the first three weeks of February and has posted those entry portions that would be posted as individual amounts. An examination of the journals and ledgers of the company as they appear in the booklet of working papers will reveal this. It will also show that, for sake of brevity, the January postings are omitted from the accounts and only the January 31 balances are shown.

During the last week of the month the following transactions were completed by the company:

Feb. 23   Received merchandise and an invoice dated February 20, terms 2/10, n/60, from Arizona Supply Company, $900.

    23   Sold merchandise on credit to Albert Getty, Invoice No. 716, $850. *The terms of all sales are 2/10, n/60.*

    25   Received a check from Albert Getty in full of the sale of February 16, less the normal 2 percent discount.

    26   Purchased several items of store supplies on credit from Store Supply Company, terms n/10 E.O.M., $85.

    27   Paid the Southwest Wholesale Company invoice of February 17, less the discount.

    28   Douglas Murphy, the proprietor, wrote a $150 check on the bank account of the company in payment of the rent on his personal residence.

    28   Paid the utility bills, $113.

    28   Paid the sales salaries for the last two weeks of the month, including a small amount of overtime, $345.

    28   Cash sales for the last half of the month, $715. (Cash sales are usually recorded daily, but are recorded only twice each month in this problem to reduce the repetitive transactions.)

Required for February:

1. Record the transactions for the last week of February.
2. Make the individual postings from the journals for this week. (Individual amounts posted from the journals are normally posted daily; but are posted only twice each month in this problem in order to simplify the problem.)
3. Make the month-end postings from the journals.

4. Prepare a February 28 trial balance and schedules of accounts receivable and accounts payable. Prepare the trial balance in the space provided in the working papers for the post-closing trial balance of Problem 7–4.
5. Double rule the date and amount columns of the columnar journals so that they may be used for recording the transaction of March.

Required for March:
1. Record the March transactions of Small Sales Company as they appear in Problem 7–4 on page 194. Post when instructed to do so.
2. Prepare a March trial balance and schedules of the accounts receivable and accounts payable.

Problem 7–5A

On page 201 is one of the special journals of Bit Different Sales Company, a journal unlike any described in your text and designed to test your knowledge of the posting principles of columnar journals.

Required:
Under the assumption that Bit Different Sales Company maintains a subsidiary Accounts Payable Ledger, describe column by column in your own words on a sheet of notebook paper how this journal would be posted.

DECISION PROBLEM 7—THE ROSE SHOP

Marty Davis and his wife operate a flower shop. The shop has prospered and employs a number of clerks, stylists and arrangers, and a deliveryman. Mrs. Davis keeps the books which consist of the following:

Cash Receipts Journal with columns for Sundry Accounts, Cr.; Sales, Cr.; Sales Taxes Payable, Cr.; and Cash, Dr.

Cash Disbursements Journal with the usual columns.

General Journal, a simple two-column journal.

General Ledger, containing among the usual accounts an account for Accounts Receivable.

These records are kept manually. The total cash sales each day is entered in the Cash Receipts Journal from a summary of the cash register readings. No sales tickets are prepared for cash sales. A credit sale is recorded on a sales ticket prepared in duplicate. The carbon copy is delivered to the customer at the time of the sale, provided the delivery of flowers sold is made directly to the buyer. (Many flowers are ordered for weddings, funerals, churches, and for special occasions not calling for delivery to the buyer.) Original copies of credit sales tickets are filed in an alphabetical file as a record of unpaid customer accounts; no further record of charge sales is made until a customer pays his account. Where payments are received on credit sales, the original copies of the sales tickets are surrendered as receipts to the customers, and the cash is entered in the cash register and included with the cash sales of the day.

At the end of each accounting period, in order to determine the total sales, cash and credit, all unpaid sales tickets in the customers' file are totaled on an

CASH DISBURSEMENTS, PURCHASES, AND PURCHASES RETURNS JOURNAL

| Debit Columns | | | | | Date | Account Titles and Explanations | F | Credit Columns | | | |
Store Supplies	Sales Salaries	Purchases	Accts. Payable	Sundry Accts.				Sundry Accts.	Accts. Payable	Pur. Discount	Cash
.....	.....	.....	.....	500.00	Dec. 1	Rent expense		.....	.....	.....	500.00
75.00	.....	525.00	.....	.....	2	Horn Supply Company		.....	600.00	.....	.....
.....	.....	850.00	.....	.....	5	Lee Co.		.....	850.00	.....	.....
.....	.....	.....	600.00	.....	10	Horn Supply Company		.....	.....	12.00	588.00
.....	.....	.....	100.00	.....	13	Lee Co. Purchases—Returns		100.00	.....	.....	.....
.....	.....	.....	750.00	.....	14	Lee Company		.....	.....	15.00	735.00
.....	.....	1,200.00	.....	.....	15	Swing Wholesale Company		.....	1,200.00	.....	.....
.....	750.00	.....	.....	.....	15	Salaries for first half of month		.....	.....	.....	750.00
.....	.....	.....	.....	175.00	18	Store equipment		.....	.....	.....	175.00
50.00	.....	1,100.00	.....	.....	23	Horn Supply Company		.....	1,150.00	.....	.....
.....	.....	.....	1,200.00	.....	24	Swing Wholesale Company		.....	.....	24.00	1,176.00
.....	750.00	.....	.....	.....	31	Salaries for last half of month		.....	.....	.....	750.00
125.00	1,500.00	3,675.00	2,650.00	675.00				100.00	3,800.00	51.00	4,674.00

adding machine and the following entry is made in the General Journal to record these receivables:

Dec.	31	Accounts Receivable..................	2,645.00	
		Sales............................		2,645.00

Then on the first day of the new accounting period the following entry is made to remove the effects of the foregoing entry from the books and to permit the continuance of the practice described for handling all collections from customers:

Jan.	2	Sales...............................	2,645.00	
		Accounts Receivable..............		2,645.00

Although Mrs. Davis does not agree, Mr. Davis feels that some sales tickets are lost. If this is the case, collections are not made on such lost tickets and, of course, these amounts never find their way into the revenue account.

Prepare a report to the Rose Shop making such comments and recommendations as you feel justified about the system for handling sales and customers accounts and detailing any improvements you would recommend.

8

Accounting for
and Controlling Cash

CASH HAS universal usefulness, small bulk for high value, and no special identification marks by which its ownership may be established. These characteristics plus the great number of cash transactions completed by the average company make procedures for controlling cash important. Obviously, cash control is very important to a business owner; but it is equally as important to employees responsible for handling cash. It is equally as important because an adequate system of cash control enables the employees to prove their work has been completed accurately and honestly.

No effort will be made here to present a complete discussion of procedures for controlling and safeguarding cash. However, adequate systems of control should be devised for handling both cash receipts and cash disbursements, and in these systems two basic principles should be observed. First, there should be a separation of duties so that the people responsible for handling cash are not the same people who make entries in the cash journals or post to the accounts in which sources and uses of cash are recorded. Second, all cash receipts should be deposited in the bank, intact; and all payments should be made by check. The one exception to this last principle is that small disbursements may be made in cash from a petty cash fund. This exception is discussed later in this chapter.

The reason for the first of the foregoing basic principles is that a division of duties necessitates collusion between two or more people if cash is to be embezzled and its theft concealed in the accounting records. As for the second, requiring that all receipts be deposited intact and all payments be made by check provides in the records kept by the bank a separate and external record of cash transactions. This external record is in addition to a company's own records, and may be used to check and prove the records kept by the company. A summary of the bank's record of a concern's cash transactions is submitted to the concern each month in a bank statement. The individual items on the statement are supported by duplicate deposit tickets and canceled checks.

THE DEPOSIT TICKET

All cash received each day should be deposited in the bank at the end of that day or early next morning. When a deposit is made, the depositor lists

Illustration 51—Deposit Ticket

Deposited for

in the
MERCHANTS NATIONAL BANK
Eugene, Oregon

_____*19*___
Please list each check separately.

	Dollars	Cents
Currency____		
Silver____		
Checks____		
Total		

Items listed above are accepted for deposit subject to collection.

the items being deposited on a form provided by the bank. This form, called a *deposit ticket*, appears as in Illustration 51. On it the depositor enters the name of the company making the deposit, its address, the date, the total amounts of currency and coins, and the amount of each individual check being deposited. Opposite the amount of each check is written the name of the local bank or the address of the out-of-town bank on which the check is drawn. Some banks prefer that the depositor list each check by the American Bankers' Association number of the bank on which the check is drawn. Every bank has a different American Bankers' Association number that readily identifies it, and most banks print this number on their checks following the bank's name.

When a deposit is made, most companies present the deposit, a deposit ticket, and a duplicate carbon copy of the deposit ticket to the receiving teller of the bank. The deposit and the original deposit ticket copy are kept by the teller. The duplicate deposit ticket is stamped "Duplicate" and returned to the depositor as acknowledgment of the deposit. At any time thereafter, if all receipts are deposited, it is possible to compare each day's individual receipts as shown by the Cash Receipts Journal with the individual items deposited as shown by the day's duplicate deposit ticket, and thus prove that every item reached the bank on the day it was received.

DEPOSITS AND THE CASH RECEIPTS JOURNAL

In a business that deposits its receipts intact and makes all payments by check, after all cash items are recorded and posted, the balance of the Cash account should be the same as the amount of money on deposit in the bank. Because of this, many companies change the name of their Cash account to the name of the bank in which the cash is deposited. They also change the names of the Cash columns in their journals. For instance, in the Cash Receipts Journal the Cash debit column and in the Cash Disbursements Journal the Cash credit column are changed to, for example, "Merchants National Bank."

Some companies depositing all cash intact each day place a double "cash" column in their Cash Receipts Journal in order to show the amount of each day's deposit. Such a double "cash" column appears as in Illustration 52 on the next page.

When a double "cash" column like the one shown is used, each day's receipts, a day's cash sales are treated as one receipt, are individually entered in the Memo column. Then, at the end of each day, the amounts entered in the Memo column that day are totaled, the cash is deposited, and the amount deposited is entered in the Debit column. The individual amounts entered in the two columns are not posted, but at the end of the month the Debit column total is debited to the "Cash" or "1st National Bank" account.

Illustration 52

CASH RECEIPTS JOURNAL

Date		Account Credited			Sales Credit	Sales Discounts Debit	1st National Bank	
							Memo	Debit
Nov.	1	Michael Doran				6.00	294.00	
	1	James McBroom				12.00	588.00	
	1	Henry Fleck				2.50	122.50	
	1	Cash Sales			1,200.00		1,200.00	2,204.50

CHECKS

Everyone is familiar with ordinary checks. A check is a written order, signed by a depositor, directing the bank to pay a specified sum of money to the person designated on its face, or to his order. Checks are widely used because they may be safely sent through the mails and also because each check acts as a receipt. Too, companies using checks for all payments secure a double record of cash payments, their own record and the record of the bank. An ordinary check with stub attached is shown in Illustration 53.

Illustration 53—Check with Stub Attached

No. 46	$196.00
Oct. 15	1966

To Acme Mfg. Co.

For Invoice 10/5

Balance	$ 687.00
Deposited	110.00
Deposited	
Total	797.00
Amt. Check	196.00
Balance	601.00

No. 46   October 15 19 66

Pingtopper Mfg. Company
1233 First Avenue, Eugene, Oregon

PAY TO THE
ORDER OF   Acme Mfg. Co. $196.00

--Exactly one hundred and ninety-six---------------------DOLLARS

Merchants National   PINGTOPPER MFG. COMPANY
Bank 26-71
      1272   *P. A. Spoke*
                        TREASURER

When checks like Illustration 53 are used, the bank balance is recalculated on the check stub as each check is drawn. When such a check is used, the stub should be filled out first to prevent making a check and overlooking the entries on its stub until after the check has been sent out and the data for the stub are no longer available. Many companies use a type of check in which a carbon copy of the check takes the place of the check stub.

Certified Check. A certified check is like an ordinary check in every way except that it has been certified by the bank upon which it was drawn.

In certifying a check, an officer of the bank upon which it is drawn certifies that the check's maker has on deposit funds sufficient to pay the check. He stamps the word "certified" and the bank's name on the check, signs his name, returns the check to its maker, and immediately orders a deduction of funds equal to the amount of the check from the maker's account. Thereafter, the bank guarantees the check's payment. Any creditor will readily accept a certified check.

Cashier's Check. A cashier's check is a bank's own check drawn by its cashier on itself. Cashier's checks are purchased from a bank and are used like postal money orders in making payments in cases where a company's own check might not be acceptable.

Bank Draft. A bank draft, like a cashier's check, is purchased from a bank and is also used in situations where a company's own check might not be acceptable. A bank draft is like a cashier's check in that it is drawn by the bank from which it is purchased, but it differs in that it is drawn upon funds the bank has on deposit in another bank.

ENDORSEMENTS

Checks received by a business are normally deposited on the day received. However, checks are also commonly transferred from person to person. Normally, when a check is transferred, it is endorsed by the person transferring it. An endorsement on a check consists of the owner's signature on the back thereof. When an owner endorses a check, he not only effects its transfer but also, if the endorsement is not qualified, guarantees the check's payment. Endorsements, like the following of John W. Evans, are of several kinds:

Blank. A blank endorsement consists of only the endorser's signature, For example:

John W. Evans

Such an endorsement makes a check or other negotiable instrument payable to bearer.

Special or Full. A special or full endorsement consists of the endorser's signature preceded by the words "Pay to the order of" and the name of the endorsee. For example:

Pay to the order of Joel E. Freeman
John W. Evans

If the endorsement just illustrated is used, Joel E. Freeman must endorse the check before title to it can be transferred again. Such an endorsement is used when a check that has already been endorsed in blank is to be sent through the mail.

Qualified. A qualified endorsement consists of the endorser's signature preceded by the words "Without recourse," or other words having the same meaning. For example:

Without recourse
John W. Evans

Such an endorsement is used when an endorser wishes to limit his liability as an endorser.

Restrictive. A restrictive endorsement ends further negotiation of a check or other negotiable instrument and appears, for example:

Pay to the order of
Allen W. Oaks only
John W. Evans

or

Pay to the order of
the U.S. National
Bank for deposit
John W. Evans

THE CHECK REGISTER

Many companies require the printer to number their checks consecutively as the checks are printed. This makes it possible to account for each check. Checks are commonly accounted for in a *Check Register.* An examination of the Check Register in Illustration 54 will show that it

Illustration 54—A Check Register

CHECK REGISTER   **Page 32**

Date	Check No.	Payee	Account Debited	F	Sundry Accounts Debit	Accts. Pay. Debit	Pur. Dis. Credit	Merchants Bank Credit
Oct. 3	42	L. & Y. Co.	Freight-In		24.50			24.50
10	43	Eugene Electric	Misc. Gen. Ex.		14.00			14.00
12	44	Voided check	Voided check					
12	45	Frank Hyatt	Purchases		25.00			25.00
15	46	Acme Mfg. Co.	Acme Mfg. Co.			200.00	4.00	196.00

differs but slightly from a Cash Disbursements Journal. The differences are:

1. The Explanation column is omitted. Any explanation needed is placed on the check stub or the carbon copy of the check.
2. A column is added for the name of each check's payee to aid in comparing canceled checks with check register entries.
3. A column is added for check numbers; and each check is entered in numerical order, making it possible to scan the numbers for omitted checks.
4. The name of the Cash credit column is changed to the name of the bank in which the cash is deposited.

When a Check Register is used, it takes the place of a Cash Disbursements Journal.

Checks are entered in the Check Register in numerical order; and if a check is spoiled in writing, many concerns require an entry such as the one on line three of the register illustrated. The spoiled check is then marked void and attached to its stub.

The Check Register is posted in exactly the same manner as a Cash Disbursements Journal.

THE BANK STATEMENT

Every month banks furnish each commercial depositor a statement of his account. The statement shows: (1) the amount on deposit at the beginning of the month, (2) checks and any other amounts deducted from the account, (3) deposits and any other amounts added to the account, and (4) the account balance at the end of the month, according to the records of the bank. If all receipts are deposited and all payments are made by check, the bank statement becomes a device for proving the depositor's cash records. A bank statement is shown in Illustration 55.

Illustration 55—Bank Statement

Valley Hardware Company *10th and Pine Sts.* *Eugene, Oregon*		*Statement of Account* *with* *MERCHANTS NATIONAL BANK* *OF EUGENE, OREGON*	
Checks in Detail	**Deposits**	**Date**	**Balance**
Balance Brought	*Forward Se*	*pt. 30 '66*	*1,578.00*
58.00		*Oct. 2 '66*	*1,520.00*
120.00 200.00		*Oct. 5 '66*	*1,200.00*
	240.00	*Oct. 6 '66*	*1,440.00*
25.00 75.00	*150.00*	*Oct. 10 '66*	*1,490.00*
	180.00	*Oct. 18 '66*	*1,670.00*
10.00 50.00		*Oct. 23 '66*	*1,610.00*
135.00	*100.00*	*Oct. 25 '66*	*1,575.00*
9.00		*Oct. 28 '66*	*1,566.00*
	198.50	*Oct. 30 '66*	*1,764.50*
			Last amount in *this column is* *your balance.*

If no error is reported within ten days this ac-
count will be considered correct.   *Vouchers Returned 9*

Banks commonly mail a commercial depositor his bank statement soon after the end of each month. Included in the envelope with the statement are the depositor's *canceled checks* and any debit or credit memoranda that have affected the account. The checks returned are the ones the bank has paid during the month. They are called "canceled checks" because they are canceled by stamping or punching to show that they have been paid. During any month, in addition to the checks the depositor has drawn, the bank may deduct from the depositor's account amounts for service charges, printing checks, items deposited that are uncollectible, and for errors. The bank notifies the depositor of each such deduction with a debit memorandum. A copy of the memorandum is always included with the monthly statement. The bank may also add amounts to the depositor's account for errors and for amounts collected for the depositor. A credit memorandum is used to notify the depositor of any such additions.

NEED FOR RECONCILING THE BANK ACCOUNT

Normally, when the bank statement arrives, the balance of cash as shown by the statement does not agree with the balance shown by the depositor's accounting records. In order to prove the accuracy of both the records of the depositor and the bank, it is necessary to reconcile and account for any differences between the two balances.

Numerous things may cause the bank statement balance to differ from the depositor's book balance of cash. Some of the more common are:

1. *Outstanding Checks.* These are checks that have been drawn by the depositor and deducted on his records but have not reached the bank for payment and deduction.
2. *Unrecorded Deposits.* Concerns often make deposits at the end of each business day, after the bank has closed. These deposits are made in the bank's night depository and are not recorded by the bank until the next business day. Consequently, the deposit of the last day of a month, if it is placed in the night depository, does not appear on the bank statement for that month.
3. *Charges for Service and Uncollectible Items.* A bank often deducts amounts from a depositor's account for services rendered and for items deposited that it is unable to collect. Insufficient funds checks are the most common of the latter. The bank notifies the depositor of each such deduction with a debit memorandum. If the item is material in amount, the memorandum is mailed to the depositor on the day of the deduction. Furthermore, in a well-managed company, each such deduction is entered in the Cash Disbursements Journal or the Check Register on the day the memorandum is received. However, occasionally there are unentered amounts near the end of the month.
4. *Collections.* Banks often act as collecting agents for their depositors, collecting for a small fee promissory notes and other items. When an item such as a promissory note is collected, the bank usually adds the

proceeds to the depositor's account and sends a credit memorandum as notification of the transaction. As soon as the memorandum is received, an entry should be made in the Cash Receipts Journal. Occasionally, there are unentered amounts near the end of the month.

5. *Errors.* Regardless of care and systems of internal control for automatic error detection, both the bank and the depositor make errors that affect the bank balance. Occasionally, these errors are not discovered until the balance is reconciled.

RECONCILING THE BANK BALANCE

The steps in reconciling the bank balance are:

1. Compare the deposits listed on the bank statement with deposits shown in the accounting records. Note any discrepancies and discover which is correct. List any errors or unrecorded items.
2. When canceled checks are returned by the bank, they are in a stack in the order in which the bank paid them and also in the order of their listing on the bank statement. While the checks are in this order, compare each check with its bank statement listing. Note any discrepancies or errors.
3. Rearrange the returned checks in numerical order, the order in which they were written. Secure the previous month's reconciliation and determine if any checks outstanding at the end of the previous month are still outstanding. If there are any, list them. Also, see that any deposits that were unrecorded by the bank at the end of the previous month have been recorded.
4. Insert among the canceled checks any bank memorandum according to their dates. Compare each check with its entry in the Check Register. If a register is not maintained, compare each check with its stub. Note for correction any discrepancies, and list any unpaid checks or unrecorded memorandum.
5. Prepare a reconciliation of the bank statement balance with the book balance of cash. Such a reconciliation is shown in Illustration 56.
6. Determine if any debits or credits appearing on the bank statement are unrecorded in the books of account. Make journal entries to record them.

ILLUSTRATION OF A BANK RECONCILIATION

To illustrate a bank reconciliation assume that Valley Hardware Company found the following when it attempted to reconcile its bank balance of October 31. The bank balance as shown by the bank statement was $1,764, and the cash balance according to the accounting records was $1,370. Check No. 124 for $150 and Check No. 126 for $200 were outstanding and unpaid by the bank. A $120 deposit, placed in the bank's night depository after banking hours on October 31, was unrecorded by the bank. Among the returned checks was a credit memorandum showing the bank had collected a note for the company on October 30, crediting the proceeds, $200 less a $2 collection fee, to the company account. Also returned with the bank statement was an NSF (not sufficient funds) check for $9. This check had been received from a customer, Frank Jones, on October 25, and had been included in that day's deposit. The collection of the note and the return of the NSF check were unrecorded on the company books. In addition, a check for $25 drawn by Valley Haberdashery was among the canceled checks returned. This check had been charged in error to the account of Valley Hardware Company. The statement reconciling these amounts is shown in Illustration 56.

Illustration 56—Bank Reconciliation
VALLEY HARDWARE COMPANY
Bank Reconciliation As of October 31, 19—

Book Balance of Cash $1,370			*Bank Statement Balance*		$1,76
Add:			*Add:*		
Proceeds of note less collection			*Deposit of 10/31* $120		
fee	198		*Valley Haberdashery*		
	$1,568		*check charged in*		
			error	25	14
					$1,96
Deduct:			*Deduct:*		
NSF check of Frank Jones	9		*Outstanding checks:*		
			No. 124 ....$150		
			No. 126	200	35
Adjusted Balance $1,559			*Adjusted Balance*		$1,55

A bank reconciliation helps locate any errors made by either the bank or the depositor; discloses any items which have been entered on the company books but have not come to the bank's attention; and discloses items that should be recorded on the company books but are unrecorded on the date of the reconciliation. For example, in the reconciliation illustrated, the adjusted cash balance, $1,559 is the true cash balance. However, at the time the reconciliation is completed, Valley Hardware Company's accounting records show a $1,370 book balance. Consequently, entries must be made to adjust the book balance, increasing it to the true cash balance. This requires two entries, the first in general journal form is:

Nov.	2	*Cash*	198.00	
		Collection Expense	2.00	
		Notes Receivable		200.00
		To record the proceeds and collection		
		charge of a note collected by the bank.		

The foregoing entry is self-explanatory. The bank collected a note receivable, deducted a collection fee, and deposited the difference to the Valley Hardware Company account. The entry increases the amount of cash on the books, records the collection expense, and reduces notes receivable.

The second entry is:

Nov.	2	*Accounts Receivable—Frank Jones*.........	*9.00*	
		Cash....................................		*9.00*
		To charge back the NSF check received from Frank Jones.		

This entry records the NSF check returned as uncollectible. The check was received from Jones in payment of his account and was deposited as cash. The bank, unable to collect the check, deducted $9 from the Valley Hardware account, making it necessary for the company to reverse the entry made when the check was received. After recording the returned check, the company will endeavor to collect the $9 from Jones. If after all legal means of collection have been exhausted and the company is still unable to collect, the amount will be written off as a loss.

NEED FOR A PETTY CASH FUND

Proper cash control requires that all receipts be deposited in the bank and that all payments be made by check. When this procedure is not followed, money from cash receipts is disbursed directly in paying obligations. This makes accounting for cash more difficult since receipts cannot be traced to the bank and canceled checks are not available to prove cash payments. However, every business must make many small payments for items such as postage, express charges, telegrams, and small items of supplies. If each small payment is made by check, many checks for trivial amounts are written. To avoid writing checks for small amounts, a *petty cash fund* is commonly used.

THE PETTY CASH FUND

When a petty cash fund is established, an estimate is made of the total small payments likely to be disbursed during a short period, usually one month. A check is drawn and debited to the Petty Cash account for an amount slightly in excess of this estimate; the check is cashed; and the money is turned over to a member of the office staff who is designated *petty cashier* and who is responsible for the petty cash and for making payments therefrom.

The petty cashier usually keeps the petty cash money in a locked box in the office safe. As each disbursement is made, a *petty cash voucher* or a *petty cash receipt,* Illustration 57, is completed. Each petty cash voucher

Illustration 57—Petty Cash Voucher

acts as a receipt and is signed by the person receiving payment. As each payment is made, the paid voucher is entered in the *Petty Cash Record* (Illustration 59) and then placed with the remaining money in the petty cashbox. Under this system, the petty cashbox should always contain paid vouchers and money equal to the amount of the fund.

Each disbursement reduces the money and increases the sum of the vouchers in the petty cashbox. When the money is nearly exhausted, the fund is reimbursed. To reimburse the fund, the petty cashier presents the paid petty cash vouchers to the company cashier who stamps each voucher "paid," retains the vouchers, and gives the petty cashier a check for their sum. When this check is cashed and the proceeds returned to the petty cashbox, the money in the box is restored to its original amount and the fund is ready to begin anew the cycle of its operations.

PETTY CASH FUND ILLUSTRATED

To avoid writing numerous checks for small amounts, a company established a petty cash fund, designating one of its office clerks, Alice Smith, petty cashier. A check for $20 was drawn, cashed, and the proceeds turned over to this clerk. The entry to record the check is shown in Illustration 58. The effect of the entry was to transfer $20 from the Cash account to the Petty Cash account.

The Petty Cash account is debited when the fund is established, but not debited or credited again unless the size of the fund is changed. If the fund is exhausted and reimbursements occur too often, the fund should be increased. This results in an additional debit to the Petty Cash account and a credit to the regular Cash account for the amount of the increase. If the fund is too large, part of the petty cash should be returned to general cash.

Illustration 58

CHECK REGISTER

Date	Chk. No.	Payee	Account Debited	F	Sundry Accts. Debit	} } }	Merchants Bank Credit
Nov. 1	58	Alice Smith, Petty Cashier	Petty Cash		20.00		20.00

During the first month of the illustrated fund's operation, the following petty cash payments were made:

Nov.	3	Collect telegram.........................	$ 1.65
	7	Purchased paper clips....................	.50
	12	Express on purchases....................	1.75
	18	Postage on sale.........................	1.80
	19	Dinner for employee working overtime....	1.60
	20	100 five-cent stamps.....................	5.00
	21	Express on purchases....................	2.80
	24	Cleaning windows........................	1.00
	27	Repair of typewriter.....................	2.50
		Total.............................	$18.60

As each amount was disbursed, a petty cash voucher or receipt was signed by the person receiving payment. Each voucher was then recorded in the Petty Cash Record and placed in the petty cashbox. The Petty Cash Record with the paid vouchers entered is shown in Illustration 59.

On November 27, after the last of the foregoing payments was made, only $1.40 in money remained in the fund. The petty cashier recognized that this would probably not cover another payment, so she gave her $18.60 of paid petty cash vouchers to the company cashier in exchange for an $18.60 check to replenish the fund. On receiving the check, she ruled and balanced her Petty Cash Record (see Illustration 59), entered the amount of the replenishing check, cashed the check, and was ready to begin anew payments from the fund.

The reimbursing check was recorded in the Check Register with the entry of Illustration 60. Information for this entry was secured from a summarization of the entries in the Petty Cash Record. Commonly, a Petty Cash Record, as in this illustration, is a supplementary record and not a book of original entry; therefore, if petty cash payments are to get to the ledger accounts, a check register entry like that of Illustration 60 is required.

Observe the debits of the entry in Illustration 60. All are to accounts affected by payments from the fund. Note that such an entry is necessary to get debits into the accounts for amounts paid from a petty cash fund. Consequently, petty cash must be reimbursed at the end of each

Illustration 59—The Petty Cash Record

PETTY CASH RECORD

Date	Explanation	Voucher No.	Receipts	Payments	Postage	Freight-In	Misc. General Expense	Sundries Account	Sundries Amount
Nov. 1	Established fund		20.00						
3	Collect telegram	1		1.65			1.65		
7	Purchased paper clips	2		.50				Office supplies	.50
12	Express on purchases	3		1.75		1.75			
18	Postage on sale	4		1.80				Delivery expense	1.80
19	Overtime meals	5		1.60			1.60		
20	100 five-cent stamps	6		5.00	5.00				
21	Express on purchases	7		2.80		2.80			
24	Cleaning windows	8		1.00			1.00		
27	Repair of typewriter	9		2.50			2.50		
	Totals		20.00	18.60	5.00	4.55	6.75		2.30
	Balance			1.40					
			20.00	20.00					
Nov. 27	Balance		1.40						
27	Replenished fund		18.60						

Distribution of Payments

Illustration 60

CHECK REGISTER

Date	Chk. No.	Payee	Account Debited	F	Sundry Accts. Debit		Mer-chants Bank Credit
Nov.	1	58	Alice Smith, Petty Cashier	Petty Cash		20.00		20.00
Nov.	27	106	Alice Smith, Petty Cashier	Postage		5.00		
				Freight-In		4.55		
				Misc. Gen. Expenses		6.75		
				Office Supplies		.50		
				Delivery Expense		1.80		18.60

accounting period, as well as at any time the money in the fund is low. If the fund is not reimbursed at the end of each accounting period, the asset petty cash is overstated and expenses and other assets are understated on the financial statements.

Occasionally, at the time of a petty cash expenditure a petty cashier will forget to secure a receipt; and by the time the fund is reimbursed, she will have forgotten the expenditure. This causes the fund to be short. If at reimbursement time the petty cash fund is short and no errors or omitted entries can be found, the shortage is recorded as an expense in the reimbursing entry with a debit to the Cash Over and Short account.

CHANGE FUND

Companies selling for cash and depositing all receipts intact should have a change fund to supply their cash registers with cash for change at the beginning of each business day. A change fund is established in much the same way as a petty cash fund. A check payable to the change fund cashier is drawn and recorded in the Check Register with an entry having a debit to the Change Fund Cash account and a credit to the general Cash account. The check is cashed and the proceeds are placed in the cash registers at the beginning of each day. Thereafter, at the end of each day, cash in the form of coins and small denomination bills equal to the amount of the change fund is removed from the registers and locked in the office safe over night. The money remaining in the registers after the change fund is removed is the proceeds from the day's cash sales and is deposited intact.

CASH OVER AND SHORT

Regardless of care exercised in making change, customers are sometimes given too much change or are shortchanged. As a result, at the end of a day the actual cash from a cash register is commonly not equal to the cash sales "rung up" on the register. When this occurs and, for example, actual cash as counted is $557 but the register shows cash sales of $556, the entry in general journal form to record sales and the overage is:

Nov.	*23*	*Cash*...	*557.00*	
		Cash Over and Short...................		*1.00*
		Sales...................................		*556.00*
		Day's cash sales and overage.		

If, on the other hand, cash is short, less cash than the amount of sales shown on the register, the entry to record the sales and shortage is:

Nov.	*24*	*Cash*...	*621.00*	
		Cash Over and Short.....................	*4.00*	
		Sales...................................		*625.00*
		Day's cash sales and shortage.		

Over a period of time cash overages should about equal cash shortages. However, customers are more prone to report instances in which they are given too little change; therefore, amounts of cash short are apt to be greater than amounts of cash over, and the Cash Over and Short account normally reaches the end of the accounting period with a debit balance. When the Cash Over and Short account has a debit balance, the balance represents an expense. It may appear on the income statement, at the end, as one of the items in the other revenue and expense section; or if the amount is small, it may be combined with other miscellaneous expenses and appear as part of the item, miscellaneous expenses. When Cash Over and Short reaches the end of the period with a credit balance, the balance represents revenue and normally appears on the income statement as part of the item, miscellaneous revenues.

INTERNAL CONTROL

Depositing receipts intact and making all payments by check aids management in controlling cash transactions and safeguarding cash. However, this is not sufficient. Procedures for handling cash must be so organized as to protect it from receipt until deposited in the bank; and additional procedures must be organized to insure that every payment is a proper payment and should be made. The organization of procedures for handling cash transactions in such a manner as to protect the cash is known as a system of *internal control* for cash. Such a system has for its purpose the automatic detection of errors and the prevention of fraud.

The essence of any internal control system is a division between several employees of the duties and responsibilities for completing and recording each transaction. The division must be made in such a manner that the work of one employee acts as a check on the work of another. This does not mean a duplication of work. Each employee performs an unduplicated portion of the whole transaction, but in such a manner that his portion acts as a check on the portion completed by a different employee.

For example, mail containing customer payments should be opened by a mail clerk who makes a list, in triplicate, of the money received. His list should give each sender's name, the purpose for which the money was sent, and the amount. The mail clerk keeps a copy of the list for his own record, sends a copy to the cashier with the money, and sends a copy to the bookkeeper. The cashier deposits the money in the bank, and the bookkeeper uses his copy for entries in the Cash Receipts Journal. Then, if the bank balance is reconciled by a fourth person, errors or fraud by the mail clerk, the cashier, or the bookkeeper will be detected. Errors will be detected because the cash deposited and the records of three different people must agree; and fraud is impossible, unless there is collusion between the employees involved. The mail clerk must report all receipts or the customers will question their account balances. The cashier must deposit all receipts because the bank balance must agree with the bookkeeper's cash balance. The bookkeeper and the person reconciling the bank account do not handle cash and therefore have no opportunity to withhold money.

The foregoing procedures for controlling cash receipts are only meant to be illustrative, since the exact procedures involved in a complete system of internal control for cash depend upon the individual business. This is because the size of a business, the number of its employees, and the types of transactions completed will affect the system's organization.

Every business needs some system of internal control. Also, the system should be extended beyond the mere protection of cash and should protect and safeguard all assets and insure that every transaction is properly recorded. In a small business, because of the limited number of employees, a division of duties is often impossible; but this does not eliminate the need for internal control; it only makes internal control more difficult. A small business must often substitute the owner's active participation in its affairs for the protection gained by a division of duties.

It is the purpose of this text to point out the need for internal control, not to present a complete discussion of the subject. Such a discussion is reserved for a course in auditing or accounting systems. However, Chapter 13 presents procedures for controlling cash payments.

QUESTIONS FOR CLASS DISCUSSION

1. Why is the control of cash important to (a) the owner of a business, and (b) the employees of a business?
2. Name and give the reason for two basic principles that should be observed in the control of cash.

3. What is meant by the phrase "all receipts should be deposited intact"?

4. Explain how a business that deposits all receipts intact can trace and prove that each cash item received actually was deposited in the bank.

5. Name and describe several forms of endorsements.

6. What changes are made in the form of the Cash Disbursements Journal of earlier chapters in order to make it into a Check Register?

7. What is a bank statement? What information appears on a bank statement?

8. Why are the bank statement balance of cash and the depositor's book balance of cash reconciled?

9. Explain how the following items cause the bank statement balance of cash to differ from the depositor's book balance of cash:

   a) Outstanding checks.
   b) Unrecorded deposits.
   c) Bank service charges.
   d) Charges for uncollectible items.
   e) Items collected for the depositor by the bank.

   In reconciling the bank balance, which of the above items is added to the bank statement balance? Which is added to the book balance of cash? Which require a journal entry on the books of the depositor?

10. Why does a firm with good cash control follow the practice of depositing receipts intact and making all payments either by check or from a petty cash fund?

11. Why are some cash payments made from a petty cash fund? Why are not all payments made by check?

12. What is a petty cash voucher? When a petty cash voucher is prepared, who signs it?

13. Explain how a petty cash fund operates.

14. Why must a petty cash fund be reimbursed at the end of each accounting period?

15. What are two results of reimbursing the petty cash fund?

16. Is the Petty Cash Record a book of original entry?

17. Which of the following statements are true? Which are false?

    a) The petty cash fund is kept in the bank.
    b) Expenses paid from a petty cash fund are not recorded in the ledger accounts until the petty cash fund is replenished.
    c) The amount of petty cash in the hands of the petty cashier should always be equal to the balance of the Petty Cash account.
    d) The Petty Cash account is debited when the petty cash fund is reimbursed.
    e) The amount of petty cash plus the petty cash vouchers should always equal the balance of the Petty Cash account.
    f) Expenses are understated if the petty cash fund is not replenished at the end of an accounting period.

18. What is the purpose of a system of internal control?

19. What is the essence of any system of internal control?

20. Why is a system of internal control important in the handling of cash transactions? Is internal control practiced only with cash transactions?

21. A company that receives remittances through the mails wishes to properly control cash transactions. Should the bookkeeper be permitted to open incoming mail? Should the mail clerk have access to the bookkeeping records? Why?

22. Is internal control important in a small business? Is a division of labor always possible in a small business? If a division of labor is not possible in a small business, what is often substituted to aid in controlling transactions?

PROBLEMS

Problem 8–1

The following information was available for use in reconciling the November 30 book balance of cash of AAA Excavators with its bank statement balance of that date:

a) After all posting was completed on November 30, the Cash account had a $2,582 debit balance. The bank statement of the same date showed a $3,208 balance.

b) Checks No. 318 for $97 and No. 323 for $214 were outstanding on the October 31 reconciliation. Check No. 323 was returned with the November checks but Check No. 318 was not.

c) The November 30 cash receipts amounted to $453. These receipts were placed in the bank's night depository after banking hours on November 30 but their amount did not appear on the bank statement.

d) In comparing the canceled checks returned with the November bank statement with the entries in the Check Register it was found that Check No. 873 for the purchase of office equipment was correctly drawn for $258 but was entered in the Check Register as though it were for $285. It was also found that Check No. 384 for $135 and Check No. 385 for $45, both drawn on November 28, were not among canceled checks returned.

e) Among the canceled checks returned was one drawn by AAA Exterminators for $89 and paid in error by the bank from the account of AAA Excavators.

f) A credit memorandum enclosed with the bank statement indicated that the bank had collected a $1,000 noninterest-bearing note for the concern, deducted a $5 collection fee, and had credited the remainder to the account of the concern.

g) A debit memorandum with a $128 NSF check received from a customer, James Watson, on November 27 and deposited was among the canceled checks returned.

h) Also among the canceled checks was a $3 debit memorandum for bank services.

Required:

1. Prepare a bank reconciliation for AAA Excavators.

2. Prepare in general journal form the entries the company would have to make to adjust its book balance of cash.

Problem 8–2

The Speedy Service Company bank account was reconciled on November 30 with two checks, No. 808 for $262 and No. 813 for $93, outstanding. The following information was available for the December 31 bank reconciliation:

Speedy Service Company 1475 North Main Street	Statement of account with THE FIRST NATIONAL BANK		

Date	Checks and Other Debits		Deposits	Balance
Dec. 1	Balance brought forward			1,834.00
2	262.00			1,572.00
3	225.00		223.00	1,570.00
5	306.00			1,264.00
6	846.00			418.00
12			945.00	1,363.00
15	51.00	117.00		1,195.00
22			649.00	1,844.00
28	321.00		748.00	2,271.00
30	240.00 NSF			2,031.00
31	1.00 SC		498.00 CM	2,528.00

Code: CM Credit Memorandum	NSF Not sufficient funds check
DM Debit Memorandum	SC Service charge

From the Cash Receipts Journal

	First National Bank	
	Memo	Debit
Dec. 3	223.00	223.00
7	310.00	
9	405.00	
12	230.00	935.00
16	193.00	
20	206.00	
22	250.00	649.00
25	508.00	
28	240.00	748.00
31	319.00	319.00
		2,874.00

From the Check Register

Check Number	First National Bank Credit
814	306.00
815	225.00
816	846.00
817	51.00
818	117.00
819	321.00
820	129.00
821	163.00
	2,158.00

From the General Ledger

Cash

Date		Explanation	F	Debit	Credit	Balance
Nov.	*30*	*Balance*	✔			*1,479.00*
Dec.	*31*		*R-8*	*2,874.00*		*4,353.00*
	31		*D-7*		*2,158.00*	*2,195.00*

The deposit ticket given to the bank on December 12 was correct. The bookkeeper prepared the deposit ticket by listing the items deposited, and he did not discover his error of that date because he failed to compare the total of the deposit ticket with the amount shown in the Cash Receipts Journal as the amount deposited. Likewise, he failed to find the error before posting because at the end of the month he also made an offsetting error in totaling the Cash Sales column in the Cash Receipts Journal.

The NSF check was received from a customer, Walter Dykes, in payment of his account. Its return was unrecorded. The credit memorandum resulted from a $500 note which the bank had collected for Speedy Service Company. The bank had deducted a $2 fee from the proceeds of the note. The collection was unrecorded.

Required:
1. Prepare a bank reconciliation for Speedy Service Company.
2. Prepare in general journal form the entries needed to record the information of the reconciliation.
3. The bookkeeper of Speedy Service Company acts as cashier. List any changes that you would make in the company's system of internal control for cash. Give a reason for each change.

Problem 8–3

Speedway Sales Company established a petty cash fund and appointed one of its office clerks, Mary Nash, petty cashier. A $25 check was drawn to establish the fund and Miss Nash completed the following transactions during the first month of its operation.

Nov. 1 Received and cashed Check No. 893. Placed the $25 proceeds in the petty cash drawer of the office safe.

  2 Paid $2.85 express charges on a small purchase of merchandise.

  4 Paid $3 to have the office windows washed.

  5 Purchased postage stamps, $5.

  8 Paid a boy $1 to deliver a package to a customer.

  13 Purchased carbon paper, $1.50.

  17 Upon the receipt of a signed petty cash voucher, gave George Lowe, the owner of Speedway Sales Company, $1 for coffee money.

  18 Paid $1.65 express charges on a purchase of merchandise.

  23 Paid $1.35 for a collect telegram.

  27 Purchased postage stamps, $5.

Nov. 27   Received replenishing Check No. 971 for $22.35 from the company cashier in exchange for the paid petty cash vouchers.

Required:
1. Prepare a Petty Cash Record and a Check Register similar to the ones illustrated in this chapter.
2. Enter the foregoing transactions in the Petty Cash Record and, where necessary, in the Check Register.
3. After recording the transactions in the Petty Cash Record, rule and balance the record and enter the replenishing check in both the Petty Cash Record and the Check Register.

Problem 8–4

Delta Company established a petty cash fund on September 30. Jane Hall was appointed petty cashier, and during September, October, and November she completed the following petty cash transactions:

Sept. 30   Received, cashed, and placed the $25 proceeds of Check No. 781 in the petty cash drawer of the office safe.

Oct.   3   Paid $5 to have the office windows washed.
        8   Paid $4.65 express on a shipment of merchandise purchased.
       11   Purchased carbon paper and paper clips, $3.85.
       17   Purchased postage stamps, $5.
       23   Paid $4.25 for minor repairs to an office chair.
       23   Received Check No. 804 to replenish the fund, $22.75.

Nov.   1   Paid express charges on merchandise purchased, $4.35.
        5   Paid $1.50 for the delivery of a package to a customer.
        9   Paid $3.95 express charges on a purchase of merchandise.
       14   Paid $2 for the delivery of a package to a customer.
       18   Paid $2.25 for a collect telegram.
       24   Purchased postage stamps, $8.
       24   After purchasing the foregoing stamps Jane Hall found she had only $1.95 in money in her petty cash fund and she could not account for the shortage. Consequently, she prepared a petty cash voucher for the amount of the shortage, had it approved by her employer, and recorded it in her Petty Cash Record. She then exchanged her paid and approved petty cash vouchers for a $23.05 Check, No. 852, to replenish the fund.

Required:
1. Prepare a Petty Cash Record and a Check Register and open the following T-accounts: Cash; Petty Cash; Office Supplies; Postage; Freight-In; Miscellaneous General Expenses; Delivery Expense; and Cash Over and Short.
2. Record the check establishing the fund, and post the Check Register as of September 30. Rule the Check Register with double rule lines.
3. Enter the October transaction in the Petty Cash Record, balance the record, and enter the replenishing check in both the Petty Cash Record

and Check Register. Post the check register entries and rule double lines across all columns of the Check Register.

4. Enter the November transactions in the Petty Cash Record. Balance the record and post the replenishing entry from the Check Register.

Problem 8–5

Perry Winkle, owner of Winkle Sales, established a petty cash fund upon the advice of his accountant. The following transactions involving the fund were completed during its first months:

Dec. 10   Drew a $25 check, No. 118, to establish the fund. Made the check payable to one of the office clerks, June West, who was appointed petty cashier.

12   Paid $4.50 express on a purchase of merchandise.

13   Purchased postage stamps, $5.

15   Purchased carbon paper and paper clips, $4.75.

18   Upon receipt of a signed petty cash voucher, gave Mr. Winkle $1 for coffee money.

19   Paid $1.50 for a collect telegram.

19   Paid $3.25 express charges on a small purchase of merchandise.

20   Paid a college student $2.50 to wash the office windows.

20   Drew Check No. 135 to replenish the fund, $22.50.

23   Paid $5.75 express charges on a purchase of merchandise.

24   Paid Cycle Delivery Service $2.50 to deliver merchandise to a customer.

29   Prepaid the express charges on a special order of merchandise shipped to a customer, $7.50.

Jan.   3   Paid $2.50 for minor repairs to an office typewriter.

5   Purchased postage stamps, $5.

5   June West, the petty cashier, observed that reimbursement of the petty cash fund was overlooked on December 31, the end of the accounting period, when the books were closed. She also noted how rapidly the cash of the fund was exhausted. Consequently, in a conference with Mr. Winkle it was decided not only to reimburse the fund for the expenditures of December and January, but also to increase its size to $50. Check No. 149 for $48.25 was drawn for these purposes.

Required:

Prepare a Petty Cash Record and a Check Register similar to the ones illustrated in this chapter, and record the foregoing transactions. Balance and rule the Petty Cash Record before entering each replenishing check. Skip a line between entries in the Check Register.

CLASS EXERCISE

Exercise 8–1

Pinetop Sales operates with annual accounting periods that end each December 31. Last December 31 the concern's bookkeeper, its petty cashier, and its sole owner, Dale Gordon, forgot to reimburse the petty cash fund at the accounting period's end. At that time there were paid petty cash vouchers in the fund for: postage, $10; freight-in, $12; and miscellaneous general expenses, $7. The oversight was discovered when petty cash was reimbursed on January 18. By that time there were additional paid vouchers in the fund for: freight-in, $9; delivery expense, $3; and office supplies, $4. Give in general journal form the January 18 entry to reimburse the petty cash fund.

ALTERNATE PROBLEMS

Problem 8–1A

The following information was available for reconciling Rapid Service Company's December 31 book balance of cash with its bank statement balance of that date:

a) The December 31 cash balance according to the accounting records was $2,779.90; but the bank statement balance of that date was $2,651.50.

b) There were two checks outstanding, No. 872 for $103.50 and No. 876 for $93.15, on the previous November 30 when the book and bank statement balances were last reconciled. Check No. 876 was returned with the December canceled checks but Check No. 872 was not.

c) Upon comparing the December canceled checks with the entries in the Check Register, it was found that Check No. 901 had been correctly drawn for $183 in payment for several items of store supplies; however, it was entered in the Check Register in error as though it were drawn for $138.

d) It was also found that Checks No. 953 for $81.25 and No. 955 for $72.10, both written and entered in the Check Register on December 30, were not among the canceled checks returned.

e) Two debit memoranda and a credit memorandum were included with the returned checks. None of the memoranda had been recorded at the time of the reconciliation. The credit memorandum showed the bank had collected a $500 note receivable for Rapid Service Company, deducted a $2 collection fee, and credited the balance to the company's account. One of the debit memoranda was for $42.35 and had attached to it an NSF check in that amount. The check had been received from a customer, Robert Small, in payment of his account. The second debit memorandum was for a special printing of checks and was for $6.40.

f) Included with the canceled checks was a check drawn by Rapid Supply Company in the amount of $71.10 and paid in error by the bank from Rapid Service Company's account.

g) The December 31 cash receipts amounted to $718.40 and had been placed in the bank's night depository after banking hours on that date; consequently, their amount did not appear on the bank statement.

Required:

1. Prepare a December 31 bank reconciliation for Rapid Service Company.
2. Prepare in general journal form the entries required to adjust the company's book balance of cash to the reconciled balance.

Problem 8–2A

Phoenix Service Company reconciled its book and bank statement balances of cash on October 31 with two checks, No. 716 for $142 and No. 717 for $275, outstanding. The following information was available for the November 30 reconciliation:

Phoenix Service Company 17th and High Streets		Statement of account with UNITED STATES NATIONAL BANK		
Date	**Checks and Other Debits**		**Deposits**	**Balance**
Nov. 1	Balance brought forward			1,912.00
2	275.00			1,637.00
3	218.00		312.00	1,731.00
5	302.00			1,429.00
9	737.00			692.00
12	75.00	132.00		485.00
14			551.00	1,036.00
18	284.00			752.00
21			512.00	1,264.00
28	343.00		472.00	1,393.00
29	43.00 NSF			1,350.00
30	3.00 SC		995.00 CM	2,342.00

Code: CM Credit Memorandum DM Debit Memorandum	NSF Not sufficient funds check SC Service charge

From the Cash Receipts Journal

	U.S. National Bank		
	Memo	**Debit**
Nov. 3	312.00	312.00
7	234.00	
11	178.00	
14	139.00	552.00
17	118.00	
19	235.00	
21	159.00	512.00
24	271.00	
25	43.00	
28	158.00	472.00
30	247.00	247.00
		2,095.00

From the Check Register

Check Number	U.S. National Bank Credit
718	218.00
719	302.00
720	75.00
721	737.00
722	132.00
723	136.00
724	284.00
725	343.00
726	53.00
	2,280.00

From the General Ledger

Cash

Date		Explanation	F	Debit	Credit	Balance
Oct.	31	Balance	✓			1,495.00
Nov.	30		R-9	2,095.00		3,590.00
	30		D-8		2,280.00	1,310.00

The deposit ticket given the bank on November 14 was correct. The bookkeeper prepared the deposit ticket by listing the items deposited, and he did not discover his error of that date because he failed to compare the deposit ticket total with the amount shown in the Cash Receipts Journal as the deposit. Likewise, he failed to discover this error before posting because at the end of the month he made a second offsetting error in totaling the Sales Discounts column in his Cash Receipts Journal.

The NSF check was received from a customer, Walter Burke, in payment of his account. Its return was unrecorded. The credit memorandum resulted from a $1,000 note collected for Phoenix Service Company by the bank, from which the bank had deducted a $5 collection fee. The collection was unrecorded.

Required:

1. Prepare a November 30 bank reconciliation for Phoenix Service Company.
2. Prepare in general journal form the entries required to adjust the book balance of cash to the reconciled balance.
3. Phoenix Service Company's bookkeeper also acts as cashier. List any changes you would make in the company's system of internal control for cash, giving the reason for each change.

Problem 8–3A

The following transactions involving petty cash were completed during December of the current year:

Dec. 3 Drew Check No. 137 to establish a $25 petty cash fund. Appointed Jane Drew, one of the office clerks, petty cashier.

4 Paid $3.85 express charges on a purchase of merchandise delivered by the express company.

7 Paid Ben Franklin Press $8 for printing advertising circulars.

8 Paid a college student $2.50 for delivering the advertising circulars to prospective customers.

11 Purchased postage stamps, $5.

12 Paid $4.25 express charges on a purchase of merchandise delivered by the express company.

12 Drew Check No. 152 to reimburse the petty cash fund; and because the fund had been so rapidly exhausted, made the check sufficiently large to increase the size of the fund to $50.

Dec. 14   Paid $5.10 express charges on a purchase of merchandise delivered by the express company.

17   Purchased postage stamps, $8.

18   The proprietor, Jack Hall, signed a petty cash voucher and took $1 from the petty cash fund for coffee money.

20   Paid $5 for repairs to a typewriter.

23   Paid $1.35 for a collect telegram.

26   Paid $3.80 express charges on a purchase of merchandise delivered by the express company.

28   Purchased postage stamps, $5.

31   Drew Check No. 172 to reimburse the petty cash fund at the end of the accounting period. There was $19.75 in cash in the fund and the cashier could not account for the shortage.

Required:

Record the foregoing transactions in a Petty Cash Record and, where required, in a Check Register similar to the ones described in this chapter. Balance and rule the Petty Cash Record at the time of each reimbursement. Skip a line between the entries in the Check Register to set them apart.

Problem 8–4A

W. A. Zapp, owner of Zapp Sales and Service, established a petty cash fund upon the advice of his accountant. During the fund's first month the following transactions were completed:

Nov. 2   Drew a $50 check, No. 562, payable to Joan Hill, petty cashier, and delivered the check plus the Petty Cash Record to Miss Hill.

4   Eight dollars of petty cash funds were used to purchase postage stamps.

5   Paid $4.35 express charges on a purchase of merchandise delivered by the express company.

8   Paid the delivery truck driver of Snowhite Laundry $2.50 upon delivery of a package of shirts Mr. Zapp had dropped off at the laundry and asked that they be laundered for him and delivered to the office.

11   Paid $5 for minor repairs to the office typewriter.

13   Paid $3.95 express charges on a purchase of merchandise.

15   Gave Mrs. Zapp, wife of the proprietor, $5 for cab fare and other personal expenses.

18   Paid Speedy Delivery $2.50 to deliver merchandise to a customer.

23   Paid $1.85 for a collect telegram.

27   Paid $4.15 express charges on a special order of merchandise shipped to a customer.

30   Drew Check No. 591 to reimburse the fund for expenditures and a $0.50 shortage.

Required:

Prepare a Petty Cash Record and a Check Register similar to the ones illustrated in this chapter and record the transactions. Balance and rule the

Petty Cash Record before entering the replenishing check. Skip a line between each check entered in the Check Register.

DECISION PROBLEM 8—JUNIOR ACCOUNTANT

You have just been employed by Morton & Harris, Certified Public Accountants, as a junior accountant. You will be assigned to prepare bank reconciliations on a number of small jobs where the clients are somewhat careless in performing this important function. As a part of your training for this assignment, the manager in charge presents you with the following problem and requests that you give him a solution with adequate explanation of how the required amounts are determined.

Problem

The following data are available from the bank statement (First National Bank) and the books of the Cactus Candy Store for June of the current year:

Information from Bank Statement:		Information from Books:	
Balance, May 31	$105	Balance per books, May 31	$98
Checks cleared during June	82	Deposits in June per books	45
Service charge	2	Balance per books, June 30	50
Collection of noninterest-bearing note (face $40, collection charge $3)	37		
Balance, June 30	100		

Assuming that there was a $12 deposit in transit on May 31; that all outstanding checks on May 31 cleared the bank in June; that no entries to adjust the Cash account were needed as the result of the May 31 bank reconciliation; and that the accounts will reconcile on June 30, answer the following questions with explanations:

1. What is the total of the deposits for June according to the bank's records, excluding the proceeds from the note collected?
2. What is the amount of the outstanding checks as of May 31?
3. What is the amount of the checks written in June?
4. What is the total of the checks written in June that also cleared the bank in June?
5. What is the total of the outstanding checks on June 30?
6. What is the amount of the deposit in transit on June 30?
7. What entry is needed on June 30 to adjust the Cash account?

Accounting for
Notes and Drafts

Some companies sell merchandise on the installment plan and commonly take promissory notes from their customers. Others, such as dealers in farm machinery, likewise often take notes. However, when companies in which the credit period is long are excepted, note transactions in comparison to other transactions are not too numerous. Nevertheless, many companies in which such transactions are not common will, at one time or another, accept a note from a customer or will give a note to a creditor. Consequently, one interested in accounting must have some knowledge of promissory notes.

PROMISSORY NOTES

A promissory note is an unconditional promise in writing to pay on demand or at a fixed or determinable future date a definite sum of money. In the note shown in Illustration 61 Hugo Brown promises to pay Frank

Illustration 61—A Promissory Note

| $100.00 | Eugene, Oregon | March 9, 1966 |

Thirty days _____ AFTER DATE ___1___ PROMISE TO PAY TO

THE ORDER OF _____ Frank Black

One hundred and no/100--DOLLARS

FOR VALUE RECEIVED WITH INTEREST AT __6%__

PAYABLE AT __First National Bank of Eugene, Oregon__

Hugo Brown

Black or his order a definite sum of money at a fixed future date. Hugo Brown is the *maker* of the note; Frank Black is the *payee*.

INTEREST

The illustrated Hugo Brown note bears interest at 6 percent. Interest is a charge for the use of money. To a borrower, interest is an expense; to a lender, it is a revenue. A note may be interest bearing or it may be noninterest bearing. If a note bears interest, the rate or the amount of interest must be stated on the note. Interest is usually stated as a percentage of the note's *principal*. If a note is noninterest bearing, no interest is collected unless the note is not paid when due. If a noninterest-bearing note is not paid when due, interest at the full legal rate may be collected from the maturity date until the date of final payment. The maturity date is the date upon which the note is due and payable.

CALCULATING INTEREST

Unless otherwise stated, the rate of interest on a note is the rate charged for the use of the principal for one year. The formula for calculating interest is:

$$\begin{array}{c} \textit{Principal} \\ \textit{of the} \\ \textit{Note} \end{array} \times \begin{array}{c} \textit{Rate of} \\ \textit{Interest} \end{array} \times \begin{array}{c} \textit{Time of the} \\ \textit{Note Expressed} \\ \textit{in Years} \end{array} = \textit{Interest}$$

For example, interest on a $1,000, 6 percent, one-year note is calculated:

$$\$1{,}000 \times \frac{6}{100} \times 1 = \$60$$

In business, most note transactions involve a period less than a full year, and this period is usually expressed in days. When the time of a note is expressed in days, the actual number of days elapsing, not including the day of the note's date but including the day on which it falls due, are counted. For example, a 90-day note, dated July 10, is due on October 8. This October 8 maturity date is calculated as follows:

Number of days in July *31*
Minus the date of the note *10*
Gives the number of days the note runs in July *21*
Add the number of days in August *31*
Add the number of days in September *30*
Total through September 30 . . . . *82*
Days in October needed to equal the time of the note, 90
days, also the due date of the note—October *8*
Total time the note runs in days *90*

Occasionally, the time of a note is expressed in months. In such cases, the note matures and is payable in the month of its maturity on the same day of the month as its date. For example, a note dated July 10 and payable three months after date is payable on October 10.

In calculating interest, banks and businessmen usually consider a year to have just 360 days. This simplifies most interest calculations. It makes the interest calculation on a 90-day, 5 percent $1,000 note as follows:

$$\textit{Principal} \times \textit{Rate} \times \frac{\textit{Exact Days}}{360} = \textit{Interest}$$

or

$$\$1,000 \times \frac{5}{100} \times \frac{90}{360} = \textit{Interest}$$

or

$$\$1,\!000 \times \frac{5}{100} \times \frac{90}{360} = \frac{25}{2} = \$12.50$$

Likewise, the interest calculation on a $1,200, 60-day, 6 percent note is:

$$\$1,\!200 \times \frac{6}{100} \times \frac{60}{360} = \$12.00$$

SIXTY-DAY, 6 PERCENT METHOD

An examination of the preceding calculation shows the interest on $1,200 at 6 percent for 60 days to be $12. Twelve dollars is 1 percent, or 0.01, of $1,200; and as in this case, the interest on any note that runs exactly 60 days and earns interest at exactly 6 percent is always 1 percent of the note's principal. This is because 60 days are $\frac{1}{6}$ of one year, and $\frac{1}{6}$ of 6 percent is 1 percent.

Therefore, it is evident that to compute the interest on any given principal at exactly 6 percent for exactly 60 days, it is only necessary to multiply the principal by 1 percent, or 0.01. And, to multiply a principal by 0.01, the decimal point is moved two places to the left in the principal. For example, the interest on $757 for 60 days at 6 percent is:

$$\$757 \times 0.01 = \$7.57$$

SIX-DAY, 6 PERCENT COUNTERPART

Six days are $\frac{1}{10}$ of 60 days. Therefore, interest at 6 percent on a given principal for six days is $\frac{1}{10}$ of 1 percent, or 0.001; and to compute interest on a given principal at 6 percent for six days, it is only necessary to move the decimal point three places to the left in the principal. For example, the interest on $1,200 at 6 percent for six days is:

$$\textit{\$1,200 } \times \textit{0.001} = \textit{\$1.20}$$

The 60-day, 6 percent method or its six-day, 6 percent counterpart may be used for any combination of days. However, either has its greatest advantage when the time is either exactly 60 days, or exactly six days, or an even combination or fraction of one or the other. For example, interest on $800 at 6 percent for 45 days is $6, and is calculated as follows:

Interest on $800 for 60 days at 6 percent is (point off two places) $8.
Forty-five days are exactly ¾ of 60 days.
Therefore, the interest for 45 days is ¾ of the interest for 60 days, or is:
¾ × $8 = $6.

Likewise, the interest on $500 at 6 percent for 42 days is $3.50, and it is calculated:

Interest on $500 for six days at 6 percent is (point off three places) $0.50.
Forty-two days are the equivalent of seven six-day periods.
Therefore, interest for 42 days is seven times the interest for six days, or is:
7 × $0.50 = $3.50.

The 60-day, 6 percent method and its six-day, 6 percent counterpart may be used for other interest rates. For example, 8 percent is 1 and ⅓ times 6 percent; and to calculate interest at 8 percent, make the calculation at 6 percent and add ⅓. Likewise, 4 percent is ⅔ of 6 percent; consequently, to calculate interest at 4 percent, make the calculation at 6 percent and take ⅔ of the result.

Actually, these short-cut methods can be used for any combination of days or for any rate of interest. However, any saving made by their use is lost when the calculation becomes complex.

NOTES PAYABLE

Notes payable result from the purchase of an asset with a note or the settlement of an account payable with a note; and they frequently arise when money is borrowed from a bank.

Giving a note to purchase an asset is not a common transaction. Occasionally, when the purchase price is high or the credit period is long, a note is given instead of making the purchase on open account. The entry for such a transaction is:

Oct.	*14*	*Store Equipment*......................	*1,600.00*	
		Notes Payable....................		*1,600.00*
		Purchased display refrigerator with a		
		one-year, 6 percent note.		

Usually, all notes payable are recorded in a single Notes Payable account. If several notes are issued, each may be identified in the account by writing the payee's name in the Explanation column on the line of the entry recording the note's issuance or payment. If a company issues many notes, an unusual situation, a supplementary record called a Notes Payable Register may be used for recording the details of each note.

NOTE GIVEN TO SECURE AN EXTENSION OF TIME ON AN ACCOUNT

A note may be given to secure an extension of time on an open account. For example, George Brock cannot pay his open account with Ajax Company when it becomes due and the company agrees to accept Brock's 90-day, 4 percent $350 note in settlement of the open account. Brock will record the transaction in his General Journal with the following entry:

Aug.	*23*	*Accounts Payable—Ajax Company*......	*350.00*	
		Notes Payable....................		*350.00*
		Gave a 90-day, 4 percent note in settle-		
		ment of our open account.		

Observe that the note does not pay the debt; it merely changes its form from an account payable to a note payable. Ajax Company prefers the note to the open account because in case of default and a lawsuit to collect, the note improves its legal position.

When the note becomes due, Brock gives Ajax Company a check for $353.50 and records the payment of the note and its interest with an entry as follows:

Nov.	*21*	*Notes Payable*.......................	*350.00*	
		Interest Expense....................	*3.50*	
		Cash............................		*353.50*
		Paid our note with interest.		

The entry just given would normally be recorded by Brock in his Check Register or Cash Disbursements Journal. However, beginning at this point and continuing through the remainder of the text almost all entries will be given in general journal form in order to simplify the illustrations. The student should realize that a company would record such entries in its Check Register or other appropriate special journal if it made use of such.

RECORDING A BANK LOAN

Banks distinguish between *loans* and *discounts*. A loan is an advance of money which is to be repaid with interest. With a loan an interest-bearing note is used, and the interest is paid when the note matures. A discount transaction differs from a loan transaction in that in a discount transaction the interest is paid in advance at the time the loan is made. When money is advanced on a discount, a noninterest-bearing note is used because the interest is calculated and deducted from the face amount of the note at the time the loan is made. With the interest deducted and paid in advance, the maker of the discounted note promises to repay only the principal. To illustrate loans and discounts, assume that Henry Green wishes to borrow $1,000 for 60 days at 6 percent.

Borrowing Money with an Interest-Bearing Note. If Green gives the bank a $1,000, 60-day, 6 percent interest-bearing note, he will record the transaction as follows:

Sept.	10	Cash...............................	1,000.00	
		Notes Payable..................		1,000.00
		Gave the bank a 60-day note.		

When the note and interest are paid, Green makes the following entry:

Nov.	9	Notes Payable.......................	1,000.00	
		Interest Expense....................	10.00	
		Cash............................		1,010.00
		Paid our 60-day, 6 percent note.		

Discounting a Note Payable. If, contrary to the situations of the previous paragraphs, it is the custom of Green's bank to collect interest in advance, the bank will take Green's noninterest-bearing $1,000 note; and from its face amount will deduct 6 percent interest for 60 days and will give Green $990. The $990 is $1,000 less the interest on $1,000 at 6 percent for 60 days and is called the *proceeds* of the discounted note. The $10 interest collected in advance is known as *bank discount*. Bank discount is interest collected in advance by a bank. To record the discounted note, Green makes the following entry:

Sept.	10	*Cash*..	990.00	
		Interest Expense......................	10.00	
		Notes Payable.....................		1,000.00
		Discounted at 6 percent our non-		
		interest-bearing note.		

When the note matures, Green pays the bank just the face amount of the note, $1,000, and records the transactions as follows:

Nov.	9	*Notes Payable*.......................	1,000.00	
		Cash...........................		1,000.00
		Paid our discounted note.		

Notice that Green does not pay interest when the discounted note is paid at maturity. No interest is due at maturity, since the full amount of interest was paid in advance when the loan was secured.

NOTES RECEIVABLE

With the exception of companies selling on the installment plan and other companies in which the credit period is long, notes receivable are not common in retail enterprises. They are more common in wholesaling and manufacturing where, when the credit period is long, notes are commonly taken in payment for merchandise or equipment. Also, in many wholesaling and manufacturing enterprises notes are taken in granting extensions on past-due accounts.

In enterprises in which the credit period is long, notes are preferred to open accounts because a note may be readily turned into cash before it is due by discounting or selling it to a bank. Notes are also preferred because a note represents a written acknowledgment by the debtor of both the debt and its amount. Also, notes are preferred because they generally earn interest.

RECORDING THE RECEIPT OF A NOTE

Notes receivable are recorded in a single Notes Receivable account. Each note may be identified in the account by writing the name of the maker in the Explanation column on the line of the entry recording its receipt or payment. Only one account is needed because the individual notes are on hand; and the maker, rate of interest, due date, and other information may be learned by examining each note. However, if note transactions are numerous, a supplementary record may be maintained to record the details of each note. This supplementary record is called a Notes Receivable Register, and as such does not change the regular journal and ledger record of notes.

A note received at the time of a sale is recorded as follows:

Dec.	5	Notes Receivable............................	500.00	
		Sales....................................		500.00
		Sold merchandise, terms six-month, 5 percent note.		

When a note is taken in granting an extension on a past-due open account, the creditor usually attempts to collect part of the past-due account in cash. This reduces the debt and requires the acceptance of a smaller note. For example, Symplex Company agrees to accept $232 in cash and a $500, 60-day, 6 percent note from Joseph Cook in settlement of his past-due account. When Symplex receives the cash and note, the following entry is made:

Oct.	5	Cash..	232.00	
		Notes Receivable.........................	500.00	
		Accounts Receivable—Joseph Cook....		732.00
		Received cash and a note in settlement of an account.		

Observe that the foregoing entry changes the form of $500 of the debt from an open account to a note receivable.

When Cook pays the note, this entry is made:

Dec.	4	Cash...	505.00	
		Notes Receivable.......................		500.00
		Interest Earned........................		5.00
		Collected the Joseph Cook note.		

DISHONORED NOTES RECEIVABLE

Occasionally, the maker of a note either cannot or will not pay his note at maturity. When a note's maker refuses to pay at maturity, the note is said to be *dishonored*. Dishonoring a note does not relieve the maker of his obligation, and every legal means should be made to collect. However, collection may require lengthy legal proceedings.

The Notes Receivable account balance should consist only of the amount of notes that have not matured. Therefore, a dishonored, past-due note is always removed from the Notes Receivable account and charged back to the account of its maker. For example, Symplex Company holds a $700, 6 percent, 60-day note of George Jones. At maturity, Mr. Jones dishonors the note. To remove the dishonored note from its Notes Receivable account, the company makes the following entry:

Oct.	14	Accounts Receivable—George Jones........	707.00	
		Interest Earned........................		7.00
		Notes Receivable.......................		700.00
		To charge the account of George Jones for his dishonored $700, 6 percent, 60-day note.		

Charging a dishonored note back to the account of its maker serves two purposes. It removes the amount of the note from the Notes Receivable account, leaving in the account only notes that have not matured; and it records the dishonored note in the maker's account. The second purpose is important because, in the future, if the maker of the dishonored note again applies for credit, his account will show all past dealings, including the dishonored note.

Observe in the foregoing entry which charged back the dishonored note of George Jones that the Interest Earned account is credited for interest earned even though it was not collected. The reason for this is that George Jones owes both the principal and the interest, and his account should reflect the full amount owed.

DISCOUNTING NOTES RECEIVABLE

Many businessmen prefer a note receivable to an open account because a note may be discounted or sold to a bank. Discounting enables the businessman to turn a note into cash without waiting until it matures. To discount a note, the owner endorses and delivers the note to the bank.

If the credit reputation of a note's endorser is good, a bank is usually willing to accept and discount a note because the endorser, by his endorsement, agrees to pay the note at maturity if it is not paid by the maker. This means that the endorser makes himself *contingently liable* for payment of the note. His *contingent liability* depends upon the note's dishonor by its maker. If the maker pays, the endorser has no liability. However, if the maker dishonors the note, then the endorser's contingent liability becomes a real liability. Contingent liabilities, because they sometimes become actual liabilities, may affect the credit standing of the one contingently liable. Consequently, when a note is discounted, the contingent liability should appear in the accounts and on the balance sheet of the person or company discounting the note.

Aside from recording the contingent liability, discounting a noninterest-bearing note receivable is similar to discounting one's own note payable. This is because there is no interest on a noninterest-bearing note. Consequently, since the bank discounting a noninterest-bearing note collects only the principal at maturity, it considers that it is lending just the principal from the *date of discount* until the date of maturity, called the *discount period;* and it discounts or collects interest in advance on just the principal for this period.

To illustrate, on April 6, Symplex Company receives a noninterest-bearing, 60-day, $800 note, dated April 5, from Frank Brown in settlement of his account. The maturity date of this note is June 4, and if Symplex Company discounts this note at its bank on April 20, the bank must wait until June 4 to collect the $800 from Brown. This is 45 days and is calculated:

> *Number of days in April* *30*
> *Date of discount* *20*
> *Days discounted in April* *10*
> *Days note discounted in May* *31*
> *Days note discounted in June* *4*
> > *Days in discount period* *45*

In this situation, the bank considers that it is lending $800 to Symplex Company for forty-five days, which is three fourths of 60 days. Furthermore, if the bank's discount rate is 6 percent, it will deduct a $6 discount from the $800 maturity value of the note ($800 × 0.01 × ¾ = $6.00), and Symplex Company will receive $800 less $6, or $794, for the note. The $794 is called the "proceeds of the note." The $6 discount is interest expense to Symplex Company.

It records the transaction:

Apr.	*20*	*Cash......................................*	*794.00*	
		Interest Expense........................	*6.00*	
		Notes Receivable Discounted..........		*800.00*
		Discounted the Brown note.		

The foregoing credit to *Notes Receivable Discounted* records the contingent liability of Symplex. After the entry is posted, the Notes Receivable and Notes Receivable Discounted accounts appear as follows:

Notes Receivable		*Notes Receivable Discounted*
(Brown note) 800		**(Brown note) 800**
(Jones note) 500		

If a balance sheet is prepared before the maturity date of the foregoing discounted note, the balances of both the Notes Receivable and Notes Receivable Discounted accounts may appear on it as follows:

Current Assets:		
Cash...............................		*$2,500*
Notes receivable......................$1,300		
Notes receivable discounted...........	*800*	*500*
Accounts receivable...................		*4,000*
Merchandise inventory...............		*8,000*
Total Current Assets.............		*$15,000*

Showing "Notes receivable discounted" on the balance sheet as a subtraction from "Notes receivable" indicates the contingent liability to a balance sheet reader.

PAYMENT OF A DISCOUNTED NOTE BY THE MAKER

When a note is discounted at a bank, the bank takes possession of the note in exchange for money. The bank will, if possible, collect the note from the maker at maturity. If the maker pays, it is only necessary for the one who discounted the note to remove the discount liability from his books. If, for example, Frank Brown pays the note discounted by Symplex Company, Symplex will make the following entry:

June	7	Notes Receivable Discounted.............	800.00	
		Notes Receivable.....................		800.00
		To remove the discount liability of the Brown note.		

In this example, the effect of the entry is to balance the Notes Receivable Discounted account and to remove the paid $800 note from the Notes Receivable account as follows:

Notes Receivable		Notes Receivable Discounted	
(Brown note) 800	(Brown note) 800	(Brown note) 800	(Brown note) 800
(Jones note) 500			

DISHONOR OF A DISCOUNTED NOTE

If it is able to do so, a bank always collects a discounted note directly from the maker; and the one who discounted the note will not hear from the bank if the note is paid at maturity. However, if a discounted note is dishonored, the bank will notify, at once, the one who endorsed and discounted the note.

If the bank is unable to collect a discounted note from its maker at maturity, it will normally *protest* the note and look to the endorser or endorsers for payment. Protesting a dishonored note fulfills one of the legal requirements necessary to hold endorsers liable. To protest a note, a *certificate of protest* is prepared and mailed to each endorser. A certificate of protest is a statement, usually attested by a notary public, that says the note was duly presented to the maker for payment and payment was refused. The cost of protesting a negotiable instrument is called a *protest fee.* The bank will look to the one who discounted a dishonored note for payment of both its maturity value and the protest fee.

For example, suppose that instead of paying the $800 note previously illustrated, Frank Brown dishonors it. As soon as the note is dishonored, the bank notifies Symplex Company by mailing a certificate of protest and a letter asking payment of the note's maturity value and protest fee. Symplex Company must pay both. If the protest fee is $1, Symplex will pay the bank $801. In recording the payment, Symplex charges the note and protest fee back to the account of Frank Brown as follows:

June	*5*	*Accounts Receivable—Frank Brown*	*801.00*	
		Cash		*801.00*
		To charge the account of Brown with his dishonored note and the protest fee.		

The dishonor changed Symplex's contingent liability to a real liability; and upon payment of the dishonored note both the real liability and the contingent liability ended. The entry just given records the payment of the real liability. The following entry is made to remove the contingent liability from the books:

June	*5*	*Notes Receivable Discounted*	*800.00*	
		Notes Receivable		*800.00*
		To remove the contingent liability on the Frank Brown note dishonored to-day.		

Of course, upon receipt of the $801, the bank will deliver to Symplex the dishonored note. Symplex Company will then make every legal effort to collect from Brown, not only the maturity value of the note and protest fee, but also interest on the maturity value and protest fee from the date of dishonor until the date of final settlement.

DISCOUNTING AN INTEREST-BEARING NOTE

Discounting an interest-bearing note receivable differs slightly from discounting a noninterest-bearing note. This is because when a bank discounts an interest-bearing note, it will collect from the maker at maturity both the note's principal and interest. As a result, the bank considers that it is lending the maturity value of the note for the discount period. Consequently, it calculates its discount on the maturity value. For example, on September 19, Symplex Company discounts the interest-bearing note of Carl Snow. The note is a $600, 4 percent, 90-day note and is dated August 20.

The maturity value of this note is $606. This is calculated:

$$\require{cancel}\cancel{600} \times \frac{\cancel{4}}{\cancel{100}} \times \frac{\cancel{90}}{\cancel{360}} = \$6.00$$

Principal of the note..............................*$600*
Interest for 90 days at 4 percent...................... __*6*__
Maturity value................................*$606*

The bank discounts the maturity value of the note for 60 days. The 60 days are calculated:

Time of the note in days................................ **90**
  Less: Time held by Symplex:
    Number of days in August...........................*31*
    Date of note..*20*
    Days held in August................................__*11*__
    Days held in September.............................*19*
  Total days held.. __*30*__
    Discount period.................................... **60**

This method of calculating the discount period differs from the one illustrated on page 240. However, either method gives the same result and is equally satisfactory.

The bank considers that it is lending Symplex Company the maturity value of the Carl Snow note for the 60-day discount period. Therefore, it deducts its discount from the $606 maturity value and gives Symplex the proceeds, $599.94. This is calculated:

Maturity value of the note.......................*$606.00*
  Less: Interest on $606 at 6 percent for 60 days
    ($606 × 0.01)................................. __*6.06*__
    Proceeds....................................*$599.94*

Symplex Company may record this transaction as follows:

Sept.	19	Cash..	599.94	
		Interest Expense.........................	6.06	
		Notes Receivable Discounted.........		600.00
		Interest Earned......................		6.00
		Discounted the Carl Snow note for 60 days at 6 percent.		

The foregoing entry records as an expense the $6.06 interest deducted by the bank. It also records as revenue the interest Symplex Company would have earned if it had held the note until maturity. A more common procedure is to offset the interest earned against the interest expense as follows:

Interest expense..*$6.06*
Interest earned.. *6.00*
      Excess of expense over revenue..................*$0.06*

Then, when the revenue and expense are offset, only the difference between them is recorded, in this manner:

Sept.	*19*	*Cash*...	*599.94*	
		Interest Expense........................	*.06*	
		Notes Receivable Discounted.........		*600.00*
		Discounted the Carl Snow note for 60		
		days at 6 percent.		

In the example just given, the proceeds of the Carl Snow note, $599.94, are less than the principal. Since the proceeds are less than the principal, the difference is debited to Interest Expense. If the proceeds of a discounted note exceed the principal, the difference is credited to Interest Earned. For example, suppose that Symplex Company held the Carl Snow note and discounted it on October 19 rather than on September 19. If the note is discounted on October 19 at 6 percent, the discount period is 30 days and the discount is $3.03. This is calculated by the 60-day, 6 percent method: $606 \times 0.01 \times \frac{1}{2} = \$3.03$. The proceeds of the note are then:

Maturity value of the note.......................*$606.00*
   Less: The bank discount........................ *3.03*
Proceeds...*$602.97*

In this case the proceeds exceed the principal, and the transaction is recorded as follows:

Oct.	*19*	*Cash*...	*602.97*	
		Notes Receivable Discounted..........		*600.00*
		Interest Earned......................		*2.97*
		Discounted the Carl Snow note at 6 per-		
		cent for 30 days.		

In either case illustrated, the bank collects the maturity value of the discounted note from Carl Snow at maturity. If within a day or so after the maturity date, Symplex does not receive notice of dishonor, it assumes that the note was paid and makes a general journal entry to cancel its discount liability.

DISCOUNTED INTEREST-BEARING NOTE DISHONORED AT MATURITY

If the Carl Snow note previously illustrated is dishonored at maturity, the bank will demand payment from Symplex of—

The maturity value of the note:		
Principal	$600.00	
Interest	6.00	*$606.00*
Protest fee (assumed amount)		*1.00*
Total		*$607.00*

Symplex must pay the $607. In recording the payment, it charges the $607 to the account of Carl Snow in the manner shown on page 243; in addition, it should cancel its discount liability.

When Symplex Company receives the dishonored note from the bank, it should make every legal effort to collect its maturity value, the protest fee, and interest on both from the date of maturity. For example, if 30 days after the dishonor, Carl Snow pays the maturity value of the dishonored note, the protest fee, and interest, he should pay:

Maturity value	*$606.00*
Protest fee	*1.00*
Interest on $607 at 4 percent for 30 days	*2.02*
Total	*$609.02*

This is recorded by Symplex Company:

Dec.	*18*	*Cash*	*609.02*	
		Accounts Receivable—Carl Snow		*607.00*
		Interest Earned		*2.02*
		Dishonored note and protest fee collected with interest.		

Interest on the dishonored Carl Snow note illustrated is calculated at 4 percent from the date of maturity, and is at the rate stated on the note. In some cases, regardless of the rate stated, interest at the maximum legal rate is collected on the maturity value and protest fee from the date of maturity. The maximum legal rate varies from 8 to 12 percent in the various states.

COLLECTING AN OUT-OF-TOWN NOTE

A promissory note is a *negotiable instrument;* and a negotiable instrument is a document to which title is readily changed, usually by endorsement and delivery, but sometimes by delivery only. Negotiable instruments readily pass from hand to hand without question because negotiable instrument laws have been written to encourage this. No effort will be made here to go into the legal aspects of negotiable instruments. That is reserved for a course in business law. For the purpose of this discussion, it is sufficient to point out that a *holder in due course* of a negotiable instrument, or one who under certain circumstances receives a negotiable instrument from a holder in due course, has the legal right to collect the instrument without proving the existence of a debt. A holder in due course is one who gives something of value for a negotiable instrument before maturity without knowledge of defects in the title of previous holders.

These legal aspects sometimes cause a problem in the collection of notes. The holder of a note will not part with the note without receiving payment, since he does not wish to part with the evidence of indebtedness. Likewise, the maker will not pay his note without gaining possession of the note, because he must pay again if the original holder transfers the note, even after receiving payment, to a holder in due course or to one with the same rights.

No problem is involved in collecting a note when both parties to the transaction live in the same city. The holder can present the note directly to its maker for payment. However, when the parties live in different cities, a problem does arise in the exchange of cash for possession of a note. This problem is usually overcome by using a bank as an agent to collect an out-of-town note. To illustrate, Symplex Company of Eugene, Oregon, holds the $1,000, 6 percent, 60-day note of Sam Small of Longview, Washington. When the note nears maturity, Symplex delivers the note to its Eugene bank for collection. The Eugene bank forwards the note to a Longview, Washington, correspondent bank, and the Longview bank notifies Sam Small that it has the note for collection. When Small pays the Longview bank, he receives possession of the note. The Longview bank transmits the proceeds of the note to the Eugene bank, and the Eugene bank credits the proceeds, less a collection fee, to the Symplex Company bank account.

Only one entry is needed to record the collection of an out-of-town note through a bank. This is made when the bank notifies that it has credited the proceeds less the collection fee. No entry is made when the note is delivered to the bank for collection. At that time it is not known if the note will be paid or dishonored. Until the note is paid, there is no change in the relationship of the parties. For example, when the Sam Small note is paid, the bank notifies Symplex that it has deposited the proceeds less the collection fee to Symplex's bank account. Symplex then makes the following entry:

Oct.	*17*	*Cash*..................................	*1,009.00*	
		Collection Expense.....................	*1.00*	
		Notes Receivable..................		*1,000.00*
		Interest Earned..................		*10.00*
		Proceeds of the Sam Small note less collection charge.		

COMMERCIAL DRAFTS

Commercial drafts are of two kinds, *sight drafts* and *time drafts*. A sight draft is payable on sight; a time draft is payable after the lapse of a period of time. Commercial drafts differ from promissory notes in that drafts arise with the creditor. Promissory notes read "I promise to pay"; they arise with

Illustration 62—A Sight Draft

$ 75.00   EUGENE, OREGON   October 10   19 66

At sight   PAY TO THE ORDER OF   Ourselves

--Seventy-five and no/100--DOLLARS

TO   Thomas Black

Portland, Oregon

Symplex Manufacturing Company

BY *W. A. Blue*

Illustration 63—A Time Draft

$ 100.00   EUGENE, OREGON   October 15,   19 66

Thirty days after sight   PAY TO THE ORDER OF   Ourselves

One hundred and no/100--DOLLARS

TO   Ralph Jones

Cottage Grove, Oregon

Symplex Manufacturing Company

BY *W. A. Blue*

the debtor or promisor. A commercial draft reads "pay to the order of"; it arises with the creditor and is a written order drawn by the creditor which orders the debtor to pay a sum of money. A sight draft is shown in Illustration 62, and a time draft is shown in Illustration 63.

SIGHT DRAFT AS A COLLECTION DEVICE

A sight draft is sometimes used in collecting a past-due account. As such it is usually much more effective than a business letter. To illustrate, assume that Thomas Black's $75 account is long past due on the books of Symplex Company. Symplex has written many letters to Black in an effort to collect but has failed to do so. Now, in a final effort, before placing the account with an attorney for collection, Symplex notifies Black that it is drawing a sight draft to be presented for collection through a bank in Black's community. If at all possible, Symplex will present the draft through the bank Black offered as a credit reference when credit was first granted. This is usually the bank with which Black does business. After notifying Black, Symplex draws a sight draft for $75, as shown in Illustration 62, and sends it to the bank in Black's community. Since Black wishes to keep a good credit reputation with his local bank, he will usually honor the sight draft. To dishonor it is to admit to his local bank that he does not pay his debts. A sight draft is honored by payment.

RECORDING SIGHT DRAFTS

No entries are made by Symplex when the sight draft against Black is drawn. At that time it is not known if Black will honor the draft, and until it is honored, the relationship of the parties is unchanged. If Black honors the draft, he pays the face amount of the draft to the bank in his community, and the bank sends this amount, less a collection charge, to Symplex. Receipt of the proceeds is Symplex's first notice of honor. Upon their receipt, Symplex makes the following entry:

Oct.	12	Cash...	74.00	
		Collection Expense...........................	1.00	
		Accounts Receivable—Thomas Black.....		75.00
		Collected the account of Thomas Black		
		with a sight draft.		

Aside from the collection expense, this is like the entry that is made when any account receivable is collected.

Black records his payment of the sight draft in the same manner that he records payment of any account payable. In effect, he has paid his account through the bank.

When a sight draft is dishonored, payment is refused and no entry is made by either party because their relationship is unchanged.

TIME DRAFTS

A time draft differs from a sight draft in that it is not payable until after the lapse of a period of time. Time drafts usually read:

Sixty days after date, pay to the order of......
or
Thirty days after sight, pay to the order of......

A draft payable 60 days after date is payable 60 days after the date of the draft. A draft payable 30 days after sight is payable 30 days after *acceptance*. A draft is accepted when the debtor agrees to pay it.

A time draft like a sight draft is drawn by the creditor, called the *drawer*. The draft orders the debtor to pay and has no effect until he agrees to pay it. The debtor, called the *drawee*, agrees to pay by writing across the face of the draft the word "accepted" and his signature. When the drawee accepts a time draft, he agrees in writing to pay a definite sum of money at a fixed future date. Consequently, a time draft upon acceptance becomes a form of promissory note; and in accounting, it is usually treated by both parties in the same manner as a promissory note.

For example, Symplex Company agrees to give Ralph Jones a 30-day extension on his $100 account if Jones will accept a 30-day time draft. Symplex draws the draft, Illustration 63, and sends it to Jones. No entry is made when the draft is drawn because it is not certain that Jones will accept it. However, he does accept and returns the accepted draft to Symplex. The accepted draft is shown in Illustration 64.

Illustration 64—An Accepted Time Draft

RECORDING TIME DRAFTS

Ralph Jones records his acceptance of the time draft as follows:

Oct.	*16*	*Accounts Payable—Symplex Company*	*100.00*	
		Notes Payable		*100.00*
		Accepted a 30-day time draft.		

When Symplex receives the accepted draft, it makes the following entry:

Oct.	*18*	*Notes Receivable*	*100.00*	
		Accounts Receivable—Ralph Jones		*100.00*
		Thirty-day time draft in settlement of		
		account.		

Notice that these are the same entries that would have been made if Jones had given Symplex a promissory note.

INTEREST, NOTES, AND DRAFTS ON THE STATEMENTS

Interest earned, interest expense, and collection expense appear on the income statement under the heading "Other revenues and expenses." Because "Other revenues and expenses" are not revenues and expenses from the regular operations of a business, they appear at the end of the statement as an addition to and a deduction from the income from operations, as follows:

Income from operation		$87,500
Other revenues and expenses:		
Interest earned	$1,200	
Interest expense	900	
Addition to income from operations		300
Net Income		$87,800

Notes and drafts receivable normally appear on the balance sheet in one amount under the caption "Notes receivable." Likewise, notes and drafts payable appear as one amount under the caption "Notes payable."

QUESTIONS FOR CLASS DISCUSSION

1. Define:

   a) Promissory note.
   b) Payee of a note.
   c) Maturity date.
   d) Dishonored note.
   e) Certificate of protest.
   f) Holder in due course.

   g) Drawee of a draft.
   h) Maker of a note.
   i) Principal of a note.
   j) Maturity value.
   k) Contingent liability.
   l) Drawer of a draft.

2. What distinction do banks make between discounts and loans?

3. Distinguish between bank discount and cash discount.

4. What are the due dates of the following notes:
   a) Ninety-day note dated November 5.
   b) Sixty-day note dated July 14.
   c) Ninety-day note dated June 5.

5. Calculate interest on the following amounts:
   a) $3,143 at 6 percent for 60 days.
   b) $1,500 at 6 percent for 24 days.
   c) $5,000 at 6 percent for 66 days.
   d) $1,800 at 4 percent for 30 days.
   e) $3,000 at 8 percent for 60 days.
   f) $2,400 at 4 percent for 90 days.
   g) $1,000 at 3 percent for 120 days.
   h) $1,200 at 7 percent for 54 days.

6. James Thumb borrows from two different banks. From the first he borrows by giving his $1,000, 60-day, 6 percent note. From the second he borrows by discounting his $1,000 note for 60 days at 6 percent. (a) Give the entries in general journal form to record the two loans on the books of Thumb. (b) Give the entries in general journal form to record the payments of the loans. (c) How do the entries differ in the two situations? (d) Which method of making loans favors the bank?

7. B. A. Lee purchased $500 worth of merchandise from Phoenix Company, terms 2/10, n/30. Lee could not pay the account when due and secured an extension of time from Phoenix Company by giving a 60-day, 6 percent, $500 note. Lee paid the note in full when due. Record this series of transactions in T-accounts (a) on the books of Lee, and (b) on the books of Phoenix Company.

8. On December 10, S. A. Starns received from a customer a $2,400, 60-day, 5 percent note dated December 8. On December 26, he discounted the note at 6 percent. The note was not protested at maturity. Give the required entries in general journal form on the books of Starns.

9. If the following accounts and balances appear in a ledger:

Notes Receivable		*Notes Receivable Discounted*	
Bal. **8,500**			**Bal.** **3,200**

   a) How many dollars of notes receivable are in the hands of the company?
   b) How many dollars of notes have been discounted?
   c) What is the contingent liability of the company?

10. How does a commercial draft differ from a promissory note?
11. Explain how a sight draft is used to collect a past-due account.
12. Why is a sight draft usually more effective as a collection device than a business letter?
13. Brown owes Green $500. The debt is past due, and Green draws a sight draft and sends it to Brown's bank for collection. Brown honors the draft. Give the required entries in general journal form (*a*) on the books of Green, and (*b*) on the books of Brown. The bank's fee was $2.50.

PROBLEMS

Problem 9–1
Part 1. On September 7 of the current year Southwest Sales sold Albert Scott $3,600 of merchandise, terms 2/10, n/60. On November 10 the concern accepted Scott's 60-day, 6 percent, $3,600 note dated that day in return for granting an additional 60 days on the amount owed. On November 25 Southwest Sales discounted the Scott note at 6 percent. The note was paid at maturity.

Required:
Prepare in general journal form entries to record the foregoing series of transactions, first on the books of Southwest Sales and then on the books of Scott.

Part 2. On December 4 Southwest Sales received an $1,800, 5 percent, 60-day note dated December 2 from Walter Giles in exchange for an extension on his slightly past-due open account. On December 26 Southwest Sales discounted the note at 6 percent, and on February 1 received notice that it had been dishonored. The concern paid the bank the maturity value of the note plus a $3 protest fee, and on March 4 received a check from Walter Giles in payment of the maturity value of the note, the protest fee, and interest at 5 percent on both for 30 days beyond maturity.

Required:
Prepare in general journal form entries to record the foregoing transactions on the books of Southwest Sales.

Problem 9–2
Prepare general journal entries to record the following transactions:
Dec. 12   Sold $1,200 of merchandise to Carl Moss, terms 2/10, n/60.
Feb. 16   Accepted a $1,200, 60-day, 6 percent note dated February 14 in granting an extension on the amount owed by Carl Moss.
    26   Discounted at 6 percent the Carl Moss note.
Apr. 18   Since a notice protesting the Carl Moss note had not been received, assumed it had been paid and canceled the discount liability.
May 2   Sold $1,500 of merchandise to Gene Nelson, terms 2/10, n/60.
July 5   Accepted a $1,500, 60-day, 4 percent note dated July 3 in granting an extension on the amount owed on open account by Gene Nelson.

July   9   Discounted the Gene Nelson note at 6 percent at the Second National Bank.

Sept.   2   Received a notice protesting the Gene Nelson note. Paid the maturity value of the note plus a $1 protest fee. Canceled the discount liability.

Oct.   1   Received a check from Gene Nelson in payment of the maturity value of his dishonored note, the protest fee, and interest at 4 percent on both for 30 days beyond maturity.

         3   Sold $1,800 of merchandise to Carl Tyler, terms 2/10, n/60.

Dec.   10   Mailed an $1,800, 6 percent, 30-day time draft to Carl Tyler who had agreed to accept the draft to secure a 30-day extension on his account balance.

        14   Received the accepted time draft mailed to Carl Tyler on the 10th.

Jan.   8   Sent the accepted time draft of Carl Tyler to the Second National Bank for collection.

        12   Received a credit memorandum from the Second National Bank, representing the proceeds of the Carl Tyler draft less a $2 collection fee.

Problem 9–3

Prepare entries in general journal form to record the following transactions:

Jan.   3   Received an $1,800, 60-day, 6 percent note dated January 2 from Paul Savoy in exchange for granting an extension of time on the amount owed on open account.

         5   Received $1,500 of merchandise from Pinetop Manufacturing Company, terms 60-day, 6 percent time draft. Accepted the draft.

         8   Sent Gene Elson an $800, 30-day, noninterest-bearing time draft which he had agreed to accept to secure a time extension on the amount owed on his open account.

        11   Drew a $900 sight draft on Richard Lyons who has ignored numerous letters written in an effort to collect his past-due account. Sent the draft to Springerville State Bank, the bank Mr. Lyons had originally given as a credit reference, for collection.

        12   Received the time draft sent Gene Elson. It was payable 30 days after sight and had been accepted on January 10.

        13   Received an $895 cashier's check from Springerville State Bank, the proceeds of the Richard Lyons sight draft less a $5 collection fee.

        20   Discounted the Paul Savoy note at 6 percent at Security Bank.

        22   Discounted at 6 percent the Gene Elson time draft.

Feb.   12   Since notice protesting the Gene Elson time draft had not been received, assumed it had been paid and canceled the discount liability.

Mar.   4   Received from Security Bank a notice protesting the Paul Savoy note. Paid the maturity value of the note plus a $2 protest fee and canceled the discount liability.

Mar.   5   Received notice from Security Bank that they held for collection the Pinetop Manufacturing Company draft. Paid the draft.

      15   Received a check from Paul Savoy in payment of his dishonored note, the protest fee, and 6 percent interest on both for 12 days beyond maturity.

Problem 9–4

Prepare entries in general journal form to record the following transactions:

Jan.   2   Received a $1,600, 6 percent, 60-day note dated December 30 from Henry Haws in granting him an extension on the amount owed on his open account.

      4   Received a $1,400, 30-day, noninterest-bearing note dated January 2 from Vernon Baker in granting an extension on the amount of his open account.

      6   Received $2,000 of merchandise from Tempe Sales, terms 60-day, 6 percent time draft. Accepted and returned the draft.

      8   Sent Roy Bodkin a $1,000, 60-day, 6 percent interest-bearing time draft for acceptance. The draft was dated January 8 and was payable 60 days after date. Mr. Bodkin had agreed to accept the draft to secure an extension on his past-due account.

      8   Discounted the Vernon Baker note at 6 percent at the First State Bank.

      9   Sold and shipped $900 of merchandise to Bruce Hart, terms 60-day, noninterest-bearing time draft dated January 9. Mailed the draft for acceptance. Recorded the sale as a sale on account and awaited the return of the accepted draft.

     12   Received the draft sent Roy Bodkin on January 8. It had been accepted.

     12   Received from Bruce Hart the draft mailed on January 9. It had been accepted.

     12   Drew a $600 sight draft addressed to George Kern, a former customer who had ignored numerous letters written in an effort to collect his past-due account. Sent the draft to the Scottsdale State Bank, Mr. Kern's bank, for collection.

     14   Discounted the Henry Haws note at 6 percent at the First State Bank.

     15   Received a $597 cashier's check from the Scottsdale State Bank. The check represented the proceeds of the George Kern sight draft less a $3 collection fee.

     15   Discounted the Bruce Hart time draft at 6 percent at the First State Bank.

     26   Discounted the Roy Bodkin time draft at 6 percent at the First State Bank.

Feb.   3   Since a notice protesting the Vernon Baker note had not been received, assumed that it had been paid and canceled the discount liability.

Mar.   1   Received a notice from the First State Bank protesting the Henry Haws note. Paid the bank the maturity value of the note plus a $1 protest fee. Canceled the discount liability.

Mar. 7 Received notice from the First State Bank that it held for collection the Tempe Sales time draft. Paid the draft.
    12 Since notice protesting the Roy Bodkin and Bruce Hart drafts had not been received, assumed both had been paid and canceled the discount liabilities.
    15 Received a check from Henry Haws for the maturity value of his dishonored note, the protest fee, and interest on both at 6 percent for 15 days beyond maturity.

CLASS EXERCISE

Exercise 9–1

On September 11 General Manufacturing Company sold Thomas Darr goods having a catalogue price of $2,000, less 20 percent and 10 percent, terms 2/10, n/60. At the end of the credit period Darr was unable to pay and was granted an extension by General Manufacturing Company upon receipt of his 60-day, 6 percent note dated November 20. General Manufacturing Company held the note until December 5. On that date the firm discounted the note at 6 percent at the First National Bank. The note was not protested at maturity.

Answer the following questions:

1. How many dollars of trade discount were granted by General Manufacturing Company?
2. How much cash discount could Darr have obtained on this purchase?
3. What was the maturity date of the note?
4. How many days were in the discount period?
5. How much bank discount was deducted by the bank?
6. What were the proceeds of the note?
7. What was the last entry made by General Manufacturing Company as a result of this series of transactions?

ALTERNATE PROBLEMS

Problem 9–1A

a) On October 6 Mesa Supply sold $1,950 of merchandise to Warren Turpin, terms 2/10, n/60. (b) On December 10 the company mailed Mr. Turpin for acceptance an $1,800, 60-day, 6 percent time draft dated December 5 and payable 60 days after date. Mr. Turpin had agreed to pay $150 of the amount he owed and to accept the draft to secure a time extension on the balance. (c) The draft was accepted by Mr. Turpin on December 12 and returned by mail along with a $150 check. Mesa Supply received both the next day. (d) On December 29 Mesa Supply discounted the Turpin draft at 6 percent at the First National Bank. (e) The draft was dishonored at maturity and on February 4 Mesa Supply paid the bank the maturity value of the draft plus a $3 protest fee, charging the account of the drawee. (f) On April 5 Mesa Supply received a check dated April 3 in payment of the maturity value of the draft, the protest fee, and interest on both at 6 percent for 60 days beyond maturity.

Required:

1. Give in general journal form Mesa Supply's entry or entries, or state that no entry is required, to record each lettered transaction or transaction portion above.
2. Give Warren Turpin's entry, or state that no entry is required, for each transaction or portion.

Problem 9–2A

Prepare entries in general journal form to record the following transactions:

July   7   Received a $2,400, 5 percent, 60-day note from Darrell Silva in exchange for granting a 60-day extension on his open account. The note was dated July 3.

       21   Discounted the Darrell Silva note at 6 percent at Security Bank.

Sept.   4   Since a notice protesting the Darrell Silva note had not been received, assumed it had been paid and canceled the discount liability.

       5   Received a $3,000, 6 percent, 30-day note dated September 2 from Walter Bowen in exchange for granting a 30-day extension on the amount he owed on open account.

     20   Discounted the Walter Bowen note at 6 percent at Security Bank.

Oct.   3   Received notice protesting the Walter Brown note. Paid Security Bank the maturity value of the note plus a $3 protest fee.

Nov.   1   Received a check from Walter Bowen in payment of his dishonored note, the protest fee, and interest at 6 percent on both for 30 days beyond maturity.

       6   Borrowed $7,500 from Security Bank by giving a 60-day, 6 percent note of this date.

       7   Borrowed $5,000 from First National Bank by discounting a noninterest-bearing note of this date at 6 percent for 60 days.

Jan.   5   Paid the amount due on the note given Security Bank on November 6.

       6   Paid the amount due on the note given First National Bank on November 7.

       7   Agreed to grant Carl Morgan a 60-day extension on his $1,200 open account in exchange for a 60-day, 5 percent time draft. Mailed the draft.

     11   Received the accepted draft sent Carl Morgan. It was payable 60 days after sight and had been accepted on January 8.

     14   Discounted the Carl Morgan draft at Security Bank at 6 percent.

Mar. 13   Since notice protesting the Carl Morgan draft had not been received, assumed it paid and canceled the discount liability.

Problem 9–3A

Prepare entries in general journal form to record the following transactions:

Nov.   3   Gave Northwest Sales a $3,000, 5 percent, 60-day note to secure a time extension on our open account of $3,234. Paid the balance in cash.

Nov. 4 Received a $2,400, 5 percent, 60-day note dated November 3, from Richard Hall in exchange for granting a time extension on his open account.

7 Received a $1,500, 6 percent, 60-day note dated November 5, from Walter Davis in exchange for a time extension on his account.

9 Discounted the Richard Hall note at 6 percent.

11 Discounted at 6 percent for 30 days our own $3,600 noninterest-bearing note.

23 Discounted the Walter Davis note at 6 percent.

28 Received a $1,600, 6 percent, 30-day note dated November 26 from Howard Bell in exchange for an extension on his account.

30 Borrowed $5,000 from Security Bank by giving a 60-day, 6 percent note.

Dec. 11 Gave Security Bank a check in payment of our note discounted on November 11.

22 Delivered the Howard Bell note to Security Bank for collection.

28 The bank returned the Howard Bell note; it had been dishonored on its due date.

Jan. 2 Received notice from Security Bank that they held for collection the note given Northwest Sales on November 3. Paid the note.

4 Since a notice protesting the Richard Hall note had not been received, assumed it had been paid.

5 Received notice from Security Bank that Walter Davis had dishonored the note discounted on November 23. Paid the bank the maturity value of the note plus $2 protest fee.

10 Received a check from Howard Bell in payment of his dishonored note with interest on the principal through January 10.

16 Received a check from Walter Davis in payment of the maturity value of his dishonored note, the protest fee, and interest on both from maturity through this date.

29 Paid the note given the bank on November 30.

Problem 9–4A

On November 10 H. H. Monti delivered to Standard Manufacturing Company a $2,400, 5 percent 60-day note of that date to secure an extension on his open account balance. Following are four unrelated things or series of things involving the note that might have happened:

a) The maker paid the note and its interest directly to the payee on its maturity date.

b) The maker dishonored the note.

c) The payee held the note 30 days and then discounted it at its bank at 6 percent. The maker paid the note and its interest on its due date. Standard Manufacturing Company canceled its discount liability three days thereafter.

d) The payee held the note 30 days and then discounted it at its bank at 6 percent. The maker dishonored the note and Standard Manufacturing

Company paid the bank the note's maturity value plus a $2 protest fee two days following its due date.

Required:

1. Give the entry for the delivery of the note, first on the books of H. H. Monti and then on the books of Standard Manufacturing Company.
2. Then give the required entry or entries on the books of H. H. Monti and then on the books of Standard Manufacturing Company for each thing or series of things that might have happened. If no entry is required, so state.

DECISION PROBLEM 9—PLAINS MACHINE COMPANY

The Plains Machine Company manufactures and sells a mechanical cotton picker. It distributes the product through retail implement dealers. It has been in business only a few years and is attempting to compete with larger and better established agricultural machinery manufacturers.

The company's mechanical pickers are somewhat less cumbersome and less complicated and, therefore, less expensive than those of its competitors. Nevertheless, the unit price on each picker is fairly substantial and, because of the custom in the industry, generous credit terms must be provided. Sales are made to dealers on account at terms of 10 percent in cash, and the balance due four months after the date of the sale. Dealers customarily give about the same terms to farmers, but since many credit extensions up to a full year are given, the dealers then must also be given a longer period to pay Plains Machine Company.

A number of other problems in financing have arisen. The company desires to schedule production more uniformly over the year but, because of the seasonal sales and the small cash inflow during the off-season, has been unable to secure the funds necessary to keep full-scale operation on a 12-month basis. Dealers also complain that customers should be given a longer credit period if competition is to be met. The company's representatives report that it is believed that dealer sales could be increased 20 percent if credit terms of nine months could be arranged.

Sales for the past year were distributed as follows:

January	*$15,000*	*July*	*$90,000*
February	*20,000*	*August*	*70,000*
March	*30,000*	*September*	*50,000*
April	*40,000*	*October*	*40,000*
May	*60,000*	*November*	*20,000*
June	*80,000*	*December*	*10,000*

At a dealers' meeting in December the vice president in charge of sales for Plains Machine Company proposed the following plan:

1. Dealers ask customers to accept noninterest-bearing drafts for balance due after 10 percent down payment. These drafts would run for nine months from dates of sales.

2. Dealers would endorse to the manufacturer customer drafts up to amounts due the company on each month's sales.
3. The company could then discount these drafts at the bank at 5 percent.

Prepare a report expressing your opinion on the vice president's proposal including the following:

1. Should dealers prefer the proposed credit plan over the current plan? Should the plan be acceptable to farmers?
2. Assuming that sales will increase 20 percent and that the cash requirement to cover production and other operating costs is 50 percent of sales, how much cash will be needed each month if production is equalized over the year?
3. Would you recommend the plan to Plains Machine Company? Explain.

Bad Debts
and Accounts Receivable;
Inventories and
Cost of Goods Sold

WHEN goods and services are sold on credit, almost always a few customers do not pay. The accounts of such customers are called *bad debts*. Keeping bad debts or uncollectible accounts to a minimum is an objective of good credit management.

GRANTING CREDIT

If losses from uncollectible accounts are to be held to a minimum, a business selling on credit must exercise great care in selecting customers to whom credit is granted. Many companies have credit departments whose duty it is to investigate the debt-paying ability and the debt-paying habits of each prospective new customer and to decide how much credit, if any, can safely be granted. In making these investigations, a credit department examines the financial statements of prospective customers, as well as credit reports secured from local and from national credit agencies, such as Dun & Bradstreet.

However, regardless of the care exercised in granting credit, there are always some accounts that can never be collected. These accounts are a loss and an expense of selling on credit. Determining the amount of this expense at the end of each accounting period is one of the problems of accounting for the revenue from charge sales.

DIRECT WRITE-OFF OF BAD DEBTS

There are two ways to account for bad debt losses, the *direct write-off method* and the *allowance method*. Of the two, the direct write-off method is the more simple and is discussed first here, although its use is limited as is explained later.

Under the direct write-off method, when it is decided that a customer's account is uncollectible, an entry like the following is made:

Nov.	*23*	*Bad Debts Expense........................*	*52.50*	
		Accounts Receivable—Dale Hall.........		*52.50*
		To write off the uncollectible account of		
		Dale Hall.		

The debit of the foregoing entry charges the bad debt loss directly to the current year's Bad Debts Expense account, and the credit removes the balance of the uncollectible account from the subsidiary ledger and controlling account.

Writing off a bad debt directly to the Bad Debts Expense account is simple, as the foregoing entry shows; however, such a write-off commonly violates *the accounting principle of matching revenues and expenses;* and, therefore, its use is permissible only in certain situations as is explained later in this chapter.

Matching Revenues and Expenses. A fundamental principle of accounting requires that on an income statement the reported revenues should be matched with expenses incurred in earning the revenues. By this is meant that when an income statement is prepared at the end of a year, it should show all revenues earned during the year, and matched against the revenues (deducted therefrom) should be all the expenses incurred in earning the revenues.

Time of a Bad Debt Loss. A bad debt loss results from an error in judgment, an error in granting credit and making a sale to a customer who will not pay. Consequently, a bad debt loss is incurred at the moment credit is granted and such a sale is made. Of course, the merchant selling to a customer who will not pay does not know at the time of the sale that he has incurred a loss, and probably will not really be sure of the loss for as much as a year or more, after he has exhausted every means of collecting. Nevertheless, final recognition does not change the time of the loss; the loss occurred at the moment of the sale.

Direct Write-off and the Mismatching of Revenues and Expenses. When it is recognized that a bad debt loss is actually incurred at the moment of a sale to a customer who will not pay, then it follows that the direct write-off of such a loss normally fails in matching revenues and expenses. It fails because the revenue from the sale is recognized in one year and the expense of the loss is usually not recognized until at least the next year, when the account is finally written off. Or, it fails because the revenue from the sale appears on the income statement of one year while the expense of the loss is deducted on the income statement of the following or a later year.

When Direct Write-off Is Permissible. Although the direct write-off method commonly fails in the matching process, it may still be used in situations where its use does not materially affect reported net income. For example, it may be used in a store where substantially all sales are for cash, and bad debt losses from a few charge sales are immaterial in relation to total sales and net income. In such a store the use of direct write-off comes under *the accounting principle of materiality*. (Under the accounting principle of materiality it is held that a strict adherence to any accounting principle, in this case the matching principle, is not required when adherence is relatively difficult or expensive and the lack of adherence does not materially affect reported net income.)

ALLOWANCE METHOD OF ACCOUNTING FOR BAD DEBTS

A company in which a large share of the sales are on credit will normally use the allowance method in accounting for bad debts. Under this method an estimate is made at the end of each accounting period of the total bad debts that are expected to result from the period's sales, and an allowance is provided for the resulting loss. This has two advantages: (1) the estimated loss is charged to the period in which the revenue is recognized, and (2) the accounts receivable appear on the balance sheet at their estimated realizable value, a more informative balance sheet amount.

Estimating Bad Debts. In making the year-end estimate of the amount of bad debts that are expected to result from the year's sales, companies commonly assume that "history will repeat." For example, over the past several years Alpha Company has experienced bad debt losses equal to one half of 1 percent of its charge sales, and during the past year its charge sales were $300,000. Consequently, if history repeats, Alpha Company can expect $1,500 of bad debt losses to result from the sales ($300,000 × .005 = $1,500).

Recording the Estimated Bad Debts Loss. Under the allowance method of accounting for bad debts, the estimated bad debts loss is recorded at the end of each accounting period with a work sheet adjustment and an adjusting entry. For example, Alpha Company will record its $1,500 estimated bad debts loss with a work sheet adjustment and an adjusting entry like the following:

Dec.	*31*	*Bad Debts Expense.....................*	*1,500.00*	
		Allowance for Bad Debts............		*1,500.00*
		To record the estimated bad debts.		

The debit of the foregoing entry causes the estimated bad debts loss to appear on the current income statement where this $1,500 expense of selling on credit is matched with the $300,000 of revenue it helped to produce.

Bad Debts in the Accounts. If at the time the foregoing bad debts adjusting entry is posted, Alpha Company has $20,000 of accounts receivable, the Accounts Receivable and Allowance for Bad Debts accounts will show the following balances:

Accounts Receivable		*Allowance for Bad Debts*	
Dec. 31 *20,000*			*Dec. 31* *1,500*

The bad debts adjusting entry reduces the accounts receivable to their estimated realizable value. However, note that the credit of the entry is to the contra account, Allowance for Bad Debts, rather than to the Accounts Receivable controlling account.

It is necessary to credit the estimated bad debts loss to the contra account, rather than the Accounts Receivable account, because at the time of the adjusting entry it is not known for certain just which customers will fail to pay. (The total loss from bad debts can be estimated from past experience; but the exact customers who will not pay cannot be known until every means of collecting from each has been exhausted.) Consequently, since the bad accounts are not identifiable, they cannot be removed from the subsidiary Accounts Receivable Ledger; and the Allowance for Bad Debts account must be credited, instead of the controlling account. The allowance account must be credited because to credit the controlling account without removing the bad accounts from the subsidiary ledger would cause the controlling account balance to differ from the sum of the balances in the subsidiary ledger.

Bad Debts on the Statements. When the balance sheet is prepared, the balance of the Allowance for Bad Debts account is subtracted thereon from the balance of the Accounts Receivable account to show the amount that is expected to be realized from the accounts, as follows:

```
                                  ASSETS

Current Assets:
  Cash . . . . . . . . . . . . . . . . . . . . . . . . . . . . . . . .        $11,300
  Accounts receivable. . . . . . . . . . . . . . . . . . . .   $20,000
    Less allowance for bad debts . . . . . . . . . . . . . .     1,500       18,500
  Merchandise inventory. . . . . . . . . . . . . . . . . . . .               27,200
  Prepaid expenses . . . . . . . . . . . . . . . . . . . . . . . .             1,100
      Total Current Assets . . . . . . . . . . . . . . . . . . . .           $58,100
```

Bad debt losses normally appear on the income statement as an administrative expense rather than as a selling expense. They appear as an administrative expense because granting credit is usually not a responsibility of the sales department; and therefore, since the sales department is not responsible for granting credit, it should not be held responsible for bad debt losses. The sales department is usually not given responsibility for granting credit because it is often feared the sales department would at times be swayed in its judgment of a credit risk by its desire to make a sale.

Writing off a Bad Debt. Occasionally, when a customer becomes bankrupt, it may be definitely known that his account is uncollectible. Otherwise, whether an account is collectible or not is usually a matter of judgment. Each account long past due must be individually judged, and those judged uncollectible are written off.

When an allowance for bad debts is provided, accounts deemed uncollectible are written off against this allowance. For example, after spending a year trying to collect, Alpha Company finally concluded the $100 account of George Vale was uncollectible, and made the following entry to write it off:

Jan.	*23*	*Allowance for Bad Debts.................*	*100.00*	
		Accounts Receivable—George Vale.....		*100.00*
		To write off the uncollectible account of George Vale.		

Posting the entry had this effect on the accounts:

Accounts Receivable				*Allowance for Bad Debts*			
Dec. 31	*20,000*	*Jan. 23*	*100*	*Jan. 23*	*100*	*Dec. 31*	*1,500*

Two points should be observed in the foregoing entry and accounts. First, although bad debts are an expense of selling on credit, the Allowance for Bad Debts account, rather than an expense account, is debited in the write-off. The allowance account is debited because the expense was recorded at the end of the period in which the sale occurred. At that time, the loss was foreseen, and the expense was recorded in the estimated bad debts adjusting entry.

Second, although the write-off removed the amount of the account from the ledgers, it did not affect the estimated realizable amount of Alpha Company's accounts receivable, as the following tabulation shows:

	Before Write-off	After Write-off
Account receivable	*$20,000*	*$19,900*
Less: Allowance for bad debts	*1,500*	*1,400*
Estimated realizable accounts receivable	*$18,500*	*$18,500*

BAD DEBT RECOVERIES

Frequently an error in judgment is made in regard to a customer's ability to pay his past-due account. As a result, accounts written off as uncollectible are later often collected in full or in part. If an account is written off as uncollectible and later the customer pays part or all of the amount previously written off, the payment should be shown in the customer's account for future credit action. The payment should be shown because when a customer fails to pay and his account is written off, the customer's credit standing is destroyed; and later, when the customer pays the amount previously written off, the payment helps restore the credit standing. When an account previously written off as a bad debt is collected, two entries are made. The first reinstates the customer's account balance and has the effect of reversing the original write-off. The second entry records the collection of the reinstated account.

For example, if the account of Dale Hall which was written off directly to the Bad Debts Expense account on page 262 is later collected in full, the following entries in general journal form are made to record the bad debt recovery:

Mar.	11	Accounts Receivable—Dale Hall...............	52.50	
		Bad Debts Expense......................		52.50
		To reinstate the account of Dale Hall written off on November 23.		
	11	Cash....................................	52.50	
		Accounts Receivable—Dale Hall.........		52.50
		In full of account.		

The first of the foregoing entries assumes collection in the year following the write-off and that the Bad Debts Expense account has a debit balance from other write-offs during the year. If the account has no balance from other write-offs and none are expected, the credit of the entry could be to a revenue account called, for example, Bad Debt Recoveries.

If the allowance method is used in accounting for bad debts, two entries are also used in recording recoveries. For example, if George Vale, whose account was written off by Alpha Company (page 265) on January 23, pays in full on August 15. The entries in general journal form to record the bad debt recovery are:

Aug.	15	Accounts Receivable—George Vale.........	100.00	
		Allowance for Bad Debts..............		100.00
		To reinstate the account of George Vale written off on January 23.		
	15	Cash...................................	100.00	
		Accounts Receivable—George Vale.....		100.00
		In full of account.		

OTHER BASES FOR ESTIMATING BAD DEBTS

As previously explained, the relationship between charge sales and past bad debt losses is often used in estimating losses from uncollectible accounts. Too, when the proportion of credit sales to cash sales remains about the same, total sales, rather than charge sales alone, may be used. Likewise, in companies where about the same percentage of accounts receivable prove uncollectible each year, a percentage of the year-end balance of the Accounts Receivable account may be set up as the estimated bad debts expense.

AGING ACCOUNTS RECEIVABLE

In estimating bad debt losses, many companies age their accounts receivable. This consists of preparing a schedule of accounts receivable with the accounts listed and their balances entered in columns according to age. Such a schedule appears as in Illustration 65. After a schedule showing account ages is prepared, responsible and experienced executives of the sales and credit departments examine each account listed thereon, and from experience and by judgment, decide which accounts are probably uncollectible. Normally, the majority of accounts appearing on the schedule are current and not past due; these are examined for possible losses but receive less scrutiny than past-due accounts. The older accounts

Illustration 65

SCHEDULE OF ACCOUNTS RECEIVABLE BY AGE

Customer's Name	Not Due	1 to 30 Days Past Due	31 to 60 Days Past Due	61 to 90 Days Past Due	Over 90 Days Past Due
Charles Abbot	45.00				
Frank Allen	53.00				
George Arden			14.00		
Paul Baum					27.00

are more apt to prove uncollectible; these receive the greatest attention. After decisions are made as to which accounts are probably uncollectible, the allowance for bad debts is adjusted to provide for them.

CORRECTING THE SIZE OF THE ALLOWANCE FOR BAD DEBTS

Regardless of care in estimating losses from bad debts, errors in judgment occur. Often, too, unforeseen changes in economic and business conditions cause a change in the amount of uncollectible accounts. When either judgment errors or changes in business conditions occur, the Allowance for Bad Debts account balance may become too large or too small. If losses are greater than anticipated, the allowance may become too small. If losses are less than anticipated, the allowance may become too large. Often, when the provision for bad debts is based on a fixed percentage of sales or accounts receivable, the passage of several accounting periods is required before it becomes apparent that the percentage is either too large or too small. In such cases, when it becomes apparent that the percentage is incorrect, an adjustment in the percentage should be made.

Sometimes, even though the amounts provided for bad debts over a number of accounting periods are approximately correct, during a single period the allowance may be exhausted by the write-off of an excessive number of uncollectible accounts. When this occurs, if additional losses are to be written off, the additional losses may be charged directly to the Bad Debts Expense account. This violates the principle of matching revenues and expenses, but is acceptable if the amounts written off are not material in amount.

Occasionally a company will permit the credit balance of its allowance account to become much greater than the amount needed to provide for losses. Two errors result from this. First, in each year that the excessive allowance is provided, the expenses of that year are overstated and the net income is understated. In addition, after the allowance becomes too large, both the accounts receivable and owner equity are understated on the balance sheet.

When it is discovered that the balance of the Allowance for Bad Debts account has become too large because of excessive provisions for bad debts, an entry to correct the situation must be made. This entry in a single proprietorship appears as follows:

Jan.	22	Allowance for Bad Debts....................	500.00	
		Frank Jones, Capital.................		500.00
		To reduce the excessive allowance for bad debts.		

The debit to the Allowance for Bad Debts account corrects the understatement of accounts receivable. The credit to the Capital account corrects the understatement of proprietorship caused by the excessive past yearly debits to the Bad Debts Expense account.

In addition to the foregoing, since each excessive debit to bad debts expense caused an understatement of income subject to income taxes, amended tax returns will probably have to be filed and additional income taxes paid.

OTHER FACTORS AFFECTING ACCOUNTS RECEIVABLE

Overpayment of an Account. Customers occasionally fail to take earned discounts or in some other manner overpay their accounts. Because of this, customer accounts with credit balances are not uncommon. When there are customer accounts with credit balances in the Accounts Receivable Ledger, the balance of the Accounts Receivable controlling account should not appear on the balance sheet as the amount of accounts receivable. In such cases, because assets and liabilities should not be offset, the accounts in the Accounts Receivable Ledger having debit balances should be added and their sum placed on the balance sheet as the amount of accounts receivable. At the same time the accounts having credit balances should be added and their sum placed on the balance sheet as a current liability under a caption such as, for example, "Credit balances in customer accounts."

Sales to and Purchases from the Same Firm. If goods are sold to and purchases are made from the same firm, two accounts should be kept, and their balances should not be offset. In such cases the amount receivable should appear on the balance sheet as part of the accounts receivable, and the amount payable should appear as part of the accounts payable.

Miscellaneous Accounts Receivable. If the caption "Accounts receivable" appears on the balance sheet without any further descriptive words or limitations, only amounts due from regular trade debtors should be included under the designation. Accounts receivable from stockholders or company officers, in the case of a corporation, or from employees should be shown separately, unless these accounts arose from sales that are collectible in accordance with the company's regular selling terms. Loans and advances to stockholders, officers, and employees may be shown as current assets under a suitable descriptive title if there is evidence that the amounts will be collected within the period normally allotted for the collection of current assets; otherwise, they should appear at the end of the asset section as, for example, "Other assets—accounts receivable from officers and employees."

INVENTORIES AND COST OF GOODS SOLD

The accounting value placed on its ending merchandise inventory is of extreme importance to a store. This is because the ending inventory amount not only appears on the balance sheet as a current asset, commonly the largest current asset, but also determines cost of goods sold and net income.

Arriving at the accounting value for an ending inventory normally involves two problems: (1) determining the quantity of each product on hand, and (2) pricing the products.

THE PROBLEM OF QUANTITY

The quantity of unsold merchandise on hand may be determined by means of a physical inventory or a perpetual or book inventory may be kept. In a physical inventory the unsold merchandise is counted, weighed, or otherwise measured to determine the units, pounds, gallons, board feet, or other measure of each product on hand. In a perpetual inventory a book record of the units of each product bought, sold, and on hand is maintained.

Physical inventories and the way in which such inventories are taken were discussed in Chapter 5; consequently, attention can be given here to perpetual inventories.

PERPETUAL INVENTORIES

Some concerns selling a limited number of different products of relatively high unit value keep perpetual or book inventories. A perpetual or book inventory makes use of a subsidiary record card for each product in stock. On these individual cards, one for each kind of product, the number of units of that product received is recorded as units are received; the number of units sold is recorded as units are sold; and after each receipt or sale, the balance remaining on hand is recorded. (An inventory card for ¼ H.P. Electric Motors is shown in Illustration 66.) At any time, each

Illustration 66

Item ¼ *H.P. Electric Motors*						Location in stock room *Bin 8*		
Maximum 25						Minimum 5		
	Received			Sold			Balance		
Date	Units	Cost	Total	Units	Cost	Total	Units	Cost	Bal-ance
1/1							10	10.00	100.00
1/5				5	10.00	50.00	5	10.00	50.00
1/8	20	10.50	210.00				{ 5	10.00	
							{ 20	10.50	260.00
1/10				3	10.00	30.00	{ 2	10.00	
							{ 20	10.50	230.00

perpetual inventory card tells the balance on hand of any one product; and the total of all cards is the amount of the inventory.

Perpetual inventories not only tell the amount of inventory on hand at any time but they also aid in controlling the total amount invested in inventory. Each perpetual inventory card may have on it the maximum and minimum amounts of that item that should be kept in stock. By keeping the amount of each item within these limits, an oversupply or an undersupply of inventory is avoided.

PERIODIC AND PERPETUAL INVENTORY SYSTEMS

A system of inventory accounting like that described in Chapter 5 is normally based upon periodic, physical inventories and is known as a periodic inventory system. As was explained in Chapter 5, cost of goods sold during an accounting period is determined under such a system by adding net cost of purchases to beginning inventory and subtracting the ending inventory. When such a system is used, a physical inventory is necessary in order to determine ending inventory and cost of goods sold.

Under a perpetual inventory system cost of goods sold during a period, as well as the ending inventory, may be determined from the accounting records without a physical inventory. Under such a system an account called "Merchandise" takes the place of and is used for recording the information entered in the periodic inventory system accounts, "Purchases" and "Merchandise Inventory." The "Merchandise" account is a controlling account that controls the numerous perpetual inventory cards described in previous paragraphs.

When merchandise is purchased by a concern using a perpetual inventory system, the acquisition is recorded as follows:

Dec.	*14*	*Merchandise...........................*	*956.00*	
		Accounts Payable—Blue Company.....		*956.00*
		Purchased merchandise on account.		

In addition to the entry recording the purchase in the Merchandise account, entries are also made on the proper perpetual inventory cards in the Received columns to show the kinds of merchandise bought.

When a sale is made, since the inventory cards show the cost of each item sold, it is possible to record both the sale and the cost of the goods sold. For example, if goods that according to the inventory cards cost $65 are sold for $100, cost of goods sold and the sale may be recorded as follows:

Dec.	*16*	*Accounts Receivable—George Black........*	*100.00*	
		Cost of Goods Sold......................	*65.00*	
		Sales.................................		*100.00*
		Merchandise........................		*65.00*
		Sold merchandise on account.		

In addition to the entry just given which credits the Merchandise account for the cost of the goods sold, the goods sold are entered in the Sold columns of the proper inventory cards.

Note the debit to Cost of Goods Sold in the entry just given. If this account is debited at the time of each sale for the cost of the goods sold, the debit balance of the account will show at the end of the accounting period the cost of all goods sold during the period.

Note also the Merchandise account as it appears in the two entries just given. If this account is debited for the cost of merchandise purchased and credited for the cost of merchandise sold, at the end of an accounting period its debit balance will show the cost of the unsold goods on hand, the ending inventory.

If cost of goods sold, as well as sales, is to be recorded in a columnar Sales Journal, an additional column is required.

Periodic inventory systems are more common than perpetual inventory systems in retail and wholesale concerns. However, perpetual inventory systems are not uncommon in concerns selling goods having a high unit cost.

THE PROBLEM OF INVENTORY PRICING

Generally inventories are priced at cost.[1] However, a departure from cost is sometimes necessary when goods have been damaged or have deteriorated. Likewise, a departure from cost is sometimes necessary when replacement costs for inventory items are less than the amounts actually paid for the items when they were purchased. This last point is discussed in more detail later in this chapter under the heading, "Cost or Market, the Lower."

ACCOUNTING FOR AN INVENTORY AT COST

Accounting for an inventory at cost is not difficult when costs remain fixed. However, when identical items were purchased during an accounting period at different costs, a problem arises as to which costs apply to the ending inventory and which apply to the goods sold. There are at least four acceptable ways of assigning costs to goods in the ending inventory and to goods sold. They are: (1) specific invoice prices; (2) average cost; (3) first-in, first-out; and (4) last-in, first-out.

To illustrate the four ways of assigning costs, assume that a company has on hand at the end of an accounting period twelve units of Article X. Also, assume that the company began the year and purchased Article X during the year as follows:

Jan. 1	*Opening inventory..10 units @ $10.00*	*=*	*$100.00*
Mar. 13	*Purchased..........15 units @ $11.50*	*=*	*172.50*
Aug. 17	*Purchased..........20 units @ $12.50*	*=*	*250.00*
Nov. 10	*Purchased..........10 units @ $12.00*	*=*	*120.00*
	Total purchases.....55 units		*$642.50*

---

[1] *Accounting Research Bulletin No. 43,* "Restatement and Revision of Accounting Research Bulletins" (New York: American Institute of Certified Public Accountants, 1953), p. 28.

Specific Invoice Prices. When it is possible to identify each item of an inventory with a specific purchase and its invoice, specific invoice prices may be used to assign costs to the inventory and to the goods sold. For example, if for purposes of illustration it is assumed that six of the twelve remaining units of Article X were from the November purchase and six were from the August purchase, then costs are assigned to the inventory and goods sold by means of specific invoice prices as follows:

Total cost of 55 units available for sale......................	*$642.50*
Less final inventory priced by means of specific invoices:	
6 units from the November purchase at $12.00 each......$72.00	
6 units from the August purchase at $12.50............. 75.00	
*12 units in ending inventory........................... *	*147.00*
Cost of goods sold..	*$495.50*

Average Cost. Under this method the prices for the units in the beginning inventory and in each purchase weighted by the number of units in the beginning inventory and in each purchase are averaged to find the average cost per unit, as follows:

$$
\begin{aligned}
10 \text{ units at } \$10.00 &= \$100.00 \\
15 \text{ units at } \$11.50 &= 172.50 \\
20 \text{ units at } \$12.50 &= 250.00 \\
10 \text{ units at } \$12.00 &= 120.00 \\
\overline{55} &\quad \overline{\$642.50}
\end{aligned}
$$

$642.50 ÷ 55 = $11.682, average cost per unit

After the average cost per unit is determined, this average cost is used to assign costs to the inventory and the units sold as follows:

Total cost of 55 units available for sale............$642.50	
Less ending inventory priced on an average cost basis	
12 units at $11.682 each......................... 140.18	
Cost of goods sold...............................$502.32	

First-In, First-Out. In a merchandising business clerks are usually instructed to sell the oldest merchandise first. Consequently, when this instruction is followed, merchandise tends to flow out on a first-in, first-out basis. When first-in, first-out is applied in pricing an inventory, it is assumed that costs also follow this pattern and, as a result, the cost of the last items received are assigned to the ending inventory and the remaining costs are assigned to goods sold. When first-in, first-out, or *Fifo* as it is often called from its first letters, is used, costs are assigned to the inventory and to the goods sold as follows:

Total cost of 55 units available for sale.....................		*$642.50*
Less ending inventory priced on a basis of Fifo:		
10 units from the November purchase at $12.00 each.....*$120.00*		
2 units from the August purchase at $12.50 each........ *25.00*		
12 units in the ending inventory......................		*145.00*
Cost of goods sold.......................................		*$497.50*

Last-In, First-Out. Under this method of inventory pricing, commonly called *Lifo,* the costs of the last goods received are matched with revenue from sales. The theoretical justification for this is that a going concern must at all times keep a certain amount of goods in stock; consequently, when goods are sold, replacements are purchased. Thus it is a sale that causes the replacement of goods; and if costs and revenues are matched, replacement costs should be matched with the sales that induced the acquisitions.

Under Lifo, costs are assigned to the twelve remaining units of Article X and to the goods sold as follows:

Total cost of 55 units available for sale.....................		*$642.50*
Less ending inventory priced on a basis of Lifo:		
10 units in the beginning inventory at $10.00 each.......*$100.00*		
2 units from the first purchase at $11.50 each........... *23.00*		
12 units in the ending inventory......................		*123.00*
Cost of goods sold.......................................		*$519.50*

Notice that this method of matching costs and revenue results in the final inventory being priced at the cost of the oldest twelve units.

Comparison of Methods. In a stable market where prices remain unchanged, the inventory pricing method is of little importance. This is true because when prices are unchanged over a period of time, all methods give the same cost figures. However, in a changing market where prices are rising and falling, each method may give a different result. This may be seen by a comparison of the costs of Article X sold as calculated by the several methods on the previous pages. These costs were:

Based on specific invoice prices...................*$495.50*
Based on average invoice prices................... *502.32*
Based on Fifo...................................... *497.50*
Based on Lifo...................................... *519.50*

All four pricing methods are used; and each under certain circumstances has its advantages. Specific invoice prices exactly match costs and revenue;

average invoice prices tend to smooth out price fluctuations; Fifo tends to associate costs and the merchandising ideal of selling the oldest merchandise first; and when prices are rising, as in the years following World War II, Lifo has certain tax advantages. However, since the method used may affect the amounts of reported ending inventory and cost of goods sold, a company should show on its statements by means of footnotes or other manner the pricing method used. Also, accountants are of the opinion that a company should select for use the method that best reflects its periodic net income.

Tax Effect of Lifo. During periods of rising prices Lifo offers a tax advantage to its users. This advantage arises because when compared with other commonly used methods the application of Lifo results in assigning greatest amounts of costs to goods sold. This in turn results in the smallest reported net incomes and income taxes.

Perpetual Inventory Situations. In the foregoing paragraphs specific invoice prices, average, Fifo, and Lifo have been applied in a periodic inventory situation. It should be noted that each may also be applied in a perpetual inventory system.

CONSISTENCY

Often a company's reported net income can be either increased or decreased simply by changing its method of inventory pricing. For this reason, although accountants hold that a company may use any accepted method that fairly reflects its periodic income, they insist that the company consistently follow the chosen method.

Often there are several acceptable ways of handling any transaction or accounting problem. Inventory pricing methods are one example, and the several methods of calculating depreciation as presented in the next chapter are another. Accountants hold that when there are several acceptable methods or procedures that may be followed in a given situation, a concern may choose any one so long as the chosen method or procedure fairly reflects periodic income and is consistently followed thereafter. Consistency is a fundamental principle of accounting. Accountants strive for consistency so that there will be a high degree of comparability in the statements prepared period after period.

In their desire for consistency, however, accountants do not hold that a method once chosen can never be changed. Rather, they agree that if upon additional consideration it is decided that a different acceptable method from the one in use will better reflect periodic net income, a change may be made. But, in such a case accountants insist that adequate disclosure of the change and its effects be reported in the company's statements.

COST OR MARKET, THE LOWER

Over the years, the traditional rule for pricing an inventory has been "the lower of cost or market." This rule gained its wide acceptance because it placed an inventory on the balance sheet at a conservative figure, the lower of cost or replacement cost on the balance sheet date.

The argument advanced in support of this conservatism was that if the replacement cost of an inventory item had declined, then its selling price would probably have to be reduced, and since this might result in a loss, the loss should be anticipated and taken in the year of the price decline. It was a good argument; however, since selling prices do not always exactly and quickly follow cost prices, the application of the rule often resulted in misstating net income in the year of a price decline and again in the succeeding year. For example, suppose that a firm purchased merchandise costing $1,000; marked it up to a $1,500 selling price; and sold one half of the goods. The gross profit on the goods sold would be calculated as follows:

Sales...	$750
Cost of goods sold..................................	500
Gross profit..	$250

However, if the $500 replacement cost of the unsold goods had declined to $450 on the inventory date, an income statement based upon the traditional application of cost or market would show:

Sales..		$750
Cost of goods sold:		
Purchases......................................	$1,000	
Less: Ending inventory....................	450	550
Gross profit......................................		$200

The $450 would be a conservative balance sheet figure for the unsold goods. However, if these goods were sold at their full price early in the following year, the $450 inventory figure would have the erroneous effect of deferring $50 of income to the second year's income statement as follows:

Sales...	$750
Cost of goods sold:	
Beginning inventory............................	450
Gross profit..	$300

Merchants are prone to be slow in marking down goods; they normally try to sell merchandise at its full price if possible. Consequently, the illustrated situation was not uncommon. For this reason the lower of cost or market rule has been modified in recent years as follows for situations in which replacement costs are below actual costs.[2]

---

[2] *Ibid.*, pp. 30 and 31.

1. Goods should be placed on an inventory at cost, even though replacement cost is lower, if there has not been and there is not expected to be a decline in selling price.
2. Goods should at times be placed on an inventory at a price below their cost but above their replacement cost. For example, suppose the cost of an item that is normally bought for $20 and sold for $30 declines from $20 to $16, and its selling price declines from $30 to $27. The normal profit margin on this item is one third of its selling price. If this normal margin is applied to $27, the item should be placed on the inventory at two thirds of $27, or at $18. This is below cost but above replacement cost.
3. At times, goods should be placed on an inventory at a price below replacement cost. For example, assume that the goods described in the preceding paragraph can only be sold for $18.50 and that the disposal costs are estimated at $3. In this case the goods should be placed on the inventory at $15.50, a price below their replacement cost of $16.

CONSERVATISM

Balance sheet conservatism was once considered one of the first principles of accounting. The objective of such conservatism was to place each item on the balance sheet at a conservative figure. This in itself was commendable; but it was often carried too far and resulted not only in the misstatement of asset values but also in unconservative income statements. For example, as shown in the foregoing paragraphs, when prices are falling, the blind application of the unmodified lower of cost or market rule to inventories may result in a conservative balance sheet figure for inventories; but it may also result in an improper deferring of net income and in inaccurate income statements. Likewise, the too rapid write-off of fixed assets to depreciation, not uncommon in the past, in order to place these assets on the balance sheet at conservative figures resulted not only in the misstatement of the asset values but also in the overstatement of expenses and in misleading income statements. Consequently, today accountants recognize that balance sheet conservatism does not outweigh other factors. Today, accountants favor practices that result in the most accurate statement of net income.

ESTIMATED INVENTORIES

Retail Method. Retailers commonly use the so-called retail inventory method in estimating inventories for interim statements; and also commonly take their end-of-the-accounting-period inventories at marked selling prices and later reduce the sum of these selling prices to a cost basis by an application of the retail inventory method.

The use of the retail method in arriving at "cost" for an ending inventory eliminates the clerical work of costing the inventory items by referring to invoices and other data.

When the retail method is used in estimating an interim inventory, the information shown in Illustration 67 at both cost and retail (selling prices)

	At Cost	At Retail
Illustration 67		
Beginning inventory	*$11,500*	*$ 19,000*
Net purchases	*47,500*	*79,000*
Freight-in	*1,000*	
Additional markups		*2,000*
Goods available for sale	*$60,000*	*$100,000*
(Observe that cost is 60 percent of retail.)		
Sales		*$ 77,000*
Markdowns		*3,000*
Total		*$ 80,000*
Ending inventory at retail ($100,000 less $80,000)		*$ 20,000*
Ending inventory at cost (60 percent of $20,000)	*$12,000*	

is required. Also, when the retail inventory method is used, the calculations of Illustration 67 are made.

Most concerns have a normal markup or a normal percentage that is added to the cost of merchandise purchased in order to arrive at its selling price. In addition to the normal markup, goods of outstanding quality or style are commonly given an additional markup; and slow-moving goods are commonly marked down if they are not sold at regular prices. Normal markups appear in Illustration 67 as the difference between "Net purchases" at cost and at retail.

It has long been customary in the use of the retail inventory method to consider additional markups but not markdowns in computing the percentage relationship between goods available for sale at cost and at retail. The justification for this was and is that a more conservative figure for the ending inventory, a figure that approaches "cost or market, the lower," results. A further discussion of this phase of the retail inventory method is reserved for a more advanced text.

In the previous paragraphs, the retail method for estimating an interim inventory was demonstrated. The retail method is also used to reduce to its cost basis a physical inventory that has been taken at the marked retail prices of the inventoried goods. When this is done:

1. *The percentage relationship between goods available for sale during the period at cost and at retail is determined:*

	At Cost	At Retail
Beginning inventory......................	*$18,000*	*$ 27,800*
Net purchases...........................	*45,000*	*70,700*
Freight-in..............................	*2,000*	
Additional markups......................		*1,500*
Goods available for sale................	*$65,000*	*$100,000*

(Relationship af cost to retail is 65 percent.)

2. *A physical inventory of the unsold goods on hand is taken at the marked retail prices of the goods.*
   Assume that the physical inventory of the unsold goods at their marked retail prices totals $30,000.
3. *The relationship of the goods available for sale at cost and at retail is applied to the inventory.*

$$\textit{\$30,000} \times \textit{65\%} = \textit{\$19,500}$$

The ending inventory at cost is $19,500.

Gross Profit Method.   Often retail price information about beginning inventory, purchases, and markups is not kept. In such cases the retail inventory method cannot be used. However, if a company knows its normal gross profit margin; has information at cost in regard to its beginning inventory, net purchases, and freight-in; and knows the amount of its sales and sales returns, the company can estimate its ending inventory by the gross profit method.

For example, on March 27, the inventory of a company was destroyed by a fire. The company's average gross profit rate was 30 percent of net sales, and on the date of the fire the company's accounts showed the following balances:

Sales..	*$31,500*
Sales returns....................................	*1,500*
Inventory, January 1, 19—.......................	*12,000*
Net purchases....................................	*20,000*
Freight-in.......................................	*500*

Since the inventory was totally destroyed by fire, it was necessary for insurance purposes to estimate the inventory by the gross profit method as shown in Illustration 68.

Illustration 68

Goods available for sale:		
Inventory, January 1, 19—.....................		$12,000
Net purchases...............................	$20,000	
Freight-in..................................	500	20,500
Goods available for sale.....................		$32,500
Less: Estimated cost of goods sold:		
Sales.......................................	$31,500	
Sales returns...............................	1,500	
Net sales...................................	$30,000	
Less: Estimated gross profit (30% of $30,000)...	9,000	
Estimated cost of goods sold..................		21,000
Estimated March 27 inventory.................		$11,500

In addition to its use in insurance cases, the gross profit method is also commonly used by accountants in checking the probable accuracy of a physical inventory taken and priced in the normal way.

QUESTIONS FOR CLASS DISCUSSION

1. What occurs when revenues and expenses are properly matched?
2. At what point in the selling-collecting procedures of a company does a bad debt loss occur?
3. Why does the direct write-off method of accounting for bad debt losses commonly fail in the matching of revenues and expenses?
4. George Jacks purchased $50 of merchandise from Company A and another $50 from Company B. He did not pay either company and one year later, on February 28, both wrote off his uncollectible accounts. Company A used the direct write-off method, and Company B used the allowance method. Give the write-off entries.
5. In estimating their bad debt losses businesses commonly assume that "history will repeat." How is the assumption that "history will repeat" used in estimating bad debt losses?
6. A company has charge sales for a year amounting to $484,000. What amount of bad debt losses may the company expect to experience from these sales if its past bad debt loss record shows losses equal to one fourth of 1 percent of charge sales? Give the entry the company would use to record its estimated bad debt losses.
7. What is a contra account? Why are estimated bad debt losses credited to a contra account rather than to the Accounts Receivable controlling account?
8. Classify the following accounts: (*a*) Accounts Receivable, (*b*) Allowance for Bad Debts, and (*c*) Bad Debts Expense.
9. Ross Company estimated on December 31, 1966, that it would lose one half of 1 percent of its 1966 charge sales as bad debts. Ross Company's

1966 charge sales were $894,000. Give the entry to record the estimated loss from bad debts.

10. On March 22, Ross Company decided the $115 account of George Thomas was uncollectible, and wrote it off as a bad debt. On September 9, they received a $115 check from Thomas in full payment of the account. Give the general journal entries required to record these transactions.

11. In an audit of the accounts of James Huggins, the auditor found the balance of the Allowance for Bad Debts account to be $5,612. He thought this excessive. After a discussion with Mr. Huggins, it was decided to reduce the account balance to $2,500. Give the required journal entry.

12. What is the effect on the balance sheet and on the income statement of an excessive provision for bad debt losses?

13. Explain the meanings of the terms "cost" and "market" as they are applied to inventory items.

14. What is the meaning of the phrase "cost or market, the lower" as it is applied to inventory items?

15. Outline the essential features of a perpetual inventory system.

16. In taking a year-end physical inventory at the end of 1966, the clerks failed to count the items on one whole shelf. The inventory value of the items was $73. What was the effect of the omission on the 1966 balance sheet and income statement? What was the effect on the 1967 statements?

17. What are the meanings of the terms "Fifo" and "Lifo"?

18. If prices are rising, will the "Lifo" or the "Fifo" method of inventory valuation result in the higher gross profit?

19. What is a "regular markup"? A "markdown"?

PROBLEMS

Problem 10–1

The Allowance for Bad Debts account of Mesa Sales and Service had a $1,415 credit balance on the first day of the 1966 accounting period. During 1966, 1967, and early 1968 the concern completed the following bad debt transactions:

1966

Mar. 15   Wrote off the $285 uncollectible account of Walter Cross.

Oct. 11   Wrote off the $355 uncollectible account of Harold Brice.

Dec. 31   Provided by means of a bad debts adjusting entry an additional allowance for bad debts equal to one fourth of 1 percent of the $398,800 of 1966 charge sales.

   31   Closed the Bad Debts Expense account.

1967

Apr. 18   Wrote off the $265 uncollectible account of James Young.

July 21   Wrote off the $350 uncollectible account of Edward Dewitt.

Nov. 5   Learned of the bankruptcy of Edward Dewitt. Made a claim on his receiver in bankruptcy for the amount written off on July 21, and on November 27 received a $70 check from the receiver. A letter accompanying the check stated the amount was a final payment on the $350 owed and that no more would be paid. Reinstated the $70 portion of the account and recorded the receipt.

Dec. 31　Provided an additional allowance for bad debts equal to one fourth of 1 percent of the $418,400 of 1967 charge sales.

31　Closed the Bad Debts Expense account.

1968

Jan. 28　Upon completion of the 1967 audit, the auditor expressed the opinion that a $1,200 allowance for bad debts would be adequate to care for any losses from the December 31, 1967, balance of accounts receivable. George Hill, the proprietor of Mesa Sales and Service, ordered the balance of the Allowance for Bad Debts account reduced to this amount.

Required:

1. Prepare entries in general journal form to record the foregoing transactions.
2. Open an Allowance for Bad Debts account and a Bad Debts Expense account. Enter the January 1, 1966, opening balance in the Allowance for Bad Debts account. Post the portions of the foregoing entries that affect these two accounts.

Problem 10–2

The perpetual inventory record card of Item A2Y showed the following transactions in the item:

Jan. 1　Balance of Item A2Y: 5 units at a cost of $5 each.

2　Received 10 units costing $5.40 each.

6　Sold 3 units.

10　Sold 8 units. (Two lines are required in Sold columns to record the sale.)

14　Received 8 units costing $6 each.

18　Sold 3 units.

28　Sold 4 units.

Required:

1. Under the assumption that the inventory record card of Item A2Y is kept on a Fifo basis, enter the beginning balance and the foregoing transactions on a perpetual inventory record card similar to the one illustrated in this chapter.
2. Under the assumption that the inventory record card of Item A2Y is kept on a Lifo basis, enter the beginning balance and the foregoing transactions on a second inventory record card.
3. Assume that the sale of January 28 was on credit to Edward Slocum, that the units were sold at $7.50 each, and give the entry in general journal form to record the sale and the cost of the goods sold on a Lifo basis.

Problem 10–3

A concern sold 1,500 units of its product during a recent accounting period.

It began the period with 300 units, costing $50 each, and it made successive purchases of the product as follows:

400 units purchased at $60 each
500 units purchased at $70 each
400 units purchased at $80 each
400 units purchased at $60 each

Required:

1. Prepare a calculation showing the number and total cost of the units for sale during the period.
2. Then, under the assumption that the concern uses periodic inventories in determining costs, prepare calculations to show the portion of the total cost that should have been assigned to the units sold and the portion assigned to the ending inventory (*a*) first on a Fifo basis, (*b*) then on a Lifo basis, and (*c*) finally on an average cost basis.

Problem 10–4

The Westbend Store uses the retail method to estimate its inventories for interim income statement purposes, and the following information for the period January 1 through October 31 is available:

	At Cost	At Retail
January 1 inventory..........................	$ 17,210	$ 23,300
Purchases....................................	142,870	204,140
Freight-in...................................	2,110	
Purchases returns...........................	1,050	1,530
Sales..		207,780
Sales returns................................		2,440
Additional markups.........................		4,290
Markdowns...................................		1,240

Required:

Prepare a statement showing the calculation of the concern's October 31 inventory by the retail method.

Problem 10–5

Valley Wholesale Company sells candy to retailers. During April of last year the manager of the company felt the inventory in the company's warehouse looked unusually low; consequently, on April 24 a surprise physical inventory was taken. It showed $23,430 of merchandise in the warehouse. Further investigation revealed that a new nightwatchman, who had been hired early in January, and a friend had joined together to loot the warehouse. Fortunately the company followed the practice of bonding all employees, so there was no loss to the company. However, in order to collect from the bonding company, it was necessary to establish the amount of the loss. The following information was available:

1. Sales from January 1 through April 24, $192,215.
2. Sales returns for the same period, $365.
3. Purchases from January 1 through April 24, $124,585.
4. Purchases returns for the same period, $235.
5. Freight-in for the same period, $2,750.

6. Merchandise inventory, January 1, $43,500.
7. Average gross profit margin for the past three years, 32 percent.

Required:
Prepare a statement showing the estimated amount of inventory that should have been in the warehouse on April 24 and the estimated amount of goods stolen.

Problem 10–6
Last year on December 5 Desert Sales purchased 1,000 units of Item A5Z at $20 per unit. It priced the units for sale at $30 each and sold 500 during the remainder of the month. On December 31, at the end of the concern's annual accounting period, the replacement cost for a unit of Item A5Z was $15. However, regardless of the price decline, Desert Sales did not reduce the selling price of the remaining 500 units of Item A5Z, and during January of this year it sold these units at $30 each.

Required:
1. Prepare for Desert Sales a partial income statement for last year and another partial income statement for this year, showing in both cases sales, cost of goods sold, and gross profit from sales of Item A5Z under the assumption that the concern priced its last year's ending inventory of Item A5Z at the lower of cost or market.
2. Prepare a second set of income statements like the foregoing, only under the assumption that Desert Sales priced its last year's ending inventory of Item A5Z at cost.
3. Write a short statement telling which of the sets of statements more nearly reflects the concern's true profit situation.

CLASS EXERCISE

Exercise 10–1
A concern had a beginning inventory and purchased its Product X-7 as follows:

Jan. *1*	*Inventory*....................	*10 units @ $9.20*
Feb. *11*	*Purchased*....................	*40 units @ $10.00*
June *3*	*Purchased*....................	*20 units @ $10.60*
Aug. *26*	*Purchased*....................	*30 units @ $11.20*
Dec. *3*	*Purchased*....................	*20 units @ $11.00*

On December 31 there were 25 units of Product X-7 in the ending inventory. Determine cost assigned to this ending inventory on (*a*) an average cost basis, (*b*) a Fifo basis, and (*c*) a Lifo basis.

ALTERNATE PROBLEMS

Problem 10–1A
On the first day of its 1966 annual accounting period the Allowance for Bad Debts account of Tiptop Sales had a $1,370 credit balance. During the next 25 months the concern completed the following bad debt transactions:

1966

Apr.   5   Wrote off the $315 uncollectible account of Walter Brown.

Aug.   13   Wrote off the $485 uncollectible account of James Ross.

Dec.   31   Provided an addition to the allowance for bad debts equal to one half of 1 percent of the $278,000 1966 charge sales.

      31   Closed the Bad Debts Expense account.

1967

Mar.   16   Wrote off the $260 uncollectible account of Samuel Huggins.

Aug.   11   Samuel Huggins whose account was written off on March 16 delivered a $100 check in partial payment of the account to our office today. In a short visit he stated that his luck had recently changed and that he now expected to pay remainder of the account within the next 60 to 90 days.

Oct.   7   Wrote off the $545 uncollectible account of Paul Teppoe.

Nov.   12   Wrote off the $235 uncollectible account of William Barr.

Dec.   31   Provided an addition to the allowance for bad debts equal to one half of 1 percent of the $281,000 1967 charge sales.

      31   Closed the Bad Debts Expense account.

1968

Jan.   23   Upon completion of the 1967 audit, the auditor expressed the opinion that a $1,250 allowance for bad debts would be adequate to absorb any losses from the December 31, 1967, balance of accounts receivable. Mr. George Tipley, the owner of Tiptop Sales, ordered the balance of the Allowance for Bad Debts account reduced to that figure.

Required:

1. Open accounts for Allowance for Bad Debts and Bad Debts Expense. Enter the $1,370, January 1, 1966, balance in the Allowance for Bad Debts account.
2. Prepare entries in general journal form to record the foregoing transactions.
3. Post the portions of the entries that affect the Bad Debts Expense and Allowance for Bad Debts accounts.

Problem 10–2A

General Sales keeps perpetual inventory records, and during January the following transactions involving its Item X3X were completed:

Jan.   1   Balance of Item X3X: 12 units costing $6 each.

      4   Received 20 units costing $7 each.

      9   Sold 10 units.

    15   Sold 15 units.

    19   Received 20 units costing $8 each.

    24   Sold 5 units.

    29   Sold 16 units.

Required:

1. Under the assumption the concern keeps its inventory records on a Fifo basis, enter the beginning balance and the foregoing transactions on a

perpetual inventory record card similar to the one illustrated in this chapter.

2. Under the assumption the concern keeps its inventory records on a Lifo basis, enter the beginning balance and the foregoing transactions on a second inventory record card.

3. Assume the 16 units sold on January 29 were sold on credit to Frank Price at $12 each, and prepare a general journal entry to record the sale and the cost of goods sold on a last-in, first-out basis.

Problem 10–4A

Part 1. A store's year-end inventory taken at marked selling prices totaled $15,900, and the store wished to convert this amount to cost. The following information was available:

	At Cost	At Retail
January 1 inventory.......................	*$ 9,680*	*$ 14,710*
Purchases...................................	*73,450*	*115,980*
Purchases returns..........................	*1,860*	*2,790*
Freight-in..................................	*3,880*	
Additional markups.........................		*3,100*
Markdowns..................................		*1,860*

Required:

Prepare a statement showing the determination of the store's inventory at cost.

Part 2. Assume management of the store of this problem's Part 1 thought there might have been a small amount of shoplifting from the store during the year, and it wished a check on the approximate amount. The following additional information was available for making this check:

	At Retail
Year's sales....................................	*$116,240*
Sales returns..................................	*3,200*
Net sales...................................	*$113,040*

Required:

Prepare a statement showing the inventory shrinkage at retail and at cost from theft or other causes.

Problem 10–5A

On the night of May 3 of last year the store of Alfred Welsch burned. Everything except the accounting records, which were in a fireproof vault, was destroyed. Mr. Welsch filed an insurance claim that listed an inventory loss of $21,500. As an insurance adjuster you are called upon to verify this claim. The following information is available from the accounting records:

1. Merchandise inventory on January 1 of last year, $23,400.
2. Sales January 1 through May 3 of last year, $94,830.
3. Sales returns for same period, $2,230.
4. Purchases from January 1 through May 3 of last year, $61,520.

5. Purchases returns for same period, $1,260.
6. Freight-in for same period, $2,660.
7. Average gross profit on sales over the past three years, 30 percent.

Required:
Prepare a statement showing an estimate of the store's May 3 inventory.

Problem 10–6A

Ratchet Sales sells a single product, and it began its 1965 annual accounting period with 200 units of this product, costing $50 each, in its inventory. It also ended each of its 1965, 1966, and 1967 accounting periods with 200 units in each of the year-end inventories. During these years it made sales as follows:

1965 sales, 1,000 units at an average sales price of $115 per unit.
1966 sales, 1,000 units at an average sales price of $133 per unit.
1967 sales, 1,000 units at an average sales price of $138 per unit.

During the same three years it made these successive purchases of the product:

1965 Purchases		1967 Purchases	
200 units @ $55 = $11,000		200 units @ $70 = $14,000	
200 units @ 50 = 10,000		400 units @ 65 = 26,000	
300 units @ 60 = 18,000		200 units @ 65 = 13,000	
300 units @ 65 = 19,500		200 units @ 75 = 15,000	
1,000	$58,500	1,000	$68,000

1966 Purchases	
500 units @ $60 = $30,000	
300 units @ 70 = 21,000	
200 units @ 70 = 14,000	
1,000	$65,000

Required:
1. Prepare a series of income statements for Ratchet Sales showing for each year the sales, calculation of cost of goods sold, and gross profit from sales under the assumption the concern prices its ending inventories on a Fifo basis.
2. Prepare a second series of income statements under the assumption the concern prices its ending inventories on a Lifo basis.
3. Answer these questions: (*a*) Which method of inventory pricing results in smaller annual income tax liabilities for the concern? (*b*) Which method of inventory pricing better synchronizes costs and revenues?

DECISION PROBLEM 10A—JERRY'S
MAN'S SHOP

Jerry's Man's Shop had been in operation for five years. Jerry Mason, the proprietor, has been aggressive in expanding the clientele and the services of the business to its customers. He began with regular credit terms of 30 days. Three years ago he decided to liberalize credit terms and advertised preseason sales with credit terms as follows: Preseason spring sales from February 15 to March 15 with customer billing on July 1; preseason fall sales from August 15 to September 15 with billing made on January 1.

Mr. Mason is now concerned about the effects of the more liberal credit policy. He notes that there has been a rapid increase in bad debts written off (he uses the direct write-off method of handling bad accounts.) He realizes that his sales have increased materially over the five-year period, but wonders if the increase in sales justifies the substantial bad debt losses which he thinks stem largely from the liberalized credit policy.

The store's markup is 40 percent on selling price. The operating expense ratio, excluding bad debts, averages 30 percent on sales. (The operating expense ratio is the ratio of total operating expenses to net sales.) Data on sales and bad debts are as follows:

Year	Credit Sales	Bad Debts Written Off	Losses by Year of Sales
1	$ 50,000	$ 500	$ 750
2	80,000	1,100	1,280
3	110,000	1,700	3,300
4	140,000	2,800	4,060
5	160,000	3,400	4,960*

Includes $750 of estimated losses on present accounts receivable.

The last column in the above summary is the result of reclassification of bad debt losses by the year the goods were sold (including estimates of losses on present accounts receivable).

Required:

a) A schedule showing percentage of bad debt to credit sales by years; (b) a schedule computing net income from credit sales by years; and (c) a report to Mr. Mason answering his concern about the new credit policy and recommending any changes you consider desirable in accounting for bad debt losses.

DECISION PROBLEM 10B—MARCY STORES

Marcy Stores, Inc., began business ten years ago. Company officials have had numerous discussions as to the inventory pricing method their store should use. A committee was appointed to study the various pricing methods and to make a report. This committee is almost evenly divided between those favoring Fifo and those favoring Lifo. The following schedule presents the inventory at the end of each of the last ten years under both methods:

	Inventory	
Dec. 31	**Fifo Cost**	**Lifo Cost**
19(*a*)	$10,000	$10,200
(*b*)	11,200	10,800
(*c*)	11,500	11,100
(*d*)	10,800	10,900
(*e*)	10,300	10,800
(*f*)	12,000	10,700
(*g*)	12,200	10,400
(*h*)	13,800	10,500
(*i*)	15,000	11,900
(*j*)	15,800	12,700

To aid the president in coming to a decision on the inventory pricing method to choose, prepare a report giving answers to the following questions:

1. Which of the inventory methods reported the lower net income for the year 19(c)? 19(d)? 19(g)? 19(j)? (Note that where other revenues and costs remain the same, net income under each of the methods will vary as does the inventory; e.g., for the year 19(b), the inventory effect on cost of goods sold for Fifo was $10,000 minus $11,200, or a net credit to cost of goods sold of $1,200; Lifo effect on cost of goods sold was $10,200 minus $10,800, or a negative effect of $600; thus Fifo produced the smaller cost of goods sold and the larger reported net income. Note that this example deducts final inventory from beginning inventory to secure net effect on cost of goods sold, since the periodic inventory system is used by the firm.)
2. Which inventory basis reported the higher total net income for the first five years? For the next five years? For the entire ten-year period?
3. The committee reported that it has observed that during years in which prices rose that Fifo yielded a net income higher than by Lifo. Explain.
4. Using the committee's conclusion in 3, in which years did prices apparently rise and in which years did prices apparently fall? Explain.

11

Accounting for
Fixed Assets
and Depreciation

A FIXED ASSET is an asset having a productive or service life longer than a single accounting period and that is held for use in the production or sale of other assets or services.

A productive or service life longer than one accounting period distinguishes a fixed asset from an item of supplies. The contribution to production of an item of supplies is or is considered to be consumed in a single accounting period, and its cost is charged to the period in which it is consumed. A fixed asset's contribution continues beyond a single period, and if revenue and expenses are matched, its cost must be allocated to the several periods of its use.

A fixed asset's use in the production or sale of other assets and services distinguishes such an asset from an item of merchandise or an investment. For example, an item of office equipment or factory machinery held for sale by a dealer is merchandise to the dealer. Likewise, land purchased and held for future expansion but presently unused is classified as a long-term investment. Neither is a fixed asset until put to use in the production or sale of other assets or services.

Fixed assets may be divided into two large classes:

a) Physical properties held more or less permanently, not for the purpose of sale, but for use in carrying out the regular activities of the business. Examples are land, buildings, furniture and fixtures, machinery, etc.

b) Natural resources subject to depletion through mining, pumping, or cutting the natural deposit or growth comprising the resource. Examples are mineral, coal, and oil deposits, growing timber, etc.

Fixed assets of the first class are the primary interest of this chapter, but both kinds are discussed.

COST OF A FIXED ASSET

The acquisition of a fixed asset is recorded by debiting a fixed asset account for its cost. Cost includes the invoice price plus any additional expenditures incurred in getting the asset in place and ready to operate or use. For example, the cost of a factory machine includes its invoice price, less any discount for cash, plus freight, truckage, and unpacking. In addition, any special concrete bases or foundations, electrical or power connections, and adjustments needed to place the machine in operation are also part of its cost. In short, the cost of a fixed asset includes all normal costs incurred in getting the asset ready to produce. All of these costs are debited to the account of the fixed asset as they are incurred.

NATURE OF DEPRECIATION

When a fixed asset is purchased, in effect a fund of usefulness that will contribute to production throughout the life of the asset is acquired. Since the life of any fixed asset (other than land) is limited, this fund of usefulness is also limited and will in effect be consumed by the end of the asset's useful life. Therefore, depreciation, as the term is used in accounting, is nothing more than the expiration of a fixed asset's fund of usefulness; and the recording of depreciation is a process of allocating and charging the cost of this fund to the accounting periods that benefit from its use.

In accounting, land as a fixed asset is considered to have an unlimited life and a fund of usefulness that remains undiminished throughout its life. Consequently, land is usually assumed not to depreciate.

PRODUCTIVE LIFE OF A FIXED ASSET

The productive or service life of a fixed asset is the period of time its owner uses it in the production or sale of other assets or services. This may not be the same as the asset's potential life. For example, typewriters have a potential ten- or twelve-year life; however, if a particular company finds from a production-cost view that it is wise to trade its old typewriters on new ones every three years, in that company typewriters have a three-year service life. Furthermore, the cost of new typewriters less their trade-in value, the cost of their fund of usefulness to this business, should be charged to depreciation expense over this three-year period.

At the time of purchase the productive life of a fixed asset must be predicted so that its depreciation may be allocated to the several periods in which it will be used. Predicting or estimating service life is sometimes difficult because several factors are often involved. Wear and tear and the action of the elements determine the useful life of some assets. However, two additional factors, *inadequacy* and *obsolescence*, often need be considered. When a business acquires fixed assets, it should acquire assets of a size and capacity to take care of its foreseeable needs; however, a business often grows more rapidly than anticipated. In such cases its fixed assets may become too small for the productive demands of the business long before they wear out. When this happens, inadequacy is said to have taken place. Inadequacy cannot easily be predicted. Obsolescence, like inadequacy, is also difficult to foretell. The exact occurrence of new inventions and improvements normally cannot be predicted; yet new inventions and improvements often cause an asset to become obsolete and make it wise to discard the obsolete asset long before it wears out.

A company that has previously used a particular type of asset may estimate the service life of a like new asset from past experience. A company without previous experience with a particular asset must depend upon the experience of others or upon engineering studies and judgment. The Bureau of Internal Revenue publishes a booklet, *Bulletin F*, that gives estimated service lives for hundreds of new assets. Many businessmen refer to this bulletin in estimating the life of a new asset.

SALVAGE VALUE

When a fixed asset has a salvage value, the cost of its fund of usefulness is its cost minus its salvage value.

The salvage value of a fixed asset is the portion of its cost that is recovered at the end of its productive life. Some assets such as typewriters, trucks, and automobiles are traded in on similar new assets at the end of their service lives. The salvage values of such assets are their trade-in values. Other assets may have no trade-in value and little or no salvage value. For example, at the end of its service life, some machinery can be sold only as scrap metal. The salvage value of such assets is the amount received from the sale of the scrap metal.

When the disposal of a fixed asset involves certain costs, as in the wrecking of a building, the salvage value is the net amount realized from the sale of the asset. The net amount realized is the amount received for the asset less its disposal cost.

Obviously, when a fixed asset is purchased, its exact salvage value is difficult to estimate. Yet, salvage value must be estimated so that depreciation can be estimated and recorded.

ALLOCATING DEPRECIATION

Many methods of allocating a fixed asset's total depreciation to the several accounting periods in its service life have been suggested and are used. Four of the more common are the *straight-line method,* the *units of production method,* the *declining balance method,* and the *sum of the years' digits method.*

Straight-Line Method.   When the straight-line method is used in allocating depreciation, the cost of the asset minus its estimated salvage value is divided by the estimated number of accounting periods in its productive life. The result of this calculation is the estimated amount the asset depreciates each period. For example, if a machine costs $550, has an estimated service life of five years, and an estimated salvage value of $50, its depreciation per year by the straight-line method is $100 and is calculated as follows:

$$\frac{Cost - Salvage}{\substack{Service\ Life \\ in\ Years}} = \frac{\$550 - \$50}{5} = \$100$$

Note that the straight-line method allocates an equal share of the cost of an asset's fund of usefulness or an equal share of its total depreciation to each accounting period in its life.

Units of Production Method.   The primary purpose of recording depreciation is to charge each accounting period in which an asset is used with a fair share of depreciation. The straight-line method charges an equal share to each period; and when fixed assets are used about the same amount in each accounting period, this method rather fairly allocates total depreciation. However, in some lines of business the use of certain fixed assets varies greatly from accounting period to accounting period. For example, a contractor may use a particular piece of construction equipment for a month and then not use it again for many months. For such an asset, since use and contribution to revenue may not be uniform from period to period, the straight-line method may not be fair. For such an asset the units of production method often more fairly allocates depreciation.

When the units of production method is used in allocating depreciation, the cost of an asset's fund of usefulness is divided by the estimated units of product it will produce during its entire service life. This division gives depreciation per unit of product. Then the amount the asset depreciates in any one accounting period is determined by multiplying the units of product produced in that period by depreciation per unit. Units of product may be expressed as units of product or in any other unit of measure such as hours of use or miles of use. For example, a delivery truck costing $4,800 is estimated to have an $800 salvage value. If it is also estimated that during the truck's service life it will be driven 50,000 miles, the depreciation per mile, or the depreciation per unit of product, is $0.08. This is calculated as follows:

$$\frac{Cost - Salvage\ Value}{Estimated\ Units\ of\ Production} = \frac{Depreciation\ per}{Unit\ of\ Product}$$

or

$$\frac{\$4,800 - \$800}{50,000\ Miles} = \$0.08\ per\ Mile$$

If these estimates are correct, and the truck is driven 20,000 miles during its first year, the depreciation for the first year is $1,600. This is 20,000 miles at $0.08 per mile. If the truck is driven 15,000 miles in the second year, the depreciation for the second year is 15,000 times $0.08, or $1,200.

Declining Balance Method. The Revenue Act of 1954 liberalized depreciation accounting by permitting depreciation methods for tax purposes which result in higher depreciation charges during the early years of a fixed asset's life. The declining balance method is one of these. Under the declining balance method, depreciation of up to twice the straight-line rate, without considering salvage value, may be applied each year to the declining book value of a new fixed asset having an estimated life of three years or more. If this method is followed and twice the straight-line rate is used, the amount charged each year as depreciation expense on a fixed asset is determined by (1) calculating a straight-line depreciation rate for the asset without considering the asset's salvage value; (2) doubling this rate; and then (3) at the end of each year in the asset's life, applying this doubled rate to the asset's remaining book value. (The book value of a fixed asset is its cost less accumulated depreciation; it is the value shown for the asset on the books.)

If this method is used to charge depreciation on a $10,000 new asset that has an estimated life of five years: (Step 1) A straight-line depreciation rate is calculated by dividing $10,000 by five (years) to determine the straight-line annual amount of depreciation, $2,000; and then dividing the $2,000 by $10,000 to determine the straight-line rate of 20 percent. Next (Step 2) this rate is doubled; and then (Step 3) annual depreciation charges are calculated as in the following table:

Year	Calculation	Annual Depreciation Expense	Remaining Book Value
1................	40% of $10,000	$4,000.00	$6,000.00
2................	40% of 6,000	2,400.00	3,600.00
3................	40% of 3,600	1,440.00	2,160.00
4................	40% of 2,160	864.00	1,296.00
5................	40% of 1,296	518.40	777.60

Under the declining balance method the book value of a fixed asset never reaches zero; consequently, when the asset is sold, exchanged, or scrapped, any remaining book value is used in determining the gain or loss on the disposal. In passing it should be noted that an asset may not be depreciated beyond its salvage value under this method.

Sum of the Years' Digits Method. Under this reducing fraction method, the years in an asset's service life are added and their sum becomes the denominator of a series of fractions used in allocating total depreciation to the periods in the asset's service life. The numerators of the fractions are the years in the asset's life in their reverse order.

For example, if the sum of the years' digits method is to be used in allocating depreciation on a machine costing $7,000, having an estimated life of five years, and having an estimated salvage value of $1,000, the sum of the years' digits in the life of the asset is calculated:

$$1 \ + \ 2 \ + \ 3 \ + \ 4 \ + \ 5 \ = \ 15$$

and then annual depreciation charges are calculated as in the following table:

Year	Calculation	Annual Depreciation Expense
1............................	5/15 of $6,000	$2,000
2............................	4/15 of 6,000	1,600
3............................	3/15 of 6,000	1,200
4............................	2/15 of 6,000	800
5............................	1/15 of 6,000	400
		$6,000

The reducing charge methods (both the declining balance and the sum of the years' digits methods) are advocated by an increasing number of accountants who claim that they give a more equitable "use charge" for long-lived fixed assets than do other methods. These accountants point out, for example, that as assets grow older, repairs and maintenance increase. Therefore, smaller amounts of depreciation computed by a reducing charge method, when added to the increasing repair costs, give a somewhat more equitable total expense charge to match against revenue than do most other methods.

Also, they point out that as an asset grows older, in some instances its revenue production is materially reduced. For example, rentals from an apartment building are normally higher in the earlier years of its life but will decline as the building becomes less attractive and less modern. Certainly in this case, a more reasonable allocation of cost would provide heavier charges in the earlier years and lighter charges in the later years of the asset's life.

The foregoing are sound reasons for the use under applicable conditions of reducing charge methods of allocating depreciation. However, a tax reason rather than sound accounting theory is probably more responsible for the increase in their popularity. The tax reason may be described as follows: Reducing charge methods of allocating depreciation normally result in the greatest amounts of depreciation expense during the early years of an asset's use. This in turn means smaller taxable incomes and taxes; and in effect it also means the interest-free use for a period of time of the amounts that would otherwise be paid in taxes under, for example, a straight-line method. Of course these interest-free amounts must in effect be repaid in higher taxes during later years of the asset's use.

RECORDING DEPRECIATION

Depreciation on the several classes of a company's fixed assets is recorded at the end of each accounting period by means of adjusting entries. This subject was discussed in an earlier chapter and needs no further amplification here.

DEPRECIATION ON THE BALANCE SHEET

In order to present as clearly as possible all the facts concerning the fixed assets of a business, both the cost of such assets and their accumulated depreciation by functional classes are commonly shown on the balance sheet. For example, the fixed assets of a merchandising concern may be shown as follows:

```
Fixed Assets:
    Store equipment . . . . . . . . .   $ 4,000
        Less: Accumulated depreciation.    1,500   $ 2,500
    Office equipment. . . . . . . . .   $ 1,800
        Less: Accumulated depreciation.      600     1,200
    Building. . . . . . . . . . . . .   $16,000
        Less: Accumulated depreciation.    1,820    14,180
    Land. . . . . . . . . . . . . . .              3,000
        Total Fixed Assets. . . . . .            $20,880
```

When fixed assets are shown in this manner, a balance sheet reader can see both the cost and the accumulated depreciation to the balance sheet date of each class of assets, and a much better picture is obtained than if only net undepreciated costs are given. When both costs and accumulated depreciation are shown, the reader can tell not only something of the physical adequacy of the assets but also something of their age. For example, $50,000 of assets with $45,000 accumulated depreciation are quite different from $5,000 of new assets. Yet, the net undepreciated cost is the same in both cases.

BALANCE SHEET FIXED ASSET VALUES

From the discussion thus far the student should recognize that the recording of depreciation is not primarily a valuing process, rather it is a process of allocating the costs of fixed assets to the several accounting periods that benefit from their use.[1] Furthermore, he should recognize that because the recording of depreciation is an allocating process rather than a valuing process, balance sheets show for fixed assets unallocated costs or undepreciated costs rather than market values.

The fact that balance sheets show undepreciated costs rather than market values seems to disturb many beginning accounting students. It should not. When a balance sheet is prepared, normally the company for which it is prepared has no intention of selling its fixed assets; consequently, the market values of these assets are of no great significance. The student should recognize that when a balance sheet is prepared, the balance sheet is prepared under the assumption the company for which it is prepared is a going concern that will continue in business long enough to recover the costs of its fixed assets through the sale of its products.

The assumption that a company is a going concern that will continue in business long enough to recover its fixed asset costs through the sale of its products is known in accounting as the *going concern concept*. It is a concept the student or any balance sheet reader should bear in mind as he reads a balance sheet.

DEPLETION

Natural resources such as timberlands, mineral deposits, and oil reserves, which are known as *wasting assets*, are carried in the accounts at cost less accumulated *depletion*. The amount such assets are depleted each year by cutting, mining, or pumping is commonly calculated on a "units of production" basis. For example, if a mine having an estimated 1,000,000 tons of available ore is purchased for $500,000, the depletion charge per ton of ore mined is $0.50 ($500,000 ÷ 1,000,000). Furthermore, if 150,000 tons of ore are mined during the first year, the depletion charge for the year is $75,000 (150,000 × $0.50); and the charge is recorded as follows:

Dec.	31	Depletion..........................	75,000.00	
		Accumulated Depletion, Mine....		75,000.00
		To record depletion of ore body resulting from mining 150,000 tons of ore.		

---

[1] *Accounting Terminology Bulletin No. 1*, "Review and Résumé" (New York: American Institute of Certified Public Accountants, 1953), p. 25.

On the balance sheet prepared at the end of the first year, the mine would appear at its $500,000 cost less $75,000 accumulated depletion.

If all of the 150,000 tons were sold by the end of the year, the entire $75,000 depletion charge would appear on the income statement as the depletion cost of the ore sold. However, if a portion remained unsold and on hand at the year-end, the depletion cost of the unsold ore would appear on the balance sheet as a portion of the cost of the unsold ore inventory, a current asset.

DISCARDING AND SELLING A FIXED ASSET

Sooner or later a fixed asset wears out, becomes obsolete, or becomes inadequate. When this occurs, the asset is discarded. If the service life and salvage value estimates were correct, the discarded asset may be sold for its salvage value. For example, a small drill press costing $900 and having an estimated four-year service life and an estimated $100 salvage value depreciates $200 each year of its life. At the end of its fourth and last year the drill press has a $100 book value, and the accounts that show its accounting history and book value appear as follows:

Machinery		*Accumulated Depreciation Machinery*	
Jan. 2, '63 *900*			*Dec. 31, '63* *200*
			Dec. 31, '64 *200*
			Dec. 31, '65 *200*
			Dec. 31, '66 *200*

If at the end of its fourth year the drill press is discarded and sold for its book value, the entry to record the sale is:

Jan.	*2*	*Cash...*	*100.00*	
		Accumulated Depreciation, Machinery.....	*800.00*	
		Machinery............................		*900.00*
		Sold machinery at book value.		

In the foregoing entry the debit to the accumulated depreciation account and the credit to the Machinery account remove the machine from the accounts and end its accounting history.

DISCARDING AND SELLING FIXED ASSETS AT A GAIN OR A LOSS

Exactly estimating salvage value or exactly estimating service life is not easy. Normally one estimate or the other is incorrect. When a fixed asset is discarded and sold, and either its salvage value or service life was incorrectly estimated, a book gain or a book loss is incurred. For example, if the drill press previously illustrated as having an estimated $100 salvage value is sold at the end of its service life for only $60, a $40 book loss is incurred. The entry to record the sale at a loss is:

Jan.	*2*	*Cash*..	*60.00*	
		Loss on the Sale of Fixed Assets.............	*40.00*	
		Accumulated Depreciation, Machinery......	*800.00*	
		Machinery...........................		*900.00*
		Sold a drill press at a loss.		

Or assume that the drill press is sold at the end of its service life for $125. If the machine is sold for $125, a $25 book gain is made. This is recorded:

Jan.	*2*	*Cash*..	*125.00*	
		Accumulated Depreciation, Machinery......	*800.00*	
		Machinery...........................		*900.00*
		Gain on the Sale of Fixed Assets........		*25.00*
		Sold a drill press at a profit.		

To illustrate further, assume that an error is made in estimating service life and the drill press previously illustrated wears out and must be discarded at the end of the third year in its estimated four-year service life. At this time the asset has a $300 book value; this is its $900 cost less three years' depreciation of $600. If the drill press is sold at the end of its third year for its estimated $100 salvage value, the entry to record the sale is:

Jan.	*2*	*Cash*..	*100.00*	
		Loss on the Sale of Fixed Assets...........	*200.00*	
		Accumulated Depreciation, Machinery....	*600.00*	
		Machinery...........................		*900.00*
		Sold a drill press at a loss.		

If, on the other hand, the life estimate of the drill press is too short, the machine will be in use after the end of its estimated service life. Normally, in such a situation, no depreciation is charged for the years after the end of the estimated life, and the asset is carried on the books at its salvage value. When the asset is finally discarded, a gain or loss is recorded if the asset is sold for more or less than its salvage value.

FIXED ASSET GAINS AND LOSSES ON THE INCOME STATEMENT

When a fixed asset is sold, it is normally sold at either a gain or loss. These gains and losses are recorded at the time of each sale in either a gain or loss account; and at the end of each period these accounts are closed to Income Summary, and their balances appear on the income statement, at the very end, in a section called "Extraneous gains and losses." Here gains are added and losses are subtracted from income from operations.

DISCARDING FIXED ASSETS BECAUSE OF DAMAGE

Occasionally, before the end of its service life, a fixed asset may be wrecked in an accident or destroyed by fire; and in such cases a loss occurs. If an uninsured asset is totally destroyed in an accident such as a fire, the entry to record the loss is:

Jan.	*3*	*Loss from Fire*............................	*500.00*	
		Accumulated Depreciation, Machinery....	*400.00*	
		Machinery...........................		*900.00*
		To record the accidental destruction of machinery.		

If the loss is partially covered by insurance, the money received from the insurance company is debited to Cash and the loss is less. The entry to record an accidental loss partially covered by insurance is:

Jan.	*3*	*Cash*...................................	*350.00*	
		Loss from Fire........................	*150.00*	
		Accumulated Depreciation, Machinery....	*400.00*	
		Machinery........................		*900.00*
		To record the destruction of machinery and the receipt of insurance compensation.		

DEPRECIATION FOR PARTIAL YEARS

In all of the illustrations thus far the assumption has been that the assets were purchased and discarded at either the beginning or end of an accounting period. This is an assumption that seldom occurs. Businessmen normally buy assets when needed and sell or discard these assets when they are no longer usable or needed; and the purchases and sales are normally made without regard for time. Because of this, depreciation must often be calculated for partial years. For example, a truck costing $2,600 and having an estimated five-year service life and a $600 estimated salvage value is purchased on October 8, 1962. If the yearly accounting period ends on December 31, depreciation for three months must be recorded on this truck. Three months are three twelfths of a year. Consequently, three months' depreciation on this truck is calculated as follows:

$$\frac{\$2,600 - \$600}{5} \times \frac{3}{12} = \$100$$

In this illustration, depreciation is calculated for a full three months, even though the asset was purchased on October 8. Depreciation is an estimate; therefore calculation to the nearest full month is usually considered sufficiently accurate. This means that depreciation is usually calculated for a full month on assets purchased before the fifteenth of the month. Likewise, depreciation for the month in which an asset is purchased is normally disregarded if the asset is purchased after the middle of the month.

The entry to record depreciation for three months on the truck purchased on October 8 is:

Dec.	*31*	*Depreciation Expense, Delivery Trucks*.....	*100.00*	
		Accumulated Depr., Delivery Trucks...		*100.00*
		To record depreciation for three months on the delivery truck.		

On December 31, 1963, and at the end of each of the following three years, a journal entry to record a full year's depreciation on this truck is made. This journal entry is:

Dec.	*31*	*Depreciation Expense, Delivery Trucks*.....	*400.00*	
		Accumulated Depr., Delivery Trucks...		*400.00*
		To record depreciation for one year on the delivery truck.		

After the December 31, 1966, depreciation entry is recorded, the accounts showing the history of this truck appear as follows:

Delivery Trucks		Accumulated Depreciation, Delivery Trucks	
Oct. 8, '62 2,600		Dec. 31, '62 100	
		Dec. 31, '63 400	
		Dec. 31, '64 400	
		Dec. 31, '65 400	
		Dec. 31, '66 400	

If this truck is disposed of during 1967, two entries must be made to record the disposal. The first records 1967 depreciation to the date of disposal, and the second records the actual disposal. For example, assume that the truck is sold for $900 on June 24, 1967. To record the disposal, depreciation for six months (depreciation to the nearest full month) must first be recorded. The entry for this is:

June	24	Depreciation Expense, Delivery Trucks.	200.00	
		Accumulated Depr., Delivery Trucks		200.00
		To record depreciation for one half year on the delivery truck.		

After making the entry to record depreciation to the date of sale, a second entry to record the actual sale is made. This entry is:

June	24	Cash..................................	900.00	
		Accumulated Depr., Delivery Trucks...	1,900.00	
		Delivery Trucks..................		2,600.00
		Gain on the Sale of Fixed Assets....		200.00
		To record the sale of a delivery truck.		

EXCHANGING FIXED ASSETS

Some fixed assets are sold at the ends of their useful lives. Others, such as machinery, automobiles, and office equipment, may be traded on new, up-to-date assets of a like nature. When a fixed asset is traded in on a new fixed asset, normally either a book gain or loss is experienced. If the trade-in allowance received is greater than the book value of the traded asset, a book gain is experienced; and if the trade-in allowance is less than the traded asset's book value, a book loss is incurred. When such gains and losses are material in amount, they should be entered in the accounts as gains and losses. Immaterial gains and losses may be absorbed into the cost basis of the new asset.

Recording Material Gains and Losses. When a material gain or loss is experienced on the exchange of a fixed asset, the gain or loss should be recognized in the accounts as a gain or a loss. For example, a machine which cost $18,000 and upon which $15,000 depreciation has accumulated is traded in at $5,500 on a like new machine having a $21,000 cash price. The book value of the old machine is $3,000. Therefore, if a $5,500 trade-in allowance is received, there is a $2,500 book gain on the transaction. The book value and gain are calculated:

> *Cost of old machine.............................$18,000*
> *Less: Accumulated depreciation................ 15,000*
> *Book value....................................... $ 3,000*
>
> *Trade-in allowance on new machine.............. $ 5,500*
> *Less: Book value of old machine................ 3,000*
> *Book gain on the exchange...................... $ 2,500*

When the exchange is made, the entry to record it is:

Jan.	5	*Machinery...................................*	21,000.00	
		Accumulated Depreciation, Machinery........	15,000.00	
		Machinery.............................		18,000.00
		Gain on the Exchange of Fixed Assets......		2,500.00
		Cash...............................		15,500.00
		Exchanged old machine and cash for a like new machine.		

Or to illustrate further, assume that the old $18,000 machine with $15,000 accumulated depreciation is traded in at $1,000 on the new machine having a $21,000 cash price. If the old machine is traded at $1,000, a $2,000 book loss is incurred. The loss is calculated:

> *Book value of old machine.........................$3,000*
> *Less: Trade-in allowance on new machine....... 1,000*
> *Book loss on the exchange.......................$2,000*

If the old machine is traded at a loss, the entry to record the exchange is:

Jan.	*5*	*Machinery*...................................	*21,000.00*	
		Loss on the Exchange of Machinery...........	*2,000.00*	
		Accumulated Depreciation, Machinery........	*15,000.00*	
		Machinery.............................		*18,000.00*
		Cash.................................		*20,000.00*
		Exchanged old machine and cash for a like new machine.		

Income Tax Method of Recording Fixed Asset Exchanges. Although a fixed asset exchange usually results in either a book gain or loss, the Internal Revenue Code does not recognize, excepting in unusual circumstances, such gains and losses as gains and losses for tax purposes. According to the Internal Revenue Code, when an old asset is traded in on a like new asset, the cost basis of the new asset is the sum of (1) the cash given plus (2) the book value of the old asset.

For example, if a typewriter which cost $180 and upon which $150 depreciation has accumulated is traded in at $45 on the purchase of a new $210 typewriter, the cost basis of the new typewriter is calculated for tax purposes as follows:

Cash paid ($210 less the $45 trade-in allowance)......$165
Book value of old typewriter ($180 less $150).......... 30
Income tax basis of new asset for depreciation, sale,
*   or disposal.......................................$195*

If this tax basis is used in recording the exchange, the entry is:

Jan.	*5*	*Office Equipment*.........................	*195.00*	
		Accumulated Depr., Office Equipment........	*150.00*	
		Office Equipment......................		*180.00*
		Cash.................................		*165.00*
		Traded old typewriter and cash for a new typewriter.		

Or to illustrate further, if rather than a $45 trade-in allowance, only a $20 allowance is received when the foregoing typewriter is exchanged, the cost basis of the new typewriter for tax purposes is:

Cash paid ($210 less a $20 trade-in allowance)........$190
Book value of old typewriter ($180 less $150).......... 30
Income tax basis of new asset for depreciation, sale,
*   or disposal.......................................$220*

And if this basis is used in recording the typewriter exchange, the entry is:

Jan.	*5*	*Office Equipment*.....................	*220.00*	
		Accumulated Depr., Office Equipment.....	*150.00*	
		Office Equipment....................		*180.00*
		Cash............................		*190.00*
		Exchanged old typewriter and cash for a new typewriter.		

When an asset having a $30 book value is traded at $45, there is a $15 book gain; likewise, there is a $10 book loss when the asset is traded at $20. However, observe in the foregoing calculations and entries that the application of the tax rule results in the nonrecognition of either the gain in the first instance or the loss in the second. The effect, when the tax rule is applied, is that the gain and the loss are absorbed into the cost basis of the new asset.

The reason for the tax rule is that it prevents a taxpayer from taking an unfair tax advantage by shifting taxable earnings from one year to the next by means of an arranged book gain or loss on an exchange. (A book loss for a taxpayer, for example, can be arranged if the dealer and the taxpayer agree to reduce by equal amounts both the normal trade-in allowance on the traded asset and the new asset's quoted price.)

At first glance it might seem that nonrecognition of gains and losses works a hardship when errors in estimating depreciation are made. However, this is usually not true. For example, when an asset is exchanged at a loss, the loss may not be counted as a loss for tax purposes; it is in fact added to the cost of the new asset. This causes the new asset to be taken into the records at a higher cost; the higher cost results in greater depreciation expense throughout the life of the new asset; and the greater depreciation expense offsets the unrecognized loss on the exchange. In the end, through greater depreciation expense, owner equity is reduced by the amount of the exchange loss. Likewise, in the end through reduced depreciation expense on the new asset, a book gain on an exchange increases owner equity by the amount of the unrecognized gain.

Materiality and the Choice of Methods. When a fixed asset is traded in on a like new asset, there is normally either a book gain or loss on the exchange; but, as previously stated, the Internal Revenue Code does not recognize such gains and losses for tax purposes. Consequently, if a gain or a loss is recorded as such at the time of an exchange, two sets of depreciation expense records must be kept throughout the life of the new asset, one for use in determining net income for accounting purposes and an additional set for determining the depreciation deduction for tax purposes.

Obviously keeping two records is more costly than one. Yet, when an exchange results in a material gain or loss, the gain or loss should be recorded and two sets of records kept. On the other hand, when an exchange results in an immaterial gain or loss, it is permissible to avoid the two sets of records by using the income tax method to record the transaction. The use of the tax method when there is a minor exchange gain or loss is permissible under the accounting *principle of materiality*.

The principle of materiality holds that strict adherence to any accounting principle is not required if the cost to adhere is proportionally great and the lack of adherence will not materially affect reported periodic net income. For example, if there is a $25 loss in trading an item of office equipment, using the income tax method to record the exchange would not materially affect the average company's statements. On the other hand, recording the loss and thereafter keeping two sets of depreciations records would be costly. Consequently, the income tax method is commonly used in such cases.

REPAIRS AND REPLACEMENTS

Fixed asset repairs and replacements fall into three classifications: (1) ordinary repairs and replacements, (2) extraordinary repairs and replacements made necessary by neglected ordinary repairs in previous accounting periods, and (3) extraordinary repairs and replacements made to extend an asset's useful life beyond that originally estimated.

Expenditures for ordinary repairs and replacements are necessary to maintain an asset in good operating condition. A building must be painted and its roof repaired or a machine must be repaired and small parts replaced. Any expenditures made to maintain a fixed asset in its normal good state of repair are considered ordinary repairs and replacements. Expenditures for ordinary repairs are current expenses and appear on the income statement as deductions from revenue.

When ordinary repairs are neglected, expenses of the accounting period of neglect are understated. Therefore, when this neglect is made good in a future period by extraordinary repairs, their cost should be debited to the proprietor's Capital account as a correction of income closed to this account during the periods in which repairs were neglected.

Sometimes extraordinary repairs and replacements are made, not because of neglected past repairs, but to extend an asset's useful life. When this occurs, the costs should be debited to the repaired asset's accumulated depreciation account under the assumption that they make good the past depreciation, add to the asset's life, and benefit future periods. Since such repairs do not increase what the asset had when new, their cost should not be debited directly to and thereby increase the balance of the fixed asset account.

BETTERMENTS

It is important not to confuse ordinary repairs and replacements with *betterments*. A betterment may be defined as the replacement of an existing asset or asset portion with an improved or superior asset or portion, usually at a cost materially in excess of the replaced item. Replacing old cast iron pipe with copper pipe, removing an old motor and replacing it with a larger, more powerful one, replacing wooden with steel beams in a building are illustrations of betterments. When a betterment is made, its cost should be debited to the improved asset's account and depreciated over the remaining service life of the asset. Also, the cost and applicable depreciation of the replaced unit or asset should be removed from the accounts.

CAPITAL AND REVENUE EXPENDITURES

A *revenue expenditure* is one that should appear on the current income statement as an expense and a deduction from the period's revenue. An expenditure for ordinary repairs is an example of such an expenditure.

Expenditures for betterments and for the kind of extraordinary repairs that lengthen the estimated life of an asset should appear on the balance sheet as increases in asset book values; and as a result, are examples of what are called *capital expenditures* or balance sheet expenditures which benefit future periods.

FIXED ASSET RECORDS

Fixed assets commonly appear on a balance sheet in functional groups. For example, on a store's balance sheet the unrecovered cost of all store equipment is commonly listed as one amount, the unrecovered cost of office equipment is listed as another amount, and the unrecovered cost of the delivery equipment is listed as still another amount. As a result, the General Ledger of such a store will normally have a separate fixed asset account and a separate accumulated depreciation account for each of its functional asset groups. It will normally have an Office Equipment account and an Accumulated Depreciation, Office Equipment account, and it will normally have a Store Equipment account and an Accumulated Depreciation, Store Equipment account. In short, the store will normally have a separate fixed asset account and a separate accumulated depreciation account for each functional group of assets it owns. Furthermore, all transactions affecting any one of the functional groups are recorded in the asset and the accumulated depreciation accounts of that group. For example, the purchase, depreciation, exchange, or sale of all office equipment is recorded in the one office equipment and its related accumulated depreciation account.

Some years ago the functional general ledger fixed asset accounts and their related accumulated depreciation accounts were often the only fixed asset records maintained by any but larger concerns. However, today because of income tax regulations any business that reports a deduction from income for depreciation or reports a gain or loss on a fixed asset sale must be able to substantiate such items with detailed records. No specific kind of records is required, but normally each general ledger fixed asset account and its related accumulated depreciation account become controlling accounts controlling detailed subsidiary records. For example, the Office Equipment account and the Accumulated Depreciation, Office Equipment account control a subsidiary ledger having a separate record for each individual item of office equipment. Likewise, the Store Equipment account and its related Accumulated Depreciation, Store Equipment account become controlling accounts controlling a subsidiary store equipment ledger. Often these subsidiary ledger records are kept on fixed asset record cards.

To illustrate these fixed asset records, assume that a store's office equipment consists of just one desk and a chair. The general ledger record of these assets is maintained in the Office Equipment controlling account and the Accumulated Depreciation, Office Equipment controlling account. Since in this case there are only two assets, only two subsidiary record cards are needed. The general ledger and subsidiary ledger record of these assets appear as shown in Illustration 69 below and on the following two pages.

Illustration 69

Office Equipment   ACCOUNT NO. *132*

DATE	EXPLANATION	FO-LIO	DEBIT	CREDIT	BALANCE
1964 July 2	Desk and chair	G-1	185 00		185 00

Accumulated Depreciation, Office Equipment   ACCOUNT NO. *132A*

DATE	EXPLANATION	FO-LIO	DEBIT	CREDIT	BALANCE
1964 Dec. 31		G-23		4 50	4 50
1965 Dec. 31		G-42		9 00	13 50
1966 Dec. 31		G-65		9 00	22 50

Illustration 69—Continued

Fixed Asset
No. 1

SUBSIDIARY FIXED ASSET AND DEPRECIATION RECORD

Item   Office chair   *General Ledger Account*   Office Equipment

Description   Office chair

Mfg. Serial No.   *Purchased from*   Office Equipment Co.

Where Located   Office

Person Responsible for the Asset   Office Manager

Estimated Life   12 years   *Estimated Salvage Value* $4.00

Depreciation per Year $3.00   *per Month* $0.25

Date	Explanation	F	Asset Record			Depreciation Record		
			Dr.	Cr.	Bal.	Dr.	Cr.	Bal.
July 2, '64		G1	40.00		40.00			
Dec. 31, '64		G23					1.50	1.50
Dec. 31, '65		G42					3.00	4.50
Dec. 31, '66		G65					3.00	7.50

Final Disposition of the Asset

Illustration 69—Continued

Fixed Asset
No. 2

SUBSIDIARY FIXED ASSET AND DEPRECIATION RECORD

General Ledger

Item Desk   *Account* Office Equipment

Description Office desk

Purchased

Mfg. Serial No.   *from* Office Equipment Co.

Where Located Office

Person Responsible for the Asset Office Manager

Estimated Life 20 years   *Estimated Salvage Value* $25.00

Depreciation per Year $6.00   *per Month* $0.50

Date	Explanation	F	Asset Record			Depreciation Record		
			Dr.	Cr.	Bal.	Dr.	Cr.	Bal.
July 2, '64		*G1*	*145.00*		*145.00*			
Dec. 31, '64		*G23*					*3.00*	*3.00*
Dec. 31, '65		*G42*					*6.00*	*9.00*
Dec. 31, '66		*G65*					*6.00*	*15.00*

Final Disposition of the Asset

The information given on the subsidiary fixed asset record cards is in the main self-evident. Note how the balance of the general ledger account, Office Equipment, is equal to the sum of the balances in the asset record section of the two subsidiary ledger cards. The general ledger account controls this section of the subsidiary ledger. Note also how the Accumulated Depreciation, Office Equipment account controls the depreciation record section of the cards. The disposition section at the bottom of the card is used to record the final disposal of the asset. When the asset is discarded, sold, or exchanged, a note telling of the final disposition is entered here. The card is then removed from the subsidiary ledger and filed for future reference.

ILLUSTRATION OF A MORE COMPLETE
INCOME STATEMENT

A number of income statement items have been introduced since this statement was last illustrated in Chapter 5. Consequently, to aid the student in placing these items on an income statement, Illustration 70 (opposite page) is presented at this point.

QUESTIONS FOR CLASS DISCUSSION

1. What are the characteristics of a fixed asset?
2. Why is not land held for future expansion a fixed asset?
3. As used in accounting, what is the meaning of the term depreciation?
4. What items enter into the cost of a fixed asset?
5. What is the cost of a fixed asset's fund of usefulness?
6. Define the following terms as they are used in accounting for fixed assets:
   a) Trade-in value.   c) Book value.   e) Inadequacy.
   b) Market value.   d) Salvage value.   f) Obsolescence.
7. A building estimated to have a useful life of 30 years was completed at a cost of $73,000. It was estimated that at the end of the building's life it would be wrecked at a cost of $1,000 and that materials salvaged from the wrecking operation would be sold for $2,000. How much straight-line depreciation should be charged on the building each year?
8. A machine costing $17,500 was installed. Its useful life was estimated at five years, after which it would have a trade-in value of $2,500. Its total life production was estimated at 50,000 units of product. During its second year the machine produced 8,000 units of product. What was the second-year charge for depreciation on the machine if depreciation were calculated on (a) a straight-line basis, (b) units of production basis, (c) a declining balance basis at twice the straight-line rate, and (d) a sum of the years' digits basis?
9. A mine having an estimated 1,000,000 tons of ore was purchased for $2,500,000. Under the assumption that 50,000 tons of ore were mined the first year, give the entry to record depletion.
10. Why do balance sheets show both cost and accumulated depreciation of each functional group of fixed assets?
11. Do balance sheets show market values for fixed assets? If not, what kind of values are shown?
12. Is it possible to keep a fixed asset in such an excellent state of repair that recording of depreciation is unnecessary?
13. A machine was purchased new on January 3, 1961, at a cost of $3,200. The machine had an estimated service life of ten years and an estimated salvage value of $200. (a) What is the annual depreciation of the machine calculated by the straight-line method? (b) Give the December 31 entry to record the annual depreciation. (c) Assume that the machine was destroyed by fire on March 2, 1966, and that there was no insurance.

Illustration 70

OKLAHOMA SALES COMPANY
Income Statement for Year Ended December 31, 19—

Revenue:			
Sales...			$114,750
Less: Sales returns........................		$ 1,250	
Sales discounts.......................		1,330	2,580
Net sales......................................			$112,170
Cost of goods sold:			
Merchandise inventory, January 1, 19—......		$12,530	
Purchases.................................	$69,370		
Less: Purchases returns...............$765			
Purchases discounts............ 980	1,745		
Net purchases..............................	$67,625		
Add: Freight-in...........................	1,840		
Net cost of purchases......................		69,465	
Goods for sale.............................		$81,995	
Merchandise inventory, December 31, 19—....		10,135	
Cost of goods sold......................			71,860
Gross profit from sales.........................			$ 40,310
Operating expenses:			
Selling expenses:			
Sales salaries............................$12,450			
Payroll taxes expense, sales salaries........	620		
Rent expense, selling space................	4,800		
Freight-out..............................	500		
Advertising expense.......................	2,165		
Personal property taxes, selling.............	205		
Store supplies used.......................	345		
Insurance expense, selling..................	215		
Depreciation of store equipment...........	835		
Total selling expenses....................		$22,135	
General and administrative expenses:			
Office salaries............................$ 3,600			
Payroll taxes expense, office salaries........	180		
Rent expense, office space.................	600		
Personal property taxes, office..............	20		
Bad debts expense........................	1,135		
Office supplies used.......................	175		
Insurance expense, office..................	25		
Depreciation of office equipment...........	195		
Total general and administrative expenses.		5,930	
Total operating expenses...............			28,065
Income from operations........................			$ 12,245
Other revenues and expenses:			
Interest earned...........................		$ 185	
Less: Interest expense......................$	60		
Cash short..........................	10	70	
Addition to income from operations........			115
Net Income...................................			$ 12,360

Give the entries required to record the loss. (*d*) Assume that there was insurance and that $1,400 was received from the insurance company to cover the fire loss. Give the entries to record the loss.

14. A machine cost $3,750. It had an estimated service life of five years and an estimated salvage value of $750. Straight-line depreciation was correctly recorded at the end of each year of the asset's life. Give the entries required under each of the following assumptions:

a) The machine was sold for $1,000 at the end of the fourth year of its life.

b) The machine was sold for $1,500 at the end of its fourth year.

c) The machine was traded at the end of its fourth year on a new machine with a list price of $4,000. A trade-in allowance of $1,000 was received. The loss on the exchange was recorded.

d) The transaction just given (*c*) was recorded by the income tax method.

e) The machine was traded in at the end of its fourth year on a new machine with a list price of $4,000. A trade-in allowance of $1,500 was received. The gain on the exchange was recorded.

f) The transaction just given (*e*) was recorded by the income tax method.

15. When an old fixed asset is traded in at a book loss on a new fixed asset of a like nature, the loss is not recognized for tax purposes. In the end this normally does not work a great hardship on the taxpayer. Why?

16. What is the difference between a capital expenditure and a revenue expenditure? Give an example of each.

17. Classify the following expenditures as either capital expenditures or revenue expenditures:

a) Repainted a building.

b) Replaced the gears in a machine and thereby doubled its normal output.

c) Replaced broken gears in a machine with like new gears.

d) Replaced a worn-out wood shingle roof with a new tile roof that is guaranteed to last the life of the building.

18. In 1966 betterments to a machine were recorded as a revenue expenditure. What was the effect of this error on the 1966 financial statements? On the 1967 and later statements?

PROBLEMS

Problem 11–1

Walter Sears organized a package delivery firm for which he completed the following transactions during a three-year period:

1966

Sept. 5 Purchased a secondhand Essex truck paying $775 cash. The remaining service life of the truck was estimated at three years with a $200 trade-in value at the end of that period.

5 Paid Service Garage $110 for a new set of tires for the Essex truck, and $35 for minor repairs to the truck's motor.

Oct. 27 Paid Service Garage $45 for repairing the rear fender and bumper of the Essex truck. Both had been damaged by the driver backing into a loading dock.

Dec. 31   Recorded straight-line depreciation on the truck.

31   Closed the expense accounts involved in the foregoing entries.

1967

Mar. 25   Purchased a new Hudson truck paying $2,525 cash. The service life of the truck was estimated at four years with a trade-in value of $730 at the end of that time.

27   Paid $125 for building special shelves and racks in the Hudson truck. The additions did not increase the truck's trade-in value.

Oct. 29   Traded the Essex truck on a new Maxwell truck having a $3,020 cash price. Received a $700 trade-in allowance; paid the balance in cash. The service life of the Maxwell truck was estimated at four years with an $800 trade-in allowance at the end of that time. (Use the income tax method.)

Dec. 21   Paid Service Garage $35 for a motor tuneup and minor repairs to the Hudson truck.

31   Recorded straight-line depreciation on the trucks.

31   Closed the expense accounts involved in the foregoing transactions.

1968

July 6   Realized the amount of business being transacted did not warrant the use of two trucks and sold the Maxwell truck for $2,300.

Required:
Prepare general journal entries to record the foregoing transactions.

Problem 11–2

On March 8, 1966, Speedy Delivery Service purchased three small trucks, paying $3,175 each. It planned to depreciate the trucks on a mileage basis under the assumption they would be driven 60,000 miles each, after which they would be traded on new trucks for an estimated trade-in allowance of $475 each. On November 29, 1966, after having been driven 11,400 miles, Truck No. 1 was totally destroyed in an accident. The insurance company paid $2,300 in full settlement of the loss claim. The destroyed truck was not replaced. On December 31, 1966, at the end of the annual accounting period, Truck No. 2 had been driven 13,200 miles and Truck No. 3 had been driven 12,800 miles. On October 16, 1967, after having been driven a total of 31,000 miles, Truck No. 2 was sold for $1,800 cash. On December 20, 1967, after having been driven 29,000 miles, Truck No. 3 was traded in on Truck No. 4. Truck No. 4 had a cash price of $3,500; a $1,900 trade-in allowance was received for Truck No. 3.

Required:
Prepare entries in general journal form to record: (1) the purchase of the three trucks, (2) the destruction of Truck No. 1 and the insurance settlement, (3) the 1966 depreciation on the remaining trucks, (4) the sale of Truck No. 2, (5) and the exchange of Trucks 3 and 4. Use the income tax method to record the exchange.

Problem 11–3

The following machines were owned by a concern the accounting periods of which end each December 31:

Asset	Pur-chased	Cost	Estimated Useful Life	Esti-mated Salvage Value	Method of De-precia-tion	Disposal Date and Details
No. 53	4/29/60	$3,500	5 years	$500	Straight-line	Traded 1/4/62 on Asset 72, trade-in allow-ance, $2,000
No. 72	1/4/62	$4,300 less trade-in allowance	5 years	$600	Sum of years' digits	Sold for $800 on 1/11/67
No. 74	1/6/62	$6,400	4 years	$400	Declining balance*	Traded on Assets No. 98, 1/5/66, trade-in allowance, $900
No. 98	1/5/66	$7,000 less trade-in allowance	12,000 units of product	$500	Units of produc-tion†	Sold for $4,000 on 5/21/67

At twice the straight-line rate.
†Asset No. 98 produced 2,500 units of product in 1966 and 500 before its sale in 1967.*

Required:

Prepare general journal entries to record: (1) the acquisition of each machine, (2) the depreciation on each machine on the first December 31 of its life, (3) the disposal of each machine. Use the income tax method to record exchanges. (Only one entry need be made to record the disposal of an old machine and acquisition of a new when the old is traded in on the new.)

Problem 11–4

During a three-year period Flagstaff Company completed the following fixed asset transactions:

1965

Jan. 7 Purchased on credit from Zippo, Inc., a Zippo calculator, $720. The serial number of the machine was X2X345. Its service life was estimated at eight years with a $144 trade-in value.

9 Purchased on credit an Accurate typewriter from Office Outfitters for $435. The machine's serial number was MMM-0156, its service life was estimated at five years, and its trade-in value at $135.

Mar. 27 Purchased a Quicko adding machine from Office Outfitters for $385. The serial number of the machine was STM-1176. Its service life was estimated at eight years with a $97 trade-in value.

Dec. 31 Record the 1965 depreciation on the office equipment.

1966

June 3 Sold the Accurate typewriter for $365 cash.

4 Purchased on credit a new Speedy typewriter for $350 from Speedway Typewriter Company. The machine's serial number was MO7781. Its service life was estimated at five years with an $80 trade-in value.

Dec. 31 Recorded the 1966 depreciation on the office equipment.

1967

Apr. 28 Traded the Zippo calculator to Office Outfitters on a new Hasty calculator having a cash price of $793. Received a $525 trade-in allowance on the old calculator and paid the balance in cash. The new calculator's serial number was WMWM178. Its service life was estimated at eight years and its trade-in value at $148.

Dec. 31   Recorded the 1967 depreciation on the office equipment.

Required:
1. Open Office Equipment and Accumulated Depreciation, Office Equipment accounts plus subsidiary fixed asset record cards as needed.
2. Prepare general journal entries to record the foregoing transactions. Post to the general ledger accounts and the subsidiary fixed asset record cards.
3. Prove the December 31, 1967, balance of the Office Equipment and Accumulated Depreciation, Office Equipment accounts by preparing with totals a schedule showing the cost and accumulated depreciation of each fixed asset owned on that date.

Problem 11–5

Redtop Sales operates with annual accounting periods that end each December 31. On December 31 of the current year a trial balance of their ledger appeared as follows:

REDTOP SALES
Trial Balance, December 31, 19—

Cash	$ 3,240	
Petty cash	25	
Accounts receivable	5,210	
Allowance for bad debts		$ 120
Merchandise inventory	11,330	
Prepaid insurance	280	
Store supplies	440	
Office supplies	260	
Store equipment	5,355	
Accumulated depreciation, store equipment		1,575
Office equipment	2,100	
Accumulated depreciation, office equipment		910
Notes payable		4,500
Accounts payable		4,750
Stanley Perkins, capital		18,440
Stanley Perkins, withdrawals	4,200	
Sales		61,430
Sales returns	930	
Sales discounts	1,060	
Purchases	42,400	
Purchases returns		670
Purchases discounts		790
Sales salaries	6,420	
Rent expense, selling space	4,800	
Advertising expense	1,170	
Office salaries	3,230	
Rent expense, office space	600	
Interest expense	135	
	$93,185	**$93,185**

Required:

1. Enter the trial balance on a work sheet form and complete the work sheet using the following information:

    a) Allowance for bad debts an additional 1 percent of sales, less sales returns and allowances.

    b) Expired insurance, $155.

    c) Store supplies inventory, $145.

    d) Office supplies inventory, $105.

    e) Depreciation of store equipment, $510; and (*f*) of office equipment, $215.

    g) Accrued sales salaries, $75; and office salaries, $45.

    h) On December 1 a $2,000, 60-day, 6 percent note payable had been given to the bank for a loan; and (*i*) on December 7 an additional $2,500 had been borrowed by discounting a $2,500 noninterest-bearing note payable for 60 days at 6 percent.

    j) December 31 merchandise inventory, $10,160.

2. From the work sheet prepare a classified income statement and a classified balance sheet.

CLASS EXERCISE

Exercise 11–1

In January of the current year, while making his initial audit of a new client's accounting records, an auditor discovered an account called "Land and Buildings." The account had a $60,000 debit balance. An investigation showed the account balance had resulted from the purchase at $8,000 of the land on which the client's warehouse had been constructed at a cost of $52,000. Further investigation revealed the warehouse site had been purchased ten years prior to the date of the audit and had been held two years before the warehouse building was erected. During this ten-year period $9,730 of property taxes had been paid on the land and its improvements and charged to an expense account called "Property Taxes." Of this amount, $270 applied to the years before the construction of the warehouse building. Examination of the expense account, Property Taxes, revealed that three years before the audit date the street beside the warehouse had been paved by the city at a cost to the client of $820. The $820 paving tax assessment had been charged to the expense account, Property Taxes. In addition to the foregoing the client had not recorded any depreciation on the warehouse during its eight-year life because "it was of concrete construction and should last forever." The building had an estimated service life of 50 years and no salvage value.

Required:

Prepare a general journal entry or entries to correct the client's accounting records through the year just ended.

ALTERNATE PROBLEMS

Problem 11–1A

Part 1. On May 6, 19—, a secondhand truck was purchased for $2,580 cash. The same day Quick-Service Garage was paid $220 for a new set of tires and for reinforcing the truck's frame so that it could carry heavier loads. Of this latter amount $140 was for tires and $80 for the reinforcing. The tires had a list price of $165, but a $25 trade-in allowance was received for the truck's old tires. Give the entries to record the purchase of the truck and the payment for the tires and reinforcing.

Part 2. At the time of purchase it was estimated the foregoing truck had a remaining service life of 50,000 miles and a $300 trade-in value at the end of that number of miles. After it was driven 20,000 miles, on June 11, 19—, the truck was retired from service. Give the entry for the retirement under each of the following assumptions: (*a*) The truck was sold for $1,850. (*b*) It was destroyed in a fire and the insurance company paid $1,600 in settlement of the loss claim. (*c*) It was traded on a new truck having a cash price of $3,400. A $1,900 trade-in allowance was received and the balance was paid in cash. (Use income tax method.)

Part 3. A mining company paid $250,000 for a tract of land under which there was an estimated 100,000 tons of Mineral A. During the first year of ownership the company mined 10,000 tons of mineral from the land. It was estimated the land would be worth $15,000 after all the mineral was removed. Give the entry to record the depletion.

Part 4. A machine having an estimated ten-year life and no salvage value was installed at a cost of $12,600. Six years later the machine was rebuilt and improved at a cost of $2,700. Of the $2,700, $1,500 was for ordinary repairs and $1,200 was for betterments. Neither the repairs nor betterments affected the salvage value or service life of the machine. Give the entry to record the depreciation on the machine for its seventh year.

Problem 11–2A

Early in January, 1958, Regal Manufacturing Company purchased a new machine for its factory. The machine, its concrete base, and power connections cost $16,000 and had an estimated 20-year service life and no salvage value. During the first week in January, 1966, the machine was repaired and rebuilt at a cost of $3,600, of which $1,200 was for ordinary repairs and $2,400 was for betterments to the machine. The betterments increased the efficiency of the machine but did not extend its useful life or increase its salvage value. On March 28, 1967, the machine was destroyed in a fire. The insurance company settled the loss claim with an $8,000 check.

Required:

Prepare entries to record the following: (1) the purchase of the machine; (2) the first year's depreciation; (3) the expenditure for repairing and rebuilding the machine; (4) the 1966 depreciation; and (5) the destruction of the machine and the receipt of the insurance company's check.

Problem 11–3A

The accounting periods of the concern owning the following machines end on December 31:

Machine No. 63. This machine was purchased on March 27, 1960, at an installed cost of $5,400. Its useful life was estimated at four years, and its trade-in value at $600. Straight-line depreciation was recorded on the machine on December 31, 1960, and on December 31, 1961. It was then traded on Machine No. 92 on January 5, 1962. A $3,000 trade-in allowance was received.

Machine No. 92. This machine was purchased on January 5, 1962, at an installed cost of $6,500 less the trade-in allowance received on Machine No. 63. Its life was estimated at five years with an $800 trade-in value. The sum of the years' digits method was used in recording depreciation on the machine on each December 31 in its life. It was sold for $1,000 on January 4, 1967.

Machine No. 94. This machine was purchased on January 8, 1962, at an installed cost of $5,000. Its useful life was estimated at five years, after which it would have a $500 trade-in value. Declining balance depreciation at twice the straight-line rate was recorded on the machine at the ends of 1962, 1963, 1964, and 1965; and on January 9, 1966, it was traded on Machine No. 127. A $1,200 trade-in allowance was received.

Machine No. 127. This machine was purchased on January 9, 1966, at a $6,552 installed cost, less the trade-in allowance received on *Machine No. 94*. It was estimated the new machine would produce 90,000 units of product during its useful life, after which it would have a $600 trade-in value. Units-of-production depreciation was recorded on the machine at the end of 1966, a year in which it produced 12,000 units of product. Between January 1 and May 3, 1967, the machine produced 5,000 more units, and on May 3 it was sold for $4,500.

Required:
Prepare general journal entries to record: (1) the purchase of each machine; (2) the depreciation recorded on the first December 31 of each machine's life; and (3) the disposal of each machine. Use the income tax method to record the exchanges. (Only one entry is required for the disposal of an old machine and the acquisition of a new one when the old is traded in on the new.)

Problem 11–4A

Service Market completed the following fixed asset transactions over a period of three years:
1965
Jan.   3   Purchased on credit a Superior scale from Alpha Equipment Company for $265. The serial number of the scale was B-23452, its service life was estimated at 20 years, and its trade-in value at $25.

       5   Purchased on credit a Coldaire refrigerated display case from Alpha Equipment Company for $3,200. The serial number of the display case was 00–23234, its service life was estimated at 16 years, and its trade-in value at $800.

Apr.   7   Purchased on credit a Regal cash register for $323 from Beta Equipment Company. The serial number of the cash register was 3–32564, its service life was estimated at 16 years, and its trade-in value at $35.

Dec.   31   Recorded the 1965 depreciation on the store equipment.

1966
Oct. 28 Sold the Regal cash register to Thomas Seay for $275 cash.
      28 Purchased on credit a new King cash register from Beta Equipment Company for $360. The serial number of the cash register was XXX-12435, its service life was estimated at 20 years, and its trade-in value at $48.
Dec. 31 Recorded the 1966 depreciation on the store equipment.
1967
May   28 Traded the Superior scale to Gamma Equipment Company on a new Rex scale having a list price of $298. Received a trade-in allowance of $200. The serial number of the new scale was MM-7678, its service life was estimated at 20 years, and its trade-in value was estimated at $34. (Use income tax method.)
Dec. 31 Recorded the 1967 depreciation on the store equipment.

Required:
  1. Open general ledger accounts for Store Equipment and Accumulated Depreciation, Store Equipment. Prepare as needed a subsidiary fixed asset ledger card for each item of equipment owned by Service Market.
  2. Prepare general journal entries to record the fixed asset transactions completed by Service Market, and post to the proper general ledger and subsidiary ledger accounts.
  3. Prove the December 31, 1967, balances of the Store Equipment and Accumulated Depreciation, Store Equipment accounts by preparing from the subsidiary fixed asset ledger cards a list showing the cost and accumulated depreciation of each store equipment item owned by Service Market on that date.

DECISION PROBLEMS 11—DAWN DAIRIES

Dawn Dairies operates a large fleet of dairy trucks. It purchases a new fleet every two years, and accounts for each fleet on a separate basis so as to determine the cost per mile of operating different kinds of trucks. Its standard policy is to replace each fleet every four years.

It has just purchased 40 new GM dairy trucks at $4,800 each. The data on the last fleet of GM trucks are as follows (averages per truck):

Year	Miles Operated	Repairs and Maintenance
1	*20,000*	*$100*
2	*18,000*	*300*
3	*15,000*	*500*
4	*12,000*	*600*

It is expected that the repair experience of the previous fleet will be repeated for the life of the new fleet. The reduction in mileage each year is largely due to the policy that operates new trucks on the better and longer lines, and takes old trucks off the regular lines and uses them as extras. After four years, old trucks are not traded in but are sold to farmers and other buyers at an average of 12½ percent of original cost.

In the past the company has used straight-line depreciation. The controller now asks that a study be made of other depreciation methods with a comparison of methods to determine which will give the most equitable expense charge for depreciation plus maintenance and repair cost as related to revenue produced by the operation of the trucks. For the purpose of this study it may be assumed that annual revenue is proportionate to the miles the trucks are operated.

Required:

1. Prepare a schedule showing straight-line depreciation, repair and maintenance cost, and total depreciation and maintenance for each of the four years; compute the percentage of each year's total expenses to the total expenses for all four years; and compute the percentage of the revenue earned each year to the total revenue for the service life of the fleet (miles per year divided by total miles for the four-year period). Compare the expense percentages with the revenue percentages.

2. Prepare similar schedules using units of production, declining balance, and sum of years' digits methods of depreciation.

3. Write a summary of conclusions, recommending the depreciation method you would use and give reason for your decision.

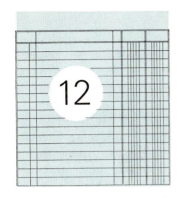

12

Adjustments,
Additional Considerations;
and Interim Statements

MOST REVENUE items are earned and collected within the time limits of a single accounting period, and as a result are credited at the time of their collection to the period in which they are earned. Likewise, most expenses are incurred and paid within a single period, and as a result are charged on payment to the period in which they are incurred. However, a revenue is sometimes earned in one accounting period and collected in a different period, and an expense is sometimes incurred in one period and paid in another. When these situations occur, a problem arises as to which period the revenue or expense should be assigned. In each case the answer depends upon the basis of accounting in use. There are two bases of accounting in common use: (1) the cash basis, and (2) the accrual basis.

THE CASH BASIS

Under the cash basis of accounting, revenues are considered to be earned at the time they are collected in cash, and expenses are considered to be incurred at the time cash is disbursed in their payment. Under this system, the gain or loss of an accounting period is the difference between revenue receipts and expense disbursements.

Under the cash basis, revenues and expenses are not necessarily matched because (1) revenues represented by receivables, (2) expenses represented by payables, and (3) cost and expense reductions represented by inventories are ignored. Consequently, the use of the cash basis is generally restricted to individuals and enterprises in which inventories, receivables, and payables are not significant. Almost all individuals who file personal income tax returns use the cash basis for calculating income subject to tax. Here the extra exactness resulting from accruing and deferring items is commonly not considered worth the extra labor required.

In accounting for a business enterprise, the cash basis has the advantage of simplicity, but it has the great disadvantage of producing financial statements that are not comparable. As an illustration, assume that a concern which prepares monthly financial statements buys its entire winter's fuel supply in August and pays for it in September. Under the cash basis this fuel supply, which is to be used over several months, is unfairly recorded as a September expense, an expense of the month of payment; and as a result, the September income statement shows a smaller net income or loss. Also, because of the extra fuel expense appearing thereon, the September income statement is not comparable with the statements of other months.

THE ACCRUAL BASIS

If comparable statements are to be obtained, revenues must be credited to the period in which they are earned and expenses must be charged to the period in which they are incurred; and this must be done regardless of when cash is received or disbursed. Under the accrual basis, this is done. Under the accrual basis, revenues are credited to the accounting period in which they are earned regardless of when payments are received, and expenses are charged to the period in which they are incurred regardless of when cash is disbursed; and as a result, under the accrual basis the gain or loss of an accounting period is the difference between revenues earned and expenses incurred. Most enterprises of any size use the accrual basis.

The obviously greater accuracy and usefulness of statements prepared under the accrual basis have been accepted from the beginning by this text. As a result, most recording procedures and adjustments necessary to allocate revenues and expenses to the proper accounting periods have already been discussed. For example, making adjustments for prepaid expenses, accrued wages, bad debts, depreciation, and inventories result in allocating items to proper accounting periods. However, several additional factors need be considered.

ACCRUED EXPENSES

Expenses are usually recorded throughout each accounting period as they are paid. Consequently, at a period end, before adjusting entries are posted, the accounts show the expenses that have been paid during the period. However, at the end of each period these paid and recorded expenses are usually not all the expenses that have been incurred.

Normally, at the end of each accounting period there are additional expenses that have been incurred but have not been paid and recorded because payment is not yet due. These unpaid and unrecorded expenses that are not yet due are called accrued expenses.

When something accrues, it grows and accumulates with the passage of time. In accounting, accrued expenses are unpaid expenses that have grown and accumulated with the passage of time. Normally they are unpaid because payment is not yet due. Accrued wages were discussed in Chapter 3 as one example of an accrued expense. Accrued interest will be used in this chapter to expand on the subject.

When a concern borrows money by issuing an interest-bearing note, interest accrues each day the note is outstanding. For example, on December 20, 1966, Alpha Company borrowed $6,000 from its bank by issuing a $6,000, 60-day, 6 percent note. Obviously, interest at the rate of $1 per day accrues on this note; and by December 31, 1966, 11 days' interest, or $11 of interest, has accrued. This $11 is unpaid on December 31 because it is not due until the note is due on February 18.

Accrued Interest Expense, Cash Basis. Under the cash basis of accounting it is almost correct to say that the method of handling accrued expenses is not a method at all. This is because under the cash basis all accrued expenses are ignored until they are paid. To illustrate, if the fiscal year of Alpha Company ends on December 31, 1966, then 11 days, or $11, of interest on the $6,000 note described in the previous paragraph is rightfully a 1966 expense, because 1966 received 11 days' benefit from the use of the borrowed money. However, under the cash basis this is ignored. Under the cash basis all interest on this note is ignored until February 18, 1967, when both the note and interest are due. On that date the 11 days of 1966 interest is added to the 49 days of 1967 interest, and both are paid without any notice that one is a 1966 expense and the other an expense of 1967. When the note and interest are paid, the entry to record the payment under the cash basis of accounting is:

Feb.	*18*	*Notes Payable*............................	*6,000.00*	
		Interest Expense.......................	*60.00*	
		Cash..................................		*6,060.00*
		Paid our $6,000, 60-day, 6 percent		
		note due today.		

The $6,000 debit of the foregoing entry records the payment of the note, and the $60 debit to Interest Expense records the payment of its 60 days' interest. Since, under the cash basis no notice was taken of the accrued interest at the end of the previous accounting period, this last debit records both the $11 of interest incurred in 1966 and the $49 of 1967 interest as an expense of 1967. Obviously this places an unfair burden on the 1967 accounting period.

Since, at the end of each accounting period, under the cash basis of accounting all accrued and deferred items are ignored as in the foregoing example, the remainder of this chapter is devoted to accounting for such items under an accrual basis.

Accrued Interest Expense, Accrual Basis. Although accrued expenses such as accrued interest are ignored under the cash basis, they are not ignored under the accrual basis. Under the accrual basis all accrued expenses such as accrued interest, accrued taxes, and accrued wages are recorded at the end of each accounting period by means of adjusting entries; and as a result these items are shown as expenses of the accounting period which receives their benefit rather than the period in which they are paid.

To illustrate accrual basis accounting for expenses such as accrued interest, assume that Beta Company whose accounting periods end each December 31 also borrowed $6,000 from its bank on December 20, 1966, by issuing a 60-day, 6 percent note. By December 31, when Beta Company's accounting period ends, 11 days, or $11, of interest expense has also accrued on this note; and under the accrual basis a work sheet adjustment and the following adjusting entry are required:

Dec.	31	Interest Expense............................	11.00	
		Accrued Interest Payable...............		11.00
		To record accrued interest on a note payable.		

Note that the debit of the foregoing entry causes the accrued interest to appear as an expense on the income statement of the accounting period ending on December 31. Note also that the credit causes the accrued interest to appear as a liability on the balance sheet of that date. After the foregoing adjusting entry is posted, the Interest Expense and Accrued Interest Payable accounts appear as follows:

Interest Expense

Date		Explanation	Dr.	Cr.	Bal.
Dec.	31	Adjusting	11.00		11.00

Accrued Interest Payable

Date		Explanation	Dr.	Cr.	Bal.
Dec.	31	Adjusting		11.00	11.00

After the statements are prepared, the Interest Expense account is closed in the usual manner. The entry to accomplish this is:

Dec.	31	Income Summary......................	11.00	
		Interest Expense..................		11.00
		To close the Interest Expense account.		

After the foregoing closing entry is posted, the Interest Expense and Accrued Interest Payable accounts appear as follows:

Interest Expense

Date		Explanation	Dr.	Cr.	Bal.
Dec.	31	Adjusting	11.00		11.00
Dec.	31	Closing		11.00	–0–

Accrued Interest Payable

Date		Explanation	Dr.	Cr.	Bal.
Dec.	31	Adjusting		11.00	11.00

Observe that the Interest Expense account is closed and has no balance but that the closing entry did not affect the Accrued Interest Payable account; it still shows the liability for the $11 of accrued interest.

To continue the illustration, on February 18, when the foregoing note becomes due, Beta Company must pay the bank $6,060. This pays both the note and its $60, or 60 days' interest. The 60 days' interest includes both the 11 days of 1966 interest and the $49 of 1967 interest. In recording the payment, under the system illustrated thus far, the bookkeeper must remember the 11 days, or $11, of 1966 interest recorded as an expense and a liability on December 31, and he must remember to divide the $60 interest payment between current 1967 interest expense and the 1966 accrued interest liability as follows:

Feb.	18	Notes Payable........................	6,000.00	
		Interest Expense......................	49.00	
		Accrued Interest Payable.............	11.00	
		Cash..............................		6,060.00
		Paid our 60-day, 6 percent note due today.		

After the entry just given is posted, the Interest Expense and Accrued Interest Payable accounts appear as follows:

Interest Expense

Date		Explanation	Dr.	Cr.	Bal.
Dec.	31	Adjusting	11.00		11.00
Dec.	31	Closing		11.00	–0–
Feb.	18	Payment	49.00		49.00

Accrued Interest Payable

Date		Explanation	Dr.	Cr.	Bal.
Dec.	31	Adjusting		11.00	11.00
Feb.	18	Payment	11.00		–0–

Observe that after the entry recording the payment of the note and interest is posted, the Accrued Interest Payable account has no balance and the Interest Expense account has a $49 debit balance. The $49 debit balance is the 1967 interest expense on the borrowed $6,000.

REVERSING ENTRIES

Recurring like transactions are usually recorded in the same way each time they occur. However, if errors are to be avoided, a bookkeeper must be alert for the recurring transaction that for some reason must be handled differently. For instance, payment of an interest-bearing note is a recurring transaction in many concerns, and payment of an interest-bearing note upon which a portion of the interest has previously been accrued is an example of a like transaction requiring a different treatment.

To illustrate, most concerns operate with accounting periods one year in length and most short-term notes of such concerns are for 30, 60, or 90 days. Therefore, since these 30-, 60-, and 90-day periods normally fall within a single accounting period, the usual entry for recording the payment of an interest-bearing note is:

June	16	Notes Payable..........................	8,000.00	
		Interest Expense......................	80.00	
		Cash.............................		8,080.00
		Paid our 60-day, 6 percent note due today.		

In the foregoing entry the entire amount of interest being paid is an expense of one accounting period. Observe that it is debited in full to the Interest Expense account. This is the normal situation and entry when a note is paid.

However, the normal entry may not apply when the life of a note being paid extended over two accounting periods and interest on the note was accrued at the end of the first period. In such a situation, under the system of handling accrued items discussed thus far, an entry like the following in which the interest payment is divided between current expense and interest accrued at the end of the previous period is required:

Feb.	18	Notes Payable.........................	6,000.00	
		Interest Expense......................	49.00	
		Accrued Interest Payable..............	11.00	
		Cash.............................		6,060.00
		Paid our 60-day, 6 percent note due today.		

When recording payment of an expense item a portion of which has previously been accrued, as in the foregoing entry, it is easy for the bookkeeper to forget to make a division between current expense and the liability accrued at the end of the previous period. This is particularly true when several weeks or months elapse between the accrual date and the payment date. Consequently, many bookkeepers like to handle accrued expenses in a manner that makes such a division unnecessary. To do so, these bookkeepers make a *reversing entry* that eliminates the need of dividing the debit recording the payment of an expense a portion of which has been previously accrued. This reversing entry reverses the adjusting entry that recorded the accrued portion of the expense, and it is made at the end of the accounting period at the time adjusting and closing entries are made. It is posted after the adjusting and closing entries have been posted and the post-closing trial balance has been prepared. Usually such reversing entries are dated the first day of the new accounting period.

The handling of accrued interest expense in Gamma Company may be used to illustrate reversing entries. On December 20, 1966, Gamma Company, like the previous Alpha and Beta companies, also borrowed $6,000 by issuing a 60-day, 6 percent note; and on December 31 the company bookkeeper made a work sheet adjustment and the following adjusting entry to record the 11 days, or $11, of accrued interest on this note:

Dec.	31	Interest Expense..............................	11.00	
		Accrued Interest Payable................		11.00
		To record the accrued interest on a note payable.		

In addition he made the following entry to close the Interest Expense account:

Dec.	31	Income Summary............................	11.00	
		Interest Expense.........................		11.00
		To close the Interest Expense account.		

After the foregoing entries were posted, the Interest Expense and Accrued Interest Payable accounts appeared as follows:

Interest Expense

Date		Explanation	Dr.	Cr.	Bal.
Dec.	31	Adjusting	11.00		11.00
Dec.	31	Closing		11.00	–0–

Accrued Interest Payable

Date		Explanation	Dr.	Cr.	Bal.
Dec.	31	Adjusting		11.00	11.00

Thus far in the illustrated procedure there is nothing new. However, the Gamma Company bookkeeper wants, when the note of this illustration is paid, to avoid having to remember to divide the $60 interest payment between current interest expense and the liability for interest accrued at the end of the previous period. Consequently, if he is to do this, he must make the following reversing entry:

Jan.	1	*Accrued Interest Payable*..................	*11.00*	
		Interest Expense.......................		*11.00*
		To reverse the accrued interest adjusting entry.		

Observe that the foregoing reversing entry is dated the first day of the new accounting period and that it is debit for credit and credit for debit the reverse of the adjusting entry used on December 31 to record the accrued interest. It should also be noted that, although reversing entries are dated the first day of the new period, they are normally made at the same time adjusting and closing entries are made. Commonly, the bookkeeper, upon completion of his adjusting and closing entries, examines the adjusting entries and reverses those the reversal of which he feels will expedite future bookkeeping.

After the foregoing reversing entry is posted, the Interest Expense and Accrued Interest Payable accounts appear as follows:

Interest Expense							Accrued Interest Payable					
Date		Explanation	Dr.	Cr.	Bal.		Date		Explanation	Dr.	Cr.	Bal.
Dec.	*31*	*Adjusting*	*11.00*		*11.00*		*Dec.*	*31*	*Adjusting*		*11.00*	*11.00*
Dec.	*31*	*Closing*		*11.00*	*–0–*		*Jan.*	*1*	*Reversing*	*11.00*		*–0–*
Jan.	*1*	*Reversing*		*11.00*	*(11.00)*							

Notice in the Accrued Interest Payable account that the reversing entry cancels the recorded liability for the accrued interest, and that after the reversing entry is posted, the $11 of accrued interest appears as a *credit* in the Interest Expense account. (Remember a red ink or an encircled balance means a balance opposite from normal.)

After posting the reversing entry which places the $11 of accrued interest in the Interest Expense account as a credit, the Gamma Company bookkeeper may on February 18, when the note is paid, ignore the fact that a portion of its interest was accrued at the end of the previous period, and he may make the following common entry for recording an interest-bearing note's payment.

Feb.	*18*	*Notes Payable*........................	*6,000.00*	
		Interest Expense.....................	*60.00*	
		Cash...........................		*6,060.00*
		Paid our 60-day, 6 percent note due today.		

The $60 debit in the foregoing entry records payment of both the $11 of 1966 interest and the $49 of 1967 interest. Yet, the entire $60 is debited to the Interest Expense account, because when the $60 debit is posted, the $11 credit from the previously posted reversing entry reduces the Interest Expense account's debit balance to $49. Thus, because of the reversing entry, the account shows only $49 of interest expense, the interest applicable to the 1967 accounting period. The Interest Expense account appears as follows after the foregoing entry is posted. Note the $49 debit balance.

Interest Expense

Date		Explanation	Debit	Credit	Balance
Dec.	*31*	*Adjusting*	*11.00*		*11.00*
Dec.	*31*	*Closing*		*11.00*	*–0–*
Jan.	*1*	*Reversing*		*11.00*	*11.00*
Feb.	*18*	*Payment*	*60.00*		*49.00*

Reversing entries are a matter of convenience that enable a bookkeeper to forget an accrued item once its adjusting entry has been reversed. They are not required. However, if a bookkeeper does not make reversing entries, he must remember to divide each entry recording the final payment of a previously accrued item between the amount accrued and the amount applicable to the period of payment.

OTHER ACCRUED EXPENSES

At the end of an accounting period, a business may have other accrued expenses such as accrued advertising or accrued taxes. If its statements are to show all of its expenses and all liabilities, adjusting entries recording each accrued expense must be made. The previously illustrated entries for accrued interest show the proper methods for handling any accrued expense.

ACCRUED REVENUE

Revenue that is earned during one accounting period but not collected until a future period because it is not due is called *accrued revenue.*

Obviously, if revenue is actually earned during an accounting period, it is unfair to credit it to a future period simply because it is collected in cash during the future period. The accrual basis recognizes this and requires that each period be given credit for the revenue actually earned during the period, regardless of when collection occurs.

Accrued interest on notes receivable may be used to illustrate accounting for accrued revenue. For example, assume that on December 12, Gamma Company receives from a customer a $15,000, 6 percent, 30-day, interest-bearing note, dated December 11. By December 31, 20 days of interest is earned on this note. Of course, the interest will not be collected until the note is collected on January 10. Nevertheless, 20 days, or $50, of interest is earned by December 31 and is December revenue. Furthermore, if Gamma Company's income statement prepared on December 31 is to show all the December revenue, this $50 of accrued interest must appear as part of the interest earned. Also, if Gamma Company's balance sheet of that date is to show all the assets, the $50 of interest earned on this note must appear as a current asset called "accrued interest receivable." Therefore, if the revenue and asset are to be shown, the following adjusting entry must be made:

Dec.	31	*Accrued Interest Receivable*..........	*50.00*	
		Interest Earned.................		*50.00*
		To record the accrued interest on a note receivable.		

This adjusting entry causes the $50 of accrued interest to appear on the December 31 income statement as interest earned. It also causes the $50 of accrued interest to appear on the balance sheet as a current asset. After the statements are prepared, the Interest Earned account is closed in the usual manner. At the time closing entries are made and posted, the Gamma Company bookkeeper may or may not choose to make reversing entries. If he does not choose to make reversing entries, he must remember when the illustrated note and interest are paid to record its 30 days or $75 of interest with credits to both Interest Earned and Accrued Interest Receivable, as follows:

Jan.	10	*Cash*..............................	*15,075.00*	
		Accrued Interest Receivable......		*50.00*
		Interest Earned.................		*25.00*
		Notes Receivable...............		*15,000.00*
		Collected a note and interest due today.		

If, on the other hand, the bookkeeper chooses to make reversing entries, he will make the following entry to reverse the accrued interest adjusting entry:

Jan.	1	*Interest Earned....................*	*50.00*	
		Accrued Interest Receivable.....		*50.00*
		To reverse the accrued interest adjusting entry.		

Notice that the reversing entry, dated the first day of the new accounting period, is debit for credit and credit for debit the reverse of the adjusting entry it reverses. After it is posted, the Accrued Interest Receivable and the Interest Earned accounts appear as follows:

Accrued Interest Receivable

Date		Explanation	Dr.	Cr.	Bal.
Dec.	31	Adjusting	50.00		50.00
Jan.	1	Reversing		50.00	–0–

Interest Earned

Date		Explanation	Dr.	Cr.	Bal.
Dec.	31	Adjusting		50.00	50.00
Dec.	31	Closing	50.00		–0–
Jan.	1	Reversing	50.00		50.00

After the reversing entry is posted, the January 10th receipt of cash in payment of the note and interest is recorded with credits to Notes Receivable and Interest Earned only, as follows:

Jan.	10	*Cash...............................*	*15,075.00*	
		Interest Earned.................		*75.00*
		Notes Receivable................		*15,000.00*
		Note and interest due today.		

The $75 credit to Interest Earned is the sum of the $50 of accrued interest earned during December and the $25 of interest earned during January. However, when the $75 credit is posted, the Interest Earned account will show only a $25 credit balance, the correct revenue for the month of January. The Interest Earned account will show only the January revenue because of the reversing entry.

PREPAID EXPENSES

Costs of goods and services that have been consumed in the business operations are called expenses, and costs of goods and services that were purchased for consumption but are unconsumed at the accounting period end are called prepaid expenses. Prepaid insurance, prepaid rent, prepaid taxes, prepaid interest, unconsumed office supplies, store supplies, and factory supplies are examples of prepaid expenses. In accounting for such items, all may be treated in either of two ways—all may be recorded at purchase either as assets or as expenses. Prepaid insurance will be used in this chapter to illustrate the two methods of treatment.

Fire, liability, workmen's compensation, and other types of insurance are paid for in advance. The amount paid is called a *premium,* and premiums paying for protection for from one to five years in advance are common. At the time of a premium payment, the entire amount paid is an asset. However, it may be recorded as an asset or it may be recorded as an expense. A premium may be recorded either way because day by day as an insurance premium expires, the amount that expires becomes an expense. Normally, if premiums are paid several years in advance, at the end of each accounting period a portion of each premium previously paid has become an expense and a portion is still an asset. Therefore, regardless of whether a premium was originally recorded as an asset or as an expense, an adjustment must be made to separate the remaining asset and the expense. If a premium was originally recorded as an asset, the adjustment removes from the asset account the amount of insurance expense. If a premium was originally recorded as an expense, the adjustment removes from the expense account the amount that is still an asset.

Recording a Prepaid Expense as an Asset. To illustrate accounting for prepaid expenses such as prepaid insurance, assume that on August 1 a $360, three-year insurance premium is paid. If the payment is recorded as an asset, the following entry in general journal form is made:

Aug.	*1*	*Prepaid Insurance.........................* 360.00	
		Cash................................	*360.00*
		Paid the premium on a three-year insurance policy.	

If the company making this entry operates with yearly accounting periods that end each December 31, by that date $50 of this $360 premium has expired and the following entry is made to remove from the asset account the $50 of expired insurance:

Dec.	*31*	*Insurance Expense........................* 50.00	
		Prepaid Insurance...................	*50.00*
		To record the expired insurance.	

After the entry is posted, the Prepaid Insurance and the Insurance Expense accounts appear as follows:

Prepaid Insurance

Date		Explanation	Dr.	Cr.	Bal.
Aug.	1	Purchase	360.00		360.00
Dec.	31	Adjusting		50.00	310.00

Insurance Expense

Date		Explanation	Dr.	Cr.	Bal.
Dec.	31	Adjusting	50.00		50.00

When the statements are prepared, the $310 debit balance of the foregoing Prepaid Insurance account appears on the balance sheet as a current asset and the $50 balance of the Insurance Expense account appears on the income statement as an expense.

After the statements are prepared, in addition to the adjusting entry to remove the expired insurance from the asset account, the following closing entry is made:

Dec.	31	Income Summary..........................	50.00	
		Insurance Expense.....................		50.00
		To close the Insurance Expense account.		

After the closing entry is posted, the Prepaid Insurance and Insurance Expense accounts appear as follows:

Prepaid Insurance

Date		Explanation	Dr.	Cr.	Bal.
Aug.	1	Purchase	360.00		360.00
Dec.	31	Adjusting		50.00	310.00

Insurance Expense

Date		Explanation	Dr.	Cr.	Bal.
Dec.	31	Adjusting	50.00		50.00
Dec.	31	Closing		50.00	–0–

When payment of any prepaid expense is initially recorded as an asset, a series of adjusting and closing entries similar to these is repeated at the end of each accounting period throughout the life of the prepaid expense.

Recording a Prepaid Expense as an Expense. Although an additional entry is required each accounting period, prepaid expenses may be originally recorded as expenses. For example, if the payment of the $360 insurance premium previously illustrated is recorded as an expense, the following entry in general journal form is made to record the payment:

Aug.	*1*	*Insurance Expense*.......................	*360.00*	
		Cash...............................		*360.00*
		To record the payment of an insurance		
		premium as an expense.		

Then, at the end of the first accounting period, $310 of the balance of the Insurance Expense account is still an asset and only $50 is an expense. Consequently, the following adjusting entry is made:

Dec.	*31*	*Prepaid Insurance*.......................	*310.00*	
		Insurance Expense....................		*310.00*
		To remove the prepaid insurance from		
		the expense account.		

The foregoing adjusting entry removes the $310 of prepaid insurance from the expense account, and after it is posted the accounts appear as follows:

Prepaid Insurance

Date		Explanation	Dr.	Cr.	Bal.
Dec.	31	Adjusting	310.00		310.00

Insurance Expense

Date		Explanation	Dr.	Cr.	Bal.
Aug.	1	Purchase	360.00		360.00
Dec.	31	Adjusting		310.00	50.00

After the foregoing adjusting entry is posted, the Insurance Expense account with a $360 debit and a $310 credit has a $50 debit balance. This $50 is the expired insurance for the period and is closed to Income Summary with the following entry:

Dec.	*31*	*Income Summary*.......................	*50.00*	
		Insurance Expense....................		*50.00*
		To close the Insurance Expense account.		

After the closing entry is posted, the Prepaid Insurance and Insurance Expense accounts appear as follows:

Prepaid Insurance

Date		Explanation	Dr.	Cr.	Bal.
Dec.	31	Adjusting	310.00		310.00

Insurance Expense

Date		Explanation	Dr.	Cr.	Bal.
Aug.	1	Purchase	360.00		360.00
Dec.	31	Adjusting		310.00	50.00
Dec.	31	Closing		50.00	–0–

At this point the $310 cost of unexpired insurance is in the Prepaid Insurance account. If it is left in this account, the account balances are the same as if the premium payment was originally recorded as an asset. If it is desired to return the unexpired insurance to the Insurance Expense account, an additional entry is required. This entry is a reversing entry; it reverses the adjusting entry that originally removed the unexpired insurance from the Insurance Expense account. It is:

Jan.	1	Insurance Expense.......................	310.00	
		Prepaid Insurance....................		310.00
		To reverse the unexpired insurance ad-		
		justing entry.		

The reversing entry returns the remaining $310 of prepaid insurance to the Insurance Expense account. After it is posted, the accounts appear as follows:

Prepaid Insurance

Date		Explanation	Dr.	Cr.	Bal.
Dec.	31	Adjusting	310.00		310.00
Jan.	1	Reversing		310.00	–0–

Insurance Expense

Date		Explanation	Dr.	Cr.	Bal.
Aug.	1	Purchase	360.00		360.00
Dec.	31	Adjusting		310.00	50.00
Dec.	31	Closing		50.00	–0–
Jan.	1	Reversing	310.00		310.00

When a prepaid expense is initially recorded as an expense, a series of adjusting, closing, and reversing entries similar to the foregoing is made at the end of each accounting period.

Choice of Methods. A prepaid expense may originally be recorded as either an asset or an expense. Both methods are correct and are used. Normally, for a prepaid item that is to be charged to expense over several accounting periods, such as prepaid insurance or supplies, the asset method is preferable. This is because the asset method requires one less entry, a reversing entry. However, for an item like prepaid interest on a discounted, short-term note payable, the expense method may be better. This is because the majority of concerns operate with accounting periods one year in length, and interest prepayments on their 30-, 60-, and 90-day notes discounted during the first nine or more months of each year, although assets at the time of payment, become interest expense before the year-end. Consequently, if interest on each note is recorded as an expense at the time the note is discounted, there is no need for a year-end adjusting entry transferring this interest from the Prepaid Interest account to Interest Expense.

UNEARNED REVENUES

Revenue collected in one accounting period but not earned until a future period is called *unearned revenue*. Unearned revenue items are liabilities until earned. Unearned subscriptions or subscriptions collected in advance by a publisher, unearned interest or interest collected in advance by a bank, and unearned rent or rent collected in advance by a landlord are examples. Such items are commonly received in one accounting period but are not entirely earned until a future period.

For example, a building rents for $100 a month, and on September 1, the building owner receives a $600 check from the tenant for six months' rent in advance. On the date of receipt, the entire $600 is unearned rent and a liability to the building owner. On that date he has the liability to furnish use of the building to the tenant for six months. Day by day as the tenant occupies the building, the liability is discharged and the rent is earned. If the building owner operates with annual accounting periods that end each December 31, by that date $400 of the $600 is earned and should appear on his income statement as revenue, and the remaining unearned $200 should appear on his balance sheet as a current liability.

Like a prepaid expense, an unearned revenue may be recorded in either of two ways. At the time of receipt, it may be recorded as a liability or as a revenue. However, regardless of which way it is recorded, at the end of each accounting period an adjustment is made to separate the unearned liability portion and the earned revenue portion. If an unearned revenue is originally recorded as a liability, the end-of-the-period adjustment removes the earned portion from the liability account. If originally recorded as revenue, the adjustment removes the unearned liability portion from the revenue account. This text favors recording as liabilities all items of unearned revenue that will be earned during a period of time extending over several accounting periods, because the liability method requires one less journal entry, a reversing entry, at the end of each accounting period.

Unearned rent may be used to illustrate the recording of all unearned revenues. For example, assume that on September 1 a landlord receives $600 from a tenant paying six months' rent in advance.

Recording Unearned Revenue as a Liability. If the landlord records the unearned rent as a liability, the following entry in general journal form is made:

Sept.	1	Cash....................................	600.00	
		Unearned Rent......................		600.00
		To record the receipt of unearned rent.		

Recording the receipt in this manner places the entire $600 in a liability account. If the landlord's annual accounting period ends on December 31, when it ends, $400 of the $600 has been earned and the following adjusting entry is required to remove the earned rent from the liability account:

Dec.	31	Unearned Rent...........................	400.00	
		Rent Earned.........................		400.00
		To remove the earned rent from the Unearned Rent account.		

This adjusting entry causes the earned $400 to appear on the income statement as revenue. The balance remaining in the Unearned Rent account then appears on the balance sheet as a liability.

After the adjusting entry is posted, the Unearned Rent and Rent Earned accounts appear as follows:

| | Unearned Rent | | | | | Rent Earned | | | |
Date	Explanation	Dr.	Cr.	Bal.	Date	Explanation	Dr.	Cr.	Bal.
Sept. 1	Receipt		600.00	600.00	Dec. 31	Adjusting		400.00	400.00
Dec. 31	Adjusting	400.00		200.00					

At the accounting period end, in addition to the adjusting entry, the following entry to close the Rent Earned account is made:

Dec.	31	Rent Earned.............................	400.00	
		Income Summary.....................		400.00
		To close the Rent Earned account.		

When an unearned revenue is initially recorded as a liability, adjusting and closing entries similar to these two are made at the end of each accounting period.

Recording Unearned Revenue as Revenue. If the landlord of the previous illustration records the receipt of the unearned rent as revenue, the following entry in general journal form is made:

Sept.	*1*	*Cash..*	*600.00*	
		Rent Earned.........................		*600.00*
		To record the receipt of unearned rent.		

This entry records the entire $600 as revenue. At the accounting period end, only $400 of the amount is earned and only $400 should appear on the income statement as revenue. Consequently, the following adjusting entry is required:

Dec.	*31*	*Rent Earned............................*	*200.00*	
		Unearned Rent.....................		*200.00*
		To remove the unearned rent from the Rent Earned account.		

This entry removes from the Rent Earned account the amount that is unearned. After it is posted, the accounts appear as follows:

Unearned Rent

Date		Explanation	Dr.	Cr.	Bal.
Dec.	*31*	*Adjusting*		*200.00*	*200.00*

Rent Earned

Date		Explanation	Dr.	Cr.	Bal.
Sept.	*1*	*Receipt*		*600.00*	*600.00*
Dec.	*31*	*Adjusting*	*200.00*		*400.00*

After the adjusting entry is posted, the Rent Earned account has a $400 credit balance and is closed to Income Summary with the following entry:

Dec.	*30*	*Rent Earned............................*	*400.00*	
		Income Summary....................		*400.00*
		To close the Rent Earned account.		

At this point the $200 amount of unearned rent is in the Unearned Rent account. If it is left there, the account balances are the same as if the receipt were originally recorded as a liability. If it is desired to return the unearned rent to the Rent Earned account, the following reversing entry is made:

Jan.	*1*	*Unearned Rent.........................*	*200.00*	
		Rent Earned........................		*200.00*
		To reverse the unearned rent adjusting		
		entry.		

This reversing entry reverses the adjusting entry that removed the unearned rent from the Rent Earned account. It also returns the unearned rent to the revenue account. After it is posted the accounts appear as follows:

Unearned Rent

Date		Explanation	Dr.	Cr.	Bal.
Dec.	31	Adjusting		200.00	200.00
Jan.	1	Reversing	200.00		–0–

Rent Earned

Date		Explanation	Dr.	Cr.	Bal.
Sept.	1	Receipt		600.00	600.00
Dec.	31	Adjusting	200.00		400.00
Dec.	31	Closing	400.00		–0–
Jan.	1	Reversing		200.00	200.00

When an unearned revenue is originally recorded as revenue, this series of adjusting, closing, and reversing entries is repeated at the end of each accounting period.

INTERIM STATEMENTS

Most concerns operate with accounting periods one year in length; and at the end of each year they prepare year-end financial statements, close their revenue and expense accounts, and begin a new cycle of operations. Also, since management in the average concern needs financial and operating data more often than once each year, in addition to their year-end statements, many concerns prepare "in-between statements" or *interim statements*. These are usually prepared each month, and commonly consist of a month-end balance sheet, an income statement for the current month, and an income statement covering operations from the first of the year to the end of the current month.

Interim statements are like the regular year-end statements in that an ordinary work sheet is used in assembling their data. They differ in that estimated inventories secured either by the gross profit or retail method are commonly used; and they also differ in that, after the statements are completed, the work sheet adjustments are not entered in the accounts and the accounts are not closed. Obviously these differences mean less work, and are the reason many concerns choose year-long accounting periods with interim statements in preference to, for example, monthly accounting periods that require a complete closing each month.

When an interim work sheet is prepared, after it is completed, the amounts in its Balance Sheet columns are the amounts for preparing the interim balance sheet. Likewise, since the accounts are not closed when interim statements are prepared, the amounts in the Income Statement columns of an interim work sheet represent revenues earned and expenses incurred from the beginning of the accounting period to the work sheet date, and are the amounts for preparing the income statement showing operating results for this period. For example, if interim statements are prepared at the end of January, at the end of February, and again at the end of March, the accounts are not closed after these statements are completed. Consequently, when the April interim work sheet is prepared, the amounts in its Income Statement columns represent revenues earned and expenses incurred from January 1 through April 30, and are the amounts for the income statement for this period.

This leaves for consideration the one-month, interim income statement, the amounts for which must be arrived at by a process of substraction. To illustrate this process, assume that an interim work sheet is prepared at the end of April. On such a work sheet the amounts in the Income Statement columns represent revenues and expenses for the four-month period, January 1 through April 30. Consequently, to arrive at the figures for the one-month, April income statement, it is necessary to subtract from each revenue amount in the Income Statement columns, the amount of that revenue applicable to the first three months of the year, and to subtract from each expense amount in the Income Statement columns, the amount of that expense applicable to the first three months of the year. The amount of each revenue and expense applicable to the year's first three months may be secured from the Income Statement columns of the March 31 interim work sheet or from the January 1–March 31 income statement.

QUESTIONS FOR CLASS DISCUSSION

1. Distinguish between the cash basis of accounting and the accrual basis. What are the advantages and disadvantages of each?
2. Richard Snyder owns a small weekly newspaper. The paper is operated with yearly accounting periods, and its receipts from subscriptions and advertising are about the same each year. Subscriptions are collected for a full year in advance, and both subscriptions and advertising receipts are considered revenue of the period in which they are collected. Would you advise that Richard Snyder accrue and defer advertising and subscriptions revenue? Why?
3. Define and give an example of (a) an accrued expense, (b) an accrued revenue, (c) a prepaid expense, and (d) an unearned revenue.
4. What is the difference between an accrued expense and a prepaid expense? An accrued revenue and an unearned revenue?

5. Classify each of the following items as (*a*) a prepaid expense, (*b*) an accrued expense, (*c*) an accrued revenue, or (*d*) an unearned revenue.
   1. Wages paid an employee in advance.
   2. Interest received by a bank on a discounted note.
   3. Subscriptions payments received by a publisher.
   4. Unpaid interest on a note given the bank.
   5. Unpaid interest on a customer's note.
   6. Insurance premiums received by an insurance company.

6. Central Sales Company closes its books annually on each December 31. On December 6 the firm gave its $6,000, 60-day, 6 percent note to the bank in order to borrow money. (*a*) Assume that the firm keeps its books on a cash basis, and give in general journal form the entries that must be made because of this note from the time it is issued until it is paid. (*b*) Assume that the firm keeps its books on an accrual basis, and give the required entries.

7. The entries marked (*a*) in the following account resulted from interest payments, and the entries marked (*b*) and (*c*) were adjusting entries. What was the nature of the entry marked (*b*)? The entry marked (*c*)? What was the nature of each of the entries marked (*d*), (*e*), and (*f*)?

Interest Expense

Date		Explanation	Debit	Credit	Balance
May	5	(*a*)	52.00		52.00
Aug.	7	(*a*)	130.00		182.00
Dec.	1	(*a*)	90.00		272.00
Dec.	31	(*b*)		30.00	242.00
Dec.	31	(*c*)	12.00		254.00
Dec.	31	(*d*)		254.00	–0–
Jan.	1	(*e*)	30.00		30.00
Jan.	1	(*f*)		12.00	18.00

8. Give in general journal form the entires to record the following:
   a) Dec. 16   Gave the bank a 60-day, 4 percent, $9,000 note.
   b) Dec. 31   Recorded the accrued interest.
   c) Jan. 1   Reversed the accrued interest adjusting entry.
   d) Feb. 14   Paid the note.
   If no reversing entry is made on January 1, what entry is required when the note is paid on February 14?

9. A company that prepares interim statements closes its books each June 30. When the company prepares an interim work sheet on April 30, the revenue and expense amounts in the Income Statement columns are revenues and expenses for what period of time?

PROBLEMS

Problem 12–1

Part 1. Boswell Sales Company borrowed $8,000 on November 16 by giving its bank a 60-day, 6 percent note for that amount. The concern's accounting periods end on December 31.

Required:

Give entries in general journal form to record the issuance and payment of the note plus any adjusting, closing, and reversing entries the concern would make under each of the following assumptions:

a) The concern keeps its accounting records on a cash basis.

b) The concern keeps its records on an accrual basis but does not make reversing entries.

c) The concern keeps its records on an accrual basis and makes reversing entries.

Part 2. On November 1, as a short-term proposition, Boswell Sales Company rented space in its warehouse to Geneva Supply Company for six months. Geneva Supply Company paid the six months' rent, $300, in advance. The accounting periods of both concerns end on December 31.

Required:

Prepare entries to record the rent receipt or payment and to adjust and close the accounts of—

1. Boswell Sales Company:

    a) First under the assumption the receipt was credited to the Rent Earned account.

    b) And then under the assumption the receipt was credited to the Unearned Rent account.

2. Geneva Supply Company:

    a) First under the assumption the payment was debited to the Rent Expense account.

    b) And then under the assumption the payment was debited to the Prepaid Rent account.

Problem 12–2

Prepare adjusting, closing, and reversing entries as required for the following groups of data under the assumption the accounting period ends on June 30.

1. The company occupies a building it purchased and moved into on February 1 of the current year. The building has an estimated 30-year life and a $15,000 salvage value. It cost $87,000.

2. On June 30 the Accounts Receivable account had a $17,515 debit balance and the Allowance for Bad Debts account had a $665 credit balance. On that date the $315 account of John Sears was deemed uncollectible and written off as a bad debt, after which the allowance for bad debts was increased to equal 5 percent of the new balance of the Accounts Receivable account. (Give the entry for the write-off too.)

3. The Interest Expense account had a $561 debit balance on June 30 before any adjustments were made. On that date the following notes payable were outstanding: (*a*) A 90-day, 6 percent, $5,000 note given the bank on April 25. (*b*) A 60-day, noninterest-bearing, $4,000 note discounted at 6 percent on June 15. (Interest Expense was debited for the discount.)

4. The Interest Earned account had a $315 credit balance before adjustments. The following notes receivable were in the company's safe: (*a*) A 60-day, 6 percent, $1,000 note dated May 19. (*b*) A 60-day, noninterest-bearing, $3,600 note dated June 10 and on which interest at 5 percent had been collected in advance and credited to the Interest Earned account.

5. The Salaries Expense account had an $18,615 debit balance before adjustments. The company's five employees are paid each Monday at the rate of $15 per day for a five-day week that ended the previous Friday. The last Friday in June fell on the 26th. One employee suffered a financial emergency on Monday, June 29, and was paid his salary in advance for the week ending on July 3. The Salaries Expense account was debited at the time of payment for the $75 paid.

Problem 12–3

On December 31, at the end of the 1966 annual accounting period, a bookkeeper made the following errors:

0. Failed to record $90 of accrued salaries.
1. A portion of the company's warehouse was rented on December 1 at $150 per month to a tenant who paid his December, January, and February rents in advance. The bookkeeper did not make an adjustment for the unearned rent on December 31, which had been credited on receipt to the Rent Earned account.
2. The bookkeeper failed to make an adjustment for the accrued interest on a customer's $2,000, 60-day, 6 percent note dated and received on November 13.
3. Through an oversight the bookkeeper failed to record $245 of depreciation on store equipment.
4. No adjustment was made to record interest accrued on a $6,000, 60-day 6 percent note given the bank December 8.
5. A machine was leased on November 1, and six months' rent, $240, was paid in advance and debited to rent expense. The bookkeeper failed to adjust for the rent prepaid on December 31.
6. The bookkeeper made an error in adding the amounts on the year-end inventory sheets which caused a $75 understatement in the merchandise inventory.

Required:

Prepare a columnar form with headings and subheadings like the following illustration. List each error by number in the column headed "Error Number." Then under the assumption that none of the errors was discovered during 1967, tell the effect of each error on the statements. In each case tell the amount of the overstatement or understatement the error would cause in the assets, liabilities, owner equity, revenue, cost and expenses, and net income. If the error had no effect on an item, write the word "none" in the proper column. The effect of the first error, numbered "0," is shown as an example.

Error Number	1966 Income Statement			December 31, 1966, Balance Sheet			1967 Income Statement		
	Revenues	Costs and Expenses	Net Income	Assets	Liab.	Owner Equity	Revenues	Costs and Expenses	Net Income
0.	*None*	*Under $90*	*Over $90*	*None*	*Under $90*	*Over $90*	*None*	*Over $90*	*Under $90*

Problem 12–4

Part 1. A concern that made disbursements for interest during 1966 totaling $535 reported the following amounts of accrued and prepaid interest on its December 31, 1965, and December 31, 1966, balance sheets:

	December 31 Balance Sheets	
	1965	1966
Prepaid interest....................................	$15	$25
Accrued interest payable.........................	60	90

Required:

Under the assumption the December 31, 1965, amounts of accrued and prepaid interest were either paid or became an expense during 1966, prepare a calculation to show the amount of interest expense the concern should have reported on its 1966 income statement.

Part 2. A company that made interest collections totaling $450 during 1966 reported the following amounts of accrued and unearned interest on its December 31, 1965, and December 31, 1966, balance sheets:

	December 31 Balance Sheets	
	1965	1966
Accrued interest receivable.......................	$85	$65
Unearned interest.................................	35	40

Required:

Under the assumption that the December 31, 1965, amounts of accrued and unearned interest were either received or earned during 1966, prepare a calculation to show how much interest should have been reported on the company's 1966 income statement as earned in that year.

Part 3. A company reported on its income statement that it earned $235 of interest during 1966. Its December 31, 1965, and December 31, 1966, balance sheets showed the following amounts of accrued and unearned interest:

December 31
Balance Sheets

	1965	1966
Accrued interest receivable	$55	$70
Unearned interest	45	35

Required:

Under the assumption that the December 31, 1965, amounts of accrued and unearned interest were either received or earned during 1966, prepare a calculation to show the amount of cash received by the company from interest during 1966.

Problem 12–5

Mesa Supply Company closes its books annually on December 31, but it prepares monthly interim statements. On July 31 of the current year a trial balance of the company's ledger appeared as follows:

MESA SUPPLY COMPANY
Trial Balance, July 31, 19—

Cash	$ 3,120	
Petty cash	50	
Accounts receivable	6,745	
Allowance for bad debts		$ 295
Merchandise inventory (January 1, 19—)	11,985	
Prepaid insurance	425	
Store equipment	12,350	
Accumulated depreciation, store equipment		1,975
Office equipment	1,670	
Accumulated depreciation, office equipment		355
Notes payable		2,500
Accounts payable		2,860
Walter Taft, capital		23,700
Walter Taft, withdrawals	3,500	
Sales		46,850
Sales returns and allowances	850	
Purchases	28,055	
Purchases returns and allowances		430
Purchases discounts		535
Sales salaries	5,530	
Rent expense, selling space	2,520	
Advertising expense	565	
Office salaries	1,750	
Rent expense, office space	280	
Interest expense	105	
	$79,500	$79,500

Required:

1. Enter the trial balance on a work sheet form and complete the January 1 through July 31, seven months' interim work sheet using the following information:

a) Allowance for bad debts, an additional 1 percent of net sales.
b) Expired insurance, $280.
c) Seven months' depreciation on store equipment, $665.
d) Seven months' depreciation on office equipment, $105.
e) Accrued sales salaries, $110.
f) The $2,500, 60-day, noninterest-bearing note payable that is outstanding was discounted at 6 percent at Guaranty Bank on July 7.
g) Estimated July 31 merchandise inventory, $10,870.

2. From the interim work sheet prepare a July 31 balance sheet and an income statement for the seven-month period ended July 31.

3. The Income Statement columns of the June 30 interim work sheet of Mesa Supply Company showed the following amounts of revenues, expenses, and net income for the six-month period, January 1 through June 30. Use these amounts plus the amounts in the Income Statement columns of the July 31 interim work sheet you have just completed to prepare an income statement for the month of July.

	Income Statement	
	Debit	*Credit*
Merchandise inventory*.....................	11,985	10,675
Sales......................................		39,225
Sales returns and allowances..............	725	
Purchases.................................	23,095	
Purchases returns and allowances..........		310
Purchases discounts.......................		440
Sales salaries.............................	4,845	
Rent expense, selling space................	2,160	
Advertising expense........................	485	
Office salaries.............................	1,500	
Rent expense, office space.................	240	
Interest expense...........................	75	
Bad debts expense.........................	385	
Expired Insurance.........................	240	
Depreciation of store equipment...........	570	
Depreciation of office equipment..........	90	
	46,395	50,650
January 1—June 30 Net Income.............	4,255	
	50,650	50,650

* *January 1, 19___, inventory, $11,985; June 30, 19___, inventory, $10,675.*

CLASS EXERCISE

Exercise 12–1

Sundown Publishing Company began publication of *Sundown*, a monthly magazine, on November 5 of the current year. Cash was received for one- and two-year subscriptions to the magazine as follows:

	One-Year Subscriptions	Two-Year Subscriptions
October.....................................	$ 4,200	$ 3,600
November.................................	5,400	4,200
December.................................	4,800	4,600
	$14,400	$12,400

Delivery of the magazine to a new subscriber was and is begun in the month following receipt of his subscription.

Required:
1. Under the assumption the subscriptions were credited upon receipt to the Unearned Subscriptions account, and the concern's accounting period ends on December 31, give the required adjusting entry.
2. Give the required adjusting entry under the assumption the subscriptions were credited upon receipt to the Subscriptions Earned account.

ALTERNATE PROBLEMS

Problem 12–1A
Part 1. On November 1 Phoenix Sales granted Joseph Douglas an extension on the due date of a debt in exchange for a $2,400, 90-day, 6 percent note dated that day. The accounting periods of Phoenix Sales end on December 31, and the note was paid when due.

Required:
Give in general journal form the entries Phoenix Sales would make in recording the receipt of the note and its payment plus any adjusting, closing, and reversing entries it would make under each of the following assumptions: (*a*) Phoenix Sales keeps its records on a cash basis; (*b*) it keeps its records on an accrual basis but does not make reversing entries; (*c*) it keeps its records on an accrual basis and makes reversing entries.

Part 2. On December 1 United Contractors rented a machine from Machinery Supply Company for six months, paying the six months' rent, $450, in advance. The accounting periods of both companies end on December 31.

Required:
1. Prepare for United Contractors the entries to record the payment of the rent and to adjust and close the accounts (*a*) first under the assumption that the payment was debited to the Equipment Rentals Expense account, and (*b*) then under the assumption that it was debited to the Prepaid Equipment Rentals account.
2. Prepare for Machinery Supply Company the entries to record the receipt of the equipment rent and to adjust and close its accounts (*a*) first under the assumption the receipt was credited to the Revenue from Equipment Rentals account, and then (*b*) under the assumption it was credited to the Unearned Equipment Rentals account.

Problem 12–2A

On December 31, at the end of its annual accounting period, Central Sales assembled the following information for year-end adjusting entries:

  a) The Store Supplies account had been debited throughout the accounting period for supplies purchased, and its year-end balance was $497. An inventory showed $127 of store supplies on hand.

  b) On December 31 there were $445 of accrued but unpaid wages.

  c) The building owned and occupied for several years by Central Sales cost $120,000 and had been depreciated under the assumption it would have a 40-year life and no salvage value.

  d) On the previous November 1, as a temporary proposition not expected to be repeated, Central Sales rented space in its building to General Supply Company. General Supply Company paid the six months' rent, $360, in advance on that date, and Central Sales credited its Rent Earned account for the amount received.

  e) Central Sales discounted its $3,000, 60-day, noninterest-bearing note payable at 6 percent at its bank on November 13, debiting Interest Expense for the discount. The note was still outstanding on December 31.

  f) Central Sales had also borrowed an additional $5,000 by giving Guaranty Bank a $5,000, 60-day, 6 percent note on December 7.

  g) A customer was granted a 60-day extension on the due date of his $2,500 account balance when he gave Central Sales a 60-day, 6 percent note for that amount dated November 25.

Required:

  1. Prepare the adjusting entries required by the foregoing information.
  2. List by letter the entries you think it would be wise to reverse.
  3. Assume the bookkeeper failed to make the adjustments required by the foregoing information and also failed to discover the omission. State for each omitted adjustment the effect of its omission on the current year's net income and the succeeding year's income.

Problem 12–3A

At the end of the 1966 annual accounting period a bookkeeper made the following errors:

  1. Failed to record accrued interest on a note payable.
  2. Failed to adjust the Rent Earned account to remove therefrom unearned rent which had been credited to this account when a tenant paid a portion of his 1967 rent in advance.
  3. Failed to adjust the Interest Expense account to remove therefrom prepaid interest on a 60-day note discounted at the bank on December 12.
  4. Failed to record interest accrued on a note receivable.
  5. Failed to record depreciation on delivery equipment.
  6. Made an error that caused an understatement of the December 31, 1966, merchandise inventory.
  7. Failed to record salaries earned by the sales employees but not paid.

Required:

Prepare a columnar form with headings and subheadings like in the following illustration. List each error by number in the column headed "Error Number." Then, under the assumption that none of the errors were discovered during 1967, list the effect of each error on the 1966 and 1967 income statements and on the 1966 balance sheet. In each case tell the effect of the error on the revenues, costs and expenses, net income, assets, liabilities, and owner equity by writing in the proper column opposite each error the word "over" to indicate an overstatement of the item, "under" to indicate an understatement, and "none" to indicate no effect. For example, the effect of the first error is shown in the illustration.

Error Num- ber	1966 Income Statement			December 31, 1966 Balance Sheet			1967 Income Statement		
	Reve- nues	Costs and Ex- penses	Net Income	Assets	Liab.	Owner Equity	Reve- nues	Costs and Ex- penses	Net Income
1.	None	Under	Over	None	Under	Over	None	Over	Under

Problem 12–4A

Scott Huff, a realtor and loan broker who has always kept his records and prepared his statements on a cash basis, prepared the following condensed income statement at the end of his 1966 annual accounting period:

SCOTT HUFF REALTOR
Income Statement for Year Ended December 31, 1966

Revenues..$41,600
Expenses.. 22,400
Net Income..$19,200

An examination of his accounting records revealed the following amounts of ignored deferred and accrued items at the ends of 1965 and 1966:

	1965	1966
Unearned revenues...............................	$1,780	$1,640
Accrued revenues...............................	1,040	1,230
Prepaid expenses...............................	1,240	870
Accrued expenses...............................	2,410	3,100

Required:
Under the assumption all the foregoing 1965 prepaid and unearned items became expenses or were earned during 1966, and all ignored 1965 accrued items were either received or paid during 1966, prepare a new condensed 1966 income statement for Scott Huff. (In other words, prepare an income statement for Scott Huff as it would appear if he kept his records and prepared his statements on an accrual basis.)

Problem 12–5A

Lakeside Sales Company closes its books annually on December 31, but it prepares monthly interim statements. On October 31 of the current year a trial balance of its ledger appeared as follows:

LAKESIDE SALES COMPANY
Trial Balance, October 31, 19—

Cash..	$ 3,630	
Petty cash......................................	50	
Accounts receivable.............................	7,115	
Allowance for bad debts........................		$ 310
Merchandise inventory (January 1, 19—)........	11,230	
Prepaid insurance..............................	325	
Store supplies.................................	440	
Store equipment................................	9,585	
Accumulated depreciation, store equipment......		1,930
Office equipment...............................	1,875	
Accumulated depreciation, office equipment.....		465
Notes payable..................................		4,000
Accounts payable...............................		2,450
Scott Huff, capital............................		19,625
Scott Huff, withdrawals........................	5,000	
Sales..		62,250
Sales returns and allowances...................	750	
Purchases......................................	35,195	
Purchases returns and allowances...............		565
Purchases discounts............................		650
Sales salaries.................................	8,550	
Rent expense, selling space....................	4,500	
Advertising expense............................	715	
Office salaries................................	2,500	
Rent expense, office space.....................	500	
Interest expense...............................	285	
	$92,245	$92,245

Required:

1. Enter the trial balance on a work sheet form and complete the October 31, ten months' interim work sheet using the following information:

   a) Allowance for bad debts, and additional 1 percent of net sales.

   b) Expired insurance for ten months, $150.

   c) Estimated inventory of store supplies, $225.

   d) Ten months' depreciation on store equipment, $600.

   e) Ten months' depreciation on office equipment, $100.

   f) Accrued sales salaries, $115.

   g) The $4,000 note payable that is outstanding is a 60-day, 6 percent note given to the bank on September 16.

   h) The estimated merchandise inventory on October 31 is $10,665.

2. From the work sheet prepare an October 31 interim balance sheet and a January 1 through October 31 interim income statement.
3. The Income Statement columns of the interim work sheet completed by Lakeside Sales Company on September 30 showed the following amounts of revenue, expenses, and net income for the period January 1 through September 30. Use these amounts and the amounts in the Income Statement columns of the October 31 work sheet you have just completed to prepare an income statement for the month of October.

| | Income Statement | |
	Debit	Credit
Merchandise Inventory*..................	11,230	10,915
Sales......................................		55,610
Sales returns and allowances.............	610	
Purchases.................................	31,720	
Purchases returns and allowances.........		490
Purchases discounts.......................		585
Sales salaries.............................	7,705	
Rent expense, selling space...............	4,050	
Advertising expense.......................	635	
Office salaries............................	2,250	
Rent expense, office space................	450	
Interest expense..........................	290	
Bad debts expense........................	550	
Insurance expense........................	135	
Store supplies used.......................	190	
Depreciation of store equipment...........	540	
Depreciation of office equipment..........	90	
	60,445	67,600
January 1—September 30 Net Income......	7,155	
	67,600	67,600

    * January 1, 19__, inventory, $11,230; September 30, 19__, inventory, $10,915.

DECISION PROBLEM 12—WILLIAMS VARIETY STORE

    Williams Variety Store has completed the second year of its operations, during which its books have been kept on an accrual basis. However, the owner of the store is curious as to how he would have fared profit-wise had his books been kept on a pure cash basis. He knows that insofar as inventories are concerned he must use an accrual basis for tax purposes; nevertheless, he has asked you to ignore this and compute the store's net income for each year both on a cash and an accrual basis, explaining how each amount on the income statement is obtained.

The summarized data for the two years follows:

	196A	196B
1. *Cash sales*	$42,000	$48,000
2. *Sales on account*	61,000	70,000
3. *Collections from customer on accounts receivable*	43,000	51,000
4. *Cash purchases of merchandise*	20,000	18,000
5. *Purchases of merchandise on account*	53,000	70,000
6. *Payments on accounts payable for merchandise purchased*	29,000	69,000
7. *Inventory of merchandise on December 31*	11,000	20,000
8. *Salaries paid (salaries accrued and unpaid at end of each year: for 196A, $800; for 196B, $420)*	15,000	16,500
9. *Mr. Williams holds a lease on the store building, dated April 1, 196A, calling for annual rental of $4,800 payable in advance each April 1. Rent of $500 per month was paid for the first quarter of 196A before the lease was negotiated. Total rent paid in cash*	6,300	4,800
10. *Paid insurance for three years on policy dated May 1, 196A*	720	
11. *Annual interest paid on 6%, three-year note payable of $5,000, dated April 1, 196A*		300
12. *Other expenses paid (includes supplies purchased, portions of which were unused at end of 196A, $200 and 196B, $300)*	1,100	1,300

13

Voucher System for Controlling Cash Disbursements; Automation

THE VOUCHER system is an internal control system for cash disbursements. The subject of internal control was introduced in Chapter 8, and a system for controlling and protecting cash receipts was described. Internal control for cash receipts is important, but equally as important is a system for controlling the incurrence and payment of obligations that result in cash disbursements. The voucher system is such a system.

WHERE A VOUCHER SYSTEM IS NEEDED

A voucher system is usually not needed in a small business. This is because the owner or manager's personal contact with all phases of the business, as a rule, provides control over cash disbursements. A small business owner or manager often makes all purchases of goods and services, hires and closely supervises all employees, and personally negotiates all contracts. Also, he normally signs all checks; and as he signs each check he knows from his own contact and observation that the assets, goods, or services for which the check pays were actually received by the business.

This is not true in a large business. In a large business duties and responsibilities have to be delegated, and personal contact with all phases of the business by the person who signs checks is not possible. For example, in a large business several department heads or individuals are delegated the duty of requesting that assets or merchandise be purchased. The purchases are made by a purchasing department, and the goods are received by a receiving department from which they are forwarded on to the original requisitioning department. Likewise, employees of a large business are hired by a personnel department, their working time recorded by a timekeeping department, and their pay calculated by a payroll department. Also, in a large business several executives may have the power to negotiate special contracts that eventually result in cash disbursements. Finally, in a large business checks in payment of the obligations incurred by all departments and individuals are signed by a company treasurer or other disbursing officer. This disbursing officer cannot possibly know from personal contact and observation that the assets, goods, and services for which the checks were issued have been received or if the items should have been purchased in the first place. Consequently, if he cannot depend upon personal contact to tell him that each obligation is a proper obligation and should be paid, he must depend upon a system of internal control. In most large companies this internal control system is a *voucher system.*

VOUCHER SYSTEM IS NOT A COMPLETE ACCOUNTING SYSTEM

The voucher system is not a complete accounting system. It has no effect on transactions other than those that result in cash disbursements. For example, it has no effect on sales or cash receipts. These are recorded in the usual manner in a Sales Journal or Cash Receipts Journal whether a voucher system is in use or not.

THE VOUCHER

The business paper around which a voucher system is organized is called a *voucher.* The dictionary defines the word "voucher" as a paper that certifies to the truthfulness of something. This is a satisfactory accounting definition. In accounting, a voucher is a business paper on which a transaction is summarized, its correctness certified, and its recording and payment are approved.

Vouchers vary somewhat from company to company; but in general, are so designed that the invoice, bill, or other documents from which they are prepared are attached to and folded inside the voucher. This makes for ease in filing. The inside of a voucher, shown in Illustration 71, usually provides spaces for (1) the date of the voucher, (2) the payee's name and address, (3) a brief summary of the transaction, and (4) the signature of the person verifying the transaction and approving it for recording and payment. The outside usually has a list of accounts commonly debited and provides spaces for the debit amounts and the amount of the credit to Vouchers Payable. It also provides spaces for (1) the voucher's due date,

Illustration 71—Inside of a Voucher

VOUCHER NO.
767

VALLEY SUPPLY COMPANY
EUGENE, OREGON

DATE ___Oct. 1, 19___

PAY TO ___A. B. Seay Wholesale Company___

CITY ___Salem___ STATE ___Oregon___

FOR THE FOLLOWING: *(ATTACH ALL INVOICES AND SUPPORTING PAPERS)*

DATE OF INVOICE	TERMS	INVOICE NUMBER AND OTHER DETAILS	AMOUNT
Sept. 30, 19___	2/10,n/60	Invoice No. C-11756	800.00
		Less Discount	16.00
		Net Amount Payable	784.00

PAYMENT APPROVED

n. C. Neal
Auditor

(2) payee, (3) a summary of the payment, (4) payment date, and (5) the paying check number. All information entered on a voucher, excepting the payment date and paying check number, is entered at the time the voucher is prepared. Information as to payment is written in later when the voucher is actually paid. The outside of a voucher is shown in Illustration 72.

THE VOUCHER SYSTEM AND CONTROL

A voucher system gains control over cash disbursements by providing a routine which (1) permits only specific departments and individuals to incur obligations that result in cash disbursements; (2) establishes procedures for incurring such obligations and for their verification, approval, and recording; and (3) permits checks to be issued only in payment of properly verified, approved, and recorded obligations.

When a voucher system is in use, control over cash disbursements begins with the incurrence of obligations that result in cash disbursements. Only specified departments and individuals are authorized to incur such obligations, and the kind each may incur is limited. For example, only the purchasing department may incur obligations by purchasing merchandise, small assets, and supplies. Likewise, only the personnel, timekeeping, and

Illustration 72—Outside of a Voucher

Voucher No.
767

ACCOUNTING DISTRIBUTION

Account Debited	Amount
Purchases	800.00
Freight-In	
Store Supplies	
Office Supplies	
Sales Salaries	
Office Salaries	
Delivery Salaries	
Advertising Expense	
Total Vouch. Pay. Cr.	800.00

Due Date   October 10, 19—

Pay to   A. B. Seay Wholesale Co.
City   Salem
State   Oregon

Summary of Charges:
Total Charges _____ 800.00
Discount _____ 16.00
Net Payment _____ 784.00

Record of Payment:
Paid _____
Check No. _____

payroll departments working together with the production department may incur obligations for ordinary wages and salaries.

Further control is gained by establishing a more or less inflexible routine to be followed in incurring each kind of obligation, providing within the routine for the production of business papers at each step, and providing a means of bringing these papers together, checking them, and using them as a basis for approving the transaction for recording and payment.

Normally the business papers are brought together in the accounting department where they are checked and become the basis for preparation of a voucher to which they are attached and folded inside. After a voucher is prepared and its business papers attached, it is sent to the person responsible for approving vouchers. Here approval is normally based upon the information in and signatures on the attached business papers.

After being approved and recorded a voucher is filed until its due date, when it is sent to the office of the company cashier or other disbursing officer for payment. Here the person responsible for issuing checks depends upon the approved voucher and its supporting papers to tell him the obligation is a proper obligation, properly incurred, and should be paid.

OPERATION OF A VOUCHER SYSTEM

The incurrence and payment of an obligation for the purchase of merchandise may be used to illustrate the operation of a voucher system. In discussing the control of purchases in Chapter 6 it was shown how a selling department manager desiring the purchase of merchandise completes a purchase requisition and sends it to the purchasing department. The purchasing department issues a purchase order to the vendor who ships the merchandise to the purchaser's receiving department and mails an invoice to the accounting department. The receiving department counts and examines the merchandise and reports to the accounting department on a receiving report. The accounting department then has in its possession:

1. A copy of the requisition listing the items requested.
2. A purchase order listing the merchandise ordered.
3. An invoice showing the goods shipped by the seller.
4. A receiving report listing the items received.

With the information contained on these business papers, the accounting department is in a position to approve the invoice for entry on the books and ultimate payment. In approving the invoice, clerks in the accounting department check and compare the information on all these papers. To facilitate the checking and comparing procedure, an invoice approval form having places for the initials of each clerk who completes a step in the checking and comparing procedure is used. After the checking and comparing procedure is completed, a voucher is prepared. This is a simple task requiring only that a clerk type the required information in the proper blank spaces on a voucher form. The information is taken from the invoice and its supporting documents. After the voucher is completed, the invoice and its supporting documents are attached to and folded inside the voucher. The voucher is then sent to the desk of the chief clerk or auditor who makes an additional check, approves the accounting distribution, and approves the voucher for recording. The voucher is then recorded in the Voucher Register.

From this point, the treatment of vouchers for so-called cash transactions and the treatment of those for credit transactions differ. If a voucher calls for immediate payment, a so-called cash transaction, after it is recorded in the Voucher Register, it is sent directly to the office of the company treasurer or disbursing officer for payment. On the other hand, if the voucher is to be paid at a later date, it is recorded in the Voucher Register and then filed in an unpaid voucher file until its due date, when it is taken from the file and sent to the office of the disbursing officer for payment.

Vouchers and the obligation they represent receive final approval and checks are written for their payment in the office of the company treasurer or other disbursing officer. Here the person responsible for paying obligations bases the issuance of each check upon a voucher and its supporting papers. A voucher and its supporting papers tell this person that an obligation is a proper obligation and should be paid.

After payment, paid vouchers are filed in a permanent, paid voucher file, normally in numerical order to aid in locating any paid voucher.

THE VOUCHER REGISTER

In a sense the Voucher Register is an expanded Purchases Journal. It is an expanded journal because all purchases, with the exception of those in which a note is given in direct settlement, whether cash or credit, whether purchases of merchandise, assets, or services, are recorded therein. As an expanded Purchases Journal, when a voucher system is in use, it replaces the purchases journals illustrated thus far.

Vouchers should always be prenumbered and entered in the Voucher Register in numerical order. If a voucher is spoiled in preparation, it should be marked void and entered without dollar amounts in its proper numerical order. In such cases the words "void" or "spoiled" are written in the register column provided for the creditor's name. Prenumbering vouchers and recording each in numerical order helps eliminate unrecorded vouchers.

Voucher Registers vary somewhat from company to company; but in general, provide columns for the date, creditor's name, voucher number, and a record of voucher payments. In addition, there is a Vouchers Payable credit column and a number of debit columns. Exact debit columns provided vary from company to company. In merchandising concerns a debit column is always provided for recording merchandise purchases; and in all companies, so long as space is available, in order that posting labor may be saved by posting column totals, special debit columns are provided for each type of expense that occurs sufficiently often to warrant a special column. In addition, a Sundry Accounts debit column is provided for those debits that do not occur often.

All information about each voucher that is entered in the register columns, with the exception of that entered in the columns used in recording the voucher's payment, is entered as soon as each voucher is approved for recording. The information as to payment date and the number of the paying check is entered later as each voucher is paid.

Sometimes a company, such as the one whose Voucher Register is shown in Illustration 73, places its expense accounts in subsidiary expense ledgers and maintains only expense controlling accounts in its General Ledger. When this is done, the usual controlling-account-subsidiary-ledger technique of posting column totals to the controlling accounts and posting individual amounts from the columns to the subsidiary expense ledgers is followed.

If individual amounts are to be posted from expense columns such as those shown in Illustration 73, it is necessary to indicate in the Voucher Register at the time each expense voucher is recorded, the subsidiary ledger account to which the amount is to be posted. The account could be indicated by placing its name in an account name column. However, often there is not sufficient room for such a column; and, as in Illustration 73, the individual subsidiary ledger expense accounts to which amounts are to be posted are commonly indicated by using account identifying code numbers. (It might be wise at this time for the student to review the discussion of code numbers in Chapter 5.) When a code number is used to identify the subsidiary ledger account to which an amount is to be posted, the code number is entered in the "Acct. Code" column at the time the amount is recorded.

A Voucher Register such as that shown in Illustration 73 is posted as follows. At the end of each month the columns are totaled and crossfooted to prove their equality. After this, the Vouchers Payable column total is credited to the Vouchers Payable account, the Purchases column total is debited to Purchases, and the Freight-In column total is debited to Freight-In. The individual amounts in these columns are not posted.

The Selling Expense and General Expense column totals are debited to these general ledger controlling accounts; and the individual amounts in the columns are debited to the subsidiary expense ledger accounts indicated by the code numbers in the "Acct. Code" columns.

The individual amounts in the Sundry Accounts column are debited to the accounts named; and the column total is not posted. If voucher register

Illustration 73

Page 32   VO

Date		Voucher No.	Payee	When and How Paid		Vouch-ers Payable Credit	Pur-chases Debit	Frei I Del
				Date	Check No.			
19—								
Oct.	1	767	A. B. Seay Co.	10/9	753	800 00	800 00	
	1	768	Daily Sentinel	10/9	754	53 00		
	2	769	Seaboard Supply Co.	10/12	756	235 00	155 00	1
	4	770	Spoiled Voucher					
	6	771	George Smith	10/6	734	65 00		
	6	772	Frank Jones	10/6	735	62 00		
	6	773	George Roth	10/6	736	70 00		
	30	998	First National Bank	10/30	972	505 00		
	30	999	Petty Cash	10/30	973	18 00		
	31	1000	Tarbell Wholesale Co.	Return—	GJ 38	235 00	235 00	
	31	1001	Office Equipment Co.	10/31	974	195 00		
						5,079 00	2,435 00	156
						(213)	(511)	(51

space is limited, account code numbers and an account code number column may be used in this section instead of account names and an Account Name column.

Although no amounts need be posted daily from the Voucher Register, the individual amounts in the Selling Expense, General Expense, and Sundry Accounts columns may be posted daily if the bookkeeper so wishes.

FILING UNPAID VOUCHERS

When a voucher system is in use, all purchases, both cash and credit, are recorded in the Voucher Register. Until after they are recorded, purchases requiring immediate cash disbursements, so-called cash transactions, are treated in the same manner as credit transactions. However, after recording, their treatment differs. The difference, as previously explained, has to do with filing and payment. A voucher for a transaction requiring an immediate disbursement is forwarded at once to the office of the disbursing officer for payment, while a voucher for a credit transaction is filed in an *unpaid voucher file* until due. On its due date, it is then taken from the file and forwarded for payment.

An unpaid voucher may be filed under the date on which it will be paid,

Illustration 73—Continued

	Selling Expenses Controlling Dr.			General Expenses Controlling Dr.			Sundry Accounts Debit		
t. le	Folio	Amount Debit	Acct. Code	Folio	Amount Debit	Account Name	Folio	Amount Debit
2	√	53 00							
						Store Supplies	117	70 00
			651	√	65 00				
1	√	62 00							
1	√	70 00							
						Notes Payable	211	500 00
						Interest Expense	721	5 00
2	√	5 00				Office Supplies	118	5 50
						Office Equipment	134	195 00
		837 00			716 00			935 00
		(600)			(650)			(√)

or it may be filed alphabetically under the name of the creditor. Each method has its advantages.

Generally unpaid vouchers are filed under the dates on which they will be paid. This aids in taking cash discounts because it automatically brings a voucher to the disbursing officer's attention on its due date. Under this system a discount is never missed because a voucher's due date was overlooked. In addition, filing vouchers by due dates aids in financial management. When vouchers are filed in this manner, it is easy for the person responsible for paying obligations to determine the total obligations maturing within a short future period. This in turn aids in forecasting short-term cash needs. Filing vouchers by due dates has one disadvantage. Under this system it is difficult to locate a particular unpaid voucher.

Filing unpaid vouchers alphabetically by creditors aids in locating individual vouchers. It also makes it easier to know the total owed each creditor. However, when vouchers are filed in this manner, a supplementary record must be maintained to tell which vouchers are due each day. This supplementary record is often a file called a *tickler file*. A tickler file for unpaid vouchers has a file with a card for each day of the month, with individual vouchers listed by creditors' names on the file card of their due date. The person responsible for paying vouchers examines the tickler file each day to determine the vouchers due that day. He then goes to the alphabetical file and removes these vouchers for payment.

All advantages of both filing methods without the complication of a tickler file may be obtained by making a carbon copy of each voucher as it is prepared. The original copies are then filed in the unpaid vouchers file by due dates and are used in making payments. After payment, the original copies are refiled numerically in a paid vouchers file. The carbon copies are filed in a permanent file, alphabetically by creditors, and become a permanent record of purchases from each creditor.

NATURE OF THE UNPAID VOUCHER FILE

When a voucher system is installed, the Vouchers Payable account and the file of unpaid vouchers are substituted for the Accounts Payable controlling account and subsidiary. Accounts Payable Ledger. In effect the unpaid vouchers file is a subsidiary ledger of creditors' accounts. Likewise, the Vouchers Payable account is in effect a controlling account controlling both the unpaid vouchers file and the vouchers listed as unpaid in the Voucher Register.

All vouchers entered in the Voucher Register result in a credit to the Vouchers Payable account, and checks drawn and entered in the Check Register in payment of vouchers result in a debit. Likewise, all vouchers entered in the Voucher Register are either paid at once or are filed in an unpaid vouchers file until paid, when they are removed. Consequently, when both the Voucher Register and Check Register are posted, the balance of the Vouchers Payable account should equal the sum of the unpaid vouchers in the unpaid vouchers file.

This equality is verified after posting is completed each month by adding the amounts of the unpaid vouchers in the unpaid vouchers file and comparing the sum with the balance of the Vouchers Payable account. Likewise, the unpaid vouchers in the file are compared with the unpaid vouchers shown in the Voucher Register's record of payments column. Since the number of each paying check and the payment date are entered in the Voucher Register's payments column as each voucher is paid, the vouchers in the register without check numbers and payment dates should be the same as those in the unpaid vouchers file.

THE VOUCHER SYSTEM CHECK REGISTER

Under a voucher system, no obligation is paid until a voucher is prepared and recorded. Furthermore, no check is drawn except in payment of a specific voucher. Consequently, as a result of these control procedures, the Check Register used in a voucher system is materially simplified. Since checks are written only in payment of vouchers, all checks result in debits to Vouchers Payable and credits to cash. If the terms of an invoice being paid provide for a discount, there is an additional credit to purchases discounts. Therefore, a voucher system Check Register needs only three money columns. It needs money columns for debits to Vouchers Payable, credits to Purchases Discounts, and credits to Cash or to the bank. Such a Check Register is shown in Illustration 74.

Not only is the design of a Check Register used with a voucher system simplified, its posting is also easier. No amounts are posted individually; all amounts are posted in the column totals at the end of the month. In posting, the Vouchers Payable debit column total is debited to the Vouchers Payable account. The Purchases Discounts credit column total is

Illustration 74—The Voucher System Check Register

CHECK REGISTER

Date		Payee	Voucher No.	Check No.	Vouchers Payable Debit	Purchases Discounts Credit	Merchants National Bank Credit
19—							
Oct.	1	C. B. & Y. RR Co.	765	728	14.00		14.00
	3	Frank Mills	766	729	73.00		73.00
	3	Ajax Wholesale Co.	753	730	250.00	5.00	245.00
	4	Normal Supply Co.	747	731	100.00	2.00	98.00
	5	Thomas McGinnin	763	732	43.00		43.00
	6	Giant Equipment Co.	759	733	342.00		342.00
	6	George Smith	771	734	65.00		65.00
	6	Frank Jones	772	735	62.00		62.00
	30	First National Bank	998	972	505.00		505.00
	30	Petty Cash	999	973	18.00		18.00
	31	Office Equipment Co.	1001	974	195.00		195.00
					6,468.00	28.00	6,440.00
					(213)	(512)	(111)

credited to Purchases Discounts, and the total of the Cash (or bank) credit column is posted to the Cash (or bank) account.

RECORDING INVOICES AT THEIR NET AMOUNTS

Thus far in this text the illustrated method for handling invoices subject to cash discounts has been to enter all such invoices in the Purchases Journal or Voucher Register at their gross amounts and to record at the time of payment any discounts taken. This is a satisfactory procedure and is commonly used. However, companies that follow the practice of taking all offered discounts also commonly use a different procedure under which invoices are recorded upon receipt at their net amounts and any discounts not taken are recorded at the time of payment as discounts lost. Actually, under this system discounts taken are not formally recorded; but discounts missed are recorded as discounts lost. For example, if a company that records invoices at their net amounts purchases $1,000 of merchandise, terms 2/10, n/30, the purchase is recorded in the company's Voucher Register with debits and credits as follows:

Dec.	*17*	*Purchases*...............................	*980.00*	
		Vouchers Payable.....................		*980.00*
		Purchased $1,000 of merchandise subject to terms of 2/10, n/30.		

If the voucher for this purchase is paid within the discount period (all vouchers should be so paid), the check register entry recording the payment has a debit to Vouchers Payable and a credit to cash for $980. However, if payment is not made within the discount period and the discount is lost, an entry like the following must be made in the General Journal when the voucher is paid:

Jan.	*15*	*Discounts Lost*............................	*20.00*	
		Vouchers Payable.....................		*20.00*
		To record a discount lost.		

In addition to the foregoing entry, a notation is placed in the When and How Paid column of the Voucher Register. The notation commonly reads "See General Journal, p. 35," or something similar. It refers a person examining the records to the entry recording the discount lost, and makes it easy to trace the entire transaction. Also, a notation as to the discount lost is placed on the voucher and a check for the full $1,000 invoice amount is drawn in its payment and entered in the Check Register.

When invoices are recorded at gross amounts, the balance of the Purchases Discounts account appears on the income statement to show discounts taken; and when invoices are recorded at their net amounts, the balance of the Discounts Lost account appears to show discounts lost. Of the two, information as to discounts lost is the more important to management, because a well-managed concern tries to take all discounts offered. If a discount is missed, someone may have failed his assigned task, and this should be called to management's attention.

THE VOUCHER SYSTEM AND PETTY CASH

Obviously a petty cash fund must be maintained when a voucher system is in use. This is because the issuance of a check under a voucher system is even more difficult, time consuming, and expensive than when a Cash Disbursements Journal or ordinary Check Register are used. Fortunately, the voucher system does not materially affect the operation of the petty cash fund. If a petty cash fund is started after a voucher system is in operation, a voucher debiting Petty Cash is prepared and recorded. A check is then drawn and cashed in its payment, and the proceeds are turned over to the petty cashier. The fund then operates in the usual manner until it must be replenished. When the fund is replenished, a voucher is prepared and approved for the amount of the replenishing check. The debits listed on the voucher are obtained in the usual manner from the petty cash record. After the replenishing voucher is recorded, a check is drawn in its payment and cashed; the proceeds are given to the petty cashier; and the fund is ready to begin anew the cycle of its operations.

UNCOMMON VOUCHER TRANSACTIONS

The voucher system provides a more or less inflexible routine of procedures for handling obligations that result in cash disbursements, which are designed to gain control over such transactions. As long as disbursement transactions follow the normal pattern, their handling and recording are a matter of routine. However, because of the system's inflexibility, uncommon transactions such as purchases returns, partial payments, notes payable, and transactions in which an error is made need special attention.

Errors. When a voucher system is in use, procedures for checking invoices, payrolls, bills, and other data should be such that an undiscovered error is a most uncommon occurrence. Yet, regardless of care, errors will occur. An error involving the amount of a voucher that is discovered before the Voucher Register is posted may be corrected by ruling a single line through the incorrect amount. The correct amount is then written in above on the same line. Care must be exercised to see that the error is corrected both in the Voucher Register and on the voucher. An error in which the wrong account is debited is corrected both in the register and on the voucher by ruling out the amount in the wrong column and on the wrong line. The amount is then written in the correct register column and on the correct line of the voucher. If proper internal control is maintained, voucher corrections must be initialed on the voucher by the persons responsible for voucher approvals.

An error discovered after the Voucher Register is posted must be corrected with a general journal entry. If, for example, the correction decreases a voucher amount, the entry is a debit to Vouchers Payable and a credit to the account originally debited. Here again care must be taken to see that the correction is made on the voucher and that it is properly approved. In addition to the correction on the voucher, a reference to the general journal entry recording the correction is made in the Voucher Register in the payments column on the upper half of the line on which the corrected voucher is recorded. The reference normally reads "See General Journal, p. 34," or something similar. The reference makes it easy for a person examining the records to trace the entire transaction.

Purchases Returns. A company with a well-organized and properly functioning routine for handling purchases makes most of its returns before vouchers are prepared. However, occasionally part of a purchase is returned after the voucher recording it is prepared and entered. Sometimes the return is even made after the Voucher Register is posted. In either case a merchandise return is recorded with a general journal entry similar to the following:

Nov.	5	*Vouchers Payable*	*15.00*	
		Purchases		*15.00*
		Credit memo No. 472 for purchase recorded		
		with Voucher No. 1000.		

In addition to the entry, a reference to the entry is made in the payments columns of the Voucher Register, on the upper half of the line for the voucher on which the return is made. This is illustrated with Voucher No. 1000 on the next to the last line of the Voucher Register shown in Illustration 73. Also, the amount of the return is deducted on the voucher. The credit memorandum and other documents verifying the return are then attached to the voucher. When the voucher is paid, a check is drawn for the corrected amount.

Notice that the return of the entry just given is credited directly to the Purchases account. This is optional; a Purchases Returns and Allowances account may be maintained, and returns may be credited to it. However, when such an account is maintained, it should be maintained to gather information about all returns and allowances; and when a voucher system is in use, most errors are found and returns are made before vouchers are prepared and approved. Consequently, in such cases, vouchers are normally prepared for the net amount purchased; and, as a result, each return is deducted from the amount of a purchase before the purchase is recorded. In such cases these returns do not appear in a Purchases Returns and Allowances account; and since the majority of returns are not recorded in a returns and allowances account, there is little gained in crediting such an account for the few returns made after vouchers are recorded. Therefore, many companies using a voucher system do not maintain a Purchases Returns and Allowances account. They maintain instead a memorandum record of returns and allowances.

Partial Payments.   Sometimes a company in a weak financial position temporarily cannot pay in full all its obligations as they mature. Often in such cases a company will make partial payments on a number of invoices in order to help maintain its credit standing. The voucher system is not designed to meet easily such a situation because under a voucher system every voucher is a unit to be paid in full with one check.

For example, assume that a company using a voucher system has recorded a $1,500 obligation with a single voucher. When the obligation becomes due, the company decides to pay the debt in two equal installments, one installment to be paid at once, and the other in 30 days. In such a case, two new vouchers for $750 each are prepared and entered in the Voucher Register. Their amounts are entered in both the Vouchers Payable credit column and the Sundry Accounts debit columns. Also, in the Sundry Accounts debit columns, the name of the account debited for each is Vouchers Payable. Consequently, as a result of this recording procedure, the Vouchers Payable account is both debited and credited for the new voucher amounts, and the recording does not change either the dollars of vouchers payable or the balance of the Vouchers Payable account. In addition to the foregoing, a reference to the new vouchers is made in the payments column of the Voucher Register on the line of the old voucher. Also the old voucher is marked "canceled," an explanation is written on it, and it is filed in the paid vouchers file. After all of this, the voucher that is to be paid at once is paid. The remaining voucher is filed until due.

If payment of a liability in installments can be anticipated at the time the obligation is incurred, the canceling of an old voucher can be avoided. In such cases all that is necessary is the preparation of a number of vouchers, one for each installment, at the time the obligation is first recorded.

Notes Payable.   If a company borrows funds by giving a note, the note is recorded in the Cash Receipts Journal as a debit to Cash and a credit to Notes Payable. Likewise, if a company purchases assets with a note, the transaction is recorded in the General Journal with a debit to the asset purchased and a credit to Notes Payable. In both cases the debt is represented by a note, and in both cases it is improper to classify the obligation as anything other than notes payable. Furthermore, neither transaction should be recorded in the Voucher Register because all voucher register entries result in credits to Vouchers Payable, and transactions in which notes are given should result in credits to Notes Payable. However, when a note matures, a voucher for its payment is prepared, since no obligation is ever paid without a voucher verifying it as a proper obligation that should be paid. The voucher is recorded in the Voucher Register with a debit to Notes Payable and a credit to Vouchers Payable, and changes the obligation in the accounting records only, from Notes Payable to Vouchers Payable.

A company in a weak financial position may give a note to a creditor to secure an extension of time on an obligation. For example, if after a voucher is prepared and recorded, it is decided to secure a time extension on an obligation by issuing a note, a general journal entry to change the obligation from a voucher payable to a note payable is made. Such an entry is similar to the following:

Nov.	*24*	*Vouchers Payable*............................	*700.00*	
		Notes Payable...........................		*700.00*
		To change the obligation of Voucher No. 983 to Notes Payable.		

In addition to the entry, a reference, see G.J. p.——, is placed in the payments column of the Voucher Register. Also, the old voucher is marked "canceled," an explanation is written on the voucher, and it is filed in the paid vouchers file. When the note becomes due, a new voucher for its payment is prepared and recorded and a check in its payment is issued.

AUTOMATION

Thus far in this text only hand-posted, pen-and-ink records have been described. This is not only because bookkeeping machines are not readily available to the vast majority of beginning students, but also because pen-and-ink methods are relatively simple and, consequently, are probably best for an introduction to record keeping. Furthermore, there is little lost motion because the principles taught with pen and ink apply directly to machine methods. Nevertheless, a student should not complete a first course in accounting without gaining an appreciation of the ability of automatic and semiautomatic machines to handle tremendous volumes of clerical work with a minimum of labor.

Electric Accounting Machines. There are many electric accounting machines on the market, some designed for a single task and others for a multiplicity of tasks. No attempt will be made here to describe these machines. In fact, only one machine will be discussed, and it for the purpose of showing how accounting machines reduce the labor needed in handling a volume of work.

Illustration 75 shows an electric accounting machine which can be used for sales accounting, cash receipts, cash disbursements, accounts payable, payroll, and any other accounting application. No attempt will be made to describe the machine's operation in each of these applications. However, when used in sales accounting, as an example, the machine will produce the invoice for each charge sale, post to the customer's account, update the statement to be sent to the customer at the end of the month, and enter

Illustration 75

Courtesy of the National Cash Register Company

the sale in the Sales Journal, all in one operation. Furthermore, it is as proficient in other applications.

In sales accounting the current page of the Sales Journal is placed in the machine at the time the operator begins processing a group of sales transactions. In Illustration 75 the Sales Journal sheet is on the tray at the back of the machine. Next, after putting the Sales Journal sheet in the machine, the operator will for each charge sale place in the machine's carriage a blank invoice form, the customer's account from the subsidiary Accounts Receivable Ledger, and the statement to be mailed to the customer at the end of the month. After this she picks up in the machine from the customer's account the amount of his previous balance. She then types the customer's name, address, terms, et cetera on the invoice. Then she types on the invoice the commodities sold. For each commodity this consists of a description, the number of units sold, and the unit price. After listing units and unit price for a commodity, the operator depresses a key and the machine multiplies units by unit price and prints the extension. After listing all items, the operator presses another key and the machine totals the invoice and prints the total on the invoice, makes the entry in the Sales Journal, and spaces over and enters the sale and the new balance on the customer's account and on the month-end statement. After this the carriage returns automatically and opens for the removal of the invoice, customer's account, and statement. It also spaces the Sales Journal sheet up one line and is ready for recording the next sale.

In addition to the foregoing, when the operator completes the processing of a day's sales, the machine will print out the dollar total of the invoices processed, which is the day's debit to the Accounts Receivable controlling account. Also, it will print out the total credit to Sales and, if any, the credit to Sales Taxes Payable. Furthermore, if the sales were entered in the machine by departments, it will break down the sales credit into totals by departments.

Illustration 76

Courtesy of International Business Machines Corporation

Punched Card Accounting. When punched cards are used in accounting, information from an invoice, check, credit memorandum, or other source document is punched into cards with a card punch like the one shown in Illustration 76. Such a punch has a keyboard similar to that of a typewriter and is operated in much the same manner, punching a hole or holes when a key is depressed. After data from a source document is punched into cards, all remaining accounting steps are automatically completed by other machines. The machines will sort the data, post it to other cards, add, multiply, divide, and subtract, select and summarize, and print accounting reports, all automatically. For example, machines will take the accounts receivable of a concern when punched into cards like the

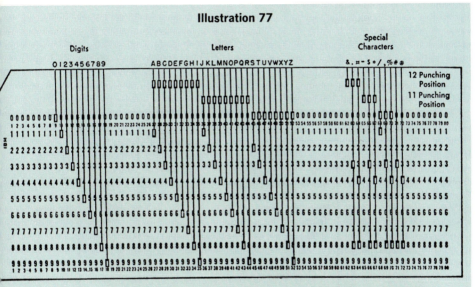

Illustration 77

© 1959 by International Business Machines Corporation

one of Illustration 79 on page 375, sort the information, and print a schedule of accounts receivable by age like the one described on page 268. Furthermore, the machine will sort the accounts (cards) at the rate of up to 2,000 cards a minute and automatically print the account amounts in columns by age at the rate of up to 100 cards per minute.

The heart of a punched card accounting system is a series of cards like the one shown in Illustration 77. The card shown has eighty vertical columns in which holes may be punched, each column having twelve punching positions, ten numbered (lines) 0 through 9 and two unnumbered positions in the upper margin. Both alphabetical and numerical information may be punched into a card, and some machines will both punch information into a card and print the information on the card. A digit of a number is recorded by punching a hole in one of the columns, for example, a five is recorded by punching a hole in one of the columns in the line of fives. A letter is recorded by punching two holes in one of the columns, for example, the letter Z is recorded by punching a hole in the 0 line and another hole in the same column in the 9 line. (At this point, for

Illustration 78

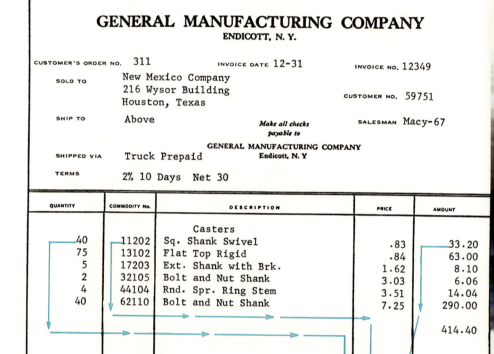

GENERAL MANUFACTURING COMPANY
ENDICOTT, N. Y.

CUSTOMER'S ORDER NO. 311	INVOICE DATE 12-31	INVOICE NO. 12349

SOLD TO New Mexico Company
216 Wysor Building
Houston, Texas

CUSTOMER NO. 59751

SHIP TO Above

Make all checks payable to

SALESMAN Macy-67

SHIPPED VIA Truck Prepaid

GENERAL MANUFACTURING COMPANY
Endicott, N. Y

TERMS 2% 10 Days Net 30

QUANTITY	COMMODITY No.	DESCRIPTION	PRICE	AMOUNT
		Casters		
40	11202	Sq. Shank Swivel	.83	33.20
75	13102	Flat Top Rigid	.84	63.00
5	17203	Ext. Shank with Brk.	1.62	8.10
2	32105	Bolt and Nut Shank	3.03	6.06
4	44104	Rnd. Spr. Ring Stem	3.51	14.04
40	62110	Bolt and Nut Shank	7.25	290.00
				414.40

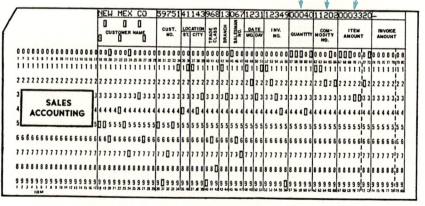

a better understanding of how digits and letters are represented by holes in a card, the student should take the information as to which holes represent which digits and letters, as shown in Illustration 77, and use this information to interpret the holes punched into the card of Illustration 78. If the student does so, he will find in the card of Illustration 78 that the two holes punched in column 18 represent an N; the two holes in column 19 represent an E; and so on.)

Illustration 78 shows a sales invoice of General Manufacturing Company with one of the cards that would be used in accounting for this sale. The one card has information punched into it as to the customer, branch, salesman, date, and invoice number, plus information as to the quantity, commodity number, and item amount of the first of the six commodities listed on the invoice. In accounting for this sale five additional commodity cards, a total of six commodity cards, one for each product listed on the invoice, are punched. Each card is punched identically as to customer, branch, salesman, date, and invoice number, and differs only as to the quantity of the product sold, commodity number, and item amount. In addition to the six commodity cards, an accounts receivable card as shown in Illustration 79 is also punched. All of these cards are produced in one

Illustration 79

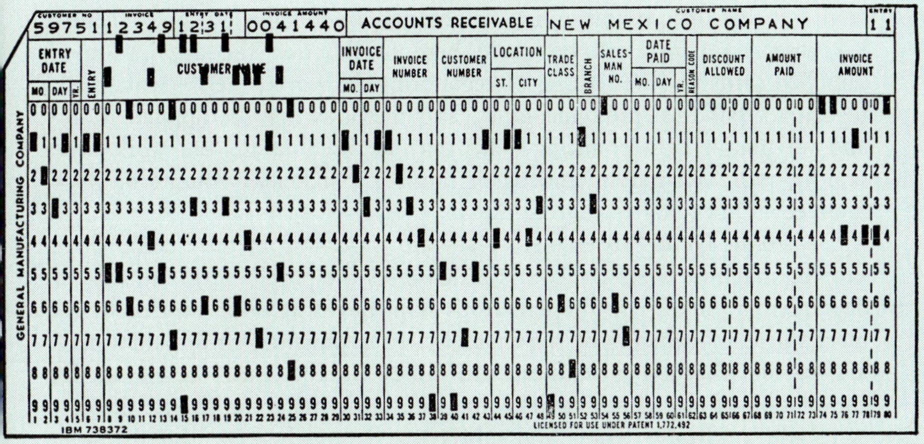

© 1958 by International Business Machines Corporation

punching operation, with the common information of the cards being reproduced from one card to the next automatically.

The six commodity cards of the Illustration 78 invoice are used in posting to the perpetual inventory records, in each case reducing the inventory record of the commodity by the units sold. The posting is done by machine automatically. Also, the commodity cards of this invoice, along with the cards of other invoices for the same period (day, week, or month), are summarized and their total, which is the amount of charge sales for the period, is debited to Accounts Receivable control and credited to Sales.

The accounts receivable card, Illustration 79, is filed in the subsidiary Accounts Receivable Ledger. Actually, this card with any other unpaid accounts receivable cards of New Mexico Company become the company's account in the subsidiary Accounts Receivable Ledger.

Observe that the accounting described in the previous two paragraphs is like that described in earlier chapters. The same debits and credits, general ledger accounts, subsidiary ledgers and controlling accounts, and the same accounting principles apply. It differs only in that it is done with cards and machines.

When accounting data is punched into cards, it is possible to secure from the cards much more information, at a reasonable cost, than is possible from traditional accounting records. For example, the six commodity cards of the Illustration 79 invoice show commodities sold, salesman, branch, city, and customer. Consequently, it is possible to take these cards and other like cards of a period such as a week or month, sort them by machine, and print reports showing total sales by commodities, by salesman, branches, territories, cities, and customers.

The foregoing discussion is given to introduce the possibilities of punched cards and punched card accounting. It is not intended to be a complete discussion; this must be deferred to a more advanced course. Likewise, no effort will be made here to describe the application of punched cards to other phases of accounting. However, the student should recognize that the cards, machines, and methods may be applied to any and all phases of accounting—and may be used to do the work more rapidly, more accurately, and when there is a sufficient volume of work, more economically.

Electronic Data Processing. Data are processed in an electric bookkeeping machine when the operator depresses the proper keys, and speed is dependent primarily on the operator's skill, but is at times limited by the mechanical movements of the machine. In a punched card system cards are passed through machines, and holes in the cards result in the completion of electrical circuits which cause the machines to sort the data or to add, multiply, divide, and subtract with punched or printed results. In a punched card operation data may be processed many times faster than with electric adding, calculating, and bookkeeping machines; however, a punched card system is slow when compared with a system that processes data electronically.

Although the phrase "processing data electronically" is commonly used, it is not always clear just when a system becomes an electronic system, because newer punched card machines make use of electronics. However, normally the phrase "processing data electronically" means using an electronic computer (Illustration 80) in processing data, with an electronic

Illustration 80

Courtesy of General Electric Company

computer being one or more machines containing from several hundred to more than a thousand vacuum tubes or transistors and being capable of, for example, from a few hundred to many thousand additions, multiplications, divisions, and subtractions per second, all completed in a predetermined sequence according to instructions stored within the machine.

No effort will be made here to explain how a computer functions. Such a discussion is beyond an elementary accounting text. Nevertheless, an accounting student should have some appreciation of what these machines can do. For example, a concern with, say, 10,000 or 12,000 employees would require five or six days each pay period to complete its payroll records and prepare the checks to pay its employees, even though a hundred or more clerks with desk calculators and other electric machines were used to speed the work. But when a computer is used on the job, it will do all the calculations, complete and print the payroll records, and print the checks in a matter of four or five hours.

For another example, a nationally known manufacturer and distributor of electrical appliances uses a computer in filling orders. The orders originate in any one of fifty-three different sales offices in as many cities, and are filled from one or more of thirty-six different warehouses scattered throughout the country. The company uses a teletype network to transmit orders from the sales offices to a central computer in Pittsburgh, Pennsylvania. The computer then takes over. It selects the best warehouse to fill the order in terms of proximity to the customer and available inventory. It prices and totals each sale, including any taxes, and updates the perpetual inventory records. In addition, the computer prepares punched cards for all accounting operations, writes the customer's invoice, and prepares punched cards for teletyping shipping instructions for each order to the warehouse selected. And, when these punched cards are placed in a teletype in Pittsburgh, they automatically reproduce for each order at the selected warehouse a bill of lading, packing lists, and shipping labels. Furthermore, the company can receive an order in one city, process it, and ship from a selected warehouse in another city in less than an hour.

Obviously, a text such as this cannot begin to describe all of the electric, punched card, and electronic machines that are used in processing data in a modern concern. However, in passing it should be observed that in this rapidly changing field there are many job opportunities for the interested student.

QUESTIONS FOR CLASS DISCUSSION

1. Why does a company install a voucher system?

2. Do all companies need a voucher system? If not, at what approximate point in a company's growth would you recommend that such a system be installed?

3. How does a voucher system aid in controlling the incurrence and payment of liabilities?

4. As it is used in a voucher system, what is the purpose of a voucher?

5. What information is usually shown (a) on the inside of a voucher, and (b) on the outside of a voucher?

6. What business papers in its support may be attached to a voucher for the purchase of merchandise? What does each of the papers tell the person responsible for signing checks?

7. A company using a voucher system prepares purchase requisitions, purchase orders, and receiving reports. Outline the steps that may be followed in this company in purchasing and paying for merchandise bought on account. Begin with the preparation of a purchase requisition and end with mailing a check.

8. Outline the steps followed in preparing, recording, and paying a voucher for (a) a so-called cash transaction, and (b) a so-called credit transaction. How do the steps differ in the two cases?

9. What is an unpaid vouchers file? What is a paid vouchers file?

10. When a company installs a voucher system, it no longer uses an Accounts Payable Ledger. What is substituted in the place of the Accounts Payable Ledger?

11. The Vouchers·Payable account may be thought of as a controlling account. If it is thought of as a controlling account, what does it control?

12. When a voucher system is installed, a Purchases Journal as described in previous chapters is no longer used. What is substituted in its place?

13. What effect, if any, does the installation of a voucher system have on the following: (a) Cash Receipts Journal, (b) Sales Journal, (c) Accounts Receivable Ledger, (d) Accounts Payable Ledger, (e) Check Register, (f) Purchases Journal, (g) General Journal, and (h) General Ledger?

14. What is the purpose of a "tickler file" when used in a voucher system?

15. Why is it important that the person responsible for approving vouchers be required to initial all error corrections on vouchers?

16. An error in the Voucher Register discovered before the register is posted may be corrected by ruling out the wrong account or amount and writing in the correct account or amount. An error discovered after the register is posted must be corrected with a general journal entry. Why is there a difference?

17. Often a company operating a voucher system credits returns directly to its Purchases account rather than to a Purchases Returns and Allowances account. Why?

18. Would you recommend a voucher system for a firm that must often make partial payments because it cannot meet its obligations in full when they are due? Why?

19. How many money columns does the Check Register have in a firm that follows the practice of recording invoices at their net amounts?

PROBLEMS

Problem 13–1

A company using a voucher system completed the following transactions:

Dec.   5   Prepared and recorded Voucher No. 2354 payable to Pinetop Wholesale Company for the purchase of merchandise having an invoice price of $2,400, terms 2/10, n/60, invoice date December 3.

    6   Prepared and recorded Voucher No. 2355 payable to Mesa Supply Company for the purchase of merchandise having an invoice price of $1,800, terms 2/10, n/60, invoice date December 4.

    9   Received a credit memorandum from Mesa Supply Company for $400 (invoice price) of merchandise received from it on December 6 and returned for credit.

   13   Issued Check No. 2349 in payment of Voucher No. 2354.

   19   Discovered that after the credit memorandum was recorded, Voucher No. 2355 had been filed in error for payment on this date. Recognized the discount had been lost and refiled the voucher for payment on the last day of its credit period, February 2.

Feb.   2   Issued Check No. 2617 in payment of Voucher No. 2355.

Required:

1. Prepare entries in general journal form to record the foregoing transactions under the assumption the invoices are recorded at their gross amounts.

2. Prepare another set of entries to record the transactions under the assumption the invoices are recorded at their net amounts.

Problem 13–2

Eastern Company uses a voucher system in which it records purchase invoices at their gross amounts. During January of the current year the company completed the following transactions affecting vouchers payable:

Jan. 2 Prepared Voucher No. 673 payable to Valley Wholesale Company for the purchase of merchandise having an invoice price of $1,800, terms 2/10, n/30.

2 Prepared Voucher No. 674 payable to Pinetop Realty Company for the January rent, $500. (Ten percent of the rent is chargeable to the office, and the remainder to the store.) Issued Check No. 670 in payment of the voucher.

4 Prepared Voucher No. 675 payable to Pacific Wholesale Company for the purchase of merchandise having an invoice price of $800, terms 2/10, n/30.

8 Prepared Voucher No. 676 for $200 and Voucher No. 677 for $500. Both vouchers were payable to Apex Equipment Company and were for the purchase of a new calculator for use in the office. The terms of the purchase were $200 cash on delivery and $500 in 30 days if the machine proved satisfactory. Issued Check No. 671 in payment of Voucher No. 676.

10 Prepared Voucher No. 678 payable to Store Supply Company for the purchase of store supplies having an invoice price of $125, terms 10 E.O.M.

12 Prepared Voucher No. 679 payable to Pacific Wholesale Company for the purchase of merchandise having an invoice price of $1,250, terms 2/10, n/30.

13 Issued Check No. 672 in payment of Voucher No. 675.

18 Prepared Voucher No. 680 payable to Mary Nance, petty cashier, to reimburse the petty cash fund. Petty cash receipts showed payments for freight-in, $12; store supplies, $7; and advertising, $10. Issued Check No. 673 in payment of the voucher.

20 Issued Check No. 674 in payment of Voucher No. 679.

26 Prepared Voucher No. 681 payable to Pioneer Wholesale Company for the purchase of merchandise having an invoice price of $600, terms 2/10, n/30.

31 Valley Wholesale Company agreed to accept $900 in cash and to grant a 30-day extension on the balance of Voucher No. 673. Canceled Voucher No. 673, and prepared Vouchers Nos. 682 and 683 for $900 each. Issued Check No. 675 in payment of Voucher No. 682.

31 Prepared Voucher No. 684 payable to Payroll for sales salaries, $800; and office salaries, $300. Issued Check No. 676 in its payment. Cashed the check and paid the employees.

Required:

1. Prepare a Voucher Register and a Check Register similar to the ones shown in Illustrations 73 and 74. Enter the transactions in the registers. Use the following account code numbers:

115 Store Supplies	611 Rent Expense, Selling Space
133 Office Equipment	612 Sales Salaries
212 Vouchers Payable	618 Advertising
511 Purchase	651 Rent Expense, Office Space
512 Freight-In	652 Office Salaries

2. Open a Vouchers Payable account, crossfoot the registers, and post the amounts that affect the Vouchers Payable account.
3. Prepare a schedule of unpaid vouchers.

Problem 13–3

Afghan Company uses a voucher system in which it records at their net amounts all invoices subject to discounts. During March of the current year the company completed the following transaction affecting vouchers payable:

Mar.   1   Prepared Voucher No. 981 payable to Basset, Inc., for the purchase of merchandise having an invoice price of $1,200, terms 2/10, n/30.

  1   Prepared Voucher No. 982 payable to Hill Realty Company for the March rent, $800. (Charge 10 percent of the rent to the office and the remainder to the store.) Issued Check No. 977 in payment of the voucher.

  5   Prepared Voucher No. 983 payable to Valley Supply Company for the purchase of store supplies having an invoice price of $200, terms 2/10, n/30.

  8   Received a credit memorandum from Basset, Inc., for merchandise having an invoice price of $150 which was received on March 1 and returned on March 5. This merchandise was defective but this was not discovered until after the voucher for the purchase was recorded.

  12   Prepared Voucher No. 984 payable to Kimwood Manufacturing Company. The invoice attached to this voucher was for the purchase of $950 of merchandise, terms F.O.B. factory, 2/10, n/30. The vendor had prepaid $60 of freight on the purchase and had added this amount to the invoice.

  14   Issued Check No. 978 in payment of Voucher No. 983.

  18   Discovered that after adjusting Voucher No. 981 for the credit memorandum received on March 8, the voucher was refiled in error for payment on March 18. Adjusted the voucher for the discount lost and refiled it for payment on the last day of its credit period, March 31. Made a general journal entry to record the discount lost.

  20   Issued Check No. 979 in payment of Voucher No. 984.

  23   Prepared Voucher No. 985 payable to Litho Printers for advertising circulars printed and delivered this day. The invoice accompanying the circulars was for $45, terms 10 E.O.M.

  27   Purchased a refrigerated display case from Commercial Refrigeration Company, terms $500 cash and $1,000 in 30 days. Prepared Voucher No. 986 for $500 and Voucher No. 987 for $1,000. Issued Check No. 980 in payment of Voucher No. 986.

  31   Issued Check No. 981 in payment of Voucher No. 981 as adjusted for the return and the discount lost.

  31   Issued Voucher No. 988 payable to Payroll for sales salaries, $1,100; and office salaries, $540. Issued Check No. 982 in payment of the voucher. Cashed the check and paid the employees.

Required:

1. Prepare a Voucher Register similar to Illustration 73. Prepare a Check Register like Illustration 74 with the exception that only one money column is needed. (Only one money column is needed because discounts are not recorded in the register; consequently, the amounts debited to Vouchers Payable are the same as the amounts credited to Cash.) Enter the transactions in the registers and, where necessary, in a two-column General Journal. Use the following account code numbers: Rent Expense, Selling Space, 611; Advertising, 612; Sales Salaries, 613; Rent Expense, Office Space, 651; and Office Salaries, 652.

2. Total and crossfoot the registers and post to a Vouchers Payable account the column totals and journal entry portions that affect this account.

3. Prepare a schedule of unpaid vouchers.

Problem 13–4

Corona Sales Company uses a voucher system in which it records invoices at their gross amounts. On October 1 of the current year the concern's unpaid voucher file contained the following unpaid vouchers:

Voucher Number	Payee	Invoice Date	Terms	Amount
607	*Town Supply Company......*	*Aug. 31*	*30 days*	*$1,600*
625	*City Wholesale Company.....*	*Sept. 10*	*1/10, n/30*	*1,750*
				$3,350

During October the company completed the following transactions affecting vouchers payable:

Oct. 1 Secured a 30-day extension on the amount owed Town Supply Company, Voucher No. 607, by giving them a 30-day, 6 percent note payable.

1 Borrowed $6,000 from Valley National Bank by giving a 30-day, 6 percent note. (Normally this transaction would be recorded in the Cash Receipts Journal; but to simplify the problem, record it with a general journal entry.)

2 Prepared Voucher No. 637 payable to P. J. Krantz Company for the purchase of merchandise, $850, terms 2/10, n/30, invoice date September 30.

5 Prepared Voucher No. 638 payable to Desert Supply Company for the purchase of store supplies, $45, and merchandise, $310, terms n/10 E.O.M.

10 Issued Check No. 633 in payment of Voucher No. 637, less the discount.

10 Entered into an agreement with City Wholesale Company to pay $750 of the amount due on Voucher No. 625 at once and to pay the balance in 30 days. Canceled Voucher No. 625 and is-

sued in its place Vouchers No. 639 and 640 for $750 and $1,000, respectively. Issued Check No. 634 in payment of Voucher No. 639.

Oct. 12   Purchased $1,250 of office equipment from Office Outfitters, terms $250 cash and $1,000 in 60 days. Prepared Vouchers No. 641 for $250 and No. 642 for $1,000. Issued Check No. 635 in payment of Voucher No. 641.

15   Prepared Voucher No. 643 payable to Valley Realtors for the October 15 to November 15 rent, $500. (Ten percent of the rent is chargeable to the office and the remainder to the store.) Issued Check No. 636 in payment of the voucher.

16   Prepared Voucher No. 644 payable to Quota Sales Company for merchandise purchased, $550, terms 2/10, n/60.

18   Received a $50 credit memorandum from Quota Sales Company for merchandise received on October 16 and returned. The merchandise had been ordered in error in the wrong sizes, and this was not discovered until after the voucher was recorded.

19   Spoiled Voucher No. 645 in preparation.

19   Prepared Voucher No. 646 to Royal Company for the purchase of merchandise, $350, terms 2/10, n/30, F.O.B. factory. Royal Company had prepaid $20 of freight on the shipment, adding this amount to the invoice, bringing its total to $370.

26   Issued Check No. 637 in payment of Voucher No. 644, less the return and discount.

29   Received notice from Valley National Bank that they held for collection the note given Town Supply Company on October 1. Prepared Voucher No. 647 in payment of the note and its $8 interest. Issued Check No. 638 in payment of the voucher.

29   Issued Check No. 639 in payment of Voucher No. 646, less the discount.

30   Issued Voucher No. 648 payable to Joan West, petty cashier, to reimburse the petty cash fund for freight on purchases, $10; advertising expense, $5; miscellaneous general expenses, $8; and store supplies, $12. Issued Check No. 640 in payment of the voucher.

31   Prepared Voucher No. 649 payable to Valley National Bank for the note given it on October 1. Issued Check No. 641 in payment of the voucher.

31   Prepared Voucher No. 650 payable to Payroll in payment of sales salaries, $825; and office salaries, $350. Issued Check No. 642 in payment of the voucher.

Required:

1. Prepare a Voucher Register and Check Register similar to the ones shown in this chapter. In addition a General Journal and a Vouchers Payable account are needed.

2. Enter the $3,350 balance in the Vouchers Payable account, and enter the two unpaid vouchers on the first two lines of the Voucher Register. Enter their amounts in the Vouchers Payable column only. These vouch-

ers were recorded in August and September and were posted in the voucher register totals of those months. They are entered at this time on the first two lines so their payment may be marked in the When and How Paid column. To prevent their being posted a second time in the October totals, rule double lines across all columns after the second line.

3. Record the October transactions in the registers and General Journal. Total and crossfoot the registers and post the voucher register and check register totals and the journal entry portions that affect the Vouchers Payable account. Use the following code numbers where necessary:

115 Store Supplies	611 Rent Expense, Selling Space
133 Office Equipment	612 Sales Salaries
211 Notes Payable	618 Advertising
212 Vouchers Payable	651 Rent Expense, Office Space
511 Purchases	652 Office Salaries
512 Purchases Discounts	659 Miscellaneous Office Expenses
513 Freight-In	711 Interest Expense

3. Prepare a schedule of vouchers payable as of October 31. Compare the schedule total with the balance of the Vouchers Payable account.

CLASS EXERCISE

Exercise 13–1

A concern that uses a voucher system completed the following transaction affecting a single voucher:

Jan. 7 Received and recorded Voucher No. 3–344 payable to Alpha-Beta Company for the purchase of merchandise having an invoice price of $1,200, terms 2/10, n/60, invoice date January 5.

10 Received a credit memorandum from Alpha-Beta Company for $200 (invoice price) of merchandise received from it on January 7 and returned for credit.

20 Discovered that Voucher No. 3–344 had been filed for payment on this date rather than on the last day of its discount period, causing the loss of the discount. Refiled it for payment on the last day of its credit period.

Mar. 6 Issued Check No. 3–401 in payment of Voucher No. 3–344.

Required:

1. Under the assumption that the invoice of Voucher No. 3–344 was recorded at its gross amount, prepare entries in general journal form to record the foregoing transactions.

2. Under the assumption that the invoice of Voucher No. 3–344 was recorded at its net amount, prepare a second set of entries to record the foregoing transactions.

ALTERNATE PROBLEMS

Problem 13–1A

Copperstate Sales Company uses a voucher system in controlling cash disbursements. During a short period it completed these transactions:

Jan. 4 Prepared and recorded Voucher No. 2119 payable to Orange Manufacturing Company for the purchase of merchandise having an invoice price of $1,400, terms 2/10, n/60, invoice date January 2.

6 Prepared and recorded Voucher No. 2123 payable to Purple Supply Company for the purchase of merchandise having an invoice price of $1,600, terms 2/10, n/60, invoice date January 3.

8 Received a credit memorandum from Purple Supply Company for $300 (invoice price) of merchandise received on January 6 and returned for credit.

12 Issued Check No. 2115 in payment of Voucher No. 2119.

18 Discovered that Voucher No. 2123 had been filed in error for payment on this date, causing the loss of the discount. Refiled the voucher for payment on the last day of its credit period, March 4.

Mar. 4 Issued Check No. 2295 in payment of Voucher No. 2123 as adjusted for the return.

Required:

1. Prepare entries in general journal form to record the foregoing transactions under the assumption the invoices were recorded at their gross amounts.
2. Prepare a second series of entries under the assumption the invoices were recorded at net amounts.

Problem 13–2A

Tucson Company uses a voucher system in which it records invoices at their gross amounts. During March of the current year it completed the following transactions affecting vouchers payable:

Mar. 1 Borrowed $5,000 from Guaranty Bank by giving a $5,000, 30-day, 6 percent note payable. (This transaction would normally be recorded in the Cash Receipts Journal. To simplify the problem, record it with a general journal entry.)

1 Prepared Voucher No. 613 payable to Phoenix Company for the purchase of merchandise having an invoice price of $1,500, terms 30 days.

3 Prepared Voucher No. 614 for $300 and Voucher No. 615 for $500. Both vouchers payable to Office Outfitters and were for the purchase of a new calculator for office use. The purchase terms were $300 cash on delivery and $500 in 60 days. Issued Check No. 613 in payment of Voucher No. 614.

9 Prepared Voucher No. 616 payable to Hippo Supply Company for the purchase of store supplies, $125, terms n/10 E.O.M.

11 Prepared Voucher No. 617 payable to Apache Wholesale Company for the purchase of merchandise having an invoice price of $750, terms 2/10, n/60.

14 Prepared Voucher No. 618 payable to Jane Orr, petty cashier, to reimburse the petty cash fund for freight-in, $15; advertising, $5; miscellaneous office expenses, $15; and store supplies, $10. Issued Check No. 614 in payment of the voucher.

Mar. 15   Prepared Voucher No. 619 payable to Dale Realty Company for the March 15 through April 15 rent, $600. (Ten percent of the rent is chargeable to the office and the remainder to the store.) Issued Check No. 615 in payment of the voucher.

18   Prepared Voucher No. 620 payable Apache Wholesale Company for the purchase of merchandise having an invoice price of $900, terms 2/10, n/60.

21   Issued Check No. 616 in payment of Voucher No. 617.

26   Prepared Voucher No. 621 payable to Pioneer Wholesale Company for the purchase of merchandise, $725; and store supplies, $25, terms 2/10, n/60.

28   Issued Check No. 617 in payment of Voucher No. 620.

31   Prepared Voucher No. 622 payable to Guaranty Bank for the note and interest due this day. (See first transaction.) Issued Check No. 618 in payment of the voucher.

31   Phoenix Company agreed to accept $500 in cash and to grant a 30-day extension on the balance of Voucher No. 613. Canceled Voucher No. 613, and prepared Vouchers Nos. 623 and 624 for $500 and $1,000, respectively. Issued Check No. 619 in payment of Voucher No. 623.

31   Prepared Voucher No. 625 payable to Payroll for sales salaries, $650; and office salaries, $300. Issued Check No. 620 in its payment. Cashed the check and paid the employees.

Required:

1. Prepare a Voucher Register and Check Register similar to the ones illustrated in this chapter. Enter the transactions in the registers and, where necessary, a two-column General Journal. Use the following code numbers as needed.

117 Store Supplies	612 Sales Salaries
133 Office Equipment	618 Advertising
211 Notes Payable	651 Rent Expense, Office Space
212 Vouchers Payable	652 Office Salaries
511 Purchases	659 Miscellaneous Office Expenses
512 Freight-In	711 Interest Expense
611 Rent Expense, Selling Space	

2. Open a Vouchers Payable account, crossfoot the registers, and post the amounts from the registers and General Journal that affect the Vouchers Payable account.

3. Prepare a schedule of unpaid vouchers.

Problem 13–3A

Del Rio Sales Company records invoices carrying cash discounts at their net amounts. During a month the concern completed the following transactions affecting vouchers payable:

Oct. 1   Prepared Voucher No. 956 payable to Rio Properties, Inc., for the October rent, $600. (Charge one twelfth to Rent Expense, Office Space and the remainder to Rent Expense, Selling Space.) Issued Check No. 952 in payment of the voucher.

Oct. 1 Prepared Voucher No. 957 payable to Hydraulic Manufacturing Company for the purchase of merchandise having an invoice price of $1,200, terms 2/10, n/30.

   1 Borrowed $5,000 from the First National Bank by giving a 30-day, 6 percent note. (Normally this transaction would be recorded in the Cash Receipts Journal. To simplify the problem you are asked to record it with a general journal entry.)

   5 Prepared Voucher No. 958 payable to Newman Wholesale Company for the purchase of merchandise having an invoice price of $800, terms 2/10, n/60.

   8 Prepared Voucher No. 959 payable to General Supply Company for the purchase of store supplies having an invoice price of $450, terms 2/10, n/30.

   15 Issued Check No. 953 in payment of Voucher No. 958.

   17 Prepared Voucher No. 960 payable to Jane Voss, petty cashier, to reimburse the petty cash fund. The paid vouchers of the petty cash fund showed expenditures of $18 for freight-in, $11 for store supplies, and $10 for advertising expenses. Issued Check No. 954 in payment of the voucher.

   18 Discovered that the discount on Voucher No. 957 had been missed because the voucher had been filed in error for payment under a due date of October 18. Added to the voucher the amount of the discount lost, and refiled it for payment on the last day of its credit period, October 31. Made an entry in the General Journal to record the discount lost.

   18 Issued Check No. 955 in payment of Voucher No. 959.

   20 Prepared Voucher No. 961 payable to Southern Sales Company for the purchase of merchandise having an invoice price of $1,400, terms 2/10, n/30.

   23 Prepared Voucher No. 962 payable to North Equipment Company for the purchase of office equipment having an invoice price of $300, terms 10 E.O.M.

   25 Prepared Voucher No. 963 payable to Swanson and Son. The invoice attached to the voucher was for $600 of merchandise, F.O.B. factory, terms 2/10, n/30. Swanson and Son had prepaid the freight amounting to $45 and had added it to the invoice, bringing the invoice total to $645.

   30 Issued Check No. 956 in payment of Voucher No. 961.

   31 Prepared Voucher No. 964 payable to the First National Bank in payment of the note and interest due this day. Issued Check No. 957 in payment of the voucher.

   31 Issued Check No. 958 in payment of Voucher No. 957 as adjusted for the discount lost.

   31 Prepared Voucher No. 965 payable to Payroll for sales salaries of $850 and office salaries of $350. Issued Check No. 959 in payment of the voucher. Cashed the check and paid the employees.

Required:

1. Prepare a Voucher Register similar to Illustration 73. Prepare a Check Register similar to Illustration 74 with the exception that only one money

column is needed. (Only one money column is needed because discounts are not recorded in the register; consequently, the amounts debited to Vouchers Payable are the same as the amounts credited to Cash.) Use the following account code numbers:

115	Store Supplies	612	Sales Salaries
133	Office Equipment	618	Advertising
211	Notes Payable	651	Rent Expense, Office Space
212	Vouchers Payable	652	Office Salaries
511	Purchases	711	Interest Expense
512	Freight-In	712	Discounts Lost
611	Rent Expense, Selling Space		

2. Enter the transactions in the registers and, where necessary, in a two-column General Journal. Crossfoot the registers and post the column totals and entry portions that affect the Vouchers Payable account.
3. Prepare a schedule of unpaid vouchers.

Problem 13–4A

Southwest Sales Company uses a voucher system in which it records at their net amounts all invoices subject to discounts. On July 1 its unpaid vouchers file contained the following unpaid vouchers:

Voucher Number	Payee	Invoice Date	Terms	Amount
389	*Northern Manufacturing Company*	*June 1*	*30 days*	*$1,600*
394	*General Wholesale Company*	*June 9*	*30 days*	*1,300*
401	*Brook Brothers*	*June 15*	*30 days*	*700*
				$3,600

During July the company completed the following transactions affecting vouchers payable:

July 1 Prepared Voucher 424 payable to Southgate Company for the purchase of merchandise having an invoice price of $750, terms 2/10, n/30.

1 Secured an extension of 30 days on the amount owed Northern Manufacturing Company, Voucher No. 389, by giving them a 30-day, 6 percent note.

5 Prepared Voucher No. 425 payable to Store Supply Company for the purchase of store supplies having an invoice price of $300, terms 2/10, n/60.

6 Southwest Sales Company discounted at 6 percent its own 15-day, noninterest-bearing $4,000 note at the bank. (Normally this transaction would be recorded in the Cash Receipts Journal. You are to record with a general journal entry.)

July   8   Purchased $1,400 of office equipment from Office Equipment Company, terms $400 cash and $1,000 in 60 days. Prepared Voucher No. 426 for $400 and Voucher No. 427 for $1,000. Issued Check No. 409 in payment of Voucher No. 426.

9   Entered into an agreement with General Wholesale Company to pay at once $700 of the amount due on Voucher No. 394 and to pay the balance in 30 days. Canceled Voucher 394 and issued Vouchers Nos. 428 and 429 for $700 and $600, respectively. Issued Check No. 410 in payment of Voucher No. 428.

10   Prepared Voucher No. 430 payable to Hill Company for the purchase of merchandise having an invoice price of $1,450, terms 2/10, n/30.

13   Spoiled Voucher No. 431 in preparation.

15   Issued Check No. 411 in payment of Voucher No. 401.

15   Issued Check No. 412 in payment of Voucher No. 425.

15   Received a credit memorandum from Hill Company for merchandise having an invoice price of $50 which was received on July 10 and returned on July 12. The merchandise of this credit memorandum was ordered in the wrong sizes, and the error was not discovered until after the voucher was recorded.

18   Prepared Voucher No. 432 payable to Madison Company. The invoice of the voucher was for merchandise having an invoice price of $650, F.O.B. factory, terms 2/10, n/30. Madison Company had prepaid the freight charges of $40 and had added this amount to the invoice, bringing the invoice total to $690.

19   Issued Check No. 413 in payment of Voucher No. 430 as adjusted for the return.

20   Discovered that Voucher No. 424 had been filed in error for payment on July 20. Added to the voucher the amount of the discount lost, and refiled the voucher for payment on the last day of its credit period, July 31. Made a general journal entry to record the discount lost.

21   Prepared Voucher No. 433 payable to the First National Bank for the note due today. Issued Check No. 414 in its payment.

25   Prepared Voucher No. 434 payable to Judy Hale, petty cashier, to reimburse the petty cash fund. Petty cash vouchers showed payments of $22 for freight-in, $10 for advertising, and $5.00 for miscellaneous office expenses, and $8 for store supplies. Issued Check No. 415 in payment of the voucher.

27   Issued Check No. 416 in payment of Voucher No. 432.

31   Issued Check No. 417 in payment of Voucher No. 424 as adjusted for the discount lost.

31   Prepared Voucher No. 435 payable to Northern Manufacturing Company in payment of the note and interest due this day. Issued Check No. 418 in payment of the voucher.

31   Prepared Voucher No. 436 payable to Payroll in payment of sales salaries, $1,410; and office salaries, $320. Issued Check No. 419 in payment of the voucher. Cashed the check and paid the employees.

Required:

1. Prepare a Voucher Register similar to Illustration 73. Prepare a Check Register similar to Illustration 74 with the exception that only one money column is needed. (Only one money column is needed because discounts are not recorded in the register; consequently, the amounts debited to Vouchers Payable are the same amounts credited to Cash.) Enter the transactions in the registers and, where necessary, in a two-column General Journal.

2. Enter the $3,600 balance in the Vouchers Payable account. Also enter the three unpaid vouchers on the first three lines of the Voucher Register. Enter the amounts in the Vouchers Payable credit column. only. These vouchers were recorded during June and were posted in the Voucher Register totals at the end of June. They are entered at this time on the first three lines of the Voucher Register so their payment may be marked in the When and How Paid column. To prevent their being posted a second time in the July totals, rule a double line after the third line of the Voucher Register.

3. Record the transactions of the month of July. Total and crossfoot the Voucher Register and the Check Register. Use the following account code numbers as required:

116 Store Supplies   611 Advertising
133 Office Equipment   612 Sales Salaries
211 Notes Payable   652 Office Salaries
212 Vouchers Payable   659 Miscellaneous Office Expenses
511 Purchases   711 Interest Expense
512 Freight-In   712 Discounts Lost

4. Open a Vouchers Payable account. Post the voucher and check register totals plus those portions of the general journal entries that affect the Vouchers Payable account.

5. Prepare a schedule of unpaid vouchers as of July 31. Compare the schedule with the balance of the Vouchers Payable account.

DECISION PROBLEM 13—ABEL BODY WORKS

Abel Body Works was founded by Jack Abel ten years ago. In the beginning his business consisted largely of repairs to severely damaged busses, trucks, and cars. Last year he accepted contracts from a fairly large school system to manufacture specially designed bodies for school busses. This new business, added to the work of his regular repair department, has doubled the volume of his sales revenue.

Tom Barton is superintendent of the new body department while Mr. Abel continues to supervise the repair department. Mr. Barton insists that he be given authority to place orders for materials and supplies. He also maintains that a system of payroll advances for workers is needed to attract and hold skilled and semiskilled laborers. These advances would amount to only a few dollars a week each for some 20 to 30 employees.

Mr. Abel is reluctant to give up his personal supervision over all expenditures. He also is uncertain as to how the advances can be made to employees without weakening his control over cash. His petty cash fund of $25 is inadequate to meet the demand for payroll advances and he hesitates to write checks in the volume demanded. The time involved in making the numerous small advances by check would also be prohibitive.

The accounting records of Abel Body Works consists of Cash Receipts and Cash Disbursements Journals, Sales and Purchases Journals, and General Journal. Only one ledger is maintained. It contains summary accounts for Accounts Receivable and Accounts Payable. Records with individual customers and creditors are kept in two alphabetical files; in the first unpaid sales invoices are kept and in the second, unpaid invoices from creditors.

You are requested to write a report to Mr. Abel making suggestions for revisions of records and procedures which will give him the control he needs but at the same time will permit Mr. Barton to exercise his judgment as to the ordering of materials and supplies and the handling of his personnel. Be specific with instructions to carry out your recommendations.

Payroll

Accounting

An understanding of payroll records and payroll accounting requires some knowledge of the laws and programs that affect payrolls. Consequently, the more pertinent of these are discussed in the first portion of this chapter before the subject of payroll records is introduced.

THE FEDERAL SOCIAL SECURITY ACT

The Federal Social Security Act provides for a number of programs, two of which materially affect payroll accounting. These are (1) a federal old-age and survivors' benefits program with medical care for the aged, and (2) a joint federal-state unemployment insurance program.

Federal Old-Age and Survivors' Benefits Program. The Social Security Act provides that a qualified worker in a covered industry who reaches the age of sixty-two and retires shall receive monthly retirement benefits for the remainder of his life, and in addition certain medical benefits after reaching sixty-five. It further provides benefits for the family of a worker covered by the act who dies either before or after reaching retirement age and benefits for covered workers who become disabled. The benefits in each case are based upon the average earnings of the worker during the years of his employment in covered industries.

No attempt will be made here to list or discuss the requirements to be met by a worker or his family to qualify for benefits. In general, any person who works for an employer covered by the act for a sufficient length of time qualifies himself and his family. All companies and individuals who employ one or more persons and are not specifically exempted are covered by the law.

Funds for the payment of old-age, survivors', and medical benefits under the Social Security Act come from payroll taxes. These taxes are imposed under a law called the Federal Insurance Contributions Act and are often called "F.I.C.A. taxes." They are also often called "old-age benefit taxes" or just "social security taxes." These F.I.C.A. taxes are imposed in like amounts on both covered employers and their employees. As presently amended, the act provides for a 1966 tax on both employers and their employees amounting to 4.2 percent of the first $6,600 paid each employee. It also provides for rate increases as follows:

Years	Tax on Employees	Tax on Employers
1967 through 1968..................4.4%		4.4%
1969 through 1972..................4.9		4.9
1973 through 1975..................5.4		5.4
1976 through 1979..................5.45		5.45
1980 through 1986..................5.55		5.55
1987 and after.....................5.65		5.65

The foregoing table shows that rate increases are scheduled. However, perhaps little effort should be made to remember rates beyond those a year or two in the future, because if history is any indication, Congress will change the future rates (probably increasing them) before they go into effect.

The Federal Insurance Contribution Act, in addition to setting rates, requires that an employer:

1. Withhold from each employee's wages each 1966 payday 4.2 percent of the wages earned. The withholding to continue during the year until 4.2 percent of $6,600 is withheld. (Observe in the table just given that the withholding rate is scheduled to increase to 4.4 percent in 1967 and to increase again in 1969, 1973, etc.)
2. Pay a payroll tax equal to the amount withheld from the wages of all employees.
3. Periodically remit both the amounts withheld from the employees' wages and the employer's tax to the Director of Internal Revenue. (Times of payment are discussed later in this chapter.)
4. Within one month after the end of each calendar quarter, file a tax information return known as Employer's Quarterly Federal Tax Return, Form 941. (See Illustration 81.)
5. Furnish each employee before January 31 following each year a Withholding Tax Statement, Form W–2, which tells the employee the amounts of his wages that were subject to F.I.C.A. and federal income taxes and the amounts of such taxes withheld. (A W–2 Form is shown in Illustration 82.)
6. Furnish the Director of Internal Revenue copies of all the W–2 Forms given the employees.

7. Keep a record for four years for each employee that shows among other things wages subject to F.I.C.A. taxes and the taxes withheld. (The law does not specify the exact form of the record; but most employers keep individual employee earnings records similar to the one shown later in this chapter.)

Illustration 81

FORM 941

EMPLOYER'S QUARTERLY FEDERAL TAX RETURN
U.S. Treasury Department—Internal Revenue Service

FEDERAL INCOME TAX WITHHELD FROM WAGES

1. AMOUNT OF INCOME TAX WITHHELD (If not required write "None")	182.10	
2. ADJUSTMENT FOR PRECEDING QUARTERS OF CALENDAR YEAR ⟶		
3. ADJUSTED TOTAL OF INCOME TAX WITHHELD		182.10

FEDERAL INSURANCE CONTRIBUTIONS ACT TAXES

4. TOTAL TAXABLE WAGES PAID (From Item 21, Schedule A)	1,950.00	
5. 3.4% OF WAGES IN ITEM 4.	163.80	
6. ADJUSTMENTS (See instructions)		
7. ADJUSTED TOTAL OF F.I.C.A. TAXES ⟶		163.80

Complete items 11-13 on reverse. If not liable for returns in succeeding quarters write "FINAL" here.

TOTALS

8. TOTAL TAXES (Item 3 plus Item 7)	345.90
9. TOTAL OF ENCLOSED DEPOSITARY RECEIPTS (From Schedule B, other side)	345.90
10. BALANCE DUE (Item 8 minus Item 9) PAY TO "INTERNAL REVENUE SERVICE"	

Under penalties of perjury, I declare that I have examined this return, including accompanying schedules and statements, and to the best of my knowledge and belief it is true, correct, and complete.

Date **April 28, 1966** Signature *John K. Jones* Title **Owner**
(Owner, President, Partner, Member, etc.)

BE SURE TO ENCLOSE REMITTANCE, DEPOSITARY RECEIPTS, AND SCHEDULE A WITH THIS RETURN.

Employer's name, address, identification number and calendar quarter. (If not correctly printed please change)

Name (as distinguished from trade name)
John K. Jones
Trade name, if any
Jones Corner Market
Address
1212 Main Street, Mesa, Arizona

Date quarter ended **March 31, 1966**
Identification No. **42 123123**

If form is not preaddressed, check type of employer—
☒ Sole owner ☐ Partnership
☐ Corporation ☐ Other (specify)

------ Entries must be made both above and below this line ------

Name (as distinguished from trade name)
John K. Jones
Trade name, if any
Jones Corner Market
Address
1212 Main Street, Mesa, Arizona

Date quarter ended **March 31, 1966**
Identification No. **42 123123**

U. S. TREASURY DEPARTMENT
District Director of Internal Revenue

OFFICIAL BUSINESS
POSTAGE AND FEES PAID

POSTMASTER: If undeliverable treat in accordance with Section 355.56 of Postal Manual

SCHEDULE A—QUARTERLY REPORT OF WAGES TAXABLE UNDER THE FEDERAL INSURANCE CONTRIBUTIONS ACT (FOR SOCIAL SECURITY)
IF WAGES WERE NOT TAXABLE UNDER THE F.I.C.A. MAKE NO ENTRIES BELOW

14. Number of persons employed (except agricultural and household employees) during pay period containing the 12th of third month in quarter.	15. Total pages of this return, including this page and any pages of Form 941a.	16. Total number of employees listed.
3	1	3

List for each employee, except agricultural employees, the WAGES taxable under the Federal Insurance Contributions Act (for Social Security) which were paid during the quarter. If you pay an employee more than $6,600 in a calendar year, report ONLY THE FIRST $6,600 of such wages.

If you have more employees than can be listed on this form, use form 941a (Rev. 10-64).

17. EMPLOYEE'S SOCIAL SECURITY ACCOUNT NUMBER (If number is unknown, see Circular E)			18. NAME OF EMPLOYEE (Please type or print)	19. TAXABLE F.I.C.A. WAGES (Paid to Employee in Quarter Before deductions)		20. See instructions on page 2
000	00	0000		Dollars	Cents	
123	12	1234	James J. Smallwood	600	00	
234	23	2345	Robert Thomas Roberts	600	00	
345	34	3456	Mary Jones Smith	750	00	

If you need more space for listing employees, use Schedule A continuation sheets, Form 941a. Total wages reported in column 19 on this page ⟶	1,950	00

21. TOTAL WAGES TAXABLE UNDER F.I.C.A. PAID DURING QUARTER
(Total wages in column 19 of this page and continuation sheets) $ **1,950 00** Enter this total in Item 4 above.

FILE THIS RETURN WITH YOUR DISTRICT DIRECTOR OF INTERNAL REVENUE.

(Form 941) Page 1

Illustration 82

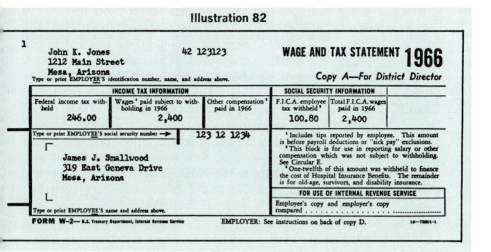

Observe that the Employer's Quarterly Federal Tax Return, Form 941 (Illustration 81) actually has two parts. (It is perforated between the two listings of the employer's name and is designed to be torn into two parts at this point.) On the first part the employer reports: (1) the total employees' federal income taxes withheld, (2) total wages that were subject to F.I.C.A. taxes (Item 4), and (3) the combined amount of the employees' and employer's F.I.C.A. taxes. (The combined employees' and employer's F.I.C.A. taxes is shown as Item 5 where it says "8.4% of wages in Item 4." The 8.4 percent is the sum of the 4.2 percent withheld from the employees' wages and the 4.2 percent levied on the employer during 1966, the year of the illustrated tax return.

On the second half of the quarterly tax return, labeled Schedule A, the employer reports each employee's social security number, name, and his wages subject to F.I.C.A. taxes. This schedule is sent to the Social Security Administration by the Director of Internal Revenue. The Social Security Administration posts the information as to each employee's wages to his social security record where it becomes the basis for determining the employee's retirement and survivors' benefits.

Joint Federal-State Unemployment Insurance Program. The federal government participates with the states in a joint federal-state unemployment insurance program. Within this joint program each state has established and now administers its own unemployment insurance program under which it pays unemployment benefits to its unemployed workers. The federal government through the Social Security Administration approves the state programs and pays a portion of their administrative expenses.

The federal money for administering the state programs is raised by a tax imposed under a law called the Federal Unemployment Tax Act. This act levies a payroll tax on employers of four or more people. Note that the tax is imposed on employers only; employees pay nothing; and also that the money from this tax is used for administrative purposes and not to pay benefits.

Historically, in 1935 when the Federal Unemployment Tax Act was first passed, only one state had an unemployment insurance program; consequently, at that time Congress passed certain sections of the Social Security Act and the Federal Unemployment Tax Act with two purposes in view. The first was to induce the individual states to create satisfactory unemployment insurance programs of their own, and the second was to provide funds to be distributed to the states for use in administering the state programs. These acts were successful in accomplishing their first purpose, all states immediately created unemployment programs; and today the acts remain in effect for their second purpose, to provide funds to be distributed to the states, and also to retain a measure of federal control over the several state programs.

The Federal Unemployment Tax Act. The Federal Unemployment Tax Act requires employers of four or more employees to—

1. Before January 31 following the end of each year, file a tax return called an "Employer's Annual Federal Unemployment Tax Return, Form 940."
2. At the time the foregoing return is filed, pay an excise tax equal to 0.4 percent of the first $3,000 in wages paid each employee.
3. Keep records to substantiate the information on the tax return. (In general the records required by other payroll laws and the regular accounting records satisfy this requirement.)

State Unemployment Insurance Programs. While the various state unemployment insurance programs differ in some respects, all have three common objectives. They are:

1. To pay unemployment compensation for limited periods to unemployed individuals. (To be eligible for benefits, an unemployed individual must have worked for a taxpaying employer covered by the law of his state. In general the various state laws cover employers of from one to four or more employees who are not specifically exempted.)
2. To stabilize employment by covered employers. (In all states this is accomplished by a so-called merit-rating plan. Under a merit-rating plan an employer who provides steady employment for his employees gains a merit rating that substantially reduces his state unemployment tax rate.)
3. To establish and operate employment facilities that assist unemployed individuals in finding suitable employment and assist employers in finding employees.

All states support their unemployment insurance programs by placing a payroll tax on employers; a few states place an additional tax on employees. At one time the basic tax rate on employers in all states was an almost uniform 2.7 percent of the first $3,000 paid each employee, and an employer could gain a merit rating that would reduce this basic rate to zero in some states by keeping his employees employed. State rates are now beginning to vary.

The states also vary as to required reports, but in general all require a tax return and payment of the required tax within one month after the end of each calendar quarter. Also, since the benefits paid an eligible unemployed individual are based upon his earnings, the tax return must usually name each employee and tell his wages.

In addition to reports and payment of taxes, all states require employers to maintain certain payroll records. These vary from state to state; but in general require, among other things, a payroll record for each pay period showing the pay period dates, hours worked, and taxable earnings of each employee. An individual earnings record for each employee is also commonly required, and each earnings record generally must show about the same information required by social security laws. In addition, information as to (1) the date an employee was hired, rehired, or reinstated after a layoff; (2) the date the employee quit, was discharged, or laid off; and (3) the reason for termination is also commonly required.

WITHHOLDING EMPLOYEES' FEDERAL INCOME TAXES

With few exceptions, employers of one of more persons are required to calculate, collect, and remit to the federal government the income taxes of their employees. Historically, although the first federal income tax law became effective in 1913, it applied to only a few individuals having high earnings, and it was not until World War II that income taxes were levied on the great masses of wage earners. At that time Congress recognized that many individual wage earners could not be expected to save sufficient money with which to pay their income taxes once each year. Consequently, Congress instituted a system of pay-as-you-go, withholding of taxes each payday at their source. This pay-as-you-go withholding of employee income taxes requires an employer to act as a tax collecting agent of the federal government.

The federal income tax to be withheld from an employee's wages is determined by his wages and the number of his exemptions. Each exemption exempts $600 of the employee's yearly earnings from income tax. For example, an employee with five exemptions and earning in one year less than $3,000 pays no tax (5 × $600 = $3,000 exempted). An employee is allowed one exemption for himself, additional exemptions if he or his wife are over sixty-five or blind, and an exemption for each dependent. Every covered employee is required to furnish his employer an employee's withholding exemption certificate, Illustration 83, showing the exemptions to which he is entitled.

Most employers use a wage bracket withholding table similar to the one shown in Illustration 84 in determining federal income taxes to be withheld

Illustration 83
Employee's Withholding Exemption Certificate, Form W-4

FORM W-4 (Rev. July 1964) U.S. Treasury Department Internal Revenue Service	**EMPLOYEE'S WITHHOLDING EXEMPTION CERTIFICATE**

Print full name ___George William Flanders___   Social Security Account Number ___307-03-2195___

Print home address ___319 East Geneva Drive___ City ___Tempe,___ State ___Arizona___

EMPLOYEE:	HOW TO CLAIM YOUR WITHHOLDING EXEMPTIONS	
File this form with your employer. Otherwise, he must withhold U.S. income tax from your wages without exemption.	1. If SINGLE, and you claim your exemption, write "1", if you do not, write "0" . . . . _____ 2. If MARRIED, one exemption each is allowable for husband and wife if not claimed on another certificate.	
	(a) If you claim both of these exemptions, write "2" ⎫ (b) If you claim one of these exemptions, write "1" ⎬ . . . . (c) If you claim neither of these exemptions, write "0" ⎭	2

EMPLOYER:
Keep this certificate with your records. If the employee is believed to have claimed too many exemptions, the District Director should be so advised.
	3. Exemptions for age and blindness (applicable only to you and your wife but not to dependents):
	  (a) If you or your wife will be 65 years of age or older at the end of the year, and you claim this exemption,
	    write "1"; if both will be 65 or older, and you claim both of these exemptions, write "2" . . . . _____
	  (b) If you or your wife are blind, and you claim this exemption, write "1"; if both are blind, and you
	    claim both of these exemptions, write "2" . . . . _____	

	4. If you claim exemptions for one or more dependents, write the number of such exemptions. (Do not claim exemption for a dependent unless you are qualified under instruction 3 on other side.)	2
	5. Add the number of exemptions which you have claimed above and write the total	4
	6. Additional withholding per pay period under agreement with employer. See Instruction 1 . . . . . $ _____	

I CERTIFY that the number of withholding exemptions claimed on this certificate does not exceed the number to which I am entitled.

(Date) ___March 15,___ , 19__66__   (Signed) _George H. Flanders_

from employees' gross earnings. The illustrated table is applicable when a pay period is one week in length. Different tables are provided for biweekly, semimonthly, and monthly pay periods.

Determining the federal income tax to be withheld from an employee's gross wages is quite easy when a withholding table is used. First the employee's wage bracket is located in the first two columns. Then the amount to be withheld is found on the line of the wage bracket in the column showing the exemptions to which the employee is entitled. The column heading numbers refer to the number of exemptions claimd by an employee on his certificate.

In addition to determining and withholding income tax from each employee's wages every payday, employers are required to—

1. Periodically remit the withheld taxes to the Director of Internal Revenue. (Times of remittance are discussed later.)
2. Within one month after the end of each quarter, file a report showing the income taxes withheld. This report is the Employer's Quarterly Federal Tax Return, Form 941, discussed previously and shown in Illustration 81. It is the same report required for F.I.C.A. taxes.
3. On or before January 31 following each year, give each employee a Withholding Statement, Form W–2, which tells the employee (1) his total wages for the preceding year, (2) wages subject to F.I.C.A. taxes, (3) in-

Illustration 84
Wage Bracket Withholding Table

Weekly Payroll period—Continued													
And the wages are—		And the number of withholding exemptions claimed is—											
At least	But less than	0	1	2	3	4	5	6	7	8	9	10 or more
		The amount of income tax to be withheld shall be—											
80	82	11.30	9.50	7.80	6.00	4.20	2.40	.60	0	0	0	0
82	84	11.60	9.80	8.00	6.20	4.40	2.60	.90	0	0	0	0
84	86	11.90	10.10	8.30	6.50	4.70	2.90	1.10	0	0	0	0
86	88	12.20	10.40	8.60	6.80	5.00	3.20	1.40	0	0	0	0
88	90	12.50	10.70	8.90	7.10	5.30	3.50	1.70	0	0	0	0
90	92	12.70	10.90	9.20	7.40	5.60	3.80	2.00	.20	0	0	0
92	94	13.00	11.20	9.40	7.60	5.80	4.00	2.30	.50	0	0	0
94	96	13.30	11.50	9.70	7.90	6.10	4.30	2.50	.70	0	0	0
96	98	13.60	11.80	10.00	8.20	6.40	4.60	2.80	1.00	0	0	0
98	100	13.90	12.10	10.30	8.50	6.70	4.90	3.10	1.30	0	0	0
100	105	14.40	12.60	10.80	9.00	7.20	5.40	3.60	1.80	0	0	0
105	110	15.10	13.30	11.50	9.70	7.90	6.10	4.30	2.50	.70	0	0

come taxes withheld, and (4) F.I.C.A. taxes withheld. A copy of this statement must also be given to each terminated employee within 30 days after his last wage payment.

4. On or before January 31 following the end of each year, send the Director of Internal Revenue carbon copies of all W–2 forms given employees.

CITY AND STATE INCOME TAXES

In addition to deducting employees' federal income taxes, employers in some cities and states must also deduct employees' city and state income taxes. When this is necessary, the city and state taxes are handled in much the same manner as federal income taxes.

FAIR LABOR STANDARDS ACT

The Fair Labor Standards Act, often called the Wages and Hours Law, sets minimum hourly wages and maximum hours of work per week for employees, with certain exceptions, of employers engaged either directly or indirectly in interstate commerce. As amended, the law at this writing sets a $1.25 per hour minimum wage and a maximum 40-hour workweek. However, although the act sets a maximum 40-hour workweek, it does not prohibit an employee from working longer hours but provides that if an employee covered by the act works more than 40 hours in one week, he must be paid for the hours in excess of 40 at his regular pay rate plus an overtime premium of at least one half his regular rate. This gives an employee an overtime rate of at least one and one half times his regular hourly rate. The act also requires employers to maintain records for each covered employee similar to the employee's individual earning record of Illustration 89.

UNION CONTRACTS

Although the Wages and Hours Law requires covered employers to pay time and one half for hours worked in excess of 40 in any one week, employers commonly operate under contracts with their employees' union that provide even better terms. For example, union contracts often provide for time and one half for work in excess of eight hours in any one day, time and one half for work on Saturdays, and double time for Sundays and holidays. When an employer is under such a union contract, since the contract terms are better than those of the Wages and Hours Law, the contract terms take precedence over the law.

In addition to specifying working hours and wage rates, union contracts often provide for the collection of employees' union dues by the employer. Such a requirement commonly provides that the employer shall deduct dues from the wages of each employee and remit the amounts deducted to the union. The employer is usually required to remit once each month and to report the name and amount deducted from each employee's pay.

OTHER PAYROLL DEDUCTIONS

In addition to the payroll deductions discussed thus far, employees may individually authorize additional deductions, such as:

1. Deductions to accumulate funds for the purchase of U.S. savings bonds.
2. Deductions to pay health, accident, hospital, or life insurance premiums.
3. Deductions to repay loans from the employer or the employees' credit union.
4. Deductions to pay for merchandise purchased from the company.
5. Deductions for donations to charitable organizations such as Boy Scouts, Girl Scouts, Community Chest, or Red Cross.

TIMEKEEPING

Compiling a record of the time worked by each employee is called *timekeeping*. In an individual company the method of compiling such a record depends upon the nature of the business and the number of its employees. In a very small business timekeeping may consist of no more than pencil notations of each employee's working time made in a memorandum book by the manager or owner. On the other hand, in a larger company a time clock or several time clocks are often used to record on clock cards each employee's time of arrival and departure. When time clocks are used, they are placed at the entrances to the office, store, or factory, and a rack for clock cards is provided beside each clock. At the beginning of each payroll period a clock card for each employee similar to Illustration 85 is placed in the rack at the entrance to be used by the

Illustration 85
A Clock Card

Clock No.		S. S. No.			
Name					
	MORNING		AFTERNOON		OVERTIME	
	In	Out	In	Out	In	Out
Mon.						
Tues.						
Weds.						
Thurs.						
Fri.						
Sat.						
Sun.						
Pay Period Ending						
Regular Time	Hours		Rate		Earnings	
Overtime						
Total Earnings for Period						

employee. Each day, as the employee enters the plant, store, or office, he takes his card from the rack and places it in a slot in the time clock. This actuates the clock to stamp the date and arrival time on the card. The employee then returns the card to the rack and proceeds to his place of work. Upon leaving the plant, store, or office at noon or at the end of the day, the procedure is reversed. The employee takes the card from the rack, places it in the clock, and stamps the time of departure. As a result, at the end of the pay period the card shows the hours the employee was on the job.

THE PAYROLL REGISTER

Each pay period the information as to hours worked as compiled on clock cards or otherwise is summarized in a Payroll Register. A pen-and-ink form of such a register is shown in Illustration 86. A payroll register for use with a bookkeeping machine would be similar. The Illustration 86 register is for a weekly pay period and shows the payroll data for each employee on a separate line. The column headings and the data recorded in the columns are in the main self-explanatory.

The columns under the heading "Daily Time" show hours worked each day by each employee. The total of each employee's hours is entered in the column headed "Total Hours." If hours worked include overtime hours, these are entered in the column headed "O.T. Hours."

The column headed "Reg. Pay Rate" is for the hourly pay rate of each employee. Total hours worked multiplied by the regular pay rate equals regular pay; overtime hours multiplied by the overtime premium rate equals overtime premium pay; and regular pay plus overtime premium pay is the gross pay of each employee.

Under the heading "Deductions," the amounts withheld from each

Illustration 86

Week

Employee	Clock Card No.	Daily Time							Total Hours	O.T. Hours	Earnings			
		M	T	W	T	F	S	S			Reg. Pay Rate	Regular Pay	O.T. Premium Pay	G$_1$ P
Robert Austin	105	8	8	8	8	8			40		2.00	80.00		8
Charles Cross	97	8	8	8	8	8	4		44	4	3.00	132.00	6.00	13
John Cruz	89	8	8	8	8	8			40		2.50	100.00		10
Howard Keife	112	8	8	0	0	0			16		2.50	40.00		4
Lee Miller	95	8	8	8	8	8			40		2.50	100.00		10
Dale Sears	53	8	8	8	8	8			40		1.50	60.00		6
Robert Smith	68	8	8	8	8	8	6		46	6	3.50	161.00	10.50	17
George Tucker	74	8	8	8	8	8			40		2.50	100.00		10
Total														78

employee's gross pay for social security or F.I.C.A. taxes are shown in the column marked "F.I.C.A. Taxes." These amounts are determined by multiplying the gross pay of each employee by the F.I.C.A. tax rate in effect. In this and the remaining illustrations of this chapter the 1967, 4.4 percent rate is used.

Observe in the F.I.C.A. Taxes column of Illustration 86 that there is no F.I.C.A. deduction for the next to last employee, Robert Smith. This is because Smith's cumulative earnings for the year have previously passed $6,600 and his wages are no longer subject to tax. (See the discussion for Illustration 90 on page 410.)

As previously stated, the income tax withheld from each employee depends upon his gross pay and exemptions. This amount is commonly determined by the use of a wage bracket withholding table and, when determined, is entered in the column headed "Federal Income Taxes."

The column headed "U.S. Savings Bonds" shows the amounts withheld from those employes who are buying bonds through payroll deductions. The total withheld from all employees for this purpose is a current liability of the business which is credited each pay period to an account called "Employees' Bond Deductions." When the amounts deducted from any one employee's wages are sufficient to purchase a bond, the bond is bought and delivered to the employee. At the same time the account Employees' Bond Deductions is debited, and Cash is credited for the bond's cost.

As previously stated, union contracts commonly require the employer to

Illustration 86—Continued

er 18, 1967

		Deductions				Payment		Distribution		
.A. es	Federal Income Taxes	U.S. Savings Bonds	Union Dues	Total Deduc- tions		Net Pay	Check No.	Sales Salaries	Office Salaries	Delivery Salaries
2	7.80	2.50		13.82		66.18	893		80.00	
7	13.90		2.50	22.47		115.53	894			138.00
0	9.00	1.25	1.50	16.15		83.85	895	100.00		
6	3.90	1.25	1.50	8.41		31.59	896	40.00		
0	10.80	2.50	1.50	19.20		80.80	897	100.00		
4	5.00	1.25		8.89		51.11	898		60.00	
	17.30	6.25		23.55		147.95	899		171.50	
0	7.20	2.50	1.50	15.60		84.40	900	100.00		
9	74.90	17.50	8.50	128.09		661.41		340.00	311.50	138.00

withhold union dues and to periodically remit the amounts withheld to the union. The total withheld for employees' union dues is a current liability until paid to the union. The column marked "Union Dues" in the illustrated Payroll Register is for this deduction.

Additional columns may be added to the Payroll Register for deductions that occur sufficiently often to warrant special columns. For example, a company that regularly deducts amounts from its employees' pay for hospital insurance may add a special column for this deduction.

An employee's gross pay less his total deductions is his net pay, and is entered in the column headed "Net Pay." The total of this column is the amount to be paid the employees. The numbers of the checks used in paying the employees are entered in the column headed "Check No."

The three columns under the heading "Distribution" are for sorting the various salaries into kinds of salary expense. Here each employee's gross salary is entered in the proper column according to the type of his work. The column totals then tell the amounts to be debited to the salary expense accounts.

RECORDING THE PAYROLL

Generally a Payroll Register such as the one shown in Illustration 86 is a supplementary memorandum record. As a supplementary record, its information is not posted directly to the accounts but is first recorded with a general journal entry, which is then posted. The entry to record the payroll shown in Illustration 86 is:

Oct.	18	Sales Salaries......................................	340.00	
		Office Salaries.....................................	311.50	
		Delivery Salaries..................................	138.00	
		F.I.C.A. Taxes Payable.........................		27.19
		Employees' Federal Income Taxes Payable......		74.90
		Employees' Bond Deductions..................		17.50
		Employees' Union Dues Payable..............		8.50
		Accrued Payroll Payable.....................		661.41
		To record the payroll of the week ended October 18.		

The debits of this entry are taken from the Payroll Register's distribution column totals, and they charge the employees' gross earnings to the proper salary expense accounts. The credits to F.I.C.A. Taxes Payable, Employees' Federal Income Taxes Payable, Employees' Bond Deductions, and Employees' Union Dues Payable record these amounts as current liabilities. The credit to Accrued Payroll Payable records as a liability the amount to be paid the employees.

PAYING THE EMPLOYEES

Almost every business pays its employees with checks. In a company having but few employees these checks are often drawn on the regular bank account. When this is done, each check is recorded in either a Check Register or a Cash Disbursements Journal. Since each check results in a debit to the Accrued Payroll Payable account, posting labor may be saved by adding an Accrued Payroll Payable debit column to the Check Register or Cash Disbursements Journal. For example, assume that a firm uses a Check Register like that described in Chapter 8, before the introduction of the voucher system. If a firm uses such a register and adds an Accrued Payroll debit column, the entries to pay the employees of the Illustration 86 payroll will appear somewhat like those in Illustration 87.

Illustration 87
An Ordinary Check Register with an Accrued
Payroll Debit Column

Date	Check No.	Payee	Account Debited	F	Sundry Accounts Debit	Accts. Pay. Debit	Accr. Pay. Debit	Pur. Dis. Credit	Bank Credit
Oct. 18	893	Robert Austin	Accrued Payroll				66.18		66.18
18	894	Charles Cross	"				115.53		115.53
18	895	John Cruz	"				83.85		83.85
18	896	Howard Keife	"				31.59		31.59
18	897	Lee Miller	"				80.80		80.80
18	898	Dale Sears	"				51.11		51.11
18	899	Robert Smith	"				147.95		147.95
18	900	George Tucker	"				84.40		84.40

Although not required by law, most employers furnish each employee an earnings statement each payday. The objective of such a statement is to inform the employee, and give him a record that may be retained, of hours worked, gross pay, deductions, and net pay. The statement usually takes the form of a detachable paycheck stub that is removed before the check is cashed. A paycheck with a detachable stub showing deductions is reproduced in Illustration 88.

Illustration 88
A Payroll Check

EUGENE SUPPLY COMPANY
EUGENE, OREGON

Employee Robert Austin

STATEMENT OF EARNINGS AND DEDUCTIONS FOR EMPLOYEE'S RECORD—
DETACH BEFORE CASHING CHECK

Total Hours	O.T. Hours	Reg. Pay Rate	Reg- ular Pay	O.T. Prem. Pay	Gross Pay	F.I.C.A. Taxes	Fed- eral In- come Taxes	U.S. Sav- ings Bonds	Union Dues	Total Deduc- tions	Net Pay
40		2.00	80.00		80.00	3.52	7.80	2.50		13.82	66.18

EUGENE SUPPLY COMPANY
2590 Chula Vista Street
Eugene, Oregon   *No.* 893

Date   October 18, 1967

Pay to the
Order of   Robert Austin $66.18

– – – – – – – Sixty-six dollars and eighteen cents – – – – – – –

EUGENE SUPPLY COMPANY

To: *Merchants National Bank*
         Eugene, Oregon

PAYROLL BANK ACCOUNT

A business with many employees normally makes use of a special payroll bank account in paying its employees. When such an account is used, one check for the payroll total is drawn on the regular bank account and deposited in the special payroll bank account. Individual payroll checks are then drawn on this special payroll account. Because only one check for the payroll total is drawn on the regular bank account each payday, a special payroll bank account simplifies reconciliation of the regular bank account. It may be reconciled without considering the payroll checks outstanding, and there may be many of these. Likewise, when the payroll bank account is separately reconciled, only the outstanding payroll checks need be considered.

Often a company with sufficient employees to need a special payroll bank account also uses a voucher system. Such a company in paying its employees completes the following steps:

1. First, it records the information shown on its Payroll Register in the usual manner with a general journal entry similar to the one illustrated on page 404. This entry causes the sum of the employees' net pay to be credited to the liability account Accrued Payroll Payable.
2. Next, a voucher payable to Payroll Bank Account for the amount of the payroll is drawn and entered in the Voucher Register. This results in a debit to Accrued Payroll Payable and a credit to Vouchers Payable.
3. Then a single check in payment of the payroll voucher is drawn, endorsed, and deposited in the payroll bank account. This transfers cash equal to the payroll total from the regular bank account to the special payroll bank account.
4. Last, individual payroll checks are drawn on the special payroll bank account and delivered to the employees. These pay the employees and, as soon as all employees cash their checks, exhaust the funds in the special account.

A special Payroll Check Register may be used in connection with a payroll bank account. However, most companies do not use such a register, but prefer to enter the payroll check numbers in their Payroll Register, making it act as a Check Register.

EMPLOYEE'S INDIVIDUAL EARNINGS RECORD

An Employee's Individual Earnings Record, Illustration 89, provides for each employee in one record a full year's summary of his working time, gross earnings, deductions, and net pay. In addition it accumulates information that—

1. Serves as a basis for the employer's state and federal payroll tax returns.
2. Tells when an employee has earned $3,000, and his wages are no longer a basis for employer's state and federal unemployment taxes.
3. Tells when an employee has earned $6,600, and his wages are no longer subject to deductions for F.I.C.A. taxes.
4. Supplies data for the Withholding Statement, Form W–2, which must be given to the employee at the end of the year.

The payroll information on an Employee's Individual Earnings Record is taken from the Payroll Register. The information as to earnings, deductions, and net pay is first recorded on a single line in the Payroll Register, from where it is posted each pay period to the earnings record.

PAYROLL TAXES LEVIED ON THE EMPLOYER

Under the previous discussion of the Federal Social Security Act, it was pointed out that F.I.C.A. taxes are levied in like amounts on both employed workers and their employers. A covered employer is required by law to deduct from his employees' pay the amounts of their F.I.C.A. taxes; but in addition, he must himself pay a tax equal to the sum of his

Illustration 89

EMPLOYEE'S INDIVIDUAL EARNINGS RECORD

Employee's Name **Robert Austin**   S.S. Acct. No. **307-03-2195**   Employee No. **105**

Home Address **111 South Greenwood**   Notify in Case of Emergency **Margaret Austin**   Phone No. **964-9834**

Employed **6/7/65**   Date of Termination _____   Reason _____

Date of Birth **June 6, 1941**   Date Becomes 65 **June 6, 2006**   Male **(X)** Female **( )**   Married **(X)** Single **( )**   Number of Exemptions **2**   Pay Rate **$2.00 hr.**

Occupation **Clerk**   Place **Office**

Date		Time Lost		Time Wk.		Reg. Pay	O.T. Prem. Pay	Gross Pay	Cumulative Pay	F.I.C.A. Taxes	Federal Income Taxes	U.S. Savings Bonds	Union Dues	Total Deductions	Net Pay	Check No.
Per. Ends	Paid	Hrs.	Reason	Total	O.T. Hours											
1/5	1/5			40		80.00		80.00	80.00	3.52	7.80	2.50		13.82	66.18	173
1/12	1/12			40		80.00		80.00	160.00	3.52	7.80	2.50		13.82	66.18	201
1/19	1/19			40		80.00		80.00	240.00	3.52	7.80	2.50		13.82	66.18	243
1/26	1/26	4	Sick	36		72.00		72.00	312.00	3.17	6.60	2.50		12.27	59.73	295
2/2	2/2			40		80.00		80.00	392.00	3.52	7.80	2.50		13.82	66.18	339
2/9	2/9			40		80.00		80.00	472.00	3.52	7.80	2.50		13.82	66.18	354
2/16	2/16			40		80.00		80.00	552.00	3.52	7.80	2.50		13.82	66.18	397
2/23	2/23			40		80.00		80.00	632.00	3.52	7.80	2.50		13.82	66.18	446
10/18	10/18			40		80.00		80.00	3,332.00	3.52	7.80	2.50		13.82	66.18	893

employees' F.I.C.A. taxes. Commonly, the tax levied on the employer is recorded at the same time the payroll to which it relates is recorded. Also, since both the employees' taxes and employer's tax are reported on the same tax return and are paid in one amount, the liability for both is normally recorded in the same liability account, the F.I.C.A. Taxes Payable account.

As previously explained, although F.I.C.A. taxes are levied on both covered employers and their employees, employers only are required to pay federal and, usually, state unemployment taxes. Most employers record all three of these payroll taxes with one general journal entry. This entry is normally made at the time the payroll to which the taxes relate is recorded. For example, the entry to record the employer's payroll taxes on the payroll of Illustration 86 is:

Oct.	18	*Payroll Taxes Expense*......................	*38.04*	
		F.I.C.A. Taxes Payable.................		*27.19*
		State Unemployment Taxes Payable......		*9.45*
		Federal Unemployment Taxes Payable....		*1.40*
		To record the employer's payroll taxes.		

The debit of this entry is to the expense account Payroll Taxes Expense. Often this one debit is broken into amounts applicable to each type of salaries and is recorded in several expense accounts such as, for example, Payroll Taxes Expense on Sales Salaries, Payroll Taxes Expense on Office Salaries, and Payroll Taxes Expense on Delivery Salaries. A division such as this makes it possible to classify on the income statement the taxes expense applicable to each type of salaries.

There are three current liability accounts credited in the foregoing entry recording the employer's payroll taxes. The credit to F.I.C.A. Taxes Payable is for $27.19. This amount is equal to and matches the total deduction from the employees' wages in the Payroll Register of Illustration 86. It is 4.4 percent of $618. The payroll total is $789.50; but since the amount previously paid in wages to one employee, Robert Smith, is in excess of $6,600, the $171.50 of his current wages is tax-exempt. The fact that Smith's current wages are not subject to F.I.C.A. taxes is determined by the person responsible for completing the Payroll Register by examining the Cumulative Pay column of Smith's individual earnings record.

The $9.45 credit to State Unemployment Taxes Payable in the employer's payroll tax entry is based on the assumption the employer's tax rate is 2.7 percent of the first $3,000 paid each employee. As previously stated, it is the duty of the one responsible for completing the Payroll Register to check the Cumulative Pay columns of the employees' individual earnings records to see when any employee's earnings reach $3,000 and are no longer subject to state and federal unemployment taxes, and when the earnings reach $6,600 and are no longer subject to F.I.C.A. taxes. In the illustrative payroll it is assumed that the employees have cumulative earnings prior to this pay period and earnings subject to the various taxes as shown in Illustration 90.

Illustration 90

Employees' Cumulative Earnings through the Last Pay Period and Earnings Subject to the Various Taxes

| Employees | Earnings through Last Pay Period | Earnings This Pay Period | Earnings Subject to— | | |
			F.I.C.A. Taxes	State Un-employment Taxes	Federal Unem-ployment Taxes
Robert Austin..	$3,252	$ 80.00	$ 80.00		
Charles Cross...	5,246	138.00	138.00		
John Cruz......	2,860	100.00	100.00	$100.00	$100.00
Howard Keife...	1,810	40.00	40.00	40.00	40.00
Lee Miller.......	880	100.00	100.00	100.00	100.00
Dale Sears......	2,400	60.00	60.00	60.00	60.00
Robert Smith...	6,674	171.50			
George Tucker..	2,950	100.00	100.00	50.00	50.00
		$789.50	$618.00	$350.00	$350.00

If the employees have prior cumulative earnings as listed in Illustration 90, then three employees have earned in excess of $3,000 and their pay is assumed, as in the majority of states, to be exempt from state unemployment taxes. One employee has previously earned $2,950 and only the first $50 of his earnings are subject to the tax, and the wages of the remaining employees are taxable in full. Consequently, the $9.45 credit to State Unemployment Taxes Payable in the entry recording the employer's payroll taxes results from multiplying $350 of wages subject to tax by the assumed 2.7 percent rate.

As the law is presently amended, an employer's federal unemployment tax is also based on the first $3,000 in wages paid each employee. Therefore, the federal unemployment tax liability in the illustrated journal entry results from multiplying $350 by the 0.4 percent rate, or is $1.40.

PAYING THE PAYROLL TAXES

Federal income and the F.I.C.A. taxes withheld each payday from the employees' pay plus the F.I.C.A. tax imposed on the employer are current liabilities until paid to the Director of Internal Revenue. If their sum is $100 or less per month, they may be paid once each quarter, when the employer files his Employer's Quarterly Tax Return, Form 941. This return is due on April 30, July 31, October 31, and January 31 following the end of each quarter, and a check for the taxes may be attached if the taxes are not more than $100 in any one month.

If the employees' F.I.C.A. and income taxes plus the employer's F.I.C.A. taxes exceed $100 in either the first or second month of a quarter, the employer is required to deposit their sum in a federal depository bank to the credit of the United States Treasury Department. This deposit, for which the employer receives a receipt, must be made within 15 days after the end of the month to which the taxes apply. For the third month of any quarter the employer may either deposit the taxes in a federal depository or he may wait until he files his Employer's Quarterly Tax Return, Form 941, and attach a check thereto for the third month's taxes.

An employer whose tax liability is less than $100 per month may use the depository procedure in paying his taxes if he so wishes.

A check attached to the employer's quarterly tax return or a check for F.I.C.A. and employees' income taxes deposited in a federal depository bank pays these taxes and should be recorded in the same manner as a check in payment of any other liability.

A deposit of a month's F.I.C.A. and withheld employees' income taxes in a federal depository bank pays these taxes. Consequently, if at the time an employer files his Employer's Quarterly Tax Return, Form 941, he has paid the taxes reported on the return by means of monthly deposits in a federal depository, he attaches his depository receipts to the return, mails it to the Director of Internal Revenue, and no bookkeeping entries are required.

When state unemployment taxes are less than $100 per month, they may normally be paid quarterly. If they exceed $100 per month, some states require monthly payments. This is similar to the federal procedures; therefore, most employers account for state unemployment taxes in the same manner as F.I.C.A. and employee income taxes.

Federal unemployment taxes are payable annually. The law requires that the return, called "Employer's Annual Federal Unemployment Tax Return, Form 940," be filed on or before January 31 following the end of a tax year. When it is filed, a check for the tax liability is attached. The check is recorded in the same manner as a check paying any other liability.

ACCRUING TAXES AND WAGES

Payroll taxes are levied on wages actually paid; consequently, there is no legal liability for taxes on accrued wages. Nevertheless, both wages and the employer's payroll taxes on the wages are, from a theoretical viewpoint, expenses of the accounting period in which the wages are earned; and if the income statement is to show all expenses of an accounting period, both accrued wages and the accrued taxes on the wages should be recorded at the end of the period.

To illustrate the entry for accruing wages and taxes on the wages, assume that (1) a company's accounting period ends on June 30, (2) its last pay period ended on June 26, (3) the company employees worked on June 28, 29, and 30 and earned sales salaries of $750 and office salaries of $250 during the three days. The adjusting entry to record these accrued wages and payroll taxes is:

June	30	Sales Salaries	750.00	
		Office Salaries	250.00	
		Payroll Taxes Expense	75.00	
		F.I.C.A. Taxes Payable		44.00
		State Unemployment Taxes Payable		27.00
		Federal Unemployment Taxes Payable		4.00
		Accrued Payroll Payable		1,000.00
		To record the accrued payroll.		

The $75 debit to Payroll Taxes Expense is the sum of the F.I.C.A., federal unemployment, and state unemployment taxes levied on the employer. The amount is based on the assumptions that all the wages were subject to taxes at a 4.4 percent F.I.C.A. tax rate, a 0.4 percent federal unemployment rate, and a 2.7 percent state unemployment rate.

Although payroll taxes on accrued wages are theoretically an expense of the accounting period in which the wages are earned, often such accrued taxes are not material in amount. Consequently, many accountants apply the rule of materiality and do not accrue such taxes.

MACHINE METHODS

Manually prepared pen-and-ink records like the ones described in this chapter are found in many small concerns, and very satisfactorily meet their needs. However, concerns having many employees commonly use machines in their payroll work. The machines vary, but are usually designed to take advantage of the fact that each pay period much the same information must be entered for each employee in the Payroll Register, on his earnings record, and on his paycheck. The machines take advantage of this and simultaneously print the information in all three places in one operation.

QUESTIONS FOR CLASS DISCUSSION

1. What are F.I.C.A. taxes? Who pays these taxes and how much must be paid? For what purposes are the funds from F.I.C.A. taxes used?

2. Company A collects from its employees approximately $83 each month in F.I.C.A. taxes and federal income taxes; Company B collects approximately $165. When must each remit these amounts to the Director of Internal Revenue?

3. What benefits are paid to unemployed workers from funds raised by the Federal Unemployment Insurance Act? Why was this act passed?

4. Who pays federal unemployment insurance taxes? What is the tax rate? When is the tax due?

5. What are the objectives of state unemployment insurance laws? Who pays state unemployment insurance?

6. What is a state unemployment merit rating? Why are such merit ratings granted?

7. What determines the amount that must be deducted from an employee's wages for federal income taxes?

8. What is a wage bracket withholding table? Use the wage bracket withholding table in Illustration 84 to find the income tax to be withheld from the wages of an employee with three exemptions who earned $85.75 in a week.

9. What does the Fair Labor Standards Act require of a covered employer?

10. How is a clock card used in recording the time an employee is on the job?

11. How is a special payroll bank account used in paying the wages of employees?

12. At the end of an accounting period a firm's special payroll bank account has a $162.35 balance because the payroll checks of two employees have not cleared the bank. Should this item appear on the firm's balance sheet? If so, where?

13. What information is accumulated on an employee's individual earnings record? Why must this information be accumulated? For what purposes is the information used?

14. What payroll taxes are levied on the employer? What taxes are deducted from the wages of an employee?

15. Paul O'Connor hires an employee and pays him $100 per week. How much do the services of the employee cost O'Connor if taxes are considered a part of the cost and O'Connor has ten employees and a state unemployment merit rating that reduces his state unemployment taxes to 1.5 percent?

PROBLEMS

Problem 14–1

The column totals of a company's Payroll Register indicated its sales employees had earned $1,800 and its office employees had earned $600 during the first pay period in January of the current year, ended January 8. The employees were to have F.I.C.A. taxes withheld from their wages at the current rate plus $215 federal income taxes, $45 United States savings bond deductions, $30 union dues, and $65 group insurance deductions.

Required:

1. Use the current rate to calculate the total of the F.I.C.A. Taxes column in the foregoing register.
2. Prepare a general journal entry to record the payroll register information.
3. Assume the company uses a voucher system and a special payroll bank account, and prepare the entries in general journal form to record the payroll voucher and its payment.
4. Prepare a general journal entry to record the payroll taxes of the company under the assumption that it has 20 employees and a state unemployment tax merit rating that reduces its state unemployment tax rate to 1.5 percent of the first $3,000 paid each employee.

Problem 14–2

On January 8 the column totals of a company's Payroll Register indicated its sales employees earned $2,260, its office employees earned $600, and its delivery employee earned $140 during the first pay period in January, 1967. The register column totals also showed F.I.C.A. tax deductions at 4.4 percent, $290 federal income taxes withheld, $50 United States savings bond deductions, $105 hospital-medical insurance deductions, and $40 union dues.

Required:

1. Determine the F.I.C.A. Taxes column total in the company's Payroll Register and prepare the general journal entry to record the information of the register.
2. Assume the company uses a voucher system and a payroll bank account in paying its employees. Assume also that it prepared Voucher No. 872 and Check No. 891 for the amount of the foregoing payroll, deposited the check in the payroll bank account, and issued Payroll Checks Nos. 2155 through 2182 to the employees for their net pay. Under these assumptions give the required voucher register and check register entries.
3. Prepare the general journal entry to record the employer's payroll taxes on the foregoing payroll under the assumption it has a merit rating that reduces its state unemployment tax rate to 0.5 percent of the first $3,000 paid each employee.

Problem 14–3

The following information was taken from a company's payroll records for the weekly pay period ended December 18:

Employees' Names	Clock Card No.	Daily Time							Pay Rate	Federal Income Taxes	U.S. Savings Bonds	Union Dues	Earnings to End of Previous Week
		M	T	W	T	F	S	S					
Andrew Bunte....	11	8	8	8	8	8	4	0	3.00	10.30	...	2.00	6,560
Edwin Globe......	12	8	8	8	8	8	0	0	2.50	7.20	2.50	1.50	5,210
Roy Hoyt.........	13	8	8	8	8	8	0	0	2.50	10.80	2.50	1.50	2,936
Suzi Lewis........	14	8	8	9	9	8	0	0	2.00	10.70	2.50	...	2,825
Robert Oliver.....	15	8	8	8	8	8	0	0	3.25	11.35	5.00	...	6,640

Required:
1. Enter the relevant information in the proper columns of a Payroll Register similar to Illustration 86. Complete the register information using a 4.4 percent rate in calculating F.I.C.A. tax withholdings. Assume the company is subject to the Fair Labor Standards Act, and also assume the first employee drives the delivery truck, the second and third are salesmen, and the last two work in the office.
2. Prepare a general journal entry to record the payroll register information.
3. Assume the concern uses a special payroll bank account and a voucher system. Prepare entries in general journal form to record the payroll voucher and the check in its payment. Assume the first payroll check is numbered 862 and enter the payroll check numbers in the Payroll Register.
4. Prepare a general journal entry to record the employer's payroll taxes expense resulting from the payroll. Assume the concern has a merit rating that reduces its state unemployment tax rate to 1.8 percent of the first $3,000 paid each employee.

Problem 14–4
The Payroll Register of Deeplake Wholesale Company for the weekly pay period ended December 6 and other records carried the following information:

Employees' Names	Clock No.	Daily Time							Pay Rate	Income Tax Exemptions	U.S. Savings Bonds	Medical Insurance	Earnings to End of Previous Week
		M	T	W	T	F	S	S					
George Abbott....	11	8	8	8	8	8	0	0	2.50	5	2.50	4.50	2,830
James Cotton.....	12	8	8	8	8	8	0	0	2.50	3	2.50		5,110
William Holm.....	13	8	8	8	8	8	0	0	2.50	5	2.50	4.50	2,912
Helen Nash.......	14	8	8	8	8	8	4	0	2.00	2		3.00	2,240
Dale Wood........	15	8	8	8	8	8	0	0	2.65	4	2.50	4.50	6,542

Required:
1. Enter the relevant information in the proper columns of a Payroll Register similar to the one shown in Illustration 86. Complete the register using a 4.4 percent rate in calculating F.I.C.A. taxes and the wage bracket withholding table of Illustration 84 in calculating federal income tax to withhold from the wages of the employees. Assume that the first three employees are sales employees, Helen Nash works in the office, and Dale Wood drives the delivery truck. Assume also that the company is subject to the Fair Labor Standards Act.
2. Prepare a general journal entry to record the information of the Payroll Register.
3. Assume that the company uses a voucher system and a special payroll bank account. Prepare entries to record the payroll voucher and its payment (Voucher No. 1373 and Check No. 1369). Enter the payroll check numbers in the Payroll Register; assume that the first payroll check number is 383.

4. Prepare a general journal entry to record the payroll taxes expense resulting from this payroll. Assume that the company has a merit rating that reduces its state unemployment tax rate to 1.2 percent of the first $3,000 paid each employee.

Problem 14–5

Payson Company has ten employees to each of whom it pays $250 per month on the last day of each month. On December 1 the following accounts and balances appeared in the concern's ledger:

> *F.I.C.A. Taxes Payable (liability for November)*.....$220.00
> *Employees' Federal Income Taxes Payable (liability for November)*............................... 120.00
> *Federal Unemployment Taxes Payable (liability for first 11 months of the year)*.................. 110.00
> *State Unemployment Taxes Payable (liability for October and November)*........................ 60.00
> *Employees' Group Insurance Premiums Payable (liability for October and November)*............ 72.00

During December and January the company completed the following payroll transactions:

Dec. 14 Prepared Voucher No. 615 payable to the First National Bank. The voucher was for $340 and was in payment of the November F.I.C.A. and employee income taxes. Issued Check No. 608 in payment of the voucher and received a federal depository receipt in return.

    31 Prepared and posted a general journal entry to record the December Payroll Register. The column totals of the register were as follows:

> *Gross pay*.................................$2,500.00
> *Employees' F.I.C.A. taxes (assumed rate 4.4 percent)*............................... 110.00
> *Employees' federal income taxes*........... 120.00
> *Group insurance deductions*................ 36.00
> *Total deductions*.......................... 266.00
> *Net pay*................................... 2,234.00
> *Shop wages*............................... 2,000.00
> *Office salaries*............................ 500.00

    31 Prepared Voucher No. 638 payable to Payroll in payment of the December payroll. Issued Check No. 623 in payment of the voucher, deposited the check in the special payroll bank account, and issued payroll checks to the employees.

Dec. 31   Prepared and posted a general journal entry to record the employer's liabilities for payroll taxes. Due to a merit rating, the company's state unemployment tax rate was 1.2 percent of the first $3,000.

Jan.   3   Prepared Voucher No. 642 payable to the Employees' Mutual Insurance Company and issued Check No. 635 in its payment. The voucher and check were for $108 and were in payment of the October, November, and December employees' group insurance premiums.

   15   Prepared Voucher No. 662 payable to the State Tax Commission for the state unemployment taxes of October, November, and December. Issued Check No. 654 in its payment. Mailed the check along with last year's fourth-quarter tax return to the State Tax Commission.

   15   Prepared Voucher No. 663 payable to the First National Bank and issued Check No. 655 in payment of the voucher. The voucher was in payment of the December F.I.C.A. and employee income taxes. Received a federal depository receipt.

   28   Prepared Voucher No. 672 payable to the Director of Internal Revenue for last year's Federal Unemployment Taxes. Issued Check No. 667 in its payment. Mailed the check and the Annual Federal Unemployment Tax Return to the Director.

   28   Mailed the Director of Internal Revenue the Employer's Quarterly Federal Tax Return reporting the F.I.C.A. taxes and the employee federal income tax deductions for the last quarter of last year. Attached federal depository receipts to show that the tax liability had been paid.

Required:

1. Prepare a Check Register similar to the one shown in Illustration 74, and prepare a Voucher Register with the following columns:

Date	Voucher No.	Payee	When and How Paid		Vouchers Payable Credit		Sundry Accounts Debited		
			Date	Check			Account Name	F	Amount

2. Enter the payroll transactions in the Voucher Register, Check Register, and a General Journal.

CLASS EXERCISE

Exercise 14–1

The following information as to earnings and deductions for a pay period ended October 12 of the current year were taken from a company's records:

Employees' Names	Gross Pay	Earnings to End of Previous Period	Federal Income Taxes	Hospital Medical Insurance Deductions
Keith Adams.......	$140.00	$6,620	$12.75	$ 4.25
Albert Burke.......	135.00	6,530	13.65	4.25
George Kohler.....	140.00	2,890	16.90	4.25
Walter Nash.......	90.00	2,840	9.20	4.25
	$505.00		$52.50	$17.00

Required:

1. Use the current rate and calculate the employees' F.I.C.A. tax withholdings, total deductions, and net pay.
2. Prepare a general journal entry to record the payroll register information. Assume all employees work in the office.
3. Prepare a general journal entry to record the employer's payroll taxes resulting from this payroll. Assume a state unemployment tax rate of 2.0 percent on the first $3,000 paid each employee.

ALTERNATE PROBLEMS

Problem 14–2A

A company's accounting period ended on June 30, 1967, and on that date the company made the following year-end adjusting entry:

June	30	Sales Salaries Expense............................	800.00	
		Office Salaries Expense............................	160.00	
		Employer's Payroll Taxes Expense..................	60.48	
		F.I.C.A. Taxes Payable.........................		42.24
		State Unemployment Taxes Payable...........		14.40
		Federal Unemployment Taxes Payable.........		3.84
		Accrued Payroll Payable.......................		960.00
		To record the accrued payroll of the last two days in June.		

The adjusting entry was not reversed; and on July 3, when the June 29 through July 3 pay period ended, the company's payroll register column totals gave the following information:

Employees' F.I.C.A. taxes payable...............$ 105.60
Employees' federal income taxes payable......... 235.44
Employees' bond deductions.................... 65.00
Sales salaries..................................... 2,000.00
Office salaries..................................... 400.00

Required:

Under the assumption no employee had earned $3,000 by July 3, give the general journal entries to record the June 29 through July 3 payroll and the payroll taxes of the employer resulting from the payroll.

Problem 14–3A

A company's payroll records carried the following information for the weekly pay period ended November 3:

Employees' Names	Clock Card No.	Daily Time							Pay Rate	Federal Income Taxes	U.S. Savings Bonds	Union Dues	Earnings to End of Previous Week
		M	T	W	T	F	S	S					
Jane Allen	12	8	8	8	8	8	0	0	2.25	10.90	2.50		2,875
Ronald Baker	13	8	8	8	8	8	3	0	3.50	16.30	5.00		6,695
Jay Gordon	14	8	8	8	8	8	0	0	2.50	7.20	1.25	1.50	1,215
Alan Morgan	15	8	8	8	8	8	0	0	2.50	5.40	1.25	1.50	2,990
Glen Scott	16	8	8	8	8	8	0	0	2.50	12.60	5.00	1.50	3,950
Ray Tanner	17	8	8	8	8	8	2	0	3.00	13.80	2.50	2.00	6,490

Required:

1. Enter the relevant information in the proper columns of a Payroll Register like Illustration 86. Complete the register information using a 4.4 percent rate in calculating F.I.C.A. tax withholdings. Assume the company is subject to the Fair Labor Standards Act. Also assume the first two employees work in the office, the next three are salesmen, and the last drives the delivery truck.
2. Prepare a general journal entry to record the payroll register information.
3. Assume the concern uses a special payroll bank account and a voucher system. Prepare entries in general journal form to record the payroll voucher and the check in its payment. Assume the first payroll check is numbered 956 and enter the payroll check numbers in the Payroll Register.
4. Prepare a general journal entry to record the employer's payroll taxes expense resulting from the payroll. Assume the concern has a merit rating that reduces its state unemployment tax rate to 2.2 percent of the first $3,000 paid each employee.

Problem 14–4A

A company's Payroll Register for the weekly pay period ended December 7 and other records carried the following information:

Employees' Names	Clock No.	Daily Time							Pay Rate	Income Tax Exemptions	U.S. Savings Bonds	Medical Insurance	Earnings to End of Previous Week
		M	T	W	T	F	S	S					
James Baker	211	8	8	8	8	8	0	0	2.25	5	2.50	4.25	2,815
William Holmes...	212	8	8	8	8	8	0	0	2.25	3	2.50	4.25	1,834
Brian Peek	213	8	8	8	8	8	0	0	2.50	5	2.50	4.25	5,145
Donald Watts	214	8	8	8	8	9	5	0	2.00	2	2.50	3.25	2,970
Terry Yale	215	0	8	8	8	8	0	0	3.00	1	2.50	...	6,525

Required:

1. Enter the relevant information in the proper columns of a Payroll Register like Illustration 86. Complete the register using a 4.4 percent tax rate in calculating F.I.C.A. taxes and the wage bracket withholding table of Illustration 84 in determining income tax amounts to withhold from the employees' wages. Assume the first three employees are sales employees, the fourth works in the office, and the fifth drives the delivery truck. Also assume the company is subject to the Fair Labor Standards Act.

2. Prepare a general journal entry to record the payroll register information.

3. Assume the company uses a voucher system and a special payroll bank account and prepare entries to record the payroll voucher and its payment (Voucher No. 2668 and Check No. 2661). Enter the payroll check numbers in the Payroll Register; assume the first payroll check number is 974.

4. Prepare a general journal entry to record the payroll taxes of the company resulting from this payroll. Assume the company has a merit rating that reduces its state unemployment tax rate to 1.5 percent of the first $3,000 paid each employee.

Problem 14–5A

A company has six employees to each of whom it pays $250 per month on the last day of each month. On December 1 the following accounts and balances appeared in the company's ledger:

a) F.I.C.A. Taxes Payable, $132. (Since the company's F.I.C.A. and employees' income taxes exceed $100 each month, the taxes must be paid each month. Consequently, the balance of this account represents the liability for both the employer and employees' F.I.C.A. taxes for November only at an assumed 4.4 per cent rate.)

b) Employees' Federal Income Taxes Payable, $85 (liability for November only).

c) Federal Unemployment Taxes Payable, $66 (liability for first eleven months of the year).

d) State Unemployment Taxes Payable, $60 (liability for October and November).

e) Employees' Bond Deductions, $58.50.

During December, the company completed the following payroll transactions:

Dec. 15   Prepared Voucher No. 882 payable to the U.S. National Bank. The voucher was for $217 and was in payment of the November F.I.C.A. and employee income taxes. Issued Check No. 875 in payment of the voucher and received a federal depository receipt in return.

31   Prepared and posted a general journal entry to record the December Payroll Register. The register column totals were as follows:

Gross Pay	F.I.C.A. Taxes	Federal Income Taxes	U.S. Savings Bonds	Total Deduc- tions	Net Pay	Sales Sala- ries	Office Sala- ries
$1,500	$66.00	$85.00	$9.00	$160.00	$1,340	$1,250	$250

Dec. 31   Prepared Voucher No. 901 payable to Payroll in payment of the December payroll. Issued Check No. 895 in payment of the voucher, deposited the check in the special payroll bank account, and issued payroll checks to the employees.

     31   Prepared and posted a general journal entry to record the employer's liabilities for payroll taxes. Due to a merit rating, the company's state unemployment tax rate was 2.0 percent of the first $3,000.

     31   Prepared Voucher No. 902 payable to the U.S. National Bank and issued Check No. 896 in its payment. The voucher and check were for $37.50 and were for the purchase of two $18.75, United States savings bonds. Delivered the bonds to the employees.

Jan. 15   Prepared Voucher No. 927 payable to the State Tax Commission for the state unemployment taxes of October, November, and December. Issued Check No. 922 in its payment. Mailed the check along with last year's fourth-quarter tax return to the State Tax Commission.

     15   Prepared Voucher No. 928 payable to the U.S. National Bank and issued Check No. 923 in payment of the voucher. The voucher was in payment of the December F.I.C.A. and employee income taxes. Received a federal depository receipt.

     31   Prepared Voucher No. 939 payable to the Director of Internal Revenue for last year's Federal Unemployment Taxes. Issued Check No. 934 in its payment. Mailed the check and the Annual Federal Unemployment Tax Return to the Director.

     31   Mailed the Director of Internal Revenue the Employer's Quarterly Federal Tax Return reporting the F.I.C.A. taxes and the employee federal income tax deductions for the last quarter of last year. Attached federal depository receipts to show that the tax liability had been paid.

Required:

1. Prepare a Check Register similar to the one shown in Illustration 74, and prepare a Voucher Register with the following columns:

Date	Voucher No.	Payee	When and How Paid		Vouchers Payable Credit		Sundry Accounts Debited		
			Date	Check			Account Name	F	Amount

2. Enter the payroll transactions in the Voucher Register, Check Register, and a General Journal.

DECISION PROBLEM 14—FRIGID AIR, INC.

Frigid Air, Inc., manufactures and sells a seasonal product which is sold in interstate commerce.

The company has an average employment of 100 factory employees. As a consequence of the seasonal nature of the product, the average employee works 40 weeks out of each calendar year and for the remaining 12 weeks is laid off. During the layoff period the employee draws unemployment compensation from the state or seeks temporary employment. Twenty to thirty percent of the employees never return to Frigid Air, thus causing a costly retraining of replacements.

During the 40 weeks he is on the payroll the average employee works 40 hours per week at a regular rate of $3.50 per hour plus time and a half for six hours per week overtime.

Due to the high layoff rate the company now pays the maximum state unemployment rate of 2.7 percent of the first $3,000 in addition to federal unemployment taxes.

The plant superintendent held a series of discussions with employee representatives of the local union and found that the employees would be willing to accept a reduction in the hourly rate from $3.50 to $3.40, provided 12 months' employment be arranged, including two weeks of paid vacation. The superintendent feels that advantages other than a reduction in employee turnover would result from scheduling year-round production and recommends to the president of the company the acceptance of the employees' proposal.

The company's attorney finds that discontinuing the 12-week layoff policy would make the company eligible for a state merit rating and a resulting reduction of its unemployment tax rate. This reduced schedule would be as follows: after one year of no layoffs, 2 percent; after two years, 1 percent; after three years, 0.5 percent. The 0.5 percent is the state's lowest rate.

Discuss the merits and disadvantages of the proposed year-round work schedule.

15

Partnership
Accounting

ABOUT HALF the states have adopted the Uniform Partnership Act to govern the formation and operation of partnerships. This act defines a partnership as "an association of two or more persons to carry on as co-owners a business for profit." A partnership has been further defined as "an association of two or more competent persons under a contract to combine some or all their property, labor, and skill in the operation of a business." And although both of these definitions tell something of its legal nature, a better understanding of a partnership as a form of business organization may be gained by examining some of its characteristics.

CHARACTERISTICS OF A PARTNERSHIP

A Voluntary Association. A partnership is a voluntary association into which a person cannot be forced against his will. This is because a partner is responsible for the business acts of his partners, when within the scope of the partnership; and too, a partner is unlimitedly liable for the debts of his partnership. Consequently, partnership law recognizes it is only fair that a person be permitted to select the people he wishes to join in a partnership, and normally a person will select only financially responsible people in whose judgment he has respect.

Based on a Contract. One advantage of the partnership form of business organization is the ease with which it may be begun. All that is required is that two or more competent people agree to be partners. Their agreement becomes a contract and should be in writing, with all possible

423

points of future disagreement covered. However, it is just as binding if only orally expressed.

Limited Life. Since a partnership is based on a contract, its life is limited. If the contract is for a definite period, the partnership ends with the period's expiration. If the contract does not specify a time period, the partnership ends when the business for which it was created is completed. Or, if no time is stated and the business for which it was created cannot be completed but goes on indefinitely, the partnership may be terminated at will by any one of the partners. In addition, death, bankruptcy, or anything that takes away the ability of one of the partners to contract automatically ends a partnership.

Mutual Agency. Under normal circumstances there is mutual agency in a partnership. By this it is meant that under normal circumstances every partner is an agent of his partnership and can bind it to any contract within the apparent scope of its business. For example, a partner in a trading business can bind his partnership to contracts to buy merchandise, lease a store building, borrow money, or hire employees, since these are all within the scope of a trading firm. On the other hand, a partner in a law firm, acting alone, cannot bind his partners to a contract to buy merchandise or rent a store building. These are not within the normal scope of a law firm's business.

Partners among themselves may agree to limit the right of any one or more of the partners to negotiate certain contracts for the partnership. However, although such an agreement is binding on the partners and on outsiders who know of the agreement, it is not binding on outsiders who are unaware of its existence. Outsiders who are unaware of anything to the contrary have a right to assume that each partner has the normal agency rights of a partner.

Mutual agency offers an important reason for care in the selection of partners. Good partners benefit all; but a poor partner can do a lot of damage. Mutual agency plus unlimited liability are the reasons most partnerships have only a few members, with two, three, or four being common numbers of partners.

Unlimited Liability. When a partnership is unable to pay its debts, the creditors may satisfy their claims from the personal assets of the partners. Furthermore, if the personal property of a partner is insufficient to meet his share, the creditors may turn to the assets of the remaining partners who are able to pay. Thus, a partner may be called on to pay all the debts of his partnership, and is said to have unlimited liability for its debts.

Unlimited liability may be illustrated as follows: Albert and Bates each invested $1,000 in a store to be operated as a partnership venture, under an agreement to share losses and gains equally. Albert has no property other than his $1,000 investment; Bates owns his own home, a farm, and has sizable savings in addition to his investment. The partners rented store space and bought $10,000 of merchandise and fixtures, paying $2,000 in cash and promising to pay the balance at a later date. However, the night before the store opened the building in which it was located burned and the merchandise and fixtures were totally destroyed. There is no insurance, all the partnership assets are lost, and Albert has no other assets. Consequently, the partnership creditors may collect the full $8,000 of their claims from Bates, although Bates may look to Albert for payment of half at a later date, if he ever becomes able to pay.

ADVANTAGES AND DISADVANTAGES OF A PARTNERSHIP

Limited life, mutual agency, and unlimited liability are disadvantages of a partnership. Yet, a partnership has advantages over both the single proprietorship and corporation forms of organization. A partnership has the advantage of being able to bring together more money and skills than a single proprietorship, and is much easier to organize than a corporation. Also, it does not have the corporation's governmental supervision and its extra burden of taxation, and partners may act freely and without the necessity of stockholders' and directors' meetings, as in a corporation.

PARTNERSHIP ACCOUNTING

Partnership accounting is exactly like that of a single proprietorship, excepting for transactions affecting owner equity. Here, because ownership rights are divided between two or more partners, there must be:

1. A Capital account for each partner.
2. A Withdrawals account for each partner.
3. An accurate measurement and division of earnings among the partners.

As for the separate Capital and Withdrawals accounts, each partner's Capital account is credited, and asset accounts showing the nature of the assets invested are debited in recording the investment of each partner. Likewise, a partner's withdrawals are debited to his Withdrawals account, and in the end-of-the-period closing procedure the Withdrawals account is credited for a partner's share of the net income. Obviously, these procedures are not new, only the added accounts are new, and they need no further consideration here. However, the matter of dividing earnings among partners does need additional discussion.

NATURE OF PARTNERSHIP EARNINGS

Because, as a member of his partnership, a partner cannot enter into an employer-employee contractural relationship with himself, a partner, like a single proprietor, cannot legally hire himself and pay himself a salary. Law and custom recognize this. Furthermore, law and custom recognize that a partner works for partnership profits and not a salary, and law and custom recognize that a partner invests his money in a partnership for earnings and not for interest.

Nevertheless, although partners have no legal right to interest on their partnership investments or salaries in payment for their partnership services, it should be recognized that partnership earnings do include a return for services, even though the return is contained within the earnings and is not a salary in a legal sense. Likewise, partnership earnings include a return on invested capital, although the return is not interest in the legal sense of the term.

Furthermore, if partnership earnings are to be fairly shared, it is often necessary to recognize that the earnings do include a return for services and a return on investments. For example, if one partner contributes five times as much capital as another, it is only fair that this be taken into consideration in the method of sharing. Likewise, if the services of one partner are much more valuable than those of another, it is only fair that some provision be made for the unequal service contributions.

DIVISION OF EARNINGS

The law provides that in the absense of a contrary agreement, all partnership earnings are shared equally. This means that if partners do not agree in advance as to the method of sharing, each partner receives an equal share. Partners may agree in advance to any method of sharing; and if they agree as to the method of sharing earnings but say nothing of losses, losses are shared in the same manner as earnings.

Several methods of sharing partnership earnings are employed. All attempt in one way or another to recognize differences in service contributions or in investments, when such differences exist. The following three methods will be discussed here:

1. On a stated fractional basis.
2. Based on the ratio of capital investments.
3. Salary and interest allowances and the remainder in a fixed ratio.

EARNINGS ALLOCATED ON A STATED FRACTIONAL BASIS

The easiest way to divide partnership earnings is to give each partner a stated fraction of the total. A division on a fractional basis may provide for an equal sharing if service and capital contributions are equal. An equal sharing may also be provided when the greater capital contribution of one partner is equalized by a greater service contribution of another. Or, if the service contributions and capital contributions are unequal, a fixed ratio may easily provide for an unequal sharing. All that is necessary in any case is for the partners to agree as to the fractional share to be given each.

For example, the partnership agreement of Morse and North may provide that each partner is to receive half the earnings; or the agreement may provide for two thirds to Morse and one third to North; or it may provide for three fourths to Morse and one fourth to North. Any fractional basis may be agreed upon as long as the partners feel earnings are thereby fairly shared. For example, assume the agreement of Morse and North provides for a two-thirds and one-third sharing, and earnings for a year are $9,000. After all revenue and expense accounts are closed, if earnings are $9,000, the partnership Income Summary account has a $9,000 credit balance. It is closed and the earnings are allocated to the partners with the following entry:

Dec.	31	Income Summary..................	9,000.00	
		A. P. Morse, Withdrawals........		6,000.00
		R. G. North, Withdrawals.......		3,000.00
		To close the Income Summary account and allocate the earnings.		

DIVISION OF EARNINGS BASED ON
THE RATIO OF CAPITAL INVESTMENTS

If the business of a partnership is of a nature that earnings are closely related to money invested, as in the investment banking business, a division of earnings based on the ratio of partners' investments offers a fair sharing method.

To see how earnings are shared in the investment ratio, assume that Chase, Davis, and Fall have agreed to share earnings in the ratio of their beginning of the year investments. If these are Chase $50,000, Davis $30,000, and Fall $40,000, and if the earnings for the year are $24,000, the respective shares of the partners are calculated as follows:

Step 1:
Chase, capital............................$ 50,000
Davis, capital............................ 30,000
Fall, capital............................ 40,000
Total invested........................$120,000

Step 2: Share of earnings to Chase $\dfrac{\$50,000}{\$120,000} \times \$24,000 = \$10,000$

Share of earnings to Davis $\dfrac{\$30,000}{\$120,000} \times \$24,000 = \$6,000$

Share of earnings to Fall $\dfrac{\$40,000}{\$120,000} \times \$24,000 = \$8,000$

The entry to allocate the earnings to the partners is then:

Dec.	31	Income Summary....................	24,000.00	
		T. S. Chase, Withdrawals........		10,000.00
		S. A. Davis, Withdrawals........		6,000.00
		R. R. Fall, Withdrawals.........		8,000.00
		To close the Income Summary account and allocate the earnings.		

SALARIES AND INTEREST AS AIDS IN SHARING

Sometimes partners' capital contributions are very unequal; and sometimes one partner devotes full time to partnership affairs and the other or others devote only part time. Too, in partnerships in which all partners devote full time, the services of one partner may be more valuable than the services of another. When these situations occur and, for example, the capital contributions are unequal, the partners may allocate a portion of the profits to themselves in the form of interest, so as to compensate for the unequal investments. Or when service contributions are unequal, they may use salary allowances as a means of compensating for unequal service contributions. Or when investment and service contributions are both unequal, they may use a combination of interest and salary allowances in an effort to fairly share earnings.

For example, Hill and Dale are partners in a business in which Hill has had much experience and could command a $9,000 annual salary working for another firm of like nature. Dale is new to the business and could expect to earn not more than $6,000 working elsewhere. Furthermore, Hill has invested $15,000 in the business and Dale has invested $5,000. Consequently, the partners have agreed that in order to compensate for the unequal service and capital contributions, they will share losses and gains as follows:

1. A share of the profits equal to interest at 8 percent is to be allowed on the partners' initial investments.
2. Annual salary allowances of $9,000 per year to Hill and $6,000 per year to Dale are to be allowed.
3. The remaining balance of income or loss is to be shared equally.

Under this agreement a year's $17,700 net income would be shared as in Illustration 91.

After the shares in the $17,700 net income are determined, the entry following Illustration 91 may be used to close the Income Summary account and carry the net income shares to the partners' Withdrawals accounts.

Illustration 91

	Share to Hill	Share to Dale	Income Allocated
Total net income.........................			$17,700
Allocated as interest:			
Hill (8 percent on $15,000)..............$ 1,200			
Dale (8 percent on $5,000)..............		$ 400	
Total allocated as interest...........			1,600
Balance of income after interest allowances.			$16,100
Allocated as salary allowances:			
Hill..	9,000		
Dale..		6,000	
Total allocated as salary allowances...			15,000
Balance of income after interest and salary allowances...............................			$ 1,100
Balance allocated equally:			
Hill..	550		
Dale..		550	
Total allocated equally..............			1,100
Balance of income.................			—0—
Shares of the Partners....................$10,750		$6,950	

Dec.	31	Income Summary.....................	17,700.00		
		Robert Hill, Withdrawals.........			10,750.00
		William Dale, Withdrawals.......			6,950.00
		To close the Income Summary account and allocate the earnings.			

Observe in the foregoing entry that the credit amounts may be taken from the first two money columns of the computation of Illustration 91.

In a legal sense, a partner does not work for a salary, nor does he invest in a partnership to earn interest; he invests and works for earnings. Consequently, when a partnership agreement provides for salaries and interest, the partners should understand that the salaries and interest are not really salaries and interest, but are only a means of sharing losses and gains.

In the illustration just completed the $17,700 net income exceeded the salary and interest allowances of the partners; but Hill and Dale would use the same method to share a net income smaller than their salary and interest allowances, or to share a loss. For example, assume that Hill and

Dale earned only $6,600 in a year. A $6,600 net income would be shared by the partners as in Illustration 92.

Illustration 92

	Share to Hill	Share to Dale	Income Allocated
Total net income.....................			$ 6,600
Allocated as interest:			
Hill (8 percent on $15,000).............$1,200	$1,200		
Dale (8 percent on $5,000)...............		$ 400	
Total allocated as interest............			1,600
Balance of income after interest allowances..			$ 5,000
Allocated as salary allowances:			
Hill.................................... 9,000	9,000		
Dale....................................		6,000	
Total allocated as salary allowances...			15,000
Balance of income after interest and salary allowances (a negative amount)........			($10,000)
Balance allocated equally:			
Hill.................................... (5,000)	(5,000)		
Dale....................................		(5,000)	
Total allocated equally...............			(10,000)
Balance of income.................			–0–
Shares of the Partners.....................$5,200	$5,200	$1,400	

The encircled items of Illustration 92 are negative items. It will be recalled that it is common practice in accounting to show negative items in red or to show them in black and encircled.

A net loss would be shared by Hill and Dale in the same manner as the foregoing $6,600 net income; the only difference being that the loss-and-gain-sharing procedure would begin with a negative amount of income, in other words a net loss, and the amount allocated equally would be a larger negative amount.

PARTNERSHIP FINANCIAL STATEMENTS

In most respects partnership financial statements are like those of a single proprietorship. However, one common difference is that the net income allocation is often shown on the income statement, at the end of the statement following the reported net income. For example, an income statement prepared for Hill and Dale might show in its last portion the allocation of the $6,600 net income of Illustration 92 as in Illustration 93.

Illustration 93

HILL AND DALE

Income Statement for Year Ended December 31, 19--

Sales.	$123,400

~~~~~~

Net Income		$ 6,600
Allocation of net income to the partners:		
Robert Hill:		
Interest at 8 percent on investment	$ 1,200	
Salary allowance	9,000	
Total.	$10,200	
Less one half the remaining deficit.	(5,000)	
Share of the net income.		$ 5,200
William Dale:		
Interest at 8 percent on investment.	$ 400	
Salary allowance	6,000	
Total.	$ 6,400	
Less one half the remaining deficit.	(5,000)	
Share of the net income.		1,400
Net Income Allocated		$ 6,600

ENDING A PARTNERSHIP

Often a partnership is terminated by the retirement of a partner. When a partner retires, he may sell his partnership interest to an outsider or to one or more of his partners, or he may withdraw his equity in the form of cash or other assets.

Sale of a Partnership Interest. Assume that Abbott, Burns, and Camp are equal partners in a $15,000 partnership that has no liabilities and the following assets and equities:

ASSETS	=	OWNER EQUITY	
Cash. . . . . $ 3,000		Abbot, capital.	$ 5,000
Merchandise 8,000		Burns, capital.	5,000
Store equipment 4,000		Camp, capital	5,000
Total $15,000		Total	$15,000

Camp's equity in this partnership is $5,000. If Camp sells his equity to Davis for $7,000, he is selling his $5,000 interest in the partnership assets. The entry on the partnership books to transfer the equity is:

Feb.	4	*Camp, Capital. . . . .*	*5,000.00*	
		Davis, Capital.		*5,000.00*
		To transfer Camp's equity in the		
		partnership assets to Davis.		

After this entry is posted, the accounting equation that shows the assets and equities of the new partnership is:

ASSETS		=	OWNER EQUITY	
Cash.	$ 3,000		Abbot, capital	$ 5,000
Merchandise	8,000		Burns, capital	5,000
Store equipment	4,000		Davis, capital	5,000
Total	$15,000		Total.	$15,000

Two points should be noted in regard to this transaction. First, the $7,000 Davis paid Camp is not recorded in the partnership books. Camp sold and transferred his $5,000 equity in the partnership assets to Davis. The entry that records the transfer is a debit to Camp, Capital and a credit to Davis, Capital for $5,000. Furthermore, the entry is the same whether Davis pays Camp $7,000 or $70,000. The amount is paid directly to Camp. It is a side transaction between Camp and Davis and does not affect partnership assets.

The second point to be noted is that Abbott and Burns must agree to the sale and transfer if Davis is to become a partner. Abbott and Burns cannot prevent Camp from selling his interest to Davis. On the other hand, Camp cannot force Abbott and Burns to accept Davis as a partner. If Abbott and Burns agree to accept Davis, a new partnership is formed and a new contract with a new loss-and-gain-sharing ratio must be drawn. If Camp sells to Davis, and either Abbott or Burns refuses to accept Davis as a partner, the old partnership must be liquidated. In such a situation, Davis acquires only the liquidation rights of Camp. (Liquidations are discussed in more detail later in this chapter.)

Withdrawal of a Partner. The best practice in regard to withdrawals is for partners to provide in advance, in their partnership contract, the procedure to be followed when a partner withdraws from the partnership. When such a procedure is agreed on in advance, it commonly provides for an audit of the accounting records and a revaluation of the partnership assets. The revaluation just prior to a retirement is very desirable because it places all assets on the books at current values and causes the retiring partner's Capital account to reflect the current value of his equity. Often, if a partnership agreement provides for an audit and asset revaluation when a partner retires, it also provides that the retiring partner is to withdraw assets equal to the book amount of his revalued equity.

For example, assume that Blue is retiring from the partnership of Smith, Blue, and Short. The partners have always shared losses and gains in the ratio of Smith, one half; Blue, one fourth; and Short, one fourth. Their partnership agreement provides for an audit and asset revaluation upon the retirement of a partner. Their balance sheet just prior to the audit and revaluation is shown in Illustration 94.

The audit and appraisal indicates the merchandise inventory is overval-

Illustration 94

SMITH, BLUE, AND SHORT
Balance Sheet, October 31, 19--

ASSETS			OWNER EQUITY	
Cash		$11,000	Smith, capital	$22,000
Merchandise inventory.		16,000	Blue, capital.	10,000
Fixed assets	$20,000		Short, capital	10,000
Less: Accum. depr. .	5,000	15,000		
Total Assets . . .		$42,000	Total Owner Equity . . .	$42,000

ued by $4,000, and that due to market changes the partnership building should be valued at $25,000 with accumulated depreciation of $8,000. The entries to record these revaluations are:

Oct.	31	Smith, Capital..................................	2,000.00	
		Blue, Capital...................................	1,000.00	
		Short, Capital..................................	1,000.00	
		Merchandise Inventory.....................		4,000.00
		To revalue the inventory.		
	31	Building..	5,000.00	
		Accumulated Depreciation, Building........		3,000.00
		Smith, Capital.............................		1,000.00
		Blue, Capital..............................		500.00
		Short, Capital.............................		500.00
		To revalue the building.		

Losses and gains from asset revaluations are always shared by the partners in their loss-and-gain-sharing ratio. The fairness of this is easy to see when it is remembered that if the partnership did not terminate, such losses and gains would sooner or later be reflected on the income statement.

In the case of Smith, Blue, and Short, after the entries revaluing the partnership assets are recorded, a balance sheet showing the new asset values and the new equities appears as in Illustration 95.

Illustration 95

SMITH, BLUE, AND SHORT
Balance Sheet, October 31, 19--

ASSETS			OWNER EQUITY	
Cash		$11,000	Smith, capital	$21,000
Merchandise inventory.		12,000	Blue, capital.	9,500
Fixed assets	$25,000		Short, capital	9,500
Less: Accum. depr. .	8,000	17,000		
Total Assets . . .		$40,000	Total Owner Equity . . .	$40,000

After the revaluation, if Blue withdraws from the partnership and takes assets equal to his equity, the entry to record his withdrawal is:

Oct.	31	Blue, Capital..	9,500.00	
		Cash...		9,500.00
		To record the withdrawal of Blue.		

In withdrawing, Blue does not have to take cash in settlement of his equity. He may take any combination of assets to which the partners agree, or he may take the new partnership's promissory note.

Needless to say, the withdrawal of Blue creates a new partnership; and consequently, a new agreement and a new loss-and-gain-sharing ratio is required. If the new partners, Smith and Short, do not agree to a new ratio, the law provides that they will share equally.

Partner Withdraws Taking Assets of Less Value than His Book Equity. Sometimes when a partner retires, the remaining partners may not wish to have the assets revalued and the new values recorded. In such cases the partners may agree, for example, that the assets are overvalued; and due to the overvalued assets, the retiring partner should, in settlement of his equity, take assets of less value than the book value of his equity. Sometimes, too, when assets are not overvalued, the retiring partner may be so anxious to retire that he is willing to take less than the current value of his equity just to get out of the partnership or out of the business.

When a partner retires taking assets of less value than his equity, he is in effect leaving a portion of his book equity in the business. In such cases, the remaining partners divide the unwithdrawn equity portion in their loss-and-gain-sharing ratio. For example, assume that Black, Brown, and Green are partners sharing gains and losses in a 2:2:1 ratio. Their assets and equities are:

ASSETS		OWNER EQUITY	
Cash.................	$ 5,000	Black, capital	$ 6,000
Merchandise	9,000	Brown, capital	6,000
Store equipment	4,000	Green, capital	6,000
Total Assets.........	$18,000	Total Owner Equity. ...	$18,000

Brown is so anxious to withdraw from the partnership that he is willing to retire if permitted to take $4,500 in cash in settlement for his equity. Black and Green agree to the $4,500 withdrawal, and Brown retires. The entry to record the retirement is:

Mar.	4	Brown, Capital......................	6,000.00	
		Cash.............................		4,500.00
		Black, Capital..................		1,000.00
		Green, Capital..................		500.00
		To record the withdrawal of Brown.		

In retiring, Brown did not withdraw $1,500 of his equity. This is divided between Black and Green in their loss-and-gain-sharing ratio. The loss-and-gain-sharing ratio of the original partnership was Black, 2; Brown, 2; and Green, 1. Therefore in the original partnership, Black and Green shared in a 2 to 1 ratio; and the unwithdrawn book equity of Brown is shared by Black and Green in this ratio.

Partner Withdraws Taking Assets of Greater Value than His Book Equity. There are two common reasons for a partner receiving upon retirement assets of greater value than his book equity. First, certain of the partnership assets may be undervalued; and second, the partners continuing the business may be so anxious for the retiring partner to withdraw that they are willing for him to take assets of greater value than his book equity.

When assets are undervalued or unrecorded and the partners do not wish to change the recorded values, the partners may agree to permit a retiring member to withdraw assets of greater value than his book equity. In such cases the retiring partner is, in effect, withdrawing his own book equity and a portion of his partners' equities. For example, assume that Jones, Thomas, and Finch are partners sharing gains and losses in a 3:2:1 ratio. Their assets and equities are:

ASSETS		OWNER EQUITY	
Cash.	$ 5,000	Jones, capital	$ 9,000
Merchandise	10,000	Thomas, capital.	6,000
Fixed assets.	3,000	Finch, capital	3,000
Total Assets.	$18,000	Total Owner Equity	$18,000

Finch wishes to withdraw from the partnership; Jones and Thomas plan to continue the business. The partners agree that certain of their assets are undervalued, but they do not wish to increase the recorded values. They further agree that if current values were recorded, the asset total would be increased $6,000 and the equity of Finch would be increased $1,000. Therefore, the partners agree that $4,000 is the proper value for Finch's equity, and that he may withdraw this amount in cash. The entry to record the withdrawal is:

May	7	*Finch, Capital*.....................	*3,000.00*	
		Jones, Capital.....................	*600.00*	
		Thomas, Capital..................	*400.00*	
		Cash........................		*4,000.00*
		To record the withdrawal of Finch.		

DEATH OF A PARTNER

A partner's death automatically dissolves and ends a partnership, and his estate is entitled to receive the value of his equity. The partnership contract should contain provisions for settlement in case a partner dies, and one provision should provide a method for determining the current value of the deceased partner's equity. This requires at least: (*a*) an immediate closing of the books to determine earnings since the end of the previous accounting period, and (*b*) a method for determining and recording current values for the assets. Upon a partner's death and after the current value of the deceased partner's equity is determined, the remaining partners and the deceased partner's estate must agree to a disposition of the equity. They may agree to its sale to the remaining partners or to an outsider, or they may agree to the withdrawal of assets in settlement. Entries for both of these procedures have already been discussed.

LIQUIDATIONS

When a partnership is liquidated, its business is ended, the assets are converted into cash, the creditors are paid, the remaining cash is distributed to the partners, and the partnership is dissolved. Although many combinations of circumstances occur in liquidations, only three are discussed here.

All Assets Realized before a Distribution, Assets Are Sold at a Profit. A partnership liquidation under this assumption may be illustrated with the following example. Ottis, Skinner, and Parr have operated a partnership for a number of years, sharing losses and gains in a 3:2:1 ratio. Due to several unsatisfactory conditions, the partners decide to liquidate as of December 31. On that date the books are closed, the income from operations is transferred to the partners' Capital accounts, and the condensed balance sheet shown in Illustration 96 is prepared.

In any liquidation the business always ends and the assets are sold. Normally, either a gain or a loss results from the sale of each group of assets. These losses and gains are called "losses and gains from realization"

Illustration 96

OTTIS, SKINNER, AND PARR
Balance Sheet, December 31, 19--

ASSETS		LIABILITIES	
Cash	$10,000	Accounts payable	$ 5,000
Merchandise inventory.	15,000		
Other assets	25,000	OWNER EQUITY	
		Ottis, capital	15,000
		Skinner, capital	15,000
		Parr, capital.	15,000
Total Assets	$50,000	Total Equities	$50,000

and are shared by the partners in their loss-and-gain-sharing ratio. If Ottis, Skinner, and Parr sell their merchandise inventory for $12,000 and their other assets for $34,000, the sales and the gain allocation are recorded as follows:

Jan.	12	Cash.	12,000.00	
		Loss or Gain from Realization	3,000.00	
		Merchandise Inventory		15,000.00
		Sold the inventory at a loss.		
	15	Cash.	34,000.00	
		Other Assets.		25,000.00
		Loss or Gain from Realization		9,000.00
		Sold the other assets at a profit.		
	15	Loss or Gain from Realization	6,000.00	
		Ottis, Capital.		3,000.00
		Skinner, Capital		2,000.00
		Parr, Capital.		1,000.00
		To allocate the net gain from reali-zation to the partners in their 3:2:1 loss-and-gain-sharing ratio.		

Careful notice should be taken of the last journal entry just shown. In a partnership termination, when assets are sold at a loss or gain, the loss or gain is allocated to the partners in their loss-and-gain-sharing ratio. Often students, in solving liquidation problems, attempt to allocate the assets to the partners in their loss-and-gain-sharing ratio. Obviously this is not correct; it is not assets but losses and gains that are shared in the loss-and-gain-sharing ratio.

After partnership assets are sold and the gain or loss allocated, the partnership cash exactly equals the combined equities of the partners and creditors. This point is illustrated for Ottis, Skinner, and Parr in the balance sheet of Illustration 97.

Illustration 97

OTTIS, SKINNER, AND PARR
Balance Sheet, January 15, 19--

ASSETS		LIABILITIES	
Cash	$56,000	Accounts payable	$ 5,000
		OWNER EQUITY	
		Ottis, capital	18,000
		Skinner, capital	17,000
		Parr, capital	16,000
Total Assets	$56,000	Total Equities	$56,000

After partnership assets are realized and the gain or loss shared, entries are made to distribute the realized cash to the proper parties. Since creditors have first claim, they are paid first. After the creditors are paid, the remaining cash is divided among the partners. Each partner has the right to cash equal to his equity or, in other words, cash equal to the balance of his Capital account. The entries to distribute the cash of Ottis, Skinner, and Parr are:

Jan.	15	Accounts Payable....................	5,000.00	
		Cash...........................		5,000.00
		To pay the claims of the creditors.		
	15	Ottis, Capital.......................	18,000.00	
		Skinner, Capital....................	17,000.00	
		Parr, Capital.......................	16,000.00	
		Cash...........................		51,000.00
		To distribute the remaining cash to the partners according to their Capital account balances.		

Notice that after losses and gains are shared and the creditors are paid, each partner receives liquidation cash equal to the balance remaining in his Capital account. This is because a partner's Capital account balance shows his equity in the partnership assets.

All Assets Realized before a Distribution, Assets Sold at a Loss, Each Partner's Capital Account Is Sufficient to Absorb His Share of the Loss. In a partnership liquidation, the assets are sometimes sold at a net loss. For example, if contrary to the assumptions of the previous illustration, the merchandise inventory of Ottis, Skinner, and Parr is sold for $9,000 and the other assets for $13,000, the entries to record the sales and loss allocation are:

Jan.	12	Cash...............................	9,000.00	
		Loss or Gain from Realization........	6,000.00	
		Merchandise Inventory...........		15,000.00
		Sold the inventory at a loss.		
	15	Cash...............................	13,000.00	
		Loss or Gain from Realization........	12,000.00	
		Other Assets.....................		25,000.00
		Sold the other assets at a loss.		
	15	Ottis, Capital.......................	9,000.00	
		Skinner, Capital....................	6,000.00	
		Parr, Capital.......................	3,000.00	
		Loss or Gain from Realization....		18,000.00
		To allocate the loss from realiza-tion to the partners in their loss-and-gain-sharing ratio.		

After the entries for the sales and the loss allocation are recorded, a partnership balance sheet appears as in Illustration 98. The balance sheet

Illustration 98
OTTIS, SKINNER, AND PARR
Balance Sheet, January 15, 19--

ASSETS		LIABILITIES	
Cash	$32,000	Accounts payable	$ 5,000
		OWNER EQUITY	
		Ottis, capital	6,000
		Skinner, capital	9,000
		Parr, capital.	12,000
Total Assets	$32,000	Total Equities	$32,000

shows the equities of the creditors and partners in the partnership cash. The following entries are required to distribute the cash to the proper parties:

Jan.	15	Accounts Payable....................	5,000.00	
		Cash............................		5,000.00
		To pay the partnership creditors.		

Jan.	15	Ottis, Capital.......................	6,000.00	
		Skinner, Capital.....................	9,000.00	
		Parr, Capital........................	12,000.00	
		Cash............................		27,000.00
		To distribute the remaining cash to the partners according to the balances of their Capital accounts.		

Notice again that after realization losses are shared and creditors are paid, each partner receives cash equal to his Capital account balance.

All Assets Realized before a Distribution, Assets Sold at a Loss, a Partner's Capital Account Is Not Sufficient to Cover His Share of the Loss. Sometimes a partner's share of realization losses is greater than the balance of his Capital account. In such cases the partner whose share of losses is greater than his capital balance must, if he can, cover the deficit by paying cash into the partnership. For example, assume contrary to the previous two illustrations that Ottis, Skinner, and Parr sell their merchandise for $3,000 and the other assets for $4,000. The entries to record the sales and the loss allocation are:

Jan.	12	Cash................................	3,000.00	
		Loss or Gain from Realization........	12,000.00	
		Merchandise Inventory...........		15,000.00
		Sold the inventory at a loss.		
	15	Cash................................	4,000.00	
		Loss or Gain from Realization........	21,000.00	
		Other Assets....................		25,000.00
		Sold the other assets at a loss.		
	15	Ottis, Capital.......................	16,500.00	
		Skinner, Capital.....................	11,000.00	
		Parr, Capital.......................	5,500.00	
		Loss or Gain from Realization....		33,000.00
		To record the allocation of the loss from realization to the partners in their loss-and-gain-sharing ratio.		

After the entry allocating the realization loss is posted, the Capital account of Ottis has a $1,500 debit balance and appears as follows:

Ottis, Capital

Date		Explanation	F	Debit	Credit	Balance
Dec.	31	Balance				15,000.00
Jan.	15	Share of loss from realization		16,500.00		(1,500.00)

Since the partnership agreement provides that Ottis is to take one half the losses or gains, and since his Capital account balance is not large enough to absorb his loss share in this case, he must, if he can, pay $1,500 into the partnership to cover his full share of the losses. If he is able to pay, the following entry is made:

Jan.	15	Cash......................................		1,500.00	
		Ottis, Capital....................			1,500.00
		To record the additional invest-			
		ment of Ottis to cover his share			
		of realization losses.			

After the $1,500 is received from Ottis, the partnership has cash amounting to $18,500; and the following entries are made to distribute the cash to the proper parties:

Jan.	15	Accounts Payable....................		5,000.00	
		Cash.......................			5,000.00
		To pay the partnership creditors.			
	15	Skinner, Capital....................		4,000.00	
		Parr, Capital.......................		9,500.00	
		Cash.......................			13,500.00
		To distribute the remaining cash			
		to the partners according to the			
		balances of their Capital ac-			
		counts.			

Often when a partner's share of partnership losses exceeds his Capital account balance, he is unable to make up the deficit. In such cases, since each member of a partnership has unlimited liability, the deficit must be borne by the remaining partner or partners. For example, assume that, contrary to the previous illustration, Ottis is unable to pay in the $1,500 necessary to cover the deficit in his Capital account. If Ottis is unable to pay, the deficit that he is unable to make good must be shared by Skinner and Parr in their loss-and-gain-sharing ratio. In the original loss-and-gain-sharing agreement, the partners shared losses and gains in the ratio of Ottis, 3; Skinner, 2; and Parr, 1. Therefore, Skinner and Parr shared in a 2 to 1 ratio; and the $1,500 that Ottis's share of the losses exceeded his Capital account balance is apportioned between them in this ratio. Normally the defaulting partner's deficit is transferred to the Capital accounts of the remaining partners. This is accomplished for Ottis, Skinner, and Parr with the following entry:

Jan.	15	Skinner, Capital.....................		1,000.00	
		Parr, Capital.......................		500.00	
		Ottis, Capital...................			1,500.00
		To transfer the deficit of Ottis to the Capital accounts of Skinner and Parr.			

After the deficit is transferred, the Capital accounts of the partners appear as in Illustration 99.

Illustration 99

Ottis, Capital

Date		Explanation	F	Debit	Credit	Balance
Dec.	31	Balance				15,000.00
Jan.	15	Share of loss from realization		16,500.00		(1,500.00)
	15	Deficit to Skinner and Parr			1,500.00	–0–

Skinner, Capital

Date		Explanation	F	Debit	Credit	Balance
Dec.	31	Balance				15,000.00
Jan.	15	Share of loss from realization		11,000.00		4,000.00
	15	Share of Ottis's deficit		1,000.00		3,000.00

Parr, Capital

Date		Explanation	F	Debit	Credit	Balance
Dec.	31	Balance				15,000.00
Jan.	15	Share of loss from realization		5,500.00		9,500.00
	15	Share of Ottis's deficit		500.00		9,000.00

After the deficit is transferred, the $17,000 of liquidation cash is distributed with the following entries:

Jan.	15	Accounts Payable....................	5,000.00	
		Cash...........................		5,000.00
		To pay the partnership creditors.		
	15	Skinner, Capital.....................	3,000.00	
		Parr, Capital......................	9,000.00	
		Cash...........................		12,000.00
		To distribute the remaining cash		
		to the partners according to their		
		Capital account balances.		

It should be understood that the inability of Ottis to meet his loss share at this time does not relieve him of liability. If at any time in the future he becomes able to pay, Skinner and Parr may collect from him the full $1,500. Skinner may collect $1,000 and Parr, $500.

QUESTIONS FOR CLASS DISCUSSION

1. Hill and Dale are partners. Hill dies and his son claims the right to take his father's place in the partnership. Does he have this right? Why?
2. Albert Gully cannot legally enter into a contract. Can he become a partner?
3. If a partnership contract does not state the period of time the partnership is to exist, when does the partnership end?
4. What is the meaning of the term "mutual agency" as applied to a partnership?
5. Jack and Jill are partners in the operation of a store. Jack without consulting Jill enters into a contract for the purchase of merchandise for resale by the store. Jill contends that he did not authorize the order and refuses to take delivery. The vendor sues the partners for the contract price of the merchandise. Will the firm have to pay? Why?
6. Would your answer to Question 5 differ if Jack and Jill were partners in a public accounting firm?
7. May partners limit the right of a member of their firm to bind their partnership to contracts? Is such an agreement binding (*a*) on the partners, and (*b*) on outsiders?
8. What is the meaning of the term "unlimited liability" when it is applied to members of a partnership?
9. Kennedy, Porter, and Foulke have been partners for three years. The partnership is dissolving, Kennedy is leaving the firm, and Porter and Foulke plan to carry on the business. In the final settlement Kennedy places an $18,000 salary claim against the partnership. His contention is that since

he devoted all of his time for three years to the affairs of the partnership, he has a claim for a salary of $6,000 for each year. Is his claim valid? Why?

10. The partnership agreement of Martin and Tritt provides for a two-thirds, one-third sharing of income but says nothing of losses. The operations for a year result in a loss. Martin claims the loss should be shared equally since the partnership agreement said nothing of sharing losses. Do you agree?

11. Blue wishes to sell Red his interest in the partnership of Blue and Green. Green refuses to have Red as a partner. Can Blue force Green to accept Red as a partner? Can Green prevent Blue from selling his interest to Red? What happens if Blue sells to Red and Green will not accept Red as a partner?

12. A, B, and C are partners with Capital account balances of $6,000 each. D gives A $7,500 for his one-third interest in the partnership. The book-keeper debits A, Capital and credits D, Capital for $6,000. D objects. He wants his Capital account to show a $7,500 balance, the amount he paid for his interest. Explain why D's Capital account is credited for $6,000.

13. After all partnership assets are converted to cash and all creditor claims paid, the remaining cash should equal the sum of the balances of the part-ners' Capital accounts. Why?

14. J, K, and L are partners. In a liquidation J's share of partnership losses exceeds his Capital account balance. He is unable to meet the deficit from his personal assets, and the excess losses are shared by his partners. Does this relieve J of liability?

PROBLEMS

Problem 15–1

Robert Orr, Thomas Parks, and James Quinn invested $15,000, $12,000, and $9,000, respectively, in a partnership. During its first year the firm earned $31,200.

Required:

1. Prepare entries to close the firm's Income Summary account and to al-locate the net income to the partners under each of the following as-sumptions:
   a) The partners failed to agree as to the method of sharing earnings.
   b) The partners had agreed to share earnings in the ratio of their be-ginning investments.
   c) The partners had agreed to share income by allowing annual salary allowances of $8,000 to Orr, $10,000 to Parks, and $6,000 to Quinn; allowing a share of the income equal to 10 percent interest on part-ners' investments; and sharing the remaining income or loss equally.
2. Prepare the section of the partners' first year income statement showing the allocation of the income to the partners under the foregoing As-sumption (c).

Problem 15–2

Robert Owen and Delbert Price are in the process of forming a partnership to which Owen will devote one third of his time and Price will devote full time. They have under discussion the following plans for sharing gains and losses:

a) In the ratio of their investments which they have agreed to maintain at $6,000 for Owen and $9,000 for Price.

b) In proportion to the time devoted to the business.

c) A salary allowance of $500 per month to Price and the balance in their investment ratio.

d) A salary allowance of $500 per month to Price, 8 percent interest on their investments, and the balance equally.

Required:

1. Prepare a schedule with columnar headings as follows:

Income-sharing Plan	$24,000 Net Income		$12,000 Net Income		$8,000 Net Loss	
	Owen	Price	Owen	Price	Owen	Price

2. List the plans by letter in the first column and show opposite each plan the shares of the partners in (a) a year's net income of $24,000, (b) a year's net income of $12,000, and (c) a year's net loss of $8,000.

Problem 15–3

Kirby, Lang, and Mohr are partners sharing losses and gains in a 2:2:1 ratio. Kirby plans to withdraw from the partnership, and on the date of his withdrawal the partners' equities in the partnership are: Kirby, $10,000; Lang, $12,000; and Mohr, $8,000.

Required:

Give in general journal form the entries for the withdrawal of Kirby under each of the following unrelated assumptions:

a) Kirby, with the consent of Lang and Mohr, sells his interest to Nash, taking from Nash $2,000 in cash and Nash's personal $10,000 note payable.

b) Kirby withdraws, taking $10,000 of partnership cash for his interest.

c) Kirby withdraws, taking $10,750 of partnership cash.

d) Kirby withdraws, taking $6,000 in cash and delivery equipment carried on the partnership books at $4,000, less $1,500 accumulated depreciation.

e) Kirby withdraws, taking $1,500 in cash and a $10,000 note payable of the new partnership.

f) Kirby transfers his interest to Lang and Mohr, taking Lang's $7,200 personal note for three fifths of his interest and Mohr's $4,800 personal note for two fifths of his interest.

Problem 15–4

Ashby, Burns, and Coope, who have always shared losses and gains in a 2:2:1 ratio, plan to liquidate their partnership. Just prior to the liquidation their balance sheet appeared as follows:

ASHBY, BURNS, AND COOPE
Balance Sheet, April 15, 19—

Cash...................	$ 2,500	Accounts payable.......	$10,500
Other assets...........	44,000	Walter Ashby, capital...	8,000
		George Burns, capital...	20,000
		Vernon Coope, capital...	8,000
	$46,500		$46,500

Required:

Under the assumption the other assets are sold and the cash is distributed to the proper parties on April 20, give the entries for the sales, the loss or gain allocations, and the distributions if—

a) The other assets are sold for $50,000.

b) The other assets are sold for $31,500.

c) The other assets are sold for $21,500, and the partner with a deficit can and does pay in the amount of his deficit.

d) The other assets are sold for $20,250, and the partners have no assets other than those invested in the business.

Problem 15–5

Mills, Nagel, and Olson are partners. Mills devotes full time to partnership affairs; Nagel and Olson devote very little time; and as a result, they share gains and losses in a 3:1:1 ratio. Of late the business has not been too profitable, and the partners have decided to liquidate. Just prior to the first realization sale, a partnership balance sheet appeared as follows:

MILLS, NAGEL, AND OLSON
Balance Sheet, October 31, 19—

Cash..........................		$ 2,500	Accounts payable.....................	$ 7,000
Accounts receivable...........		9,500	Albert Mills, capital.................	6,000
Merchandise inventory........		16,000	Robert Nagel, capital................	12,000
Equipment..................$12,000			Donald Olson, capital...............	12,000
Less, Accumulated depr..... 3,000		9,000		
		$37,000		$37,000

The assets were sold, the creditors were paid, and the remaining cash was distributed to the partners on the following dates:

Nov. 4 The accounts receivable were sold for $6,500.
     8 The merchandise inventory was sold for $11,000.
   11 The equipment was sold for $5,000.
   12 The creditors were paid.
   12 The remaining cash was distributed to the partners.

Required:
1. Prepare general journal entries to record the asset sales, the allocation of the realization loss, and the payment of the creditors.
2. Under the assumption that the partner with a deficit can and does pay in the amount of his deficit on November 12, give the entry to record the receipt of his cash and the distribution of partnership cash to the remaining partners.
3. Under the assumption that the partner with a deficit cannot pay, give the entry to allocate his deficit to his partners. Then give the entry to distribute the partnership cash to the remaining partners.

CLASS EXERCISES

Exercise 15–1

The partnership agreement of Ross and Sears provides that income be shared by allowing salary allowances of $8,000 per year to Ross and $6,000 per year to Sears and then sharing any remaining balance equally. At the end of their first year in business, when a work sheet was prepared, it was discovered the partnership had earned just $5 during the year. Sears suggested that the $5 be given to the office boy as a bonus, thereby increasing the expenses of the year and causing the partnership to exactly break even. He further suggested that the partnership could then forget the sharing of gains and losses for the first year, since there would be none. If his suggestions are followed, who gains most and how much does he gain?

Exercise 16–2

Abbot, Birch, and Collins entered into a partnership. Abbot invested $9,000, Birch invested $6,000, and Collins invested $3,000. They agreed to share gains and losses equally. Their business lost heavily, and at the end of the year they decided to liquidate. After converting all the partnership assets to cash and paying all creditor claims, $6,000 of partnership cash remained.

Required:
Prepare a general journal entry to distribute the cash to the partners.

ALTERNATE PROBLEMS

Problem 15–1A

The partnership of Abel, Brock, and Cody earned $24,300 during its first year in business.

Required:

1. Prepare entries to close the firm's Income Summary account and to allocate the net income to the partners under each of the following assumptions:

   a) The partners had not agreed on a method of sharing earnings.

   b) The partners shared earnings in the ratio of their beginning investments which were Abel, $16,000; Brock, $12,000; and Cody, $8,000.

   c) The partners shared earnings by allowing salary allowances of $500 per month to Abel, $600 per month to Brock, and $800 per month to Cody, plus interest at 10 percent annually on beginning investments, and the balance of income or loss equally.

2. Prepare the income statement section showing the allocation of the year's income to the partners under Assumption *(c)* above.

Problem 15–2A

Robert Kemp and Walter Lott are forming a partnership to which Kemp is to devote one half of his time and Lott is to devote full time. They have discussed the following plans for sharing gains and losses:

a) In the ratio of their investments which are to be $12,000 for Kemp and $8,000 for Lott.

b) In proportion to the time devoted to the business.

c) A salary allowance of $500 per month to Lott and the balance in the investment ratio.

d) A salary allowance of $500 per month to Lott, 8 percent interest annually on their investments, and the balance equally.

Required:

1. Prepare a schedule with columnar headings as follows:

Income-sharing Plan	$30,000 Net Income		$15,000 Net Income		$9,000 Net Loss	
	Kemp	Lott	Kemp	Lott	Kemp	Lott

2. List the plans for sharing gains and losses by letter in the first column. Then opposite each plan show the partners' shares in a $30,000 annual net income, a $15,000 net income, and a $9,000 net loss.

Problem 15–3A

Paul Drake is retiring from the partnership of Drake, Ellis, and Folk. The partners have always shared losses and gains in a 2:3:1 ratio; and on Drake's retirement date they have Capital account balances as follows: Paul Drake, $12,000; Eugene Ellis, $15,000; and Robert Folk, $10,000.

Required:
Using the current date, give in general journal form the entries for the retirement of Drake under each of the following unrelated assumptions:

a) Drake retires and withdraws from the business, taking $2,000 in partnership cash and the note of the new partnership of Ellis and Folk for $10,000.

b) Drake withdraws, taking $13,600 of partnership cash in full settlement for his equity.

c) Drake retires, taking $8,000 in partnership cash and delivery equipment carried on the partnership books at its $4,000 cost, less $1,000 of accumulated depreciation.

d) Drake sells his partnership interest to Glenn Geer, with the consent of Ellis and Folk, taking from Geer $5,000 in cash and Geer's personal $10,000 note payable.

e) Drake sells and transfers his interest to Ellis and Folk, taking from Ellis a $10,000 personal note payable for two thirds of his interest and taking $5,000 in cash from Folk for one third of his interest.

Problem 15–4A LiKE quiz
Hart, Ivor, and Jaco plan to liquidate their partnership. They have always shared losses and gains in a 5:3:2 ratio, and just prior to the liquidation their balance sheet appeared as follows:

HART, IVOR, AND JACO
Balance Sheet, March 31, 19—

Cash......................	$ 3,500	Accounts payable........	$13,500
Other assets............	45,000	Allen Hart, capital......	10,000
		Floyd Ivor, capital......	20,000
		Alvin Jaco, capital......	5,000
	$48,500		$48,500

Required:
Prepare general journal entries to record the sale of the other assets and the distribution of the cash to the proper parties under each of the following assumptions:

a) The other assets are sold for $50,500.

b) The other assets are sold for $30,000.

c) The other assets are sold for $22,000, and the partner with the deficit can and does pay in the amount of his deficit.

d) The other assets are sold for $20,000, and the partners have no assets other than those invested in the business.

Problem 15–5A
Until March 2 of the current year Knox, Lacy, and Mann were partners sharing losses and gains in their capital ratio. On that date Knox suffered a heart attack and died. Lacy and Mann immediately ended the business operations and prepared the following adjusted trial balance:

KNOX, LACY, AND MANN

Adjusted Trial Balance, March 2, 19—

Cash...	$ 4,500	
Accounts receivable.........................	10,500	
Allowance for bad debts......................		$ 500
Merchandise inventory.......................	23,000	
Store equipment..............................	13,500	
Accumulated depreciation, store equipment....		3,500
Land..	4,500	
Building......................................	50,000	
Accumulated depreciation, building...........		9,500
Accounts payable.............................		3,000
Mortgage payable, land and building..........		10,000
John Knox, capital...........................		30,000
Robert Lacy, capital.........................		30,000
George Mann, capital.........................		15,000
John Knox, withdrawals.......................	1,000	
Robert Lacy, withdrawals.....................	1,000	
George Mann, withdrawals.....................	1,000	
Revenues.....................................		39,000
Expenses.....................................	31,500	
	$140,500	$140,500

Required:

1. Prepare entries to close the revenue, expense, income summary, and withdrawals accounts of the partnership.
2. Assume the estate of Knox agreed to accept the land and building and assume the mortgage thereon in settlement for its claim against the partnership assets, and that Lacy and Mann planned to continue the business and rent the building from the estate. Give the entry to transfer the land, building, and mortgage and to settle with the estate.
3. Assume that in the place of the foregoing the estate of Knox demanded a cash settlement and the business had to be sold to a competitor who gave $68,000 for the noncash assets and assumed the mortgage but not the accounts payable. Give the entry to transfer the noncash assets and mortgage to the competitor, and give the entries to allocate the loss to the partners and to distribute the partnership cash to the proper parties.

DECISION PROBLEM 15—BAKER, HOOD, AND TAYLOR

A year has passed since Tom Baker, Jim Hood, and Bill Taylor formed a partnership as consulting engineers. A written agreement detailing provisions of the partnership contract was signed. This agreement was adequate in all respects except for the following provision:

"It is agreed that profits and losses shall be distributed in proportion to the respective *total* contributions of the several partners. In order to evaluate more accurately the total contributions of the partners, the division will be determined after one year of operations."

The public accounting firm, of which you are a member, has been requested to make recommendations to the partners on a plan for distributing net income in accordance with the partnership agreement and in as equitable a manner as possible. The following is a summary of the data compiled by the accounting firm:

Tom Baker: Invested $30,000 of the partnership capital; devoted full time to the partnership; previously employed as consulting engineer at a salary of $20,000 per year.

Jim Hood: Invested $10,000 capital; gave full time to the business; is a graduate engineer but has had only four years' experience since finishing college; earned $7,500 per year at the time the partnership was formed.

Bill Taylor: Invested $100,000 capital; is a building contractor and is able to turn considerable business to the partnership; he devotes to the business of the partnership only about two days per month to help in formulating policy.

Write the section of the accounting firm's report outlining the plan you would recommend for distribution of the partnership net income, giving your reasons for the recommendations.

Corporations:
Organization
and Operation

THE THREE common types of business organizations are single proprietorships, partnerships, and corporations. Of the three, corporations are fewer in number than are either of the other two. Yet, in dollar volume, they transact more business than do the other two combined. Thus, because of their business volume and also because almost every person reading this paragraph will at some time either work for or own an interest in a corporation, an understanding of corporations and their accounting is important. And, a start on this understanding may well be made by examining some of the advantages and disadvantages of the corporate form of business organization.

ADVANTAGES OF THE CORPORATE FORM

Separate Legal Entity. From Chief Justice John Marshall's long ago (1818) definition and description of a corporation as "an artificial being, invisible, intangible, and existing only in the contemplation of the law" has grown the doctrine that a corporation is a legal entity, separate and distinct from the persons who own it. The owners are called *stockholders;* they own the corporation, but they are not the corporation. The corporation, in a legal sense, is an artificial person, separate and distinct from its stockholders.

Separate legal entity is the most important characteristic of a corporation, since it gives a corporation all the rights and responsibilities of a person, excepting those only a natural person may exercise, such as the right to vote or marry. Because of its separate legal entity, a corporation may buy, own, and sell property in its own name. It may sue and be sued in its own name. It may enter into contracts with both outsiders and its own stockholders. In short, through its agents, a corporation may conduct its affairs as a legal person with the rights, duties, and responsibilities of a person.

Lack of Liability of Its Stockholders. As a separate legal entity a corporation is responsible for its own acts and its own debts, and its stockholders have no liability for either. From the viewpoint of an investor, this is perhaps the most important advantage of the corporate form.

Ease of Transferring Ownership Rights. Ownership rights in a corporation are represented by shares of stock. And, all that is necessary to convey these rights is a transfer of ownership of the stock. Furthermore, since a corporation is a legal entity, the transfer has no effect on the corporation, and a stockholder may transfer and dispose of his stock at will.

Continuity of Life. The death, incapacity, or withdrawal of a stockholder does not affect the life of a corporation. A corporation's life depends on its charter, and may continue for the time stated in the charter. Furthermore, this period may be of any length permitted by the laws of the state in which the corporation is organized; and at the expiration of the stated time, the charter may normally be renewed and the period extended. Thus, a perpetual life is possible for a successful corporation.

No Mutual Agency. Mutual agency does not exist in a corporation. A corporation stockholder, acting as a stockholder, does not have the power to bind the corporation to contracts. His participation in the affairs of the corporation is limited to the right to vote in the stockholders' meetings. Consequently, stockholders need not exercise the care of partners in selecting people with whom they associate themselves in the ownership of a corporation.

Ease of Capital Assembly. Lack of stockholder liability, lack of mutual agency, and the ease with which an interest may be transferred make it easy for a corporation to assemble large amounts of capital from the combined investments of many stockholders. Actually, a corporation's capital-raising ability is, as a rule, limited only by the profitableness with which it can employ the funds of its stockholders. This is very different from a partnership. In a partnership, capital-raising ability is always limited by the number of partners and their individual wealth; and the number of partners is in turn usually limited by mutual agency and unlimited liability.

DISADVANTAGES OF THE CORPORATE FORM

Governmental Control and Supervision. Corporations are created by fulfilling the requirements of a state's laws. Because of this, corporations are said to be "creatures of the state," and as such are subject to much closer state control and supervision than are single proprietorships and partnerships.

In addition, the rights, powers, and duties of corporations, their stockholders, and officials are derived from corporation laws. There would be no objection to this if the laws were simple and easy to understand; but unfortunately, they are notoriously diverse, complicated, and in some cases vague; and as a result the exact rights, duties, and responsibilities of corporations, their directors, and stockholders vary from state to state and are often difficult to define precisely.

Taxation.   The greatest disadvantage of the corporate form is usually considered its extra burden of taxes. Corporations as business units are subject to all the taxes of single proprietorships and partnerships, and in addition, are subject to several not levied on either of the other two. The most important of these are state and federal income taxes which together commonly exceed 50 percent of a corporation's income. However, insofar as the owners of a corporation are concerned, the burden does not end here. The income of a corporation is taxed twice, first as corporation income and again as personal income when distributed to the stockholders as dividends. This differs from single proprietorships and partnerships, which as business units are not subject to income taxes, and whose income is taxed only as the personal income of their owners.

Lack of Liability of the Stockholders.   A page back, lack of stockholder liability was listed as an advantage of the corporate form. In a small corporation, when an attempt is made to borrow money or secure credit, it may also be a disadvantage, since lack of stockholder liability reduces a corporation's credit. This is because, when stockholders have no liability, a creditor may look only to the assets of the corporation for satisfaction of his claims. Consequently, credit is normally limited to an amount for which the corporation assets furnish adequate security. This differs from a partnership. If a partnership becomes bankrupt, and its assets are not sufficient to meet creditor claims, the creditors may look to the partners' personal assets for satisfaction. Consequently, other things being equal, a partnership with, say, $50,000 in capital can often borrow more money than can a corporation with equal capital.

Of course the effect on a small corporation's credit of no stockholder liability can be and often is overcome by having a stockholder of means endorse the corporation's notes or agree to make good its obligations. However, the stockholder must be willing to back the corporation, since the effect of his endorsement or agreement is to remove the limitation on his liability.

ORGANIZING A CORPORATION

A corporation is created by securing a charter from one of the fifty states or the federal government. Federal charters are limited to national banks, savings and loan associations, and quasi-government corporations, such as the Federal Deposit Insurance Corporation. Consequently, the majority of corporations are chartered by the states.

At one time corporation charters were granted by special acts of state legislatures. Today, in the various states, this power has been delegated to the secretary of state or some other state official; and in delegating the power, the various state legislatures have passed laws setting forth the requirements to be met by persons seeking such a charter. These requirements vary with the states, but in general call for filing several copies of a charter application. Normally, the application must be signed by three or more subscribers to the prospective corporation's stock who are called "incorporators." The application usually must include:

1. The name of the corporation and its legal address within the state.
2. The purpose for which the corporation is organized.
3. The period of time during which the proposed corporation is to exist.
4. The amount of stock authorized and its par value, if any.
5. If there is to be more than one kind of stock, the amount of each.
6. If the stock is to be divided into different kinds or classes, a statement must be made as to the preferences, qualifications, limitations, restrictions, and rights of each class.
7. The names and addresses of the subscribers and the amount of stock subscribed by each.

Normally the secretary of state or other designated state officer is required to see that the application complies with the law. If it does and all fees, taxes, and charges have been paid, the charter is issued. In many states a copy of the application is approved and returned as the corporation charter. In any case, the corporation comes into existence with the issuance of its charter.

After the corporation comes into existence, usually at the first meeting of its stockholders, bylaws to govern the conduct of its affairs are adopted. Bylaws normally include among other things:

1. The time, place, manner of calling, and rules for conducting meetings of the stockholders and board of directors.
2. The number, qualifications, duties, powers, and length of office of the directors.
3. The appointment, duties, powers, compensations, and length of office of corporation officers other than directors.
4. Any proper rules and regulations to govern the acts of the directors and officers.

The bylaws together with the charter give the basic rules for conducting the corporation affairs. It is important that all acts of the stockholders, directors, and officers conform with the regulations in both.

ORGANIZATION COSTS

The costs of organizing a corporation, such as costs of printing stock, legal fees, promoters' fees, and amounts paid the state to secure a charter, are called organization costs, and are debited on incurrence to an account called Organization Costs. Theoretically, the sum of these costs represents an intangible asset from which the corporation will benefit throughout its life; and theoretically these costs should be written off like a prepaid expense over the corporation's life. However, since the number of years a corporation will remain in existence cannot be foretold, many accountants favor writing off such costs during a corporation's early years. There is no good reason for this, other than being conservative. Nevertheless, to be conservative, organization costs are commonly written off over, for example, the first five years of a corporation's life.

Before 1954, when organization costs were written off, the resulting expense could not be deducted in calculating federal income taxes. However, since that date, the Internal Revenue Code has provided that such costs may be deducted proportionally over the first five or more years of a corporation's life.

When a balance sheet is prepared for a corporation having organization costs, the amount of this asset appears thereon as an intangible asset in the intangible asset section of the statement. The intangible assets section follows immediately after the fixed asset section on a balance sheet.

MANAGEMENT OF A CORPORATION

Although ultimate control of a corporation rests with its stockholders, this control is exercised only indirectly through the election of the board of directors. The individual stockholder, as a stockholder, does not actively participate in management. His right as a stockholder to participate begins and ends with his vote in the stockholders meeting, where he has one vote for each share of stock owned.

Normally stockholders meet once each year to elect directors and transact such other business as is provided in the bylaws. Theoretically, stockholders owning or controlling the votes of 50 percent plus one share of a corporation's stock can elect the board and control the corporation. Actually, because many stockholders do not attend the annual meeting, a much smaller percentage is frequently sufficient for control. Commonly, stockholders who do not attend the annual meeting delegate to an agent their voting rights. This is done by signing a legal document called a *proxy*, which gives the agent the right to vote the stock.

A corporation's board of directors is responsible and has final authority for the direction of corporation affairs; but it may act only as a collective body, an individual director, as a director, has no power to transact corporation business. And, as a rule, although it has final authority, a board will limit itself to establishing policy, delegating the day-by-day direction of corporation business to the corporation's administrative officers whom it selects and elects.

A corporation's administrative officers are commonly headed by a president who is normally the chief executive officer and is directly responsible to the board for managing, controlling, and supervising the corporation's business. To aid the president, many corporations have one or more vice presidents who are vested with specific managerial powers and duties by the president and the directors. In addition, the corporation secretary keeps the minutes of the meetings of the stockholders and directors, and in a small corporation may also be responsible for keeping a record of the stockholders and the changing amounts of their stock interests. The treasurer is custodian of corporation funds.

Illustration 100 shows the organizational chart of a corporation. Note its

Illustration 100

Organization Chart of a Corporation

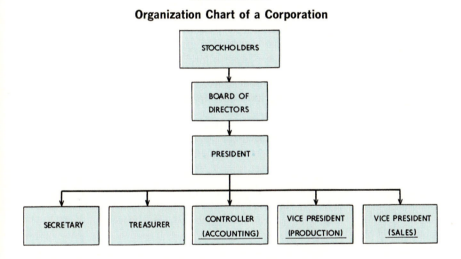

lines of authority extending from the stockholders through the board and on to the administrative officers.

CORPORATION ACCOUNTING

A corporation's accounting records are, as a rule, like those of an equal-size single proprietorship or partnership, and generally its accounting differs only for transactions directly affecting the stockholder equity accounts. Here a difference results because a distinction is always made in corporation accounting between invested capital and capital from earnings retained in the business.

On this score, it will be recalled that in a single proprietorship or partnership no distinction is made between invested capital and capital from earnings. Furthermore, an owner's investment plus changes in his equity resulting from gains and losses are recorded in the same account, the owner's Capital account. However, in a corporation this differs. In a corporation, due to the distinction that is and should be made between invested capital and retained earnings, there are two kinds of proprietary accounts: (1) *contributed capital accounts* and (2) *retained earnings accounts*. The contributed capital accounts show the amounts originally invested in the corporation by its stockholders, and the retained earnings accounts show earnings retained in the business.

Separate contributed capital and retained earnings accounts are used in corporation accounting to preserve in the accounts a record of the amount paid a corporation by its stockholders for its stock. This record is necessary because in most states a corporation may not legally pay a dividend when to do so reduces the stockholders' equity below the amount paid the corporation for its stock.

State laws prohibiting the payment of a dividend by a corporation, when to do so reduces the stockholders' equity below the amount paid the corporation for its stock, were written to protect corporation creditors. The reasoning behind these laws is as follows:

1. Since a corporation's stockholders have no liability for its debts, the corporation's creditors may look only to corporation assets for payment of their claims.
2. When a corporation pays cash or other assets to its stockholders in the form of dividends, it reduces in equal amounts both its assets and the stockholders' equity.
3. Consequently, if dividends may not be paid when to do so reduces the stockholders' equity below the amount originally paid the corporation for its stock, then a fund of assets equal to this original investment is kept in the business for the protection of the creditors and the payment of their claims.

When state laws establish rules like the foregoing to govern the payment of dividends, the laws also normally make directors personally liable for repayment to the corporation of a dividend declared and paid in violation of the rules. A director who votes against such a dividend is not held liable; consequently, directors are usually careful not to vote for an illegal dividend.

CORPORATION OWNER EQUITY ACCOUNTS ILLUSTRATED

To demonstrate the use of separate accounts for contributed capital and retained earnings as found in corporation accounting, and to contrast their use with a single capital account in a sole proprietorship, assume that on January 5, 1966, a single proprietorship and a corporation having five stockholders were formed. Assume further that $25,000 was invested in each. In the sole proprietorship the owner, John Ohm, invested the entire amount; and in the corporation five stockholders each bought 500 shares of its $10 par value common stock at $10 per share. Without dates and explanations, the entries to record the investments are:

Single Proprietorship		Corporation	
Cash...............25,000		Cash...............25,000	
John Ohm, Capital	25,000	Common Stock....	25,000

And after the entries were posted, the owner-equity accounts of the two concerns appeared as follows:

Single Proprietorship
John Ohm, Capital

Date	Dr.	Cr.	Bal.
Jan. 5, '66		25,000	25,000

Corporation
Common Stock

Date	Dr.	Cr.	Bal.
Jan. 5, '66		25,000	25,000

To continue the illustration, it will be recalled that in a single proprietorship, when the Income Summary account is closed, the amount of gain or loss is transferred from the Income Summary account to the Capital account of the owner. In a corporation this differs; in a corporation the gain or loss is carried to the Retained Earnings account. For example, if in the two concerns under discussion, each earned $8,000 during the first year and retained the earnings for use in carrying on their operations, after the Income Summary accounts were closed, the owner equity of each appeared in its accounts as follows:

Single Proprietorship
John Ohm, Capital

Date	Dr.	Cr.	Bal.
Jan. 5, '66		25,000	25,000
Dec. 31, '66		8,000	33,000

Corporation
Common Stock

Date	Dr.	Cr.	Bal.
Jan. 5, '66		25,000	25,000

Retained Earnings

Date	Dr.	Cr.	Bal.
Dec. 31, '66		8,000	8,000

And the owner equity of each appeared on its balance sheet as follows:

Single Proprietorship Owner Equity	Corporation Stockholders' Equity
John Ohm, capital, January 1, 1966...................$25,000	Common stock, $10 par value, authorized and issued 2,500 shares......$25,000
Add: Net income........... 8,000	Retained earnings.......... 8,000
John Ohm, capital, December 31, 1966...............$33,000	Stockholders' equity........$33,000

To continue the illustration, assume that the two concerns each lost $11,000 during their second year. If there were no withdrawals in the single proprietorship or additional investments in either concern, the owner-equity accounts of each appeared at the end of the second year as follows:

Single Proprietorship

John Ohm, Capital

Date	Dr.	Cr.	Bal.
Jan. 5, '66		25,000	25,000
Dec. 31, '66		8,000	33,000
Dec. 31, '67	11,000		22,000

Corporation

Common Stock

Date	Dr.	Cr.	Bal.
Jan. 5, '66		25,000	25,000

Retained Earnings

Date	Dr.	Cr.	Bal.
Dec. 31, '66		8,000	8,000
Dec. 31, '67	11,000		(3,000)

Observe that the Retained Earnings account of the corporation has a debit balance of $3,000. A corporation is said to have a *deficit* when it has a debit balance in its Retained Earnings account, as in this illustration. A deficit is in effect a negative amount of retained earnings.

At the end of the second year the owner-equity sections from the balance sheets of the two concerns appeared as follows:

Single Proprietorship	Corporation
Owner Equity	**Stockholders' Equity**
John Ohm, capital, January 1, 1967.................$33,000	*Common stock, $10 par value, 2,500 shares authorized and issued......$25,000*
Deduct: Net loss.......... 11,000	*Deduct: Deficit........... 3,000*
John Ohm, capital, December 31, 1967.............$22,000	*Stockholders' equity........$22,000*

During their second year both the corporation and the proprietorship suffered losses, which in each case reduced the equities of their owners to $22,000. Notice in the illustration just given how the $22,000 equity in the corporation is shown by listing the amount of stock and deducting therefrom the $3,000 deficit.

The corporation of the preceding simplified illustrations had only one kind of stock and only one contributed capital account, its Common Stock account. It should be noted that a corporation may have several contributed capital accounts; for example, if a corporation issues more than one kind or class of stock, it will have a separate account for the transactions in each class. Likewise, for reasons of law or management, a corporation may use more than one retained earnings account.

CASH DIVIDENDS AND RETAINED EARNINGS

A dividend is a distribution made to its stockholders by a corporation. Dividends are declared or voted by the board of directors, and courts have generally held that the board is final judge of when, if at all, a dividend should be paid. Dividends may be distributed in cash, other assets, or in a corporation's own stock. Cash dividends are the most common, and such a dividend is normally stated in terms of so many dollars or cents per share of stock. For example, a corporation may declare a dividend of one dollar per share on its outstanding common stock. If it does so, an owner of one hundred shares will receive one hundred dollars.

In many states a dividend may be declared and paid only if earnings equal to or greater than the amount of the dividend have been accumulated. For this reason, it is often said that dividends are paid from retained earnings. In a sense this is true. However, it should be recognized that the declaration and payment of a cash dividend reduces in equal amounts both cash and retained earnings.

Since a corporation's stockholders change, a dividend is normally declared on one date to be paid on a future date to the *stockholders of record* (stockholders according to the corporation's records) of a specified third date. For example, a board of directors may declare a dividend on December 28, to be paid on January 25 to the stockholders of record of

January 20. Of the three dates involved here, December 28 is called the *date of declaration*, January 20 is the *date of record*, and January 25 is the *date of payment*. Declaring a dividend on one date to be paid to the stockholders of record on a future date gives new purchasers of the stock an opportunity to have their ownership recorded in time to receive the dividend.

A stockholder has no right to a dividend until it is declared by the board of directors. However, as soon as a cash dividend is declared, it becomes a liability of the corporation, normally a current liability, and must be paid. Furthermore, the stockholders have the right to sue and force payment of a cash dividend once it is declared. Since dividends are usually declared on one date to be paid on a future date, two entries are used to record the declaration and payment of each dividend. The first entry, which is made at the time of the declaration, reduces the stockholders' equity and records the liability of the dividend; and the second records its payment. The two entries commonly appear as follows:

Dec.	*28*	*Retained Earnings*....................	*25,000.00*	
		Common Dividend Payable.......		*25,000.00*
		To record the declaration of a $1 per share dividend on the 25,000 shares of outstanding common stock.		
Jan.	*25*	*Common Dividend Payable*...........	*25,000.00*	
		Cash.........................		*25,000.00*
		To record payment of the dividend declared on December 28.		

DIVIDEND POLICY

Since a corporation is a legal entity, the profits it earns belong to the corporation. The stockholders own the corporation; but they have no legal right to its profits, until the board declares a dividend; and the board is the final judge of when such a dividend should be declared. In deciding upon a dividend, the board normally considers both its legality and the wisdom of its declaration.

Although the answer varies somewhat from state to state, generally, a dividend is legal when it does not reduce the stockholders' equity below the amount paid to the corporation for its stock. As to the wisdom of a dividend, the directors must decide whether the corporation can spare the cash needed for its payment, or when cash is available, if the cash cannot be used to better advantage in expanding the corporation's operations for greater profits in the future. Many large corporations follow the policy of paying out in dividends around 70 percent of earnings, and retaining the balance to finance expansion and growth.

RIGHTS OF STOCKHOLDERS

If a corporation issues only one kind of stock, the stock is known as *common stock*. When individuals buy such stock, they acquire all the specific rights granted by the corporation's charter to its common stockholders; and they also acquire the general rights granted stockholders by the laws of the state in which the corporation is organized. The laws vary, but in general all common stockholders have the following rights:

1. The right to vote in the stockholders' meetings.
2. The right to sell or otherwise dispose of their stock.
3. The right of first opportunity to purchase any additional shares of common stock issued by the corporation. (This is called the *preemptive right* of common stockholders. It gives a common stockholder the opportunity to protect his interest in the corporation. For example, if a stockholder owns one fourth of the common stock of a corporation, he has first opportunity to buy one fourth of any new common stock issued. This enables him to maintain his one-fourth interest.)
4. The right to share pro rata with other common stockholders in any dividends declared.
5. The right to share, if the corporation is liquidated, in any assets remaining after creditors are paid.

PREFERRED STOCK

A corporation may issue more than one kind or class of stock. If two classes are issued, one is generally known as common stock and the other as *preferred stock*. Preferred stock is so called because of the preferences granted its owners. These commonly include a preference as to payment of dividends, and may include a preference as to the return of the stock's par value in a liquidation.

A preference as to dividends does not give an absolute right to dividends. Rather it gives the preferred stockholders the right, if dividends are declared, to receive their preferred dividend before the common stockholders are paid a dividend. In other words, if dividends are declared, a dividend must be paid the preferred stockholders before a dividend may be paid to the common stockholders. However, if the directors are of the opinion that no dividends should be paid, then neither the preferred nor the common stockholders receive a dividend.

Dividends on the majority of preferred stocks are limited to a fixed maximum amount. For example, a share of $100 par value, 6 percent, nonparticipating preferred stock has a preference each year to a dividend of 6 percent of its par value, or $6; but the dividend is limited to that amount.

Although dividends on the majority of preferred stocks are limited in amount, dividends on a corporation's common stock are unlimited, except by the earning power of the corporation and the judgment of its board of directors.

While dividends on most preferred stocks are limited to a fixed basic percentage or amount, some preferred stocks have the right, under certain circumstances, to dividends in excess of a fixed basic percentage or amount. Such preferred stocks are called *participating preferred stocks*. Participating preferred stocks may be fully participating, or their participation may be limited to a fixed maximum amount. The exact terms of participation depend in each case on the preferred stock contract. For example, if a corporation issues a fully participating, 6 percent, $100 par value, preferred stock, the owners of such stock have a preference to dividends each year of $6 per share. Then, each year, after the common stockholders receive a 6 percent dividend on the par value of their shares, the preferred stockholders have the right to participate with the common stockholders in any additional dividends declared. The participation is usually on the basis of an equal additional percentage-per-share dividend to each group of stockholders.

Often when preferred stock is participating, participation is limited. For example, a $100 par value, 5 percent, preferred stock may be issued with the right of participation in dividends to 10 percent of its par value. Such a stock has a preference to dividends of 5 percent each year. It also has a right, after the common stockholders receive a 5 percent dividend, to participate in additional dividends until it has received 10 percent, or $10, per share. Its participation rights end at this point.

In addition to being participating or nonparticipating, preferred stocks are either *cumulative* or *noncumulative*. A cumulative preferred stock is one on which any undeclared dividends accumulate each year until paid. A noncumulative preferred stock is one on which the right to receive dividends is forfeited in any year in which dividends are not declared.

The accumulation of dividends on cumulative preferred stocks does not guarantee their payment. Dividends cannot be guaranteed because earnings from which they are paid cannot be guaranteed. However, when a corporation issues cumulative preferred stock, it does agree to pay its cumulative preferred stockholders both their current dividends and any unpaid back dividends, called *dividends in arrears*, before it pays a dividend to its common stockholders.

In addition to the preferences it receives, preferred stock carries with it all the rights of common stock, unless such rights are specifically denied in the preferred stock contract. Commonly, preferred stock is denied the right to vote in the meetings of the stockholders, as in the example in the following section that tells why preferred stock is issued.

Preferred Dividends in Arrears on the Balance Sheet Date. A liability for a dividend does not come into existence until the dividend is declared by the board of directors. Consequently, if on the dividend date a corporation's board fails to declare a dividend on its cumulative preferred stock, the dividend in arrears is not a liability and does not appear on the balance sheet as such. However, if there are preferred dividends in arrears, this information should appear on the balance sheet, and normally such information is given in a balance sheet footnote. For example, if three years' dividends have been missed, such a footnote might read, "Dividends for the current and two past years are in arrears on the preferred stock." When a balance sheet does not carry such a footnote, a balance sheet reader has the right to assume that all current and back dividends on the preferred stock have been paid.

WHY PREFERRED STOCK IS ISSUED

Two common reasons why preferred stock is issued can best be shown by means of an example. Suppose that three men with a total of $100,000 to invest wish to organize a corporation requiring $200,000 of capital. If they sell and issue $200,000 of common stock, they will have to share control with other stockholders. However, if they sell and issue $100,000 of common stock to themselves, and sell to outsiders $100,000 of 6 percent, cumulative preferred stock having no voting rights, they can retain control of the corporation for themselves.

Also, suppose the three promoters expect their new corporation to earn an annual after-tax return of $20,000. If they sell and issue $200,000 of common stock, this will mean a 10 percent return; but if they sell and issue $100,000 of each kind of stock, retaining the common for themselves, they can increase their own return to 14 percent, as follows:

Net after-tax income..............................$20,000
Preferred dividends at 6 percent................... 6,000
Balance to common stockholders (equal to 14 percent on their $100,000 investment)..............$14,000

The foregoing is an example of what is known as securing a *leverage* on an investment. The common stockholders secure a leverage, or greater return, on their investment because the dividends on the preferred stock are less than the amount that can be earned through the use of the preferred stockholders' money.

In the foregoing example the preferred stock carries a cumulative preference as to dividends. The exact preference granted in this and every other case always depend on what must be granted to sell the stock. As a rule, nothing is granted beyond what is necessary.

STOCK VALUES

Several values apply to stock. For instance, a stock may have a par value, a book value, a market value, and a redemption value.

Par Value. Par value is the arbitrary value established for a share of stock in the charter of its issuing corporation and printed on the face of each stock certificate. Par value does not establish worth, and its main significance is a legal one that is discussed in more detail in the next chapter.

Book Value. The book value of a share of stock measures the equity of one share of the stock in the assets of its issuing corporation. If a corporation issues only one kind of stock, common stock, the book value or equity of all the outstanding common shares is equal to the sum of the corporation's contributed and retained capital; and consequently, the book value of one share is equal to the sum of the contributed and retained capital divided by the number of shares outstanding. For example, a corporation has the following contributed and retained capital:

Common stock (1,000 shares, $25 par)	*$25,000*
Retained earnings	*6,100*
Total stockholders' equity	*$31,100*

Thus, in this instance the book value of a share of the corporation's common stock is $31,100 divided by 1,000 shares, or $31.10 per share.

When a corporation issues both common and preferred stock, the book value of each depends on the preferences granted the preferred stockholders. For example, assume a corporation has the following capitalization:

Preferred stock (1,000 shares, $100 par)	*$100,000*
Common stock (20,000 shares, $10 par)	*200,000*
Retained earnings	*40,000*
Total stockholders' equity	*$340,000*

If the preferred stock is nonparticipating and there are no dividends in arrears, its book value is equal to its par value of $100 per share. Under these circumstances all the retained earnings are allotted to the common stock, because the preferred stockholders having received all their dividends have no further claim on past earnings as represented by the balance of the Retained Earnings account. Furthermore, in this situation the book value of the common stock is $240,000 divided by 20,000 shares, or $12 per share. In cases where preferred dividends are in arrears, available retained earnings equal to the dividends in arrears are allotted and added to the book value of the preferred stock; and any remaining retained earnings then go to the common stock.

Market Value. The market value of a share of stock is the price at which a share can be sold. Market values are influenced by earnings, dividends, book value, and general market conditions.

Redemption Value. Redemption values apply to preferred stocks. Often corporations issuing preferred stock reserve the right to redeem the stock by paying the preferred stockholders the par value of their stock plus a premium. The amount a corporation agrees to pay to redeem a share of its preferred stock is called the "redemption value" of the stock. Normally, a corporation reserves the right to either redeem or permit the stock to remain outstanding, as it chooses.

INCORPORATION OF A PARTNERSHIP

Often, in order to avoid unlimited liability, or to gain a more permanent organization, or additional funds, partnerships are incorporated. When a partnership is incorporated, if it has been in existence long, its assets commonly require revaluation before they are taken over by the corporation, because—

1. There may have been errors in keeping the books. (Often it is wise to call in a certified public accountant to perform an audit in order that he may express an opinion as to the amounts shown for the assets and liabilities.)
2. Fixed assets purchased several years previous to the reorganization may be grossly overvalued or undervalued due to price changes and market fluctuations.
3. The business may have goodwill. (Goodwill may be defined as the value of a business over and beyond the value of its physical assets, with the best evidence of its existence being a rate of return in excess of the normal rate for other firms in the same business.)

Incorporation of a Partnership Illustrated. To illustrate the reorganization of a partnership into a corporation, assume that Hill, Dale, and Knob, who have always shared earnings in the ratio of 2:2:1, decided to expand their business and to reorganize it into a corporation to be known as Apex Corporation. A condensed balance sheet of the partnership just prior to the reorganization is shown in Illustration 101.

In planning the reorganization, the partners agree that—

1. The assets are to be revalued as follows: (*a*) The allowance for bad debts is to be increased to $500 to allow for certain doubtful accounts. (*b*) The merchandise inventory is to be written down $800 to allow for damaged and shopworn goods. (*c*) The building is to be written up to its present replacement cost of $30,000, and the accumulated depreciation increased to show the building to be one-third depreciated.

Illustration 101

HILL, DALE, AND KNOB
Balance Sheet, May 30, 19--

ASSETS			LIABILITIES		
Cash		$ 2,500	Accounts payable. . .	$ 9,300	
Accounts receivable.	$ 6,000		Mortgage payable. . .	7,000	
Allow. for bad debts	300	5,700	Total Liabilities .		$16,300
Merchandise inventory		25,000			
Store equipment. . .	$ 4,800		PROPRIETORSHIP		
Accumulated depr.. .	1,200	3,600			
Building	$18,000		Hill, capital	$13,500	
Accumulated depr.. .	6,000	12,000	Dale, capital	15,000	
Land		2,500	Knob, capital	6,500	
			Total Proprietorship		35,000
Total Assets . .		$51,300	Total Liab. and Prop.		$51,300

2. The assets and liabilities are to be taken over by the new corporation; and each partner is to accept $10 par value common stock of the corporation at par in exchange for his partnership equity.

The following entries are required to revalue the partnership assets and to allocate losses and gains from revaluation to the partners:

May	30	*Loss or Gain from Revaluation*.	200.00	
		Allowance for Bad Debts.		200.00
		To increase the allowance for bad debts to allow for additional probable losses.		
	30	*Loss or Gain from Revaluation*.	800.00	
		Merchandise Inventory.		800.00
		To revalue the merchandise inventory.		
	30	*Building*.	12,000.00	
		Accumulated Depreciation, Building.		4,000.00
		Loss or Gain from Revaluation.		8,000.00
		To revalue the building at replacement cost and to show it to be one-third depreciated.		
	30	*Loss or Gain from Revaluation*.	7,000.00	
		Hill, Capital.		2,800.00
		Dale, Capital.		2,800.00
		Knob, Capital.		1,400.00
		To allocate the net gain from revaluation to the partners in their loss-and-gain-sharing ratio.		

Losses or gains from revaluation may be allocated to the partners as each asset is revalued. However, if there are many assets, it is easier to place the loss or gain from each revaluation in a loss or gain account and then to allocate the account balance.

After the entries revaluing the assets of Hill, Dale, and Knob are posted, a trial balance of the partnership ledger lists the amounts for the revalued assets and owner equity shown in Illustration 102.

Illustration 102

HILL, DALE, AND KNOB
Trial Balance, May 30, 19--

Cash	$ 2,500	
Accounts receivable	6,000	
Allowance for bad debts		$ 500
Merchandise inventory	24,200	
Store equipment	4,800	
Accumulated depreciation, store equipment		1,200
Building	30,000	
Accumulated depreciation, building		10,000
Land	2,500	
Accounts payable		9,300
Mortgage payable		7,000
Hill, capital		16,300
Dale, capital		17,800
Knob, capital		7,900
	$70,000	$70,000

After the assets are revalued, the additional entries required by the reorganization depend upon whether the partnership books are to be retained and used by the corporation or new books are to be opened. Commonly, if the partnership books have been well kept, they are retained. Consequently, in this illustration assume that the books of Hill, Dale, and Knob are to be retained for use by the corporation.

If the partnership books are retained, after the assets, are revalued and the gain transferred to the partners' Capital accounts, only one additional entry is required to change the partnership books into the books of the corporation. The entry closes the partners' Capital accounts and opens the corporation's Common Stock account. In this case it appears as follows:

May	*30*	*Hill, Capital*	*16,300.00*	
		Dale, Capital	*17,800.00*	
		Knob, Capital	*7,900.00*	
		Common Stock		*42,000.00*
		To record the distribution of stock to the partners in exchange for their equities.		

After the foregoing entry is posted, the books of Hill, Dale, and Knob are the records of Apex Corporation. Of course, at the time the entry is prepared and posted, the shares of stock representing the interest in the new corporation of each former partner should be delivered to him.

QUESTIONS FOR CLASS DISCUSSION

1. List (a) the advantages and (b) disadvantages of the corporation form of business organization.
2. A corporation is said to be a separate legal entity. What is meant by this?
3. What effect does a separate legal existence have upon the ability of a corporation to enter into contracts with its stockholders? What effect does a corporation's separate legal existence have on the liability of its stockholders for the corporation's debts?
4. How may lack of stockholder liability be both an advantage and a disadvantage to a small corporation?
5. Before it will loan money to a small corporation, a bank insists that a large stockholder of the corporation, S. T. Larr, personally endorse the corporation's note. Why does the bank ask for the endorsement of Larr? Would the bank demand this endorsement if the business were organized as a partnership and Larr were a partner?
6. What are organization costs? List several.
7. What is a proxy?
8. What are the two kinds of proprietary accounts used in corporation accounting? Why are the two kinds of proprietary accounts used?
9. In corporation accounting, what is a deficit?
10. What is the reasoning behind laws that prohibit the payment of dividends by a corporation when to do so would reduce the stockholders' equity in the corporation to a point below the amount originally invested in the corporation by its stockholders?
11. The Income Summary account of a corporation shows an $82,000 net income. Give the entry to close the account. How does the entry differ from the entry to close the Income Summary account of a single proprietorship or partnership?
12. What are the three dates involved in the declaration and payment of a cash dividend?
13. Laws place no limit on the amounts partners may withdraw from a partnership. On the other hand, laws regulating corporations place definite limits on the amounts that may be withdrawn by the owners of corporations in the form of dividends. Why is there a difference?
14. At the annual meeting of the stockholders of a corporation the president reported that the corporation had earned during the year $450,000 after taxes. Then he told the stockholders that the directors were of the opinion that the corporation could pay only $90,000 in cash dividends. Can you offer a reason for this corporation's ability to pay only $90,000 in dividends when it has earned five times that amount?

15. On December 21 the Green Corporation declared a cash dividend of $2.50 per share on its 5,000 shares of outstanding common stock. The dividend was to be paid on January 20 to stockholders of record of January 15. Give the entries for the declaration and payment of the dividend.

16. List the rights of common stockholders.

17. What is the preemptive right of common stockholders?

18. What are the meanings of the following words when applied to stock: (a) preferred, (b) participating, (c) nonparticipating, (d) cumulative, and (e) noncumulative?

19. What are the meanings of the following terms when applied to stock: (a) par value, (b) book value, (c) market value, and (d) redemption value.

PROBLEMS

Problem 16–1

On January 11, 1965, Charles Abbey, William Betts, and George Cabot associated themselves in the operation of a business in which they each invested $15,000. During 1965 the business lost $5,100, and during 1966 it earned $19,200. On January 5, 1967, the three men agreed to pay themselves $12,000 of the accumulated earnings, and on January 10, 1967, the $12,000 was paid out.

Required:

1. Under the assumption the business is a partnership in which the partners share losses and gains equally, give the entries (a) to record the investments and (b) to close the Income Summary account to the Withdrawals accounts and to close the Withdrawals accounts to the Capital accounts at the end of 1965 and again at the end of 1966. (c) Under the additional assumption that the partners were each paid $4,000 on January 10, give the entry to record the payment.

2. Under the assumption the business is a corporation and $10 par value common stock was issued at par, give the entries (a) to record the investments, (b) to close the Income Summary account at the end of 1965 and again at the end of 1966, and (c) to record the distribution of the retained earnings. (Ignore corporation income taxes.)

Problem 16–2

Stetson Corporation has outstanding 1,000 shares of $100, 6 percent preferred stock and 20,000 shares of $10 par value common stock. The preferred stock is cumulative and nonparticipating. During a seven-year period the corporation paid out the following amounts in dividends:

1960	*$18,000*
1961	*–0–*
1962	*–0–*
1963	*16,000*
1964	*14,000*
1965	*24,000*
1966	*30,000*

Required:

1. *a*) Prepare a form with columnar headings as follows:

Year	Total Paid to Preferred	Balance Due Preferred	Total Paid to Common	Dividend per Share Preferred	Dividend per Share Common	Percent on Par Preferred	Percent on Par Common

b) In the first column enter the years 1960 through 1966. Then determine and fill in the information opposite each year in the remaining columns. (In the last two columns indicate the percent on par paid in dividends on each class of stock. Assume there were no dividends in arrears in 1960 and in any year in which the corporation paid a dividend, it always paid the full amount of current and back dividends due the preferred stockholders before paying anything to the common stockholders.)

2. Prepare and complete a second form according to the foregoing directions under the assumption that rather than being cumulative and nonparticipating, the preferred stock of the corporation is noncumulative and nonparticipating.

3. Prepare and complete a third form according to the foregoing directions under the assumption the preferred stock of the corporation is cumulative and fully participating.

Problem 16–3

Part 1. The common stock of Standard Corporation is selling on the stock exchange today at $7.50 per share, and a just published balance sheet shows the stockholders' equity in the corporation as follows:

Stockholders' Equity

Preferred stock, 7 percent, cumulative and nonparticipating, $10 par value, 10,000 shares issued and outstanding..$100,000
Common stock, $5 par value, 50,000 shares issued and outstanding........ 250,000
Retained earnings........ 79,000
Total stockholders' equity........$429,000

Required:

Answer these questions: (1) What is the market value of the corporation's common stock? (2) What are the par values of its (*a*) common stock and (*b*) preferred stock? (3) If there are no dividends in arrears, what are the book values of the (*a*) common stock and (*b*) preferred stock? (4) If two years' dividends are in arrears on the preferred stock, what are the book values of (*a*) the common stock and (*b*) the preferred stock?

Part 2. The stockholders' equity sections from the balance sheets of three corporations follow:

1. Stockholders' Equity:

Cumulative and nonparticipating, $100 par value, 6 per-	
cent, preferred stock, authorized and issued 1,000 shares..$	100,000
Common stock, $25 par value, 10,000 shares authorized and	
issued..	250,000
Retained earnings...	64,000
Total stockholders' equity.........................$	414,000

2. Stockholders' Interest:

Preferred stock, $100 par value, 7 percent cumulative and	
nonparticipating, 500 shares authorized and issued.....$	50,000*
Common stock, $100 par value, 500 shares authorized and	
issued..	50,000
Retained earnings...	6,000
Total stockholders' interest.......................$	106,000

* *The current year's dividend is unpaid on the preferred stock.*

3. Stockholders' Equity:

Cumulative and nonparticipating, $10 par value, 7 percent	
preferred stock, 100,000 shares authorized and issued....$1,000,000*	
Common stock, $25 par value, 100,000 shares authorized	
and issued...	2,500,000
Total contributed capital............................$3,500,000	
Deficit..	540,000
Stockholders' equity..................................$2,960,000	

* *Three years' dividends are in arrears on the preferred stock.*

Required:

Prepare a schedule showing the book value per share of the preferred and common stock of each corporation.

Problem 16–4

XL Corporation has outstanding 2,000 shares of $100 par value common stock, all owned by five men who are also the corporation's board of directors. The corporation is in a position to expand; but to do so it needs $300,000 additional capital which its present owners are unable to supply. Consequently, the board of directors is considering the issuance of 3,000 shares of $100 par value, 6 percent, cumulative and nonparticipating, preferred stock to gain the additional capital, and it has asked you to prepare a report showing the return to the two classes of stockholders from the following amounts of before-tax profit:

a) $25,000 or a 5 percent before-tax return on the $500,000 invested.
b) $50,000 or a 10 percent before-tax return on the $500,000 invested.
c) $75,000 or a 15 percent before-tax return on the $500,000 invested.
d) $100,000 or a 20 percent before-tax return on the $500,000 invested.

Required:

1. Prepare a form with columnar headings as follows:

Before-Tax Earnings	Federal Income Taxes	After-Tax Earnings		Preferred Dividends		Common Dividends	
		Amount	Percent Return on Investment	Total Paid to Preferred	Percent Return on Investment	Total Paid to Common	Percent Return on Investment

2. Enter the amounts of before-tax profit in the first column.
3. Calculate the federal income tax applicable to each level of earnings and enter in the second column. (Corporations are required (1965) to pay a 22 percent federal income tax on the first $25,000 of their earnings and 48 percent on any earnings over $25,000. Thus, the federal income tax on $50,000 of earnings is 22 percent of the first $25,000 plus 48 percent on the second $25,000, or a total of $17,500.)
4. Complete the information of the form under the assumption that all after-tax earnings are paid out in dividends.
5. Observe that this corporation earns a 20 percent before-tax return on its stockholders' $500,000 investment when it earns $100,000. Then observe that at this level of earnings the after-tax return to the common stockholders is 20.25 percent. Explain why the common stockholders' after-tax rate of return is greater than the corporation's before-tax rate.

Problem 16–5

Edwin Brand and Dennis Cahill operate a building supply firm, Knothole Suppliers, as partners sharing losses and gains in a 3 to 2 ratio. They have just entered into an agreement with John Decker to reorganize their firm into a corporation. On the date of the reorganization, March 3 of the current year, a trial balance of the partnership ledger appears as follows:

KNOTHOLE SUPPLIERS

Trial Balance, March 3, 19—

Cash	$ 4,140	
Accounts receivable	18,300	
Allowance for bad debts		$ 350
Merchandise inventory	37,250	
Store equipment	10,000	
Accumulated depreciation, store equipment		2,000
Office equipment	2,300	
Accumulated depreciation, Office equipment		950
Building	32,000	
Accumulated depreciation, building		8,000
Land	6,000	
Accounts payable		6,370
Mortgage payable		12,000
Edwin Brand, capital		48,170
Dennis Cahill, capital		32,150
	$109,990	$109,990

The agreement between the partners and Decker carries the following provisions:

1. The accounting records of the old business are to be continued for the new corporation, which is to be known as Knothole Suppliers, Inc.
2. The partnership assets are to be revalued as follows:
    a) The $300 account receivable of Valley Contractors is known to be uncollectible and is to be written off as a bad debt. After the write-off the allowance for bad debts is to be increased to 5 percent of the remaining accounts receivable.
    b) The merchandise inventory is to be written down to $35,000.
    c) Insufficient depreciation has been taken in the past on the store equipment; consequently, the book value of the store equipment is to be decreased to $6,500 by increasing the balance of the accumulated depreciation account.
    d) The recorded value of the building is to be increased to its replacement cost, $40,000, and the amount of accumulated depreciation is to be increased to show the building one-fourth depreciated.
3. The corporation is to issue 20,000 shares of $5 par value common stock.
4. After the partnership assets are revalued, the partners are to accept shares of the corporation's stock at par in exchange for their partnership equities.
5. Any remaining stock is to be bought by John Decker at par for cash.

Required:
1. Prepare entries in general journal form to change the partnership into a corporation and to reflect the foregoing provisions.
2. Prepare a balance sheet for the corporation.

CLASS EXERCISE

Exercise 16–1
Information as to the assets, liabilities, and stockholders' equity in each of Corporations A, B, and C follow:

	Corporation A	Corporation B	Corporation C
Assets	$232,000	$287,000	$?
Liabilities	41,000	?	71,000
Common stock	100,000	200,000	50,000
Retained earnings or deficit	?	?	?

Required:
Under the assumptions that (1) the corporations each have the same number of shares of stock outstanding and (2) the book value of Corporation A's shares is the same as the book value of Corporation B's shares and also the same as Corporation C's shares, determine the missing amounts indicated by the question marks.

ALTERNATE PROBLEMS

Problem 16–1A

Paul Curry, George Dawson, and James Elliott began a new business on February 3, 1965. They invested $15,000, $20,000, and $25,000, respectively. During its first year, 1965, the business lost $4,800, and during its second year, 1966, it earned $26,400. On January 3, 1967, the men agreed to pay out to themselves $18,000 of the accumulated earnings of the business, and on January 12, the $18,000 was paid out.

Required:

1. Under the assumption that the business is a partnership in which the partners share losses and gains in the ratio of their beginning investments, give the entries to record the partners' investments and to close the Income Summary account to the partners' Withdrawals accounts and to close the Withdrawals accounts to the Capital accounts at the end of 1965 and again at the end of 1966. Under the additional assumption that the $18,000 paid to the partners on January 12, 1966, was paid in the investment ratio, give the entry to record the payment.
2. Under the assumption that the business is a corporation and that $5 par value common stock was issued at par, give the entries to (a) record the investments, (b) close the Income Summary account at the end of 1965 and again at the end of 1966, and (c) record the distribution of the retained earnings. (Ignore corporation income taxes.)

Problem 16–2A

Mesa Corporation has outstanding 2,000 shares of $100, 6 percent preferred stock and 12,000 shares of $25 par value common stock. The preferred stock is cumulative and nonparticipating. During a seven-year period the corporation paid out the following amounts in dividends:

$$
\begin{array}{lr}
1960\ldots\ldots\ldots\ldots\ldots\ldots\ldots\ldots\ldots\ldots\ldots\ldots & \$30,000 \\
1961\ldots\ldots\ldots\ldots\ldots\ldots\ldots\ldots\ldots\ldots\ldots\ldots & -0- \\
1962\ldots\ldots\ldots\ldots\ldots\ldots\ldots\ldots\ldots\ldots\ldots\ldots & -0- \\
1963\ldots\ldots\ldots\ldots\ldots\ldots\ldots\ldots\ldots\ldots\ldots\ldots & 30,000 \\
1964\ldots\ldots\ldots\ldots\ldots\ldots\ldots\ldots\ldots\ldots\ldots\ldots & 36,000 \\
1965\ldots\ldots\ldots\ldots\ldots\ldots\ldots\ldots\ldots\ldots\ldots\ldots & 48,000 \\
1966\ldots\ldots\ldots\ldots\ldots\ldots\ldots\ldots\ldots\ldots\ldots\ldots & 42,000 \\
\end{array}
$$

Required:

1. *a)* Prepare a form with columnar headings as follows:

Year	Total Paid to Preferred	Balance Due Preferred	Total Paid to Common	Dividend per Share Preferred	Dividend per Share Common	Percent on Par Preferred	Percent on Par Common

b) In the first column enter the years 1960 through 1966. Then determine and fill in the information opposite each year in the remaining columns. (In the last two columns indicate the percent on par paid in dividends on each class of stock. Assume no dividends were in arrears in 1960 and in any year in which the corporation paid a dividend, it always paid the full amount of current and back dividends due the preferred stockholders before paying anything to the common stockholders.)

2. Prepare and complete a second form according to the foregoing directions under the assumption that rather than being cumulative and nonparticipating, the preferred stock of the corporation is noncumulative and nonparticipating.

3. Prepare and complete a third form according to the foregoing directions under the assumption the preferred stock of the corporation is cumulative and fully participating.

Problem 16–3A

Palmtop Corporation has had outstanding since it was organized 100,000 shares of $5 par value common stock and 1,000 shares of $100 par value, 6 percent preferred stock. The current year's and two prior years' dividends have not been paid on the preferred stock. However, the company has recently prospered, and the board of directors wants to know how much cash will be required for dividends if a $0.50 per share dividend is paid on the common stock.

Required:

Prepare a schedule for the board of directors showing the amounts of cash required for dividends to each class of stockholders under each of the following assumptions:

a) The preferred stock is noncumulative and nonparticipating.
b) The preferred stock is cumulative and nonparticipating.
c) The preferred stock is cumulative and fully participating.
d) The preferred stock is cumulative and participating to 9 percent.

Problem 16–4A

EZ Corporation has outstanding 10,000 shares of $10 par value common stock, all owned by four men who are also the corporation's board of directors. The company needs $150,000 additional capital for expansion purposes which its owners are unable to supply. Consequently, they are considering the issuance of 1,500 shares of $100 par value, 6 percent, cumulative and nonparticipating preferred stock to gain the additional capital, and they have asked you to prepare a report showing the return to the two classes of stockholders from the following amounts of before-tax profit:

a) $12,500 or a 5 percent before-tax return on the $250,000 invested.
b) $25,000 or a 10 percent before-tax return on the $250,000 invested.
c) $37,500 or a 15 percent before-tax return on the $250,000 invested.
d) $50,000 or a 20 percent before-tax return on the $250,000 invested.

Required:
1. Prepare a form with columnar headings as follows:

		After-Tax Earnings		Preferred Dividends		Common Dividends	
Before-Tax Earnings	Federal Income Taxes	Amount	Percent Return on Investment	Total Paid to Preferred	Percent Return on Investment	Total Paid to Common	Percent Return on Investment

2. Enter the amounts of before-tax profit in the first column.
3. Calculate the federal income tax applicable to each level of earnings and enter in the second column. (Corporations are required (1965) to pay a 22 percent federal income tax on the first $25,000 of their earnings and 48 percent on any earnings over $25,000. Thus, the federal income tax on $37,500 of earnings is 22 percent of the first $25,000 plus 48 per cent on the next $12,500, or a total of $11,500.)
4. Complete the information of the form under the assumption that all after-tax earnings are paid out in dividends.
5. Explain why at any pretax earnings level above $25,000 the after-tax rate of return to the common stockholders of this corporation is greater than the after-tax rate of return earned by the corporation as a whole.

Problem 16–5A

Hunt and Isley have operated Mesa Sales for a number of years as partners sharing losses and gains in a 3 to 2 ratio. They have just entered into an agreement with Cecil Jarvis to reorganize their business into a corporation to be known as Mesa Sales, Inc. Just prior to the reorganization a balance sheet of the partnership appeared as follows:

MESA SALES
Balance Sheet, February 23, 19 —

Assets			*Liabilities*		
Cash........................		$ 3,050	Accounts payable.............		$ 9,700
Accounts receivable..........$15,150			Mortgage payable............		20,000
Allowance for bad debts....	325	14,825	Total Liabilities............		$29,700
Merchandise inventory.......		38,375			
Store equipment............$11,875			*Owner Equity*		
Accumulated depreciation..	4,750	7,125			
Building...................$42,000			Gary Hunt, capital..........$42,925		
Accumulated depreciation..	10,500	31,500	Ray Isley, capital.............	27,250	
Land......................		5,000	Total Owner Equity........		70,175
Total Assets.............		$99,875	Total Equities............		$99,875

The partners and Jarvis agree that—
1. The partnership is to issue 10,000 shares of $10 par value common stock.
2. The partnership books are to be retained and used by the corporation.

3. The assets of the partnership are to be revalued as follows:
   a) The allowance for bad debts is to be increased $1,500, after which $850 of accounts known to be uncollectible are to be written off as bad debts.
   b) The merchandise inventory is to be written down to $35,000 to allow for shopworn and damaged merchandise.
   c) The recorded value of the building is to be increased to the building's replacement cost, $50,000; and the accumulated depreciation on the building is to be increased to show the building to be one-fourth depreciated.
   d) The recorded value of the land is to be increased to its present estimated market value of $10,000.
4. The stock of the new corporation is to be issued in 100-share units. Consequently, after the assets and partnership equities are revalued, each partner is to withdraw sufficient cash from the partnership to reduce his Capital account to the nearest $1,000 multiple.
5. After the Capital account balances are reduced to the nearest $1,000 multiple, the partners are to accept shares of the corporation's stock equal in par value to their equities.
6. The remaining stock is to be purchased by Cecil Jarvis for cash.

Required:
1. Prepare general journal entries to change the partnership to a corporation, giving effect to the foregoing provisions.
2. Prepare a balance sheet for the new corporation.

DECISION PROBLEM 16—POTTER ENTERPRISES, INC.

Tom Potter has developed a new technique for improving low-yield oil well production. He has patented the process so that others may not use it without royalty payments to the patent holder. Mr. Potter employed a firm of geophysicists and petroleum engineers to test his process and to estimate the income potential of its commercial use. This firm estimates an annual $60,000 after-tax income with prospects of increasing this amount materially as the process becomes better known.

Nolle, Graber & Associates, investment bankers, have been consulted on plans for raising the capital considered necessary to launch the new enterprise. The following data appear reliable:

a) The new firm, to be known as Potter Enterprises, Inc., will need $500,000 total capital to exploit the new process fully.
b) It is recognized that considerable risk will attach to investments in the new firm, which is generally true of most promotional ventures.
c) Sufficient asset security and reasonable income prospects should support the sale of 6 percent preferential stock at par value up to $200,000.
d) Mr. Potter and his immediate associates desire to retain voting control over the firm, but are unable to raise more than $250,000 of the required capital. The $250,000 includes $50,000 allowed Mr. Potter for his patent rights, his consultants' fees, etc.

e) The investment banking firm would be willing to invest up to $100,000 under the following conditions: $60,000 if the projected annual after-tax income is at least 15 percent; $100,000 if the projected return is 20 percent or more.

Prepare a report giving the following: (1) A capitalization plan using preferred and common stock and stating the planned distribution of the common stock; (2) a projection of the return on common stock using the $60,000 estimated annual after-tax net income; (3) the percentage of voting control to be retained by Potter and associates under your plan; and (4) the leverage which would accrue to common stockholders if the actual net income for the first year of operations were $55,000, and for the second year, $96,000.

Corporations:
Stock Transactions

THE REORGANIZATION of the partnership of Hill, Dale, and Knob into Apex Corporation was used in Chapter 16 to illustrate the formation of a corporation through the reorganization of a partnership. The situation presented was a simple one, and a minimum of entries were used in recording it. This chapter introduces additional situations commonly encountered when corporations are organized and their stock is sold.

AUTHORIZATION OF STOCK

A corporation is authorized in its charter to issue a certain amount of stock. The stock may be of one kind, common stock, or both common and preferred stock may be authorized; but regardless, the corporation may issue only the amount of each authorized by its charter. Often a corporation will secure an authorization to issue more stock than it plans to sell at the time it is organized. This enables the corporation to expand at any time in its future through the sale of the additional stock, and without the need of applying to the state for the right to issue more stock. For example, a corporation needing $300,000 to begin its operations may secure the right to issue $500,000 of stock, but then issue only $300,000 of the stock, keeping the remainder until a future date when it may wish to sell the stock and expand without applying to the state for the right to issue more stock.

At the time a corporation receives its charter, it is common practice to make memorandum entries in the accounts to show the amounts of each class of stock authorized, as follows:

Common Stock

Date	Explanation	F	Debit	Credit	Balance
Authorized on June 10, 19—, to issue			*1,000 shares of $100 par value common stock.*		

Preferred Stock

Date	Explanation	F	Debit	Credit	Balance
Authorized on June 10, 19—, to issue			*1,000 shares of $100 par value preferred stock.*		

SELLING STOCK FOR CASH

When stock is sold for cash and immediately issued, an entry in general journal form like the following is commonly used to record the sale and issuance:

June	15	Cash............................		75,000.00	
		Common Stock...............			75,000.00
		Sold and issued 750 shares of $100 par value common stock.			

And after the entry is posted the Common Stock account appears as follows:

Common Stock

Date	Explanation	F	Debit	Credit	Balance
Authorized on June 10, 19—, to issue			*1,000 shares of $100 par value common stock.*		
19—					
June 15				*75,000.00*	*75,000.00*

AUTHORIZED AND ISSUED STOCK ON THE BALANCE SHEET

After authorized stock has been sold and issued, it is common practice to show on the balance sheet both the stock authorized and the stock issued, as follows:

```
                    STOCKHOLDERS' EQUITY

Preferred stock, $100 par value per
  share, authorized 1,000 shares, is-
  sued 650 shares . . . . . . . . .     $65,000
Common stock, $100 par value per share,
  authorized 1,000 shares, issued 750
  shares. . . . . . . . . . . . . .      75,000
         Total stock issued. . . . . .          $140,000
```

STOCK SUBSCRIPTIONS

Often corporations sell their stock for cash and immediately issue the stock. Often, too, when stock is first sold, especially in the organization of a new corporation, it is sold by means of *subscriptions*. When stock is sold by means of subscriptions, a person wishing to become a stockholder signs a subscription blank or a subscription list on which he subscribes to a certain number of shares and agrees to pay for the stock either in one amount or in installments. When the subscription is accepted by the corporation, it becomes a contract.

When a prospective stockholder signs a corporation's subscription list or one of its subscription blanks, and the corporation accepts the subscription, the corporation acquires an asset, the right to receive payment from the subscriber; and at the same time, its stockholder equity is increased by the amount the subscriber agrees to pay. The increase in assets is recorded in an account for common stock, called *Subscriptions Receivable Common Stock*; and the increase in stockholder equity is recorded in an account for common stock, called *Common Stock Subscribed*. Both accounts are of a temporary nature. The subscriptions receivable will be turned into cash or other assets when the subscriber pays for his stock. Likewise, when payment is completed, the stock subscribed will be issued and will become outstanding stock. Normally subscribed stock is not issued until paid for.

If a corporation receives subscriptions to both common and preferred stock, separate subscriptions receivable and stock subscribed accounts must be kept for each. If the number of subscribers becomes large, the subscriptions receivable accounts often become controlling accounts that control subsidiary Subscribers' Ledgers that have an account with each subscriber. The controlling account for each class of subscriptions receivable and its Subscribers' Ledger operate in the same manner as, for example, the Accounts Receivable controlling account and the Accounts Receivable Ledger discussed in a previous chapter.

When unpaid subscriptions exist on the balance sheet date, the intention is normally to collect the amounts within a relatively short period. Therefore, unpaid subscriptions normally appear on the balance sheet as current assets under the title "Subscriptions Receivable, Common Stock" or "Subscriptions Receivable Preferred Stock."

SALE OF STOCK THROUGH SUBSCRIPTIONS, WITH COLLECTIONS IN INSTALLMENTS

Corporations selling stock through subscriptions may collect the subscriptions in one amount or in installments. To illustrate the sale of stock through subscriptions collected in installments, assume that on June 7, 19—, Northgate Corporation received a charter authorizing the issuance of 10,000 shares of $10 par value common stock. On the same day it accepted subscriptions to 5,000 of the shares at par, under subscription contracts calling for a 10 percent down payment to accompany the subscriptions and the balance in two equal installments due in 30 and 60 days.

The subscriptions were recorded with the following entry:

June	7	Subscriptions Receivable, Common Stock....	50,000.00	
		Common Stock Subscribed.............		50,000.00
		Accepted subscriptions to 5,000 shares of common stock at par.		

Receipt of the down payments and the two installment payments were recorded with these entries:

June	7	Cash..	5,000.00	
		Subscriptions Receivable, Common Stock		5,000.00
		Collected the down payments on the common stock subscribed.		
July	6	Cash..	22,500.00	
		Subscriptions Receivable, Common Stock		22,500.00
		Collected the first installment payments on the common stock subscribed.		

Aug.	5	*Cash*	*22,500.00*	
		Subscriptions Receivable, Common Stock		*22,500.00*
		Collected the second installment payments		
		on the common stock subscribed.		

When stock is sold through subscriptions, the stock is paid for as soon as the subscriptions are paid in full; and as soon as the subscriptions are paid, the stock is issued. The entry to record the issuance of the Northgate common stock appeared as follows:

Aug.	5	*Common Stock Subscribed*	*50,000.00*	
		Common Stock		*50,000.00*
		Issued 5,000 shares of common stock sold		
		through subscriptions.		

MINIMUM LEGAL CAPITAL

Par value is an arbitrary value that a corporation places on a share of its stock at the time of authorization. Normally a corporation may choose a par value of any amount; but stocks with pars of $100, $50, $25, $10, $5, and $1 are common. Early corporation laws required all stocks to have a par value. Today, all states permit the issuance of stock having no-par value.

When a corporation issues par value stock, the par value is printed on each certificate and is used in accounting for the stock. Also, in many states, when a corporation issues par value stock, it establishes for itself a *minimum legal capital* equal to the par value of the issued stock. For example, if a corporation issues 1,000 shares of $100 par value stock, it establishes for itself a minimum legal capital of $100,000.

Laws establishing minimum legal capital normally require stockholders to invest in a corporation, assets equal in value to minimum legal capital or be liable to the corporation's creditors for the deficiency. In other words, these laws require stockholders to give a corporation par value for its stock or be liable for the deficiency. In addition, when corporation laws set minimum legal capital requirements, they normally also make illegal any payments to stockholders for dividends or their equivalent when these payments reduce owner equity below minimum legal capital.

Corporation laws governing minimum legal capital were written in an effort to protect corporation creditors. The authors of these laws reasoned somewhat as follows: A corporation's creditors may look only to the assets of the corporation for satisfaction of their claims. Consequently, when a corporation is organized, its stockholders should provide it with a fund of assets equal to its minimum legal capital. Thereafter, this fund of assets should remain with the corporation and should not be returned to the stockholders in any form until all creditor claims are paid.

Although par value helps establish minimum legal capital and is used in accounting for par value stock, it does not establish a stock's worth or the price at which a corporation must issue the stock. If purchasers are willing to pay more than par, a corporation may sell and issue its stock at a price above par. Likewise, in some states, if purchasers will not pay par, a corporation may issue its stock at a price below par. Normally a corporation's potential earning power and the supply of investment funds determine whether purchasers will pay par, less than par, or more than par.

STOCK PREMIUMS AND DISCOUNTS

Premiums. When a corporation sells and issues stock at a price above its par value, the stock is said to be issued at a *premium*. A premium is an amount in excess of par paid by the purchasers of newly issued stock. For example, if a corporation sells and issues its $100 par value stock for $109 per share, the $9 in excess of par is called a "premium." Although a premium is an amount in excess of par paid by purchasers of newly issued stock, it is not considered a profit to the issuing corporation. Rather a premium is part of the investment of the stockholders who pay more than par for their stock. When stock is issued at a premium, stockholders invest more than the legal minimum of capital; consequently since premiums are amounts in excess of minimum legal capital, they should be accounted for separately from the par value of the stock to which they apply.

Some states permit the payment of a "dividend" from amounts received as stock premiums, but others do not. Nevertheless, and regardless of legality, accountants are opposed to calling such a distribution a "dividend." Their opposition stems from the fact that such a distribution is obviously a return of invested capital and should be labeled clearly as such. Calling it a "dividend" might lead an uninformed person to believe the payment was from earnings.

Discounts. In many states it is illegal for a corporation to sell and issue stock for less than par. However, in some states, stock may be sold for less than par. When a corporation sells and issues its stock at a price below par, the stock is said to be issued at a *discount*. For example, a corporation that sells and issues its $100 par value stock at $89 per share is said to issue the stock at a discount of $11 per share. A discount is the difference between par and the price paid when the price is less than par. When stock is sold at a discount, the discount is not considered a loss to the issuing corporation, rather, the corporation's stockholders are investing less than minimum legal capital. In such cases, in most states, the stockholders are contingently liable for the investment deficiency. This contingent liability is called a *discount liability*.

Careful notice should be taken that stockholders owning stock issued at a discount are not contingently liable to the issuing corporation; they are contingently liable to the corporation's creditors. Insofar as the issuing corporation is concerned, stock issued at a discount is paid for in full. However, if at any time after stock is issued at a discount the issuing corporation becomes bankrupt, its creditors may in many states force the current owners to pay to the corporation the amount of the discount, if the current owners knew at the time they purchased the stock that it was originally issued at a discount. The money paid is then used for the satisfaction of the creditor claims. It should be noted from the foregoing that if the ownership of specific shares originally issued at a discount can be traced from one owner to the next, and the owners knew of the discount, then the discount liability follows the stock from owner to owner.

Since a stock discount represents an investment deficiency, it should be accounted for separately from the par value of the stock to which it applies.

ENTRIES FOR STOCK SOLD AT A PREMIUM

When, for example, common stock is sold at a premium and the stock is immediately issued, the transaction may be recorded as follows:

Dec.	*1*	*Cash*......................................	*110,000.00*	
		Common Stock........................		*100,000.00*
		Premium on Common Stock...........		*10,000.00*
		To record the sale of 1,000 shares of $100 par value common stock at $110 per share.		

If subscriptions are taken for stock at a premium, the subscriptions collected, and the stock issued, the following entries are used:

Dec.	*2*	*Subscriptions Receivable, Common Stock*...	*10,250.00*	
		Common Stock Subscribed.............		*10,000.00*
		Premium on Common Stock...........		*250.00*
		Accepted subscriptions to 100 shares of $100 par value common stock at $102.50 per share.		

Jan.	2	Cash...	10,250.00	
		Subscriptions Receivable, Common Stock		10,250.00
		Collected subscriptions in full.		
	2	Common Stock Subscribed..................	10,000.00	
		Common Stock..........................		10,000.00
		Issued stock to fully paid subscribers.		

Notice that the subscriptions receivable account is debited at the time the subscription is accepted for the sum of the stock's par value and premium; this is the amount the subscribers agree to pay. Notice, too, that the stock subscribed account is credited for par value and that the premium is credited to a premium account at the time the subscriptions are accepted.

ENTRIES FOR STOCK SOLD AT A DISCOUNT

Since in many states it is illegal to sell and issue stock at a discount and in those states in which stock may be sold and issued at a discount a discount liability attaches to such stock, corporations seldom sell and issue stock at a discount. However, if stock is sold for cash at a discount and immediately issued, the transaction may be recorded with an entry similar to the following:

Mar.	5	Cash...	8,900.00	
		Discount on Common Stock..................	1,100.00	
		Common Stock..........................		10,000.00
		Sold and issued 100 shares of $100 par value common stock at $89 per share.		

If stock is subscribed at a discount and later paid for and issued, the following series of entries may be used to record the transactions:

Mar.	10	Subscriptions Receivable, Common Stock.....	950.00	
		Discount on Common Stock..................	50.00	
		Common Stock Subscribed...............		1,000.00
		Accepted subscriptions to ten shares of $100 par value common stock at $95 per share.		

Apr.	*10*	*Cash.................................*	*950.00*	
		Subscriptions Receivable, Common Stock		*950.00*
		Collected subscriptions in full.		
	10	*Common Stock Subscribed..................*	*1,000.00*	
		Common Stock..........................		*1,000.00*
		Issued stock to fully paid subscribers.		

PREMIUMS, DISCOUNTS, AND STOCK SUBSCRIBED ON THE BALANCE SHEET

Stock premiums and discounts help measure the capital contributions of stockholders, and on the balance sheet are commonly added to or are deducted from the stock to which they relate, as in Illustration 103.

Illustration 103
SHAREHOLDERS' EQUITY

```
Preferred stock, $100 par value, 6 percent
  cumulative and nonparticipating, 2,500
  shares authorized, 1,500 shares issued. . . . .$150,000
    Add premium on preferred stock. . . . . . . .   7,500
    Amount paid in. . . . . . . . . . . . . .            $157,500
Common stock, $10 par value, 25,00 shares
  authorized, 20,000 shares issued. . . . . . .$200,000
Unissued common stock subscribed, 5,000 shares. .  50,000
    Total common stock issued and subscribed. .$250,000
    Add premium on common stock . . . . . . . .  20,000
    Deduct discount on common stock . . . . . .  (2,500)
    Amount paid in and subscribed . . . . . .            267,500
        Total contributed capital . . . . . . .           $425,000
Retained earnings . . . . . . . . . . . . . .            123,000
        Total Shareholders' Equity. . . . . . .                   $548,000
```

Under the laws of some states a subscriber becomes a stockholder upon acceptance of his signed subscription contract, and under the laws of these states a subscriber receives all the rights of a stockholder as soon as his subscription contract is accepted, even though the stock is not paid for and the stock certificate is not issued. Consequently, if stock is subscribed but unissued on the balance sheet date, the amount of such stock should be disclosed on the balance sheet as in Illustration 103.

PAR VALUE, BOOK VALUE, AND WORTH

As previously stated, par value is the arbitrary value that a corporation places on a share of its stock, and it has a legal significance in that it helps establish minimum legal capital. However, since stock may be issued at a premium or at a discount, even in a newly organized corporation a stock's par value may have little relation to its book value, its market value, or worth; and in an older corporation, after earnings or losses, a stock's par value may have still less relation. The lack of relation between par value and book value may be easily demonstrated with the stockholders' equity sections from the balance sheets of corporations A and B, which follow:

```
                           CORPORATION A

Common stock, par value $100, authorized and issued 1,000
    shares. . . . . . . . . . . . . . . . . . . . . . . . . $100,000
Retained earnings . . . . . . . . . . . . . . . . . . . .     50,000
         Total capital stock and retained earnings . . . . . . .      $150,000

                           CORPORATION B

Common stock, par value $100, authorized and issued 1,000
    shares. . . . . . . . . . . . . . . . . . . . . . . . . $100,000
Deficit . . . . . . . . . . . . . . . . . . . . . . . . .  ( 30,000)
         Total capital stock and deficit . . . . . . . . . . .        $70,000
```

Notice that the common stocks of both corporations have $100 par values. However, Corporation A has retained earnings of $50,000, and the book value per share of its stock is $150. At the same time, Corporation B has a deficit of $30,000, and the book value per share of its stock is only $70. This is an $80 difference in book values for stocks, the par values of which are the same.

Although it cannot be so easily demonstrated, the difference in market values of these stocks is probably much more than $80 per share. This is because earnings affect market value, and obviously the earnings of these two corporations have not been equal. Corporation A has retained earnings of $50,000; its operations have apparently been profitable. On the other hand, Corporation B's operations have apparently been unprofitable because it has a deficit of $30,000.

NO-PAR STOCK

Once all stocks were required to have a par value; but today, all states permit the issuance of so-called no-par stock or stock without par value. The primary advantage of no-par stock is that, since it does not have a par value, it may be issued at any price without a discount liability attaching.

When no-par-value stock is issued, the issuance may be recorded in one of two ways. The choice depends upon the laws of the state of incorporation and the wishes of the board of directors. Some state laws require that a corporation must credit the entire proceeds from the sale of no-par stock to a no-par stock account. In other states, when no-par stock is issued, the board may choose to place a *stated value* on the stock. When a stated value is placed on no-par stock and the stock is sold for more than stated value, the no-par stock account is credited for stated value and the remainder is credited to a contributed capital account called, for instance, "Contributed Capital in Excess of Stated Value of No-Par Stock." To illustrate the two methods of recording no-par stock, assume that a corporation sells and issues 1,000 shares of its authorized no-par common stock at $42 per share.

If the corporation is organized in a state in which the entire amount received from the sale of no-par stock must be credited to a no-par stock account, it will record the sale as follows:

Sept.	20	Cash..	42,000.00	
		No-Par Common Stock.................		42,000.00
		To record the sale and issuance of 1,000 shares of no-par common stock at $42 per share.		

If the corporation is organized in a state in which the directors may place a stated value on no-par stock, accounting for the sale of the no-par stock is similar to accounting for par value stock. For example, if the directors place a stated value of $25 per share on the stock, its sale and issuance is recorded as follows:

Sept.	20	Cash..	42,000.00	
		No Par Common Stock.................		25,000.00
		Contributed Capital in Excess of Stated Value of No Par Stock..................		17,000.00
		To record the sale at $42 per share of 1,000 shares of no par stock having a stated value of $25 per share.		

From the foregoing it is obvious that when a stated value is placed on no-par stock, the accounting treatment for such stock is similar to that for par value stock. However, a sharp distinction should be made between a par value and a stated value; they are not synonymous. A par value is more formal than a stated value. A par value is established by a corporation at the time of its organization. It appears in the corporation's charter and normally can be changed only by an application to the state. A stated value is more flexible. The directors of a corporation establish a stock's stated value by resolution. Normally, at any time, they may also change it by passing an additional resolution.

NO-PAR STOCK AND LEGAL CAPITAL

State laws permitting the issuance of no-par stock vary as to minimum legal capital requirements for corporations issuing such stock. Most states require the entire amount received by a corporation from the sale of its no-par stock be considered minimum legal capital and as such be made unavailable for dividend payments. A few states permit a corporation issuing no-par stock to establish its minimum legal capital at the stock's stated value and to pay out as "dividends" any amount above stated value received from the sale of such stock.

EXCHANGING STOCK FOR ASSETS OTHER THAN CASH

Corporations often accept assets other than cash in exchange for their stock. When they do so, the transaction is recorded in somewhat the following manner:

Apr.	3	Machinery...............................	10,000.00	
		Buildings...............................	25,000.00	
		Land..................................	5,000.00	
		Common Stock........................		40,000.00
		Exchanged 400 shares of common stock at par for machinery, building, and land.		

When a corporation accepts assets other than cash for its stock, it is the duty of the board of directors to place a fair market value on the accepted assets. If the assets are fairly valued, such transactions are perfectly proper. Nevertheless, when par value stock is exchanged for assets other than cash and a discount is not recorded, outsiders may question the value placed on the assets and whether they are really worth the par value of the stock given. If the value of the assets is not equal to the par value of the stock exchanged, a discount should be recorded. However, such discounts are seldom recorded because as a rule, unless fraud is evident, courts will accept the judgment of a board of directors as to the value placed on assets taken in exchange for stock. Consequently, boards are prone to inflate the value of such assets in order, when necessary, to avoid recording a discount. Such inflation is unnecessary when no-par stock is exchanged for assets other than cash.

STOCK SPLITS

Sometimes, when a corporation's stock is selling at a high price, the corporation will call it in and issue two, three, four, five, or more new shares in the place of each old share previously outstanding. For example, a corporation having outstanding $100 par value stock selling for $375 a share may call in the old shares and issue to the stockholders two shares of $50 par, or four shares of $25 par, or ten shares of $10 par, or any number of shares of no-par stock in exchange for each $100 share formerly held. This is known as a *stock split* or a *stock split-up*, and its usual purpose is to effect a reduction in the market price of the stock and, consequently, to facilitate trading in the stock.

A stock split has no effect on total stockholders' equity, the equities of the individual stockholders, or on the balances of any of the contributed or retained capital accounts. Consequently, all that is required in recording a stock split is a memorandum entry in the stock account reciting the facts of the split. For example, such a memorandum might read, "Called in the outstanding $100 par value common stock and issued ten shares of $10 par value common stock for each old share previously outstanding."

STOCK DIVIDENDS

A stock dividend is a distribution by a corporation without consideration of shares of its own common stock to its common stockholders. Usually the distribution is prompted by a desire to give the stockholders some evidence of their interest in retained earnings without distributing cash or other corporation assets which the board of directors thinks it wise to retain in the business.

A clear distinction should be made between a cash dividend and a stock dividend. Cash is distributed in a cash dividend; and as was pointed out in a previous section, such a dividend reduces both assets and stockholders' equity. A stock dividend differs in that shares of the corporation's own stock, rather than cash, are distributed; and such a dividend has no effect on assets, total capital, or the amount of any stockholder's equity.

A stock dividend has no effect on corporation assets, total capital, and the amount of any stockholder's equity because such a dividend involves nothing more than a transfer of retained earnings to contributed capital. To illustrate this assume that Northwest Corporation has the following capital stock and retained earnings:

```
              CAPITAL STOCK AND RETAINED INCOME

Common stock, $100 par value, authorized 1,500
   shares, issued and outstanding 1,000 shares   $100,000
Capital contributed by stockholders in excess
   of the par value of their shares . . . . . .      8,000
      Total contributed captial. . . . . . . . .  $108,000
Retained earnings. . . . . . . . . . . . . . .      35,000
      Total contributed and retained capital .    $143,000
```

Assume further that on December 28 the directors of Northwest Corporation declared a 10 percent or 100-share stock dividend distributable on January 20 to the January 15 stockholders of record.

If the fair market value of Northwest Corporation's stock on December 28 is $150 per share, the following entries may be made to record the dividend declaration and distribution:

Dec.	28	*Retained Earnings*...........................	*15,000.00*	
		Common Stock Dividend Distributable....		*10,000.00*
		Premium on Common Stock.............		*5,000.00*
		To record the declaration of a 100-share common stock dividend.		
Jan.	20	*Common Stock Dividend Distributable*.......	*10,000.00*	
		Common Stock..........................		*10,000.00*
		To record the distribution of a 100-share common stock dividend.		

Note that the foregoing entries change $15,000 of stockholders' equity from retained earnings to contributed capital, or as it is commonly said, $15,000 of retained earnings are capitalized. Note also that the retained earnings capitalized are equal to the fair market value of the 100 shares issued ($150 × 100 shares = $15,000).

As previously pointed out, a stock dividend does not distribute funds from retained earnings to the stockholders, nor does it affect in any way the corporation assets. Likewise, it has no effect on total capital and on the individual equities of the stockholders. To illustrate these last points, assume that Johnson owned ten shares of Northwest Corporation's stock prior to the dividend. The corporation's total contributed and retained capital before the dividend and the book value of Johnson's ten shares were as follows:

Common stock (1,000 shares).....................$100,000
Premium on common stock......................   8,000
Retained earnings.............................   35,000
    Total contributed and retained capital.......$143,000

$143,000 ÷ 1,000 Shares Outstanding = $143 per Share Book Value
$143 × 10 = $1,430 for the Book Value of Johnson's Ten Shares

A 10 percent stock dividend gives a stockholder one new share for each ten shares previously held. Consequently, Johnson received one new share; and after the dividend, the contributed and retained capital of the corporation and the book value of Johnson's holdings are as follows:

```
Common stock (1,100 shares)....................$110,000
Premium on common stock.....................   13,000
Retained earnings..............................   20,000
      Total contributed and retained capital.......$143,000
```

$143,000 ÷ 1,100 Shares Outstanding = $130 per Share Book Value
$130 × 11 = $1,430 for the Book Value of Johnson's Eleven Shares

Before the stock dividend, Johnson owned 10/1,000 or 1/100 of the Northwest Corporation stock and his holdings had a $1,430 book value. After the dividend, he owned 11/1,100 or 1/100 of the corporation and his holdings still had a $1,430 book value. In other words, there was no effect on his equity other than that it was repackaged from ten units into eleven. Likewise, the only effect on corporation capital was a permanent transfer to contributed capital of $15,000 in retained earnings. Consequently, insofar as both the corporation and Johnson are concerned, there was no shift in equities or corporation assets.

Why Stock Dividends Are Distributed.   If a stock dividend has no effect on corporation assets and stockholder equities, other than to repackage the equities into more units, why are such dividends declared and distributed?

Insofar as a corporation is concerned, a stock dividend enables it to give its shareholders some evidence of their interest in retained earnings without the necessity of distributing corporation cash or other assets to them. Consequently, stock dividends are often declared by corporations that have used the funds from earnings in expanding and, consequently, do not feel they have sufficient cash with which to pay a cash dividend.

Stockholders also commonly benefit from a small stock dividend, although they own no greater share in the issuing corporation after the dividend than before. They benefit because, as a rule, a small stock dividend has little or no effect on the market price per share of the issuing corporation's stock. Consequently, since each stockholder has more shares after the dividend, if the price per share is unchanged, the total market value of his holdings is increased.

Amount of Retained Earnings Capitalized.   In the entry on page 494 retained earnings equal to the fair market value of the dividend stock were capitalized in recording the stock dividend. The reason for this is best explained by quoting the American Institute's Committee on Accounting Procedure, as follows:

. . . "a stock dividend does not, in fact, give rise to any change whatsoever in either the corporation's assets or its respective shareholders' proportionate interests therein. However, it cannot fail to be recognized that, merely as a consequence of the expressed purpose of the transaction and its characterization as a *dividend* in related notices to shareholders and the public at large, many recipients of stock dividends look upon them as distributions of corporate earnings and usually in an amount equivalent to the fair value of the additional shares received. Furthermore, it is to be presumed that such views of recipients are materially strengthened in those instances, which are by far the most numerous, where the issuances are so small in comparison with the shares previously outstanding that they do not have any apparent effect upon the share market price and, consequently, the market value of the shares previously held remains substantially unchanged. The committee therefore believes that where these circumstances exist the corporation should in the public interest account for the transaction by transferring from . . ." retained earnings to contributed capital "an amount equal to the fair value of the additional shares issued. Unless this is done, the amount of earnings which the shareholder may believe to have been distributed to him will be left, except to the extent otherwise dictated by legal requirements, in . . ." retained earnings and "subject to possible further similar stock issuances or cash distributions."[1]

The Committee on Accounting Procedure described a small stock dividend as being one of "say, 20% to 25% of the previously outstanding shares."[2]

Large Stock Dividend. Although a small stock dividend may have little or no effect on the market price of a company's shares, a large dividend normally does. Consequently, the Committee on Accounting Procedure has said in regard to a large stock dividend:

"Where the number of additional shares issued as a stock dividend is so great that it has, or may reasonably be expected to have, the effect of materially reducing the share market value, the committee believes that the implications and possible constructions discussed in the preceding paragraph are not likely to exist and that the transaction clearly partakes of the nature of a stock split-up. . . ." "Consequently, the committee considers that under such circumstances there is no need to capitalize . . ." retained earnings, "other than to the extent occasioned by legal requirements."[3]

Capitalizing retained earnings to the extent of legal requirements means in most states that a corporation may record a large dividend (over 25 percent) by debiting retained earnings and crediting the stock account for the par value of the shares issued.

Stock Dividends on the Balance Sheet. Since a stock dividend is "payable" in stock rather than in assets, it is not a liability to its issuing corporation. Therefore, if a balance sheet is prepared between the declaration and distribution dates of a stock dividend, the amount of the dividend distributable should appear thereon in the contributed capital section.

---

[1] *Accounting Research Bulletin No. 43*, "Restatement and Revision of Accounting Research Bulletins" (New York: American Institute of Certified Public Accountants, 1953), pp. 51 and 52.

[2] *Ibid.*, p. 52.

[3] *Ibid.*, p. 52.

STOCK CERTIFICATES AND THE TRANSFER OF STOCK

When an investor buys stock in a corporation, he receives a stock certificate as evidence of the shares purchased. Commonly, in a small corporation only one certificate is issued for each block of stock purchased, the one certificate may be for any number of shares. For example, the certificate of Illustration 104 is for 50 shares. Large corporations commonly use preprinted 100-share denomination certificates in addition to blank certificates that may be made out for any number of shares.

Illustration 104

Number
98

Shares
- 50 -

Incorporated under the laws of the State of Illinois

WESTFIELD PUBLISHING COMPANY

This Certifies that, _____ Robert Wetzel _____

is the owner of _____ - fifty - _____ fully paid and non-assessable $100.00 par value shares of the Common Capital Stock of the Westfield Publishing Company transferable on the books of the corporation in person or by duly authorized attorney upon surrender of this Certificate properly endorsed.

IN WITNESS WHEREOF the said company has caused this Certificate to be signed by its duly authorized officers and its corporate seal to be hereunto affixed this __10th__ day of __March__ , A. D. 19 **55** .

WESTFIELD PUBLISHING COMPANY

By _Perry A. Greenleaf_
President

ATTEST:
S. A. Small
Secretary

An owner of stock may transfer at will either part or all the shares represented by a stock certificate. To do so he completes the endorsement on the reverse side of the certificate and sends the certificate to the corporation secretary in a small corporation or to the corporation's transfer agent in a large one. For example, assume that Robert Wetzel, the owner of the certificate for 50 shares shown in Illustration 104, sells ten of the shares to William Morris. To do so Wetzel completes the endorsement on the back of the certificate, as shown in Illustration 105, signs his name in the presence of a witness, and sends it to the corporation secretary or transfer agent. The old certificate is canceled and retained and two new certificates are issued in its place. One for ten shares is sent to Morris and the other for 40 shares is sent to Wetzel.

Illustration 105
Stock Certificate (Reverse Side) Showing
Endorsement for Transferred Stock

For value received, _____ hereby sell, assign and transfer unto

William Morris

ten (10) _____ Shares of the
Capital Stock represented by the within Certificate and do hereby irrevocably constitute and appoint *Sylvia Wingard*
Attorney, to transfer the said stock on the books of the within-named Corporation,
with full power of substitution in the premises.

DATED *January 1, 1966*

Robert Wetzel

In presence of:

Charles Blackburn

Stock Certificate Book. When it is organized, a corporation must have
a supply of stock certificates printed. In a small corporation the certificates
often have stubs attached, and the certificates and stubs are bound in a
Stock Certificate Book in the manner of a checkbook. As each stock
certificate is issued, the name of its owner, the number of shares, and the
date of issuance are entered on a blank certificate, and the certificate is
signed by the proper corporation officials. At the same time, the name and
address of the stock owner, the number of shares, and the date are entered
on the certificate stub. The certificate is then removed and delivered to its
owner.

When stock is returned for transfer, the old certificate is marked
canceled, attached to its stub in the Stock Certificate Book, and one or
more new certificates are issued in its place. Consequently, as a result of
these procedures, the Stock Certificate Book of a small corporation
contains a current record of the shares owned by each stockholder.

If a small corporation issues both common and preferred stock, it uses
separate stock certificate books as well as separate stock accounts for each.

Transfer Agent and Registrar. A large corporation, one whose stock is
listed on a major stock exchange, must have a registrar and a transfer agent
who are assigned the responsibilities of transferring the corporation's stock,
keeping its stockholder records, and preparing the official lists of stockholders for stockholders' meetings and for payment of dividends.

Assigning the duties of transferring stock and keeping stockholder records to a transfer agent and a registrar helps insure that only the proper amount of stock is issued and that the stock records are honestly and accurately kept. Usually registrars and transfer agents are large banks or trust companies.

When the owner of stock in a corporation having a registrar and a transfer agent wishes to transfer his stock to a new owner, he completes the endorsement on the back of his certificate and, usually through a stockbroker, sends the certificate to the transfer agent. The transfer agent cancels the old certificate and issues one or more new certificates which he sends to the registrar. The registrar enters the transfer in the stockholder records and sends the new certificate or certificates to the proper owners.

Banks and trust companies acting as registrars and transfer agents commonly so act for a number of corporations; and consequently, are in a position to make use of punched card and electronic equipment in keeping stockholder records for each.

ACCOUNTING TREATMENT OF CORPORATION INCOME TAXES

As previously stated, of the three common types of business organizations, the corporation alone as a business unit is subject to federal income taxes. Single proprietorships and partnerships as business units are not required to pay federal income taxes and normally are not required to pay state income taxes. Insofar as federal tax laws are concerned and most states laws, the income of single proprietorships and partnerships is taxed as the personal income of the single proprietor or the partners.

Federal and, where applicable, state income taxes are an expense of doing business as a corporation. However, as a rule, no attempt is made to classify the expense on the income statement; rather it is commonly listed at the end of the statement as in Illustration 106.

On the work sheet prepared for a corporation, state and federal income taxes are commonly treated in the nature of an adjustment in the

---

Illustration 106

Section from a Corporation Income Statement Showing Treatment of Income Taxes

THE EXCEL MANUFACTURING COMPANY
Income Statement for Year Ended December 31, 19--

Revenue from sales:
  Sales $310,000

Income before state and federal income taxes	$ 78,700
Less: State and federal income taxes. . . .	32,600
Net Income.	$ 46,100

Adjustments columns as is shown in the work sheet on pages 616 and 617. When state and federal income taxes are so treated, after the work sheet is completed an adjusting entry like the following is used to record the taxes:

Dec.	*31*	*State and Federal Income Tax Expense*.......	*32,600.00*	
		State and Federal Income Taxes Payable...		*32,600.00*
		To record the liability for income taxes.		

QUESTIONS FOR CLASS DISCUSSION

1. What are the balance sheet classifications of the accounts: (*a*) Subscriptions Receivable Common Stock, (*b*) Common Stock Subscribed, (*c*) Premium on Common Stock, and (*d*) Discount on Common Stock?

2. What is a stock premium? What is a stock discount?

3. Differentiate between discount on stock and discount on a note given to a bank in order to borrow money.

4. Does a corporation earn a profit by selling its stock at a premium? Does it incur a loss by selling its stock at a discount?

5. Why do corporation laws make purchasers of stock at a discount contingently liable for the discount? To whom are such purchasers contingently liable?

6. On May 1 the Renolds Corporation received subscriptions to 1,000 shares of its $100 par value common stock at $105 per share. The subscription contract called for a 10 percent down payment to accompany the contract and the payment of the balance in two equal installments due in 30 and 60 days. Give the entries to record (*a*) the receipt of the subscription, (*b*) the receipt of the down payment, (*c*) the receipt of the installment payments, and (*d*) the issuance of the stock.

7. On April 3 the Morgan Corporation received subscriptions to 1,000 shares of its $100 par value common stock at $96 per share. The subscriptions contracts called for a 20 percent down payment to accompany the subscriptions contracts and the payment of the balance 30 days thereafter. Give the entries to record (*a*) the receipt of the subscriptions, (*b*) the receipt of the down payment, (*c*) the receipt of the balance due, and (*d*) the issuance of the stock.

8. What advantage is claimed for no-par stock?

9. On April 1 Mason Corporation sold and issued 1,000 shares of its no-par common stock for $63,000. No stated value was placed on the stock. Give the entry for the sale of the stock.

10. Assume that the Mason Corporation (Question 9) placed a stated value of $50 per share on its no-par stock. Give the entry for the sale of the stock.

11. What is the effect in terms of assets and stockholders' equity of the declaration and distribution of (*a*) a cash dividend and (*b*) a stock dividend?

12. What is the difference between a stock dividend and a stock split?
13. Courts have held that a dividend in the stock of the corporation distributing the dividend is not taxable income to its recipients. Why?
14. If a balance sheet is prepared between the date of declaration and the date of distribution of a dividend, how should the dividend be shown if it is to be distributed in (*a*) cash and (*b*) stock?
15. What are the duties and responsibilites of a corporation's registrar and transfer agent?

PROBLEMS

Problem 17–1

Royal Plaza Corporation was organized to construct and lease an apartment building. It received a charter granting the right to issue 2,000 shares of $100 par value, 6 percent, cumulative and nonparticipating, preferred stock and 200,000 shares of $10 par value common stock. It then completed the following additional transactions:

Mar. 3 Accepted subscriptions to 2,000 shares of preferred stock at $105 per share. The subscriptions were accompanied by 10 percent down payments.

3 Accepted subscriptions to 100,000 shares of common stock at $12.50 per share. Ten percent down payments accompanied the subscription contracts.

5 Exchanged 12,000 shares of common stock for land valued by the board of directors at $150,000.

5 Gave the promoters of the corporation 1,000 shares of common stock for their services in organizing the corporation. The board of directors placed a value of $12.50 per share on the stock.

6 Paid the engraver's bill for engraving and printing the stock certificates, $750.

Apr. 2 Received payment in full of the unpaid balance on the March 3 preferred subscriptions. Issued the stock.

2 Received payment in full of the unpaid balance on the March 3 common subscriptions. Issued the stock.

15 Accepted subscriptions and 10 percent down payments on 50,-000 shares of common stock at $12.75 per share.

Required:
1. Prepare general journal entries to record the foregoing transactions.
2. Prepare the stockholders' equity section of a balance sheet for the company as it would appear at the close of business on April 15.

Problem 17–2

Mulberry Corporation received a charter granting the right to issue 2,000 shares of $100 par value, 6 percent cumulative and nonparticipating, preferred stock and 20,000 shares of no-par common stock on which the board of directors voted to place a $10 per share stated value. The corporation then completed the following transactions involving stock:

Apr. 2 Accepted subscriptions to 1,000 shares of preferred stock at $97 per share. The subscription contracts were accompanied by 10 percent down payments.

Apr. 3 Accepted subscription contracts to 15,000 shares of common stock at $12 per share. The contracts were accompanied by 25 percent down payments.

9 Issued 500 shares of common stock to each of the two promoters of the corporation for their services in organizing and promoting the business. The shares were valued at $12 each.

May 2 Collected the balance due on the preferred stock and issued the stock.

3 Collected in full the subscriptions to 10,000 of the common shares subscribed on April 3, and collected $6 per share from the subscribers to the remaining 5,000 shares. Issued the stock of the fully paid subscribers.

15 Exchanged 2,500 shares of common stock for land on which the board of directors placed a $30,000 value.

31 Sold and immediately issued 1,500 shares of common stock at $12.50 per share.

Required:

1. Open T-accounts for Cash; Subscriptions Receivable Preferred Stock; Subscriptions Receivable Common Stock; Land; Organization Costs; Preferred Stock; Discount on Preferred Stock; Preferred Stock Subscribed; No-Par Common Stock; Excess Contributed Over Stated Value, No-Par Common Stock; and No-Par Common Stock Subscribed.

2. Enter the transactions directly in the T-accounts.

3. Prepare a classified balance sheet for Mulberry Corporation as of May 31.

Problem 17–3

On June 27, 1966, and again on December 28 Mesa Corporation declared the regular $3 per share semiannual dividend on its preferred stock and a $0.60 per share dividend on its common stock. These were the only dividends declared by the corporation during the year. The December 28 dividends were unpaid on December 31 when the stockholders' equity in the corporation appeared as follows:

Stockholders' Equity

Preferred stock, $100 par value, 6 percent cumulative and nonparticipating, 5,000 shares authorized, 2,500 shares issued	...........$250,000	
Add: Premium on preferred stock	 12,500	
Amount paid in		$ 262,500
Common stock, $10 par value, 100,000 shares authorized, 60,000 shares issued	.........$600,000	
Add: Premium on common stock	 120,000	
Amount paid in		720,000
Total contributed capital		$ 982,500
Retained earnings		223,000
Total stockholders' equity		$1,205,500

During 1967 the corporation completed the following stock-related transactions:

Jan. 20   Paid to the January 15 stockholders of record the dividends declared on December 28 of the previous year.

Mar. 15   Accepted subscriptions to 10,000 shares of common stock at $16 per share. Twenty-five percent down payments accompanied the subscription contracts.

Apr. 14   Received the balance due on the common stock subscriptions of March 15 and issued the stock.

June 26   Declared the regular $3 per share semiannual dividend on the preferred stock and a $0.60 per share dividend on the common stock.

July 20   Paid to the July 15 stockholders of record the dividends declared on June 26.

Oct. 24   Declared a 10 percent common stock dividend distributable on November 20 to the November 15 stockholders of record. The October 24 stock market quotation for Mesa Corporation common stock was $16.50 per share, and the board of directors voted to use this quotation in recording the dividend.

Nov. 20   Distributed the stock dividend declared on October 24.

Dec. 29   Declared the regular $3 per share semiannual dividend on the preferred stock and a $0.55 per share dividend on the common stock.

Required:

1. Prepare general journal entries to record the foregoing transactions.
2. Gary Sears purchased 100 shares of Mesa Corporation common stock on June 12, 1966, becoming a stockholder of record on June 23. Since becoming a stockholder, he has sold none of his Mesa Corporation stock. If he continues to hold this stock until after the December 29, 1967, dividend is paid, will his cash from dividends declared by the corporation during 1967 exceed the cash he received from dividends declared by the corporation during 1966? Present figures to prove your answer.

Problem 17-4

Deeplake Corporation is a rapidly growing and profitable young company. During the five years of its existence it has used all assets from earnings in expanding and has not declared a dividend. Consequently, at its January 18 meeting the board of directors, feeling that the corporation should distribute to its stockholders some evidence of its prosperity, but recognizing the corporation needed all its cash in further expansion moves, voted to distribute a 5 percent stock dividend on February 25 to its February 20 stockholders of record.

On January 18 Deeplake Corporation's stock was selling at $8 per share, and on that date the capital section of its balance sheet appeared as follows:

Stockholders' Equity

Common stock, $5 par value, authorized 500,000
   shares, issued and outstanding 300,000 shares..$1,500,000
Premium on common stock.....................   225,000
    Total contributed capital...................$1,725,000
Retained earnings.............................   543,000
    Total stockholders' equity.................$2,268,000

Required:

1. Prepare entries to record the declaration and distribution of the dividend.
2. Prepare the stockholder equity section of the corporation's February 25 balance sheet as it will appear after the dividend distribution.
3. Harold Burton owned 500 shares of Deeplake Corporation stock on February 20. Present a calculation of the book value of his holdings before the dividend and another calculation of the book value after the dividend.

Problem 17–5

Salt River Corporation received a charter granting the right to issue 2,500 shares of 6 percent, cumulative and nonparticipating, $100 par value, preferred stock and 50,000 shares of $10 par value common stock. During the first day of its existence the corporation completed a number of transactions, and at the end of the day prepared the following trial balance:

SALT RIVER CORPORATION

Trial Balance, March 31, 19—

Cash	*$133,500*	
Subscriptions receivable preferred stock	*84,000*	
Subscriptions receivable common stock	*200,000*	
Land	*52,500*	
Preferred stock		*$ 50,000*
Premium on preferred stock		*7,500*
Preferred stock subscribed		*100,000*
Common stock		*50,000*
Premium on common stock		*62,500*
Common stock subscribed		*200,000*
	$470,000	*$470,000*

Required:

Reproduce in general journal form the entries that resulted in the foregoing trial balance. Assume that (1) all transactions in each class of stock were at the same price per share, (2) the outstanding preferred stock was issued without subscriptions for the land, and (3) the outstanding common stock was issued without subscriptions for cash.

CLASS EXERCISE

Exercise 17–1

J. J. Bonzer, Inc., was incorporated in 1959 to take over the going business of J. J. Bonzer, a single proprietorship. At the time of incorporation it was authorized to issue 15,000 shares of $10 par value common stock, of which 10,000 were immediately issued. On March 1 of the current year the president of the corporation, J. J. Bonzer, owned 9,000 of the corporation's 10,000 outstanding shares; and on that date, in order to supply the corporation with additional capital, he bought at $12 per share the 5,000 shares of previously unissued stock. After the sale was recorded, the bookkeeper prepared the following statement showing stockholders' equity in the corporation:

J. J. BONZER, INC.
Statement of Stockholders' Equity, March 1, 19—

Common stock, $10 par value, 15,000 shares
* authorized and issued.........................$150,000*
Premium on common stock...................... 10,000
* Total contributed capital....................$160,000*
Retained earnings................................. 48,500
*   Total Stockholders' Equity...............$208,500*

Upon hearing of the sale to the president, the minority stockholders protested their rights had been ignored and they had suffered a loss as a result. The president acknowledged their protest and agreed to pay to the minority stockholders the book value of their loss.

Required:
1. Name the right of the minority stockholders that was ignored.
2. Prepare a statement showing the calculation of the book value of the loss suffered by the minority stockholders.

ALTERNATE PROBLEMS

Problem 17–1A
Valley Ridge Corporation was organized to manufacture a mechanical product. It received a charter granting the right to issue 1,000 shares of $100 par value, 7 percent cumulative and nonparticipating, preferred stock and 50,000 shares of $10 par value common stock. It then completed the following transactions involving stock:

Mar. 1 Accepted subscription contracts and $107,500 in down payments on 30,000 shares of common stock at $10.75 per share. The contracts called for one third of the subscription price on acceptance of the contracts and the balance in 30 days.

   2 Accepted subscription contracts and $34,000 in down payments on 1,000 shares of preferred stock at $102 per share. The contracts called for one-third down and the balance in 30 days.

  25 Exchanged 5,000 shares of common stock for land valued by the board of directors at $52,500.

  25 Gave the corporation's lawyers 500 shares of common stock, valued at $5,250, in full for their services in securing the corporation charter and getting the corporation organized.

  31 Received the balance due on the March 1 common stock subscriptions. Issued the stock.

Apr. 1 Received the balance due on the preferred stock subscriptions of March 2. Issued the stock.

  30 Received one-third down payments and subscription contracts for 12,000 shares of common stock at $9.75 per share. The contracts called for one third down and the balance in 30 days.

Required:
1. Prepare general journal entries to record the foregoing transactions.
2. Prepare the stockholders' equity section of a balance sheet for the company as it would appear on April 30.

Problem 17–2A

Glenn Oak Corporation was organized to construct and operate a factory. It received a charter which authorizes it to issue 2,500 shares of $100 par value, 6 percent cumulative and nonparticipating, preferred stock and 25,000 shares of no-par common stock on which the board of directors voted to place a $5 stated value. After receiving the charter the corporation completed the following transactions involving stock:

Mar. 10   Accepted subscriptions to 2,000 shares of preferred stock at $97.50 per share and to 20,000 shares of common stock at $12 per share. Each subscription contract was accompanied by a 10 percent down payment.

   10   Exchanged 2,000 shares of common stock for a plant site upon which the board of directors placed a $24,000 value.

   10   Issued 500 shares of common stock at $12 per share to the corporation's promoters for their services in organizing and promoting the business.

Apr. 9   Collected the balance due on the preferred stock subscriptions and issued the stock.

    9   Collected the balance due on the common stock subscriptions and issued the stock.

   30   Accepted subscriptions, accompanied by 10 percent down payments, to 2,000 shares of common stock at $12.50 per share.

Required:

1. Open T-accounts for Cash; Subscriptions Receivable Preferred Stock; Subscriptions Receivable Common Stock; Land; Organization Costs; Preferred Stock; Discount on Preferred Stock; Preferred Stock Subscribed; No-Par Common Stock; Excess Contributed Over Stated Value, No-Par Common Stock; and No-Par Common Stock Subscribed.
2. Enter the transactions directly in the T-accounts.
3. Prepare a classified balance sheet for Glen Oak Corporation.

Problem 17–3A

On December 31 of last year the stockholders' equity section from Phoenix Corporation's balance sheet appeared as follows:

Stockholders' Equity

Preferred stock, $100 par value, 6 percent cumulative and nonparticipating, 2,500 shares authorized, 1,000 shares issued............		*$100,000*
Common stock, $10 par value, 100,000 shares authorized, 50,000 shares issued...........	*$500,000*	
Add: Premium on common stock............	*75,000*	
Amount paid in........................		*575,000*
Total contributed capital..............		*$675,000*
Retained earnings...........................		*225,000*
Total stockholders' equity.............		*$900,000*

During the current year the corporation completed the following stock-related transactions:

Mar. 25   Declared the regular semiannual $3 per share dividend on the preferred stock and a $0.50 per share dividend on the common stock.

Apr. 20   Paid to the April 15 stockholders of record the dividends declared on March 25.

      30   Accepted subscriptions to 10,000 shares of common stock at $17.50 per share. Ten percent down payments accompanied the subscription contracts.

May 30   Received the balance due on the April 30 subscriptions and issued the stock.

Sept. 24   Declared the regular semiannual $3 per share dividend on the preferred stock and a $0.50 per share dividend on the common stock.

Oct. 20   Paid to the October 15 stockholders of record the dividends declared on September 24.

Dec. 20   Declared a 10 percent common stock dividend distributable on January 20 to the January 15 common stockholders of record. The December 20 stock market quotation for Phoenix Corporation's common stock was $18 per share, and the board of directors voted to use this quotation in recording the dividend.

Dec. 31   Closed the Income Summary account for the year. The year's after-tax net income was $109,000.

Required:

1. Prepare general journal entries to record the foregoing transactions.
2. Under the assumption that Jerry Payne owns 100 shares of Phoenix Corporation common stock which he plans to hold until after the distribution of the stock dividend declared on December 20, (*a*) prepare a calculation of the book value of his 100 shares as of December 31, and (*b*) another calculation of the book value of his total shares after the dividend distribution.

Problem 17–4A

The December 31, year-end balance sheet of Lonepine Corporation showed the following stockholders' equity:

Stockholders' Equity

Preferred stock, $100 par value, 6 percent cumulative and nonparticipating, 5,000 shares authorized, 2,500 shares issued...	*$ 250,000*
Common stock, $10 par value, 500,000 shares authorized, 250,000 shares issued........$2,500,000	
Add: Premium on common stock......... 600,000	
Amount paid in.....................	*3,100,000*
Total contributed capital...........	*$3,350,000*
Retained earnings.......................	*995,000*
Total shareholders' equity..........	*$4,345,000*

The preferred stockholders are entitled to a $1.50 per share quarterly dividend. There are no preferred dividends in arrears. The last dividend on this stock was declared and recorded on December 28, three days prior to the preparation of the above stockholders' equity section, and is payable on January 21 to the January 14 preferred stockholders of record.

In the six years of its existence the corporation, although its operations have been profitable, has not paid any dividends on its common stock. The directors have discussed the wisdom of a common dividend, but have not declared such a dividend because they felt that all assets from earnings, beyond the amount needed to pay preferred dividends, should be kept in the business and used to expand operations.

During January and February of the current year the corporation completed the following stock-related transactions:

Jan. 21 Paid the $1.50 per share quarterly dividend declared on the preferred stock on the previous December 28.

25 At its meeting held this day the board of directors recognized the corporation's common stockholders should be given some evidence of their company's profitable operations; but it also recognized that all assets from previous earnings were needed in the company's operations. Consequently, it voted to distribute a 4 percent stock dividend on February 20 to the February 15 common stockholders of record. The corporation's common stock was selling at $17.50 per share on January 25 and the board voted to follow the American Institute of Certified Public Accountant's recommendations in recording the dividend.

Feb. 20 Distributed the stock dividend declared on January 25.

Mar. 27 Declared the regular quarterly $1.50 per share dividend on the preferred stock.

Apr. 21 Paid to the April 14 preferred stockholders of record the preferred dividend declared on March 27.

Required:

1. Prepare general journal entries to record the foregoing transactions.
2. Prepare a balance sheet stockholders' equity section as it would appear on February 20 after the distribution of the stock dividend.
3. George Sutton owned 500 shares of Lonepine stock on February 15 and received his dividend stock. Prepare a calculation showing the book value of his shares before the dividend declaration and another calculation showing the book value of his shares after the distribution of the dividend stock.

DECISION PROBLEM 17—POLO-FANT CORPORATION

F. W. Polo and L. D. Fant operated a partnership for a number of years until Mr. Polo's death five years ago. At that time the firm was incorporated with Mrs. Polo receiving a large block of stock for her husband's interest. Data relative to the capitalization at the present date are:

Common stock, $20 par value, 15,000 shares
authorized, 10,000 shares issued...............$200,000
Retained earnings.............................. 115,000
Total stockholders equity...................$315,000

The corporation has been very profitable, its stock is presently selling at $40 per share; but it has been expanding at such a rapid rate that no dividends have been paid during the five years of its life. Mrs. Polo, at the last stockholders' meeting, insisted upon the payment of a cash dividend. Mr. Fant pointed out that the company would have to borrow the money to pay the dividend since "profits" have been used in expanding the business. The board of directors agreed with Mr. Fant and consequently no dividend was declared.

However, it is now agreed that some form of share distribution (stock dividend or stock split) will be made which will permit Mrs. Polo to sell new shares for an amount equal to the expectations which she has had for income on her investment. Specifically new shares are to be issued in an amount that will permit Mrs. Polo as well as other stockholders to realize from their sale approximately 6 percent for each of the five years, or a total of 30 percent on the par value of the shares held. It is hoped that the shareholders will be able to sell the new shares without reducing the market value of their remaining holdings.

Three proposals have been made for the new share distribution:

1. Distribute a 50 percent stock dividend. Each stockholder who wishes may sell enough shares to realize in cash the 30 percent cumulative dividend.
2. Distribute a stock dividend approximately equal in market value to 30 percent of the $200,000 par value of the shares outstanding.
3. Issue a two for one stock split.

Prepare a report analyzing each of the three proposals, giving your opinion as to the kind of share distribution that should be made to accomplish the purposes desired.

Corporations:
Contributed
and Retained Capital

STOCKHOLDER EQUITY in a corporation arises from (1) issuance of stock in exchange for assets; (2) further dealings by a corporation in its own stock, called treasury stock transactions; (3) donations of assets to the corporation by stockholders and outsiders; and from (4) retaining in the business assets from earnings. Equity from the first three sources is called *contributed capital* and that from the fourth is *retained earnings*. Both have been discussed in previous chapters, but further discussion is needed.

TREASURY STOCK

Corporations often reacquire shares of their own stock. Sometimes a corporation will purchase its own stock on the open market to be given to employees as a bonus. Sometimes shares are bought in order to maintain a favorable market for the stock. Occasionally a corporation in a poor financial position will receive shares of its own stock as a gift from its stockholders. Regardless, if a corporation reacquires shares of its own stock, such stock is known as *treasury stock*. Treasury stock is a corporation's own stock that has been issued and then reacquired either by purchase or gift. Notice that the stock must be the corporation's own stock; the acquisition of stock of another corporation does not create treasury stock. Furthermore, the stock must have been once issued and then reacquired; only stock issued and reacquired qualifies as treasury stock. This last point distinguishes treasury stock from unissued stock, and the distinction is important because stock once issued at par and then reacquired as treasury stock may be legally reissued at a discount without discount liability.

As just pointed out, treasury stock differs from unissued stock in that it may be sold at a discount without discount liability. However, in other respects it has the same status as unissued stock. Both are equity items rather than assets. Both are subtracted from authorized stock to determine outstanding stock when such things as book values are calculated. Neither receives dividends nor has a vote in the stockholders' meetings.

PURCHASE OF TREASURY STOCK[1]

When a corporation purchases its own stock, it reduces in equal amounts both its assets and its stockholders' equity. To illustrate this, assume that on May 1 of the current year the condensed balance sheet of Curry Corporation appears as in Illustration 107.

Illustration 107

CURRY CORPORATION
Balance Sheet, May 1, 19--

ASSETS		CAPITAL	
Cash	$ 30,000	Common stock, $100 par value, authorized and issued 1,000	
Other assets	95,000	shares	$100,000
		Retained earnings.	25,000
Total Assets	$125,000	Total Capital.	$125,000

If on May 1 Curry Corporation purchases 100 shares of its outstanding stock at $115 per share, the transaction is recorded as follows:

May	1	Treasury Stock, Common....................	11,500.00	
		Cash.................................		11,500.00
		Purchased 100 shares of treasury stock at $115 per share.		

The debit in the foregoing entry records a reduction in the equity of the stockholders; and the credit to Cash records a reduction in assets. Both are equal to the cost of the treasury stock; and after the entry is posted, a new balance sheet will show the reductions as in Illustration 108.

Notice in the second balance sheet that the cost of the treasury stock appears in the stockholders' equity section as a deduction from common stock and retained earnings. In comparing the two balance sheets, notice that the treasury stock purchase reduces both assets and stockholders' equity by $11,500.

Notice also on the second balance sheet that the dollar amount of issued

---

[1] There are several ways of accounting for treasury stock transactions. This text will discuss the so-called cost basis, which seems to be the most widely used, and it will leave a discussion of other methods to a more advanced text.

Illustration 108

CURRY CORPORATION
Balance Sheet, May 1, 19--

ASSETS		CAPITAL	
Cash	$ 18,500	Common stock, $100 par value, authorized and issued 1,000 shares of which 100 are in the treasury. . . .	$100,000
Other assets	95,000	Retained earnings of which $11,500 is restricted by the purchase of treasury stock.	25,000
		Total.	$125,000
		Less: Cost of treasury stock	11,500
Total Assets	$113,500	Total Capital.	$113,500

stock remains at $100,000 and is unchanged from the first balance sheet. The amount of *issued stock* is not changed by the purchase of treasury stock. However, the purchase of treasury stock does reduce *outstanding stock*. In Curry Corporation, the purchase reduced the outstanding stock from 1,000 to 900 shares.

There is a distinction between issued stock and outstanding stock. Issued stock is stock that has been issued; it may or may not be outstanding. Outstanding stock is stock that has been issued and is outstanding. Only outstanding stock is effective stock, receives dividends, is given a vote in the meetings of stockholders, and enters into such things as the calculation of book values.

Restricting Retained Earnings by the Purchase of Treasury Stock. When a corporation purchases treasury stock, the effect on its assets and stockholders' equity is the same as a cash dividend. When a corporation purchases treasury stock or declares a cash dividend, it transfers corporation assets to its stockholders and thereby reduces both assets and stockholders' equity. Consequently, since the effect is the same, most states place limitations upon treasury stock purchases, just as they place limitations on dividends. These limitations usually provide that a corporation may purchase treasury stock only to the extent of retained earnings available for dividend charges, after which the retained earnings become restricted and legally unavailable for dividends. This means that (1) only a corporation with retained earnings available for dividends may purchase treasury stock; and (2) it may either purchase treasury stock to the extent of such earnings or it may use the earnings as a basis for dividends, but it may not do both. In other words, a corporation may not purchase treasury stock to the extent of its retained earnings available for dividend charges and then use the same retained earnings again as a basis for the declaration of dividends. Or again, it may not by the purchase of treasury stock transfer corporation assets to its stockholders to the extent of retained earnings available for dividends and then transfer more assets by means of cash dividends.

Notice in Illustration 108 how the restriction of retained earnings is shown on the balance sheet. It may also be shown by means of a footnote.

Treasury Stock as an Asset. Treasury stock has appeared on corporation balance sheets as an asset. This is an error. The acquisition of treasury stock reduces in equal amounts both assets and stockholders' equity. Consequently, it is generally agreed that it should appear on the balance sheet as a deduction in the equity section.

REISSUANCE OF TREASURY STOCK

When treasury stock is reissued, it may be reissued at cost, above cost, or below cost.

Reissuance of Treasury Stock at Cost. When treasury stock is reissued at cost, the entry to record the transaction is the reverse of the one used to record its purchase. For example, assume that Curry Corporation sells at cost ten of the hundred treasury shares, the purchase of which at 115 was previously illustrated. The entry to record this is:

May	27	Cash...	1,150.00	
		Treasury Stock, Common.................		1,150.00
		Reissued ten shares of treasury stock at its cost price of $115 per share.		

Notice that the sale of the ten shares at cost restores to the corporation the same amount of assets and stockholder equity taken away when these shares were purchased.

Reissuance of Treasury Stock at a Price above Cost. Although treasury stock may be sold at cost, it is commonly sold at a price either above or below cost. When sold at a price above cost, the amount received in excess of cost is commonly credited to a contributed capital account called "Contributed Capital, Treasury Stock Transactions." For example, assume that Curry Corporation sells for $120 per share an additional ten shares of the treasury stock purchased at $115. The entry to record the transaction appears as follows:

June	3	Cash...	1,200.00	
		Treasury Stock, Common.................		1,150.00
		Contributed Capital, Treasury Stock		
		Transactions...........................		50.00
		Sold at $120 per share treasury stock that cost $115 per share.		

Reissuance of Treasury Stock at a Price below Cost. When treasury stock is reissued at a price below cost, the entry to record the sale normally depends upon whether there is contributed capital from previous transactions in treasury stock. If a corporation has such contributed capital, a "loss" on the sale of treasury stock may be debited to the account of this capital. For example, assume that after having sold ten of its one hundred treasury shares at $115 and ten at $120, Curry Corporation sells ten shares at $110. The entry to record the transaction is:

July	7	Cash...	1,100.00	
		Contributed Capital, Treasury Stock Transactions..	50.00	
		Treasury Stock, Common.....................		1,150.00
		Sold at $110 per share ten shares of treasury stock purchased at $115.		

If a corporation selling treasury stock below cost does not have contributed capital from previous treasury stock transactions, the "loss" on the sale is normally debited to retained earnings. For example, if Curry Corporation sells its remaining 70 shares of treasury stock at $110 per share, the following entry is made to record the transaction:

July	10	Cash...	7,700.00	
		Retained Earnings.............................	350.00	
		Treasury Stock, Common.....................		8,050.00
		Sold treasury stock purchased at $115 per share for $110 per share.		

DONATED TREASURY STOCK

Stockholders sometimes return to a corporation as a gift a portion of their stock. Such donations occur when a corporation is in need of additional assets and the donated stock is to be resold to provide them.

When its stockholders donate to a corporation a portion of their stock, the stock is secured without cost. Consequently, since the acquisition does not decrease the corporation's assets nor increase its liabilities, it has no effect on stockholder equity. On the other hand, although the acquisition of donated treasury stock does not affect assets and equities, its sale increases both. These points may be demonstrated with Bell Corporation.

On June 1 Bell Corporation, having experienced a series of losses, finds itself in the need of additional assets to carry on its operations. In order to secure the assets the company's stockholders decide to donate to the corporation a portion of their stockholdings which are to be sold to outsiders for cash. A balance sheet of the corporation before the donation appears as in Illustration 109.

Illustration 109

BELL CORPORATION
Balance Sheet, June 1, 19--

ASSETS		CAPITAL	
Cash	$ 1,000	Common stock, $100 par value,	
Other assets	103,000	authorized and issued 1,000	
		shares	$100,000
		Retained earnings.	4,000
Total Assets	$104,000	Total Capital.	$104,000

If Bell Corporation stockholders donate pro rata a hundred shares of their stock, the donation may be recorded with a memorandum entry in the General Journal somewhat as follows:

June	1	*Received on this date from the stockholders as a donation 100 shares of $100 par value common stock.*	

Such an entry cannot be posted in the sense that dollar amounts are entered in the accounts. However, when treasury stock is received as a donation, a treasury stock account is opened in the ledger and the number of shares received is shown in the account by means of a memorandum. This memorandum is in effect a posting of the journal memorandum recording the receipt of the stock.

After Bell Corporation receives the foregoing shares from its stockholders, a new balance sheet showing its financial position appears as in Illustration 110.

A comparison of the balance sheets prepared before and after the

Illustration 110

BELL CORPORATION
Balance Sheet, June 1, 19--

ASSETS		CAPITAL	
Cash	$ 1,000	Common stock, $100 par value,	
Other assets	103,000	authorized and issued 1,000	
		shares of which 100 are in	
		the treasury	$100,000
		Retained earnings.	4,000
Total Assets	$104,000	Total Capital.	$104,000

donation shows that the donation did not affect either total assets or the amount of stockholder equity.

Although the receipt of donated treasury stock does not increase or decrease assets and stockholders' equity, its sale increases both. For example, if Bell Corporation sells its hundred shares of donated treasury stock for $92 per share, both assets and the stockholders' equity are increased $9,200, and the transaction is recorded:

June	7	*Cash*	*9,200.00*	
		Contributed Capital, Sale of Do-		
		nated Treasury Stock		*9,200.00*
		Sold 100 shares of donated treasury		
		stock at $92 per share.		

After the treasury stock is sold and the transaction recorded, a balance sheet showing the new financial position of Bell Corporation appears as in Illustration 111.

Illustration 111

BELL CORPORATION
Balance Sheet, June 7, 19--

ASSETS			CAPITAL	
Cash	$ 10,200		Common stock, $100 par value,	
Other assets	103,000		authorized and issued 1,000	
			shares	$100,000
			Retained earnings.	4,000
			Contributed capital, sale of	
			donated treasury stock . .	9,200
Total Assets	$113,200		Total Capital.	$113,200

Observe in the balance sheet prepared after the sale that both assets and stockholder equity are increased $9,200 by the sale. The increase in assets is in cash; the increase in stockholder equity appears as contributed capital from the sale of donated treasury stock.

DONATIONS OF CAPITAL BY OUTSIDERS

Sometimes a corporation will receive a gift or a donation from some person or persons other than its stockholders. For example, a corporation may, as an inducement to locate a plant in a particular city, receive a plant site as a gift. Such a donation increases both assets and stockholders' equity by the fair market value of the contributed asset. The increase in stockholders' equity is contributed capital, capital contributed by others than the stockholders.

CONTRIBUTED CAPITAL IN THE ACCOUNTS
AND ON THE STATEMENTS

Numerous accounts are required in recording contributed capital. Actually a separate account is needed for each kind or source. Furthermore, in addition to separate accounts, each kind of contributed capital may be shown on the balance sheet, as in Illustration 112.

Illustration 112

CONTRIBUTED CAPITAL AND RETAINED EARNINGS

Common stock, $10 par value, 10,000 shares authorized, issued, and outstanding . . .	$100,000
Capital contributed by stockholders in excess of the par value of their shares.	11,500
Contributed capital, treasury stock transactions	3,000
Total capital contributed by stockholders	$114,500
Other contributed capital:	
Contributed capital from the donation of a plant site by the Tri-City Chamber of Commerce	22,000
Total contributed capital	$136,500
Retained earnings	56,100
Total contributed capital and retained earnings.	$192,600

In Illustration 112, the second item is "Capital contributed by stockholders in excess of the par value of their stock, $11,500." This item resulted from common stock premiums. At the time the amounts originated they were probably credited to an account called "Premium on Common Stock." However, as in Illustration 112, it is common practice to show an item such as this on the balance sheet under a more descriptive caption than the name of the account in which it is recorded.

CONTRIBUTED CAPITAL AND DIVIDENDS

Under the laws of some states, contributed capital may not be returned to stockholders as dividends. However, one reason for separate contributed capital accounts is that, under the laws of some states, dividends may be debited or charged to certain contributed capital accounts. Seldom may dividends be charged against the par or stated value of the outstanding stock; however, the exact contributed capital accounts to which a corporation may charge dividends depend upon the laws of the state of its incorporation. For this reason it is usually wise for a board of directors to secure competent legal advice before voting to charge dividends to any contributed capital account.

RETAINED EARNINGS

Retained earnings, as the name implies, is stockholder equity that has arisen from retaining assets from earnings in the business. The retained income includes earnings from normal operations as well as gains from such transactions as the sale of fixed assets or investments.

Retained earnings may be free and unappropriated, or they may be "earmarked" or appropriated for some special purpose. Generally, only the amount of free or unappropriated retained earnings is considered immediately available for dividends. Of course, what is meant by the phrase "available for dividends" is that a credit balance exists in the Retained Earnings account and dividends may be debited thereto.

It should be remembered that dividends are normally paid in cash, and their payment reduces in like amounts both cash and stockholders' equity. The existence of accumulated earnings, as evidenced by a credit balance in the Retained Earnings account, makes the payment of dividends legally possible. However, whether dividends are paid also depends upon the availability of cash with which to pay them. If cash or assets that will shortly become cash are not available, a board may think it wise to forego the declaration of dividends, even though retained earnings exist. Often the directors of a corporation having a large balance in its Retained Earnings account will not declare a dividend because all current assets are needed in the operation of the business

APPROPRIATIONS OF RETAINED EARNINGS

Although the entire balance of a corporation's Retained Earnings account is usually available to absorb debits from dividend declarations, it is normally not wise to exhaust the balance for this purpose. Earnings are a source of assets. Some assets from earnings should be paid out in dividends; but some should be retained for emergencies, for distribution as dividends in years in which earnings are not sufficient to pay normal dividends, and for use in expanding operations. The last reason is an important one. If a corporation is to expand and grow, it may sell additional stock to secure the assets needed in expansion; however, it may also expand by using assets acquired through earnings. Ford Motor Company is a good example of a company that has made use of the latter method. Less than $100,000 was originally invested in Ford Motor Company, and the company has gorwn to its present size primarily from retaining in the business assets from earnings.

When a corporation expands by retaining assets from earnings, the earnings are invested in plant, equipment, merchandise, et cetera, and are not available for dividends. Many stockholders do not understand this; and upon seeing a large amount of retained earnings reported on the balance sheet, agitate for dividends that cannot be paid because the assets from earnings are invested in the business.

Although the practice is not now as common as it once was, some corporations earmark or appropriate retained earnings as a means of informing their stockholders that earnings equal to the appropriations are unavailable for dividends. Retained earnings are appropriated by a resolution passed by the board of directors; and the appropriations are recorded in the accounts and reported on the balance sheet as, for example, like in Illustration 113.

Appropriations of retained earnings are often called "reserves of retained earnings" and may appear on the balance sheet under captions such as "Reserve for plant expansion," Reserve for working capital," and "Reserve for bonded indebtedness."

Illustration 113
STOCKHOLDERS' EQUITY

Common stock, $1 par value, 5,000,000 shares			
authorized and issued			$5,000,000
Retained earnings:			
Appropriated retained earnings:			
Appropriated for plant expansion.	$200,000		
Appropriated for working capital.	250,000		
Appropriated for bonded indebtedness. . . .	75,000		
Total appropriated retained earnings. . .		$525,000	
Unappropriated retained earnings.		350,000	
Total retained earnings			875,000
Total contributed and retained capital			$5,875,000

Voluntary and Contractual Appropriations. Appropriations of retained earnings may be voluntarily made or they may be required by contract. Retained earnings appropriated for plant expansion or for working capital are examples of voluntary appropriations. The first is made to show that assets from earnings are being kept in the business for use in expanding the plant, and the second to show that the company is supplying a portion of its working capital needs from earnings. (Working capital is the excess of current assets over current liabilities.)

The two foregoing appropriations are known as discretionary appropriations. Both are made at the discretion of the board of directors; and since they are voluntary and discretionary, the board may at any time reverse its judgment and return these appropriations or any like appropriations to unappropriated retained earnings.

Illustration of a Retained Earnings Appropriation. To illustrate an appropriation of retained earnings, assume the directors of Deeplake Corporation recognize that in five years their plant will need to be expanded by the construction of a $1,000,000 addition. To finance the expansion, the board discusses the possibility of waiting until the addition is needed and then securing the required funds through the sale of additional stock. They also discuss the possibility of financing the expansion through the annual retention for each of the succeeding five years of $200,000 of assets from earnings. Income in excess of this amount is earned each year, and the directors decide this is the better plan.

In order each year to retain in the business $200,000 of assets from earnings, the directors recognize it is only necessary to refrain from paying out earnings equal to this amount in dividends. However, the board also recognizes that if earnings are retained, the Retained Earnings account and the amount reported on the balance sheet under the caption "Retained earnings" will grow each year and will create a demand by some stockholders for more dividends. Consequently, the board decides that in addition to retaining the assets from earnings, it will at the end of each of the succeeding five years vote an appropriation and transfer of $200,000 of retained earnings from the Retained Earnings account to the Retained Earnings Appropriated for Plant Expansion account. Also, it will show the appropriations on the balance sheet.

If the board follows through on this plan and votes the yearly appropriations, the entry to record each appropriation is:

Dec.	28	*Retained Earnings*..................	*200,000.00*	
		Retained Earnings Appropri-		
		ated for Plant Expansion.......		*200,000.00*
		To record the appropriation of		
		retained earnings.		

When a retained earnings appropriation is recorded, a portion of the balance of the Retained Earnings account is transferred to the proper appropriated retained earnings account, as in the foregoing entry. This reduces the balance of the Retained Earnings account but does not reduce total retained earnings. It merely changes a portion from free, unappropriated retained earnings to appropriated retained earnings.

Before going on, it should be observed in the foregoing situation that the transfer of $200,000 each year from the Retained Earnings account to the Retained Earnings Appropriated for Plant Expansion account does not provide funds for the expansion. Earnings provided the funds; the appropriations do nothing more than inform the stockholders of the board's intention to retain in the business assets from earnings equal to the amount appropriated.

Disposing of an Appropriation of Retained Earnings. The purpose for which an appropriation of retained earnings was made is at times accomplished or passes, and there is no longer a need for the appropriation. When this occurs, the appropriated retained earnings should be returned to the (unappropriated) Retained Earnings account. For example, when bonds mature and are paid and there is no longer a need for an appropriation of retained earnings for bonded indebtedness, the balance of the Retained Earnings Appropriated for Bonded Indebtedness account should be returned to the Retained Earnings account.

American Accounting Association on Appropriations of Retained Income. The American Accounting Association's Committee on Concepts and Standards Underlying Corporate Financial Statements does not favor showing retained earnings appropriations on published balance sheets as in Illustration 113 on page 519. Rather, the Committee feels the entire amount of a corporation's retained earnings should be shown on its balance sheet in one amount and, if portions are appropriated, the stockholders should be informed of this by balance sheet footnotes.[2]

It is of interest to note that the Committee on Concepts and Standards in its discussion of retained income appropriations says:

Appropriations of retained income which purport to reflect managerial policies relative to earnings retention are ineffective, and frequently misleading, unless all retained income which has in fact been committed to operating capital is earmarked. Partial appropriation fosters the implication that retained earnings not earmarked are available for distributions.[3]

In other words, the Committee is of the opinion that income appropriations are both ineffective and often misleading, because balance sheet readers are apt to think that funds from unappropriated earnings are available for dividends when often a major share of such funds is also invested in assets used in the business.

SURPLUS

The terms "contributed capital" and "retained earnings" have been in common use for about 15 years. Prior to the early nineteen-fifties stockholder equity was commonly shown on published balance sheets under two main headings: (1) Capital stock, and (2) Surplus. Under "Capital stock" was shown the portion of stockholder equity represented by the par or stated value of the corporation's outstanding stock, and under "Surplus" was shown the remainder of the equity.

"Surplus," as the word was used on these balance sheets, was defined as "that part of the stockholders' equity not represented by the par or stated value of the corporation's outstanding stock." Furthermore, "surplus" was divided into "earned surplus," which was defined as earnings retained in the business, and "capital surplus," which was surplus from all sources other than earnings. And each of these was in turn divided and subdivided

---

[2] *Reserves and Retained Income, Supplementary Statement No. 1,* Committee on Concepts and Standards Underlying Corporate Financial Statements (Columbus, Ohio: American Accounting Association, 1950), p. 1.

[3] *Ibid.,* p. 1.

Illustration 114

OUTLINE IN WHICH NEW DIVISIONS AND TERMINOLOGY ARE USED IN SHOWING SOURCES AND INTENDED USES OF STOCKHOLDER EQUITY

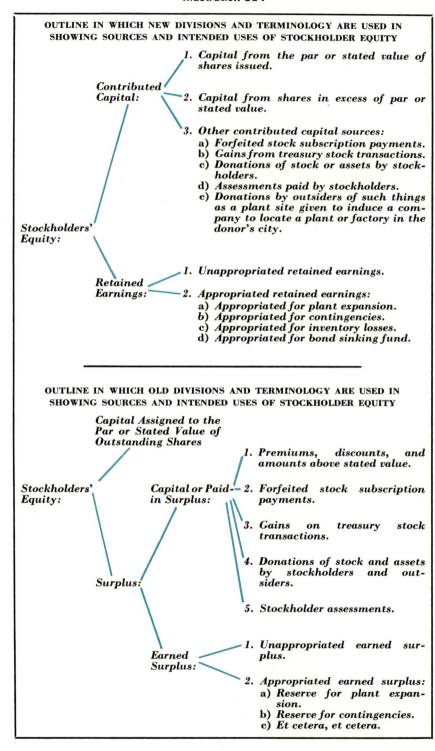

Stockholders' Equity:

Contributed Capital:

1. *Capital from the par or stated value of shares issued.*

2. *Capital from shares in excess of par or stated value.*

3. *Other contributed capital sources:*
   a) *Forfeited stock subscription payments.*
   b) *Gains from treasury stock transactions.*
   c) *Donations of stock or assets by stockholders.*
   d) *Assessments paid by stockholders.*
   e) *Donations by outsiders of such things as a plant site given to induce a company to locate a plant or factory in the donor's city.*

Retained Earnings:

1. *Unappropriated retained earnings.*

2. *Appropriated retained earnings:*
   a) *Appropriated for plant expansion.*
   b) *Appropriated for contingencies.*
   c) *Appropriated for inventory losses.*
   d) *Appropriated for bond sinking fund.*

OUTLINE IN WHICH OLD DIVISIONS AND TERMINOLOGY ARE USED IN SHOWING SOURCES AND INTENDED USES OF STOCKHOLDER EQUITY

Stockholders' Equity:

Capital Assigned to the Par or Stated Value of Outstanding Shares

Surplus:

Capital or Paid-in Surplus:

1. *Premiums, discounts, and amounts above stated value.*

2. *Forfeited stock subscription payments.*

3. *Gains on treasury stock transactions.*

4. *Donations of stock and assets by stockholders and outsiders.*

5. *Stockholder assessments.*

Earned Surplus:

1. *Unappropriated earned surplus.*

2. *Appropriated earned surplus:*
   a) *Reserve for plant expansion.*
   b) *Reserve for contingencies.*
   c) *Et cetera, et cetera.*

to show the capital surplus sources and intended uses of earned surplus. These divisions, as they were commonly given, are shown in the lower half of Illustration 114 where the sources of stockholder equity are presented in outline form, first using present-day divisions and terminology and then repeated with old divisions and terminology.

The student should examine carefully the outline of Illustration 114; and should add an understanding of the terms "surplus," "capital surplus," "paid-in surplus," and "earned surplus" to his fund of accounting knowledge. An understanding of these terms is important, because, although their use is being discontinued on current financial statements, they are still found in the literature of accounting and on an occasional published report.

It is well that the use of the word "surplus" is being abandoned. Actually the term has a general connotation of an "excess" of something; however, this was not and is not its meaning in accounting. Certainly in accounting the term "surplus" was and is not meant to convey the idea that there was or is an excess of corporate capital, or cash, or assets of any kind. The term, properly qualified with descriptive adjectives, did and does purport to show the source or sources of some of the corporate assets. Fortunately, to avoid any misunderstanding, new and more meaningful terminology has been developed.

RETAINED EARNINGS STATEMENT

At the end of each accounting period, in addition to a balance sheet and an income statement, it is customary to prepare for a corporation a retained earnings statement or, if old terminology is used, an earned surplus statement. A retained earnings statement is prepared to show the changes that have occurred in retained earnings during an accounting period, and may be simple or complex, as the following pages will show.

Illustration 115 is a reasonably simple retained earnings statement and was prepared from the information shown in the following two Westwood Corporation accounts:

Retained Earnings

Date	Explanations	Debit	Credit	Balance
Jan. 1, '66	Balance			180,250
Mar. 24, '66	Quarterly dividend	3,000		177,250
June 21, '66	Quarterly dividend	3,000		174,250
Sept. 27, '66	Quarterly dividend	3,000		171,250
Dec. 20, '66	Quarterly dividend	3,000		168,250
Dec. 20, '66	Stock dividend	20,000		148,250
Dec. 20, '66	Appropriation for plant expansion	25,000		123,250
Dec. 31, '66	Net income after taxes		53,400	176,650

Retained Earnings Appropriated for Plant Expansion

Date	Explanations	Debit	Credit	Balance
Dec. 22, '65			*25,000*	*25,000*
Dec. 20, '66			*25,000*	*50,000*

When the retained earnings statement of Illustration 115 is compared with the information shown in the corporation's Retained Earnings and Retained Earnings Appropriated for Plant Expansion accounts, it is apparent the statement is nothing more than a report of the changes recorded in the accounts.

CORRECTION OF ERRORS AND RECORDING NONRECURRING ITEMS

Sometimes an error affecting income is made in one accounting period and is not discovered until a later period. Since income is closed to the Retained Earnings account, errors of this kind cause either an overstate-

---

Illustration 115
WESTWOOD CORPORATION
Statement of Retained Earnings
For Year Ended December 31, 1966

Unappropriated Retained Earnings:
Balance of unappropriated retained
earnings, January 1, 1966 . . . $180,250
Additions:
Net income after state and fed-
eral income taxes   53,400
Total $233,650
Deductions and appropriations:
Quarterly cash dividends. . . . $12,000
Dividend in common stock . . .   20,000
Retained earnings appropriated
for plant expansion   25,000
Total Deductions and Appro-
priations   57,000
Balance of unappropriated retained
earnings, December 31, 1966 . . $176,650

Appropriated Retained Earnings:
Appropriated for plant expansion,
balance, January 1, 1966 · · · $25,000
Appropriated during 1966 · · · · · 25,000
Appropriated for plant expansion,
December 31, 1966 · · · · · ·   50,000
Total Retained Earnings Appropriated
and Unappropriated. $226,650

ment or an understatement of retained earnings. Once such errors were corrected almost exclusively by direct debits or credits to the Retained Earnings account. Today, there are two schools of thought on their corrections, as well as on the handling of extraneous and nonrecurring items such as material gains and losses from fixed asset sales and losses from catastrophes not ordinarily covered by insurance such as wars, riots, floods, and earthquakes.

Of the two schools of thought, one would handle such transactions and corrections by direct debits and credits to the Retained Earnings account. Under this treatment the items would appear only on the retained earnings statement. The other school insists such corrections and items should be taken through the Income Summary account and should appear on the income statement of the period in which they occur or are discovered. The two schools are the opposing sides of a debate as to whether the income statement should report *only regular operating results of the current period* or should be an *all-inclusive statement.*

To illustrate the opposing positions, assume that on December 28, 1965, the Dale Corporation bookkeeper in error recorded as machinery repairs the purchase of a $5,000 machine. The error caused a $5,000 overstatement of expenses and a $5,000 understatement of 1965 income carried to retained earnings and was not discovered until February 23, 1966. In addition to the foregoing, during the last week in February, Green Creek overflowed its banks and swept away a small uninsured building carried in the accounts at $8,000.

Current Operating Performance Income Statement. Accountants who think the income statement should report only the results of current operations would record the foregoing error correction and flood loss as follows:

Feb.	23	*Machinery*......................................	*5,000.00*	
		Retained Earnings......................		*5,000.00*
		To correct a previous accounting period error in which the purchase of machinery was recorded as an expense.		
	28	*Retained Earnings*...........................	*8,000.00*	
		Accumulated Depreciation, Building..........	*2,000.00*	
		Building.................................		*10,000.00*
		To record the destruction of a building by a flood.		

The foregoing items are extraneous and nonrecurring; and when handled in the manner shown, they do not appear on any income statement.

Illustration 116

DALE CORPORATION
Statement of Retained Earnings
For Year Ended December 31, 1966

Retained earnings, January 1, 1966		$117,800
Correction of errors of prior years:		
Add:		
Understatement of 1965 income resulting from charging the purchase of machinery to machinery repairs		5,000
Corrected balance of retained earnings, January 1, 1966		$122,800
Current operations:		
Add:		
Net income after state and federal income taxes		43,000
Total		$165,800
Deduct:		
Loss resulting from the destruction of a building by flood .	$ 8,000	
Cash dividends.	20,000	28,000
Retained Earnings, December 31, 1966.		$137,800

However, they would appear on the 1966 statement of retained earnings as shown in Illustration 116.

All-Inclusive Income Statement. Accountants who favor an all-inclusive income statement would record the correction and flood loss as follows:

Feb.	23	*Machinery*...............................	5,000.00	
		Correction of Prior Year's Income........		5,000.00
		To correct a previous accounting period error in which the purchase of machinery was recorded as an expense.		
	28	*Loss from Flood*...........................	8,000.00	
		Accumulated Depreciation, Building.........	2,000.00	
		Building...............................		10,000.00
		To record the destruction of a building by a flood.		

When extraneous and nonrecurring items are recorded as in the last two entries, the accounts Loss from Flood and Corrections of Prior Years' Income are closed to Income Summary and the items appear on the income statement as in Illustration 117.

Illustration 117

DALE CORPORATION

Income Statement for Year Ended December 31, 1966

Revenue from sales	$600,000
Less: Cost of goods sold	350,000
Gross profit from sales.	$250,000
Operating expenses	165,000
Income from operations	$ 85,000
Add: Correction of understatement of 1965 income resulting from recording the purchase of a machine as machinery repairs.	5,000
Total.	$ 90,000
Deduct: Loss from flood.	8,000
Income before state and federal income taxes	$ 82,000
State and federal income taxes	31,000
Net Income Carried to Retained Earnings. . .	$ 51,000

When an income statement is prepared, as in Illustration 117, under the all-inclusive concept, all error corrections affecting prior years' income and all extraneous items are reported on the income statement. Likewise, only the net income plus any deductions for dividends and changes resulting from retained earnings appropriations appear on the retained earnings statement.

Proponents of the all-inclusive income statement argue that all income and loss items should appear on the income statement of the period in which they occur and that at no time should the income statement be bypassed and items affecting either current or prior years' income be taken directly to retained earnings. They point out that as a result of this procedure, if the net incomes reported on all income statements prepared by a corporation during its life are added, the sum will exactly equal the income the corporation has earned during its life. They also claim that this procedure gives a better and more complete earnings picture.

Accountants who favor the current operating performance statement point out that stockholders and investors are primarily interested in the item reported on the income statement as "net income," and that these people do not always carefully note the items added and deducted in arriving at reported "net income." Consequently, if extraneous and nonrecurring items are carried to the income statement, some stockholders and investors may be misled as to a corporation's earning power. They feel that when extraneous and nonrecurring items are carried directly to retained earnings, the income statement gives a better picture of earning capacity.

The Committee on Accounting Procedure of the American Institute of Certified Public Accountants seems to favor the current operating performance income statement. The Committee has recommended, where such items are material in amount and would tend to impair the significance of reported net income, the recording of nonrecurring items and error corrections be by direct debits and credits to retained earnings.[4]

Of course the recommendation of the Committee does not settle the argument, and until such time as authoritative opinions are more in agreement, a student or an instructor is justified in accepting either view.

QUESTIONS FOR CLASS DISCUSSION

1. What are the two main sources of stockholders' equity in a corporation?
2. While examining a corporation balance sheet, a businessman observed that the various items in the stockholders' equity section really showed sources of assets. Was this observation correct?
3. What is treasury stock? How is it like unissued stock? How does it differ from unissued stock? What is the legal significance of this difference?
4. General Plastics Corporation bought 1,000 shares of Capital Steel Corporation stock and turned it over to its treasurer for safekeeping. Is this treasury stock? Why or why not?
5. What is the effect of a treasury stock purchase in terms of assets and stockholders' equity? What is the effect on a corporation's assets and stockholders' equity of a treasury stock donation?
6. Distinguish between issued stock and outstanding stock.
7. Why do state laws place limitations on the purchase of treasury stock?
8. Give the accounting meanings of the terms: (a) surplus, (b) earned surplus, (c) capital surplus, and (d) paid-in surplus.
9. Why do accountants feel that the word "surplus" should not be used in published balance sheets as a term to describe a portion of the stockholders' equity?
10. Under what descriptive headings and subheadings is the equity of the stockholders in a corporation shown on most present-day balance sheets?
11. Why are retained earnings sometimes appropriated?
12. Does the appropriation and transfer of retained earnings to retained earnings appropriated for plant expansion provide funds for the expansion? How do such appropriations aid in accumulating funds for a plant expansion?
13. How does a corporation dispose of a retained earnings appropriation such as retained earnings appropriated for plant expansion?
14. Explain why the American Accounting Association's Committee on Concepts and Standards Underlying Corporate Financial Statements does not favor showing appropriations of retained earnings on published balance sheets.
15. How may an "all-inclusive income statement" differ from a "current operating performance income statement"?

---

[4] *Accounting Research Bulletin No. 43*, "Restatement and Revision of Accounting Research Bulletins" (New York: American Institute of Certified Public Accountants, 1953), p. 63.

PROBLEMS

Problem 18–1

The stockholders' equity section from a corporation balance sheet follows:

Capital Stock and Surplus

Preferred stock, $100 par value, 6 percent cumulative and nonparticipating, 2,500 shares authorized and issued.....		*$250,000*	
Common stock, $10 par value, authorized 50,000 shares, issued 40,000 shares................................		*400,000*	
Total stock issued..................			*$ 650,000*
Capital surplus:			
Premium on preferred stock..........	*$ 37,500*		
Premium on common stock..........	*14,300*		
Treasury stock surplus...............	*6,200*		
Donated surplus......................	*15,000*		
Total.............................	*$ 73,000*		
Less: Discount on common stock...	*1,600*		
Total capital surplus.............		*$ 71,400*	
Earned surplus:			
Appropriated:			
Reserve for plant expansion.........	*$100,000*		
Reserve for working capital.........	*50,000*		
Total...........................	*$150,000*		
Unappropriated earned surplus.......	*174,100*		
Total earned surplus.............		*324,100*	
Total surplus....................			*395,500*
Total capital stock and surplus...			*$1,045,500*

Required:

Rearrange and restate this equity section to conform with the proposals of the American Institute of Certified Public Accountants and the American Accounting Association. (The donated surplus arose from the donation of a plant site, and the treasury stock surplus from the purchase and sale of treasury stock.)

Problem 18–2

Plastic Products Corporation received a charter granting the right to issue 50,000 shares of $10 par value common stock. It then completed the following transactions:

a) Accepted subscriptions to 25,000 shares of stock at $11.50 per share.

b) Received factory land as a donation from Tri-City Chamber of Commerce in return for locating its plant on the site. The fair market value of the property was $15,000.

c) Collected the subscriptions of Transaction (a) and issued the stock.
d) Gave a contractor $65,750 in cash and 500 shares of stock for erecting a factory building. The contract price for the building was $71,625; but upon its completion the contractor agreed to accept the cash and stock in full settlement.
e) Paid $175,000 for factory machinery.
f) During the first year's operations sold $615,600 of products for cash and paid $527,100 in operating expenses.
g) Made an adjusting entry to record depreciation on machinery, $17,300, and depreciation on factory building, $1,200. (Debit Operating Expenses Controlling.)
h) Made an adjusting entry to record state and federal income taxes payable, $28,000. (Debit the expense account State and Federal Income Taxes Expense.)
i) Closed the Sales, Operating Expenses Controlling and State and Federal Income Taxes Expense accounts to Income Summary, and close the Income Summary account.
j) Declared a $0.10 per share quarterly cash dividend.
k) Declared a 5 percent stock dividend. The stock was selling at $12 per share on the day of the declaration.
l) Paid the cash dividend.
m) Distributed the stock dividend.
n) Purchased 1,000 shares of treasury stock at $12.25 per share.
o) Sold 500 shares of treasury stock at $12.75 per share.
p) Paid the state and federal income taxes payable.
q) Declared a quarterly cash dividend of $0.20 per share.

Required:
1. Open the following T-accounts: Cash; Subscriptions Receivable Common Stock; Machinery and Equipment; Accumulated Depreciation, Machinery and Equipment; Building; Accumulated Depreciation, Building; Land; State and Federal Income Taxes Payable; Cash Dividend Payable; Common Stock; Premium on Common Stock; Common Stock Subscribed; Contributed Capital from Treasury Stock Transactions; Contributed Capital from Plant Site Donation; Retained Earnings; Stock Dividend Distributable; Treasury Stock; Income Summary; Sales; Operating Expenses Controlling; and State and Federal Income Taxes Expense.
2. Enter the transactions directly in the accounts, using the transaction letters to identify the amounts.
3. Prepare the stockholders' equity section of a balance sheet reflecting the foregoing transactions.

Problem 18–3

At the end of last year Dale Corporation had outstanding 25,000 shares of $10 par value common stock issued at par. Also at that time, after several unprofitable years, the corporation had a $32,500 deficit and was in need of additional working capital. Consequently, to supply the additional working capital the corporation's stockholders agreed to donate pro rata one fifth of their shares to the corporation to be sold for cash. On January 20 the stock was donated, and on January 25 it was sold at $8.50 per share.

Required:
1. Give the entries to record the donation and sale of the stock.
2. Calculate the book value per share of the outstanding stock: (*a*) before the donation; (*b*) after the donation but before the sale of the treasury shares; and (*c*) after the sale of the treasury shares.
3. Calculate for a stockholder who owned 100 shares before the donation the book value of his shares (*a*) before the donation, and (*b*) after the sale of the treasury stock.

Problem 18–4

On January 1 of the current year the stockholders of Arizona Corporation had a $327,350 equity in the corporation. The equity had resulted from the issuance of 20,000 shares of $10 par value common stock at $11.50 per share and the retention over a period of years of $97,350 of assets from earnings. During the first six months of the year the corporation completed these transactions:

Jan. 12 The board of directors, anticipating the loss of a lawsuit, voted to place $50,000 of retained earnings in an appropriation for possible lawsuit loss. (Credit the account Retained Earnings Appropriated for Possible Lawsuit Loss.)

      12 In the place of the normal cash dividend, the board declared a 5 percent stock dividend payable on February 15 to the February 10 stockholders of record. The stock of the corporation was selling at $17.50 per share on this day.

Feb. 15 Distributed the stock dividend declared on January 12.

Apr. 10 Purchased 1,000 shares of treasury stock at $17.50 per share.

May   21 Sold 500 of the treasury shares at $18.50 per share.

June 14 The corporation lost the lawsuit as anticipated by its board of directors in January, and it paid the plaintiff the $35,000 damages ordered by the court.

      25 Sold 200 of the remaining treasury shares at $17 per share.

      30 The board of directors voted to return the balance of the Retained Earnings Appropriated for Possible Lawsuit Loss account to unappropriated retained earnings.

Required:
1. Prepare general journal entries to record the foregoing transactions.
2. Prepare the stockholders' equity section of the corporation's June 30 balance sheet under the assumption the corporation is authorized to issue 25,000 shares of $10 par value common stock.

Problem 18–5

The condensed Income Summary and Retained Earnings accounts of Desert Hills Corporation follow:

Income Summary

1966			1966		
Dec. 31 *Cost of goods sold*	*620,000*		Dec. 31 *Revenue from sales*	*1,080,000*	
31 *Operating expenses*	*360,000*				
31 *Income taxes*	*42,000*				

Retained Earnings

1966		1966	
Mar. 23 *Cash dividend*	*8,000*	Jan. 1 *Balance*	*143,500*
June 25 *Cash dividend*	*8,000*		
Sept. 28 *Cash dividend*	*8,000*		
Dec. 28 *Cash dividend*	*8,000*		
28 *Stock dividend*	*12,000*		

All events and transactions affecting the two accounts are reflected therein with the following exceptions:

a) On January 18, 1966, the company's auditor discovered that on December 22, 1965, a $9,850 check in payment for betterments to the company building had been debited in error to the Building Repairs Expense account.

b) On November 17, 1966, the company building suffered $7,500 in damages to its roof as a result of a windstorm. Repairs were made, and since the company's insurance did not cover the loss, a check was issued on December 29 in payment for the repairs. However, the bookkeeper was unsure of the proper account to debit; consequently, he had not recorded the check.

Required:

1. Under the assumption that management thinks the corporation's income statement should reflect only current operating performance, prepare:

   a) Entries to record the error correction and the uninsured loss and to close the Income Summary account.

   b) A condensed 1966 income statement and a statement of retained earnings.

2. Under the assumption that management thinks the corporation's income statement should be an all-inclusive statement, prepare:

   a) Entries to record the error correction and the uninsured loss and to close the Income Summary account.

   b) A condensed 1966 income statement and a statement of retained earnings.

Problem 18–6

Triangle Corporation's December 31, 1965, balance sheet showed the following retained earnings:

Retained earnings:
  Retained earnings appropriated for plant
    expansion.................................*$100,000*
  Unappropriated retained earnings............ *364,500*
    Total retained earnings.....................*$464,500*

The corporation's management believes the concern's income statement should reflect only current operating performance and that unusual and non-recurring items should be carried directly to the Unappropriated Retained Earnings account. Consequently, at the end of 1966 the company's Unappropriated Retained Earnings account appeared as follows:

Unappropriated Retained Earnings

Date		Explanation	Debit	Credit	Balance
1966					
Jan.	*1*	*Balance*			*364,500*
	27	*Correction of a 1965 income understatement due to an overstatement of the 1965 depreciation on machinery*		*2,400*	*366,900*
	27	*Correction of a 1965 income overstatement due to an overstatement of the December 31, 1965, inventory*	*1,700*		*365,200*
Mar.	*23*	*Quarterly cash dividend*	*6,000*		*359,200*
May	*17*	*Cost of lawsuit lost*	*23,400*		*335,800*
June	*25*	*Quarterly cash dividend*	*6,000*		*329,800*
Sept.	*24*	*Quarterly cash dividend*	*6,000*		*323,800*
Dec.	*27*	*Stock dividend*	*24,500*		*299,300*
	27	*Quarterly cash dividend*	*6,000*		*293,300*
	27	*Appropriation for plant expansion*	*25,000*		*268,300*
	31	*Net income after state and federal taxes*		*105,200*	*373,500*

Required:
  1. Prepare a statement of retained earnings for Triangle Corporation that reflects the entries in the foregoing account.
  2. Prepare a second statement of retained earnings for the company as it would appear if the company's management preferred an all-inclusive income statement rather than a current operating performance statement.

CLASS EXERCISE

Exercise 18–1

During a short period of time Brookside Corporation received a charter and completed the following transactions:

    a) Began business by selling and issuing $12,000 of common stock for cash.

    b) Purchased $10,000 of equipment for cash.

    c) Sold and delivered $30,000 of services on credit.

    d) Collected $27,000 of accounts receivable.

    e) Paid $25,000 of operating expenses.

    f) Purchased $7,000 of additional equipment, giving $4,000 in cash and a $3,000 promissory note payable.

    g) Closed the Revenue from Services, Operating Expenses, and Income Summary accounts.

Required:

1. Open the following T-accounts on a sheet of ordinary notebook paper: Cash, Accounts Receivable, Equipment, Notes Payable, Common Stock, Retained Earnings, Income Summary, Revenue from Services, and Operating Expenses.

2. Record the transactions directly in the T-accounts.

3. Answer these questions:

    a) Does the corporation have retained earnings?

    b) Does it have any cash?

    c) If the company has retained earnings, why does it not also have cash?

    d) Can Brookside Corporation declare a legal cash dividend?

    e) Can it pay the dividend?

    f) In terms of assets, what does the balance of the Notes Payable account represent?

    g) In terms of assets, what does the balance of the Common Stock account represent?

    h) In terms of assets, what does the balance of the Retained Earnings account represent?

ALTERNATE PROBLEMS

Problem 18–2A

Pinion Corporation received a charter granting the right to issue 50,000 shares of $5 par value common stock. It then completed these transactions:

    a) Accepted subscriptions to 15,000 shares of common stock at $5.50 per share.

    b) Gave Corona Corporation 25,000 shares of stock for the following assets: machinery, $35,000; factory building, $85,000; and land, $17,500.

    c) Collected the subscriptions of Transaction (*a*) and issued the stock.

    d) Purchased additional machinery for cash, $65,000.

    e) During its first year sold $628,500 of products for cash, and paid $550,300 of operating expenses.

f) Made an adjusting entry to record depreciation on machinery, $10,700, and depreciation on factory building, $2,500. (Debit Operating Expenses Controlling.)

g) Made an adjusting entry to record state and federal income taxes payable, $25,000. (Debit State and Federal Income Taxes Expense.)

h) Closed the Sales, Operating Expenses Controlling, State and Federal Income Taxes Expense, and Income Summary accounts.

i) Declared a $0.10 per share quarterly dividend.

j) Paid the dividend previously declared.

k) Paid the state and federal income taxes payable.

l) Purchased 1,000 shares of treasury stock at $5.75 per share.

m) Sold 500 of the treasury shares at $6 per share.

n) Declared a 10 percent stock dividend. The stock was selling for $6 per share on the day of the declaration.

o) Distributed the stock dividend.

p) Declared a $0.10 per share quarterly cash dividend.

q) The local chamber of commerce purchased and gave to the corporation a plot of land immediately to the west of the present factory building. The land had a fair market value of $15,000 and was to be used in expanding the factory and its payroll.

Required:
1. Open the following T-accounts: Cash; Subscriptions Receivable Common Stock; Machinery and Equipment; Accumulated Depreciation, Machinery and Equipment; Building; Accumulated Depreciation, Building; Land; State and Federal Income Taxes Payable; Cash Dividend Payable; Common Stock; Premium on Common Stock; Common Stock Subscribed; Contributed Capital from Treasury Stock Transactions; Contributed Capital from Plant Site Donation; Retained Earnings; Stock Dividend Distributable; Treasury Stock; Income Summary; Sales; Operating Expenses Controlling; and State and Federal Income Taxes Expense.
2. Enter the transactions directly in the accounts, using the transaction letters to identify the amounts.
3. Prepare the stockholders' equity section of a balance sheet reflecting the foregoing transactions.

Problem 18–4A

The board of directors of South Mountain Corporation voted on December 21 of last year to appropriate $40,000 of retained earnings and to retain in the business assets equal to the appropriation for use in expanding their plant. This was the fifth of such appropriations; and after it was recorded, the corporation had the following retained and contributed capital:

> *Common stock, $5 par value, 500,000 shares*
> *authorized, 350,000 shares issued* *$1,750,000*
> *Retained earnings appropriated for plant*
> *expansion* *200,000*
> *Unappropriated retained earnings* *76,450*
> *$2,026,450*

On February 2 of the current year the board signed a contract for construction of the plant addition for which the earnings were appropriated; and on October 23, upon completion of the addition, the contractor was paid $197,-350, the contract price.

At their December 22 meeting the board voted to return the balance of the Retained Earnings Appropriated for Plant Expansion account to unappropriated retained earnings. It also voted a 35,000-share stock dividend distributable on January 20 to the January 17 stockholders of record. The company's stock was selling for $5.75 per share on the day the dividend was declared.

Required:
1. Prepare entries to record the December 21 appropriation, the payment of the contractor, the return of the appropriated retained earnings to unappropriated retained earnings, the declaration of the stock dividend, and its distribution.
2. Prepare the stockholders' equity section of the corporation's balance sheet reflecting the foregoing transactions.

Problem 18–5A

Following are the condensed Income Summary and Retained Earnings accounts of Sandlot Sales Corporation:

Income Summary

1966			1966		
Dec. 31 *Cost of goods sold*	*635,250*		Dec. 31 *Revenue from sales*		*985,500*
31 *Operating expenses*	*250,250*				
31 *Income taxes*	*44,000*				

Retained Earnings

1966			1966		
Mar. 5 *Cash dividend*	*5,000*		Jan. 1 *Balance*		*185,500*
June 7 *Cash dividend*	*5,000*				
Sept. 3 *Cash dividend*	*5,000*				
Dec. 6 *Cash dividend*	*5,000*				
6 *Stock dividend*	*10,000*				

All events and transactions affecting the two accounts are reflected therein excepting the following:
a) On January 17, 1966, the company's auditor discovered that on December 24, 1965, $2,500 of ordinary repairs to machinery was debited in error to the asset account, Machinery.
b) In 1964 the company purchased for $25,000 land at the edge of town as a future warehouse site. The warehouse was not built and 1966 zoning

changes made use of the land for this purpose impossible. However, on December 27, 1966, the land was sold as a motel site for $40,000. The bookkeeper was unsure of the proper account to credit for this nonrecurring gain; consequently, the check for the sale was unrecorded.

Required:
1. Under the assumption that management thinks the corporation's income statement should be an all-inclusive statement, prepare:
    a) Entries to record the error correction and the land sale and to close the Income Summary account.
    b) A condensed 1966 income statement and a statement of retained earnings.
2. Under the assumption that management thinks the corporation's income statement should be a current operating performance statement, prepare:
    a) Entries to record the error correction and the land sale and to close the Income Summary account.
    b) A condensed 1966 income statement and a statement of retained earnings.

Problem 18–6A
The Income Summary and Retained Earnings accounts of Copperstate Corporation follow:

Income Summary

1967			1967		
Dec. 31	Cost of goods sold	385,500	Dec. 31	Revenue from sales	550,750
31	Operating expenses	139,250			
31	Income taxes	6,000			

Retained Earnings

1967			1967		
Mar. 11	Cash dividend	2,000	Jan. 1	Balance	83,750
June 15	Cash dividend	2,000			
Sept. 14	Cash dividend	2,000			
Dec. 15	Cash dividend	2,000			
15	Stock dividend	8,000			

At the end of every year the bookkeeper of Copperstate Corporation enters depreciation on each item of office equipment on the item's fixed asset record card. He then totals the entries on the cards to secure the amount for the adjusting entry used in recording depreciation on office equipment. In totaling the amounts entered on the cards at the end of 1966 an error was made that resulted in a $1,000 understatement of 1966 depreciation. The error has not been corrected.

Required:

1. Under the assumption that management of Copperstate Corporation prefers a current operating performance income statement, ignore any tax effects of the error and prepare:

   a) Entries to correct the error and close the Income Summary account.

   b) A condensed 1967 income statement and a statement of retained earnings.

2. Under the assumption that management prefers an all-inclusive income statement, ignore any tax effect of the error and prepare:

   a) Entries to correct the error, to close the Correction of Prior Years' Errors account, and to close the Income Summary account.

   b) A condensed 1967 income statement and a statement of retained earnings.

DECISION PROBLEM 18—SPAR ELECTRONICS, INC.

Sarah Lee

Naney Brooks owns 100 shares of stock in Spar Electronics *Larabee & Co.* She is concerned because she has received such small dividends on the stock. From the last stockholders' report she has concluded that there are ample funds available for much larger dividends. In addition to cash in banks, the corporation's balance sheet shows the following items which she believes represents cash funds:

1. A large "Paid-in surplus."
2. Plenty of "Undivided profits" (retained earnings).
3. A large "Reserve for general contingencies."
4. A substantial "Reserve for depreciation."
5. A large "Reserve for plant expansion."

Obviously the company's balance sheet contains some old terminology. In simple, nontechnical language,(1) explain the nature of the items which Mrs. Brooks Lee has confused with cash.(2) Also indicate more meaningful terminology which should be used in the balance sheet, so that that statement might be less confusing to the reader.

Long-Term
Liabilities
and Investments

WHEN A BUSINESS borrows money that is not to be repaid for a relatively long period of time, it may borrow by means of a mortgage, by means of bonds, or by issuing long-term notes.

BORROWING MONEY WITH A MORTGAGE

A business may borrow by placing a mortgage on some or all of its fixed assets. A mortgage actually involves two legal documents. The first is a kind of promissory note called a *mortgage note*, which is secured by a second legal document called a *mortgage* or a *mortgage contract*. In the mortgage note the mortgagor, the one who mortgages property, promises to repay the money borrowed. The mortgage or mortgage contract requires a number of things of the mortgagor. Normally, among other things, the mortgagor must keep the property in a good state of repair, carry adequate insurance, pay the interest on the mortgage note, and, often, make payments to reduce the mortgage liability. These duties and responsibilities are always set forth in the mortgage contract, which also grants the mortgage holder certain rights. Among these is the right to foreclose in case the mortgagor fails in any of the pledged duties, such as paying interest, keeping the property in repair, or carrying adequate insurance. In a foreclosure a court takes possession of the mortgaged property for the mortgage holder and may order its sale. If the property is sold, the proceeds go first to pay the claims of the mortgage holder, after which any money remaining is paid to the former owner of the property.

When a business borrows by means of a mortgage, the transaction commonly involves the business and one bank or one insurance company. Since a bank or insurance company may normally loan a single borrower no more than an amount equal to 10 percent of the bank or insurance company's net worth, there is always a limitation on the size of a mortgage loan. Consequently, large companies often cannot find a single lender who wishes to and may legally lend to one borrower the amount they wish to borrow. In such cases, in the place of a mortgage loan, bonds are often issued. Bonds make possible the division of a large loan into portions that may be sold to many small investors.

BORROWING MONEY BY ISSUING BONDS

Borrowing money by issuing bonds is similar to borrowing by issuing a mortgage. Actually in many cases the only real difference is that a number of bonds, often in denominations of $1,000, are issued in the place of a single mortgage note. For all practical purposes each bond is a promissory note, promising to pay a definite sum of money to its holder, or owner of record, at a fixed future date. Like promissory notes, bonds bear interest; and like a mortgage note, are often secured by a mortgage. However, since bonds may be owned and transferred during their lives by a number of people, they differ from promissory notes in that they do not name the lender.

When a company issues bonds secured by a mortgage, it normally sells the bonds to an investment firm, known as the *underwriter*, which in turn resells the bonds to the public. In addition to the underwriter, the company issuing bonds selects a trustee to represent the bondholders. In most cases the trustee is a large bank or trust company to whom the company issuing the bonds executes and delivers the mortgage which acts as security for the bonds. It is the duty of the trustee to see that the company fulfills all the pledged responsibilities of the mortgage contract, or as it is often called the deed of trust. It is also the duty of the trustee to foreclose if any pledges are not fulfilled.

WHO MAY ISSUE BONDS

Most large companies are organized as corporations, and corporations have made extensive use of bonds as a means of financing. However, the sale of bonds is not a privilege limited to corporations. The federal government issues bonds, and most state and local governmental units make wide use of bonds in financing projects. However, this text, as most accounting texts, limits its consideration of bonds to corporate bonds.

CLASSIFICATION OF BONDS

Over the years corporation lawyers and financiers have created a wide variety of bonds, each with slightly different combinations of characteristics. As a result, a single method of classifying bonds is impossible, and bonds are classified in a number of ways. Two common ways are: (1) as to the method of paying principal, and interest, and (2) as to type of security.

Bonds Classified as to Payment of Principal and Interest. When bonds are classified as to method of paying the principal, they may be *serial bonds* or *sinking fund bonds*. When serial or term bonds are issued, portions of the issue become due and are paid in installments over a period of years. For example, a corporation may issue $5,000,000 of serial bonds with the provision that $500,000 of the bonds become due and are to be paid each year until all are paid. Sinking fund bonds provide in their deed of trust that a sinking fund be created to pay the bonds at maturity. Sinking funds are discussed in more detail later in this chapter.

Bonds may be issued without provision for either installment payments or a sinking fund. Such bonds are normally payable at maturity and are often to be paid with funds from the sale of a new bond issue.

When bonds are classified as to method of interest payment, they are either *registered bonds or coupon bonds*. Ownership of registered bonds is registered or recorded with the issuing corporation, which offers some protection from loss or theft. Title to such bonds is transferred in much the same manner as title to stock is transferred. Interest payments are usually made by checks mailed to the registered owners.

Coupon bonds secure their name from the interest coupons attached to each bond. Each coupon calls for payment on the interest payment date of the interest due·on the bond to which it is attached. The coupons are detached as they become due and are deposited with a bank for collection in much the same manner as an out-of-town note is deposited for collection. Often ownership of a coupon bond is not registered. Such unregistered bonds are payable to bearer or are bearer paper, and ownership is transferred by delivery. Sometimes bonds are registered as to principal with interest payments by coupons.

Bonds Classified as to Security. Bonds may be secured or unsecured. Unsecured bonds are called *debentures* and depend upon the general credit standing of their issuing corporation for security. Only financially strong corporations are able to sell unsecured bonds. When bonds are secured, they are normally secured by mortgages or liens on assets. Such bonds are often classified according to the type of assets pledged for their security. Some of the more common classifications are *real estate mortgage bonds,* *equipment trust bonds,* and *collateral trust bonds*. An issue of real estate mortgage bonds is normally secured by a mortgage on a portion or all of the issuing corporation's plant and equipment. Equipment trust bonds are commonly issued by railroads and are secured by a mortgage on rolling stock. Collateral trust bonds are secured by stocks, bonds, and other negotiable instruments deposited with a trustee.

WHY A CORPORATION ISSUES BONDS

A corporation in need of long-term funds may secure these funds by issuing either additional common stock, preferred stock, or bonds. Each has it advantages and disadvantages.

Stockholders are the owners of a corporation, and bondholders are creditors. Issuing additional common stock spreads control of management over a larger number of owners and spreads earnings over more shares. As creditors, bondholders do not share in either management or earnings. Furthermore, since bonds are usually secured by a mortgage or lien and interest payments are fixed in amount, the interest rate paid on bonds is usually less than the dividend rates on either common or preferred stocks.

As owners, stockholders receive dividends only when income sufficient for their payment has been earned. Whenever sufficient income has not been earned, stockholders receive no dividends and must wait for dividends until sufficient income is earned. This is not true of bondholders. Interest payments to bondholders must be made when due whether any income is earned or not, because if interest payments are not made when due, the bondholders may foreclose and take the assets pledged for their security.

In this age of high corporation income taxes, taxes are also always a factor in a decision between issuing stocks or bonds. Bond interest is a deductible expense in calculating income subject to taxes, while dividends are a sharing of income and are not a deductible expense. Because of this the federal income tax is often one of the most important factors in a decision between issuing preferred stock or bonds. The importance of this factor is demonstrated in Illustration 118 where the results of three methods of securing additional funds are shown.

Often the deciding factor between issuing additional stocks or issuing bonds is the estimated amount of future earnings and their probable stability. If the earnings rate per dollar invested is expected to be greater than the bond interest rate or the rate of dividends on preferred stock, and is also expected to be stable, it is usually to the advantage of the common stockholders to issue either bonds or preferred stock. On the other hand, if the expected earnings rate is less than the bond interest rate or the rate of dividends on preferred stock, the common stockholders receive a greater return if additional common stock rather than either bonds or preferred stock is issued.

For example, assume that the Apex Corporation which has $2,000,000 of common stock outstanding wishes to raise an additional $2,000,000 for expansion. The results of three methods of securing the additional funds are shown in Illustration 118. This table shows the results first with an

Illustration 118

	Operating Income of $540,000			Operating Income of $70,000		
	Plan No. 1	Plan No. 2	Plan No. 3	Plan No. 1	Plan No. 2	Plan No. 3
Common stock, $100 par (20,000 shares).................	$2,000,000	$2,000,000	$2,000,000	$2,000,000	$2,000,000	$2,000,000
Additional common stock, $100 par (20,000 shares)...........................	2,000,000			2,000,000		
Preferred stock, 6 percent cumulative.................		2,000,000			2,000,000	
5 percent bonds..........................			2,000,000			2,000,000
Total capitalization......................	$4,000,000	$4,000,000	$4,000,000	$4,000,000	$4,000,000	$4,000,000
Operating income before federal income tax......	$ 540,000	$ 540,000	$ 540,000	$ 70,000	$ 70,000	$ 70,000
Deduct: Bond interest expense......................			100,000			100,000
Income (or deficit*) after bond interest expense...	$ 540,000	$ 540,000	$ 440,000	$ 70,000	$ 70,000	$ 30,000*
Deduct: Federal and state income taxes of 50 percent.................	270,000	270,000	220,000	35,000	35,000	–0–
Net income (or deficit*) after federal taxes........	$ 270,000	$ 270,000	$ 220,000	$ 35,000	$ 35,000	$ 30,000*
Preferred dividends....................		120,000			120,000	
Income (or deficit*) after taxes and preferred dividends or bond interest................	$ 270,000	$ 150,000	$ 220,000	$ 35,000	$ 85,000*	$ 30,000*
Income (or deficit*) per share of common stock....	$6.75	$7.50	$11.00	$0.875	$4.25*	$1.50*

assumed $540,000 operating income and then with an assumed operating income of $70,000 per year. Plan No. 1 assumes Apex Corporation issues an additional $2,000,000 of common stock which brings its common stock outstanding to 40,000 shares. Plan No. 2 assumes the additional funds are raised by issuing $2,000,000 of 6 percent, cumulative preferred stock. Plan No. 3 assumes $2,000,000 of 5 percent bonds are sold. Obviously, Plan No. 3 is to the advantage of the original common stockholders if earnings are sufficiently large. However, when earnings are less than the interest on the bonds, Plan No. 1 offers the best return to the original stockholders.

Notice the effect on the three financing methods of the assumed 50 percent combined federal and state income tax rate. Actually, since corporation rates have reached this level, a choice between issuing stock and issuing bonds is normally a choice between common stock and bonds. Preferred stock might be issued, but normally only if the issuing corporation expected that during the life of a bond issue there might be several years during which it would not have sufficient pretax earnings to pay the bond interest. In such a case, if preferred stock were issued, the dividends on the stock could be postponed during these years.

RECORDING BOND TRANSACTIONS

A decision to issue bonds rests with the board of directors. However, many corporations provide in their charters that such a decision must be approved by the stockholders.

When bonds are to be issued, after the resolution for their issuance is passed by the board and approved by the stockholders, the bonds are printed, and the deed of trust is drawn and deposited with the trustee of the bondholders. The deed of trust always states the total amount of bonds that is secured by it and that may be issued and sold. When the deed of trust is deposited, an entry is made to record the authorization of the bond issue. The entry is usually a memorandum entry and appears somewhat as follows:

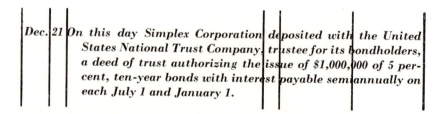

Dec. 21   On this day Simplex Corporation deposited with the United States National Trust Company, trustee for its bondholders, a deed of trust authorizing the issue of $1,000,000 of 5 percent, ten-year bonds with interest payable semiannually on each July 1 and January 1.

In addition to the memorandum entry in the General Journal, a memorandum as to the amount of bonds authorized is also placed in the Bonds Payable account in the ledger.

Often when an issue of bonds is authorized, more bonds are authorized than are to be immediately issued. For example, if a corporation has an immediate need for only $750,000 but the property it is mortgaging is ample to secure a $1,000,000 bond issue, a deed of trust is drawn for the larger amount, and $1,000,000 of bonds are authorized. Then only $750,000, the amount necessary to cover immediate needs, is sold. The remaining bonds are held in reserve to be sold when additional funds are needed. In such a situation where only $750,000 is presently needed but the property being mortgaged is sufficient to secure a $1,000,000 issue, if the deed of trust were drawn for only the $750,000 immediately needed, it would be necessary to use a second mortgage as security if an additional loan of $250,000 were later needed. Issuing a second mortgage would be undesirable because the claims of the first mortgage would take priority over those of the second, causing the second mortgage to be less desirable, and normally making a higher rate of interest necessary on it.

After the deed of trust is deposited with the trustee of the bondholders, a corporation may sell its bonds. For example, if on January 1 Simplex Corporation sells $750,000 of the bonds, the authorization of which was previously illustrated, the entry to record the sale is:

Jan.	1	Cash..............................	750,000.00	
		Bonds Payable................		750,000.00
		Sold $750,000 of 5 percent bonds.		

When a corporation with bonds outstanding prepares a balance sheet, it should show both the amount of bonds authorized and the amount issued and outstanding. For example, if Simplex Corporation prepares a balance sheet immediately after the bond sale just recorded, it may show the liability as follows:

Long-Term Liabilities:

First-mortgage, 5 percent bonds payable, due December 31, 1984:
    Authorized $1,000,000
    Unissued   250,000
    Issued and outstanding $750,000

When both bonds authorized and bonds issued are shown on the balance sheet, owners of the bonds are in a better position to judge whether the assets pledged as security are ample to cover the entire issue.

Authorized but unissued bonds may be sold and issued whenever funds are needed. For example, if after issuing $750,000 of its $1,000,000 of authorized bonds Simplex Corporation finds itself in need of additional funds, it may issue the remaining bonds. When it does so, it will make the following entry:

July	*1*	*Cash*................................	*250,000.00*	
		Bonds Payable...............		*250,000.00*
		Issued the remaining authorized 5 percent bonds.		

On each July 1 and January 1 thereafter, when Simplex Corporation pays the semiannual interest on its outstanding bonds, the following entry is made:

Jan.	*1*	*Bond Interest Expense*..............	*25,000.00*	
		Cash.........................		*25,000.00*
		Made the semiannual interest payment on $1,000,000 of 5 percent bonds.		

At the end of their ten year life, when the bonds are paid and retired, the entry to record their retirement is:

Dec.	*31*	*Bonds Payable*...............	*1,000,000.00*	
		Cash....................		*$1,000,000.00*
		To record the retirement of $1,000,000 of 5 percent bonds.		

BONDS SOLD BETWEEN INTEREST DATES

When bond certificates are printed, they promise to pay a designated amount of interest on each specified interest date. Sometimes bonds are sold on their interest dates; more often they are sold between interest dates. When bonds are sold between interest dates, it is customary to charge purchasers for interest accrued since the previous interest payment and to return this accrued interest to the purchasers on the next interest date. For example, assume that on March 1, a corporation sells $100,000 of 4½ percent bonds on which interest is payable semiannually on each January 1 and July 1. The entry to record the sale between interest dates is:

Mar.	1	Cash..........................	100,750.00	
		Bond Interest Expense.........		750.00
		Bonds Payable...............		100,000.00
		To record the sale of $100,000 of bonds on which two months' interest has accrued.		

At the end of four months, on the July 1 semiannual interest payment date, the purchasers of these bonds are paid a full six months' interest. This payment includes four months' interest earned by the bondholders after March 1 and the two months' accrued interest collected from them at the time the bonds were sold. The entry to record the payment is:

July	1	Bond Interest Expense............	2,250.00	
		Cash.......................		2,250.00
		To record payment of the semi-annual interest on the bonds.		

After this entry is posted, the Bond Interest Expense account has a $1,500 debit balance and appears as follows:

Bond Interest Expense

July 1	(Payment)	2,250.00	Mar. 1 (Accrued interest)	750.00

The $1,500 debit balance is the interest on the $100,000 of bonds at 4½ percent for the four months from March 1 to July 1.

BOND INTEREST RATES

When a corporation borrows by issuing bonds, the interest rate it must pay depends upon its credit standing, the security offered, and upon the current *market rate for bond interest*. The market rate for bond interest is the rate that borrowers are willing to pay and lenders are willing to take for the use of money. It fluctuates from day to day as the supply and demand for investment funds fluctuate.

When a corporation issues bonds, it specifies in the deed of trust and on each bond the interest rate it will pay. This rate is called the *contract rate*.

Normally, when a board of directors authorizes a bond issue, it estimates the interest rate the market will demand and offers a contract rate equal to its estimate. However, a period of time always elapses between the authorization of a bond issue and its sale, and during this period bond interest rates fluctuate. Consequently, when bonds are finally sold, their contract rate seldom coincides with the market rate.

BONDS SOLD AT A DISCOUNT

When a corporation offers a bond issue with a contract rate of interest below the prevailing market rate, the bonds can be sold only at a discount. For example, assume that a corporation offers $100,000 of 4 percent, ten-year bonds on which interest is payable semiannually. Assume further that on the day the bonds are offered the prevailing interest rate for like bonds is slightly in excess of 4 percent, and as a result the highest bid for the bonds is $99,000. If the corporation accepts this bid and sells the bonds, the entry to record the sale is:

Jan.	1	Cash..............................	99,000.00	
		Discount on Bonds Payable........	1,000.00	
		Bonds Payable................		100,000.00
		Sold bonds at a discount.		

The corporation of this illustration receives $99,000 that it may use for ten years. For the use of the $99,000 it agrees to repay $100,000 and to pay $4,000 interest during each of the ten years, a total of $40,000. Or, in other words, to the corporation the cost of using the $99,000 for ten years is the difference between the amount received and the amounts to be paid, or is:

> *Amounts to be paid:*
> Face of the bonds............................$100,000
> Interest (4 percent annually for ten years)..... 40,000
> Total to be paid............................$140,000
> *Amount received:*
> Bid price for the bonds........................ 99,000
> Cost of the $99,000 for ten years..............$ 41,000

If the $41,000 cost is divided equally over the ten-year life of the issue, the annual cost is $4,100. Furthermore, if the $4,100 is expressed as a percentage of the $99,000, the annual interest rate is in effect 4.14+ %

($4,100 ÷ $99,000 = 0.0414+). Obviously, then, a discount has the effect of adjusting and increasing an offered contract rate.

The corporation of this illustration receives $99,000 for its bonds, but in ten years must repay $100,000. The $1,000 discount is a cost of using the $99,000 which must be paid at maturity. However, since each year in the life of the issue benefits from the use of the $99,000, it is only fair that each should bear a fair share of the $1,000 discount.

The accounting procedure for dividing a discount and charging a fair share to each accounting period in the life of the applicable bond issue is called *amortizing* a discount. There are several methods of amortizing a discount, a common one is the straight-line method. With this method, a discount is divided equally and an equal portion is charged to each accounting period in the life of the bond issue to which it applies. For example, if the $1,000 discount on the bonds of this illustration is amortized by the straight-line method, each year in the ten-year life of the issue must bear $100. Furthermore, if each year bears $100, then each semiannual interest period must bear $50. Thus, if the $1,000 discount is amortized by the straight-line method, the following entry is made on each semiannual interest payment date to record the interest payment and the discount amortization:

July	*1*	*Bond Interest Expense.............*	*2,050.00*	
		Cash.......................		*2,000.00*
		Discount on Bonds Payable.....		*50.00*
		To record payment of six months'		
		interest and amortization of one		
		twentieth of the discount.		

The $50 discount amortization at the time of each interest payment increases recorded bond interest expense $50 each six months, and $100 each year. Also, the $50 amortization each six months completely writes off the $1,000 discount by the end of the issue's ten-year life.

BONDS SOLD AT A PREMIUM

When a corporation offers an issue with a contract rate higher than the market rate, purchasers will normally pay more than par, and the bonds will be sold at a premium. For example, assume that a corporation offers $100,000 of 5 percent, ten-year bonds on which interest is payable semiannually. Assume further that the market rate on similar bonds is below 5 percent on the day the bonds are offered and as a result they are sold at a premium, for $102,000. The entry to record the sale is:

Jan.	1	Cash...........................	102,000.00	
		Premium on Bonds Payable....		2,000.00
		Bonds Payable...............		1 00,000.00
		Sold bonds at a premium.		

The corporation of this illustration received $102,000 that it may use. To this corporation, like the previous one, the cost of using the $102,000 is the difference between the amount received and the amounts to be paid, or is:

Amounts to be paid:
Face of the bonds..........................$100,000
Interest (5 percent annually for ten years).....   50,000
Total to be paid..........................$150,000
Amount received.............................. 102,000
Cost of the $102,000 for ten years.............$ 48,000

And, if the $48,000 cost is divided equally over the ten years of the issue, the annual cost is $4,800, or in effect 4.70+% (4,800 ÷ $102,000 = 0.0470+) per year. Obviously, then, a premium like a discount is also an adjustment of an offered contract rate. However, a premium has the effect of decreasing an offered contract rate.

When bonds are sold at a premium, since the premium is in effect an adjustment of the contract rate, the premium should be amortized if each accounting period in the issue's life is to bear its fair share of the borrowed money's cost. If a premium is amortized on a straight-line basis, an equal amount is written off each period. For example, if the $2,000 premium of this illustration is amortized on a straight-line basis, $200 must be written off each year or $100 must be written off with each interest payment. If $100 is written off with each payment, the entry to record the payment and the premium amortization is:

July	1	Bond Interest Expense.............	2,400.00	
		Premium on Bonds Payable........	100.00	
		Cash......................		2,500.00
		To record payment of six months' interest and the amortization of one twentieth of the premium.		

Observe in the foregoing entry that the premium amortization has the effect of reducing the recorded interest expense from the $2,500 paid the bondholders to $2,400.

ACCRUED BOND INTEREST EXPENSE

Often when bonds are sold, the bond interest periods do not coincide with the issuing company's accounting periods. In such cases it is necessary at the end of each accounting period to make an adjustment for interest accrued. For example, on March 1, 1967, a corporation having yearly accounting periods which end on December 31, sells $100,000 of 4½ percent, 20-year bonds for $101,200. The interest on the bonds is to be paid semiannually on each March 1 and September 1. The entry to record the September 1 semiannual interest payment is:

Sept.	1	Bond Interest Expense...............	2,220.00	
		Premium on Bonds Payable........	30.00	
		Cash..........................		2,250.00
		To record payment of interest on the bonds and amortization of the premium.		

On December 31, 1967, and on each December 31 thereafter throughout the life of this issue, there are always four months' accrued interest on these bonds. The interest will not be paid until the following March 1; therefore, at each year-end an adjusting entry like the following is required:

Dec.	31	Bond Interest Expense.............	1,480.00	
		Premium on Bonds Payable........	20.00	
		Bonds Interest Payable........		1,500.00
		To record four months' accrued interest.		

This adjusting entry may be reversed at the beginning of the new accounting period. If it is reversed, the normal interest payment and premium amortization entry is made when interest is paid on March 1.

PREMIUMS AND DISCOUNTS ON BONDS OUTSTANDING LESS THAN THEIR FULL TERM

The bonds previously illustrated were either 10- or 20-year bonds and were assumed to be outstanding in each case a full 10 or 20 years. Often bonds are not outstanding the full term of years in their authorized lives. For example, assume that in November, 1966, a $1,000,000 20-year bond issue dated January 1, 1967, and due January 1, 1987, was authorized. Assume further that interest is payable semiannually on the issue on each January 1 and July 1 and that the issue was sold on March 1, 1967, at a $47,600 discount.

Between January 1, 1967, and January 1, 1987, is a period of 20 years, or 240 months; but between March 1, 1967, and January 1, 1987, is only 238 months. Consequently, since the bonds will be outstanding only 238 months, the discount must be amortized over this shorter period. Therefore, when interest is paid on July 1, 1967, four months' discount, or $800 ($47,600 × $\frac{4}{238}$ = $800), should be written off; and on January 1, 1968, and at the end of each six months thereafter, six months' discount, or $1,200 ($47,600 × $\frac{6}{238}$ = $1,200), should be amortized.

DISCOUNTS AND PREMIUMS ON THE BALANCE SHEET

The trend in balance sheet presentation is to show bond premiums and discounts somewhat as follows:

Long-Term Liabilities:		
First 5 percent real estate mortgage bonds, due in 1978.	$2,500,000	
Add: Unamortized premium.	30,000	$2,530,000
Collateral trust 4 percent bonds, due in 1980	$1,000,000	
Deduct: Unamortized discount.	22,000	978,000

It was once not uncommon for bond discount to be placed on the balance sheet as an asset under a long-term prepaid expense classification called "Deferred charges" and for bond premium to be shown as a "Deferred credit." However, general opinion now rejects the idea that bond discount is a prepaid expense; rather this opinion holds that bond discount is "unpaid interest expense," payable when the bonds mature. This expense accrues over the life of the bonds. Therefore, on the balance sheet, bond discount should be deducted from the maturity value of the bonds to reduce the maturity value for the discount not yet earned by investors and not yet an actual liability to the issuing corporation. Similarly premium on bonds should be added to maturity value, since the premium represents a liability to pay interest in excess of the market rate over the remaining life of the bonds.

COSTS OF A BOND ISSUE

When bonds are issued, there are certain costs such as attorneys' fees, printing, and so on. Often their sum is material in relation to the bond issue; and theoretically, they are prepaid expenses that should be set up in a separate account and written off over the life of the issue. However, as a practical measure such costs are commonly added to the discount, if the bonds are sold at a discount, or are deducted from the premium, if sold at a premium, and are then written off with the premium or discount. This treatment is not theoretically accurate; however, it is long established and has the same effect as the more accurate treatment of such costs as a separate prepaid item.

REDEMPTION OF BONDS

Bonds are commonly issued with the provision that they may be redeemed at the issuing corporation's option, usually upon the payment of a premium. Such bonds are known as *callable bonds*. Corporations commonly insert redemption clauses in deeds of trust because if interest rates decline, it may be advantageous to call and redeem outstanding bonds and issue in their place new bonds paying a lower interest rate.

Not all bonds have a provision giving their issuing company the right to call. However, even though the right is not provided, a company may secure the same effect by purchasing its bonds on the open market. Often such action is wise when a company has funds available and its bonds are selling at a price below par plus their unamortized premium or at a price below par minus unamortized discount. For example a company has outstanding on their interest date $1,000,000 of bonds on which there is $12,000 unamortized premium. The bonds are selling at 98.5 percent of par value, and the company decides to buy and retire one tenth of the issue. The entry to record the purchase and retirement is:

Apr.	*1*	*Bonds Payable.............................*	*100,000.00*	
		Premium on Bonds Payable.................	*1,200.00*	
		Gain on the Retirement of Bonds.......		*2,700.00*
		Cash.....................................		*98,500.00*

The retirement results in a $2,700 gain. This gain is the difference between the cash given and the retired bonds' par value plus the applicable premium.

CONVERTIBLE BONDS

To make an issue more attractive, bond owners may be given the right to exchange their bonds for a fixed number of shares of the issuing company's common stock. Such bonds are known as convertible bonds. They offer investors initial investment security and, if the issuing company prospers, an opportunity to share in the prosperity by converting their bonds to stock. Conversion is always at the bondholders' option and is not exercised except when to do so is to their advantage.

When bonds are converted into stock, the conversion changes creditor equity into ownership equity. The generally accepted rule for measuring the contribution for the issued shares is that the book value of the liability becomes the book value of the capital contributed for the new shares. For example, assume that (1) a company has outstanding $1,000,000 of bonds upon which there is $8,000 unamortized discount; (2) the bonds are convertible at the rate of a $1,000 bond for 18 shares of $50 par value common stock; and (3) $100,000 in bonds have been presented on their interest date for conversion. The entry to record the conversion is:

May	1	Bonds Payable....................	100,000.00	
		Discount on Bonds Payable.....		800.00
		Common Stock................		90,000.00
		Premium on Common Stock....		9,200.00
		To record the conversion of bonds.		

Note in the foregoing entry that the bonds' $99,200 book value sets the accounting value for the capital contributed. Usually when bonds have a conversion privilege, it is not exercised until the stock's market value and normal dividend payments are sufficiently high to make the conversion profitable to the bondholders.

BOND SINKING FUND

Although bonds normally offer a smaller return than either common or preferred stocks, they appeal to a portion of the investing public. Normally the appeal results from their fixed return and greater security. Security is commonly important to bond investors. A corporation issuing bonds may offer investors a measure of security by placing a mortgage on certain of its assets. Often it will give additional security by agreeing in its deed of trust to create a *bond sinking fund*. A bond sinking fund is a fund of assets accumulated to pay the bondholders at maturity.

When a corporation issuing bonds agrees to create a bond sinking fund, it normally agrees to create the fund by making periodic cash deposits with a sinking fund trustee. It is the duty of the trustee to safeguard the cash, to invest it in good sound securities, and to add the interest or dividends earned to the sinking fund. Generally, when the bonds become due, it is also the duty of the sinking fund trustee to sell the sinking fund securities and to use the proceeds to pay the bondholders. The sinking fund trustee may or may not be the trustee with whom the deed of trust is deposited.

When a sinking fund is created, the amount that must be deposited periodically in order to provide a sum sufficiently large to retire a bond issue at maturity will depend upon the net rate of compound interest that can be earned on the invested funds. The rate is a compound rate because earnings are continually reinvested by the sinking fund trustee to earn an additional return, and it is a net rate because the trustee commonly deducts the fee for his services from the earnings.

To illustrate the operation of a sinking fund, assume a corporation issues $1,000,000 of ten-year bonds and agrees to deposit with a sinking fund trustee at the end of each year in the issue's life sufficient cash to create a fund large enough to retire the bonds at maturity. If the trustee is able to invest the funds in such a manner as to earn a 4 percent net return, $83,290.95 must be deposited each year and the fund will grow to maturity as shown in Illustration 119.

Illustration 119

End of Year	Amount Deposited	Interest Earned on Fund Balance	Balance in Fund after Deposit and Interest
1..........	$83,290.95	-0-	$ 83,290.95
2..........	83,290.95	$ 3,331.64	169,913.54
3..........	83,290.95	6,796.54	260,001.03
4..........	83,290.95	10,400.04	353,692.02
5..........	83,290.95	14,147.68	451,130.65
6..........	83,290.95	18,045.23	552,466.83
7..........	83,290.95	22,098.67	657,856.45
8..........	83,290.95	26,314.26	767,461.66
9..........	83,290.95	30,698.47	881,451.08
10..........	83,290.95	35,258.04	1,000,000.00

Calculating the amount that must be deposited each year in order that the deposits and their interest will produce a fund of a required size is a problem reserved for a course in mathematics of finance or advanced accounting. It is deemed sufficient here that the student understand how such a fund operates.

When a sinking fund is created, by periodic deposits, the entry to record the amount deposited each year appears as follows:

Dec.	31	Bond Sinking Fund..................	83,290.95	
		Cash...........................		83,290.95
		Deposited cash with sinking fund trustee.		

Each year the sinking fund trustee invests the amount deposited, and each year collects and reports the earnings on the investments. His earnings report results in a journal entry to record the sinking fund income. For example, if $83,290.95 is deposited at the end of the first year in the sinking fund, the accumulation of which is shown in Illustration 119, and 4 percent is earned, the entry to record the sinking fund earnings at the end of the second year is:

Dec.	31	Bond Sinking Fund..................	3,331.64	
		Sinking Fund Earnings...........		3,331.64
		To record the sinking fund earnings.		

Sinking fund earnings appear on the income statement as financial revenue in the "other revenues and expenses section."

When bonds payable mature, it is usually the duty of the sinking fund trustee to convert the fund's investments into cash and pay the bondholders. Normally if the sinking fund securities, when sold, produce the amount needed to pay the bondholders, the trustee pays them and notifies the corporation. When the corporation receives notice that its bonds have been paid, it makes the following entry:

Jan.	3	Bonds Payable..................	1,000,000.00	
		Bond Sinking Fund.........		1,000,000.00
		To record the payment of our bonds by the sinking fund trustee.		

Sinking fund investments normally earn slightly more or less than anticipated. Consequently, when a sinking fund is liquidated, there is always either a little more or a little less cash in the fund than is needed to pay the bondholders. If there is more cash than needed, after the bondholders are paid, the excess is returned to the corporation by the trustee. The entry to record receipt of returned sinking fund cash is:

Jan.	3	Cash..................................	3,105.00	
		Bond Sinking Fund.............		3,105.00
		Unused sinking fund balance returned by sinking fund trustee.		

If there is insufficient cash in a sinking fund with which to pay the bondholders when bonds become due, the debtor corporation must pay the shortage into the fund. The entry to record this is:

Jan.	3	Bond Sinking Fund..................	1,382.20	
		Cash.............................		1,382.20
		To record payment of cash to the sinking fund trustee to cover the fund's deficit.		

RESTRICTION ON DIVIDENDS DUE TO OUTSTANDING BONDS

If a corporation disburses in dividends all assets acquired each year through earnings and pays out still more assets in sinking fund deposits, it may find itself within a few years without sufficient assets, particularly current assets, to operate and unable either to pay dividends or make sinking fund deposits. To prevent this, a deed of trust may restrict the dividends a corporation may pay while its bonds are outstanding.

When dividends are restricted by a deed of trust, the restriction may say the corporation may pay dividends in any year only to the extent that the year's earnings exceed sinking fund requirements. Or the restriction may require the corporation to appropriate retained earnings each year equal to the year's sinking fund requirements. If the latter method is used, its purpose is to reduce dividend payments by reducing the balance of the Retained Earnings account available to absorb dividend charges.

To illustrate the appropriation each year of retained earnings equal to the year's sinking fund requirements, assume that the corporation whose bond fund accumulations are shown in Illustration 119 must make such appropriations. Assume further that the corporation is required by its deed of trust to appropriate an amount of retained earnings each year equal to the sum of its sinking fund deposit plus the year's sinking fund earnings. If the corporation makes the appropriations, it will appropriate $83,290.95 the first year and will record the appropriations as follows:

Dec.	*31*	*Retained Earnings..........................*	*83,290.95*	
		Retained Earnings Appropriated for		
		Bonded Indebtedness...................		*83,290.95*
		To record the appropriation of retained earnings equal to the deposit in the bond sinking fund.		

Only $83,290.95 must be appropriated the first year because the sinking fund deposit of the year was made at the year's end and, consequently, there were no sinking fund earnings. However, if the sinking fund earns a 4 percent return, at the end of the second year the corporation must appropriate $86,622.59 of retained earnings. This is the sum of the second year's deposit and the second year's sinking fund earnings. Furthermore, if 4 percent is earned, the third year's appropriation will be $90,087.49 ($83,290.95 + $6,796.54 = $90,087.49) and the appropriations will continue to grow throughout the life of the bond issue.

After a bond issue has been paid, the appropriations have served their purpose and the amount appropriated during the life of the issue is returned to unappropriated retained earnings with an entry like this:

Jan.	*15*	*Retained Earnings Appropriated for Bonded*		
		Indebtedness.............................	*1,000,000.00*	
		Retained Earnings....................		*1,000,000.00*
		To return the retained earnings appropriated for bonded indebtedness to unappropriated retained earnings.		

Terminology. When a corporation is required by a deed of trust to appropriate retained earnings each year equal to the year's sinking fund requirements, the total of such appropriations may appear on its balance sheet in the retained earnings section as "Retained earnings appropriated for bonded indebtedness." However, if the corporation uses older terminology, such appropriations may appear under a caption such as "Reserve for bond sinking fund" or "Sinking fund reserve." The latter captions are not good, since many balance sheet readers get the mistaken idea from them that something, cash, for example, is held in reserve. Nevertheless, they are still occasionally seen on published balance sheets.

LONG-TERM NOTES

When bond interest rates are temporarily unfavorable and funds are available from four or five large banks or insurance companies, often long-term notes maturing in two, three, or five years are issued instead of bonds. Also, in some instances, in order to avoid the costs of issuing bonds and dealing with several thousand bondholders, long-term notes maturing in ten, twenty, or more years are issued instead of bonds.

Long-term notes whether maturing in two or three years or in ten or more years are often secured by mortgages. Too, those maturing in ten or more years may provide for sinking funds. Consequently, long-term notes take on the characteristics of both mortgages and bonds. Ordinarily they differ only in that they are placed with a few lenders, usually at par. Insofar as accounting is concerned, long-term notes receive the same treatment as mortgages or bonds.

STOCKS AND BONDS AS INVESTMENTS

A business may buy stocks and bonds as investments; and such investments are classified as either *temporary investments* or *long-term investments*. The classification depends in each case upon whether the stocks and bonds are readily marketable and upon the intention of the investing company. If readily marketable and the investing company intends to keep the securities for only a short period, the investment is classified as a temporary investment, a current asset. If the intention is to keep the stocks and bonds for a long period, usually more than a year, the investment is classified as a long-term investment.

Temporary or short-term investments are often made by a company whose business is seasonal in nature. Normally, in such a company during the busy season, much of the current assets is invested in inventories and accounts receivable; and during the slack or off season these inventories and accounts are turned into cash through sales and collections. Often during the slack season, in order to earn additional income, this temporarily idle cash is invested in high-grade securities which at the beginning of the next busy season are converted back to cash.

Long-term investments differ from temporary investments in that they are to be kept for a longer period. Long-term investments include funds earmarked for special purposes, such as bond sinking funds and building funds, as well as real estate and other long-term assets owned but not employed in the regular business operations. Such investments appear on the balance sheet in a classification of their own under the title of "Long-term investments," which appears on the balance sheet immediately following the current asset section.

Stocks and bonds purchased as investments are normally bought through brokers who charge a commission for their services. Brokers acting as agents for their customers buy and sell stocks and bonds on stock exchanges such as the New York Stock Exchange. Five or six million shares of stock and several thousand bonds are bought and sold each day on stock exchanges, and each day the sales prices are published on the financial pages of many newspapers. Stock prices are quoted on the basis of dollars and ⅛ dollars per share. For example, a stock quoted at 46⅛ sold for $46.125 per share, and stock quoted at 25½ sold for $25.50 per share. Bonds are normally issued in $1,000 denominations, but their prices are quoted on a percentage basis. For example, a $1,000 bond quoted at 98⅛ sold at 98⅛ percent of $1,000, or $981.25, and a $1,000 bond quoted at 86¼ sold for $862.50.

Temporary Investments. When stocks and bonds are bought as temporary investments, they are recorded at their total cost, which includes the commission paid the broker. For example, 1,000 shares of American Sales Corporation common stock are purchased as a temporary investment at 23¼ plus a $200 broker's commission. The entry to record the transaction is:

Sept.	*10*	*American Sales Corporation Stock*............	23,450.00	
		Cash....................................		23,450.00
		Purchased 1,000 shares of stock for $23,250		
		plus a $200 broker's commission.		

When dividends are received on stocks held as either temporary or long-term investments and interest is received on bonds held as short-term investments, an entry similar to the following is made:

Oct.	*5*	*Cash*.....................................	1,000.00	
		Dividends Earned.......................		1,000.00
		Received a $1 per share dividend on the		
		American Sales Corporation stock.		

When interest is received on bonds held as a long-term investment, a different method is commonly used in recording the earnings. This method is discussed later in this chapter under long-term investments.

When a temporary investment in stocks or bonds is sold, normally a gain or a loss is incurred. If the amount received is greater than the original cost of the investment plus the commission on the sale and other costs, there is a gain. For example, if the 1,000 shares of American Sales Corporation common stock, the purchase of which at $23,450 was recorded above, are sold at 25¾ less a commission and taxes on the sale amounting to $205, there is a $2,095 gain, and the transaction is recorded:

Jan.	*7*	*Cash...*	*25,545.00*	
		American Sales Corporation Stock........		*23,450.00*
		Gain on the Sale of Investments.........		*2,095.00*
		Sold 1,000 shares of stock for $25,750 less a		
		$205 commission and other costs.		

When stocks and bonds held as temporary investments are sold at a price less than their cost plus the sale costs, a loss is incurred. For example, if the American Sales Corporation stock of the previous illustrations is sold at 22½ less a commission and taxes of $196, a $1,146 loss is incurred, and the transaction is recorded:

Jan.	*7*	*Cash...*	*22,304.00*	
		Loss on the Sale of Investments..............	*1,146.00*	
		American Sales Corporation Stock........		*23,450.00*
		Sold 1,000 shares of stock for $22,500 less a		
		$196 commission and other costs.		

When an income statement is prepared, bond interest and dividends earned plus any gains or losses on investment sales are listed at the end in the "other revenues and expenses section."

If a balance sheet is prepared while temporary investments are held, such investments should appear as a current asset immediately following cash. Since temporary investments are current assets, they are normally valued on the balance sheet at lower of cost or market. However, both cost and market prices should be shown as follows:

```
Current Assets:
   Cash . . . . . . . . . . . . . . . .      $23,000
   Temporary investments, at cost (present
      market value, $14,700) . . . . . . . .    13,250
   Notes receivable . . . . . . . . . . . .     2,500
```

Long-Term Investments. Stocks purchased as a long-term investment are accounted for in the same manner as a temporary stock investment. Likewise, the entry to record bonds purchased as a long-term investment is similar to the ·entry for a temporary stock investment. However, since bonds purchased as a long-term investment are normally purchased at either a premium or discount and are often held to maturity, the entry to record interest earned on such bonds differs from the entry for interest on a temporary bond investment.

To illustrate the entries for bonds purchased as a long-term investment, assume that ten $1,000, 4 percent, 20-year bonds on which interest is paid semiannually are purchased on their interest date 15 years before maturity at 98¼. The commission on the purchase is $25, bringing the total cost to $9,850. The entry to record the purchase is:

Jan.	1	Zest Corporation Bonds................	9,850.00	
		Cash.............................		9,850.00
		Purchased ten bonds for $9,825 plus a		
		$25 commission.		

Bonds differ from stocks in that sooner or later they mature and are normally redeemed at face value. For example, if the Zest Corporation bonds just illustrated are held to maturity and are redeemed at face value, they will be redeemed for $1,000 each. Consequently, if these bonds are held to maturity, they produce 4 percent interest each year plus a $150 gain, at the end of 15 years. The gain is the difference between their cost and maturity value. This difference, although a combination of discount and commission, is called a discount and is treated as an adjustment of the bond interest earned. Normally a portion is amortized on each interest payment date. If a portion of the $150 is amortized each semiannual interest payment date, the entry to record the interest receipt and the discount amortization is:

July	1	Cash................................	200.00	
		Zest Corporation Bonds...............	5.00	
		Bond Interest Earned.............		205.00
		Received the interest on the Zest Cor-		
		poration bonds and amortized one		
		thirtieth of the discount.		

In the entry just given, the $5 debit to the bond investment account increases the book value of the Zest Corporation bonds. After the entry is posted, the bond investment account appears as follows:

Zest Corporation Bonds

Date	Explanation	Debit	Credit	Balance
Jan. 1, '66	Purchase	9,850.00		9,850.00
July 1, '66	Discount amortization	5.00		9,855.00

If these bonds are held to maturity, and the account balance is increased $5 on each semiannual interest date, when the bonds mature, they will be shown in the account at their full $10,000 maturity value.

Bonds purchased as long-term investments may be sold before maturity. If the Zest Corporation bonds are held three years and then sold, the bond investment account just prior to the sale will show a $9,880 value for the bonds and will appear as follows:

Zest Corporation Bonds

Date	Explanation	Debit	Credit	Balance
Jan. 1, '66	Purchase	9,850.00		9,850.00
July 1, '66	Discount amortization	5.00		9,855.00
Jan. 1, '67	Discount amortization	5.00		9,860.00
July 1, '67	Discount amortization	5.00		9,865.00
Jan. 1, '68	Discount amortization	5.00		9,870.00
July 1, '68	Discount amortization	5.00		9,875.00
Jan. 1, '69	Discount amortization	5.00		9,880.00

If the bonds are sold after three years for $9,975 less a $25 commission, the entry to record the sale is:

Jan.	1	Cash....................................	9,950.00	
		Zest Corporation Bonds..........		9,880.00
		Gain on Sale of Investments.....		70.00
		Sold Zest Corporation bonds for $9,975 less a $25 commission.		

Bonds may be purchased as long-term investments at a cost greater than their maturity value. In such cases the bonds are recorded at cost with the difference between cost and maturity value, called a premium, being treated as an interest rate adjustment and amortized over the remaining life of the bonds. For example, twenty $1,000, 4 percent bonds are purchased ten years before maturity at a total cost of $20,250. The entry to record the purchase is:

Jan.	1	Able Corporation Bonds.............	20,250.00	
		Cash...........................		20,250.00
		Purchased 20 bonds at a premium.		

If the interest on these bonds is paid semiannually, the entry to record its receipt and to record the premium amortization is:

July	1	Cash..............................	400.00	
		Able Corporation Bonds..........		12.50
		Bond Interest Earned............		387.50
		Received interest and amortized		
		one twentieth of the premium.		

Unless there is a material decline in market prices, long-term investments in stocks are shown in the accounts and on the balance sheet at cost, and long-term investments in bonds are shown at cost adjusted for any premium or discount amortized. Since these investments are not for sale, minor fluctuations in market prices are normally ignored.

Bonds Purchased between Interest Dates.   Often bonds are purchased between interest dates. In such cases the purchaser pays the interest accrued since the last interest payment. For example, if a $1,000, 4½ percent bond on which interest is paid semiannually on January 1 and July 1 is purchased on March 1, at par, the entry to record the purchase is:

Mar.	1	Best Corporation Bonds.............	1,000.00	
		Bond Interest Earned...............	7.50	
		Cash...........................		1,007.50
		Purchased a bond with two		
		month's accrued interest.		

On July 1, the semiannual receipt of interest on this bond is recorded:

July	*1*	*Cash*...............................	*22.50*	
		Bond Interest Earned...........		*22.50*
		Received interest on the Best Cor-		
		poration bond.		

The net effect of these two entries on the Bond Interest Earned account is a $15 credit. This is the equivalent of four months' interest, March 1 to July 1, on $1,000 at 4½ percent.

THE CORPORATION BALANCE SHEET

Corporation balance sheets are normally longer and more complicated than those of either single proprietorships or partnerships. In this and the three previous chapters a number of isolated corporation balance sheet sections have been illustrated. In order to bring all of these together, the balance sheet of Best Corporation is shown in Illustration 120.

THE CORPORATION EARNINGS STATEMENT

The detail presented in the income statement or earnings statement, as well as in the balance sheet, depends upon the use for which the statement is prepared, or upon the class of readers to which the statement is to be presented. Statements to management must contain considerably more detail than those presented to stockholders and the general public. Actually, the basic statements to all groups should be compact and concise; and where considerable detail must be reported, this should be done in supplementary schedules. The principal statements should be reasonably short, each being contained on a single page, or in the case of the balance sheet, on not more than two facing pages.

Income statements illustrated so far in this text have been multiple-step statements; i.e., cost of goods sold is deducted in one step, then operating expenses, then income taxes, etc. This implies a preferential order for the recovery of costs and expenses. Actually, in theory, there is no such preferential order for there can be no net income unless all costs and expenses are recovered.

To avoid some of the implications of the multiple-step statement, the single-step form of income statement is being used more and more in published reports. This form of statement may be in considerable detail, but generally when employed for the published statement, it is condensed, as in Illustration 121. This illustration is adapted from a recent annual report to stockholders by the National Dairy Products Corporation (amounts and footnotes are omitted as not being essential to illustration of form).

Illustration 120

BEST CORPORATION
Balance Sheet, December 31, 19--

ASSETS

Current Assets:			
Cash		$ 15,000	
Able Corporation common stock.		5,000	
Accounts receivable.	$ 50,000		
Less: Allowance for bad debts.	1,000	49,000	
Merchandise inventory.		115,000	
Subscriptions receivable common stock.		15,000	
Prepaid expenses		1,000	
Total Current Assets			$200,000
Long-Term Investments:			
Bond sinking fund.		$ 15,000	
Toledo Corporation common stock.		5,000	
Total Long-Term Investments.			20,000
Fixed Assets:			
Land		$ 28,000	
Buildings.	$190,000		
Less: Accumulated depreciation	30,000	160,000	
Store equipment.	$ 85,000		
Less: Accumulated depreciation	20,000	65,000	
Total Fixed Assets			253,000
Intangible Assets:			
Goodwill			23,000
Deferred Charges:			
Unamortized moving costs			4,000
Total Assets			$500,000

LIABILITIES

Current Liabilities:			
Notes payable.	$ 10,000		
Accounts payable	24,000		
State and federal income taxes payable	16,000		
Total Current Liabilities.		$ 50,000	
Long-Term Liabilities:			
First 5% real estate mortgage bonds, due in 1979 .	$100,000		
Deduct: Unamortized discount	2,000	98,000	
Total Liabilities.			$148,000

CONTRIBUTED CAPITAL AND RETAINED EARNINGS

Contributed Capital:			
Common stock, $100 par value per share, author-			
ized 2,500 shares, issued 2,000 shares		$200,000	
Unissued common stock subscribed, 250 shares . . .		25,000	
Capital contributed by the stockholders in excess			
of the par value of their shares		33,000	
Total Contributed Capital.		$258,000	
Retained Earnings:			
Appropriated retained earnings:			
Appropriated for bonded indebtedness . . $15,000			
Appropriated for plant expansion 10,000	$ 25,000		
Unappropriated retained earnings	69,000		
Total Retained Earnings.		94,000	
Contributed Capital and Retained Earnings. .			352,000
Total Liabilities and Capital.			$500,000

Illustration 121

NATIONAL DAIRY PRODUCTS CORPORATION

Statement of Earnings for the Year Ended December 31, 19—

Revenue:

   Sales less discounts allowed .... $.....
   Dividends, interest, and other income .... $.....

     Total .... $.....

Revenue Deductions:

   Cost of products .... $.....
   Delivery expenses ....
   Selling expenses ....
   General and administrative expenses ....
   Miscellaneous charges—net ....
   Interest on long-term debt ....
   Provision for federal and Canadian taxes on income .....

     Total .... $.....

Net Earnings for the Year .... $.....

QUESTIONS FOR CLASS DISCUSSION

1. What two legal documents are involved when a company borrows by giving a mortgage? What is the purpose of each?

2. What is the primary difference between a share of stock and a bond?

3. What is a deed of trust? What are some of the provisions commonly contained in a deed of trust?

4. Define or describe: (*a*) registered bonds, (*b*) coupon bonds, (*c*) serial bonds, (*d*) sinking fund bonds, (*e*) redeemable bonds, (*f*) convertible bonds, and (*g*) debenture bonds.

5. Company A issued $1,000,000 of 5 percent, ten-year bonds and sold them at 104; Company B issued $1,000,000 of 4 percent, ten-year bonds and sold them at 96. Which company incurred the higher rate of interest for its borrowed funds?

6. On its January 1 date of issue Blue Corporation sold at 98½ a $1,000,000, 4½ percent, ten-year bond issue on which interest is payable each July 1 and January 1. Give the entries for (*a*) the bond sale, (*b*) the semiannual payment of interest and amortization of discount, and (*c*) the retirement of the bonds at maturity.

7. On April 1, three months after its date of issue, Green Corporation sold a $1,000,000, 5 percent, ten-year bond issue on which interest is payable each July 1 and January 1. The corporation received $1,018,350 from the

sale. Give the entries for (*a*) the bond sale, (*b*) the first interest payment and amortization of discount, (*c*) the second interest payment and amortization of discount, and (*d*) the retirement of the bonds.

8. On its February 1 date of issue Brown Corporation sold at 97 a $1,000,-000, 4½ percent, ten-year bond issue on which interest is payable on each August 1 and February 1. Give (*a*) the entry to record the first payment of interest and amortization of discount, (*b*) the adjusting entry required each December 31 to record accrued interest on the issue, (*c*) the entry to reverse the accrued interest adjusting entry, and (*d*) the February 1 payment of bond interest and amortization of discount.

9. On their January 1 date of issue, Standard Corporation sold $1,000,000 of 5 percent, ten-year bonds at par. In its deed of trust the corporation agreed to create a bond sinking fund by making annual deposits with a trustee that with the interest earned would create a fund sufficient to retire the bonds at maturity. Assume that the trustee can invest the funds so as to earn 4 percent, that $83,290.95 is deposited at the end of each year, and that the fund grows to maturity as shown in Illustration 119. (*a*) Give the entry to record the deposit made at the end of the first year in the life of the bond issue. (*b*) Give the entry to record the second-year sinking fund earnings. (*c*) Give the entry to record the deposit made at the end of the fifth year. (*d*) Give the entry to record the fifth-year sinking fund earnings.

10. Assume the bond sinking fund of Question 9 earns slightly more than 4 percent and at the end of the tenth year has a balance of $1,002,915. Give the entries to record (*a*) the payment of the bonds by the sinking fund trustee, and (*b*) the return of the fund balance to Standard Corporation.

11. What purpose is served by creating a bond sinking fund?

12. What is the balance sheet classification of a bond sinking fund?

13. What purpose is served by requiring a corporation to appropriate retained earnings each year equal in amount to its sinking fund deposit plus the sinking fund earnings?

14. Assume that in addition to the bond sinking fund Standard Corporation (Question 9) also agreed to appropriate retained earnings each year during the life of its bond issue equal to the sum of the annual sinking fund deposit plus the sinking fund earnings of that year. Under the assumption that the fund earns a return each year equal to the assumed earnings of the table in Illustration 119, give the entries for the appropriations at the ends of the (*a*) second, and (*b*) fifth years in the life of the bond issue.

15. A company purchased 1,000 shares of American Corporation common stock at 44¼ plus a $450 brokerage commission. Later the company sold the stock at 51⅜ less a $520 brokerage commission. Give the entries to record the transactions.

16. On March 1, a firm purchased ten $1,000, 4½ percent, 20-year bonds of the Daul Corporation as a temporary investment at 98¼ plus accrued interest and a commission of $25. Interest is payable on the bonds semiannually on each July 1 and January 1. Give the entries for (*a*) the purchase of the bonds, and (*b*) the July 1 semiannual receipt of interest.

17. On September 1 the firm of Question 16 sold the ten $1,000 bonds at

99¼ plus accrued interest and less a commission of $25. Give the entry to record the sale.

18. Hite Corporation purchased as a long-term investment on their interest payment date, ten years before maturity, ten $1,000, 5 percent bonds of Blue Company at 102¼ plus a $25 commission. The corporation held the bonds for five years and sold them on their interest payment date at 100½ less a $25 commission. Give the entries to record (a) the purchase, (b) the receipt of a semiannual interest payment, and (c) the sale of the bonds.

19. How does the single-step income statement differ from the multiple-step form?

PROBLEMS

Problem 19–1

A corporation has outstanding 100,000 shares of $10 par value common stock which was issued at the time it was organized. Over the years the corporation has prospered and now needs additional capital for expansion. Its board of directors estimates that with an additional $1,000,000 the company can expect to earn $300,000 per year before bond interest and income taxes. The corporation's combined state and federal income tax rate is expected to continue at its present 50 percent. Three methods of securing the additional capital have been suggested. They are the issuance of 100,000 additional shares of $10 par value common stock; the issuance of 10,000 shares of $100 par value, 6 percent cumulative and nonparticipating preferred stock, or the issuance of $1,000,000 of 5 percent, 20-year bonds.

Required:

Calculate the earnings per share that will accrue to the original common stockholders of the corporation if (a) additional common stock is issued, (b) the preferred stock is issued, and (c) bonds are issued. (Assume the preferred stock and bonds are issued at par.)

Problem 19–2

On April 17, 1963, Random Corporation deposited a deed of trust with Western Trust Company which authorized it to issue $1,000,000 of 4½ percent, 20-year bonds dated May 1, 1963, and paying interest on each May 1 and November 1. It then completed these transactions:

1963
June   1   Sold the entire bond issue for $994,025 plus accrued interest.
Nov.   1   Paid the semiannual interest on the bonds.
Dec. 31   Recorded the accrued interest on the bonds.
1964
Jan.   1   Reversed the accrued interest adjusting entry.
May   1   Paid the semiannual interest on the bonds.
1967
May   1   Paid the semiannual interest on the bonds, and purchased in the open market and retired $100,000 of the bonds. The purchase price was $98,500, including the commission.

Required:
Prepare general journal entries to record the foregoing transactions.

Problem 19–3

On December 8, 1962, a corporation deposited a deed of trust with the trustee of its bondholders which authorized it to issue $1,000,000 of 5 percent, ten-year, convertible bonds, dated January 1, 1963, and upon which interest is payable on each January 1 and July 1. The conversion clause in the deed of trust granted the bondholders the right to convert their bonds before January 1, 1968, into shares of the company's common stock at the rate of 85 shares of $10 par value common stock for each $1,000 bond.

Required:
Give entries in general journal form to record the following transactions:
a) Sold the entire bond issue at 102 on January 1, 1963.
b) Paid the interest and amortized the premium on July 1, 1963.
c) After paying the interest on January 1, 1964, converted bonds having a $100,000 par value to common stock.
d) Paid the interest and amortized the premium on July 1, 1964.
e) On January 1, 1967, purchased on the open market and retired bonds having a $100,000 par value. The total cash outlay was $99,750.
f) Paid the interest and amortized the premium on July 1, 1967.

Problem 19–4

South Mountain Corporation deposited a deed of trust with Western Trust Company on December 14, 1962, which authorized it to issue $2,000,000 of 5 percent, four-year bonds. (Four years are an unrealistically small number of years for a bond issue; however, by using such a number, all entries for a bond sinking fund may be required without the necessity of many repetitive entries.)

In the deed of trust South Mountain Corporation agreed to create a bond sinking fund by depositing with a trustee $470,980 at the end of each year in the life of the bond issue. It was assumed the sinking fund investments would earn 4 percent net and the fund would grow to maturity as follows:

End of Year	Amount Deposited	Interest Earned on Fund Balance	Balance in Fund after Deposit and Interest
1.................	$470,980	$ –0–	$ 470,980
2.................	470,980	18,840	960,800
3.................	470,980	38,432	1,470,212
4.................	470,980	58,808	2,000,000

In addition to the sinking fund, South Mountain Corporation agreed in its deed of trust to appropriate retained earnings each year equal to the sum of its sinking fund deposit plus the sinking fund earnings of that year.

After depositing the deed of trust, the corporation completed these transactions:

1963
Jan. 1 Sold the entire bond issue at par.
Dec. 31 Made the first annual sinking fund deposit.
     31 Appropriated retained earnings as required by the deed of trust.

1964
Dec. 31 Made the second annual sinking fund deposit.
     31 Received the sinking fund trustee's report showing the sinking fund had earned $18,840 during the year.
     31 Appropriated retained earnings as required by the deed of trust.

1965
Dec. 31 Made the third annual sinking fund deposit.
     31 Received the sinking fund trustee's report showing the fund had earned $38,402. (This is slightly less than was anticipated the fund would earn. However, it is not enough to warrant a change in the deposit required of South Mountain Corporation.)
     31 Appropriated retained earnings equal to the sum of the sinking fund deposit and sinking fund earnings.

1966
Dec. 31 Made the fourth annual sinking fund deposit.
     31 Received the sinking fund trustee's report showing the fund had earned $58,985.
     31 Appropriated retained earnings equal to the sum of the sinking fund deposit plus the year's sinking fund earnings.

1967
Jan. 12 Received a report from the sinking fund trustee showing the bonds had been paid in full. Attached to the report was a check for the excess earnings in the sinking fund.
     15 The board of directors voted to return the retained earnings appropriated for bonded indebtedness to unappropriated retained earnings.

Required:
Prepare general journal entries to record the foregoing transactions.

Problem 19–5

A concern completed these investment transactions:

Feb.   1 Purchased as a long-term investment ten Delta Corporation, $1,000, 5 percent, 20-year bonds on their interest date six years before maturity. The purchase price was 102¾ plus a $25 commission.
Mar. 15 Purchased as a temporary investment 1,000 shares of Knox, Inc., common stock at 22¼ plus a $225 commission.
Apr.   1 Purchased as a temporary investment ten El Paso Corporation, $1,000, 4½ percent, 20-year bonds on which interest is payable each February 1 and August 1. The purchase price was 98¼ plus a $25 commission and two months' accrued interest.
June   7 Received a $0.30 per share dividend on the Knox, Inc., stock.

Aug. 1 Received a check for the semiannual interest on the Delta Corporation bonds, and amortized a portion of the premium paid when the bonds were purchased.

1 Received a check for the semiannual interest on the El Paso Corporation bonds.

Oct. 10 Sold the Knox, Inc., common stock at 28 less a $280 commission and other sale costs.

12 Purchased as a long-term investment 500 shares of Rudy Corporation common stock at 52½ plus a $265 commission.

Dec. 1 Sold the El Paso Corporation bonds at 99½ plus four months' accrued interest and less a $25 commission.

Feb. 1 Received a check for the semiannual interest on the Delta Corporation bonds, and amortized a portion of the premium.

1 After holding the Delta Corporation bonds for one year, changed the investment policy toward them and sold them at 103 less a $25 commission.

Required:
Prepare general journal entries to record the foregoing transactions.

CLASS EXERCISE

Exercise 19–1

Walter Nash purchased 1,000 shares of Fenner Corporation $10 par value common stock on June 3 of the current year, paying 12⅝ plus a $125 commission. One month later he received an additional 500 shares of the stock from Fenner Corporation as a stock dividend and two months later he sold 600 of his shares, receiving 10¼ less a $65 commission.

Required:
Prepare general journal entries to record the foregoing transactions.

ALTERNATE PROBLEMS

Problem 19–1A

The outstanding stock of a corporation consists of 20,000 no-par common shares which were issued when the corporation was organized. The corporation has grown and now needs additional capital. Its board of directors estimates that with an additional $1,000,000 in capital the company can expect to earn $450,000 annually before bond interest and income taxes. The corporation's combined state and federal income tax rate is expected to continue at its present 50 percent. Three methods for securing the additional capital have been suggested. They are the issuance of 10,000 additional shares of no-par common stock at $100 per share, the issuance at par of 10,000 shares of $100 par value, 6½ percent cumulative and nonparticipating, preferred stock, and the issuance at par of $1,000,000 of 5 percent, 20-year bonds.

Required:
Calculate the earnings per share that will accrue to the corporation's original common stockholders if (*a*) the common stock is issued, (*b*) the preferred stock is issued, and (*c*) the bonds are issued.

Problem 19–2A

On February 11, 1964, Bluelake Corporation deposited a deed of trust with Guaranty Trust Company which authorized it to issue $3,000,000 of 5 percent, 20-year bonds dated March 1, 1964, and paying interest on each September 1 and March 1. It then completed these transactions:

1964
Apr.   1   Sold $2,400,000 of the bonds for $2,447,800 plus accrued interest.
Sept. 1   Paid the semiannual interest on the bonds.
Dec. 31   Recorded the accrued interest on the bonds.
1965
Jan.   1   Reversed the accrued interest adjusting entry.
Mar. 1   Paid the semiannual interest on the bonds.
1967
Mar. 1   Paid the semiannual interest on the bonds, and purchased in the open market and retired $300,000 of the bonds. The purchase price was $298,000, including the commission.

Required:
Prepare general journal entries to record the foregoing transactions.

Problem 19–3A

On February 11, 1963, a corporation deposited a deed of trust with the trustee of its bondholders which authorized it to issue $1,000,000 of 4½ percent, ten-year, convertible bonds, dated March 1, 1963, and upon which interest is payable each March 1 and September 1. The conversion clause in the deed of trust granted the bondholders the right to convert their bonds before March 1, 1968, into shares of the company's common stock at the rate of 150 shares of $5 par value common stock for each $1,000 bond. The corporation then completed these transactions:

1963
Mar.   1   Sold the entire bond issue at 98½.
Sept. 1   Paid the interest on the bonds and amortized the discount.
Dec. 31   Recorded the accrued interest on the bonds.
1964
Jan.   1   Reversed the accrued interest adjusting entry.
Mar. 1   Paid the interest on the bonds and amortized the discount.
1965
Mar. 1   After paying the semiannual interest on the bonds, converted bonds having a $300,000 par value to common stock.
1967
Mar. 1   Purchased on the open market and retired bonds having a $100,-000 par value. The total cash outlay was $97,500.

Sept. 1 Paid the interest and amortized the discount on the outstanding bonds.

Required:
Prepare general journal entries to record the foregoing transactions.

Problem 19–4A

A corporation deposited with the trustee of its bondholders a deed of trust authorizing the issuance of $3,000,000 of 5 percent, 20-year, convertible bonds, dated May 1, 1963, and paying interest on each November 1 and May 1. The conversion clause in the deed of trust granted the bondholders the right to convert their bonds before May 1, 1968, into shares of the company's stock at the rate of 80 shares of $10 par value common stock for each $1,000 bond.

Required:
Prepare general journal entries to record the following:
a) The company sold the entire issue on July 1, 1963, receiving $3,096,400 in cash.
b) Made the first semiannual interest payment.
c) Recorded the accrued interest on December 31, 1963.
d) Reversed the accrued interest adjusting entry.
e) Made the second semiannual interest payment.
f) At the option of the bondholders, after paying the interest on May 1, 1966, converted $1,000,000 par value of bonds to common stock.
g) On November 1, 1967, purchased on the open market and retired $500,-000 par value of the outstanding bonds. The purchase price was $497,-500, including the commission.

Problem 19–5A

Prepare general journal entries to record the following transactions:
1966
Jan. 10 Purchased as a long-term investment 1,000 shares of Maple Corporation $10 par value common stock, paying 24½ plus a $250 commission.
Mar. 3 Received a $0.25 per share quarterly dividend on the Maple Corporation common stock.
June 5 Received a 100-share common stock dividend from Maple Corporation.
6 Sold the 100 shares of Maple Corporation stock received as a dividend in the previous transaction, receiving 23 less a $25 commission.
July 1 Purchased as a temporary investment 100 shares of Oak Corporation common stock, paying 79¾ plus an $80 commission.
Sept. 1 Purchased as a temporary investment ten Walnut Corporation, 4½ percent, 20-year bonds on which interest is payable semiannually on each November 1 and May 1. The purchase price was 97 plus four months' accrued interest and a $25 commission.
Nov. 1 Received a check for the semiannual interest on the Walnut Corporation bonds.

1967

Jan.   1   Sold the Walnut Corporation bonds at 98¼ plus two months' accrued interest and less a $25 commission.

Mar.   1   Purchased as a long-term investment ten Hickory Corporation, 5 percent, 20-year bonds on their interest date ten years before maturity. The purchase price was 102¾ plus a $25 commission.

Sept. 1   Received a check for the semiannual interest on the Hickory Corporation bonds and amortized a portion of the purchase premium.

Mar.   1   Received a check for the semiannual interest on the Hickory Corporation bonds and amortized a portion of the premium.

       1   Changed the investment policy toward the Hickory Corporation bonds and sold them at 101½ less a $25 commission.

DECISION PROBLEM 19—BELL
MANUFACTURING COMPANY

The board of directors of the Bell Manufacturing Company has employed you as a consultant to advise the board on a problem which has caused considerable dissention among the members.

Twenty-five years ago the company issued 40-year, first-mortgage bonds. The deed of trust provided that "a sinking fund for the retirement of said bonds be set up by equal annual payments" from corporation earnings. On the advice of attorneys both a sinking fund and a reservation of retained earnings have been established and maintained. At the end of the twenty-fifth year these balances appear on the company's balance sheet:

Bond sinking fund...........................$ 8,269,587

Reserve for bond sinking fund (retained earn-
     ings appropriated for bonded indebtedness).. 12,180,500

Approximately $4,000,000 of the par value of the bonds have been purchased on the open market when prices were favorable and their cost paid from the sinking fund. The bonds so purchased have been canceled. This accounts for the difference between the "reserve" and the "fund."

The question raised by the board members is whether the "Reserve" should be adjusted downward to equal the "Fund," with the excess returned to Retained Earnings and used in the payment of cash dividends. Also, they would like to know if it is now necessary to retain in the "Reserve" amounts of retained earnings covering bonds already retired? (Answers should be based on the purpose of reserving earnings and of course should not consider any possible legal implications.)

Write a report giving your opinion as to the correct answers to the questions raised. Explain in nontechnical language the purposes of both the bond sinking fund and the reservation of retained earnings.

Departmentalization
and Control

A BUSINESS is departmentalized or divided into departments for managerial purposes, with each department commonly being placed in charge of a manager who, under perfect circumstances, is responsible for both the output of the department and the resources expended in attaining that output. Output may be in units of product manufactured, dollars of sales achieved, or services performed; and resources expended may be goods sold, raw materials consumed, wages paid, depreciation, heat, lights, et cetera. And, ideally the output should be obtained with the smallest expenditure of resources.

When a business is departmentalized, if management is to know how well each department is performing, it is necessary for the accounting system to supply information by departments as to resources expended and outputs achieved. Such an accounting system is a departmental system.

DEPARTMENTAL INFORMATION IS NORMALLY FOR MANAGEMENT'S USE ONLY

Before examining the manner in which departmental accounting systems function, it should be observed that departmental operating details, when gathered, are generally not made public. Rather such information is for the use of management in controlling operations, appraising performances, allocating resources, and in taking remedial actions. For example, if one of several departments is particularly profitable, perhaps it should be expanded. Or if a department is in trouble, information as to its revenues, costs, and expenses may point to a proper remedial action.

BASIS FOR DEPARTMENTALIZATION

In every departmentalized business there are two basic kinds of departments, *productive departments* and *service departments*. In a factory the productive departments are those engaged directly in manufacturing operations, and in a store they are the departments making sales. In either type of business the service departments are such departments as the general office, advertising, purchasing, payroll, and personnel departments. Obviously, the service departments are so called because they assist or perform services for the productive departments.

The division of a factory into productive departments is commonly based on manufacturing processes employed or products or components manufactured. The division in a store is usually based on kinds of goods sold, with each selling or productive department being assigned the sale of one or more kinds of merchandise. However, in dividing a store into selling departments several principles should be observed. First, the goods included in each department should be related in nature and so located as to be convenient for one person to supervise and control. In addition, all the goods in one department should have approximately the same markup percentage or gross profit margin; because if goods having different profit margins are put in the same department, one kind with a high profit margin may carry another that produces little or no profit.

DEPARTMENTAL GROSS PROFITS

Accumulating information as to sales, purchases, and inventories by departments, so that departmental gross profits may be calculated, is the usual starting point in measuring departmental results in a store. This information may be gathered in several ways, and normally a store's size, the goods it sells, and the number of its departments determine the methods and procedures used.

Two common devices for gathering information needed in calculating departmental gross profits are (1) separate departmental accounts, and (2) departmental analysis sheets.

Separate Departmental Accounts. A store having only a few departments may provide in its General Ledger a separate set of merchandise accounts for each. If it does so, it accumulates information until the end of an accounting period as to each department's sales, sales returns, purchases, and purchases returns in the department's own accounts. Then at the end of the period it takes inventories by departments, and using the information in the several separate sets of departmental accounts, calculates cost of goods sold and gross profits by departments.

Departmental Analysis Sheets. Although a store having only a few departments may readily provide a separate set of merchandise accounts for each, a store with many departments may find its ledger rather large and awkward if it follows this procedure. As a result, a store with many departments, instead of opening separate accounts for each, often secures departmental information as to sales, sales returns, purchases, and purchases returns by using departmental analysis sheets.

When a store uses departmental analysis sheets, it provides only one undepartmentalized general ledger account for all sales, another account for sales returns, another for purchases, and another for purchases returns; and it then records its transactions and posts to these accounts as though it were not departmentalized. But, in addition to this, each day it also summarizes its merchandise transactions by departments and records the summarized amounts on analysis sheets. For example, a concern using analysis sheets, in addition to recording charge sales in the usual manner in a Sales Journal, will sort and total each day's charge tickets by departments and enter the totals in the proper departmental columns of a sales analysis sheet like the one of Illustration 122. Also, it will determine daily cash sales by

Illustration 122

DEPARTMENTAL SALES ANALYSIS SHEET

Date		Type of Sales	Men's Wear Dept.	Boys' Wear Dept.	Men's Shoe Dept.	Men's Hat Dept.	Women's Wear Dept.
May	1	Cash sales	257.00	110.00	155.00	37.00	197.00
		Charge sales	102.00	82.00	58.00	76.00	105.00
	2	Cash sales	138.00	97.00	127.00	58.00	222.00
		Charge sales	127.00	103.00	82.00	62.00	189.00
	3	Cash sales	152.00	72.00	97.00	73.00	205.00

departments and in addition to recording these sales in the usual manner in a Cash Receipts Journal, will also enter the amounts on the analysis sheet. As a result, at the end of a month or other period the column totals on the sales analysis sheet will tell sales by departments, and the grand total of all columns should equal the balance of the Sales account.

When a store uses departmental analysis sheets, it uses an analysis sheet for recording sales, another analysis sheet for recording sales returns, another for purchases, and still another for purchases returns; and at the end of a period the several analysis sheets give departmental breakdowns of the store's sales, sales returns, purchases, and purchases returns.

RECORDING TRANSACTIONS BY DEPARTMENTS

The use of separate accounts or the use of analysis sheets is one variation in accounting procedures found in departmentalized merchandising concerns. There are many others. For example, a concern having only a few transactions may use columnar pen-and-ink journals in recording transactions by departments, or a concern with more transactions may use electric bookkeeping machines, punched cards, or punched paper tape.

Pen-and-Ink Records. Pen-and-ink journals are adapted to departmental transactions by the simple procedure of increasing the columns in each journal, a separate column is added in each journal for each department. Illustration 123 shows a Purchases Journal for use in a departmentalized

Illustration 123

PURCHASES JOURNAL

Date		Account Credited	F	Accounts Payable Credit	Purchases Debit		
					Men's Dept.	Boys' Dept.	Shoe Dept.
Feb.	1	Acme Mfg. Co.......		250.00	250.00		
	1	N. A. Green Co......		110.00			110.00
	2	Horn Supply Co....		275.00	200.00	75.00	

concern having three departments. Each invoice recorded in this journal is entered on a separate line, with the invoice amount entered in the Accounts Payable credit column and distributed to the proper departmental purchases columns according to the items purchased. The credits to individual creditor accounts entered in the Accounts Payable column are posted daily, and the column totals are posted to the Accounts Payable controlling account and the proper departmental purchases accounts at the end of the month.

Obviously, this additional-columns technique is applicable to any journal or register such as, for example, a Sales Journal or Voucher Register.

Electric Bookkeeping Machines. Illustration 75 on page 371 shows a modern electric bookkeeping machine. It was explained beginning on page 370 that this machine could be used for sales accounting, purchases, cash receipts, or any other accounting application; and it was also explained how the machine could, for example, for each charge sale produce the customer's invoice, post to the customer's account, update the customer's month-end statement, and enter the sale in the Sales Journal. In addition to this, if the machine is properly set and the right keys are depressed in the sales invoice preparation procedure, the machine will accumulate information as to sales by departments and will print out departmental sales totals after the last sales invoice is prepared each day. It will also, when used for recording purchases or returns, accumulate departmental totals for these transactions.

Punched Cards.   Illustration 124 shows a type of pin-punched price tag

Illustration 124

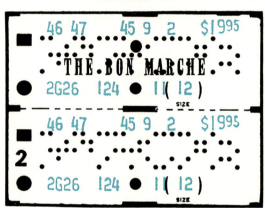

used by many large department stores. Such tags show the price of an item of merchandise and are an essential part of the inventory control system in a store using them, an inventory control system that makes it easy to accumulate information as to sales and returns by items, colors, sizes, manufacturers, et cetera, as well as in dollar amounts by departments.

Pin-punched price tags get their name from the pin-size holes punched in the tags. These holes carry information in the code arrangement of their punching as to an item's price, size, color, and so on. The machine used to punch the holes also prints the punched information on the tag for visual reading.

When an item of merchandise is sold, the lower half of the tag is removed by the salesclerk and placed on a spindle beside the cash register, and the upper half is left attached to the item sold. At the end of each day the spindled tag portions are taken to the accounting department and run through a tag converter, a machine that electronically repunches each tag's information into a regular full-size punched card like the ones described and illustrated in earlier chapters. After being punched, the full-size cards are automatically sorted and resorted by machine and are used to produce rapidly information as to sales by departments as well as other useful data.

When merchandise is returned, the customer is instructed to return with the merchandise the price tag portion left attached at the time of sale. These returned tag portions are spindled until the end of each day when they too are run through the tag converter to produce the full-size punched cards used in accounting for returns.

Punched Paper Tape.   Some stores use punched paper tape in recording information about sales as to departments, prices, items, et cetera. The punched paper tape, which is approximately one inch in width, is produced by the cash registers on which salesclerks "ring up" sales. A sample of this tape is shown in Illustration 125.

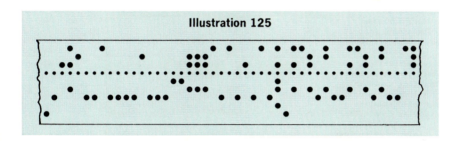

Illustration 125

In producing such paper tape, all that is required of the salesclerk is that he depress the proper cash register keys in "ringing up" a sale, causing the register to punch the sale information into the tape. At the end of each day the tape produced in each register is run through a tape to card converter which electronically converts the punched information on the tape to regular punched cards. The punched cards are then used in producing all desired summaries and reports.

INCOME STATEMENT SHOWING DEPARTMENTAL GROSS PROFITS

Accumulating information and arriving at a gross profit figure for each selling department in a departmentalized business is not too difficult, as the foregoing pages reveal. However, to go beyond this and arrive at reliable net income figures is a little more difficult; consequently, many concerns make no effort to calculate more than gross profits by departments. Illustration 126 shows an income statement prepared for such a concern. The statement sets out departmental gross profits and combines these figures to arrive at a combined gross profit figure, a figure from which the unallocated operating expenses are deducted to arrive at the store's net income.

Observe in Illustration 126 that in addition to showing gross profits in dollar amounts, gross profits are also expressed as percentages of net sales. These percentages make departmental comparisons easier.

Illustration 126

VALLEY HABERDASHERY
Income Statement
For Year Ended December 31, 19--

	Men's Clothing	Boys' Clothing	Shoes	Combined
Revenue from sales:				
Sales	$46,000	$34,000	$20,000	$100,000
Less: Sales returns . .	750	425	350	1,525
Net sales	$45,250	$33,575	$19,650	$ 98,475
Cost of goods sold:				
Inventory, Jan. 1	$ 7,400	$ 4,200	$ 3,350	$14,950
Purchases	30,000	21,700	11,800	63,500
Freight-in. . . .	150	125	75	350
Goods for sale. .	$37,550	$26,025	$15,225	$78,800
Inventory, Dec. 31	8,100	3,500	4,150	15,750
Cost of goods sold. . . .	29,450	22,525	11,075	63,050
Gross profits . . .	$15,800	$11,050	$ 8,575	$ 35,425
Gross profit percentages	(34.9%)	(32.9%)	(43.5%)	(36.0%)

Operating expenses:		
Selling expenses:		
Sales salaries	$7,000	
Sales commissions.	5,000	
Advertising.	550	
Sales supplies used.	200	
Depreciation of store equipment.	700	
Total selling expenses		$13,450
General and administrative expenses:		
Office salaries.	$3,800	
Office supplies used.	250	
Expired insurance	300	
Bad debts.	210	
Depreciation of office equipment	150	
Depreciation of building	1,200	
Property taxes	900	
Total general and administrative expenses.		6,810
Total operating expenses		20,260
Net Income		$ 15,165

ALLOCATING FREIGHT-IN

Freight-in is a factor in calculating cost of goods sold. When possible, payments for freight should be analyzed and charged to individual departments so that a more accurate gross profit figure may be calculated for each. Either separate accounts or analysis sheets may be used.

In many stores the goods in a shipment are often consigned to a single department, and the freight on such a shipment may readily be charged to the responsible department. However, a shipment sometimes contains merchandise for several departments; and when this happens, it is necessary to allocate the shipment's freight charges between the departments on some fair basis, such as, for example, size and weight of the articles received.

ALLOCATING EXPENSES

If a concern goes beyond the calculation of departmental gross profits and attempts to arrive at a net income figure for each selling department, it must charge each department with its *direct expenses* and allocate to the departments any *indirect expenses*. The direct expenses of a department are those incurred for the sole benefit of that department, for example, the salary of an employee who works in only one department is a direct expense of that department. Indirect expenses are expenses incurred for the joint benefit of more than one department, for example, rent, heat, and lights. The entire amount of a direct expense may be charged directly to the department benefited by its incurrence. However; an indirect expense can only be allocated on some fair basis such as, for example, the amount of floor space occupied, as in the allocation of janitorial expenses.

When an indirect expense is allocated, portions are assigned to each department, preferably on the basis of benefits received. For example, a jewelry store purchases janitorial services from an outside firm and allocates the cost among its three departments according to the floor space occupied. If the cost of janitorial services for a period is $140 and the amounts of floor space occupied are:

> *Jewelry department*............................*250 sq. ft.*
> *Watch repair department*......................*125*
> *China and silver department*..................*500*
> *Total*.......................................*875 sq. ft.*

The departmental shares of the janitorial expense are:

$$\textit{Jewelry Department:} \qquad \frac{250}{875} \times \$140 = \$40$$

$$\textit{Watch Repair Department:} \qquad \frac{125}{875} \times \$140 = \$20$$

$$\textit{China and Silver Department:} \ \frac{500}{875} \times \$140 = \$80$$

BASES FOR ALLOCATING EXPENSES

In the following paragraphs bases for allocating a representation of indirect expenses are discussed. In the discussions no hard-and-fast rules are given because several factors are often involved in an expense allocation, and the importance of the factors vary from situation to situation. Consequently, judgment rather than hard-and-fast rules is required.

Wages and Salaries. An employee's wages may be either a direct or an indirect expense. If an employee spends all of his time in one department, his wages are a direct expense of the benefited department; but if an employee works in more than one department, his wages become an indirect expense that may be allocated between or among the benefited departments. Normally, working time spent in each department is a fair basis for allocating wages.

A supervisory employee at times supervises more than one department, and in such cases the time spent in each department is usually a fair basis for allocating his salary. However, since a supervisory employee is frequently on the move from department to department, the time spent in each is often difficult to measure. Consequently, some companies allocate the salary of such an employee to his departments on the basis of employees in each department, while others make the allocation on the basis of the supervised departments' sales. When a supervisor's salary is allocated on the basis of employees, it is assumed that he is supervising people and the time spent in each department is related to the number of employees in each. When a supervisory employee's salary is allocated on the basis of sales, it is assumed that the time devoted to each department is related to the department's productiveness.

Rent. Rent expense is normally allocated to benefited departments on the basis of the amount and value of the floor space occupied by each.

Since all customers who enter a store must pass the departments by the entrance and only a fraction of these people go beyond the first floor, ground floor space is more valuable for retail purposes than is basement or upper floor space, and space near the entrance is more valuable than is space in an out-of-the-way corner. Yet since there is no exact measure of floor space values, all such values and the allocations of rent based on such values must depend on judgment. Nevertheless, if good judgment, statistics as to customer traffic, and the opinions of experts who are familiar with current rental values are used, fair allocations can normally be made.

Advertising. When a store advertises a department's products, if the advertising is effective, people come into the store to buy the products. However, at the same time they also often buy other unadvertised products. Consequently, advertising benefits all departments, even those the products of which are not advertised; and as a result, many stores treat advertising as an indirect expense and allocate it on the basis of sales. When advertising costs are allocated on a sales basis, a department producing one fifteenth of the total sales is charged with one fifteenth of the advertising cost and a department producing one sixth of the sales is charged with one sixth.

Although in many stores advertising costs are allocated to departments on the basis of sales, in others advertising is treated as a direct expense and charged directly to the departments. When advertising is charged directly, each advertisement is analyzed and the cost of the column inches of newspaper space or minutes of TV or radio time devoted to the products of a department is charged to the department.

Since advertising is treated by some stores as a direct expense and by others as an indirect expense, both treatments appear in the illustrations that follow.

Depreciation. Depreciation on equipment used solely in one department is a direct expense of that department; and if adequate fixed asset records are kept, the depreciation applicable to each department may be learned by examining the records. Where adequate records are not maintained, depreciation must be treated as an indirect expense and allocated to the departments on the basis of the value of the equipment in each.

Building depreciation, when the building is owned, is normally allocated like rent.

Taxes and Insurance. Taxes and insurance are indirect expenses and are allocated to departments on the basis of the insured and taxable property in each. Taxes and insurance on the building are allocated in the same manner as rent.

Lights. Lighting expense is an indirect expense that is normally allocated on the basis of the number, size, and burning time of the lights in each department.

Heat. Heating costs are often allocated to the various floors of a building on the basis of the amount of radiation on each floor. Usually the first floor requires more radiation because of heat lost through the doors as customers enter and leave. After heating expense is allocated to the various floors, the amount allocated to each floor is assigned to the departments on the floor according to floor space occupied.

Delivery Expense. The cost of delivering packages depends upon the number, size, and weight of the packages. Usually, it is impossible to consider all three factors in a single allocation basis. Consequently, the most important one is often used. Sometimes all three factors, number, size, and weight, are ignored, and delivery expenses are allocated on a sales basis. Often, too, where the number, size, and weight of packages are closely related to sales, such a basis is fair.

MECHANICS OF ALLOCATING AND CHARGING EXPENSES

It would be possible in most cases to analyze each indirect expense incurred and to allocate and charge it to departmental expense accounts at the time of incurrence or payment. However, this is seldom done because it involves too many allocations and too much work. Instead, expense amounts paid or incurred, both direct and indirect, are commonly accumulated in undepartmentalized expense accounts until the end of a period, when a *departmental expense allocation sheet* is used to allocate and charge each expense to the benefited departments. A departmental expense allocation sheet is shown in Illustration 127 and is discussed in more detail later in this chapter.

Illustration 127

TEMPE HARDWARE COMPANY
Departmental Expense Allocation Sheet
Year Ended December 31, 19—

Undepartmentalized Expense Accounts and Service Departments	Bases of Allocation	Expense Account Balances	Allocations of Expenses to Departments					
			General Office Dept.	Purchasing Dept.	Cleaning and Maintenance	Hardware Dept.	Housewares Dept.	Appliances Dept.
Salaries expense	Direct, payroll records	$39,050	$7,250	$6,400	$3,000	$10,200	$4,800	$7,400
Rent expense	Amount and value of space	7,200	360	360	40	3,200	814	2,426
Advertising	Sales	2,070				920	460	690
Expired insurance	Insured property	320	50	30	12	132	24	72
Depreciation of equipment	Direct, property records	1,200	200	125	50	350	175	300
Lighting expense	Wattage of lights	226	18	18	5	90	40	55
Heating expense	Floor space	960	48	48	8	424	144	288
Supplies used	Direct, requisitions	625	102	63	125	133	54	148
Total Expenses by Departments		$51,651	$8,028	$7,044	$3,240	$15,449	$6,511	$11,379
Allocation of service department expenses:								
General office	Sales		8,028			3,568	1,784	2,676
Purchasing department	Purchases			7,044		3,166	1,761	2,117
Cleaning and maintenance	Floor space				3,240	1,605	545	1,090
Total Expenses Applicable to Selling Departments		51,651				$23,788	$10,601	$17,262

ALLOCATING SERVICE DEPARTMENT EXPENSES

In order that they may sell their products, selling departments must have the services provided by the service departments just as they must have building space, heat, and lights. Therefore, service department operating expenses are in effect indirect expenses of the selling departments; and if net incomes are calculated, the cost of operating each service department should be allocated to the selling departments it serves. The following are commonly used bases for these allocations:

Departments	Expense Allocation Bases
General office department	*Number of employees in each department or sales.*
Personnel department	*Number of employees in each department.*
Payroll department	*Number of employees in each department.*
Advertising department	*Sales or amounts of advertising charged directly to each department.*
Purchasing department	*Dollar amounts of purchases or number of purchase invoices.*
Cleaning and maintenance department	*Square feet of floor space occupied.*

DEPARTMENTAL EXPENSE ALLOCATION SHEET

As previously stated, it would be possible to allocate and charge most indirect expenses to departments as they are incurred or paid; but this is seldom done. Rather, expenses are commonly accumulated in undepartmentalized expense accounts until the end of an accounting period when a departmental expense allocation sheet is used, not only to allocate the accumulated expenses to the benefited departments, but also to allocate to the productive departments the costs of operating the service departments. Illustration 127 shows such an allocation sheet.

To prepare an expense allocation sheet, the account names of the to-be-allocated expenses are entered in the sheet's first column along with the names of the service departments. Next the bases of allocation are entered in the second column, and the account balances are entered in the third. Then, each expense account balance is allocated according to the basis shown, and the allocated portions are entered in the departmental columns. After this the departmental columns are totaled, and the service department column totals are allocated in turn to the productive departments.

Upon completion, the amounts in the columns of an expense allocation sheet are available for preparing departmental income statements showing net incomes by departments. Such a statement for the appliances department of the firm of Illustration 127 is shown in Illustration 128.

Illustration 128

TEMPE HARDWARE COMPANY
Appliance Department Income Statement
For Year Ended December 31, 19--

Sales		$84,464
Cost of goods sold.		59,321
Gross profit from sales		$25,143
Operating expenses:		
Sales salaries.	$7,400	
Rent expense.	2,426	
Advertising	680	
Expired insurance	72	
Depreciation of equipment	300	
Lighting expense.	55	
Heating expense	288	
Supplies used	148	
General office expenses	2,666	
Purchasing department expenses.	2,117	
Cleaning and maintenance expenses . . .	1,095	
Total operating expenses.		17,247
Appliance Department Net Income		$ 7,896

ELIMINATING AN UNPROFITABLE DEPARTMENT

The management of a store in which departmental net incomes are calculated is often confronted with a situation in which one or more departments shows a loss. When this occurs, consideration is often given to eliminating the unprofitable department or departments; and when such consideration is given, what are known as escapable and inescapable expenses are encountered. Escapable expenses are those that would end with an unprofitable department's elimination; inescapable expenses are those that would continue even though the department were eliminated.

Illustration 129

JOE M. HARDT COMPANY
Income Statement for Year Ended December 31, 19--

	Department A	Department B	Combined
Sales	$42,100	$63,150	$105,250
Cost of goods sold.	31,400	37,800	69,200
Gross profits from sales.	$10,700	$25,350	$ 36,050
Operating expenses:			
Selling expenses:			
Sales salaries. . . . . $ 6,000		$10,000	$16,000
Advertising 600		900	1,500
Store supplies used 150		280	430
Depreciation of store equipment . 240		410	650
Rent expense. 1,600		3,200	4,800
Total selling expenses . . . . $ 8,590		$14,790	$23,380
General and admin. expenses:			
Expired insurance . . . . $ 200		$ 350	$ 550
Bad debts expense 150		225	375
Share of general office expenses. 2,580		3,870	6,450
Total general and adminis-			
trative expenses. . . . . . $ 2,930		$ 4,445	$ 7,375
Total operating expenses. . .	11,520	19,235	30,755
Net Income or Loss (*).	$ 820*	$ 6,115	$ 5,295

For example, Joe M. Hardt Company is contemplating the elimination of its Department A. The company's income statement for the past year is shown in Illustration 129.

Joe M. Hardt Company's Department A incurred an $820 net loss for the year; however, an examination of its expenses reveals the following escapable and inescapable expenses:

	Escapable Expenses	Inescapable Expenses
Sales salaries...............................	$6,000	
Advertising......................................	600	
Store supplies used............................	150	
Depreciation of store equipment................		$ 240
Rent expense...................................		1,600
Expired insurance (merchandise and equip-		
ment)..	180	20
Bad debts expense..............................	150	
Share of the general office expenses.............	350	2,230
Total.......................................	$7,430	$4,090

If Department A is discontinued, its $4,090 of inescapable expenses will have to be borne by Department B; thus, until Department A's annual loss exceeds $4,090 or until a more profitable department can be substituted, Joe M. Hardt Company is better off continuing the unprofitable department.

Aside from inescapable expenses, unprofitable departments are also often continued because they bring business to other profitable departments.

DEPARTMENTAL CONTRIBUTIONS TO OVERHEAD

Many people, particularly department heads whose efficiencies are judged and whose salaries depend on the amounts of "net income" earned by their departments, are critical when such net income figures are used in making decisions as to departmental efficiencies. Their critical attitude arises from the fact that departmental net income figures are always affected by the assumptions made in allocating expenses.

People who are critical of departmental net income figures often suggest the substitution of *departmental contributions to overhead* when decisions are to be made. A department's contribution to overhead is the amount its revenues exceed its direct costs and expenses. In other words, a department's contribution to overhead is the amount of revenue remaining after direct items are charged but before indirect and service department expenses are allocated. Illustration 130 is a departmental income statement showing contributions to overhead.

Illustration 130

SMITHFIELD MEN'S STORE
Departmental Income Statement for Year Ended December 31, 19--

	Men's Department	Boys' Department	Shoe Department	Combined
Revenue from sales.	$100,000	$ 40,000	$ 20,000	$160,000
Cost of goods sold.	65,000	24,000	12,000	101,000
Gross margin on sales	$ 35,000	$ 16,000	$ 8,000	$ 59,000
Direct expenses:				
Sales salaries.	$ 18,000	$ 8,500	$ 3,500	$ 30,000
Advertising	1,000	500	300	1,800
Depreciation.	700	400	300	1,400
Supplies used	300	200	100	600
Total direct expenses	$ 20,000	$ 9,600	$ 4,200	$ 33,800
Departmental contributions to				
overhead.	$ 15,000	$ 6,400	$ 3,800	$ 25,200
Indirect expenses:				
Rent.			$ 6,000	
Heating and lighting.			800	
Taxes and insurance			1,200	
Total indirect expenses			$ 8,000	
Expenses of administrative departments			10,500	18,500
Net Income.				$ 6,700

APPRAISING DEPARTMENTAL EFFICIENCIES

Net income figures are used in some stores in judging departmental efficiencies; and contributions to overhead are used for the same purpose in others. But, is either a net income figure or a contribution to overhead a good index of how well a department has performed? Some people hold that neither is. These people say that, since many expenses entering into the calculation of a department's net income or into its contribution to overhead are beyond the control of the department's manager, neither net income nor contribution to overhead should be used in judging how well the department has operated.

People who oppose the use of net incomes and departmental contributions in appraising efficiencies are of the opinion that only a department's *controllable costs and expenses* should be used in judging how well the department has operated. A department's controllable costs and expenses are those over which the department's manager has some control as to the amounts expended. They are not the same as direct costs and expenses. Direct costs and expenses are those chargeable directly to a department; the amounts expended may or may not be under the control of the manager. For example, a manager often has little or no control over the amount of equipment in his department and its resulting depreciation, but he commonly has some control over the employees and the amount of work they do.

When controllable costs and expenses are used in judging a department's efficiency, statistics are prepared showing the department's output and its controllable costs and expenses. The statistics do not necessarily show either net income or contribution to overhead.

At this point a beginning student may ask, "Which best measures departmental efficiencies, net income figures, departmental contributions, or controllable costs and expenses?" The answer is that the concepts of departmental contributions and of controllable costs and expenses are newer; but no one of the three may be applied without judgment, each is helpful, and each is used.

JOINT COSTS

Joint costs which are encountered in some manufacturing concerns have much in common with indirect expenses. A joint cost is a single cost incurred to secure two or more essentially different products. For example, a meat-packer incurs a joint cost when he buys a pig from which he will get bacon, hams, shoulders, liver, heart, hide, pig feet, and a variety of other products in portions which he cannot alter. Likewise, a sawmill incurs joint costs when it buys a log and saws it into unalterable portions of Clears, Select Structurals, No. 1 Common, No. 2 Common, and other grades of lumber. In both cases, as with all joint costs, the problem is one of allocating the costs to the several joint products.

A joint cost may be, but is not commonly, allocated on some physical basis, such as the ratio of pounds, square feet, or gallons of each joint product to total pounds, square feet, or gallons of all joint products flowing from the cost. The reason this method is not commonly used is that the cost allocations resulting from its use may be completely out of keeping with the market values of the joint products, and thus may cause certain of the products to sell at a profit while others always show a loss.

The usual method of allocating a joint cost is *in the ratio of the market values of the joint products at the point of separation.* For example, a sawmill buys for $30,000 a number of logs which when sawed produce a million board feet of lumber in the following grades and amounts:

Grade	Board Feet	Market Price per 1,000 Board Feet	Market Value of Production of Each Grade	Ratio of Market Value of Each Grade to Total
Structural............	*100,000*	*$120*	*$12,000*	*12/50*
No. 1 Common.........	*300,000*	*60*	*18,000*	*18/50*
No. 2 Common.........	*400,000*	*40*	*16,000*	*16/50*
No. 3 Common.........	*200,000*	*20*	*4,000*	*4/50*
	1,000,000		*$50,000*	

If the foregoing ratios of market values by grades to the total market value of all grades is used in allocating the $30,000 joint log cost, the cost is apportioned between the grades as follows:

$$
\begin{aligned}
\textit{Structural:} \quad & \$30,000 \times 12/50 = \$\ 7,200 \\
\textit{No. 1 Common:} \quad & \$30,000 \times 18/50 = 10,800 \\
\textit{No. 2 Common:} \quad & \$30,000 \times 16/50 = 9,600 \\
\textit{No. 3 Common:} \quad & \$30,000 \times 4/50 = 2,400 \\
\hline
& \$30,000
\end{aligned}
$$

Note that there are 1,000,000 board feet of lumber involved in these illustrations and the portion of No. 3 Common is 2/10 of the total. If the No. 3 Common were allocated 2/10 of the $30,000 log cost, it would be allocated $6,000 ($30,000 × 2/10 = $6,000). This is more than the grade's $4,000 market value and would cause this grade to show a loss.

Now observe that if the No. 3 Common is allocated a share of the $30,000 joint cost based on market values by grades, it is allocated $2,400 of the $30,000. Furthermore, when the $2,400 is subtracted from the grade's $4,000 market value, $1,600 remains to cover other costs and perhaps a profit.

STANDARD COSTS

Thus far all costs discussed have been actual or historical costs, historical in the sense that they had been incurred and were history by the time they were recorded. Another kind of costs called *standard costs* is commonly used in judging efficiencies and in placing responsibilities.

A standard cost is a cost that should be incurred under normal conditions in producing a given product or part or in performing a particular service. Standard costs are established by means of engineering and accounting studies made before the product is produced or the service is performed, and are then used to judge actual costs incurred when the product or service is produced. In other words, standard costs (what costs should be) are used to judge actual costs (what costs were).

Great care and the combined efforts of people in accounting, engineering, personnel administration, and other management areas are required in establishing standard costs. Time and motion studies are made of each labor operation in a product's production or in the performance of a service to learn both the best way to perform the operation and the standard labor time required under normal conditions for performance. Exhaustive investigations are also made of the quantity, grade, and cost of each material required; and machines and other productive equipment are subject to detailed studies in an effort to achieve maximum efficiencies and to learn what costs should be.

However, regardless of care exercised in establishing standard costs and in revising them as conditions change, actual costs incurred in producing a given product or service are apt to vary on occasion from standard costs. When this occurs, the difference in total cost is likely to be a composite of several cost differences. For example, the quantity, or the cost, or both the quantity and cost of the material used may have varied from standard; and the labor time, or the labor cost, or both the time and cost of labor may have varied. Likewise, the quantity and cost of the overhead may have varied. (Costs such as rent, taxes, depreciation, heat, and lights are known as overhead.)

When actual costs vary from standard costs, the differences are called *variances*. Variances may be favorable or unfavorable. A favorable variance is one in which actual cost is below standard cost, and an unfavorable variance is one in which actual cost is above standard.

When variances occur, they are isolated and studied for possible remedial action and to place responsibilities. For example, if the standard material cost for producing 2,000 units of Product A is $800, but material costing $840 was used in producing the units, the $40 variance may have resulted from paying a price higher than standard for the material, or a greater quantity of material than standard may have been used. The price paid for a material is a purchasing department responsibility; consequently, if the variance was caused by a price greater than standard, responsibility rests with the purchasing department. On the other hand, since the production department is usually responsible for the amount of material used, if a quantity greater than standard was used, responsibility normally rests with the production department. However, if more than a standard amount of material was used because the material was of a grade below standard, causing more than normal waste, responsibility is back on the purchasing department for buying a substandard grade.

Isolating Variances. As previously stated, when variances occur, they are isolated and studied for possible remedial action and to place responsibilities. For example, assume a company has established four pounds of material costing $0.25 per pound as the standard amount and cost of material required in manufacturing one unit of its Product Z. Assume further that the company has just completed 1,000 units of Product Z, using 4,100 pounds of material costing $0.26 per pound, or $1,066. Under these assumptions the actual and standard material costs for the 1,000 units are:

Actual cost: *4,100 pounds @ $0.26..............$1,066*
Standard cost: *4,000 pounds @ $0.25.............. 1,000*
            Excess of Actual over Standard.................$ 66

Observe that actual material cost is $66 above standard. This cost variation is isolated as to causes in the following manner:

QUANTITY VARIANCE
   Actual units at the standard price..4,100 lbs. @ $0.25 = $1,025
   Standard units at the standard price.4,000 lbs. @ $0.25 = 1,000
     Variance (unfavorable)............ 100 lbs. @ $0.25 =   *$25*

PRICE VARIANCE

Actual units at the actual price.....4,100 lbs. @ $0.26 = $1,066
Actual units at the standard price..4,100 lbs. @ $0.25 =   1,025
Variance (unfavorable)............4,100 lbs. @ $0.01 =   *41*
Excess Material Cost............   *$66*

The foregoing analysis shows that $25 of the excess material cost resulted from using 100 more units than standard, and $41 resulted from a unit price $0.01 above standard. With this information management can go to the responsible individuals for explanations.

Labor cost in manufacturing a given part or in performing a service depends on a composite of the number of hours worked (quantity) and the wage rate paid (price). Therefore, when labor cost for a task varies from standard, it too may be analyzed into a quantity variance and a price variance.

Overhead costs are subject to quantity and price variances also. However, since establishing overhead standards and analyzing overhead variances is somewhat complicated, a discussion of these points is deferred to a more advanced text.

Management by Exception. When standard costs are used, a control technique known as *management by exception* is commonly practiced. Under this technique management gives its attention only to a relatively small number of variances, those in which actual costs are significantly different from standard, and gives little or no attention to the relatively large number of cost situations in which performance is satisfactory. In other words, management concentrates its attention on the exceptional or irregular situations and pays little attention to the normal.

QUESTIONS FOR CLASS DISCUSSION

1. Why is a business divided into departments?
2. Differentiate between productive departments and service departments.
3. Name several service departments of a department store.
4. What are the productive departments of (a) a factory, and (b) a store?
5. What is the purpose of a departmental sales analysis sheet? How is a sales analysis sheet used in determining sales by departments?
6. What is a pin-punched price tag? How is such a tag used in determining sales by departments?
7. How is punched paper tape used in determining sales by departments?
8. Differentiate between direct and indirect expenses.
9. Suggest a basis for allocating each of the following expenses to departments: (a) salary of a supervisory employee, (b) rent, (c) heat, (d) electricity used for lighting, (e) janitorial services, (f) advertising, (g) expired insurance, and (h) taxes.

10. How is a departmental expense allocation sheet used in allocating expenses to departments?
11. How reliable are the amounts shown as net incomes for the various departments of a store when expenses are allocated to the departments?
12. As the terms are used in departmental accounting, what are (a) escapable expenses, and (b) inescapable expenses?
13. How is a department's contribution to overhead measured?
14. What are a department's controllable costs and expenses?
15. What is a joint cost? How is such a cost normally allocated?
16. What is a standard cost? For what are standard costs used?
17. In standard cost accounting, what are variances?

PROBLEMS

Problem 20–1

Valley Sales carries on its operations in three selling departments, A, B, and C, and two service departments, general office and purchasing. At the end of an annual accounting period the accountant of the company prepared the following adjusted trial balance:

VALLEY SALES

Adjusted Trial Balance, December 31, 19—

Cash..	$ 7,875	
Merchandise inventory, Department A..........	9,300	
Merchandise inventory, Department B..........	18,200	
Merchandise inventory, Department C..........	14,500	
Supplies.......................................	620	
Equipment.....................................	36,940	
Accumulated depreciation, equipment..........		$ 10,135
Jerry Collingsworth, capital....................		72,925
Jerry Collingsworth, withdrawals...............	9,000	
Sales, Department A............................		52,400
Sales, Department B............................		104,200
Sales, Department C............................		68,400
Purchases, Department A.......................	34,400	
Purchases, Department B.......................	79,300	
Purchases, Department C.......................	41,700	
Salaries expense...............................	36,855	
Rent expense..................................	7,500	
Advertising expense............................	5,625	
Expired insurance..............................	500	
Heating and lighting expense...................	1,200	
Depreciation of equipment......................	1,820	
Supplies used..................................	1,125	
Janitorial services.............................	1,600	
	$308,060	$308,060

Required:

1. Prepare a departmental expense allocation sheet for Valley Sales, using the following information:

    a) Valley Sales treats salaries, supplies used, and depreciation of equipment as direct departmental expenses. The payroll, requisition, and fixed asset records show the following amounts of these expenses by departments:

	Salaries Expense	Supplies Used	Depr. of Equipment
General office...............	$10,295	$ 145	$ 250
Purchasing department...........	7,040	130	220
Department A................	4,660	275	425
Department B................	8,320	315	615
Department C................	6,540	260	310
	$36,855	$1,125	$1,820

   b) The company treats the remainder of its expenses as indirect and allocates them as follows:

    1. Rent expense on the basis of the amount and value of floor space occupied. The general office occupies 600 square feet and the purchasing department occupies 400 square feet on a balcony at the rear of the store. This space is not as valuable as space on the main floor; therefore, the store allocates $500 of its rent to these two departments on the basis of space occupied and allocates the remainder to the selling departments on the basis of the main-floor space they occupy. The selling departments occupy main-floor space as follows: Department A, 2,000 square feet; Department B, 3,500 square feet; and Department C, 1,500 square feet.
    2. Advertising expense on the basis of sales.
    3. Insurance expense on the basis of the book values of the equipment in the departments, which are: general office, $2,500; purchasing, $2,000; Department A, $6,500; Department B, $9,500; and Department C, $4,500.
    4. Heating and lighting and janitorial services on the basis of floor space occupied.

   c) The company allocates general office department expenses to the selling departments on the basis of sales, and it allocates purchasing department expenses on the basis of purchases.

2. Prepare a departmental income statement for the store showing sales, cost of goods sold, expenses, and net incomes by departments and for the entire store. The year-end inventories were: Department A, $11,600; Department B, $23,400; and Department C, $13,400.

3. Prepare a second income statement for the store showing departmental contributions to overhead and overall net income.

Problem 20–2

Krueger Company is considering the elimination of its unprofitable Department B. The company's last year income statement appears as follows:

KRUEGER COMPANY

Income Statement for Year Ended December 31, 19—

	Dept. A	Dept. B	Combined
Sales.....................................	$76,500	$45,900	$122,400
Cost of goods sold........................	46,750	34,325	81,075
Gross margin on sales....................	$29,750	$11,575	$ 41,325
Operating expenses:			
Direct expenses:			
Advertising........................	$ 1,175	$ 895	$ 2,070
Store supplies used...................	325	215	540
Depreciation of store equipment......	850	475	1,325
Total direct expenses..............	$ 2,350	$ 1,585	$ 3,935
Allocated expenses:			
Sales salaries........................	$11,050	$ 6,630	$ 17,680
Rent expense........................	2,625	1,575	4,200
Bad debts expense....................	380	230	610
Office salaries.......................	2,600	1,560	4,160
Insurance expense....................	200	150	350
Miscellaneous office expenses........	325	200	525
Total allocated expenses...........	$17,180	$10,345	$ 27,525
Total expenses..................	$19,530	$11,930	$ 31,460
Net Income (Loss)......................	$10,220	$ (355)	$ 9,865

If Department B is eliminated:

1. The company has one office clerk who earns $80 per week or $4,160 per year and four salesclerks each of whom earns $85 per week or $4,420 per year. At present the salaries of two and one-half salesclerks are charged to Department A and one and one-half salesclerks to Department B. It is the opinion of management that two salesclerks may be dismissed if Department B is eliminated, leaving only two full-time clerks in Department A, and making up the difference by assigning the office clerk to part-time sales work in the department. It is felt that although the office clerk has not devoted half of her time to the office work of Department B, if she devotes the same amount of time to selling in Department A during rush hours as she has to the office work of Department B, it will be sufficient to carry the load.

2. The lease on the store building is long term and cannot be changed; therefore, the space presently occupied by Department B will have to be used by and charged to Department A. Likewise, Department A will have to make whatever use of Department B's equipment it can, since the equipment has little or no sales value.

3. The elimination of Department B will eliminate the Department B advertising expense, losses from bad debts, and store supplies used. It will also eliminate 80 percent of the insurance expense, the portion on merchandise, and 25 percent of the miscellaneous office expenses presently allocated to Department B.

Required:

1. List in separate columns the amounts of Department B's escapable and inescapable expenses.
2. Under the assumption that Department A's sales and gross profit will not be affected by the elimination of Department B, prepare an income statement showing what the company can expect to earn from the operation of Department A after Department B is eliminated.

Problem 20–3

Salt River Supply Company began its operations one year ago with two selling departments and one office department. Following are the year's operating results:

SALT RIVER SUPPLY COMPANY

Departmental Income Statement
For Year Ended December 31, 19—

	Dept. A	Dept. B	Combined
Revenue from sales......................	$80,000	$50,000	$130,000
Cost of goods sold.......................	52,000	30,000	82,000
Gross profit from sales...................	$28,000	$20,000	$ 48,000
Direct expenses:			
Sales salaries.........................	$10,500	$ 6,000	$ 16,500
Advertising..........................	900	675	1,575
Store supplies used...................	400	200	600
Depreciation of equipment.............	1,075	575	1,650
Total direct expenses.................	$12,875	$ 7,450	$ 20,325
Allocated expenses:			
Rent expense.........................	$ 4,800	$ 2,400	$ 7,200
Heating and lighting expense..........	1,200	600	1,800
Share of office department expenses.....	4,800	3,000	7,800
Total allocated expenses..............	$10,800	$ 6,000	$ 16,800
Total expenses.....................	$23,675	$13,450	$ 37,125
Net Income...........................	$ 4,325	$ 6,550	$ 10,875

The company plans to open a third selling department which it estimates will produce $30,000 in sales with a 35 percent gross profit margin and requiring the following direct expenses: sales salaries, $4,500; advertising, $450; store supplies, $175; and depreciation of equipment, $350.

A year ago, when operations began, it was necessary to rent store space in excess of requirements. This extra space was assigned to and used by Departments A and B during the year; but when the new department, Department C, is opened it will take one fourth of the space presently assigned to Department A and one sixth of the space assigned to Department B.

The company allocates its general office department expenses to its selling departments on the basis of sales, and it expects the new department to cause a $525 increase in general office department expenses.

The company expects Department C to bring new customers into the store who, in addition to buying goods in the new department, will also buy sufficient merchandise in the two old departments to increase their sales by 5 percent each. And, although the old departments' sales are expected to increase, their gross profit percentages are not expected to change. Likewise, their direct expenses, other than supplies, are not expected to change. The supplies used will increase in proportion to sales.

Required:
Prepare a departmental income statement showing the company's expected operations with three selling departments.

Problem 20–4

The Arizona Store sells both men's and women's clothing and shoes. It has a men's clothing department, a men's shoe department, and four other departments selling women's clothing and shoes. Walter Deskin does all the window decorating for the store. However, this takes only a portion of his time; and when all window decorating is done, he spends the remainder of his time selling in the men's clothing and men's shoe departments. His work in the two selling departments consists of waiting on customers in turn as they enter either department, and also in straightening and rearranging merchandise in either department as needed after the merchandise has been shown to customers.

The store allocates a portion of Deskin's $6,000 annual salary to Advertising and Display Expense and divides the remainder between the two selling departments in which he works. The three-way salary division was based last year on a sample of the time the employee spent in window decorating and in working in the two selling departments. To gain the sample, observations were made on several days throughout the year of the manner in which the employee spent his time while at work. Following are the results of these observations:

Observed Manner in Which Employee Spent His Time	Elapsed Time in Minutes
Window decorating	*1,800*
Selling in men's clothing department	*1,850*
Straightening and rearranging merchandise in men's clothing department	*350*
Selling in shoe department	*1,425*
Straightening and rearranging merchandise in shoe department	*375*
Doing nothing while waiting for a customer to enter one of the selling departments	*200*

Required:
Prepare a calculation showing the share of the employee's salary to be allocated to Advertising and Display Expense and the shares to be allocated to the selling departments.

Problem 20–5

Hillside Development Company bought ten acres of hilly land at $4,000 per acre, spent $37,000 putting in streets and sidewalks, and divided the land into 30 building lots of equal size. Since some of the lots sloped downhill from the streets and some sloped uphill and some had trees and some did not, the lots were not of equal value. Therefore, five lots were marked for sale at $5,000 each, ten at $4,000 each, and fifteen at $3,000 each. During the first accounting period three of the $5,000 lots, five of the $4,000 lots, and ten of the $3,000 lots were sold. Selling expenses amounted to 10 percent of the selling price of each lot sold.

Required:

Prepare an income statement showing sales, cost of sales, selling expenses, and net income from the sale of the 18 lots.

Problem 20–6

PikNik Furniture Company manufactures outdoor furniture. It has just completed an order consisting of 300 units of its deluxe picnic table. The cost records for the tables show 14,500 board feet of lumber costing $3,045 and 610 hours of labor costing $1,525 were used in their manufacture. The company has established the following standards for manufacturing one unit of this particular table:

Materials: 50 board feet of lumber at $0.20 per board foot.
Labor: 2 hours at $2.50 per hour.

Required:

1. Prepare a calculation showing the isolation of the material variances and labor variances incurred in manufacturing the tables.
2. Tell who is normally responsible for each isolated variance.

Problem 20–7

A. Farmer produced and marketed a million pounds of potatoes last year, and at the year-end he prepared the following statement to show the results:

A. FARMER
Income from the Production and Sale of Potatoes
For Year Ended December 31, 19—

	Results by Grades			Combined
	No. 1	No. 2	No. 3	
Sales by grades:				
No. 1, 300,000 lbs. @ $0.045 per lb.	*$13,500*			
No. 2, 500,000 lbs. @ $0.04 per lb......		*$20,000*		
No. 3, 200,000 lbs. @ $0.03 per lb......			*$6,000*	
Combined........................				*$39,500*
Costs:				
Land preparation, seed, planting, and cultivating @ $0.01422 per lb...	*$ 4,266*	*$ 7,110*	*$2,844*	*$14,220*
Harvesting, sorting, and grading @ $0.01185 per lb....................	*3,555*	*5,925*	*2,370*	*11,850*
Marketing @ $0.00415 per lb.........	*1,245*	*2,075*	*830*	*4,150*
Total costs......................	*$ 9,066*	*$15,110*	*$6,044*	*$30,220*
Net Income or (Loss).................	*$ 4,434*	*$ 4,890*	*$ (44)*	*$ 9,280*

On the foregoing statement A. Farmer divided his costs among the grades on a per pound basis. He did this because, with the exception of marketing costs, his records did not show costs per grade. As to marketing costs, the records did show that $4,020 of the $4,150 was the cost of placing the No. 1 and No. 2 potatoes in bags and hauling them to the warehouse of the produce buyer. Bagging and hauling costs were the same for both grades. The remaining $130 of marketing costs was the cost of loading the No. 3 potatoes into trucks of a potato chip factory that bought these potatoes in bulk and picked them up at the farm.

Required:
Prepare an income statement that will show better the results of producing and marketing the potatoes.

CLASS EXERCISE

Exercise 20–1
Moore, Neal, and Otto formed a partnership to carry out a real estate venture. Moore invested $2,000 in cash, Neal invested land valued at $15,000, and Otto invested $13,000 in cash. The partners installed streets and water mains costing $15,000 and divided the land into 14 building lots. They priced Lots 1, 2, 3, and 4 for sale at $3,000 each; Lots 5, 6, 7, 8, 9, 10, 11, and 12 at $3,500 each; and Lots 13, and 14 at $4,000 each. The partners agreed that

Moore could take Lot 13 at cost for his personal use. The remaining lots were sold and the partnership dissolved.

Required:

Give the general journal entry to distribute the partnership cash to the partners.

ALTERNATE PROBLEMS

Problem 20–1A

Desert Sales has three selling departments, X, Y, and Z, and two service departments, general office and purchasing. At the end of an accounting period its bookkeeper brought together the following information for use in preparing the year-end statements:

Sales, Purchases, and Inventories:

	Dept. X	Dept. Y	Dept. Z
Sales...........................	*$95,400*	*$51,200*	*$73,400*
Purchases.......................	*67,900*	*35,300*	*41,800*
January 1 (beginning) inventory...	*12,300*	*8,500*	*10,200*
December 31 (ending) inventory....	*14,500*	*9,400*	*7,300*

Direct Departmental Expenses:

Desert Sales treats salaries, supplies used, and depreciation as direct departmental expenses. The payroll, requisition, and fixed asset records showed the following amounts of these expenses by departments:

	Salaries Expense	Supplies Used	Depr. of Equipment
General office......................	*$ 9,345*	*$ 235*	*$ 625*
Purchasing department.............	*6,160*	*195*	*375*
Department X......................	*10,360*	*385*	*850*
Department Y......................	*5,510*	*215*	*450*
Department Z......................	*8,140*	*295*	*500*
	$39,515	*$1,325*	*$2,800*

Indirect Expenses:

The concern incurred the following amounts of indirect expenses:

Rent expense..	*$6,600*
Advertising expense.............................	*5,500*
Expired insurance................................	*750*
Heating and lighting expense....................	*1,750*
Janitorial expense..............................	*2,100*

Desert Sales allocates the foregoing expenses to its departments as follows:

a) Rent expense on the basis of the amount and value of floor space occupied. The general office and purchasing departments occupy space in the rear of the store which is not as valuable as space in the front; consequently, $600 of the total rent is allocated to these two departments in proportion to the space occupied by each. The remainder of the rent is divided between the selling departments in proportion to the space occupied. The five departments occupy these amounts of space: General Office, 600 square feet; Purchasing Department, 400 square feet; Department X, 3,000 square feet; Department Y, 1,500 square feet; and Department Z, 1,500 square feet.

b) Advertising expense on the basis of sales.

c) Expired insurance on the basis of equipment book values. The book values of the equipment in the departments are: General Office, $3,500; Purchasing Department, $2,000; Department X, $9,000; Department Y, $5,000; and Department Z, $5,500.

d) Heating and lighting and janitorial expenses on the basis of floor space occupied.

Service Department Expenses:

Desert Sales allocates its general office department expenses to its selling departments on the basis of sales, and it allocates purchasing department expenses on the basis of purchases.

Required:

1. Prepare a departmental expense allocation sheet for the concern.
2. Prepare a departmental income statement showing sales, cost of goods sold, expenses, and net incomes by departments and for the entire store.
3. Prepare a second departmental income statement showing departmental contributions to overhead and overall net income.

Problem 20–3A

South Mountain Sales Company began business last year with two selling departments and a general office department. It had the following results for the year:

SOUTH MOUNTAIN SALES COMPANY

Departmental Income Statement
For Year Ended December 31, 19—

	Dept. 1	Dept. 2	Combined
Sales..............................	$120,000	$60,000	$180,000
Cost of goods sold...................	84,000	36,000	120,000
Gross profit from sales..............	$ 36,000	$24,000	$ 60,000
Direct expenses:			
Sales salaries.....................	$ 12,500	$ 7,200	$ 19,700
Advertising expense...............	1,125	750	1,875
Store supplies used...............	600	300	900
Depreciation of equipment........	1,025	550	1,575
Total direct expenses............	$ 15,250	$ 8,800	$ 24,050

SOUTH MOUNTAIN SALES COMPANY—Cont.

	Dept. 1	Dept. 2	Combined
Allocated expenses:			
Rent expense.....................$	5,400	$ 3,600	$ 9,000
Heating and lighting expense......	1,080	720	1,800
Share of general office expenses....	7,000	3,500	10,500
Total allocated expenses........$	13,480	$ 7,820	$ 21,300
Total expenses................$	28,730	$16,620	$ 45,350
Net Income.......................$	7,270	$ 7,380	$ 14,650

The company plans to add a third selling department which it estimates will produce $40,000 in sales with a 35 percent gross profit margin. The new department will require the following estimated direct expenses: sales salaries, $4,500; advertising expense, $450; store supplies, $250; and depreciation on equipment, $525.

When the company began its operations, it was necessary to rent a store room having selling space in excess of requirements. This extra space was assigned to and used by Departments 1 and 2 during the year; but when Department 3 is opened, it will take over one third the space presently assigned to Department 1 and one sixth the space assigned to Department 2. The space reductions are not expected to affect the operations or sales of the old departments.

The company allocates its general office department expenses to its selling departments on the basis of sales. It expects the new department to cause a $950 increase in general office department expenses.

The company expects the addition of Department 3 to bring new customers to the store who, in addition to buying Department 3 merchandise, will also do sufficient buying in the old departments to increase their sales by 5 percent each. It is not expected the increase in sales in the old departments will affect their gross profit percentages or any of their direct expenses other than supplies. It is expected the supplies used will increase in proportion to sales.

Required:

Prepare a departmental income statement showing the company's expected operations with three selling departments.

Problem 20–4A

Cactus Sales has three selling and two service departments, and it allocates personal property taxes to the departments on the basis of taxable property. The taxable property in the service departments consists of equipment, and in the selling departments it consists of both inventory and equipment. The inventories vary somewhat throughout the year; however, for purposes of allocation the company assumes an average of the beginning and ending inventories in each department is a fair representation of the inventory in each department throughout the year. Following are the book values of the equipment in the departments and last year's beginning and ending inventories:

Departments	Book Value of Equipment	January 1 Inventory	December 31 Inventory
Office department..............*$5,600*			
Purchasing department........ *4,000*			
Department X................. *5,800*		*$20,400*	*$19,200*
Department Y................. *5,100*		*18,600*	*17,200*
Department Z................. *4,200*		*16,400*	*18,800*

Required:

Under the assumption that the concern incurred $1,320 personal property taxes last year, prepare a calculation showing the allocation of the taxes to the departments.

Problem 20–6A

Office Furniture Company has just completed an order for 1,000 identical typewriter tables. The records show 10,100 board feet of lumber costing $3,939 and 2,250 hours of labor costing $5,715 were used in manufacturing the tables. The company's established material and labor standards for one unit of this type of table are ten board feet of lumber costing $0.40 per board foot and 2.2 hours of labor at $2.50 per hour.

The company has several job classifications the wage rates of which vary. Due to a number of employee illnesses during the time the foregoing tables were in process, it was necessary to temporarily use higher-paid employees on jobs normally performed by lower-paid employees. The higher-paid employees drew their regular wages while on the temporary jobs.

Required:

Prepare calculations to isolate the material and labor variances in manufacturing the foregoing tables.

DECISION PROBLEM 20—THE HOUSE OF
MAPLE

F. W. Dodd and Tom Pryor have been partners in the furniture business for 20 years. Mr. Dodd wishes to retire from active participation in the business. He feels that, since he has been largely responsible for sales promotion, some measures must be taken to counter the loss of his services in this area if the business is to continue without a sales revenue loss and a net income reduction.

He proposes that department heads be given, in addition to their present salaries, 10 percent of the net income of their respective departments. This bonus is to be determined on net income computed after deduction of the bonus as an expense but before any distribution to the partners by way of salary, interest on capital, etc. Mr. Dodd will forego his $25,000 per year salary after his retirement but Mr. Pryor's salary will remain at $20,000. Mr. Pryor will agree to the proposal provided you find that his share of the profit based on last year's operations would not be materially less under Mr. Dodd's plan.

The sales departments are: Furniture; Floor Coverings; Draperies and Pictures; Electrical Appliances; and Customer Services. Some changes in accounting for expenses must be made, for the firm has never attempted to departmentalize operating expenses. The firm's ledger reveals the following expense accounts:

a) Sales Salaries and Commissions.

b) Salaries and Wages, Customer Services Department.

c) Office Salaries.

d) Depreciation, Taxes, and Insurance on Office Furniture and Equipment.

e) Building Occupancy Expense (depreciation, repairs, insurance, taxes, utility expense, custodial expense, and other occupancy expenses).

f) Advertising.

g) Supplies Used (includes materials, supplies, and parts used in the Customer Services Department, some of which are sold to customers).

h) Delivery Expenses (includes cost of trucks used by Customer Services).

i) Taxes and Insurance on Merchandise, Fixtures, and Equipment in Sales Departments.

j) Bad debts.

k) Telephone Expense.

The Customer Services Department lays carpets, repairs furniture and electrical appliances including television and radio sets; custom-makes draperies; and, furnishes other services to customers at the request of the sales departments. Where no charge for the service is made to the customer, the sales department requesting the service is charged.

Prepare a report to Mr. Pryor giving your opinion of how the proposal may affect Mr. Pryor's share of future net income. This report should include:

1. Recommendations as to the bases that may be used for departmentalizing operating expenses.

2. A schedule based on the previous year's figures showing by departments (a) net income before bonus to the department head, (b) bonus, and (c) net income. (For purposes of this schedule assume that your recommendations in (1) above were applied to the previous year's revenues and expenses and the application resulted in the following departmental net incomes before bonuses to department heads: Furniture, $120,000; Floor Coverings, $40,000; Draperies and Pictures, $25,000; Electrical Appliances, $50,000; and Customer Services, $28,000.)

3. A second schedule showing the allocation of last year's total net income to the partners. In this schedule show in one set of columns the net income and its allocation as actually made and in the second set of columns the net income and allocation that would have been made had Mr. Dodd's proposals been in effect. (In this schedule assume that in addition to partners' salary allowances, interest is allowed on partners' investments as follows: Dodd, interest amounting to $30,000; and Pryor, $18,000. And that remaining income is shared 60 percent to Dodd and 40 percent to Pryor.)

21

Manufacturing
Accounting

IN PREVIOUS CHAPTERS consideration has been given to the accounting problems of service-type and merchandising concerns. In this and the next two chapters some of the accounting problems of manufacturing enterprises are examined.

Manufacturing and merchandising concerns are alike in that both depend for revenue upon the sale of one or more commodities or products. However, they differ in that a merchandising company buys the products it sells in the finished state in which they are sold, while a manufacturing concern buys raw materials which it manufactures into the finished products it sells. For example, a shoe store buys shoes and sells them in the same form in which they are purchased; but a manufacturer of shoes buys leather, cloth, glue, nails, and dye and turns these items into salable shoes.

Some of the similarities and differences in accounting for merchandising and manufacturing concerns are readily apparent when their income statements are compared. For example, compare the Nelson Hardware Company income statement, Illustration 25, on page 118, with that of Excel Manufacturing Company, Illustration 131 on page 614. Notice that the revenue, selling expense, and general and administrative expense sections of the two statements are similar. However, when the cost of goods sold sections are compared, a difference readily becomes apparent. To emphasize this difference, the cost of goods sold section from a merchandising concern's income statement is condensed and reproduced on the next page beside that of a manufacturing company.

Merchandising Company		*Manufacturing Company*	
Cost of goods sold:		*Cost of goods sold:*	
Merchandise inventory............$14,200.00		Finished goods inventory........$ 11,200.00	
Purchases........................ 34,150.00		Cost of goods manufactured	
Goods available for sale...........$48,350.00		(see Manufacturing Schedule).. 170,500.00	
Merchandise inventory............ 12,100.00		Goods available for sale.........$181,700.00	
Cost of goods sold................$36,250.00		Finished goods inventory........ 10,300.00	
		Cost of goods sold..............$171,400.00	

Notice in the costs of goods sold section from the manufacturing company's income statement that the inventories of goods for sale are called *finished goods inventories* rather than merchandise inventories. Notice too that the "Purchases" element of the merchandising company becomes "Cost of goods manufactured (see Manufacturing Schedule)" on the manufacturer's statement. These differences result because the merchandising company buys its goods ready for sale, while the manufacturer creates its salable products from raw materials.

The words "see Manufacturing Schedule" refer the income statement reader to a separate schedule called a "Schedule of the Cost of Goods Manufactured." This manufacturing schedule or manufacturing statement (see page 615) shows the costs of manufacturing the products created by a manufacturing company. The records and techniques used in accounting for these costs are the distinguishing characteristics of manufacturing accounting.

SYSTEMS OF ACCOUNTING IN MANUFACTURING CONCERNS

The accounting system used by a manufacturing company may be either a so-called general accounting system or a cost accounting system. A general accounting system is a noncost system. It uses periodic physical inventories of raw materials, goods in process, and finished goods; and it has as its goal the determination of the total cost of all goods manufactured during each accounting period. A cost accounting system differs in that it uses perpetual inventories, and has as its goal the determination of the unit cost of manufacturing a product or performing a service. General accounting or noncost accounting systems are the subject of this chapter; cost accounting systems are discussed in the next two chapters.

ELEMENTS OF MANUFACTURING COSTS

A manufacturer takes *raw materials* and by applying *direct labor* and *factory overhead* converts these materials into finished products. Raw materials, direct labor, and factory overhead are the "elements of manufacturing costs."

Raw Materials. Raw materials are the commodities that enter directly into and become a part of a finished product. Such items as leather, dye, cloth, nails, and glue are raw materials of a shoe manufacturer. Raw materials are often called *direct materials*. Direct materials are materials the costs of which are chargeable directly to the product or products manufactured, and are distinguished from *indirect materials* or factory supplies which are such items as grease and oil for the machinery, cleaning fluids, etc. Indirect materials are accounted for as factory overhead.

The raw materials of a manufacturer are called "raw materials," even though they may not necessarily be in their natural raw state. For example, leather is manufactured from hides, nails from steel, and cloth from cotton. Nevertheless, leather, nails, and cloth are the raw materials of a shoe manufacturer even though they are finished goods to a previous manufacturer.

Direct Labor. Direct labor is labor, the cost of which is chargeable directly to the product or products manufactured. It is often described as the labor of those people who work, either with machines or hand tools, directly on the materials converted into finished products. In manufacturing, direct labor is distinguished from *indirect labor*. Indirect labor is the labor of superintendents, foremen, millwrights, engineers, janitors, and others who do not work directly on the finished products. Indirect labor aids in production; often it makes production possible, but does not enter directly into the finished product. Indirect labor is accounted for as a factory overhead cost.

In a noncost system, an account called *Direct Labor* is debited each payday for the wages of those workers who work directly on the product. Likewise, each payday, the wages of indirect workers are debited to one or more indirect labor accounts. Also, at the end of each period, the amounts of accrued direct and indirect labor are recorded in the direct and indirect labor accounts by means of adjusting entries. From this it can be seen that a manufacturing company's payroll accounting is similar to that of a merchandising company. When a cost accounting system is not involved, no new techniques are required, and only the new direct and indirect labor accounts distinguish the payroll accounting of a manufacturer from that of a merchandising company.

Factory Overhead. Factory overhead, often called *manufacturing overhead or factory burden*, includes all manufacturing costs other than direct material and direct labor costs. Overhead may include:

Indirect labor.	Heat, lights, and power.
Factory supplies.	Depreciation of plant and equipment.
Repairs to buildings and equipment.	Patents written off.
Insurance on plant and equipment.	Small tools written off.
Taxes on plant and equipment.	Workmen's compensation insurance.
Taxes on raw materials and work in process.	Payroll taxes on the wages of the factory workers.

Factory overhead does not include selling and administrative expenses. These are not a part of factory overhead because they are not incurred in the manufacturing operations. They are not incurred in order to produce the manufactured products.

Payroll taxes on the wages of factory workers are an overhead cost and an important item. However, no new techniques in addition to those presented in Chapter 14 are required in accounting for these taxes; consequently, in order to simplify the situations of this and the next two chapters, payroll taxes are omitted in the illustrations.

All factory overhead costs are accumulated in overhead cost accounts which vary from company to company, with the exact accounts depending in each case upon the nature of the company and the information desired. For example, one indirect labor account or several accounts, such as Indirect Labor—Superintendence, Indirect Labor—Engineering, Indirect Labor—Building Maintenance, may be opened in the ledger. Or, to illustrate further, one account called "Expired Insurance on Plant Equipment" may be maintained, or an expired insurance account each for buildings and the different kinds of equipment may be used. But regardless of accounts, overhead costs are recorded with the same types of journals as are selling and administrative expenses. Some, such as indirect labor and light and power, are recorded in a Voucher Register or a Cash Disbursements Journal as they are paid and are then posted to the accounts. Others, such as depreciation and expired insurance, reach the accounts from the General Journal where they are first recorded with adjusting entries.

Two overhead costs mentioned in the list previously given require special attention at this point. They are *patents written off* and *small tools written off*.

PATENTS

Patents are granted by the federal government to encourage the invention of new machines and mechanical devices. A patent gives its owner the exclusive right to manufacture the patented machine or device for 17 years. All costs of developing a patented machine or device, or the costs of acquiring patent rights of others, are debited to an asset account called "Patents," which is classified for balance sheet purposes as an *intangible asset*.

Although a patent gives its owner the exclusive right to manufacture a patented device for 17 years, its cost should be written off over a shorter period if its useful life is estimated to be less than 17 years. For example, if a patent costing $20,000 has an estimated useful life of only ten years, the following adjusting entry is made at the end of each full accounting year in its life:

Dec.	31	Patents Written Off.....................	2,000.00	
		Patents............................		2,000.00
		To write off one tenth of the patent		
		cost.		

The entry's debit causes the $2,000 patents cost to appear on the manufacturing statement as a factory overhead cost. The credit directly reduces the balance of the Patents account. Normally, patents are written off directly to the Patents account as in this entry.

SMALL TOOLS

Small tools such as hammers, wrenches, and drills which have low individual costs and are easily lost, broken, or stolen are normally either charged directly to an overhead cost account at the time of purchase or are accounted for on an inventory basis. This is because it is impracticable to set up individual records to account for such items on a depreciation basis.

Under the accounting principle of materiality, if small tools costng about the same amount are purchased each year to replace those lost, broken, or stolen, their costs may be charged directly to an overhead cost account at the time of purchase. However, if the amounts purchased vary from year to year and are material, an inventory basis becomes a better means of accounting for them.

When small tools are accounted for on an inventory basis, the cost of tools on hand at the beginning of a period is represented by a debit balance in the Small Tools account; and as tools are purchased during the period, their cost is debited to this account. At the end of the period a physical inventory of usable tools on hand in the factory is taken; and the inventory amount is subtracted from the end-of-the-period balance of the Small Tools account to determine the cost of tools lost, broken, and stolen during the period. This cost is then charged to overhead by an adjusting entry similar to the following:

Dec.	31	Small Tools Written Off...............	200.00	
		Small Tools.......................		200.00
		To record the cost of the tools lost,		
		broken, and stolen.		

The debit of the foregoing entry records as an overhead item the cost of tools lost, broken, or stolen during the period. The credit reduces the balance of the Small Tools account to the cost of the usable tools on hand.

Since the lives of small tools are relatively short, when an inventory is taken at the end of an accounting period, normally all usable tools are placed on the inventory at cost.

ACCOUNTS PECULIAR TO A MANUFACTURING COMPANY

Because of the nature of its operations, a manufacturing concern's ledger normally contains more accounts than that of a merchandising concern. However, some of the same accounts are found in the ledgers of both, for example, Cash, Accounts Receivable, Sales, and many selling and administrative expenses. Nevertheless, although there are accounts in common, many accounts are peculiar to a manufacturing company. For instance, accounts such as Machinery and Equipment, Accumulated Depreciation of Machinery and Equipment, Factory Supplies, Factory Supplies Used, Raw Materials Inventory, Raw Material Purchases, Goods in Process Inventory, Finished Goods Inventory, and Manufacturing Summary are normally found only in the ledgers of manufacturing concerns. Some of these accounts merit special attention.

Raw Material Purchases Account. When a general accounting system is in use, the cost of all raw materials purchased is debited to an account called Raw Material Purchases. Often a special column is provided in the Voucher Register or other journal for the debits of the individual purchases, thus making it possible to periodically post these debits in one amount, the column total.

Raw Materials Inventory Account. When a noncost system is in use, the raw materials on hand at the end of each accounting period are determined by a physical inventory; and through a closing entry the cost of this inventory is debited to the Raw Materials Inventory account where it becomes a record of the materials on hand at the end of one period and the beginning of the next.

Goods in Process Inventory Account. All manufacturing concerns, excepting those in which the manufacturing process is instantaneous, normally have on hand at any time partially processed products called *goods in process* or *work in process*. These are products in the process of being manufactured, products that have received a portion or all of their materials and have had some direct labor and overhead applied but that are not completed.

In a manufacturing concern using a general accounting system the amount of goods in process at the end of each accounting period is determined by a physical inventory; and through a closing entry the cost of this inventory is debited to the Goods in Process Inventory account where it becomes a record of the goods in process at the end of one period and the beginning of the next.

Finished Goods Inventory Account. The finished goods of a manufacturer are the equivalent of a store's merchandise; they are products in their completed state ready for sale. Actually, the only difference is that a manufacturing concern creates its finished goods from raw materials, while a store buys its merchandise in a finished, ready-for-sale state.

In a noncost system the amount of finished goods on hand at the end of each period is determined by a physical inventory; and through a closing entry the cost of this inventory is debited to the Finished Goods Inventory account as a record of the finished goods at the end of one period and the beginning of the next.

The three inventories of a manufacturing company, raw materials, goods in process, and finished goods, are current assets for balance sheet purposes.

INCOME STATEMENT OF A MANUFACTURING COMPANY

As previously stated, the income statement of a manufacturing company normally differs from that of a merchandising concern only in the cost of goods sold section. Here, the item "Cost of goods manufactured" replaces "Purchases," and finished goods inventories take the place of merchandise inventories, as can be seen by examining the income statement of Excel Manufacturing Company shown in Illustration 131.

Observe in the cost of goods sold section of Excel Manufacturing Company's income statement that only the total cost of goods manufactured is shown. It would be possible to expand this section to show the detailed costs of the materials, direct labor, and overhead entering into the cost of goods manufactured. However, if this were done, the income statement would be long and unwieldy. Consequently, the common practice is to show only the total cost of goods manufactured and to attach a supporting schedule showing the details. This supporting schedule is called a "schedule of the cost of goods manufactured" or a "manufacturing statement."

MANUFACTURING STATEMENT

The cost elements of manufacturing are raw materials, direct labor, and factory overhead; and a manufacturing statement is normally constructed in such a manner as to emphasize these elements. Notice in Illustration 132 that the first section of the statement shows the cost of raw materials used. Also observe the manner of presentation is the same as that used on the income statement of a merchandising company to show cost of goods purchased and sold.

Illustration 131
THE EXCEL MANUFACTURING COMPANY
Income Statement for Year Ended December 31, 19--

Revenue:			
Sales			$310,000
Cost of goods sold:			
Finished goods inventory, January 1, 19--		$ 11,200	
Cost of goods manufactured (see Manu-			
facturing Schedule)		170,500	
Goods available for sale.		$181,700	
Finished goods inventory, December 31, 19--		10,300	
Cost of goods sold.			171,400
Gross profit.			$138,600
Operating expenses:			
Selling expenses:			
Sales salaries.	$18,000		
Advertising expense	5,500		
Delivery salaries	12,000		
Shipping supplies used.	250		
Delivery equipment insurance expired. .	300		
Depreciation of delivery equipment. . .	2,100		
Total selling expenses		$ 38,150	
General and administrative expenses:			
Office salaries	$ 3,700		
Officers' salaries.	12,000		
Miscellaneous general expense	200		
Bad debts expense	1,550		
Office supplies used.	100		
Depreciation of office equipment. . . .	200		
Total general and administrative			
expenses		17,750	
Total operating expenses.			55,900
Operating income.			$ 82,700
Financial expense:			
Bond interest expense			4,000
Net income before state and federal income			
taxes			$ 78,700
Less: State and federal income taxes . . .			32,600
Net Income.			$ 46,100

The so-called second section shows the cost of the direct labor applied to production, and the third section shows factory overhead costs. If overhead accounts are not too numerous, the balance of each is often listed in this third section, as in Illustration 132. However, if overhead accounts are numerous, only the total of all may be shown; and in such cases the total is supported by a separate attached schedule showing the amount of each cost.

In the last section the calculation of cost of goods manufactured is completed. Here the beginning goods in process inventory is added to the sum of the manufacturing costs to show the cost of all goods in process during the period. Then, from the cost of all goods in process, the cost of the goods still in process at the end is subtracted to show cost of the goods manufactured.

Illustration 132

THE EXCEL MANUFACTURING COMPANY
Schedule of the Cost of Goods Manufactured
For Year Ended December 31, 19--

Raw materials:			
Raw materials inventory, January 1, 19--		$ 8,000	
Raw materials purchased.	$85,000		
Freight on raw materials purchased	1,500		
Delivered cost of raw materials purchased. . . .		86,500	
Raw materials available for use.		$94,500	
Raw materials inventory, December 31, 19--		9,000	
Raw materials used			$ 85,500
Direct labor			60,000
Factory overhead costs:			
Indirect labor		$ 9,000	
Supervision		6,000	
Power		2,600	
Repairs and maintenance.		2,500	
Factory taxes.		1,900	
Factory supplies used.		500	
Factory insurance expired.		1,200	
Small tools written off.		200	
Depreciation of machinery and equipment.		3,500	
Depreciation of building		1,800	
Patents written off		800	
Total factory overhead costs			30,000
Total Manufacturing Costs.			$175,500
Add: Goods in process inventory, January 1, 19--			2,500
Total Goods in Process during the Year . . .			$178,000
Deduct: Goods in process inventory, December 31,			
19--			7,500
Cost of Goods Manufactured			$170,500

The manufacturing statement is prepared from the Manufacturing Statement columns of a work sheet. The items that appear on the statement are summarized in these columns, and all that is required in constructing the statement is a rearrangement of the items into the proper statement order. The manufacturing work sheet is shown in Illustration 133.

WORK SHEET FOR A MANUFACTURING COMPANY

In examining Illustration 133, it should be recalled that a work sheet is a tool of the accountant on which he—

1. Achieves the effect of adjusting the accounts before entering the adjustments in the accounts.
2. Sorts the adjusted account balances into columns according to the financial statement upon which they appear. And
3. Calculates and proves the mathematical accuracy of the net income.

With the foregoing in mind, the primary difference between the work sheet of a manufacturing company and that of a merchandising company is an additional set of columns. Insofar as the adjustments are concerned,

Illustration 133

THE EXCEL MANUFACTURING COMPANY

Manufacturing Work Sheet for Year Ended December 31, 19—

Account Titles	Trial Balance Dr.	Trial Balance Cr.	Adjustments Dr.	Adjustments Cr.	Mfg. Statement Dr.	Mfg. Statement Cr.	Income Statement Dr.	Income Statement Cr.	Balance Sheet Dr.	Balance Sheet Cr.
Cash	11,000								11,000	
Accounts receivable	32,000								32,000	
Allowance for bad debts		300		(a) 1,550						1,850
Raw materials inventory	8,000				8,000	9,000			9,000	
Goods in process inventory	2,500				2,500	7,500			7,500	
Finished goods inventory	11,200						11,200	10,300	10,300	
Office supplies	150			(b) 100					50	
Shipping supplies	300			(c) 250					50	
Factory supplies	750			(d) 500					250	
Prepaid insurance	1,800			(e) 1,500					300	
Small tools	1,300			(f) 200					1,100	
Delivery equipment	9,000								9,000	
Accumulated depreciation of delivery equipment		2,400		(g) 2,100						4,500
Office equipment	1,700								1,700	
Accumulated depreciation of office equipment		1,200		(h) 200						1,400
Machinery and equipment	132,000								132,000	
Accumulated depr. of machinery and equip.		15,000		(i) 3,500						18,500
Factory building	190,000								190,000	
Accumulated depreciation of factory building		18,000		(j) 1,800						19,800
Land	9,500								9,500	
Patents	12,000			(k) 800					11,200	
Accounts payable		14,000								14,000
First-mortgage bonds payable		100,000								100,000
Common stock		150,000								150,000
Retained earnings		33,660								33,660
Sales		310,000						310,000		
Raw material purchases	85,000				85,000					
Freight on raw materials	1,500		(l) 400		1,500					
Direct labor	59,600		(l) 60		60,000					
Indirect labor	8,940				9,000					

Account	Trial Balance Dr	Trial Balance Cr	Adjustments Dr	Adjustments Cr	Manufacturing Dr	Manufacturing Cr	Income Statement Dr	Income Statement Cr	Balance Sheet Dr	Balance Sheet Cr
Supervision	6,000				6,000					
Power expense	2,600				2,600					
Repairs and Maintenance	2,500				2,500					
Factory taxes	1,900				1,900					
Sales salaries	18,000						18,000			
Advertising expense	5,500						5,500			
Delivery salaries	11,920		(l) 80				12,000			
Office salaries	3,700						3,700			
Officers' salaries	12,000						12,000			
Miscellaneous general expense	200						200			
Bond interest expense	2,000		(m) 2,000				4,000			
	644,560	644,560								
Bad debts expense			(a) 1,550				1,550			
Office supplies used			(b) 100				100			
Shipping supplies used			(c) 250				250			
Factory supplies used			(d) 500		500					
Factory insurance expired			(e) 1,200		1,200					
Delivery equipment insurance expired			(e) 300				300			
Small tools written off			(f) 200		200					
Depreciation of delivery equipment			(g) 2,100				2,100			
Depreciation of office equipment			(h) 200				200			
Depreciation of machinery and equipment			(i) 3,500		3,500					
Depreciation of building			(j) 1,800		1,800					
Patents written off			(k) 800		800					
Accrued wages payable				(l) 540						540
Bond interest payable				(m) 2,000						2,000
State and federal income taxes expense			(n) 32,600				32,600			
State and federal income taxes payable				(n) 32,600						32,600
			47,640	47,640		16,500				
Cost of goods manufactured to Income Statement columns						170,500	170,500			
					187,000	187,000	274,200	320,300	424,950	378,850
Net Income							46,100			46,100
							320,300	320,300	424,950	424,950

they are made in the same way on both kinds of work sheets. Also, the mathematical accuracy of the net income is proved in the same way. However, since an additional accounting statement, the manufacturing statement, is prepared for a manufacturing company, the work sheet of such a company has an additional set of columns, the Manufacturing Statement columns, into which are sorted the items appearing on the manufacturing statement.

PREPARING A MANUFACTURING COMPANY'S WORK SHEET

A manufacturing company's work sheet is prepared in the same manner as that of a merchandising concern. First a trial balance is entered in the Trial Balance columns in the usual manner. Next information for the adjustments is assembled, and the adjustments are entered in the Adjustments columns just as for a merchandising company. The adjustments information for the work sheet shown in Illustration 133 is as follows:

a) Estimated bad debt losses ½ percent of sales, or $1,550.
b) Office supplies used, $100.
c) Shipping supplies used, $250.
d) Factory supplies used, $500.
e) Expired insurance on factory, $1,200; and expired insurance on the delivery equipment, $300.
f) The small tools inventory shows $1,100 of usable small tools on hand.
g) Depreciation of delivery equipment, $2,100.
h) Depreciation of office equipment, $200.
i) Depreciation of factory machinery and equipment, $3,500.
j) Depreciation of factory building, $1,800.
k) Yearly write-off of one seventeenth of the cost of patents, $800.
l) Accrued wages: direct labor, $400; indirect labor, $60; delivery salaries, $80. All other employees paid monthly on the last day of each month.
m) One-half year of bond interest expense accrued, $2,000.
n) State and federal income taxes payable, $32,600.

After the adjustments are completed, the amounts in the Trial Balance columns are combined with the amounts in the Adjustments columns and are sorted to the proper Manufacturing Statement, Income Statement, or Balance Sheet columns, according to the statement on which they appear. No new techniques are required here. However, certain of the trial balance items merit special attention.

Notice that the beginning raw materials and goods in process inventories (trial balance amounts) are sorted to the Manufacturing Statement debit column. Then the $9,000 ending raw materials inventory and the $7,500 ending goods in process inventory are directly entered in the Manufacturing Statement credit column and in the Balance Sheet debit column.

These procedures have the effect of adding the beginning raw materials and goods in process inventories to the costs of manufacturing and of deducting the ending inventories. Observe also that the beginning finished goods inventory (trial balance amount) is sorted to the Income Statement debit column and the $10,300 ending finished goods inventory is directly entered in the Income Statement credit column and in the Balance Sheet debit column. This is the identical treatment given the merchandise inventories of a merchandising company.

Many beginning accounting students have difficulty getting the inventories of a manufacturing company in the proper work sheet columns. This difficulty will not arise if it is remembered that raw materials and goods in process have to do with manufacturing, appear on the manufacturing statement, and go into the Manufacturing Statement columns; and that the finished goods inventory is the equivalent of a merchandise inventory and is treated in the same manner.

Note that in addition to the raw materials and goods in process inventories, direct labor and manufacturing overhead costs also appear on the manufacturing statement and go into the Manufacturing Statement columns.

After the raw materials, goods in process, direct labor, and overhead costs are sorted to and entered in the manufacturing columns, the columns are totaled and the difference between the totals is the cost of the goods manufactured. This cost of goods manufactured amount is entered in the Manufacturing Statement credit column in order to make the debit and credit columns equal; and it is also carried into the Income Statement debit column in the same debit position as the Purchases account balance of a merchandising company.

The Income Statement columns and Balance Sheet columns of a manufacturing work sheet, as well as the items in these columns, are treated in the same manner as on the work sheet of a merchandising company. Consequently, these columns need no further attention here.

ADJUSTING ENTRIES

The adjusting entries of a manufacturing company are prepared in the same way as those of a merchandising concern. An adjusting entry is entered in the General Journal for each adjustment appearing in the work sheet Adjustments columns. No new techniques are required here.

CLOSING ENTRIES

The accounts the balances of which enter into the calculation of cost of goods manufactured show manufacturing costs for a particular accounting period and must be closed and cleared at the end of each period. Normally they are closed and cleared through a Manufacturing Summary account, which is in turn closed and cleared through the Income Summary account.

The entries to close and clear the manufacturing accounts of Excel Manufacturing Company are as follows:

Dec.	31	Manufacturing Summary....................	187,000.00	
		Raw Materials Inventory................		8,000.00
		Goods in Process Inventory.............		2,500.00
		Raw Material Purchases.................		85,000.00
		Freight on Raw Materials...............		1,500.00
		Direct Labor...........................		60,000.00
		Indirect Labor.........................		9,000.00
		Supervision............................		6,000.00
		Power Expense..........................		2,600.00
		Repairs and Maintenance...............		2,500.00
		Factory Taxes..........................		1,900.00
		Factory Supplies Used..................		500.00
		Factory Insurance Expired..............		1,200.00
		Small Tools Written Off................		200.00
		Depr. of Machinery and Equipment.....		3,500.00
		Depreciation of Building...............		1,800.00
		Patents Written Off....................		800.00
		To close those manufacturing accounts having debit balances.		
	31	Raw Materials Inventory....................	9,000.00	
		Goods in Process Inventory.................	7,500.00	
		Manufacturing Summary..............		16,500.00
		To set up the ending raw materials and goods in process inventories and to remove their balances from the Manufacturing Summary account.		

The foregoing entries are taken from the information in the Manufacturing Statement columns of the Illustration 133 work sheet. Compare the first entry with the information shown in the Manufacturing Statement debit column. Note how the debit to the Manufacturing Summary account is taken from the column total, and how each account having a balance in the column is credited to close and clear it. Also observe that the second entry has the effect of subtracting the ending raw materials and goods in process inventories from the manufacturing costs shown in the debit column.

The effect of the foregoing entries is to cause the Manufacturing Summary account to have a debit balance equal to the $170,500 cost of goods manufactured. This $170,500 balance is closed to the Income Summary account along with the cost and expense accounts, the balance of which appear in the Income Statement debit column. Observe the last credit in the following entry which is used to close the accounts, the balances of which appear in the Income Statement debit column of the Illustration 133 work sheet.

Dec.	31	Income Summary...............................	274,200.00	
		Finished Goods Inventory.................		11,200.00
		Sales Salaries.............................		18,000.00
		Advertising Expense......................		5,500.00
		Delivery Salaries.........................		12,000.00
		Office Salaries...........................		3,700.00
		Officers' Salaries........................		12,000.00
		Miscellaneous General Expense............		200.00
		Bond Interest Expense....................		4,000.00
		Bad Debts Expense.......................		1,550.00
		Office Supplies Used......................		100.00
		Shipping Supplies Used...................		250.00
		Delivery Equipment Insurance Expired.....		300.00
		Depreciation of Delivery Equipment........		2,100.00
		Depreciation of Office Equipment.........		200.00
		State and Federal Income Taxes Expense...		32,600.00
		Manufacturing Summary.................		170,500.00
		To close the income statement accounts having debit balances.		

After the foregoing entry, the remainder of the income statement accounts of Illustration 133 are closed as follows:

Dec.	31	Finished Goods Inventory.....................	10,300.00	
		Sales...	310,000.00	
		Income Summary.......................		320,300.00
		To close the Sales account and to bring the ending finished goods inventory on the books.		
	31	Income Summary............................	46,100.00	
		Retained Earnings.......................		46,100.00
		To close the Income Summary account.		

INVENTORY VALUATION PROBLEMS OF A MANUFACTURER

In a manufacturing company using a noncost system, at the end of each period, an accounting value must be placed on the inventories of raw materials, goods in process, and finished goods. No particular problems are encountered in valuing raw materials because the items are in the same form in which they were purchased and a cost or market price may be applied. However, placing an accounting value on goods in process and finished goods is generally not so easy. This is because items of goods in process and finished goods consist of raw materials to which certain amounts of labor and overhead have been applied. They are not items in the same form in which they were purchased. Consequently, a price paid a previous producer cannot be used to measure their inventory value. Instead, their inventory value must be built up by adding together estimates of the raw materials, direct labor, and overhead costs applicable to each item.

Estimating raw material costs applicable to a goods in process or finished goods item is usually not too difficult. Likewise, from its state of completion, a responsible plant official can normally make a reasonably accurate estimate of the direct labor applicable to an item. However, estimating overhead costs presents more of a problem, which is often solved by assuming that overhead costs are closely related to direct labor costs, and this is often a fair assumption. Often there is a close relation between direct labor costs and such things as supervision, power, repairs, depreciation, etc. Furthermore, when this relation is used to apply overhead costs, it is assumed that the relation of overhead costs to the direct labor costs in each goods in process and finished goods item is the same as the relation between total overhead costs and total direct labor costs.

For example, an examination of the manufacturing statement in Illustration 132 will show that Excel Manufacturing Company's total direct labor costs were $60,000 and its overhead costs were $30,000. Or, an examination will show that during the year the company applied in the production of all its products $2 of direct labor for each $1 of overhead costs. Or, during the year the company's overhead costs were 50 percent of direct labor cost.

Overhead Costs, $30,000 ÷ Direct Labor, $60,000 = 50 Percent

Consequently, in estimating the overhead applicable to a goods in process or finished goods item, Excel Manufacturing Company may assume that this 50 percent overhead rate is applicable. It may assume that if in all its production the overhead costs were 50 percent of the direct labor costs, then in each goods in process and finished goods item this relationship also exists.

If Excel Manufacturing Company makes this assumption and its goods in process inventory consists of 1,000 units of Item X with each unit containing $3.75 of raw material and having $2.50 of applicable direct labor, then the goods in process inventory is valued as shown in Illustration 134.

Illustration 134

Product	Raw Materials Cost	Direct Labor Applicable	Overhead (50 Percent of Direct Labor)	Estimated Total Unit Cost	No. of Units	Total Inventory Valuation
Item X	$3.75	$2.50	$1.25	$7.50	1,000	$7,500.00

Excel Manufacturing Company may use the same procedure in placing an accounting value on the items of its finished goods inventory.

QUESTIONS FOR CLASS DISCUSSION

1. How does the income statement of a manufacturing company differ from the income statement of a merchandising company?

2. What are the three elements of manufacturing costs?

3. What are (a) direct labor, (b) indirect labor, (c) direct material, (d) indirect material, and (e) factory overhead costs?

4. Name several items that are accounted for as factory overhead costs by a manufacturing company.

5. What is a patent? What is the legal life of a patent? Is the legal life of a patent the same as its useful or economic life?

6. Standard Company has a patented device that cost $3,600 to develop. Give the entry to record the yearly expiration of the patent on this device under the assumption that the patent will have a useful or economic life of 12 years.

7. Explain why small tools are often accounted for on an inventory basis.

8. Name several accounts that are often found in the ledgers of both manufacturing and merchandising companies. Name several accounts that are found only in the ledgers of manufacturing companies.

9. What three new inventory accounts appear in the ledger of a manufacturing company?

10. How are the raw material inventories handled on the work sheet of a man-

ufacturing company? How are the goods in process inventories handled? How are the finished goods inventories handled?

11. Which inventories of a manufacturing company receive the same work sheet treatment as the merchandise inventories of a merchandising company?

12. Which inventories of a manufacturing company appear on its manufacturing statement? Which appear on the income statement?

13. What accounts are summarized in the Manufacturing Summary account? What accounts are summarized in the Income Summary account?

14. What are the three manufacturing cost elements emphasized on the manufacturing statement?

15. What kind of items are carried into the Manufacturing Statement columns of the manufacturing work sheet? What kind of items are carried into the Income Statement columns? What kind of items are carried into the Balance Sheet columns?

16. Why is the cost of goods manufactured entered in the Manufacturing Statement credit column of a work sheet and again in the Income Statement debit column?

17. May prices paid a previous manufacturer for items of raw materials determine the balance sheet value of the items of the raw materials inventory? Why? May such prices also determine the balance sheet values of the goods in process and finished goods inventories? Why?

18. Standard Company used an overhead rate of 80 percent of direct labor cost to apply overhead to the items of its goods in process inventory. If the manufacturing statement of the company showed total overhead costs of $72,800, how much direct labor did it show?

19. The manufacturing statement of a company showed the following costs: materials, $52,000; direct labor, $60,000; and overhead costs $90,000. (a) If the company's overhead rate was based on direct labor cost, what was the overhead rate? (b) If the company's $10,000 ending goods in process inventory had direct labor costs of $3,000, what was its direct material costs?

PROBLEMS

Problem 21–1

Following are the Manufacturing Statement columns from the work sheet of Webster Manufacturing Company as of the end of the past year:

	Manufacturing Statement	
	Debit	**Credit**
Raw materials inventory..................	21,200	18,600
Goods in process inventory...............	18,700	26,500
Raw materials purchased..................	82,600	
Discounts on raw materials purchased......		1,200
Direct labor.............................	100,000	
Factory supervision......................	12,000	
Indirect labor...........................	16,900	
Heat, light, and power...................	16,200	
Machinery repairs........................	5,100	
Rent of factory..........................	12,000	
Property taxes, machinery................	1,800	
Factory insurance expense................	3,200	
Factory supplies used....................	7,600	
Depreciation of factory machinery.........	15,200	
	312,500	46,300
Cost of goods manufactured to income statement.............................		266,200
	312,500	312,500

Required:
Prepare a manufacturing statement for the concern.

Problem 21–2

The work sheet of S. L. French, Manufacturer is reproduced on the next page.

Required:

1. From the work sheet prepare an income statement supported by a schedule of cost of goods manufactured.
2. Prepare compound closing entries for the company.

S. L. FRENCH MANUFACTURER
Manufacturing Work Sheet for Year Ending December 31, 19—

Account Titles	Trial Balance Dr.	Trial Balance Cr.	Adjustments Dr.	Adjustments Cr.	Mfg. Statement Dr.	Mfg. Statement Cr.	Income Statement Dr.	Income Statement Cr.	Balance Sheet Dr.	Balance Sheet Cr.
Cash	6,000								6,000	
Accounts receivable	17,500								17,500	
Allowance for bad debts		200		(a) 350						550
Raw materials inventory	18,600				18,600	19,100			19,100	
Goods in process inventory	5,300				5,300	8,400			8,400	
Finished goods inventory	10,700						10,700	10,500	10,500	
Factory supplies	1,450			(b) 1,200					250	
Prepaid factory insurance	800			(c) 650					150	
Small tools	3,250			(d) 550					2,700	
Machinery and equipment	72,400								72,400	
Accumulated depreciation, machinery and equipment		18,700		(e) 3,600						22,300
Patents	10,200			(f) 800					9,400	
Accounts payable		3,700								3,700
Mortgage notes payable		30,000								30,000
S. L. French, capital		84,900								84,900
S. L. French, withdrawals	10,000								10,000	
Sales		138,000				138,000				
Raw material purchases	47,200				47,200					
Direct labor	26,700		(g) 600		27,300					
Factory rent	6,000				6,000					
Indirect labor	4,700		(g) 150		4,850					
Supervision	6,000				6,000					
Power	2,400				2,400					
Repairs to machinery	1,600				1,600					
Selling expenses	14,300						14,300			
General and administrative expenses	10,400		(a) 350				10,750			
	275,500	275,500								
Factory supplies used			(b) 1,200		1,200					
Factory insurance expired			(c) 650		650					
Small tools written off			(d) 550		550					
Depreciation of machinery and equipment			(e) 3,600		3,600					
Patents written off			(f) 800		800					
Wages payable				(g) 750						750
			7,900	7,900	126,050	27,500				
Cost of goods manufactured to income statement						98,550	98,550			
					126,050	126,050	134,300	148,500	156,400	142,200
Net Income							14,200			14,200
							148,500	148,500	156,400	156,400

Problem 21–3

Following are the items from the Manufacturing Statement columns of Cactus Manufacturing Company's work sheet prepared at the end of last year. The illustrated columns show the items as they appeared after all adjustments were completed but before the ending work in process inventory was calculated and entered and before the cost of goods manufactured was calculated.

Cactus Manufacturing Company makes a single product called Cacto. On December 31, at the end of last year, the goods in process inventory consisted of 5,000 units of Cacto with each unit containing an estimated $0.80 of raw materials and having had an estimated $2 of direct labor applied:

	Manufacturing Statement	
	Debit	Credit
Raw materials inventory.....................	21,200	19,300
Goods in process inventory..................	17,800	?
Raw materials purchased....................	81,400	
Direct labor...............................	100,000	
Indirect labor..............................	16,900	
Factory supervision.........................	12,000	
Heat, light, and power......................	8,600	
Machinery repairs..........................	6,300	
Rent of factory.............................	7,200	
Property taxes, machinery...................	1,900	
Factory insurance expired...................	3,300	
Factory supplies used.......................	7,400	
Depreciation expense, factory machinery....	16,900	
Small tools written off.....................	500	
	301,400	?
Cost of goods manufactured................		?
	301,400	301,400

Required:

1. Calculate the relation between direct labor and factory overhead costs and use this relation to determine the value of the ending goods in process inventory.
2. After placing a value on the ending goods in process inventory, determine the cost of goods manufactured.
3. Prepare a manufacturing statement for Cactus Manufacturing Company.
4. Prepare entries to close the manufacturing accounts and to summarize their balances in the Manufacturing Summary account.
5. Prepare an entry to close the Manufacturing Summary account.

Problem 21–4

Mesa Manufacturing Company's trial balance as of December 31, 19—, appeared as follows:

MESA MANUFACTURING COMPANY
Trial Balance, December 31, 19—

Cash...	$ 17,500	
Raw materials inventory........................	13,300	
Goods in process inventory.....................	15,300	
Finished goods inventory.......................	16,600	
Prepaid factory insurance......................	4,200	
Factory supplies...............................	6,400	
Factory machinery.............................	175,500	
Accumulated depreciation, factory machinery..		$ 28,800
Small tools....................................	3,700	
Patents..	4,500	
Common stock.................................		100,000
Retained earnings.............................		34,400
Sales..		359,700
Raw material purchases........................	61,800	
Discounts on raw material purchases...........		1,000
Direct labor...................................	89,100	
Indirect labor.................................	13,300	
Factory supervision...........................	11,800	
Heat, light, and power.........................	17,900	
Machinery repairs.............................	4,400	
Rent of factory................................	7,200	
Property taxes, machinery.....................	800	
Selling expenses controlling...................	31,400	
Administrative expenses controlling...........	29,200	
	$523,900	$523,900

Additional Information:
1. Expired factory insurance, $2,200.
2. Factory supplies used, $6,300.
3. Depreciation of factory machinery, $9,900.
4. Small tools written off, $700.
5. Patents written off, $1,300.
6. Accrued wages payable: (a) direct labor, $900; (b) indirect labor, $500; and (c) factory supervision, $200.
7. Ending inventories: (a) raw materials, $12,800; (b) goods in process consisted of 4,000 units of product with each unit containing an estimated $1.40 of materials and having had an estimated $1 of direct labor applied; and (c) finished goods consisted of 3,000 units of product with each unit containing an estimated $1.96 of raw materials and having an estimated $2.40 of direct labor applied.
8. Estimated state and federal income taxes expense, $29,000.

Required:
1. Enter the trial balance on a work sheet form and make the adjustments from the information given. Then sort the items to the proper Manufacturing Statement, Income Statement, and Balance Sheet columns.

2. After the Direct Labor and factory overhead cost accounts have been adjusted and carried into the Manufacturing Statement columns, determine the relation between direct labor and overhead costs and use this relation to determine the overhead applicable to each unit of goods in process and finished goods. After the amounts of overhead applicable to the units of goods in process and finished goods are determined, calculate the balance sheet values of these inventories, enter these inventory amounts on the work sheet, and complete the work sheet.
3. From the work sheet prepare a manufacturing statement and an income statement.
4. Prepare compound closing entries.

Problem 21–5

On January 1 of the current year a trial balance of Sun Valley Manufacturing Company's ledger appeared as follows:

SUN VALLEY MANUFACTURING COMPANY
Trial Balance, January 1, 19—

Cash...	$ 32,100	
Accounts receivable...........................	73,800	
Allowance for bad debts.......................		$ 1,200
Raw materials inventory.......................	37,100	
Goods in process inventory....................	34,400	
Finished goods inventory......................	48,700	
Prepaid factory insurance.....................	1,200	
Factory supplies..............................	1,600	
Machinery....................................	226,700	
Accumulated depreciation, machinery.........		78,400
Accounts payable.............................		21,100
Common stock................................		250,000
Retained earnings............................		104,900
	$455,600	$455,600

During the year the company completed the following transactions:
1. Sold $692,500 of finished goods on account.
2. Wrote off $1,000 of accounts receivable as uncollectible.
3. Collected $689,100 of accounts receivable.
4. Purchased on account:

a) Factory supplies...............................	$ 11,500
b) Machinery.....................................	60,800
c) Raw materials.................................	185,100
	$257,400

5. Made cash disbursements in payment of—

a) Factory insurance premiums.....................$ 2,900
b) Accounts payable............................... 253,200
c) Direct labor.................................... 159,500
d) Indirect labor.................................. 36,600
e) Heat, light, and power.......................... 13,600
f) Machinery repairs...............................   9,400
g) Selling expenses................................ 81,200
h) General and administrative expenses............ 72,500
                                                      $628,900

The following inventory and adjustments information was available at the year-end:

6. Allowance for bad debts to be increased to a year-end balance of $1,700. (Debit General and Administrative Expenses Controlling.)
7. An examination of insurance policies showed $1,000 of factory insurance prepaid at the year-end.
8. An inventory of factory supplies showed $3,400 of supplies on hand.
9. Estimated depreciation on factory machinery, $31,300.
10. Accrued wages:
    a) Direct labor, $500.
    b) Indirect labor, $300.
11. Estimated state and federal income taxes expense, $37,500.
12. Inventories:

    a) Raw materials, $36,700.
    b) Goods in process consisted of 3,200 units of product with each unit containing $3.65 of materials and having had $4.00 of direct labor applied. (Use the relation of direct labor cost, after adjustments, to factory overhead costs, after adjustments, to determine overhead costs applicable to each unit of goods in process and finished goods.)
    c) Finished goods inventory consisted of 3,000 units of product with each unit containing an estimated $7.50 of materials and having had an estimated $6 of direct labor applied.

Required:
1. Open skeleton balance column accounts and enter the January 1 trial balance amounts.
2. Record the condensed transactions directly in the accounts.
3. Prepare a trial balance of the accounts on a work sheet form. Complete the work sheet.
4. Prepare a manufacturing statement, an income statement, and a balance sheet.
5. Enter adjusting and closing entries directly in the accounts and prepare a post-closing trial balance.

CLASS EXERCISE

Exercise 21–1

An end-of-the-accounting-period trial balance of a manufacturing company follows. To simplify the problem and to save time the trial balance is in numbers of not more than two integers.

Required:
1. Prepare a manufacturing work sheet form on ordinary notebook paper.
2. Copy the trial balance on the work sheet form and complete the work sheet using the following information:

   a) Ending inventories:

   Raw materials, $3.

   Goods in process, $5.

   Finished goods, $2.

   Factory supplies, $1.

   b) Allowance for bad debts an additional $2.

   c) Expired factory insurance, $1.

   d) Depreciation of factory machinery, $3.

   e) Accrued payroll:

   Direct labor, $4.

   Indirect labor, $2.

   Office salaries, $1.

SOUTHERN MANUFACTURING COMPANY
Trial Balance, December 31, 19—

Cash...	$ 4	
Accounts receivable..................................	5	
Allowance for bad debts.............................		$ 1
Raw materials inventory..............................	2	
Goods in process inventory...........................	4	
Finished goods inventory.............................	3	
Factory supplies......................................	3	
Prepaid factory insurance............................	4	
Factory machinery....................................	23	
Accumulated depreciation, factory machinery..........		2
Common stock..		20
Retained earnings....................................		5
Sales...		81
Raw material purchases..............................	15	
Freight on raw materials.............................	1	
Direct labor..	12	
Indirect labor..	3	
Power..	5	
Machinery repairs....................................	2	
Rent of factory.......................................	8	
Selling expenses control..............................	9	
Administrative expenses control.......................	6	
	$109	$109

ALTERNATE PROBLEMS

Problem 21–1A

The following alphabetically arranged items were taken from the Manufacturing Statement and Income Statement columns of Tempest Manufacturing Company's year-end work sheet:

Advertising..................	$ 1,200		Goods in process, Decem-	
Depreciation, machinery....	2,100		ber 31...................	$ 7,500
Depreciation, office equip-			Finished goods, January 1	10,500
ment.....................	500		Finished goods, Decem-	
Depreciation, selling equip-			ber 31..................	8,400
ment.....................	600		Miscellaneous factory ex-	
Direct labor.................	38,800		penses...................	500
Factory supplies used........	1,100		Office salaries..............	4,200
Federal income taxes expense	8,100		Raw material purchases....	51,500
Freight on raw materials....	1,500		Rent of factory building....	4,800
Heat and power, factory.....	2,000		Rent of office space.........	1,400
Indirect labor...............	3,500		Rent of selling space........	1,600
Inventories:			Repairs to machinery......	1,800
Raw materials, January 1.	9,800		Sales.....................	180,100
Raw materials, December			Sales discounts............	3,400
31.....................	10,100		Sales salaries..............	17,500
Goods in process,			Superintendence, factory...	7,200
January 1...............	8,200			

Required:

Prepare an income statement and a schedule of cost of goods manufactured.

Problem 21–2A

The following items appeared in the Manufacturing Statement and Income Statement columns of the work sheet prepared for Southwest Manufacturing Company on December 31, 19—, at the end of an annual accounting period:

	Mfg. Statement		Income Statement	
	Debit	Credit	Debit	Credit
Raw materials inventory.........	12,600	12,100	....	....
Goods in process inventory.......	14,800	12,900	....	....
Finished goods inventory........	....	....	16,100	18,800
Sales.........................	....	....	....	361,500
Raw material purchases........	59,000	....	....	....
Discounts on raw material pur-				
chases......................	....	800	....	....
Totals forward.................	86,400	25,800	16,100	380,300

	Mfg. Statement		Income Statement	
	Debit	**Credit**	**Debit**	**Credit**
Totals brought forward........	86,400	25,800	16,100	380,300
Direct labor....................	90,000	....	....	....
Indirect labor..................	13,800	....	....	....
Factory supervision............	12,000	....	....	....
Heat, light, and power..........	18,400	....	....	....
Machinery repairs..............	4,500	....	....	....
Rent of factory.................	7,200	....	....	....
Property taxes, machinery.......	1,700	....	....	....
Selling expenses controlling.....	....	....	30,800	....
Administrative expenses controlling.........................	....	....	28,900	....
Expired factory insurance.......	2,400	....	....	....
Factory supplies used...........	6,100	....	....	....
Depreciation, factory machinery.	10,500	....	....	....
Small tools written off..........	400	....	....	....
Patents written off..............	2,500	....	....	....
State and federal income taxes expense.....................	....	....	29,500	....
	255,900	25,800	....	....
Cost of goods manufactured.....	....	230,100	230,100	....
	255,900	255,900	335,400	380,300
Net Income...................			44,900	....
			380,300	380,300

Required:
1. Prepare for Southwest Manufacturing Company an income statement supported by a schedule of cost of goods manufactured.
2. Prepare compound closing entries.

Problem 21–3A

The following information appears on the records of a manufacturing firm:

Inventories	Beginning	Ending
Finished goods..............................	$10,500	$11,200
Goods in process............................	6,500	5,700
Raw materials..............................	16,000	18,000

Cost of goods sold................................	$56,000
Direct labor......................................	10,000
Factory overhead costs...........................	5,800

Required:
On the basis of the information given determine for the accounting period:

1. Cost of goods manufactured.
2. Total manufacturing costs incurred.
3. Cost of raw materials used.
4. Cost of raw materials purchased.

(Hint: It may be helpful to set up the manufacturing statement and the cost of goods sold section of the income statement.)

Problem 21–4A

A trial balance of Bluelake Manufacturing Company's ledger as of December 31, 19—, the end of an annual accounting period, appeared as follows:

BLUELAKE MANUFACTURING COMPANY
Trial Balance, December 31, 19—

Cash...	$ 14,800	
Raw materials inventory.......................	13,700	
Goods in process inventory....................	12,500	
Finished goods inventory......................	15,100	
Prepaid factory insurance.....................	3,600	
Factory supplies..............................	6,800	
Factory machinery............................	163,200	
Accumulated depreciation, factory machinery..		$ 31,300
Small tools....................................	4,100	
Patents.......................................	6,700	
Common stock.................................		100,000
Retained earnings.............................		16,700
Sales...		370,000
Raw material purchases.......................	62,000	
Discounts on raw material purchases..........		1,200
Direct labor..................................	98,400	
Indirect labor................................	12,100	
Factory supervision...........................	11,700	
Heat, light, and power........................	17,900	
Machinery repairs.............................	4,200	
Rent of factory...............................	6,000	
Property taxes, machinery.....................	1,700	
Selling expenses controlling..................	31,400	
General and administrative expenses controlling..	28,300	
	$519,200	$519,200

Additional Information:
1. Expired factory insurance, $2,400.
2. Factory supplies used, $5,900.
3. Depreciation of factory machinery, $10,200.
4. Small tools written off, $500.
5. Patents written off, $1,400.
6. Accrued wages payable:
   a) Direct labor, $1,600.

    b) Indirect labor, $700.
    c) Factory supervision, $300.
7. Ending inventories:
    a) Raw materials, $13,200.
    b) Goods in process consisted of 2,500 units of product with each unit containing an estimated $1.10 of raw materials and having had an estimated $2 of direct labor applied.
    c) Finished goods consisted of 2,000 units of product with each unit containing an estimated $2.60 of raw materials and having had an estimated $3.60 of direct labor applied.
8. Estimated state and federal income taxes payable, $30,000.

Required:
   1. Enter the trial balance on a work sheet form. Make the adjustments from the information given. Sort the items to the proper Manufacturing Statement, Income Statement, and Balance Sheet columns.
   2. After the Direct Labor account and the factory overhead cost accounts have been adjusted and carried into the Manufacturing Statement columns, determine the relation between overhead costs and direct labor cost and use the relation to determine the amount of overhead applicable to each unit of goods in process and finished goods. After overhead applicable to each unit of goods in process and finished goods is determined, calculate the inventory values of the goods in process and finished goods inventories. Enter these inventory amounts on the work sheet and complete the work sheet.
   3. From the work sheet prepare a manufacturing statement and an income statement.
   4. Prepare closing entries.

DECISION PROBLEM 21A—MARTIN
TRIMMERS, INC.

Martin Trimmers manufactures and sells a single product, an electric grass trimmer. The company has been in operation for three years and has increased its sales substantially each year. However, R. C. Martin, the president, does not understand why the larger sales volume has not increased net income. He believes that the responsibility lies with his production manager.

A preliminary investigation disclosed the following:
   1. During the last three years all units of product sold were sold at $40 each through manufacturers' agents. No discounts were allowed and there was no change in sales price during the three years.
   2. Number of units sold were: 5,000 in 1965; 7,000 in 1966; and 8,000 in 1967.
   3. Number of units in the final finished goods inventory were: 500 in 1965; 1,500 in 1966; and 2,000 in 1967.
   4. Finished goods inventories have been priced at 50 percent of selling price, or $20 per unit.
   5. A condensed income statement for the three years shows:

	1965	1966	1967
Sales..........................	$200,000	$280,000	$320,000
Cost of goods sold:			
Finished goods, January 1........$	0	$ 10,000	$ 30,000
Cost of goods manufactured......	165,000	248,000	272,000
Goods for sale....................	$165,000	$258,000	$302,000
Finished goods, December 31......	10,000	30,000	40,000
Cost of goods sold...............	$155,000	$228,000	$262,000
Gross margin on sales.............	$ 45,000	$ 52,000	$ 58,000
Selling and general expenses........	15,000	21,700	28,000
Net Income.....................	$ 30,000	$ 30,300	$ 30,000

Prepare a report to Mr. Martin supplying answers to the following questions: How many trimmers have been manufactured each year? Has the production cost of the trimmer increased? Has the inventory method affected the reported net income? Using the first-in, first out method of pricing, what was the net income per year? The net income per unit sold? What was the average selling and general expenses per trimmer sold during each of the three years? Express an opinion as to why reported net income has not kept pace with the rising sales volume, and make any recommendations you feel will assist Mr. Martin.

DECISION PROBLEM 21B—B M QUARRIES

Jack Bailey and C. L. Moyer entered into a partnership agreement for the purpose of quarrying and selling granite. The actual quarrying operations have been under way for one month. Between 40 and 50 hourly workers have been used in the quarry and six workers in sales and in the office.

Mr. Bailey's daughter, Mary, has kept records which yield the following first-month trial balance:

Cash..	$ 4,100	
Receivables.................................	8,650	
Land..	150,000	
Machinery (includes trucks, earthmovers, air compressors, drills, small tools, milling equipment, office equipment, etc.)................	35,000	
Notes payable...............................		$ 35,000
Accounts payable............................		6,500
Jack Bailey, capital.........................		79,500
C. L. Moyer, capital.........................		78,750
Sales.......................................		26,000
Expenses...................................	28,000	
	$225,750	$225,750

The partners are quite disappointed in the results of the first month's operations. They realize, however, that more precise accounting for expenses and the recognition of the cost of unsold granite would undoubtedly change the profit picture somewhat. You are asked to make recommendations for improvement in the accounting; to prepare an income statement and a statement of the cost of granite mined for the month; and to indicate any improvement needed in the accounts being used.

Upon analysis the following data are determined:

1. The land consists entirely of granite fields. Approximately one half of 1 percent of the total cost should be set up as depletion for the first month. (Treat depletion as a cost similar to the raw material cost of a fabricating concern.)
2. Depreciation may be approximated at 12 percent per annum; of the monthly total, $30 is on office equipment. (The assets have varying service life periods ranging from three to twenty years. For the purpose of the first month's statement the blanket 12 percent annual rate will have to be used.)
3. The notes payable bear interest at 6 percent and were dated as of the first of the month just passed.
4. Expenses of $28,000 were paid in cash for—

> *Labor*..*$19,000*
> *Office salaries*.......................................　*850*
> *Sales commissions*...................................　*2,100*
> *Other quarry expenses*...............................　*6,050*

Ignore payroll taxes in computing expenses.
5. Approximately 25 percent of the granite taken from the quarry during the month has not been sold.

Job Order
Cost Accounting

Cost accounting is not something distinct and entirely different from the general accounting described in previous chapters. It differs primarily in its emphasis which is upon the unit costs to produce a given product, process, or service and upon the control of these costs. Actually, cost accounting represents only an adaptation and expansion of general accounting, made in such a manner as to aid in collecting and controlling costs.

COST ACCOUNTING SYSTEMS

There are two general types of cost accounting systems: (1) job order cost systems, and (2) process cost systems. However, of the two there are an infinite number of variations and combinations.

In cost accounting a *job* is often a single turbine, machine, or other product manufactured especially for and to the specifications of a customer. A job may also be a single construction project of a contractor. A *job lot* is a quantity of identical items, such as five hundred typewriters, manufactured in one lot as a job or single order. And a *job order cost system* is one in which costs are assembled in terms of jobs or job lots of product. Such a system is commonly found in a manufacturing concern in which the products are individually different in the sense that each unit, such as a turbine, or each lot of product, such as five hundred typewriters, is sufficiently unique to be identifiable.

A *process* is a step in manufacturing a product, for example, the cutting of clay into bricks in a brickyard is a step in manufacturing bricks; and a *process cost system* is one in which costs are assembled in terms of processes or manufacturing steps. Process cost systems are commonly found in companies in which production is characterized by a steady flow of materials into and through a series of processes to produce a uniform product, as in the manufacture of paint, flour, and petroleum products.

Job order cost accounting is the subject of this chapter; process cost accounting is dealt with in the next.

PERPETUAL INVENTORIES AND THE FLOW OF COSTS IN A JOB COST SYSTEM

Two characteristics distinguish a job order cost system from a general accounting system as described in the previous chapter. They are: (1) the more extensive use in the cost system of perpetual inventory controlling accounts; and (2) the flow of costs through the accounts in the cost system.

Cost accounting is distinguished by its use of inventory controlling accounts. For example, in a cost system the purchase and use of all materials are recorded in a perpetual inventory account called Materials which controls a subsidiary ledger having a separate ledger card for each different kind of materials used. Likewise, in a job cost system the Goods in Process and Finished Goods accounts are also perpetual inventory accounts controlling subsidiary ledgers.

In addition to perpetual inventory controlling accounts, job cost accounting is also distinguished by the flow of manufacturing costs from the Materials, Factory Payroll, and Overhead Costs accounts into and through the Goods in Process and Finished Goods accounts and on to the Cost of Goods Sold account. This flow is diagrammed in Illustration 135 on the next page. An examination of the diagram and a moment's thought will show that costs flow through the accounts in the same way materials, labor, and overhead are placed in production in the factory, move on to become finished goods, and finally are sold.

THE GOODS IN PROCESS ACCOUNT

The goods in process account and its subsidiary ledger of *job cost sheets*, called the *Job Cost Ledger*, are the heart of a job cost system. The Goods in Process account is used in accumulating total material, labor, and overhead costs of all jobs; and the individual cost sheets, one for each job, are used in accumulating cost applicable to each job.

In addition to being a controlling account, the Goods in Process account is also a perpetual inventory account operating somewhat as follows: At the beginning of a cost period the cost of any unfinished jobs in process is shown by the debit balance of the Goods in Process account. Throughout the cost period materials, labor, and overhead are placed in production in

Illustration 135
Diagram Showing the Flow of Costs in a Job Cost System

Materials

Debited for the cost of all materials purchased | Credited for direct materials placed in process

Credited for indirect materials charged to overhead

Goods in Process

Debited for the cost of direct materials, direct labor, and overhead placed in production | Credited for the cost of goods completed as each job is completed

Finished Goods

Debited for the cost of the goods completed as each job is completed | Credited for the cost of goods sold as each job or lot of goods is sold

Cost of Goods Sold

Debited for the cost of goods sold as each job or lot of goods is sold

Factory Payroll

Debited for wages paid | Credited for direct labor charged to production

Credited for indirect labor charged to overhead

Overhead Costs

Debited for indirect materials, indirect labor, and other overhead costs paid and expired | Credited for overhead costs charged to production the factory; and periodically their costs are debited to the Goods in Process account (note the last three debits in the Goods in Process account that follows). Also, throughout the period the cost of each job completed (the sum of the job's material, labor, and overhead costs) is credited to the Goods in Process account as each job is finished. Consequently, as a result of these procedures the Goods in Process account is a perpetual inventory account the debit balance of which shows, after all posting is completed, and without a physical inventory, the cost of the unfinished jobs still in process. For example, the following Goods in Process account shows a $12,785 March 31 ending inventory of unfinished jobs in process.

Goods in Process

Date		Explanation	Debit	Credit	Balance
Mar.	1	*Balance, beginning inventory*			*2,850*
	10	*Job 7449 completed*		*7,920*	*5,070*
	18	*Job 7448 completed*		*9,655*	*14,725*
	24	*Job 7450 completed*		*8,316*	*23,041*
	29	*Job 7452 completed*		*279*	*23,320*
	29	*Job 7451 completed*		*6,295*	*29,615*
	31	*Materials used*	*17,150*		*12,465*
	31	*Labor applied*	*10,100*		*2,365*
	31	*Overhead applied*	*15,150*		*12,785*

In addition to the foregoing discussion, it should be pointed out that the Goods in Process account and its subsidiary ledger of cost sheets operate in the usual manner of controlling accounts and subsidiary ledgers. The material, labor, and overhead costs debited to each individual job on its cost sheet must be individually or in totals debited to the Goods in Process account. Likewise all credits to jobs on their cost sheets must be credited individually or in totals to the Goods in Process account.

JOB COST SHEETS

Observe in Illustration 136 how a job cost sheet is designed to accumulate the costs applicable to a job. Although this accumulation is discussed in more detail later, it may be summarized as follows. When a job is begun, information as to the customer, job number, and job description is filled in on a blank cost sheet and the cost sheet is placed in the Job Cost Ledger. The job number identifies the job and makes easier the charges to it for materials, labor, and overhead. As materials are required for the job, they are transferred from the materials storeroom and are used to complete the job. At the same time their cost is charged to the

Illustration 136

JOB COST SHEET

Customer's Name   Cone Lumber Company   Job. No.   7452

Address   Eugene, Oregon

Job Description   10 H.P. electric motor to customer's specifications

| Date Promised 4/1 | | | Date Started 3/23 | | Date Completed 3/29 | | |

Date	Materials		Labor		Overhead Costs Applied		
	Requisition No.	Amount	Time Ticket No.	Amount	Date	Rate	Amount
19— Mar. 23	1-003	53.00	C-3422	8.00	3/29	150 per-cent of the direct labor	$123.00
24			C-3478	16.00			
			C-3479	6.00			
25	1-079	21.00	C-4002	16.00			
26			C-4015	16.00	**Summary of Costs**		
					Materials		$ 74.00
27			C-4032	12.00	Labor		82.00
28			C-4044	8.00	Overhead		123.00
					Total Cost of the job		279.00
					Remarks: Completed and shipped 3/29		
	Total	74.00	Total	82.00			

job in the Materials column of the job's cost sheet. Labor used on the job is likewise charged to the job in the Labor column; and when the job is finished, the amount of overhead applicable is entered in the Overhead Costs Applied column. After this, the cost totals are summarized to determine the job's total cost.

ACCOUNTING FOR MATERIALS UNDER A JOB COST SYSTEM

Acquisition of Materials. In a cost accounting system the purchase and use of all materials are accounted for in a perpetual inventory account called Materials. This account is a controlling account controlling the subsidiary Materials Ledger. The Materials Ledger has a separate card for each kind, size, style, and grade of material used in the factory. Each card shows for its kind of material the amounts received, the amounts issued, and the balance on hand. A subsidiary materials ledger card is reproduced in Illustration 137.

Illustration 137

MATERIALS LEDGER CARD

Item   Armature core   Stock No.   C–347   Location in Storeroom   Bin 137

Maximum   400   Minimum   150   Number to Reorder   200

	Received				Issued				Balance		
Date	Receiving Report No.	Units	Unit Price	Total Price	Requisition No.	Units	Unit Price	Total Price	Units	Unit Price	Total Price
3/1									180	1.00	180.00
3/5					4345	20	1.00	20.00	160	1.00	160.00
3/11					4416	10	1.00	10.00	150	1.00	150.00
3/12	C-114	200	1.00	200.00					350	1.00	350.00

When materials are purchased, their acquisition is recorded in a Voucher Register, if such a register is used, with an entry like this:

Mar.	12	Materials...............................	200.00		
		Vouchers Payable....................		200.00	
		Purchased raw materials.			

In addition to the foregoing entry, the units and costs of materials purchased and received are entered in the Received columns of the proper materials ledger cards. These last entries keep the sum of the materials ledger account balances in agreement with the Materials controlling account.

Use of Materials. Under a cost system, in order to control the use of materials, all materials are placed in a materials storeroom as they are purchased and received. The storeroom is the responsibility of a storeroom keeper whose duty it is to store and care for all materials until they are needed in production, to issue materials to the factory for use as needed.

and to inform the purchasing department by means of a purchase requisition when the supply of an item is low and an order for a new supply should be placed.

When materials are needed in the factory, a materials requisition (Illustration 138) is prepared and signed by a foreman, superintendent, or

Illustration 138
A Materials Requisition

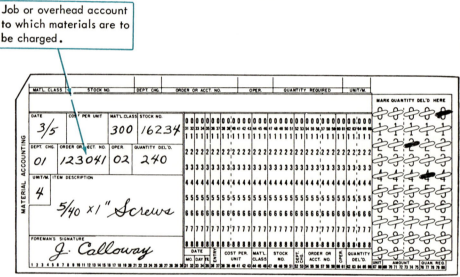

Job or overhead account to which materials are to be charged.

other responsible person. A materials requisition is prepared by entering on a requisition form information as to the quantity, description, and stock number of the material needed. Normally, the foreman or other person responsible for requesting materials does not know the unit price of an item requisitioned; consequently, the blank for this information is not filled in until the requisition reaches the accounting department. However, the persons responsible for requisitioning materials do know the particular job or overhead cost for which the material is to be used, and they are definitely responsible for filling in the job number or overhead cost account to which the material is to be charged. This information is very important since it enables the accounting department to charge each requisition to the proper job or overhead account.

When a material requisition is presented to the storeroom keeper, he examines it to see that it is properly prepared, makes certain that the overhead cost account or job number to which the material is to be charged is shown, and that the requisition is signed by a person with authority to sign. If the requisition is in order, he delivers the material and forwards the requisition on to the accounting department. Normally, requisitions are forwarded to the accounting department in batches; an entire day's requisitions are a common batch.

In the accounting department each requisition is first priced. Prices are obtained from the inventory cards in the Materials Ledger. These are the cards like Illustration 137 that show for each kind of material the amounts received, the amounts issued, and the balance on hand. Normally, at the time a requisition is priced the material that was requisitioned and issued on the basis of the requisition being priced is recorded as being issued in the "Issued" column of the proper materials ledger card.

After a batch of requisitions are priced and recorded in the Materials Ledger, they are sorted[1] by jobs and overhead accounts and are charged to the proper jobs and overhead accounts. Requisitions for direct materials are charged to jobs in the Materials columns of cost sheets in the Job Cost Ledger. Requsitions for indirect materials are charged to overhead accounts. Often these overhead accounts are kept in a subsidiary Overhead Costs Ledger which is controlled by an Overhead Costs controlling account in the General Ledger. If the requisitions are few in number, they may be individually entered on the cost sheets and in the overhead accounts. However, if they are numerous, they are totaled by jobs and accounts and only the totals are entered.

After a batch of requisitions is charged to the proper jobs and overhead accounts, they are resorted into two groups. In one group are placed the direct material requisitions which were charged to jobs; in the other group are placed the indirect material requisitions that were charged to overhead accounts. Both groups are then separately totaled, and the totals are entered on a materials used summary similar to Illustration 139. Then

Illustration 139

MATERIALS USED SUMMARY

Date		Remarks	Direct Materials	Indirect Materials
Mar.	1		653 00	
	2		210 00	18 50
	3		907 00	
	31		156 50	
	31	Totals	17,150 00	320 00

---

[1] The materials requisition shown in Illustration 138 is designed to be punched and sorted in a card sorter. Requisitions requiring hand sorting are also used.

periodically, once a week, once a month, or at the end of a cost period, the summary is totaled and an entry like the following is made to record the materials used:

Mar.	*31*	*Goods in Process*.....................	*17,150.00*	
		Overhead Costs....................	*320.00*	
		Materials.......................		*17,470.00*
		To record the materials used.		

Observe in the foregoing entry that the first debit is equal to the sum of all the direct material requisitions charged to jobs and summarized on the materials used summary. When the entry is posted, it helps keep the Goods in Process account balance equal to the sum of the costs entered on the job cost sheets in the Job Cost Ledger. Likewise, posting the second debit, which is the sum of the indirect material requisitions charged to overhead accounts, helps keep the Overhead Costs controlling account balance equal to the sum of the overhead account balances in the subsidiary Overhead Costs Ledger.

Note that the credit of the entry under discussion is equal to the sum of all the material requisitions issued during the period covered by the entry. Since these requisitions were individually recorded as materials issued, (credits) in the "Issued" columns of the materials ledger cards, this credit to the Materials account helps keep its balance equal to the sum of the balances on the materials ledger cards in the Materials Ledger.

ACCOUNTING FOR LABOR IN A JOB COST SYSTEM

Paying for Labor Purchased. Time clocks, clock cards, a Payroll Register, and a general journal entry similar to those described in Chapter 14 are commonly used in a factory to record the hours and cost of the work of each direct and indirect labor employee. The employees daily record their working time on clock cards as they enter and leave the plant; and the cards are summarized in a Payroll Register. Then, at the end of a payroll period the information of the Payroll Register is recorded with a general journal entry, and the employees are paid.

Without the complications of payroll taxes, income taxes, and other deductions, the entries to record a factory's Payroll Register and the payment of its employees are as follows:

Mar.	7	Factory Payroll.......................	2,900.00	
		Vouchers Payable.................		2,900.00
		To record the factory payroll.		
	7	Vouchers Payable....................	2,900.00	
		Cash............................		2,900.00
		Paid the employees.		

In a factory the entries just given are repeated at the end of each pay period. Consequently, at the end of a month or other cost period the Factory Payroll Account has a series of debits (see Illustration 141) like the debit of the first of the foregoing entries, and the sum of these debits is the total amount paid the direct and indirect labor employees during the cost period.

Use of Labor. The clock cards just discussed are a record of hours worked each day by each employee, but they do not show how the employees spent their time or the specific jobs and overhead tasks on which they worked. Consequently, if the hours worked by each employee are to be charged to specific jobs and overhead accounts, another record called a *labor time ticket* must be made. Labor time tickets like the one shown in Illustration 140 tell how an employee spent his time while at work.

Illustration 140—A Time Ticket

The time ticket of Illustration 140 is a "pen-and-ink" ticket and is suitable for use in a plant in which only a small number of such tickets are prepared and recorded each day. In a plant in which many tickets are prepared, a time ticket that can be made into a punched card similar to Illustration 138 would be more suitable.

Labor time tickets serve as a basis for charging jobs or overhead accounts for an employee's wages. Throughout each day a labor time ticket is prepared each time an employee is changed from one job or overhead task to another. The tickets may be prepared by the worker or his foreman. If the employee works on only one job all day, only one ticket is prepared. If he works on more than one job, a separate ticket is made for each. At the end of a day all the tickets of that day are sent to the accounting department.

In the accounting department the time tickets are priced, sorted by jobs and overhead accounts, and are charged to the proper jobs in the Job Cost Ledger or overhead accounts in the Overhead Costs Ledger. After this they are regrouped into direct labor tickets and indirect labor tickets, totaled by groups, and the totals are entered on a labor cost summary similar to the materials used summary of Illustration 139.

At the end of a month or other period, after all the tickets of the period have been charged to jobs and overhead accounts, summarized on the labor cost summary, and the summary columns totaled, the column totals show the total direct and the total indirect labor used during the period. These totals become the basis for a general journal entry to charge the labor used to the Goods in Process and Overhead Costs controlling accounts. The entry appears as follows:

Mar.	31	*Goods in Process*...................	*10,100.00*	
		Overhead Costs....................	*2,500.00*	
		Factory Payroll.................		*12,600.00*
		To record the labor cost summary.		

Accrued Wages. When time tickets and a labor cost summary are used in recording factory wages, an accrued payroll adjusting entry at the end of the cost period is unnecessary. This is because the time tickets of all the

Illustration 141

Factory Payroll

Date		Explanation	Debit	Credit	Balance
Mar.	7	*Weekly payroll payment*	*2,900*		*2,900*
	14	*Weekly payroll payment*	*2,950*		*5,850*
	21	*Weekly payroll payment*	*3,105*		*8,955*
	28	*Weekly payroll payment*	*3,040*		*11,995*
	31	*Labor cost summary*		*12,600*	*605*

days in the cost period, including those after the last full pay period, are summarized on the labor cost summary. Consequently, the journal entry which records the summary records both wages earned and paid during the period and wages earned but unpaid at the end of the period. This is shown in the Factory Payroll account of Illustration 141.

In the Factory Payroll account of Illustration 141 the four debits are the amounts paid the employees at the ends of the four weekly pay periods in the March cost period. The one $12,600 credit is the cost of the labor used, and the $605 credit balance is the accrued payroll.

ACCOUNTING FOR OVERHEAD IN A JOB COST SYSTEM

Incurrence of Overhead. Overhead costs include all manufacturing costs other than for direct material and direct labor. Commonly, in a job cost system an account called Overhead Costs and a subsidiary Overhead Costs Ledger having a separate account for each kind of overhead cost are used in recording overhead.

Entries recording the incurrence of overhead items normally arise from four sources:

1. *Indirect Materials Used.* All indirect materials used are an overhead item. Each day requisitions for indirect materials are recorded in the Indirect Materials account in the Overhead Costs Ledger and are summarized on the materials used summary. At the end of a cost period the total indirect materials used as shown on the summary is debited to the Overhead Costs account.
2. *Indirect Labor Used.* Indirect labor is also an overhead item. Each day time tickets for labor classified as overhead are recorded in the Indirect Labor account in the subsidiary Overhead Costs Ledger and are summarized on the labor cost summary. At the end of the cost period the amount of indirect labor used as shown by the labor cost summary is debited to the Overhead Costs account.
3. *Miscellaneous Payments.* Throughout a cost period vouchers are prepared for miscellaneous overhead items such as repairs by outsiders, telephone, light, and power. Normally a special column in the Voucher Register headed "Overhead Costs, debit" is provided to collect the debits resulting from these items. The individual items are posted to the proper accounts in the Overhead Costs Ledger, and the column total is debited to the Overhead Costs controlling account.
4. *Accrued and Prepaid Items.* At the end of each cost period adjusting entries are made in the General Journal to record such overhead items as depreciation, expired insurance, and taxes. These entries are posted to both subsidiary overhead cost accounts and to the Overhead Costs controlling account.

Before going on, turn to page 652 and observe the four debit items in the Overhead Costs controlling account of Illustration 143. These debits represent the indirect materials, indirect labor, miscellaneous payments, and accrued overhead items just discussed.

Application of Overhead. In a job cost system, in order that the cost of each job may be determined as soon as the job is finished, it is necessary to identify with each job the costs of the materials, labor, and overhead used in its manufacture. No difficulties arise in identifying material and labor costs with specific jobs. Material costs are identified with jobs by means of material requisitions, and labor costs are identified by means of labor time tickets. However, identifying and charging overhead to jobs is not so easy. In the first place, overhead items apply to all jobs and cannot definitely be identified with any particular job; and in the second place, the exact cost of certain overhead items, such as machinery repairs, cannot be known until the end of an accounting period or some other future date, which is usually days, weeks, or even months after many jobs are completed. Consequently, in a job cost system overhead is applied to jobs as they are finished by means of a *predetermined overhead application rate*.

A predetermined overhead application rate for applying overhead to jobs is established before a cost period begins. It may be established by (1) estimating in advance for the period about to begin the total overhead that will be incurred during the period; (2) estimating, for example, the cost of direct labor that will be applied to production during the period; then (3) calculating the ratio, expressed as a percentage, of the estimated overhead to the estimated direct labor cost. For example, if a cost accountant estimates a factory will incur $180,000 of overhead during the year about to begin, estimates that $120,000 of direct labor will be applied to production in the factory during this period, and these estimates are used in establishing an overhead application rate, the rate is 150 percent of direct labor cost and is calculated as follows:

$$\frac{\textit{Next Year's Estimated Overhead Costs, \$180,000}}{\textit{Next Year's Estimated Direct Labor Costs, \$120,000}} = \textit{150 Percent}$$

After a predetermined overhead application rate like the foregoing is established, it is used throughout the year to apply overhead to jobs as they are finished. Overhead is assigned to each job, and the cost of each job is calculated in the following manner: (1) As each job is completed the total cost of the materials used on the job is determined by adding the amounts in the Materials column of the job's cost sheet. Then (2) the cost of the labor applicable to the job is determined by adding the amounts in the Labor column of the cost sheet. After this, (3) the overhead applicable to the job is calculated by multiplying the job's labor cost, as shown by the Labor column total, by the predetermined overhead application rate. The overhead cost thus calculated is then (4) entered in the Overhead Costs Applied column on the job's cost sheet. After this, (5) the job's material, labor, and overhead cost totals are entered in the summary section of the cost sheet and totaled to determine the cost of the job.

In addition to the foregoing and at the same time overhead is entered on a job's cost sheet, the overhead assigned to the job is also entered on an overhead applied summary similar to Illustration 142.

Illustration 142

OVERHEAD APPLIED SUMMARY

Date		Job Number	Remarks	Overhead Applied	
Mar.	*10*	*7449*		*3,114*	*00*
	31	*7452*		*123*	*00*
	31	*7451*		*2,568*	*00*
	31		*Total*	*15,150*	*00*

When overhead is applied to jobs on the basis of a predetermined overhead rate based upon direct labor costs as in the foregoing discussion, it is assumed that the overhead applicable to a particular job bears the same relation to the job's direct labor cost as the total estimated overhead of the factory bears to the total estimated direct labor costs. This assumption may not be proper in every case. However, when the ratio of overhead to direct labor cost is approximately the same for all jobs, an overhead rate based upon direct labor cost offers an easily calculated and fair basis for assigning overhead to jobs. In those cases in which the ratio of overhead to direct labor cost does not remain the same for all jobs, some other relationship must be used. Often overhead rates based upon the ratio of overhead to direct labor hours or overhead to machine hours are used. However, a discussion of these is reserved for an advanced cost accounting course.

Charging Overhead to Unfinished Jobs. Overhead costs incurred during a period benefit all jobs worked on during the period, both jobs finished and those still in process at the period end. Therefore, in completing the accounting work at the end of a cost period, overhead is charged to any jobs still in process at that time. The predetermined application rate and the direct labor charged to each unfinished job up to the end of the cost period are used in the same manner as with completed jobs in assigning overhead to each job still in process. The amounts assigned are charged to each job on its cost sheet and also on the overhead applied summary.

Recording the Total Overhead Applied. At the end of a cost period, after applicable overhead is applied to jobs in process and entered on the overhead applied summary, the summary total shows the overhead applied to all jobs. This total is recorded in the accounts with an entry like the following:

Mar.	31	*Goods in Process*...................	*15,150.00*	
		Overhead Costs................		*15,150.00*
		To record overhead applied to jobs as shown by the overhead applied summary.		

After the foregoing entry is posted, the overhead applied appears as a credit in the Overhead Costs controlling account as in Illustration 143.

Illustration 143

Overhead Costs

Date		Explanation	F	Debit	Credit	Balance
Mar.	31	*Indirect materials*	*G24*	*320*		*320*
	31	*Indirect labor*	*G24*	*2,500*		*2,820*
	31	*Miscellaneous payments*	*V89*	*3,306*		*6,126*
	31	*Accrued and prepaid items*	*G24*	*9,056*		*15,182*
	31	*Applied*			*15,150*	*32*

In the Overhead Costs account shown in Illustration 143 the actual overhead costs incurred are represented by four debits. The first is the indirect materials cost from the materials used summary, and the second debit is the indirect labor cost from the labor used summary. The third is the total of the miscellaneous overhead costs for which vouchers were prepared; and the fourth (normally there would be several such items) represents the many accrued and expired overhead items, such as depreca-tion, expired insurance, and taxes. The sum of the four debits is, as nearly as it can be measured, the overhead incurred. The one credit to the account is the estimated amount of overhead applied to jobs and was taken from the total of the overhead applied summary.

Overapplied and Underapplied Overhead. If, as explained in the previous paragraph, the actual overhead costs incurred during a month or other cost period are debited to the Overhead Costs account and the estimated overhead applied to jobs is credited, the Overhead Costs controlling account will seldom be in balance at the end of a month or other cost period. Some months overhead actually incurred and debited to the account will exceed estimated overhead applied to jobs and credited. Other months estimated overhead applied to jobs and credited will exceed overhead incurred and debited. When the Overhead Costs account has a debit balance at the end of a period (actual overhead incurred greater than overhead applied), the balance is known as *underapplied overhead*; and when the balance is a credit balance (actual overhead less than overhead applied), it is called *overapplied overhead*. The under- or overapplied balance is usually left in the account until the end of a year. If the balance is small and fluctuates from debit to credit throughout the year, it indicates the predetermined overhead rate is very nearly accurate. However, if a large debit balance builds up in the account, it indicates the rate is too low and should be increased. If a large credit balance builds up, it indicates the rate is too high.

At the end of each year the Overhead Costs account balance is commonly closed to the Cost of Goods Sold acccount as an adjustment of the cost of goods manufactured and sold during the year.

RECORDING THE COMPLETION OF A JOB

When a job is completed, its cost is transferred from the Goods in Process account to the Finished Goods account with an entry like the following which transfers the cost of the job the cost sheet of which appears on page 642:

Mar.	29	*Finished Goods*............................	*279.00*	
		Goods in Process.....................		*279.00*
		To transfer the cost of Job No. 7452 to		
		Finished Goods.		

In addition to the foregoing entry, and at the same time it is made, the completed job's cost sheet is removed from the Job Cost Ledger, marked "completed," and filed away. This is in effect the equivalent of posting a credit to the Job Cost Ledger equal to the credit to the Goods in Process controlling account.

In a concern gathering costs for job lots of product with a job cost system, the Finished Goods account often becomes a perpetual inventory controlling account controlling a subsidiary Finished Goods Ledger having a separate account card for each kind of finished goods kept on hand. As a perpetual inventory account its balance shows, at any time posting is completed, the amount of finished goods on hand. As a controlling account the Finished Goods account and its subsidiary Finished Goods Ledger operate in the usual manner of controlling accounts and subsidiary ledgers.

RECORDING COST OF GOODS SOLD

When a cost system is in use, the cost to manufacture a job or job lot of product is known as soon as the goods are finished. Consequently, when goods are sold, since their cost is known, the cost can be recorded at the time of sale. For example, if goods costing $279 are sold for $450, the cost of the goods sold may be recorded with the sale as follows:

Mar.	29	Accounts Receivable—Cone Lumber Co....	450.00	
		Cost of Goods Sold......................	279.00	
		Sales...............................		450.00
		Finished Goods.....................		279.00
		Sold for $450 goods costing $279.		

When cost of goods sold is recorded at the time of each sale as in the foregoing entry, the balance of the Cost of Goods Sold account shows at the end of an accounting period the cost of goods sold during the period.

OPERATING STATEMENTS UNDER A JOB COST SYSTEM

When an income statement is prepared for a company using a job cost system, information for the cost of goods sold section is obtained from an analysis of the Finished Goods account. The beginning balance of the account is the beginning inventory of finished goods; the debits transferring the costs of finished goods to the account show the cost of goods manufactured; and the ending balance is the ending inventory of finished goods. The remainder of the income statement is prepared in the usual manner.

The schedule of cost of goods manufactured or manufacturing statement of a company using a job cost system is commonly less complicated than that of a company using a general accounting system. It may be prepared monthly from an analysis of the Goods in Process account. Such a monthly statement appears as in Illustration 144.

Illustration 144

APEX MANUFACTURING COMPANY
Manufacturing Statement for Month Ended March 31, 19--

Direct materials requisitioned.	$17,150
Direct labor applied to production.	10,100
Overhead costs applied to production at a pre-	
determined rate of 150 per cent	15,150
Total	$42,400
Add beginning inventory of goods in process	2,850
Total	$45,250
Deduct ending inventory of goods in process	12,785
Cost of Goods Manufactured Using a Predetermined	
Overhead Application Rate	$32,465

The ease with which a manufacturing statement like that of Illustration 144 may be prepared from an analysis of the Goods in Process account becomes apparent when the statement of Illustration 144 is compared with the information in the Goods in Process account on page 641.

The manufacturing statement of Illustration 144 is for one month. A statement for a year is similar excepting the item, cost of goods manufactured, is adjusted at the end of the statement for the over- or underapplied overhead as follows:

Cost of goods manufactured using a predetermined	
overhead application rate	$430,230
Add underapplied overhead	1,320
Cost of Goods Manufactured at Actual Cost	$431,550

QUESTIONS FOR CLASS DISCUSSION

1. The emphasis of cost accounting differs from the emphasis of general accounting. What is emphasized in cost accounting?
2. What are the two main types of cost accounting systems? Which system generally best fits the needs of a manufacturer (a) who manufactures machinery to his customers' specifications, (b) who manufactures adding machines in lots of 500, and (c) who manufactures paint?
3. Give the cost accounting meanings of the following:
   a) Job order cost system.   f) Labor time ticket.
   b) Process cost system.   g) Materials requisition.
   c) Job.   h) Materials used summary.
   d) Job lot.   i) Labor cost summary.
   e) Job cost sheet.   j) Summary of overhead costs applied.
4. What two important characteristics distinguish a manufacturing cost accounting system from a general accounting system for a manufacturer?
5. What are the subsidiary ledgers controlled by each of the following accounts: (a) Materials, (b) Goods in Process, and (c) Finished Goods?
6. How is the inventory of goods in process determined in a general accounting system? How may this inventory be determined in a job cost system?

7. What is the purpose of a job cost sheet? What is the ledger containing the job cost sheets of unfinished jobs in process? What controlling account controls this ledger?

8. What are the sources of the job cost sheet entries for (*a*) materials, and (*b*) for labor?

9. Refer to the job cost sheet shown in Illustration 136. How was the overhead charged to this job determined?

10. Outline a procedure that may be used in a job cost system to account for the use of materials.

11. In a job cost system, what is the purpose of the materials used summary?

12. At the end of a cost period the Direct Materials column of a materials used summary totaled $51,625 and the Indirect Materials column totaled $5,210. (*a*) What amount of materials was charged to jobs during the cost period? (*b*) What amount of materials was charged to overhead cost accounts? (*c*) Give the general journal entry to record the materials used during the cost period.

13. Outline a procedure that may be used in a job cost system to account for the use of labor.

14. At the end of a cost period a labor cost summary's Direct Labor column totaled $43,215 and the Indirect Labor column totaled $8,329. (*a*) How much labor was charged directly to jobs during this cost period? (*b*) How much labor was charged to overhead cost accounts? (*c*) Give the general journal entry to record the labor used during the period.

15. When a cost accounting system is in use, why is it unnecessary to make an end-of-the-period adjusting entry to record the accrued factory wages?

16. What are the four common sources of entries recording overhead cost items?

17. At the end of a cost period after all entries have been posted: (*a*) What does the sum of the items debited to the Overhead Costs controlling account represent? (*b*) What is credited to the Overhead Costs controlling account? (*c*) What does the balance of the account represent?

18. How is a predetermined overhead rate established? Why is a predetermined overhead rate used in a job cost system to charge overhead to jobs?

19. In December of 1966 the Universal Company accountant estimated his company would incur overhead in the amount of $300,000 during 1967. He also estimated that during 1967 his company would use $200,000 of direct labor. If these estimates were used to establish an overhead rate based upon direct labor cost, what was the rate?

20. Assume that Universal Company of Question 19 established its overhead rate based upon the estimates of $300,000 of overhead costs and $200,000 of direct labor. Assume further that during 1967, Job No. 2147 was completed by the company. The job's cost sheet showed $2,625 of direct materials used and $3,200 of direct labor charged. What was the cost of Job No. 2147?

21. What does the total of the overhead costs applied summary show at the end of a cost period?

22. Why does a company using a job cost system normally have either overapplied or underapplied overhead at the end of each cost period?

23. At the end of a cost period the Overhead Costs controlling account has a credit balance. Is this overapplied or underapplied overhead?

24. A company sold for $3,200 a job, the cost sheet of which showed a total cost of $2,173. Give the entires to record the sale and the cost of the goods sold.

PROBLEMS

Problem 22–1

A portion of the transactions completed during a cost period by a company using a job cost system and a voucher system follow:

a) Purchased materials on account, $145,000.
b) Paid freight on materials, $2,100.
c) Paid factory wages, $109,000.
d) Paid $4,700 for repairs to factory machinery.
e) Made an adjusting entry to record: depreciation of factory building, $18,500; depreciation of machinery, $29,000; expired insurance, $2,400; and accrued factory taxes, $3,700.
f) Recorded the materials used summary. The column totals were:

> *Direct materials*.................................$128,000
> *Indirect materials*..............................   7,000
>   **$135,000**

g) Recorded the labor cost summary. The column totals were:

> *Direct labor*.....................................$102,000
> *Indirect labor*..................................   11,500
>   **$113,500**

h) Recorded the summary of overhead costs applied. Overhead was applied to jobs during the cost period on the basis of direct labor cost. The rate was 75 percent.
i) Recorded jobs finished and transferred to finished goods, $254,000.
j) Recorded the sale at $302,000 of jobs that cost $223,000.

Required:
1. Prepare general journal entries to record the summarized transactions.
2. Open T-accounts for Materials, Goods in Process, Finished Goods, Factory Payroll, Overhead Costs, and Cost of Goods Sold. Post those portions of the general journal entries that affect the T-accounts.
3. After posting the entries, list the T-accounts and tell what the balance of each represents.

Problem 22–2

Stonevalley Manufacturing Company uses a job cost system. On the first day of April the concern's Goods in Process account had a $16,500 debit balance and at the end of the month, after all posting was completed, it had a $25,200 debit balance and appeared as follows:

Goods in Process

Date		Explanations	F	Debit	Credit	Balance
Apr.	1	Balance				16,500
	12	Job 785 completed			31,600	(15,100)
	18	Job 783 completed			35,400	(50,500)
	19	Job 784 completed			53,300	(103,800)
	24	Job 786 completed			46,500	(150,300)
	28	Job 782 completed			43,600	(193,900)
	30	Materials charged		61,400		(132,500)
	30	Labor charged		83,000		(49,500)
	30	Overhead charged		74,700		25,200

Required:
1. From the information in the Goods in Process account prepare a manufacturing statement for Stonevalley Manufacturing Company.
2. Under the assumption that the direct labor cost of Job No. 782 was $16,500, determine the cost of its materials.

Problem 22–3
Dandee Manufacturing Company makes on special order a small machine called a "solidifier." During a cost period the following jobs were in process:

Job No.	Product	Customer
872	8 H.P. solidifier	Hidden Valley Mine
873	3 H.P. solidifier	Deephole Mine
874	5 H.P. solidifier	Hiltop Mine

Materials were delivered by the storeroom keeper to the factory on the following materials requisitions:

Requisition No.	Amount	Charge to Job	Charge to Subsidiary Overhead Account
1521	82.00	872	
1522	60.00	872	
1523	64.00	873	
1524	68.00	874	
1525	12.00		Machinery lubricants
1526	16.00	872	
1527	47.00	874	
1528	8.00	872	
1529	52.00	873	
1530	14.00	873	
1531	10.00	874	
1532	24.00		Building repairs

The following labor time tickets were received in the accounting department:

Time Ticket No.	Amount	Charge to Job	Charge to Subsidiary Overhead Account
2112	16.00	872	
2113	18.00	872	
2114	16.00	873	
2115	8.00		Machinery repairs
2116	12.00	874	
2117	20.00	874	
2118	20.00	872	
2119	18.00	873	
2120	16.00	872	
2121	20.00	873	
2122	16.00	874	
2123	12.00	872	
2124	20.00	873	
2125	6.00		Building repairs
2126	12.00		Building repairs

Jobs 872 and 873 were completed during the cost period. Overhead was assigned to each job upon completion. The overhead rate used was 200 percent of direct labor cost.

Overhead was also assigned to Job No. 874 which was still in process at the end of the cost period.

Required:
1. Prepare job cost sheets for Job Nos. 872, 873, and 874.
2. Prepare a materials used summary, a labor cost summary, and a summary of overhead costs applied.
3. Enter the requisitions for direct materials in the materials columns of the proper job cost sheets. Enter all requisitions on the materials used summary. (Normally, requisitions for indirect materials are debited to the Indirect Materials account in the subsidiary Overhead Costs Ledger. This step is omitted here in order to shorten and simplify the problem.)
4. Enter the time tickets for direct labor in the labor columns of the proper job cost sheet. Enter all time tickets on the labor cost summary. (Normally, time tickets for indirect labor are debited to the Indirect Labor account in the subsidiary Overhead Costs Ledger. This step is omitted here in order to shorten and simplify the problem.)
5. Calculate the overhead applicable to each job. Enter the overhead on the job cost sheets and on the overhead costs applied summary.
6. Prepare general journal entries to record the (a) materials used summary, (b) labor cost summary, (c) overhead costs applied summary, and (d) the jobs completed.

7. Open T-accounts for Goods in Process and Finished Goods. Post the portions of the journal entries applicable to these accounts. Prove the account balances.

Problem 22–4

Hyhill Manufacturing Company completed the following transactions, among others, during a cost period:

a) Purchased materials on account, $13,000.
b) Paid factory wages, $12,400.
c) Paid miscellaneous factory overhead items, $800.
d) Materials requisitions were used during the cost period to charge jobs with materials. The requisitions were then entered on a materials used summary. (Instructions for recording the summary are given in Item j.) An abstract of the requisitions showed the following materials charged to jobs. (Charge the materials to the jobs by making entries directly in the job T-accounts in the subsidiary Job Cost Ledger.)

Job No. 1	$ 2,600
Job No. 2	1,300
Job No. 3	2,800
Job No. 4	3,000
Job No. 5	600
	$10,300

e) Labor time tickets were used to charge jobs with direct labor. The time tickets were then entered on a labor cost summary. (Instructions for recording the summary are given under Item k.) An abstract of the tickets showed the following labor charged to the several jobs. (Charge the labor to the jobs by making entries directly in the job T-accounts in the Job Cost Ledger.)

Job No. 1	$2,400
Job No. 2	1,400
Job No. 3	2,600
Job No. 4	2,800
Job No. 5	400
	$9,600

f) Job Nos. 1, 3, and 4 were completed and transferred to finished goods. A predetermined overhead application rate of 150 percent of direct labor cost was used to apply overhead to each job upon its completion. (Enter the overhead in the job T-accounts; mark the jobs "completed"; and make a general journal entry to transfer their costs to the Finished Goods account.)

g) Job Nos. 1 and 3 were sold on account for a total of $24,000.

h) At the end of the cost period, charged overhead to the uncompleted jobs at the rate of 150 percent of direct labor cost. (Enter the overhead in the job T-accounts.)

i) At the end of the cost period, made an entry to record: depreciation on the factory building, $2,300; depreciation on the machinery, $4,100; expired factory insurance, $600; and accrued taxes payable, $1,200.

j) Recorded the information of the materials used summary. The column totals were:

$$\begin{array}{ll}
\textit{Direct materials}\dots\dots\dots\dots\dots\dots\dots\dots & \$10,300 \\
\textit{Indirect materials}\dots\dots\dots\dots\dots\dots\dots\dots & \underline{2,000} \\
& \underline{\$12,300}
\end{array}$$

k) Recorded the information of the labor cost summary. The column totals were:

$$\begin{array}{ll}
\textit{Direct labor}\dots\dots\dots\dots\dots\dots\dots\dots\dots & \$\ 9,600 \\
\textit{Indirect labor}\dots\dots\dots\dots\dots\dots\dots\dots & \underline{3,100} \\
& \underline{\$12,700}
\end{array}$$

l) Recorded the information of the overhead applied summary. (See Items *f* and *h* for the amount of overhead applied.)

Required:

1. Open the following general ledger T-accounts: Materials, Goods in Process, Finished Goods, Factory Payroll, Overhead Costs, and Cost of Goods Sold.
2. Open an additional T-account for each of the five jobs. Assume that each job's T-account is a job cost sheet in a subsidiary Job Cost Ledger.
3. Prepare general journal entries to record the applicable information of Items *a, b, c, f, g, i, j, k,* and *l*. Post the entry portions that affect the general ledger accounts opened.
4. Enter the applicable information of Items *d, e, f,* and *h* directly in the T-accounts that represent job cost sheets.
5. Present statistics to prove the balances of the Goods in Process and Finished Goods accounts.
6. List the general ledger accounts and tell what is represented by the balance of each.

CLASS EXERCISE

Exercise 22–1

The Goods in Process account of a concern using a job order cost system had a $4,200 debit balance at the beginning of a cost period. During the period the concern's cost accountant prepared and posted the following four entries:

Goods in Process......................	62,100.00	
Overhead Costs.......................	5,800.00	
Materials.......................		67,900.00
To record the materials used.		
Goods in Process......................	50,500.00	
Overhead Costs.......................	12,700.00	
Factory Payroll..................		63,200.00
To record the labor used.		

Goods in Process............................	40,400.00	
Overhead Costs......................		40,400.00
To record the overhead applied to jobs.		
Finished Goods.............................	142,100.00	
Goods in Process.....................		142,100.00
To transfer to Finished Goods the costs of all jobs finished.		

Required:

Under the assumption there was only one job in process at the end of the cost period and that it had $6,100 of material charged to it, determine the amounts of labor and overhead charged to the job.

ALTERNATE PROBLEMS

Problem 22–1A

Redtop Manufacturing Company uses a job cost system and a voucher system. During its first year it completed the following condensed transactions:

a) Purchased materials on account, $183,800.
b) Returned $1,700 of materials purchased.
c) Paid freight on materials, $2,100.
d) Paid factory wages, $168,000.
e) Paid for repairs to factory machinery, $8,000.
f) Made a year-end adjusting entry to record: depreciation of factory building, $18,000; depreciation of machinery, $28,000; expired factory insurance, $3,500; accrued factory taxes payable, $10,500.
g) Recorded the labor cost summary. Its column totals were:

> Direct labor................................$141,000
> Indirect labor............................. 33,000
> $174,000

h) Recorded the materials used summary. Its column totals were:

> Direct materials...........................$154,500
> Indirect materials........................ 11,000
> $165,500

i) Recorded the overhead applied summary. Overhead was applied to jobs during the period on the basis of direct labor cost. The rate was 80 percent.
j) Recorded the costs of the jobs finished and transferred to finished goods, $312,000.
k) Recorded the sale at $405,000 of jobs that cost $270,000.
l) At the end of the year, closed the Overhead Costs account.

Required:

1. Prepare general journal entries to record the foregoing transactions.
2. Open T-accounts for Materials, Goods in Process, Finished Goods, Factory Payroll, Overhead Costs, and Cost of Goods Sold. Post the journal entry portions that affect the accounts.
3. Prepare a manufacturing statement for the concern.
4. List the balance of each T-account and tell what the balance represents.
5. Give, also, the balance of the Overhead Costs account before it was closed, and tell what this balance represented.

Problem 22–2A

A cost accountant estimated before a year began that his small company would incur during the year the direct labor cost of 20 men working 2,000 hours each at an average rate of $3 per hour. He also estimated the concern would incur the following overhead costs during the year:

Indirect labor	*$15,750*
Superintendence	*12,000*
Rent of factory building	*7,200*
Heat, lights, and power	*4,800*
Insurance expense	*3,400*
Depreciation of machinery	*24,200*
Machinery repairs	*3,000*
Supplies expense	*1,500*
Miscellaneous factory expenses	*1,350*
Total	*$73,200*

At the end of the year for which the estimates were made the cost records showed the company had actually incurred $73,350 of overhead costs and had completed and sold five jobs which had direct labor costs as follows: Job No. 603, $25,400; Job No. 604, $23,200; Job No. 605, $21,700; Job No. 606, $22,800; and Job No. 607, $24,900. In addition Job No. 608 was in process at the period end and had had $2,500 of direct labor and its share of overhead costs charged.

Required:

Under the assumption the concern used a predetermined overhead application rate based on the foregoing overhead and direct labor estimates, determine: (1) the predetermined application rate used, (2) the total overhead applied to jobs during the year, and (3) the over- or underapplied overhead at the year-end. Under the further assumption the concern closed its over- or underapplied overhead to Cost of Goods Sold as an adjustment of the cost of jobs sold, (4) give the entry to close the Overhead Costs account.

Problem 22–3A

A company manufacturing to the special order of its customers a small machine called a "smasher" had the following jobs in process during a cost period:

Job No.	Product	Customer
402	7 lb. smasher	Electronics, Inc.
403	15 lb. smasher	Research Associates
404	8 lb. smasher	Data Search, Inc.

Materials were delivered by the storeroom keeper to the factory on the following material requisitions:

Requisition No.	Amount	Charge to Job	Charge to Subsidiary Overhead Account
2007	$34.00	402	
2008	46.00	402	
2009	74.00		Machinery repairs
2010	72.00	403	
2011	36.00	403	
2012	28.00		Machinery lubricants
2013	26.00	402	
2014	40.00	403	
2015	42.00	404	
2016	18.00	403	
2017	10.00	404	

The following labor time tickets were received in the accounting department:

Time Ticket No.	Amount	Charge to Job	Charge to Subsidiary Overhead Account
3307	$12.00	402	
3308	18.00	403	
3309	24.00	403	
3310	20.00	403	
3311	22.00		Machinery repairs
3312	18.00		Building repairs
3313	24.00	402	
3314	16.00	402	
3315	8.00	403	
3316	20.00	402	
3317	20.00	403	
3318	16.00	404	
3319	18.00	403	
3320	16.00		Building maintenance

Job Nos. 402 and 403 were completed during the cost period, and overhead was assigned to each upon completion. The overhead rate used was 200 percent of direct labor cost.

Overhead was also assigned to Job No. 404 which was still in process at the period end.

Required:

1. Prepare job cost sheets for Job Nos. 402, 403, and 404.
2. Prepare a materials used summary, a labor cost summary, and a summary of overhead costs applied.
3. Enter the materials requisitions for direct materials in the materials columns of the proper job cost sheets. Enter all material requisitions on the materials used summary, placing the requisition numbers in the Explanation column. (Normally, material requisitions for indirect materials are debited to the Indirect Materials account in the subsidiary Overhead Costs Ledger. This step is omitted here in order to shorten and simplify the problem.)
4. Enter the time tickets for direct labor in the labor columns of the proper job cost sheets. Enter all labor time tickets on the labor cost summary, placing the time ticket numbers in the Explanation column. (Normally labor time tickets for indirect labor are debited to the Indirect Labor account in the subsidiary Overhead Costs Ledger. This step is omitted here in order to shorten and simplify the problem.)
5. Calculate the amount of overhead applicable to each job. Enter the overhead on the job cost sheets and on the summary of overhead costs applied.
6. Prepare general journal entries to record the (*a*) materials used summary, (*b*) labor cost summary, (*c*) summary of overhead costs applied, and (*d*) the jobs completed.
7. Open T-accounts for Goods in Process and Finished Goods. Post the portions of the journal entries applicable to these accounts. Prove the balances of the accounts.

DECISION PROBLEM 22A—MASON REPAIR CENTER

John Mason operates a general repair center catering to fairly large repair jobs on furniture and equipment. He desires to bid on a contract offer by the city school board to repair and refinish all furniture and equipment in five of the city's high schools.

Although his records have been fairly complete in the past, he has never attempted to compute the cost of each job. However, he feels that he has not priced all jobs correctly, that probably he has incurred losses on some jobs, and has lost other contracts by overbidding.

A summary of expenses affecting production costs for the past year follows:

Salaries and wages..	*$70,000*
Materials...	*9,000*
Service truck expense.................................	*8,000*
Small tool expense...................................	*900*
Depreciation...	*5,600*
Other indirect production expenses...............	*8,700*
Shop expenses (indirect)............................	*25,800*

An analysis of "Salaries and Wages" shows that it consisted of $60,000 direct labor and $10,000 indirect labor. You find that there has been a fairly consistent relationship in the past five years between direct labor and overhead costs. Mr. Mason has estimated direct labor costs of $30,000 and materials of $7,000 on the school contract. He feels that if the school contract is secured, overhead costs, exclusive of depreciation, will increase by 40 percent. Depreciation will increase $600 because of greater wear and tear on equipment that will be used on the school contract.

Prepare a report to Mr. Mason giving consideration to the following:

1. Would a job order cost system be applicable to each repair job?
2. Explain how the cost of each job may be determined upon the completion of the job.
3. Compute the overhead rate that would have been used last year. Compute the overhead rate which would be used if the school contract is obtained. (Compute rates to the nearest one tenth of 1 percent.)
4. What is the estimated total cost to complete the school job?
5. What other expenses should be taken into account in determining the bid price on the school job?

DECISION PROBLEM 22B—BELL FURNITURE, INC.

Tom Bell and associates operate a small furniture manufacturing company producing tables and occasional chairs. He desires to place a bid on a large contract offered by a drug chain for display tables and cases. His plant and facilities are adequate for present business plus the production required by the drug chain contract. The new contract would not affect present business.

Bell has a job order cost system. The drug chain contract offer is for 1,900 tables and 1,600 cases. The specifications indicate the following cost estimates per unit:

	Tables	Cases
Direct material....................................	*$68*	*$130*
Direct labor..	*30*	*50*

An overhead rate (based on direct labor cost) of 60 percent has been used for the past several years.

The following schedule shows the actual overhead incurred during the past year and also the projected increases if the new contract is undertaken.

	Past Year	Projected Increase if New Contract Undertaken
Superintendence............................	$10,800	$ 8,000
Indirect labor...............................	18,600	6,000
Indirect materials..........................	3,700	4,300
Repairs and maintenance..................	6,100	4,800
Depreciation................................	8,900	900
Other factory expenses....................	7,750	5,300
	$55,850	$29,300

Direct labor cost for the year totaled $91,800. For the past five years the underapplied overhead has averaged 1½ percent of the total overhead incurred.

Prepare a report to Mr. Bell giving consideration to the following:

1. Comment upon the situation with respect to the continued presence of underapplied overhead.
2. What overhead rate (to the nearest one tenth of 1 percent) would you estimate for next year, if the drug chain contract is taken? Give probable explanation for any substantial change in this rate over the 60 percent rate in use last year.
3. What is the production cost which should enter into Mr. Bell's bid?
4. Explain how the material and labor cost were probably obtained.
5. What other expenses and costs (nonmanufacturing) should be taken into account in preparing the bid?
6. Comment on the effect on the profitableness of present business of gaining the drug chain contract.

Process
Cost Accounting

In the production of a product, a *process* is a manufacturing operation or step; a *processing department* is a physical grouping of men and machines required to complete a process; and a *process cost system* is one in which costs are assembled in terms of processes or manufacturing steps.

Process cost systems are commonly found in companies manufacturing products such as sugar, paper, cement, bricks, and similar products. In such companies the product results from the completion in turn of a series of processes, with each process advancing the product one stage toward completion, as in a brickyard where clay is dug from clay pits, ground and mixed with other ingredients, cut into bricks, and baked in kilns, and where finished bricks result from the completion in turn of the mining, grinding and mixing, cutting, and baking processes.

BASIC DIFFERENCE BETWEEN PROCESS AND JOB ORDER COST ACCOUNTING

A cost center is a unit or activity for which costs are collected; and a difference in cost centers is the basic difference between process, and job order cost accounting. In a job cost system the cost centers are jobs, and costs are collected on job cost sheets by jobs. In a process cost system there are no jobs or job cost sheets; the cost centers are the processes through which the product pass; and costs are collected in separate goods in process accounts, one for each process.

Differences in products and in manufacturing procedures are responsible for the difference in cost centers in the two systems. In a company to which a job cost system is applicable there are identifiable jobs individually manufactured. In a company to which a process cost system is applicable there are no jobs and production is normally on a more or less continuous basis for an inventory from which customers' orders are filled. Furthermore, in a company to which a process cost system is applicable, the products are standardized in the sense that the units of any one product are assumed to have the same amounts of material, labor, and overhead and are assumed to have been processed in the same manner in each processing department through which they passed.

NATURE OF A PROCESS COST SYSTEM

In a process cost system: (1) Material, labor, and overhead costs are recorded for each process or processing department for a uniform cost period, such as a month. (2) During the period, in addition to cost records, records are also kept of the number of units of product processed in each department. (3) At the end of each cost period, as an aid in controlling costs, material, labor, and overhead costs per unit of product processed are calculated for each department. And (4) at the end of each cost period the accumulated costs of processing a product are transferred and advanced in turn from the goods in process account of one department to the goods in process account of the next and on to the Finished Goods account, just as the product itself was transferred and advanced in the manufacturing procedure from department to department and on to the finished goods warehouse.

Each of the foregoing characteristics of a process cost system are discussed in the pages that follow and are illustrated with the accounts and procedures of Delta Processing Company.

RECORDING COSTS BY DEPARTMENTS

Material Costs. Material requisitions summarized on a materials used summary having a column for each processing department may be used in collecting material costs by departments. However, when only a few different kinds of materials are used, and kinds not likely to be misappropriated, material requisitions are sometimes eliminated and a record of the materials issued to each department, which is kept by the storeroom keeper, is substituted. In such a case the materials chargeable to each department are reported by the storeroom keeper at the end of each cost period by means of a *consumption report.*

At the end of each cost period the materials issued as shown by the materials used summary or consumption report are charged to the departments with a journal entry. For example, at the end of the April cost period the column totals of Delta Processing Company's materials used summary showed the following materials issued to its three processing departments:

Grinding department...........................$ 9,900
Mixing department............................. 2,040
Packaging department......................... 1,515
   Total Materials Issued.......................$13,455

The information of this summary was recorded with the following entry:

Apr.	*30*	*Goods in Process, Grinding Department*......	9,900.00	
		Goods in Process, Mixing Department........	2,040.00	
		Goods in Process, Packaging Department.....	1,515.00	
		Materials.............................		13,455.00
		To record the materials issued to the departments.		

In a process cost system each processing department's material, labor, and overhead costs are recorded in a separate goods in process account as in the foregoing entry. Consequently, a concern like Delta Processing Company, which has three processing departments, has three goods in process accounts. Concerns using process cost systems commonly do not differentiate between direct and indirect materials used in production; and as in Delta Processing Company, they commonly record requisitions for both kinds of materials on their materials used summaries without a distinction as to kind.

Labor Costs. In a process cost system time tickets summarized on a labor cost summary having a column for each processing department are commonly used in accumulating labor costs by departments. Labor costs as shown by the time tickets are entered on the summary each day, generally without a distinction as to direct and indirect labor; and at the end of a cost period the column totals of the summary show the labor cost applicable to each department. These totals are charged to the goods in process accounts of the departments with an entry like the following:

Apr.	*30*	*Goods in Process, Grinding Department*......	5,700.00	
		Goods in Process, Mixing Department........	3,570.00	
		Goods in Process, Packaging Department.....	909.00	
		Factory Payroll........................		10,179.00
		To charge the departments with the labor applied to production.		

In a concern in which each employee spends all his time in the same department it is possible to dispense with time tickets and a labor cost summary and to secure departmental labor cost information directly from the payroll records.

Overhead Costs. It is possible in a concern using a process cost system to provide a separate account for each department for each kind of overhead cost incurred, for example, separate insurance expense accounts, one for each department, and periodically to charge overhead costs to these departmental accounts as the costs are paid, accrue, and expire. However, a more common system is to provide one set of undepartmentalized overhead accounts, to record overhead costs in these accounts without regard as to amounts applicable to each department, and to allocate the recorded overhead to the several departments at the end of each cost period.

When overhead costs are recorded in undepartmentalized accounts and allocated at the end of a cost period, an overhead allocation sheet like Illustration 145 is often used.

Illustration 145
DELTA PROCESSING COMPANY
Departmental Overhead Costs Allocation Sheet
For Month Ended April 30, 19—

Undepartmentalized Cost Accounts	Basis of Allocation	Cost Account Balance	Allocations of Cost		
			Grinding Dept.	Mixing Dept.	Packaging Dept.
Superintendent's Salary	Number of employees	$1,000	$ 600	$ 250	$ 150
Expired insurance	Value of equipment	522	348	79	95
Property taxes	Value of equipment	816	544	123	149
Depreciation of machinery	Value of equipment	1,920	1,280	288	352
Depreciation of building	Floor space	1,845	1,220	204	421
Power costs	Meters	404	283	76	45
Total		$6,507	$4,275	$1,020	$1,212

When an allocation sheet like Illustration 145 is used, overhead costs, as previously explained, are recorded in undepartmentalized accounts throughout each cost period. At the period end the account balances are entered in the Cost Account Balance column of the allocation sheet and are allocated to the departments on some fair bases, with the allocated shares being entered in the proper departmental columns of the sheet.

In allocating costs an effort is always made to pick bases of allocation the application of which will fairly share the costs between the departments. For example, in allocating the superintendent's salary, the first item allocated in Illustration 145, it is assumed the superintendent devotes his time to supervising employees and the ratio of employees in the department is a fair basis for allocating his salary. Therefore, since the concern's grinding department has twelve employees, the mixing department five, and the packaging department three, a total of twenty employees, the superintendent's $1,000 salary is divided among the departments in a 12:5:3 ratio; and the amounts charged to the departments are determined as follows:

$$\textit{Mixing department's share:}\ \$1,000 \times \frac{12}{20} = \$600$$

$$\textit{Grinding department's share:}\ \$1,000 \times \frac{5}{20} = \$250$$

$$\textit{Packaging department's share:}\ \$1,000 \times \frac{3}{20} = \$150$$

Ratio of employees is a fair basis for allocating a cost such as superintendence. Likewise, ratio of floor space occupied is a fair basis for allocating rent or building depreciation; and ratio of equipment values is a fair basis for insurance, taxes, and equipment depreciation.

Sometimes in allocating costs more precise bases than ratios are used. For example, Delta Processing Company has separate meters for measuring the shares of electric power (last item in Illustration 145) consumed in its departments.

When an overhead costs allocation sheet is used in allocating overhead, the completed sheet becomes the basis for an entry to close the undepartmentalized overhead accounts and transfer the costs recorded in these accounts to the goods in process accounts of the departments. For example, the following entry taken from the allocation sheet of Illustration 145 closes the overhead accounts of Delta Processing Company and transfers the costs recorded in these accounts to the concern's goods in process accounts:

Apr.	30	*Goods in Process, Grinding Department*........	4,275.00	
		Goods in Process, Mixing Department.........	1,020.00	
		Goods in Process, Packaging Department.......	1,212.00	
		Superintendent's Salary..................		1,000.00
		Expired Insurance.......................		522.00
		Property Taxes..........................		816.00
		Depreciation of Machinery................		1,920.00
		Depreciation of Building.................		1,845.00
		Power Costs.............................		404.00
		To close the overhead accounts and transfer the overhead recorded therein to the departmental goods in process accounts.		

The debits in the foregoing entry were taken from the allocation column totals of Illustration 145; the credits are Delta Processing Company's undepartmentalized overhead account balances as shown in the Cost Account Balance column of the sheet.

RECORDING NUMBERS OF UNITS PROCESSED

In a factory using a process cost system, daily output records are commonly maintained in each processing department. Sometimes meters are attached to machines, and the meter readings are the basis of the daily records; other times each department foreman is made responsible for a daily production count. In either case the meter readings or daily counts are summarized at the end of each month or other cost period in a report called a department production report. (A production report of Delta Processing Company's grinding department is shown in Illustration 146.) Such a report commonly shows for a department: (1) the units of product that were in process in the department at the beginning of the cost period,

Illustration 146

DEPARTMENT PRODUCTION REPORT

Department   Grinding   *Month* April , 19

Quantity to Be Accounted for:		
Units in process at the beginning of month....	30,000	
Units placed in process during month........	90,000	
Total to be accounted for....................		120,000
Accounted for as Follows:		
Units completed and transferred to Mixing Department.................	100,000	
Units completed and on hand in department..	0	
Unfinished units in process at end of month....	20,000	
Total units accounted for...................		120,000

Stage of completion of the units in process at the beginning of the month as to:	Stage of completion of the unfinished units in process at the end of month as to:
Materials Completed	Materials Completed
Labor 1/3	Labor 1/4
Overhead 1/3	Overhead 1/4

(2) the number that were finished and transferred to the next department or to finished goods, and (3) the inventory of units still in process at the end of the period. In addition (4) the report commonly shows the stages of completion of the beginning and ending inventories of goods in process.

CALCULATING UNIT PROCESSING COSTS

As an aid in controlling costs, companies using process cost systems commonly calculate for each processing department material, labor, and overhead costs per unit of product processed. These calculations are simple in departments in which there are no beginning or ending goods in process inventories. In such a department, unit costs are only a matter of dividing in turn the material, labor, and overhead costs charged to the department during a period by the number of units processed in the department during the period. For example, if during a cost period a brickyard's clay mining department was charged with $1,200 of materials, $6,000 of labor, and $4,800 of overhead, and during the same period the department mined 20,000 yards of clay, the $1,200, $6,000, and $4,800 are each divided by 20,000 to secure a $0.06 materials cost, a $0.30 labor cost, and a $0.24 overhead cost, per yard of clay mined.

EQUIVALENT FINISHED UNIT COSTS

When a processing department begins and ends a cost period with work in process inventories, portions of the materials, labor, and overhead charged to the department are used: (1) to finish the beginning work in process inventory, (2) to start and finish the units begun and finished in the department during the period, and (3) to begin the ending goods in process inventory. Consequently, in such a case the material, labor, and overhead costs charged to the department have to be allocated between the inventories and the units begun and finished.

Commonly material, labor, and overhead costs are allocated to the inventories and units started and finished on the bases of equivalent finished units. Also, in such a case unit processing costs are calculated on the bases of equivalent finished units and thereby become equivalent unit processing costs.

An equivalent finished unit of material, of labor, and of overhead are in each instance amounts of material, labor, and overhead equivalent to that required to complete the processing of one unit of product in the department for which the equivalent units are calculated. Furthermore, the use of equivalent finished units in allocating costs is based on the assumption that the same amount of material is required to give each of four units of product one fourth of their material as is required to give a single unit all its material, or that it takes the same labor and overhead to process each of three units of product one third the way to completion as it takes to finish a single unit.

Allocating labor costs to the inventories and units started and finished in Delta Processing Company's grinding department may be used to illustrate the use of equivalent finished units in allocating costs. For this illustration the following information is available:

a) The grinding department was charged with $5,700 of labor during the April cost period.

b) It is assumed that labor is applied evenly throughout the department's process. In other words, it is assumed that product one-third processed has received one third the labor that will be applied to it in the department, that product one-half processed has received one half its labor, and so on.

c) The goods in process in the department at the beginning of the cost period consisted of 30,000 units of product that were one-third completed when the period began.

d) The goods finished in the department consisted of 100,000 units. These in turn consisted of the foregoing 30,000 beginning units plus 70,000 units started and finished during the period.

e) The department's ending inventory of goods in process consisted of 20,000 units, one-fourth finished when the period ended.

In arriving at the portions of the $5,700 labor cost to be assigned to each inventory and to the goods started and finished, three calculations are required. Under the assumptions just listed they are:

Calculation One: *The equivalent finished units and the sum of equivalent finished units of labor assigned to each inventory and to the goods started and finished are calculated as follows:*

	Units Involved	Fraction of a Unit of Labor Added during This Period	Equivalent Units of Labor Added during This Period
Inventory of 30,000 units one-third completed at the beginning	*30,000*	*⅔*	*20,000*
Units started and finished	*70,000*	*1*	*70,000*
Inventory of 20,000 units one-fourth completed at the end	*20,000*	*¼*	*5,000*
Total Equivalent Units...			*95,000*

<u>Calculation Two:</u> *The department's labor cost is divided by its total equivalent units of labor to secure the cost of an equivalent unit of labor in the department, as follows:*

$5,700 of Labor ÷ 95,000 Equivalent Units = $0.06 per Equivalent Unit

<u>Calculation Three:</u> *The equivalent units of labor added to the inventories and goods started and finished are then multiplied in turn by the cost of an equivalent unit of labor to determine the shares of labor cost chargeable to each. The shares in this case are:*

Beginning inventory (20,000 equivalent units at $0.06)..........$1,200
Units started and finished (70,000 equivalent units at $0.06)...... 4,200
Ending inventory (5,000 equivalent units at $0.06).............. 300
    Total labor charged to the department....................$5,700

The 30,000 units in this department's beginning goods in process inventory were one-third completed when the cost period began. Consequently, they received two thirds of their labor and were two-thirds completed during the period. If it is assumed that it takes *one unit* of labor to begin and complete a unit of product, then these 30,000 units should each be charged with two thirds of a unit of labor. Notice in the first of the foregoing calculations that these units are assigned two thirds of a unit of labor. Observe also that the 70,000 units that were started and finished are each assigned a full unit and that the 20,000 units that were started but only one-fourth finished are charged with one-fourth unit. Notice in the first calculation that the units involved in each inventory and the goods started and finished are multiplied by the fraction of a unit of labor applied to each to determine the portions of the total labor cost, measured in equivalent finished units, that are applicable to each.

The calculations just illustrated show the use of the idea of equivalent finished units in allocating labor cost to inventories and to goods started and finished. Calculations similar to these also used in allocating material and overhead costs.

PROCESS COST ACCOUNTING ILLUSTRATED

Several characteristics of a process cost system have been illustrated and discussed thus far in this chapter. On this and the next few pages these individual illustrations are brought together and expanded into a more complete illustration, the cost system of Delta Processing Company, a manufacturer of a single product, a patented home remedy called Noxall.

It is assumed in the illustration that the manufacturing procedure for Noxall is as follows: Material AAA is finely ground in the grinding department of Delta Processing Company, after which it is transferred to the mixing department where materials BBB and CCC are added, and the resulting mixture is thoroughly mixed. The mixing process results in the product Noxall, which is transferred upon completion to the packaging department. In the packaging department Noxall is packaged in paper boxes, packed in cartons, and then transferred to the finished goods warehouse until sold.

Delta Processing Company assumes:

a) That all material AAA placed in process in the grinding department is placed in process at the time the department's process is first begun.

b) That all materials BBB and CCC placed in process in the mixing department are placed in process evenly throughout the process. In other words, the company assumes that when product is one-third processed in this department, it has received one third its materials BBB and CCC, and that when the product is three-fourths processed, it has received three fourths of its materials.

c) That three fifths of the packaging department materials are used at the beginning of the process and that two fifths are used at the end. However, this has no effect because the company follows the practice of packaging all Noxall finished each day, and as a result, there is never an inventory of partially processed product in the department.

d) That labor and overhead applied in each process are applied evenly throughout the process.

At the end of the April cost period the cost accountant of the company used the following entries (each has been previously discussed) to record the concern's materials used summary, labor cost summary, and overhead cost allocation sheet:

Apr.	30	*Goods in Process, Grinding Department*........	*9,900.00*	
		Goods in Process, Mixing Department..........	*2,040.00*	
		Goods in Process, Packaging Department.......	*1,515.00*	
		Materials................................		*13,455.00*
		To record the materials issued to the departments.		
	30	*Goods in Process, Grinding Department*........	*5,700,00*	
		Goods in Process, Mixing Department..........	*3,570.00*	
		Goods in Process, Packaging Department.......	*909.00*	
		Factory Payroll..........................		*10,179.00*
		To charge the departments with the labor applied to production.		

Apr.	*30*	*Goods in Process, Grinding Department*........	*4,275.00*	
		Goods in Process, Mixing Department..........	*1,020.00*	
		Goods in Process, Packaging Department.......	*1,212.00*	
		Superintendent's Salary..................		*1,000.00*
		Expired Insurance.......................		*522.00*
		Property Taxes..........................		*816.00*
		Depreciation of Machinery...............		*1,920.00*
		Depreciation of Building.................		*1,845.00*
		Power Costs.............................		*404.00*
		To close the overhead cost accounts and transfer the overhead recorded therein to the departmental goods in process accounts.		

After the foregoing entries were posted, the goods in process accounts of the concern's three processing departments appeared as follows:

Goods in Process, Grinding Department

Date		Explanation	Debit	Credit	Balance
Apr.	*1*	*Beginning inventory*			*4,250*
	30	*Materials*	*9,900*		*14,150*
	30	*Labor*	*5,700*		*19,850*
	30	*Overhead*	*4,275*		*24,125*

Goods in Process, Mixing Department

Date		Explanation	Debit	Credit	Balance
Apr.	*1*	*Beginning inventory*			*3,785*
	30	*Materials*	*2,040*		*5,825*
	30	*Labor*	*3,570*		*9,395*
	30	*Overhead*	*1,020*		*10,415*

Goods in Process, Packaging Department

Date		Explanation	Debit	Credit	Balance
Apr.	*30*	*Materials*	*1,515*		*1,515*
	30	*Labor*	*909*		*2,424*
	30	*Overhead*	*1,212*		*3,636*

On April 30, the production reports prepared by the department foremen gave the following information in regard to inventories and goods started and finished in each department during the month:

	Grinding Department	Mixing Department	Packaging Department
Units in the beginning inventories of goods in process..	*30,000*	*16,000*	*-0-*
Stage of completion at beginning of the period of the beginning inventories of goods in process.......	*⅓*	*¼*	
Units started in process and finished during period.....	*70,000*	*85,000*	*101,000*
Total units finished and transferred to next department or to finished goods..	*100,000*	*101,000*	*101,000*
Units in the ending inventories of goods in process..	*20,000*	*15,000*	*-0-*
Stage of completion of ending inventories of goods in process.................	*¼*	*⅓*	

After receiving the production reports, the company's cost accountant prepared a process cost summary, Illustration 147, for the grinding department. A process cost summary is a report peculair to a processing company; a separate one is prepared for each processing department and shows: (1) the costs charged to the department, (2) the department's equivalent unit processing costs, and (3) the costs applicable to the department's goods in process inventories and its goods started and finished.

Observe in Illustration 147 that a process cost summary has three sections. In the first, headed Costs Charged to the Department, are summarized the costs charged to the department. Information for this section comes from the department's goods in process account. Compare the first section of Illustration 147 with the goods in process account of the grinding department as shown on page 678.

The second section of a process cost summary shows the calculation of equivalent unit costs. The information for this section as to units involved and fractional units applicable to the inventories comes from the department's production report (Illustration 146). Information as to material, labor, and overhead costs comes from the first section of the summary.

Notice in the second section of Illustration 147 that two separate equivalent unit calculations are made. Two calculations are required

Illustration 147

DELTA PROCESSING COMPANY
Process Cost Summary, Grinding Department
For Month Ended April 30, 19--

COSTS CHARGED TO THE DEPARTMENT:

Material requisitioned	$ 9,900
Labor charged.	5,700
Overhead costs incurred.	4,275
	$19,875
Goods in process at the beginning of the month	4,250
Total Costs to Be Accounted for.	$24,125

EQUIVALENT UNIT PROCESSING COSTS:

Material:	Units Involved	Fraction of a Unit Added	Equivalent Units Added
Beginning inventory	30,000	-0-	-0-
Units started and finished	70,000	1	70,000
Ending inventory	20,000	1	20,000
			90,000

Unit processing cost for material: $9,900 ÷ 90,000 = $0.11

Labor and Overhead:	Units Involved	Fraction of a Unit Added	Equivalent Units Added
Beginning inventory	30,000	2/3	20,000
Units started and finished	70,000	1	70,000
Ending inventory	20,000	1/4	5,000
			95,000

Unit processing cost for labor: $5,700 ÷ 95,000 = $0.06
Unit processing cost for overhead: $4,275 ÷ 95,000 = $0.045

COSTS APPLICABLE TO THE WORK OF THE DEPARTMENT:

Goods in Process, One-third Processed at the Beginning of April:

Costs charged to the beginning inventory of goods in process during previous month	$4,250	
Material added (all added during March).	-0-	
Labor applied (20,000 x $0.06)	1,200	
Overhead applied (20,000 x $0.045)	900	
Cost to process.		$ 6,350

Goods Started and Finished in the Department during April:

Material added (70,000 x $0.11).	$7,700	
Labor applied (70,000 x $0.06)	4,200	
Overhead applied (70,000 x $0.045)	3,150	
Cost to process.		15,050
Total cost of the goods processed in tne department and transferred to the mixing department (100,000 Units at $0.214 Each)		$21,400

Goods in Process, One-fourth Processed at the End of April:

Material added (20,000 x $0.11).	$2,200	
Labor applied (5,000 x $0.06).	300	
Overhead applied (5,000 x $0.045).	225	
Cost to one-fourth process		2,725
Total Costs Accounted for.		$24,125

because material added to the product and labor and overhead added are not added in the same proportions and at the same stages in the processing procedure of this particular department. As previously stated, all material is added at the beginning of this department's process, and labor and overhead are added evenly throughout the process. Consequently, the number of equivalent units of material added is not the same as the number of equivalent units of labor and overhead added.

Observe in the second section of Illustration 147, in the calculation of equivalent finished units for materials, that the beginning inventory is assigned no material. In the grinding department all material placed in process is placed there at the beginning of the process. The 30,000 beginning inventory units were one-third completed at the beginning of April. Consequently, these units received all their material during March when their processing was first begun, and should bear none of the $9,900 cost of material issued to the department during April.

Notice in the calculation of equivalent finished units of labor and overhead that the beginning inventory units which were one-third completed at the beginning, are each assigned two thirds of a unit of labor and overhead. If these units were one-third completed on April 1, then they were two-thirds completed during the April cost period. Beginning accounting students often have difficulty at this point. In a situation such as this, they are apt to assign only an additional one-third unit of labor and overhead when two thirds is required.

A process cost summary's third section shows how the material, labor, and overhead costs charged to a department are assigned to its inventories and goods started and finished. Notice in Illustration 147, for example, how costs are assigned to the beginning work in process inventory. The first amount charged is the $4,250 beginning inventory costs. This amount represents the material, labor, and overhead costs used to one-third complete the inventory during March, the previous cost period. Normally, the second charge to a beginning inventory is for additional material assigned to it. However, in the grinding department no additional material costs are assigned during April to the beginning inventory because these units received all of their material when their processing was first begun during the previous month. The second charge to the beginning inventory is for labor. The $1,200 portion of applicable labor costs is calculated by multiplying the number of equivalent finished units of labor used in completing the beginning inventory by the cost of an equivalent finished unit of labor (20,000 equivalent finished units of labor at $0.06 each). The third charge to the beginning inventory is for overhead. The applicable $900 portion is determined by multiplying the equivalent finished units of overhead used in completing the beginning inventory by the cost of an equivalent finished unit of overhead (20,000 × $0.045).

After costs are assigned to the beginning inventory, the procedures used in assigning these costs are repeated in assigning costs to the work started and finished and to the ending inventory.

Notice in the second section of the grinding department's process cost summary that the equivalent finished unit cost for material is $0.11, for labor is $0.06, and for overhead is $0.045. The total of these three costs is $0.215. Notice, however, in the third section of the summary that the unit cost of the 100,000 units finished and transferred is $0.214. The cost of the units finished and transferred is $0.214, which is less than $0.215, because unit costs were less in the department during the previous month, and the 30,000 beginning units were one-third processed at these lower costs during the previous month.

After completing the grinding department's cost summary, the accountant prepared the following entry to transfer from the goods in process account of the grinding department to the goods in process account of the mixing department the cost of the 100,000 units processed in the department and transferred to the mixing department during April. Information for the entry as to the cost of the units transfer was taken from the third section of the process cost summary reproduced in Illustration 147.

Apr.	30	*Goods in Process, Mixing Department.........*	*21,400.00*	
		Goods in Process, Grinding Department...		*21,400.00*
		To transfer the cost of the 100,000 units of product transferred to the mixing department.		

Posting the foregoing entry had the effect on the accounts shown in Illustration 148. Observe that the effect is one of transferring and advancing costs from one department to the next just as the product is transferred and advanced in the manufacturing procedure.

After posting the entry transferring to the mixing department the grinding department costs of processing the 100,000 units transferred, the cost accountant prepared a process cost summary for the mixing department. Information required in its preparation was taken from the mixing department's goods in process account and production report. The summary appeared as in Illustration 149.

Two points in Illustration 149 require special attention. The first is the calculation of equivalent finished units. Since the materials, labor, and overhead of the mixing department are all added to the product evenly throughout the process of this department, only a single equivalent unit calculation is required. This differs from the grinding department, the previous department, where it will be recalled that two equivalent unit calculations were required. Two were required because material placed in

Illustration 148

Goods in Process, Grinding Department

Date		Explanation	Debit	Credit	Balance
Apr.	1	Beginning inventory			4,250
	30	Materials	9,900		14,150
	30	Labor	5,700		19,850
	30	Overhead	4,275		24,125
	30	Units to mixing department		21,400	2,725

Goods in Process, Mixing Department

Date		Explanation	Debit	Credit	Balance
Apr.	1	Beginning inventory			3,785
	30	Materials	2,040		5,825
	30	Labor	3,570		9,395
	30	Overhead	1,020		10,415
	30	Units from grinding department	21,400		31,815

process and the labor and overhead placed in process were not placed in process at the same stages in the processing procedure.

The second point needing special attention in the mixing department cost summary is the method of handling the grinding department costs transferred to this department. During April, 100,000 units of product with accumulated grinding department costs of $21,400 were transferred to the mixing department. Of these 100,000 units, 85,000 were started in process in the department, finished, and transferred to the packaging department. The remaining 15,000 were still in process in the department at the end of the cost period.

Notice in the first section of Illustration 149 how the $21,400 of grinding department costs transferred to the mixing department are added to the other costs charged to the department. Compare the information in this first section with the mixing department's goods in process account as it is shown on page 678 and again in Illustration 148.

Notice again in the third section of the mixing department's process cost summary how the $21,400 of grinding department costs are apportioned between the 85,000 units started and finished and the 15,000 units still in process in the department. The 16,000 beginning goods in process units received none of this $21,400 charge because they were transferred from the grinding department during the previous month. Their grinding department costs are included in the $3,785 beginning inventory costs.

Illustration 149

DELTA PROCESSING COMPANY
Process Cost Summary, Mixing Department
For Month Ended April 30, 19--

COSTS CHARGED TO THE DEPARTMENT:

Materials requisitioned	$ 2,040
Labor charged	3,570
Overhead costs incurred	1,020
Total Processing Costs.	$ 6,630
Goods in process at the beginning of the month.	3,785
Costs transferred from the grinding department (100,000 units at $0.214) each)	21,400
Total Costs to Be Accounted for	$31,815

EQUIVALENT UNIT PROCESSING COSTS:

Materials, Labor, and Overhead:	Units Involved	Fraction of a Unit Added	Equivalent Units Added
Beginning inventory	16,000	3/4	12,000
Units started and finished.	85,000	1	85,000
Ending inventory.	15,000	1/3	5,000
Total equivalent units.			102,000

Unit processing cost for materials: $2,040 ÷ 102,000 = $0.02
Unit processing cost for labor: $3,570 ÷ 102,000 = $0.035
Unit processing cost for overhead: $1,020 ÷ 102,000 = $0.01

COSTS APPLICABLE TO THE WORK OF THE DEPARTMENT:

Goods in Process, One-Fourth Completed at the Beginning of April:

Costs charged to the beginning inventory of goods in process during previous month	$ 3,785	
Materials added (12,000 x $0.02).	240	
Labor applied (12,000 x $0.035)	420	
Overhead applied (12,000 x $0.01)	120	
Cost to process		$ 4,565

Goods Started and Finished in the Department during April:

Costs in the grinding department (85,000 x $0.214).	$18,190	
Materials added (85,000 x $0.02).	1,700	
Labor applied (85,000 x $0.035)	2,975	
Overhead applied (85,000 x $0.01)	850	
Cost to process		23,715
Total accumulated cost of goods transferred to the packaging department (101,000 units at $0.28)		$28,280

Goods in Process, One-Third Processed at the End of April:

Costs in the grinding department (15,000 x $0.214).	$ 3,210	
Materials added (5,000 x $0.02)	100	
Labor applied (5,000 x $0.035).	175	
Overhead applied (5,000 x $0.01).	50	
Cost to one-third process		3,535
Total Costs Accounted for		$31,815

The third section of the mixing department's process cost summary shows that 101,000 units of product with accumulated costs of $28,280 were completed in the department during April and transferred to the packaging department. The cost accountant used the following entry to transfer the accumulated cost of these 101,000 units from the mixing department's goods in process account to the goods in process account of the packaging department.

Apr.	*30*	*Goods in Process, Packaging Department.....*	*28,280.00*	
		Goods in Process, Mixing Department....		*28,280.00*
		To transfer the accumulated grinding department and mixing department costs of the 101,000 units transferred to the packaging department.		

Posting the foregoing entry had the effect shown in Illustration 150. Observe that again the effect is one of transferring and advancing costs from the goods in process account of one department to that of the next just as the product was transferred and advanced in the manufacturing procedure.

After posting the entry transferring the $28,280 of accumulated grinding department and mixing department costs to the goods in process account of the packaging department, the cost accountant prepared for the packaging department the process cost summary of Illustration 151.

Since there were no beginning or ending goods in process inventories in the packaging department, the process cost summary of Illustration 151 is much simplified. The lack of goods in process inventories makes an

Illustration 150

Goods in Process, Mixing Department

Date		Explanation	Debit	Credit	Balance
Apr.	*1*	*Beginning inventory*			*3,785*
	30	*Materials*	*2,040*		*5,825*
	30	*Labor*	*3,570*		*9,395*
	30	*Overhead*	*1,020*		*10,415*
	30	*Units from grinding department*	*21,400*		*31,815*
	30	*Units to packaging department*		*28,280*	*3,535*

Goods in Process, Packaging Department

Date		Explanation	Debit	Credit	Balance
Apr.	*30*	*Materials*	*1,515*		*1,515*
	30	*Labor*	*909*		*2,424*
	30	*Overhead*	*1,212*		*3,636*
	30	*Units from mixing department*	*28,280*		*31,916*

Illustration 151

DELTA PROCESSING COMPANY
Process Cost Summary, Packaging Department
For Month Ended April 31, 19--

```
Costs Charged to the Department:
  Materials requisitioned . . . . . . . . .      $ 1,515
  Labor charged . . . . . . . . . . . . .            909
  Overhead costs incurred . . . . . . . .          1,212
    Total processing costs. . . . . . . .        $ 3,636
  Costs transferred from the mixing depart-
    ment (101,000 units at $0.28 each). . .       28,280
    Total Costs Charged to the 101,000
    Units Received in the Department,
    Packaged and Transferred to Finished
    Goods (101,000 Units at $0.316 Each)         $31,916
```

```
Unit Processing Costs:
  101,000 units of product were received in
  this department, processed and trans-
  verred to finished goods. There were no
  inventories of goods in process.
    Unit processing cost for materials: $1,515 ÷
      101,000 = $0.015
    Unit processing cost for labor: $909 ÷ 101,000 =
      $0.009
    Unit processing cost for overhead: $1,212 ÷
      101,000 = $0.012
```

equivalent finished unit calculation unnecessary. Also, since there were no inventories, all costs charged to the department were applicable to the 101,000 units of product received in the department, packaged, and transferred to finished goods. Consequently, there was no need of a so-called third section on the summary to apportion costs between inventories and units started and finished.

After completing the cost summary for the packaging department, the cost accountant prepared and posted the following entry to transfer from the goods in process account of the packaging department to the Finished Goods account the $31,916 accumulated costs of the goods completed by the company in April.

Apr.	*30*	*Finished Goods*.....................................	31,916.00	
		Goods in Process, Packaging Department......		31,916.00
		To transfer to Finished Goods the accumulated		
		costs of goods completed during April.		

Posting the foregoing entry has the effect shown in Illustration 152.

Illustration 152

Goods in Process, Packaging Department

Date	Explanation	Debit	Credit	Balance
Apr. 30	*Materials*	*1,515*		*1,515*
30	*Labor*	*909*		*2,424*
30	*Overhead*	*1,212*		*3,636*
30	*Units from mixing department*	*28,280*		*31,916*
30	*Units to finished goods*		*31,916*	*–0–*

Finished Goods

Date	Explanation	Debit	Credit	Balance
Apr. 30	*Units from packaging depart-ment*	*31,916*		*31,916*

Observe that again the effect is one of transferring and advancing costs.

STANDARD COSTS

Many large concerns use cost accounting systems based on standard costs. As was explained in Chapter 20, a standard cost is a cost established by engineering and accounting studies and is the cost that should be incurred under normal conditions in producing a given product or part. When a concern uses standard costs, both its standard costs and its actual costs are commonly taken into the accounts. This requires some rather complicated bookkeeping, and your authors think it wise to defer a discussion of this to an advanced cost accounting course.

QUESTIONS FOR CLASS DISCUSSION

1. What is the basic difference between process cost accounting and job order cost accounting?

2. During a cost accounting period the molding department of a manufacturing firm using a process cost system had charged to it $2,100 of materials, $4,130 of labor, and $1,750 of overhead. During the period the department produced 100,000 units of finished product. What was the cost per unit for materials, labor, and overhead?

3. The materials used summary of a company using a process cost system shows the following costs for materials issued to its three processing departments during a cost period:

Melting department..............................$2,350
Molding department.............................. 1,875
Finishing department............................ 600
                                                $4,825

Give the general journal entry to record the information of the summary.

4. The labor cost summary of a company using a process cost system shows the following costs for labor in its departments:

Melting department..............................$ 3,400
Molding department.............................. 2,150
Finishing department............................ 4,725
                                                $10,275

Give the general journal entry to record the information of the summary.

5. The Gamma Company operates a process cost accounting system. The company follows the practice of charging all overhead items to undepart-

DEPARTMENT OVERHEAD COSTS ALLOCATION SHEET
For Period Ended May 31, 19—

Undepartmentalized Cost Accounts	Basis of Allocation	Cost Account Balance	Allocation of Costs		
			Melting Dept.	Molding Dept.	Finishing Dept.
Factory supervision	*Number of employees*	*$3,800*	*$1,000*	*$1,000*	*$1,800*
Personal property taxes	*Value of property*	*900*	*200*	*300*	*400*
Expired insurance	*Value of property*	*450*	*100*	*150*	*200*
Depreciation of machinery	*Value of property*	*1,350*	*300*	*450*	*600*
Light and power	*Meters*	*750*	*50*	*100*	*600*
Rent of building	*Floor space*	*1,000*	*200*	*300*	*500*
		$8,250	*$1,850*	*$2,300*	*$4,100*

mentalized cost accounts. At the end of each cost accounting period the company prepares a departmental overhead costs allocation sheet to determine the overhead applicable to each of its departments. The allocation sheet for the cost period ending May 31 is shown above. Prepare a general journal entry to close the undepartmentalized cost accounts and to charge the overhead to the processing departments.

6. What is a production report? What information is commonly shown on a production report?

7. What is an equivalent finished unit of (*a*) labor, (*b*) materials, and (*c*) overhead? Why are equivalent finished units calculated for a processing department?

8. Compute the output of a department measured in equivalent finished units under the following assumptions:

a) Beginning goods in process inventory, 12,000 units, three-fourths completed at the beginning of the cost period.

b) Goods started and finished during the period, 63,000 units.

c) Ending goods in process inventory, 9,000 units, two-thirds completed.

9. A department of a processing firm had charged to it during a cost period $54,000 of labor. At the beginning of the cost period the department had in process 15,000 units of product that were two-thirds finished. During the period the department started and finished an additional 18,000 units of product. At the end of the period the department had 8,000 units of product that were one-half finished. How much of the $54,000 of labor should be charged to each inventory and to the goods started and finished? (Assume that labor is added to the product evenly throughout the process.)

10. How many equivalent finished unit calculations are required in the preparation of a process cost summary for each of the following departments?

Department A In Department A all materials, labor, and overhead are added to the product of the department evenly throughout the process.

Department B In Department B all materials are added at the beginning of the process, and labor and overhead are added evenly throughout the process.

Department C In Department C all materials are added at the beginning of the process. One half the labor added to the product in this department is added evenly throughout the first one third of the process, and the other half is added evenly throughout the last two thirds of the process. Overhead is added evenly throughout the entire process.

11. Differentiate between a department production report and a department process cost summary.

12. The process cost summary of a department normally has three sections. What is shown in each section?

PROBLEMS

Problem 23–1

Cactus Processing Company manufactures a product on a continuous basis in a single processing department. During a cost period the department had $20,125 of labor charged to it and during the same period 23,800 units of product were finished in the department and transferred to finished goods. Of the 23,800 units finished, 8,000 were in process at the beginning of the cost period and 15,800 were begun and finished during the period. The 8,000 units in process at the beginning were two-fifths complete as to labor when the period began. In addition to the foregoing units, 7,200 units were in process in the department, one-third complete as to labor when the period ended.

Required:

Calculate the equivalent units of labor applied to the product of the department, the cost of an equivalent unit of labor, and the amounts of labor cost applicable to the goods started and finished and to the department's beginning and ending goods in process inventories.

Problem 23–2

The product of Sage Processing Company is produced on a continuous basis in a single processing department in which material, labor, and overhead are added to the product evenly throughout the manufacturing process.

At the end of the current May cost period, after the material, labor, and overhead costs were charged to the Goods in Process account of the single processing department, the account appeared as follows:

Goods in Process

May	1	Balance	1,362	
	31	Materials	5,325	
	31	Labor	10,863	
	31	Overhead	15,194	
			32,744	

During the cost period the company finished and transferred to finished goods 72,000 units of the product, of which, 9,000 were in process at the beginning of the period and 63,000 were begun and finished during the period. The 9,000 that were in process were one-third processed when the period began. In addition to the foregoing units, 8,000 additional units were in process and were one-fourth completed at the end of the cost period.

Required:
1. Prepare a process cost summary for the department.
2. Draft the general journal entry to transfer to Finished Goods the cost of the product finished in the department during the month.

Problem 23–3

Hardrock Processing Company manufactures a simple product on a continuous basis in one department. All materials are added in the manufacturing process of this product when the process is first begun. Labor and overhead are added evenly throughout the process.

During the current April cost period the company completed and transferred to finished goods 43,000 units of the product. These consisted of 5,000 units that were in process at the beginning of the period and 38,000 units begun and finished during the period. The 5,000 beginning goods in process units were complete as to materials and four-fifths complete as to labor and overhead when the period began.

In addition to the foregoing units, 6,000 additional units were in process at the end of the period, complete as to materials and one-half complete as to labor and overhead.

Since the company has only one processing department, it has only one Goods in Process account. At the end of the period, after entries recording material, labor, and overhead had been posted, the account appeared as follows:

Goods in Process

Apr. 1	*Balance*	*5,333*
30	*Materials*	*27,060*
30	*Labor*	*9,744*
30	*Overhead*	*14,868*
		57,005

Required:

Prepare a process cost summary and the entry to transfer to Finished Goods the cost of the product completed in the department during April.

Problem 23–4

Ringo Processing Company manufactures on a continuous basis a product that is processed in two departments, Department A and Department B. At the end of the May cost period, after entries recording material, labor, and overhead costs were posted, the goods in process accounts of the two departments appeared as follows:

Goods in Process, Department A

May 1	*Balance*	*3,095*
31	*Materials*	*7,500*
31	*Labor*	*6,050*
31	*Overhead*	*3,850*

Goods in Process, Department B

May 1	*Balance*	*5,950*
31	*Materials*	*17,700*
31	*Labor*	*16,320*
31	*Overhead*	*6,720*

The May departmental production reports gave the following information:

	Department A	Department B
May 1 inventory of goods in process........................	*15,000 units*	*12,000 units*
State of completion on May 1....	*⅓*	*¼*
Product started and finished.....	*40,000 units*	*47,000 units*
May 31 inventory of goods in process........................	*10,000 units*	*8,000 units*
Stage of completion on May 31	*½*	*½*

Ringo Processing Company assumes all material placed in process in Department A is placed in process when the department's process is first begun. It further assumes labor and overhead applied to the product of the department are applied evenly throughout the process.

The company also assumes all material, labor, and overhead added to the product in Department B are added evenly throughout the department's process.

At the end of the May cost period, after charging each department with its share of material, labor, and overhead costs, and after receiving the department production reports, the cost accountant of the company prepared the following process cost summary for Department A.

RINGO PROCESSING COMPANY
Process Cost Summary, Department A
For Month Ended May 31, 19—

Costs Charged to the Department:

Materials requisitioned......................	$ 7,500.00
Labor charged...............................	6,050.00
Overhead costs incurred....................	3,850.00
	$17,400.00
Goods in process at the beginning of the	
month...................................	3,095.00
Total Costs to Be Accounted for.............	$20,495.00

Equivalent Unit Processing Costs:

Material:	Units Involved	Fraction of a Unit Added	Equivalent Units Added
Beginning inventory.......	15,000	–0–	–0–
Units started and finished.	40,000	1	40,000
Ending inventory..........	10,000	1	10,000
			50,000

Unit processing cost for material: $7,500 ÷ 50,000 = $0.15

Labor and Overhead:	Units Involved	Fraction of a Unit Added	Equivalent Units Added
Beginning inventory.......	15,000	⅔	10,000
Units started and finished.	40,000	1	40,000
Ending inventory..........	10,000	½	5,000
			55,000

Unit processing cost for labor: $6,050 ÷ 55,000 = $0.11
Unit processing cost for overhead: $3,850 ÷ 55,000 = $0.07

Costs Applicable to the Work of the Department:

Goods in Process, One-third Processed at the Beginning of May:

Cost charged to beginning inventory of
goods in process during the previous
month..............................$3,095.00
Materials added (all added during April)..   –0–
Labor applied (10,000 × $0.11)............ 1,100.00
Overhead applied (10,000 × $0.07)........ 700.00
      Cost to process (carried forward)..... $ 4,895.00

Goods Started and Finished in the Department during May:

Materials added (40,000 × $0.15).........$6,000.00
Labor applied (40,000 × $0.11)............ 4,400.00
Overhead applied (40,000 × $0.07)........ 2,800.00
      Cost to process.....................   13,200.00
Total Cost of the Goods Processed in the
Department and Transferred to De-
partment B (55,000 Units at $0.329
Each)................................ $18,095.00

Goods in Process, One-half Processed at the End of May:

Materials added (10,000 × $0.15).........$1,500.00
Labor applied (5,000 × $0.11)............. 550.00
Overhead applied (5,000 × $0.07)......... 350.00
      Cost to one-half process.............   2,400.00
Total Costs Accounted for................ $20,495.00

Required:
1. Prepare the general journal entry to transfer to Department B the cost of the 55,000 units processed in Department A and transferred during May.
2. After completing Requirement 1, prepare a process cost summary for Department B.
3. Prepare the general journal entry to transfer to the Finished Goods account the costs of the product finished in Department B.

CLASS EXERCISE

Exercise 23–1

Forty-eight thousand units of product were completed in Department Z and transferred to finished goods during a cost period. Of these 48,000 units, 12,000 were in process and were one-third completed at the beginning of the period and 36,000 units were begun and completed during the period. In addition to the foregoing units, 10,000 more units were in process in the department, three-fifths processed at the period end.

Required:
Calculate the equivalent units of material added to the product processed in Department Z during the period under each of the following unrelated assumptions:

a) All the materials added to the product of the department are added when the department's process is first begun.

b) The materials added to the product of the department are added evenly throughout the department's process.

c) One half the materials added in the department are added when the department's process is first begun and the other half is added when the process is three-fourths completed.

ALTERNATE PROBLEMS

Problem 23–1A

In the burnishing department of a processing concern labor is added to the department's product evenly throughout its processing. During a cost period 50,000 units of product were finished in this department and transferred to finished goods. Of these 50,000 units, 15,000 were in process at the beginning of the period and 35,000 were begun and completed during the period. The 15,000 beginning goods in process units were one-fifth completed when the period began. In addition to the foregoing units, 9,000 additional units were in process and were one-third completed at the period end.

Required:
Under the assumption that $13,800 of labor was charged to the burnishing department during the period, determine: (1) the equivalent units of labor applied to the department's product, (2) the cost of an equivalent unit of labor, and (3) the shares of the $13,800 that should be charged to the beginning inventory, the units started and finished, and the ending inventory.

Problem 23–2A

Two operations, mixing and finishing, and two departments are used in the manufacturing procedure of Mountain Processing Company. The procedure is begun in the mixing department and completed in the finishing department.

At the beginning of the May cost period there were 5,000 units of product in the mixing department which were three-fifths processed. These units were completed during the period and transferred to the finishing department. Also, the processing of 31,000 additional units were begun in the mixing department during the period. Of these 31,000 units, 23,000 were finished and transferred to the finishing department. The remaining 8,000 units were in the department in a one-half processed state at the end of the period.

It is assumed that the material, labor, and overhead applied in the mixing department are applied evenly throughout the process of the department.

At the end of the cost period, after entries recording materials, labor, and overhead were posted, the Goods in Process, Mixing Department account of the company appeared as follows:

Goods in Process, Mixing Department

May 1	Balance	2,901	
31	Materials	9,280	
31	Labor	12,209	
31	Overhead	6,090	
		30,480	

Required:
1. Prepare a process cost summary for the mixing department.
2. Prepare the journal entry to transfer to the finishing department the cost of the goods completed in the mixing department and transferred.

Problem 23–3A

Hidden Valley Company makes a product that is processed in two departments. All the materials of the product are added in the first department, Department One, and labor and overhead are applied. The product is then complete insofar as Department One is concerned and it is transferred to Department Two. In Department Two more labor and overhead are applied and the product is completed and transferred to finished goods.

At the end of a cost period after entries charging Department Two with its labor and overhead costs and the cost of the units transferred to it from Department One were posted, the goods in process account of the department appeared as follows:

Goods in Process, Department Two

Date		Explanations	Debit	Credit	Balance
Apr.	1	Balance (1,200 units ⅔ processed)			2,640
	30	Labor	3,500		6,140
	30	Overhead	5,400		11,540
	30	12,000 units transferred from			
		Department One	19,200		30,740
	30	10,200 units transferred to			
		Finished Goods		?	?

Required:
1. Under the assumptions (a) there were no units lost or spoiled in Department Two during the period, (b) the units in the department's ending inventory were one-fifth processed at the period end, and (c) labor and overhead added to the product of the department are added evenly throughout the department's process, prepare a process cost summary for Department Two.

2. After preparing the process cost summary, prepare the entry to transfer to finished goods the cost of the units finished in the department and transferred.

DECISION PROBLEM 23A—RED CLAY BRICK COMPANY

Pat Day and associates purchased land with abundant clay deposits several years ago. Red Clay Brick Company was organized and started manufacturing bricks in sufficient quantities to supply local demands. Expanding business and a desire to enter wider markets have made Mr. Day, president of the company, realize that better cost and inventory figures are needed.

The production process may be described as follows. Clay and sand are mined from the clay field and delivered by trams to the clay shed. There the clay and sand are mixed with other ingredients such as manganese and red oxide to provide appropriate texture and colorization. The mixture and water provide a "stiff mud." This mud is forced through machines which mold the bricks. These bricks are taken by hand from a conveyor belt and placed on small trucks and pushed on a small rail track to drying sheds. Here most of the moisture is evaporated from the bricks which remain on the small trucks. These are then pushed by hand to kilns and loaded into various kilns for the purpose of burning. After the burning process, the bricks are loaded either directly into trucks and railroad cars or are carted to the brickyard where they will await sale.

At any time inventories of work in process are to be found in the drying sheds and in the kilns. Up to this time no attempt has been made to determine the cost of any of the several manufacturing processes. A substantial inventory of finished bricks is usually on hand in the brickyard. This inventory will vary considerably from month to month and from year to year, depending upon the market.

Write a report to Mr. Day with special attention to the following:

1. Your outline of the cost system which would facilitate determining the cost of bricks manufactured. What departments would you suggest as cost centers? Name or describe these departments so that each can be identified.
2. In your opinion, approximately how could the cost of in-process inventory be determined in each department?
3. How would the cost per 1,000 bricks produced be determined?
4. What aids should the cost system provide management?

DECISION PROBLEM 23B—MILL TOWN FEED COMPANY

Bill Dodd and Tom Planty have operated a feed mill for several years. Two kinds of feed are manufactured and sold, one a mixture of small maize grain and ground bulk material (alfalfa, etc.) and the other based on low-grade peanuts with bulk materials of peanut stick, hay, etc. A small amount of vitamins and minerals are added to both feed mixtures.

Both feeds are manufactured by approximately the same processes. The materials are first stored in the warehouse and in grain elevators. From there they are carried by small trams or automatic conveyors to a screening process, from there to grinding and mixing, next to sacking and labeling, and finally to storage or directly to trucks or freight cars. Little or no work in process remains when the mill is shut down after each day's operation.

In the past the actual costs of these feeds have not been determined until the end of each year. Finished feed has been priced for sale at 1.6 times the cost of the basic grain or nuts. Thus feed prices have varied throughout the year as the cost of the basic grain or nuts changed.

The widening market demands more accurate cost information for pricing purposes. Mr. Dodd and Mr. Planty also recognize that increasing labor costs are not taken into account by their present pricing formula.

They are not familiar with cost systems but feel that some kind of cost system is needed by their firm. You are asked to write a report outlining your recommendations for an adequate costing method which would give better pricing information. Include in your recommendations brief descriptions of the kind of cost methods available giving specific instructions as to the accumulation of the costs and the determination of the manufacturing costs of the two finished feeds under each system.

Management's
Use of Accounting Data

ALTHOUGH management uses in many ways information gathered by means of accounting; almost all the uses may be grouped under three main headings: (1) reporting the effects of past decisions, (2) controlling operations, and (3) planning.

The balance sheet, the income statement, and their related schedules, such as the manufacturing statement, are formal reports used by management to show the effects of past decisions. The collection of data for and the preparation and use of these reports were subjects of several earlier chapters, and their analysis and interpretation is the subject of Chapter 26. Likewise, the use of accounting as a tool in controlling operations was illustrated with the discussion of controlling sales and purchases in Chapter 6 and controlling cash receipts and cash disbursements in Chapters 8 and 13. Consequently, these phases of management's use of accounting will be passed over for now, and this and the next chapter will be devoted to a discussion of the use of accounting data in planning.

PLANNING

A plan is a procedure or course of action; and planning is the process of examining several alternative courses and deciding which is best. Planning always requires decisions as to future actions.

Planning may involve one small part of a business, or it may involve the entire enterprise; consequently, in studying the use of accounting data in planning, it is best to consider as separate subjects: (1) period planning, and (2) project planning.

Period planning is better known as budgeting. It is the process of planning the entire activity of a business for a future period, usually one year, although many companies project their plans in a general way for from five to ten years ahead. Period planning is of vital interest to businessmen and is discussed in the next chapter.

Although period planning and project planning tend to merge into one another and period planning always involves project plans, project planning has to do primarily with decisions about small segments of a business or about individual projects such as buying or building new fixed assets, increasing business volume by entering new markets, increasing or decreasing the sales price of a product, and numerous others.

PURCHASE OF NEW INCOME-PRODUCING ASSETS

Plans involving the acquisition of new income-producing assets are among the most important faced by management. They are important not only because large sums of money are often involved but also because fixed assets, once acquired, may affect business operations for a long time.

Normally, when management considers the purchase of new income-producing assets, its problem is to choose between several alternate investment proposals. For example, a company may buy Machine A and produce and market the machine's product, or it may buy Machine B and produce and market a totally different product; but commonly, with limited funds, it cannot do both. In such cases, to help management compare and choose between alternate proposals, the *payback period* for each investment and the *rate of return on the average investment* in each proposal are calculated for purposes of comparison.

To illustrate these calculations, assume that Murray Company is considering several alternate fixed asset investments. Among the proposals is the purchase of a machine to be used in manufacturing a new product called Product 2XY. The new machine will cost $16,000, have an eight-year service life, and no salvage value. The company management estimates that 10,000 units of Product 2XY will be sold each year and the sales will result in an annual $1,800 profit, as shown in Illustration 153.

Illustration 153

PROFIT FROM PRODUCT 2XY SALES

Annual sales of Product 2XY.....................		*$30,000*
Deduct:		
Cost of materials, labor, and overhead other than depreciation on the new machine.......	*$15,500*	
Depreciation on new machine..................	*2,000*	
Additional selling and administrative expenses..	*8,900*	*26,400*
Annual before taxes profit from sale of product....		*$ 3,600*
Income taxes (assumed rate 50%)...............		*1,800*
Annual after taxes profit from product sales......		*$ 1,800*

Payback Period. Through the annual sale of 10,000 units of Product 2XY, Murray Company expects to gain $30,000 of revenue. The $30,000 is sufficient to recover all costs of producing and selling the 10,000 units and to leave an $1,800 profit. Among the costs recovered each year in the $30,000 of revenue is $2,000 depreciation on the new machine. Consequently, $3,800 ($2,000 depreciation plus the $1,800 profit) is available each year to "pay back" the machine's cost. Therefore the payback period on the $16,000 investment in this new machine is 4.21+ years and is calculated:

$$\$16,000 \quad \div \quad \$3,800 \quad = \quad 4.21+ \text{ Years to Recover Cost}$$

When other things are equal, in choosing between investment possibilities, the one having the shortest payback period is the best. However, other things must be equal, and the payback period should never be the only factor considered. This is because the payback period ignores the length of time revenue will continue to be earned after the end of the payback period. For example, one investment may pay back its cost in three years and cease to produce revenue at that point, while a second investment may require five years to pay back its cost but will continue to produce income for another 15 years.

Rate of Return on Average Investment. The rate of return on the average investment in a machine is calculated by dividing the after-tax profit from the sale of the machine's product by the average investment in the machine. For example, Murray Company estimates it will earn an $1,800 after-tax profit from selling the product of the $16,000 machine it proposes to buy. As to average investment, each year depreciation will reduce the book value of the machine $2,000; consequently, the company may assume it will have $16,000 invested in the machine during its first year, $14,000 during the second, $12,000 during the third, and so on for the machine's eight-year life. Or, in other words, the company may assume it will have an amount equal to the machine's book value invested each year. If it makes this assumption, then the average amount it will have invested during the eight-year life is the average of the machine's book values. This is $9,000 and may be calculated as follows:

Year	Book Value		
1................	$16,000		
2................	14,000		
3................	12,000	$\dfrac{\$72,000}{8}$	= $9,000 **Average Book Value**
4................	10,000		**and Average Investment**
5................	8,000		
6................	6,000		
7................	4,000		
8................	2,000		
Total........	$72,000		

In the foregoing calculation the eight yearly book values were averaged to determine average investment. A shorter way to the same answer is to average the book values of the machine's first and last years, in this manner:

$$\frac{\$16,000 + \$2,000}{2} = \$9,000$$

And since the answer is the same either way the calculation is made, the shorter calculation is preferable.

After average investment is determined, the rate of return on average investment is calculated, as previously stated, by dividing the estimated annual after-tax profit from the sale of the machine's product by average investment, as follows:

$$\$1,800 \div \$9,000 = 20\% \; Return \; on \; Average \; Investment$$

At this point students commonly want to know what is considered a good return on average investment. To this there is seldom a definite answer because an investment return is good or bad only when it is related to other investment returns. Also, factors other than return, such as risk, are always involved in an investment decision. However, when average investment returns are used in comparing and deciding between several fixed asset investments, the one having the least risk, the shortest payback period, and the highest return for the longest time is usually the best.

REPLACEMENT OF FIXED ASSETS

The replacement of obsolete equipment often gives management some of its most difficult problems. For example, Allen W. Oaks Company has a machine which it has used for two years. The machine cost $36,000, and its life was estimated when new at 12 years with no salvage value. An equipment salesman has offered the company a $5,000 trade-in allowance for this machine on a new semiautomatic machine having a $40,000 price. The new machine's life is estimated at ten years with no salvage value. The capacities of both the old and the new machines are the same; however, the equipment salesman in his efforts to sell the new machine offers the following statistics to show the annual savings **he claims** will result from purchasing the new equipment:

Operating Costs	Keep Old Machine	Buy New Machine
Labor to operate machine......................	$ 5,400	$1,800
Supplies...	450	500
Repairs..	200	300
Taxes..	350	400
Power..	1,200	1,250
Depreciation....................................	3,000	4,000
Total Operating Costs.....................	$10,600	$8,250

From the salesman's statistics the new semiautomatic machine appears to offer a $2,350 savings in total operating costs each year. However, in the statistics is a $3,000 charge for depreciation on the old machine, and since this is a *sunk cost*, it is irrelevant.

A sunk cost is a cost growing out of a past irrevocable decision. In this case the $3,000 annual depreciation charge grows from the decision made two years ago to buy the old machine. The company paid $36,000 for the machine and in two years has charged off $6,000 of the cost to depreciation. Consequently, at this point it may either keep the machine and absorb the remaining $30,000 of its cost in annual depreciation charges or it may trade the machine at a loss. Either way there is a sunk cost and this cost should not enter into the replacement decision.

Actually, insofar as the company is concerned the important consideration is: How can the product of these machines be gotten for the next ten years with the smallest outlay of additional funds, called *out-of-pocket costs?* A comparison of the estimated out-of-pocket costs of operating the two machines follows:

Out-of-Pocket Operating Costs	Keep Old Machine	Buy New Machine
Labor to operate machine.....................	$5,400	$1,800
Supplies......................................	450	500
Repairs.......................................	200	300
Taxes...	350	400
Power...	1,200	1,250
For recovery of additional capital..............		3,500
Interest on average additional investment......		1,155
Total Out-of-Pocket Operating Costs.........	$7,600	$8,905

The new machine sells for $40,000 less a $5,000 trade-in allowance, or it requires a $35,000 cash outlay. In the table of out-of-pocket costs, this $35,000 is spread over the life of the new machine by the annual $3,500 charge for recovery of additional capital.

If the company spends (takes out of its pocket) the $35,000 for the new machine and recovers this amount at the rate of $3,500 per year, an average of $19,250 additional capital (($35,000 + $3,500) ÷ 2 = $19,250) will be invested in the new machine during its life. And, regardless of where the funds are secured, the purchase will result in a sacrifice of interest. Consequently, if, say, 6 percent is the going interest rate, $1,155 in interest should be added to the new machine's other out-of-pocket costs.

Allen W. Oaks Company can get the product it sells from either the old or, if purchased, the new machine; and an examination of the table of out-of-pocket costs shows that $1,305 more out-of-pocket costs will be required annually in getting the product if the old machine is replaced with the new. Thus, the company will be better off keeping the old machine.

OUT-OF-POCKET AND SUNK COSTS

An out-of-pocket cost, as encountered in the previous section, is a cost requiring a current outlay of funds; while a sunk cost is a cost growing from a past irrevocable decision. Wages, power, supplies, and taxes are examples of out-of-pocket costs; and the unrecovered book value of a fixed asset is an example of a sunk cost.

As previously stated, sunk costs do not enter into a fixed asset exchange decision. However, management sometimes has difficulty recognizing this and is often reluctant to take the book loss involved in such an exchange. For example, if an obsolete machine having a $30,000 book value is salable or tradable for only $5,000, management may be reluctant to take the $25,000 book loss. However, it should not be. In reality, the $25,000 has been lost whether or not the asset is sold or traded; and the only reason the books do not show the asset at its $5,000 salvage value is that a judgment error was made in establishing its depreciation rate—the rate was not set sufficiently high to write off the obsolescence, which could have been unpredictable, that has occurred.

SCRAP OR REBUILD DEFECTIVE UNITS

The cost to manufacture a product that does not pass inspection is an additional example of a sunk cost, and like other sunk costs should not enter into a decision as to whether the product should be sold for scrap or rebuilt to pass inspection. For example, a concern has 10,000 defective units of product that cost $1 per unit to manufacture. The defective units can be sold as they are for $0.40 each, or they can be rebuilt for $0.80 per unit, after which they can be sold for their full price of $1.50 per unit. Should the company rebuild the units or should it sell them as they are? Obviously, the original $1 per unit cost does not enter into the decision; and the comparative returns from scrapping or rebuilding, based on the information given, are:

	As Scrap	Rebuilt
Sale of defective units................................	$4,000	$15,000
Less cost to rebuild.................................		8,000
Net Return..	$4,000	$ 7,000

From the foregoing it appears that rebuilding is the better decision, and this is true if the rebuilding does not interfere with normal operations.

However, suppose that in order to rebuild the defective units the company must forego manufacturing 10,000 new units that will cost $1 per unit to manufacture and can also be sold for $1.50 per unit. In this situation the comparative returns become:

	As Scrap	Rebuilt
Sale of defective units..........................	*$ 4,000*	*$15,000*
Less cost to rebuild............................		*8,000*
Sale of new units..............................	*15,000*	
Less cost to manufacture.......................	*10,000*	
Net Return....................................	*$ 9,000*	*$ 7,000*

If the defective units are sold without rebuilding, then the new units can be manufactured and sold, and the total net return will be $9,000 as shown in the first column above. Obviously this is better than foregoing the manufacture of the new units and rebuilding the defective units for a $7,000 net return.

PRODUCT PRICING

Prices are commonly not determined entirely by competition; most companies, as a rule, have some control over the prices at which they sell their products. This is true because, with the exception of certain raw materials, few similar products are exactly alike. Quality and style often differ. Also, services furnished by sellers of like products commonly vary. Consequently, similar products often sell at different prices.

Similar products can be sold at different prices because they are not exactly alike. And because similar products are not exactly alike, many companies in pricing a product can and do add a fair profit to the cost of the product's materials, labor, and overhead at the normal rate of production, and then by aggressive advertising and selling get the price asked.

In setting a product's price, many factors are usually involved. Two factors commonly involved are: (1) if demand is elastic, the number of units sold will vary with the price; and (2) when production volume varies, some expenses vary with volume and some remain fixed.

The first of the above factors stated in another way is: When demand for a product is elastic, and its price is lowered, at each successive lower price more units will be sold; and if the price is increased, at each successive higher price fewer units will be sold.

For a better understanding of the second factor just given, consider the following expenses incurred in driving an automobile 8,000 miles per year:

Expenses That Vary with Mileage		Annual Fixed Expenses	
Gasoline and oil	$210	Depreciation	$400
Tires	28	Insurance	72
Lubrication	16	License fee	10
Repairs	20		$482
	$274		

The lists show the expenses incurred in driving a car 8,000 miles per year. If the car were driven 12,000 miles in a year rather than 8,000, the expenses incurred for gasoline, oil, tires, lubrication, and repairs would increase in proportion to the increase in miles. However, the annual fixed expenses would remain more or less fixed and unchanged.

Just as there are expenses that remain fixed and expenses that vary with the miles a car is driven, there are also expenses that remain fixed and expenses that vary with the number of units of product manufactured in a factory. And, as will be shown, these fixed and variable expenses are often a factor in setting product prices.

In setting a product's price, management normally tries to set the price at an amount that will result in the greatest reasonable profit. The profit must be within reason or new competition and, sometimes, government intervention are invited. Normally, the greatest profit results from the price that produces the greatest *marginal revenue*. Marginal revenue is revenue from sales less variable expenses or expenses that vary with sales. For example, in setting the price for a new portable radio on which the variable expenses are $10 per set, management of Electronics, Inc., prepared the estimates of Illustration 154.

Obviously, from Illustration 154, the price that will produce the greatest marginal revenue is $17.50. At this price 30,000 sets can be sold and $225,000 in marginal revenue earned. The $17.50 price pays all variable expenses of its volume and leaves $225,000 in marginal revenue to cover the fixed expenses and provide a profit.

Illustration 154

Suggested Sales Price per Set	Units That Can Be Sold	Sales Revenue	Variable Expenses	Marginal Revenue
$20.00	10,000	$200,000	$100,000	$100,000
17.50	30,000	525,000	300,000	225,000
15.00	36,000	540,000	360,000	180,000
12.00	48,000	576,000	480,000	96,000
11.00	60,000	660,000	600,000	60,000

If a company manufactures more than one product, its pricing problems become more complicated and are often affected by capacity to produce. For example, Taplett Company manufactures two products, Product M having variable expenses of $12 per unit and Product S having variable expenses of $16 per unit. The products are similar but noncompetitive; and although the materials from which they are manufactured differ, the machines and methods used in their manufacture are almost identical. Taplett Company has the capacity to produce either 10,000 Product M units, or 10,000 Product S units, or a number of Product M units plus a number of Product S units, the sum of which is 10,000. In setting prices, Taplett Company prepared the Illustration 155 estimates.

Illustration 155

Suggested Sales Price per Unit	Units That Can Be Sold	Sales Revenue	Variable Expenses	Marginal Revenue
Product M				
$25.00	3,000	$ 75,000	$ 36,000	$39,000
20.00	5,000	100,000	60,000	40,000
18.00	6,000	108,000	72,000	36,000
16.00	8,000	128,000	96,000	32,000
15.00	10,000	150,000	120,000	30,000
Product S				
$30.00	2,000	$ 60,000	$ 32,000	$28,000
25.00	5,000	125,000	80,000	45,000
23.00	7,000	161,000	112,000	49,000
22.00	8,000	176,000	128,000	48,000
21.00	9,500	199,500	152,000	47,500

An examination of Illustration 155 shows that Taplett Company can gain the greatest marginal revenue from each product at prices of $20 for Product M and $23 for Product S. However, these prices require production of 5,000 Product M units and 7,000 Product S units, a total of 12,000 units. Consequently, since Taplett Company can produce only 10,000 units, the greatest revenue, within its capacity to produce, will be gained at prices of $25 for Product M and $23 for Product S.

Obviously pricing problems are usually more complicated than the ones in the foregoing simplified situations. For example, in the foregoing situations the fact that some expenses are neither fixed nor variable is ignored. Nevertheless, and regardless, factors of demand and fixed and variable expenses are present in almost all pricing situations; and if management is to maximize profits, it must know as much as possible about the fixed, the semifixed, and the variable expenses of manufacturing and marketing each of its products.

COST OF AN ADDITIONAL VOLUME OF BUSINESS

When a cost accounting system is in use, the per unit costs obtained from the system are average costs. Cost systems are designed to give average costs; and these average costs are useful in pricing a product and for many other purposes. However, when there are decisions as to the wisdom of obtaining an additional volume of business, average costs are not necessarily the important costs. Often, the important costs are the added costs, called *incremental costs* or *differential costs*. For example, a firm operating at its normal capacity, which is approximately 80 percent of full capacity, has annually been producing and selling approximately 100,000 units of product with these results:

Sales (100,000 units @ $10.00)................		*$1,000,000*
Materials (100,000 units @ $3.50)..............$350,000		
Labor (100,000 units @ $2.20)................	*220,000*	
Overhead (100,000 units @ $1.10).............	*110,000*	
Selling expenses (100,000 units @ $1.40).......	*140,000*	
Administrative expenses (100,000 units @		
$0.80).....................................	*80,000*	*900,000*
Operating Profit.........................		*$ 100,000*

The firm's sales department reports it has a customer who has offered to buy 10,000 units of product at $8.50 per unit. The sale to the new customer is several times larger than any previous sale made by the company, and it would not affect other business since it is in an entirely new territory. In considering the wisdom of accepting the order, management of the company asked its accounting department to prepare statistics to show the probable profit or loss that would result from the sale. The accounting department prepared the following estimates based upon the average costs previously given:

Sales (10,000 units @ $8.50).......................		*$85,000*
Materials (10,000 units @ $3.50).................$35,000		
Labor (10,000 units @ $2.20)......................	*22,000*	
Overhead (10,000 units @ $1.10)..................	*11,000*	
Selling expenses (10,000 units @ $1.40)............	*14,000*	
Administrative expenses (10,000 units @ $0.80)....	*8,000*	*90,000*
Operating Loss..............................		*$ 5,000*

If a decision were based solely on the foregoing estimates, the new business would likely be rejected. However, before rejecting the order, the costs of the new business were examined more closely and the following additional information obtained. (1) Manufacturing 10,000 additional units of product would require materials and labor at $3.50 and $2.20 per unit just as with normal production. (2) However, the 10,000 units could be manufactured with overhead costs in addition to those already incurred of only $5,000 for power, packing, and handling labor. (3) Commissions and other selling expenses resulting from the sale would amount to $2,000 in addition to the selling expenses already incurred. And (4) $1,000 additional administrative expenses in the form of clerical work would be required if the order were accepted. Based on this added information, the statement of Illustration 156 showing the effect of the additional business on the company's normal business was prepared.

Illustration 156

	Present Business	Additional Business	Present Plus the Additional Business
Sales.............	$1,000,000	$85,000	$1,085,000
Materials..........	$350,000	$35,000	$385,000
Labor.............	220,000	22,000	242,000
Overhead..........	110,000	5,000	115,000
Selling expenses....	140,000	2,000	142,000
Administrative expenses.........	80,000	1,000	81,000
Total...........	900,000	65,000	965,000
Operating Profit........	$ 100,000	$20,000	$ 120,000

It is obvious from Illustration 156 that when present business is charged with all present costs and the additional business is charged only with its incremental or differential costs, accepting the additional business at $8.50 per unit will apparently result in $20,000 additional profit.

Incremental or differential costs always apply to a particular situation at a particular time. For example, adding units to a given production volume might or might not increase depreciation expense. If the additional units require more machines and more space, depreciation expense is increased. Likewise, if present machines are used but the additional units shorten their life, more depreciation expense results. However, if present machines are used and their depreciation depends more on the passage of time or obsolescence, rather than on use, additional depreciation expense might not result from the added units of product.

BUY OR MAKE

Incremental or differential costs are often a factor in a decision as to whether a given part or product should be bought or made. For example, a manufacturer has idle machines upon which he can make Part 417 of his product. This part is presently purchased at a $1.20 delivered cost per unit. The manufacturer estimates that to make Part 417 would cost $0.45 for materials, $0.50 for labor, and an amount of overhead. At this point a question arises as to how much overhead should be charged. If the normal overhead rate of the department in which the part would be manufactured is 100 percent of direct labor cost, and this amount is charged against Part 417, then the unit costs of making Part 417 would be $0.45 for materials, $0.50 for labor, and $0.50 for overhead, a total of $1.45. At this cost, the manufacturer would be better off to buy the part at $1.20 each.

However, on a short-run basis the manufacturer might be justified in ignoring the normal overhead rate and in charging Part 417 for only the added overhead costs resulting from its manufacture. Among these added overhead costs might be, for example, power to operate the machines that would otherwise be idle, depreciation on the machines if the part's manufacture resulted in additional depreciation, and any other overhead that would be added to that already incurred. Furthermore, if these added overhead items total less than $0.25, the manufacturer might be justified on a short-run basis in manufacturing the part. However, on a long-term basis, Part 417 should be charged a full share of all overhead.

Any amount of overhead less than $0.25 per unit results in a total cost for Part 417 that is less than the $1.20 per unit purchase price. Nevertheless, in making a final decision as to whether the part should be bought or made, the manufacturer should consider in addition to costs such things as quality, the reactions of customers and suppliers, and other intangible factors. When these additional factors are considered, small cost differences may become a minor factor.

As a final note it should be observed that while the situations described in this chapter are only a sample of situations encountered and are in many cases oversimplified, they serve their purpose when they bring some of the factors involved in project planning to the student's attention.

QUESTIONS FOR CLASS DISCUSSION

1. If depreciation is an expense, explain why, when a machine's product is sold at a profit, the portion of the machine's cost recovered each year through the sale of the product includes both the profit from the product's sale and the year's depreciation.

2. During its life, what is the average amount invested in a machine that cost $12,000, has an estimated five-year service life, and an estimated $1,500 trade-in value?

3. Differentiate between a "sunk cost" and an "out-of-pocket cost."

4. When a company is contemplating the purchase of a new fixed asset to replace an obsolete fixed asset, which is usually more significant the costs "sunk" in the obsolete asset or the out-of-pocket costs necessary to acquire and operate the new asset?

5. Differentiate between fixed costs, semifixed costs, and variable costs.

6. A company manufactures and sells in the United States 500,000 units of a product at $5 per unit. Its manufacturing costs are $3 per unit, and its selling expenses are $1.50 per unit. Can you describe a situation under which the company may be willing to sell an additional 100,000 of the units abroad at $2.90 per unit?

7. Within a given marketing area, is the demand for gasoline elastic or inelastic? Should a service station operator who is about to start a price war by cutting his pump price for gasoline, give some consideration to the elasticity of the demand for gasoline? Why?

8. Six years ago a company purchased for $1,000,000 the mineral rights to an ore body containing 1,000,000 tons of ore. The company invested an additional $1,000,000 in mining machinery designed to exhaust the mine in ten years. During its first five years the mine produced 500,000 tons of ore that were sold at a profit. During its sixth year 100,000 tons of ore were mined; but due to technological changes in the manufacturing processes of the customers to whom the ore was normally sold, there was little demand for the ore and it was sold at a $1 per ton loss. If during the next four years the remaining 400,000 tons of ore could be mined and sold at a $1 per ton loss, and there was no prospect of ever doing better, would you recommend that the ore be mined and sold at a loss or would you recommend that the mine be closed so that there would be no loss from mining and selling the remaining ore?

9. A lumber mill buys logs at $45 per thousand board feet and manufactures them into a line of products including packing crates that are made from lumber that would be burned as waste if the crates were not manufactured. The cost accountant of the firm has produced statistics to show the crates are manufactured and sold at a loss. In his statistics he charges the crates with the lumber used in their manufacture at $45 per thousand board feet. If you were the manager of this firm, what information would you want before discontinuing the manufacture of the crates?

10. A company that normally manufactures 100,000 units of a product annually is considering the manufacture and sale of an additional 20,000 units annually. In discussing the costs of manufacturing the additional units, the term "differential costs" is used. What is meant by this term?

PROBLEMS

Problem 24–1

A company is considering the addition of a new product to its line. Production of the product will make use of factory space not presently in use and will require the purchase of new machinery costing $180,000 and having a 12-

year life and no salvage value. The following additional information is available:

Estimated annual sales of the new product.......$165,000	
Estimated costs:	
Materials......	*37,500*
Direct labor......	*41,000*
Overhead including depreciation on the new	
machinery......	*22,500*
Selling and administrative expenses......	*22,000*
State and federal income taxes......	*50%*

Required:

Calculate (1) the payback period on the investment in the new machinery, and (2) the rate of return on the average investment in new machinery.

Problem 24–2

Three years ago Roxbury Company purchased at a $20,000 total cost a stamping machine for use in its factory. Since that time a new semiautomatic machine that does the same work at a considerable savings in operating costs has come on the market. The company has received a $3,000 trade-in offer for its old machine on one of the new semiautomatic ones. The following statistics comparing the machines are available:

	Old Machine	**New Machine**
Cost of old machine and selling		
price of new......	*$20,000*	*$27,000*
Estimated life new......	*15 years*	*12 years*
Estimated salvage value......	*None*	*None*
Capacity in units per hour......	*2,000 units*	*2,000 units*
Maintenance, supplies, etc., per		
year......	*$1,700*	*$1,500*
Power costs per year......	*$ 400*	*$ 450*
Operating labor costs per year....	*$6,000*	*$1,800*

Roxbury Company is negotiating a $100,000 to $150,000, 5 percent, long-term loan. The funds are to be used in modernizing and expanding the plant. The larger, $150,000 loan is sufficient to cover the cost of the new machine; consequently, funds to purchase the machine are no problem.

Required:

Prepare statistics to show whether or not it would be wise for Roxbury Company to trade in its old machine on the new semiautomatic one.

Problem 24–3

Drexel Company's plant will produce 75,000 units of the company's product annually when running at capacity. The company is presently making and selling 60,000 units at $18 per unit. At this production level costs and expenses are as follows:

Manufacturing costs:
Fixed..*$4.50*
Variable.. *9.00*
Selling expenses:
Fixed.. *1.50*
Variable.. *.25*
Administrative expenses:
Fixed.. *1.00*
Variable.. *.20*

The company would like to increase output and sales to capacity; and the sales manager is of the opinion that capacity output can be sold if (*a*) the selling price is reduced to $17.50 per unit and (*b*) a sustained advertising campaign that will increase fixed selling expenses $25,000 annually is instituted.

Required:
Prepare a comparative income statement showing operating results with present sales in the first set of columns and expected results after the price reduction and advertising campaign in the second set of columns.

Problem 24–4

Como Company annually sells at $10 per unit 100,000 units of its product 3KT which cost $9 per unit to manufacture and sell. In producing and selling 100,000 of the units the company has the following costs and expenses:

Fixed manufacturing overhead costs.............*$100,000*
Fixed selling expenses........................... *50,000*
Fixed administrative expenses.................... *60,000*
Variable costs and expenses:
    Materials ($2 per unit)........................ *200,000*
    Labor ($2.50 per unit)......................... *250,000*
    Manufacturing overhead ($1.50 per unit)........ *150,000*
    Selling expenses ($0.50 per unit).............. *50,000*
    Administrative expenses ($0.40 per unit)........ *40,000*

All the units the company presently sells are sold in this country. However, recently an exporter has offered to buy 10,000 units of 3KT for sale abroad; but he will pay only $8.90 per unit, which is below the company's present $9 per unit manufacturing and selling costs.

Required:
Prepare an income statement that shows (1) in one set of columns the revenue, costs, expenses, and income from selling 100,000 units of the product in this country; (2) in a second set of columns the additional revenue, costs, expenses, and income from selling 10,000 units to the exporter; and (3) in a third set of columns the combined results from both sources. (Assume that acceptance of the new business will not increase any of the company's fixed costs and expenses nor change any of the variable costs and expenses.)

Problem 24–5

Whitter Company sells at $16 per unit a product having variable manufacturing and selling costs, other than advertising, of $10 per unit. The fixed costs of manufacturing and selling the product are $50,000. The company is presently spending $15,000 annually for advertising and is selling 17,000 units of the product each year. The advertising manager has suggested an increase in the product's advertising budget and he has developed the following statistical relations between advertising expenditures and unit sales:

An Annual Advertising Expenditure of —	Will Result in the Annual Sale of —
$10,000	14,000 units
15,000	17,000 units
20,000	20,000 units
25,000	22,000 units
30,000	23,000 units
35,000	23,800 units
40,000	24,500 units

Required:

Prepare a form with column headings as follows: Units Sold, Revenue Earned, Fixed Costs, Variable Costs, Advertising Costs, Total Costs, Profit Earned. Enter the expected sales in units in the first column and complete the information of the form to determine the advertising level that will produce the most profit.

Problem 24–6

Last year Mucho Company sold 10,000 units of its Product E2T. The units were produced on three two-year-old machines that cost $20,000 each, had an estimated ten-year life new (eight years remaining), and no salvage value. The units were sold at $10 each with the following results:

MUCHO COMPANY

Income from Sales of E2T, Year Ended December 31, 19—

Sales...		$100,000
Less:		
Cost of goods sold (other than depreciation on the three machines).....................	$55,000	
Depreciation on the three machines...........	6,000	
Selling and administrative expenses...........	20,000	81,000
Income before taxes..........................		$ 19,000
State and federal income taxes (50 percent)......		9,500
Net Income from Sale of E2T....................		$ 9,500

The company can expand the sale of E2T to 12,500 units per year at $10 per unit; but since its three machines are producing at capacity, it will be necessary to either (a) buy an additional machine like one of the three presently in use or (b) trade one of the machines presently in use on a machine having twice the capacity of the traded machine. If a machine like one presently in use is purchased, it will cost $20,000 and have a ten-year life and no salvage value. If the machine of twice the capacity is purchased, it will cost $34,000, less a $10,000 trade-in allowance on the used machine and will also have a ten-year life and no salvage value.

Since certain of the company's costs are fixed, if production and sales are increased to 12,500 units, cost of goods sold, other than depreciation on the machines, will increase 20 percent. Likewise, selling and administrative expenses will increase 20 percent.

Required:

1. Prepare a comparative income statement showing in one set of columns the expected operating results using four machines of the capacity of the three now in use and in the second set of columns the results using two present capacity machines plus the double-capacity machine. Use the income tax method for the exchange in calculating depreciation on the new larger machine.
2. Calculate the time required for the extra profits and extra depreciation to pay back the additional investment in each new machine.

CLASS EXERCISE

Exercise 24–1

A product selling for $6.50 per unit has the following variable costs: materials, $1.75; labor, $1.50; manufacturing overhead, $0.75; and variable selling and administrative expenses, $0.50. The fixed costs of manufacturing and selling the product are $140,000.

Required:

Calculate the number of units of the product that must be sold to produce a $40,000 after-tax (50 percent rate) net income.

ALTERNATE PROBLEMS

Problem 24–1A

A company is considering the addition of a new product to its line. It estimates it can sell 30,000 units of the product annually at $5.30 per unit; but to manufacture the units will require new machinery having an estimated ten-year life, no salvage value, and costing $80,000. This additional information is also available: (a) material cost per unit of product, $1.80; (b) direct labor cost per unit, $0.70; (c) annual manufacturing overhead other than depreciation on the new machinery, $28,000; (d) selling and administrative expenses per unit, $0.80; and (e) income tax rate 50 percent.

Required:

Calculate (1) the payback period on the investment in new machinery, and (2) the return on the average investment in new machinery.

Problem 24–2A

Pepe Stamping Company produces and sells 20,000 units of Product X3X annually which it produces on two 10,000-unit capacity, four-year-old machines that cost $6,000 each and which have been depreciated under the assumption they would have no salvage value at the end of an expected ten-year life. The company has an opportunity to expand its operations from 20,000 units to 30,000 units annually. However, to do so it must either: (1) purchase a new and larger machine having a 35,000-unit capacity, ten-year life with no salvage value, and costing $38,000, less a $1,000 trade-in allowance each on the two old machines; or (2) purchase for $1,200 installed a secondhand machine of the same age, 10,000-unit capacity, and having the same remaining expected useful life as the old machines. Material costs will be the same whether three old machines or the new 35,000-unit machine is used. However, since each old machine and also the new machine requires an operator, the new machine offers an annual savings of two operators' wages. This and other savings are evident from examining the following table showing operating costs for three old machines and the one new machine:

	Three 10,000-Unit Machines	One 35,000-Unit Machine
Labor...................	$15,000	$5,000
Maintenance, supplies, etc...........	600	950
Power....................	750	600
Insurance, taxes, etc......	300	1,500

Required:

Prepare statistics to aid the company management in its decision between purchasing the additional secondhand machine or the new 35,000-unit machine. Assume the company must pay 5 percent interest for the use of long-term capital.

Problem 24–3A

Rosa Company manufactured and sold 100,000 units of one of its products at $5 per unit during the past year. The 100,000 units are the maximum number the company can make on a one-shift basis, and the company is considering an additional shift.

Per unit manufacturing and selling costs for the 100,000 units manufactured and sold during the past year were: materials, $1.50; direct labor, $1; manufacturing overhead, $1; selling expenses, $0.40; administrative expenses, $0.30; and a 50 percent income tax rate.

The production manager estimates a second shift would produce an additional 100,000 units; but due to slight second shift inefficiencies and a wage differential required by the union contract, direct labor costs for these units would be 10 percent higher than for the units produced on the first shift. The production manager also estimates that 60 percent of present overhead costs is fixed at any production level from zero to 300,000 units and 40 percent varies with volume.

The purchasing department estimates that if materials for 200,000 units of product are purchased during a year, a quantity discount would reduce material costs 5 percent on all units.

The office manager estimates that for any level of production from zero to 250,000 units, two thirds of administrative expenses remain fixed and one third varies with production volume.

The sales manager is certain that with a 10 percent reduction in the unit selling price and a 25 percent increase in selling expenses the 200,000 units can be sold.

Required:

Prepare a comparative income statement showing in the first set of columns the operating results on a one-shift basis and in the second set of columns the estimated results on a two-shift basis.

Problem 24–4A

Snapit Company manufactures a small tool it sells to wholesalers at $3 each. During a normal year the company manufactures and sells approximately 100,000 of the tools, and data on a normal year's costs for manufacturing and selling this number of tools are as follows:

Materials.......................................	*$ 60,000*
Direct labor....................................	*50,000*
Manufacturing overhead.........................	*75,000*
Selling expenses................................	*30,000*
Administrative expenses........................	*25,000*
	$240,000

A mail-order concern has offered to buy 10,000 of the tools at $2.25 each to be marketed under the mail-order concern's trade name. If accepted, the order is not expected to affect sales through present channels.

A study of normal costs and their relation to the new business reveals: (a) Material costs are 100 percent variable. (b) The per unit direct labor costs for the additional units will be 50 percent greater than normal since their production will require overtime at time and one half. (c) Of a normal year's manufacturing overhead costs, two thirds will remain fixed at any production level from zero to 150,000 units and one third will vary with volume. (d) There will be no additional selling costs if the new business is accepted. (e) Acceptance of the new business will increase administrative costs $1,500.

Required:

Prepare a comparative income statement that shows (1) in one set of columns the operating results and operating income of a normal year, (2) in the second set of columns the operating results and income that may be expected from the new business, and (3) in the third set of columns the combined results from normal and the expected new business.

Problem 24–5A

Since its product is patented, Mulligan Company has a monopoly on its manufacture and sale. Variable costs in manufacturing and selling the product are $24 per unit for any number up to 15,000 units. If more than 15,000 units are produced and sold, because of the economies of volume purchasing, variable costs are reduced to $20 per unit. Fixed costs are $200,000 for any production level up to 15,000 units. Then because more machines, employees, and supervision are required, fixed costs increase to $350,000 for any production level between 15,000 and 30,000 units; and fixed costs increase to $480,000 for any production level between 30,000 and 45,000 units. Estimated sales at various prices per unit are as follows:

Selling Price	Estimated Salable Units
$100	2,000
80	5,000
60	10,000
50	20,000
40	35,000
30	45,000

Required:

Prepare a form with the following column headings: Selling Price, Salable Units, Sales Revenue, Variable Costs, Fixed Costs, Total Costs, and Profit. Enter the selling prices in the first column and complete the form to show the profit at each selling price.

DECISION PROBLEM 24—MAGNUM METALS, INC.

Magnum Metals, Inc., operates an aluminum plant at Stone Center. This is one of ten plants owned by the company and is the only one earning less than the expected return on investment. An engineering appraisal disclosed that the following factors contributed to the poor return on this plant: The distance from raw material sources, a relatively high electric power cost, and lack of modern machines.

A new plant is under consideration, to be located nearer raw material supplies and close to hydroelectric power at greatly reduced cost. This move would necessitate abandonment of plant buildings and much of the machinery and equipment at Stone Center. The president of the company favors the move; however, the chairman of the board is not convinced that the Stone Center plant should be abandoned in view of the great loss.

You have been asked to make recommendations concerning the proposed abandonment of the Stone Center location and construction of the new plant. Data developed during the course of your analysis include the following:

1. *Book Value of Plant and Equipment at Stone Center:*

> **Plant buildings and land, less depreciation......$1,200,000**
> **Machinery and equipment, less depreciation.....3,800,000**

Abandonment would result in a $1,000,000 loss on sale of the plant buildings and land plus an 80 percent loss on the machinery and equipment.

2. *Investment in New Plant:*

The projected investment in the new plant is $12,000,000. The estimated average life of all new plant assets is 20 years, and the investment in modern facilities will double the 25,000-ton capacity of the Stone Center plant. It is estimated the 50,000 tons produced by the new plant can be sold without a price reduction.

3. *Costs per Ton of Product:*

	Stone Center Plant	New Plant (Estimated)
Material, labor, and plant expenses (exclusive of depreciation)	$325	$275
Depreciation	20	12
Total Costs per Ton	$345	$287

Production costs at Stone Center together with applicable nonfactory costs such as selling and administrative expenses have been at break even (no profit nor loss) on sales.

Prepare a report analyzing the advantages of the move including your recommendations relative to the proposal. Present any pertinent analyses based on the data given.

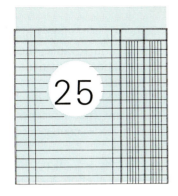

Budgets
and Budgeting

THE MANAGEMENT of any business plans. It is impossible to conceive of a business in which objectives have not been set and plans made to reach the objectives. For example, with an act so simple as purchasing an item of supplies, there must be a plan to use the supplies.

Although every company management plans, the ways in which various managements plan differ. Some managements are very informal in their planning; all planning is done on scraps of paper or in the heads of management and remains there. Other managements commit their plans to paper in an orderly manner and are said to prepare *budgets*. A budget is a *plan* of future action, and budgeting is the process of *planning* future action. The key words in the foregoing sentence are "plan" and "planning."

BUDGETS AND THEIR OBJECTIVES

Why do managements plan? It is easy to say the purpose of planning is to maximize profits. This is true; but planning or budgeting benefits reach beyond this and may be grouped under several headings as follows:

Planning. When a firm plans, it may be assumed that its actions are based upon thorough investigations, study, and research. Not only should this result in the best conceivable plans but it should also instill in executives the habit of basing decisions upon investigations and study.

Controlling. A budget aids in controlling business operations. It does this by influencing the actions of people. For example, when a department manager knows that his department's expenses will be compared with the planned expenses of a budget, he is influenced toward keeping the expenses at the planned level.

Coordinating. Coordination requires that a business be operated as a whole rather than as a group of separate departments. When a budget plan is prepared, each department's objectives are determined in advance; these objectives are coordinated; and, for example, the production department is scheduled to produce what the selling department can sell.

Communicating. When a budget is prepared, the budget becomes a means of informing the organization not only of plans that have been approved by management but also of budgeted actions management wishes the organization to take during the budget period.

Motivating. When obtainable budgeted objectives are set, all persons responsible can normally be depended upon to make every effort to attain or exceed the objectives for which they are personally responsible.

THE BUDGET PERIOD

Budget periods normally coincide with accounting periods. This means that in most companies the budget period is one year in length. However, in addition to their annual budgets, many companies prepare long-range budgets setting forth major objectives for from three to five or ten years in advance. Such long-range budgets are often used as the framework into which each annual budget is fitted.

Although most budgets are prepared for a year, yearly budgets are commonly broken down into quarterly or monthly budgets. Short-term budgets of a quarter or a month are useful yardsticks for measuring the degree of accomplishment toward the total results desired.

When an annual budget is broken down into monthly budgets, monthly budget reports like that of Illustration 157 are normally prepared to compare actual achievements with the budgeted plan.

PREPARING A BUDGET

A company's budget is commonly the work of a budget committee which may be made up of the president who acts as chairman, the sales manager, the production manager, and other department heads, depending upon the nature of the company.

Sales Budget. The budget committee's first major task is the sales budget. An estimate of goods to be sold and revenue to be derived from sales is the starting point in preparing most budgets. This is because the plans of all departments are related to sales and expected revenues.

The sales budget commonly grows from a reconciliation of forecasted business conditions, plant capacity, proposed selling expenses, such as advertising, and estimates of expected sales. As to expected sales, in a concern having traveling salesmen each salesman is commonly asked to submit through his sales manager an estimate of expected sales for his territory; and, for example, in a department store each department manager is commonly asked to forecast sales for his department. The final

Illustration 157

CONSOLIDATED STORES, INC.
Income Statement with Variations from Budget
For Month Ended April 30, 19--

	Actual	Budget	Variations
Sales	$63,500	$60,000	$+ 3,500
Less: Sales returns and allowances.	1,800	1,700	+ 100
Sales discounts	1,200	1,150	+ 50
Net sales	$60,500	$57,150	$+ 3,350
Cost of goods sold:			
Merchandise inventory, April 1, 19--.	$42,000	$44,000	$- 2,000
Purchases, net.	39,100	38,000	+ 1,100
Freight-in.	1,250	1,200	+ 50
Goods for sale.	$82,350	$83,200	$- 850
Merchandise inventory, April 30, 19--	41,000	44,100	- 3,100
Cost of goods sold.	$41,350	$39,100	$+ 2,250
Gross profit.	$19,150	$18,050	$+ 1,100
Operating expenses:			
Selling expenses:			
Sales salaries.	$ 6,250	$ 6,000	$+ 250
Advertising expense	900	800	+ 100
Store supplies used	550	500	+ 50
Depreciation of store equipment	1,600	1,600	
Total selling expenses.	$ 9,300	$ 8,900	$+ 400
General and administrative expenses:			
Office salaries	$ 2,000	$ 2,000	
Office supplies used.	165	150	$+ 15
Rent.	1,100	1,100	
Expired insurance	200	200	
Depreciation of office equipment.	100	100	
Total general and administrative expenses .	$ 3,565	$ 3,550	$+ 15
Total operating expenses	$12,865	$12,450	$+ 415
Income from Operations.	$ 6,285	$ 5,600	$+ 685

sales budget is then based on these estimates as reconciled with forecasted business conditions, selling expenses, and so on.

The reason for having sales estimates submitted by salesmen or department managers is that these people are familiar with their territories and departments; and, also, they normally feel a greater responsibility for reaching goals they have had a hand in setting.

Merchandising, Production, and Material Purchases Budgets. In a store, merchandise must be purchased before it is sold, and in a factory it must be produced. As a result, once sales estimates are completed it is necessary to plan merchandise purchases or product production.

Merchandising Budget. Monthly departmental merchandising forecasts are the usual starting point in building a store's merchandising budget. Illustration 158 shows such a forecast for Department A of Consolidated Stores. The sales figure in Illustration 158 is the budgeted February sales from the concern's previously prepared sales budget. Then since the markup in this department is 40 percent (based on sales), cost of goods sold is 60 percent of budgeted sales; and if planned inventories for the department are known, budgeted departmental purchases can be determined as in the illustration.

To produce a storewide merchandising budget, a budget similar to

Illustration 158
CONSOLIDATED STORES, INC.
Merchandising Budget for Department A, Month of February, 19--

Sales at planned selling prices (see sales budget). . . . . $ 6,800
Budgeted purchases for February:
  Cost of goods to be sold during February (60 percent of $6,800). $ 4,080
  Planned February 28th inventory   8,000
  Total merchandise required. $12,080
  Inventory on February 1   7,600
    Budgeted Purchases for February . . . . $ 4,480

Illustration 158 is prepared for each department. Then all the departmental budgets are combined for a monthly merchandising budget for the entire store and the monthly budgets are combined again for the year's budget.

Production and Material Purchases Budgets. The production budget for a manufacturing concern is prepared in much the same way as a store's merchandising budget. To begin, an estimate of the units of each product to be manufactured is made, often as in Illustration 159.

Illustration 159
THE MARNE PRODUCTION COMPANY
PRODUCTION BUDGET
Planned Quantity of Goods to Be Manufactured
For the Year Ending December 31, 1967

Units of product required to meet sales estimates . . . 62,300
Planned inventory, December 31, 1967. 8,600
    Total units required. 70,900
Units in inventory, January 1, 1967 8,100
Number of Units to Be Manufactured. 62,800

After the production budget and the number of units of each product to be manufactured are determined, the next step is to set up the material purchases budget. To do this a materials specification sheet showing kinds and quantities of materials needed for proposed production is prepared. From this an estimate of materials to be purchased can be made as in Illustration 160 (assume in this illustration for sake of brevity that only one kind of material is needed and that two units of it are used to make each unit of finished goods).

After the material purchases budget is completed, labor costs and factory overhead are estimated. Then all estimates are assembled in a statement of budgeted cost of goods to be manufactured.

Expense Budget. As soon as a tentative sales estimate is made, it is communicated to department heads such as the sales manager and office manager who are asked to make expense estimates for their departments.

Illustration 160

THE MARNE PRODUCTION COMPANY
MATERIAL PURCHASES BUDGET
Planned Quantity and Cost of Raw Material to Be Purchased
For the Year Ending December 31, 1967

```
Required units of material for goods to be manufactured (62,800 x 2). . 125,600
Planned inventory, December 31, 1967. . . . . . . . . . . . . . . . . .  21,200
       Total units of material required. . . . . . . . . . . . . . . . 146,800
Units in January 1, 1967, material inventory. . . . . . . . . . . . . .  18,600
Units to be purchased . . . . . . . . . . . . . . . . . . . . . . . . . 128,200
Estimated unit cost . . . . . . . . . . . . . . . . . . . . . . . . . .    x $2
Estimated Cost of Material to Be Purchased. . . . . . . . . . . . . . .$256,400
```

The department heads normally base their estimates on the previous year's expenses, adjusted for increases or decreases in service expected of them, changes in wage scales, changes in supply costs, and other pertinent data. Their estimates must meet the approval of the budget committee or be increased or decreased; however, asking for estimates from department heads helps secure their cooperation in carrying out the final budget.

Plant and Equipment Budget. The plant and equipment budget lists equipment to be scrapped and additional equipment to be purchased if the proposed production program is carried out. The purchase of additional equipment requires funds; and anticipating equipment additions in advance normally makes it easier to provide the funds.

At times estimated production may exceed plant capacity. Budgeting makes it possible to anticipate this and either revise the production schedule or increase plant capacity.

Cash Budget. After tentative sales, expenses, production, and equipment budgets have been set, the cash budget is prepared. This budget is important. A company should have at all times enough cash to meet needs but not too much. Too much cash is undesirable because it often cannot be profitably invested.

A cash budget requires management to forecast cash receipts and disbursements, and usually results in better cash management. Also, it enables management to arrange well in advance for loans to cover any anticipated inadequacies.

In preparing the cash budget, anticipated receipts are added to the beginning cash balance, and anticipated expenditures are deducted. Annual cash budgets are usually broken down into monthly budgets. Illustration 161 shows a monthly cash budget for Consolidated Stores, Inc.

Master Budget. After the sales, expense, production, equipment, and cash budgets are coordinated and completed, they are combined into a master budget. The master budget is then approved by the board of directors and transmitted to the organization as the approved objectives for the budget period.

Illustration 161

CONSOLIDATED STORES, INC.
Cash Budget for January, 19--

Cash balance, January 1, 19-- . . .		$32,500
Add estimated cash receipts:		
Cash sales	$43,200	
Collections of accounts receivable	18,650	
Interest on investments.	750	
Property rentals	1,800	64,400
Available cash		$96,900
Deduct estimated disbursements:		
Accounts payable	$41,300	
State and federal taxes.	2,750	
Payrolls	8,250	
Building repairs	15,300	
Dividends.	4,000	
Miscellaneous items.	1,200	72,800
Estimated Cash Balance, January 31,		
19--		$24,100

ACCOUNTING AND BUDGETING

Preparing and carrying out a budget involves all departments; consequently, it is not primarily an accounting function. However, the task of assembling data and translating it into financial terms often falls to the accounting department. Furthermore, the accounting department, since it is in charge of accounting records and is constantly dealing with actual transactions, is well qualified to deal with budget data.

One budget task the accounting department is commonly called upon to perform is to prepare from the budget an estimated income statement for the budget year and an estimated balance sheet as it will appear at the end of the budget year, if budget plans are carried out. This task is, in a sense, actually one of accounting for events before they happen. It differs but little from accounting for events after they happen.

PREPARING ESTIMATED STATEMENTS

Normally, when the accounting department is called on to prepare an estimated balance sheet and an estimated income statement as they will appear at the end of the budget period, it is called upon to do so a month or more before the budget period begins. For example, the accounting department may be given a copy of the budget during the last week of November and be requested to prepare estimated statements for the year beginning the following January 1.

During the last week in November, the accounting department does not know what the following December 31 post-closing or January 1 opening trial balance amounts will be. Consequently, its first task is to project the company's account balances ahead and arrive at the December 31, estimated, post-closing trial balance for the current year.

After arriving at this December 31, estimated, post-closing trial balance, the estimated, post-closing trial balance is commonly entered in the first two money columns of a work sheet. Next the budgeted transactions are entered in the second pair of work sheet columns in the same manner as adjustments are entered on an ordinary work sheet. For example, if the budget calls for sales on account of $250,000 the name of the Sales account is entered on the work sheet in the Account Titles column below the names of the estimated trial balance accounts; and then Sales is credited and Accounts Receivable is debited for $250,000 in the second pair of money columns in the same manner that an adjustment is entered on an ordinary work sheet.

After all budgeted transactions are entered on the work sheet, the estimated trial balance amounts in the first pair of money columns are combined with the budget amounts in the second pair of columns and are sorted to the proper Income Statement and Balance Sheet columns of the work sheet. After this, the estimated income statement and estimated balance sheet are prepared from the information in the Income Statement and Balance Sheet columns in the same manner as an ordinary income statement or balance sheet.

FIXED AND VARIABLE BUDGETS

Some concerns prepare what are known as "fixed" budgets; others prepare so-called "variable" or "flexible" budgets.

The budgets discussed thus far have been of the fixed variety. When a fixed budget is prepared, the best information available is used to arrive at an estimate of the actual operating level expected during the budget year. All plans are then based on this one "fixed" level of activity. A fixed budget, in other words, assumes a single level of activity, and cost and expense estimates are made for this one level only.

The weakness of a fixed budget is that it makes no provision for an operating level different from that planned; and there are often years in which, for unforeseen reasons, the actual operating level varies substantially from the budget plan. Furthermore, when this occurs, good management requires that costs and expenses be adjusted to fit the new unplanned activity level; and under a fixed budget, for lack of planning, these adjustments have to be made on a "best-guess" basis. True, these best guesses may prove satisfactory; but planning in advance for several activity levels should produce both better cost control and more precise guidance for management.

A variable budget differs from a fixed budget in that it provides cost and expense estimates for varying rates of operating activity. For example, a concern preparing a variable budget may estimate it will sell during the coming budget year, depending upon economic conditions, from 100,000 to 160,000 units of product. It then provides in its flexible budget, for instance, a set of cost and expense estimates for the 100,000-unit level, another set for the 110,000-unit level, another for 120,000 units, still another for 130,000, and so on up to 160,000 units. In other words, when a flexible budget is prepared, cost and expense estimates are made for each of the several production levels that may be experienced. Then, as the year progresses and the actual operating level becomes known, the budget costs and expenses for that level are compared with the actual costs and expenses. Any variations provide cost control data for managerial action.

A variable budget, like a fixed budget, is departmentalized; and each department head has the responsibility of meeting the goals set out in the budget for his department. Reports are prepared frequently, usually monthly, to permit review of operating performance; and variations from budgeted costs at the operating level achieved constitute an objective measure of the responsible official.

FIXED AND VARIABLE EXPENSES AND BREAK-EVEN POINTS

Companies that prepare variable budgets normally make studies of costs, expenses, and sales at various production levels. One commonly made study is a break-even point analysis. The break-even point for a company is the point at which revenue from sales exactly equals cost of goods sold plus expenses. It is the point where there is neither a profit nor a loss. It is the point at which the company exactly breaks even.

For example, a company sells for $100 a unit a single product having $70 variable expenses per unit sold. If the fixed expenses involved in selling the product are $24,000, the company breaks even on the product as soon as it sells 800 units or as soon as its sales volume reaches $80,000. This break-even point may be determined as follows:

1. Each unit sold at $100 pays its $70 variable expenses and contributes $30 toward the fixed expenses.
2. The fixed expenses are $24,000; consequently, 800 units ($24,000 ÷ $30 = 800) must be sold to pay the fixed expenses.
3. And 800 units at $100 each produces an $80,000 sales volume.

The $30 amount that the sales price of this product exceeds variable expense per unit is called the *marginal contribution per unit*. In other words the marginal contribution per unit is the amount that the sale of one unit contributes toward payment of the fixed expenses and a profit.

Also, the marginal contribution of a product expressed as a percentage of the sales price is the *marginal contribution rate* of the product. For instance, the marginal contribution rate of the $100 product of this illustration is 30 percent ($30 ÷ $100 = 30%).

And with marginal contribution and marginal contribution rate defined, it is possible to set up the following formulas for calculating a break-even point in units and in dollars:

$$\textit{Break-even Point in Units} = \frac{\textit{Fixed Expenses}}{\textit{Marginal Contribution}}$$

$$\textit{Break-even Point in Dollars} = \frac{\textit{Fixed Expenses}}{\textit{Marginal Contribution Rate}}$$

Application of the second formula to figures for the product of this illustration gives this result:

$$\textit{Break-even Point in Dollars} = \frac{\$24,000}{30\%}$$

or

$$\frac{\$24,000}{.30} = \$80,000$$

BREAK-EVEN CHART

A break-even point may be charted as in Illustration 162. Such a chart makes it easier to visualize the relation of sales, fixed and variable expenses, and the break-even point. Note in Illustration 162 how the line representing sales begins at zero and moves upward. Note also how the line representing costs and expenses begins at the $24,000 fixed expense level and intersects the sales line at $80,000. This intersection point is the break-even point. When sales go above $80,000, increasing profits are earned as is shown by the increasing spread between the lines; and when sales fall below this point, a loss is incurred.

CALCULATING THE SALES REQUIRED FOR A DESIRED NET INCOME

A slight extension of the concept behind the break-even calculation will produce a formula that may be used in determining the sales level necessary to produce a desired net income. The formula is:

$$\textit{Sales at Desired Income Level} = \frac{\textit{Fixed Expenses} + \textit{Net Income} + \textit{Income Taxes}}{\textit{Marginal Contribution Rate}}$$

To illustrate the formula's use, assume the company of the previous section, the company having $24,000 of fixed expenses and a 30 percent marginal contribution rate, has set a $20,000 after-tax income goal for itself. Assume further that in order to have a $20,000 net income, the

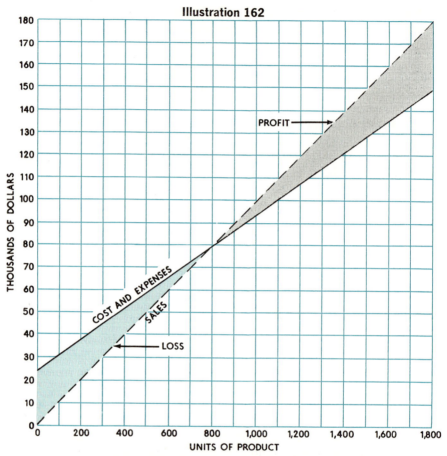

Illustration 162

company must earn $28,500 and pay $8,500 in taxes. Under these assumptions, $175,000 of sales are necessary to produce a $20,000 net income. This is calculated as follows:

$$\text{Sales at Desired Income Level} = \frac{\text{Fixed Expenses} + \text{Net Income} + \text{Income Taxes}}{\text{Marginal Contribution Rate}}$$

$$\text{Sales at Desired Income Level} = \frac{\$24,000 + \$20,000 + \$8,500}{30\%}$$

$$\text{Sales at Desired Income Level} = \frac{\$52,500}{30\%} = \$175,000$$

The break-even and profit situations just described represent an oversimplification of what is normal. The company of the illustration has only one product, while most companies have many products, the sales of which result in different amounts of fixed and variable expenses. Also, in the illustrated situation it is assumed that expenses are either fixed or variable.

Some expenses are fixed, some vary directly with sales, and some vary with sales but not in the same proportion as sales. Nevertheless, the illustrated situation will serve to introduce break-even and profit-level calculations, and complicated situations may be left to an advanced course.

MANAGERIAL EVALUATION OF ALTERNATIVES

Budgeting and related techniques can provide a great deal of help to management in its consideration of alternative courses of action. Budgeted statements based on careful estimates can be used to compare income before putting into effect a contemplated course of action with the estimated income after the action. Techniques such as break-even analysis may point up certain risks involved in contemplated action, or the comparative risks involved in alternative actions which are under considerations. For example, perhaps a new plant is proposed. If it is built, new break-even points will result because of increased fixed costs. Generally in such a case, the closer the break-even point is to the anticipated sales volume, the greater the risk.

Differential cost analysis as discussed in the previous chapter may also have considerable influence on management's choice of alternatives. Differential cost analysis and other budgeting techniques should aid in answering such managerial problems as these:

1. Should selling prices be reduced in order to stimulate demand?
2. Could greater profits be made by reducing selling prices and increasing production?
3. Should new markets be cultivated even at the expense of substantial reductions in selling prices?
4. Should additional product lines be undertaken if no new plant facilities are required in their manufacture?
5. Should a machine or other fixed asset be constructed by the concern or should it be purchased from an outside supplier?

The answers to these and many other questions are aided by break-even analyses, the preparation of estimated income statements and balance sheets, by differential cost analyses, and by other applications of budgeting techniques. Always, when the tools of accounting and budgeting are brought to bear on any problem in business which affects the basic objectives of profit maximization or the financial welfare of the business, considerable aid to management in choosing proper alternatives will result.

QUESTIONS FOR CLASS DISCUSSION

1. What does a company gain by preparing a budget?
2. What is the normal length of a budget period?
3. What are some advantages of having a budget prepared by a budget committee made up of department heads?

4. What is a sales budget? An expense budget? A production budget? An equipment budget? A cash budget? A master budget?

5. A manufacturing firm plans to begin a budget year with 1,680 units of its product on hand; it plans to sell 48,000 units during the year and to end the year with an 1,800-unit inventory. If production is to be at a uniform rate throughout the year, how many units should the firm plan to produce each month?

6. Differentiate between a fixed budget and a variable budget.

7. What happens at the break-even point in terms of fixed expenses, variable expenses, and profit?

8. A firm's cost of goods sold and variable expenses are 60 percent of each sales dollar, and its fixed expenses are $72,000. What is its break-even point?

9. Often several months before a budget year begins, an accounting department is asked to prepare an estimated income statement for the budget year and an estimated balance sheet to show the effect of carrying out the budget plans. Describe how such estimated statements can be prepared.

10. A company president said he thought his company benefited from having its department heads meet before the beginning of a new year to discuss the new year's prospects but that any time spent preparing a formal budget was wasted. Express your opinion on this subject.

PROBLEMS

Problem 25–1

Amigo Company manufactures a steel product called a "cosa." Each "cosa" requires 75 pounds of steel and is produced in a single operation by a stamping process. The concern's management estimates there will be 1,600 units of the product and 60 tons of steel on hand on March 31 of the current year, and that 12,000 units of the product will be sold during the year's second quarter. Management also believes that due to the possibility of a strike in the steel industry, the concern should begin the third quarter with a 150-ton steel inventory and 2,000 finished "cosas."

Required:

Prepare for the company an April 1 through June 30 production budget and a steel purchases budget that shows the number of tons of steel to be purchased.

Problem 25–2

During the latter part of February, Joel Huff, owner of Huff and Puff Sales approached his bank for a $10,000 loan to be made on April 1 and repaid 60 days thereafter with interest at 6 percent. He planned to increase his concern's inventory by $10,000 during March and needed the loan to pay for the merchandise during April. The bank's loan officer was interested in Mr. Huff's ability to repay the loan and asked him to forecast his concern's May 31 cash position.

On February 28 Huff and Puff Sales expected to have a $3,400 cash balance, an accounts receivable balance of $28,000, and $13,900 accounts payable. Its budgeted sales, purchases, and cash expenditures for the following three months are:

	March	April	May
Sales..........................	$24,000	$25,000	$23,000
Merchandise purchases.......	25,500	15,000	14,000
Payroll.......................	2,400	2,400	2,400
Rent.........................	1,000	1,000	1,000
Other cash expenses...........	1,200	1,100	1,300
Repayment of bank loan......			10,100

The budgeted March purchases include the inventory increase. All sales are on account; and past experience indicates 80 percent is collected in the month following the sale, 15 percent in the next month, 4 percent in the next, and the remainder is not collected. Application of this experience to the February 28 accounts receivable balance indicates $22,500 of the $28,000 will be collected during March, $4,000 during April, and $1,000 during May.

Required:
Prepare cash budgets for March, April, and May for Huff and Puff Sales under the assumption the bank loan will be paid on May 31.

Problem 25–3
A company manufactures two products that sell for $1,000 per unit each; but beyond that they have little in common, as the following data shows:

	Product A	Product B
Sales price per unit........................	$ 1,000	$ 1,000
Variable manufacturing and selling		
costs per unit...........................	600	400
Fixed manufacturing and selling costs.....	240,000	360,000

Required:
1. Calculate the break-even point of each product in dollars.
2. Prepare a break-even chart for each product.
3. Assume a 50 percent income tax rate for the company and calculate the sales volumes necessary to produce a (a) $50,000, (b) $100,000, and (c) $150,000 after-tax profit from each product.

Problem 25–4
Last year Able Company sold 40,000 units of its Product 23X at $10 per unit. To manufacture and sell the product required $100,000 of fixed manufacturing overhead and $20,000 of fixed selling and administrative expenses. Last year's per unit variable costs and expenses for Product 23X were:

Material A..	$4.00
Direct labor (paid on a piece-rate basis).............	1.50
Variable manufacturing overhead costs..............	.30
Variable selling and administrative expenses........	.20

The company's engineers have discovered that the material cost in producing the product can be cut in half if Material B is substituted for Material A. The substitution has no affect on the product's quality; but it gives the company a choice in pricing the product. (1) The company can maintain the present per unit price, sell the same number of units, and make a $2 per unit greater profit as a result of the substitution. Or (2) it can reduce the product's price $2 per unit, an amount equal to the material savings, and because of the lower price, increase the units sold by 50 percent. If the latter choice is made, the fixed overhead, selling, and administrative expenses will remain fixed and the variable labor, overhead, selling, and administrative expenses will vary with volume.

Required:
1. Calculate the break-even point in dollars for each alternative.
2. Prepare a break-even chart for each.
3. Prepare an income statement showing sales, variable costs, fixed costs, income taxes (50 percent rate), and net income for each alternative.

Problem 25–5

Assume it is the first week in December and the accounting department of Beagle Manufacturing Company has been asked to prepare a set of estimated statements as they will appear at the end of the year beginning next January 1. The accounting department has projected ahead the November 30 account balances of the current year and has arrived at the following December 31 post-closing trial balance:

BEAGLE MANUFACTURING COMPANY
Estimated Post-closing Trial Balance, December 31 19—

Cash..	$ 29,500	
Accounts receivable...........................	35,000	
Allowance for bad debts.......................		$ 3,100
Raw materials inventory.......................	19,800	
Goods in process inventory....................	15,200	
Finished goods inventory......................	22,700	
Prepaid factory insurance.....................	1,200	
Factory supplies..............................	2,900	
Factory machinery............................	182,000	
Accumulated depreciation, factory machinery..		50,600
Accounts payable.............................		16,500
State and federal income taxes payable........		21,000
Dividends payable............................		3,000
Common stock, $100 par value................		150,000
Premium on common stock....................		15,000
Retained earnings............................		49,100
	$308,300	$308,300

Beagle Manufacturing Company's budget plans call for the following condensed transactions to be completed during the coming year:

1. *Sales (all on account)*..............................   *$360,000*
2. *Purchases (all on account):*
      Raw materials...................................*$ 62,000*
      Factory supplies..............................   *5,000*
      Factory machinery (on October 1).............. *85,000*   *152,000*
3. *Cash receipts:*
      Collection of accounts receivable................*$355,000*
          ($3,100 of accounts receivable will be written off
          as bad debts.)
      Sale during October of 500 shares of $100 par value
      common stock at $140 per share................. *70,000*   *425,000*
4. *Cash disbursements:*
      Payment of accounts payable....................*$153,500*
      Payment of insurance premiums (debit prepaid
          factory insurance)............................   *3,600*
      Dividend payments.............................   *12,000*
      State and federal income taxes payable..........   *21,000*
      Direct labor....................................   *90,000*
      Factory supervision............................   *12,000*
      Indirect labor.................................   *9,500*
      Heat, light, and power.........................   *18,700*
      Machinery repairs..............................   *5,400*
      Rent of factory building........................   *12,000*
      Property taxes, machinery.......................   *1,600*
      Sales salaries..................................   *28,200*
      Advertising....................................   *4,200*
      Officers' salaries...............................   *20,000*
      Office salaries.................................   *11,000*   *402,700*
5. *End of the budget year adjustments will be required*
    for:
      a) Estimated bad debts expense..................*$ 3,600*
      b) Expired factory insurance....................   *3,800*
      c) Factory supplies used........................   *5,400*
      d) Depreciation on factory machinery............   *18,200*
      e) State and federal income taxes expense........   *21,500*
6. *End of the budget year inventories are expected to*
    be:
      Raw materials..................................   *20,800*
      Goods in process...............................   *14,900*
      Finished goods.................................   *21,200*
7. *Quarterly dividends at $2 per share are expected to*
    be declared on the stock outstanding on March
    31, on June 30, on September 30, and on De-
    cember 31.

Required:
   1. Enter the December 31, estimated trial balance in the Trial Balance
     columns of a work sheet.

2. Enter the budgeted transaction in the work sheet's Adjustments columns in the same manner adjustments are entered.
3. Enter the budgeted adjustments on the work sheet and complete it.

Problem 25-6
From the work sheet of Problem 25–5 prepare an estimated manufacturing statement, an estimated income statement, and an estimated balance sheet for the budget year.

CLASS EXERCISE

Exercise 25-1
Last year Yuba Company incurred a loss selling 8,000 units of its product at $50 per unit. Last year's fixed costs for the product's sale were $121,500, and the variable costs per unit of product sold were $35. The concern's management feels that a sustained advertising campaign costing $15,000 annually would sufficiently increase sales at $50 per unit to show a profit.

Required:
Under the assumptions the foregoing fixed costs will remain fixed, the company spends the $15,000 annually for advertising, and the variable costs continue at $35 per unit, (1) calculate the concern's break-even point, and (2) prepare an income statement showing sales, fixed, and variable expenses at the break-even point.

ALTERNATE PROBLEMS

Problem 25-1A
Tri-Products sells three products which it purchases in their finished ready-for-sale state. The products' March 31 inventories are: Product A, 3,000 units; Product B, 3,800 units; and Product C, 6,500 units. The concern's manager is disturbed because each product's March 31 inventory is excessive in relation to immediately expected sales. Consequently, he has set as a goal a month-end inventory for each product that is equal to one half the following month's expected sales. Expected sales in units for April, May, June, and July are:

	Expected Sales in Units			
	April	May	June	July
Product A..................	4,000	4,600	5,000	3,800
Product B..................	2,800	2,800	3,400	3,600
Product C..................	6,000	5,400	5,200	5,800

Required:
Prepare an April, a May, and a June purchases budget in units for the three products.

Problem 25–2A

Mucho Sales Company expects to have a $6,300 cash balance on December 31 of the current year. It also expects to have a $35,500 balance of accounts receivable and $21,400 of accounts payable. Its budgeted sales, purchases, and cash expenditures for the following three months are:

	January	February	March
Sales...............................	$24,000	$18,000	$27,000
Purchases..........................	14,000	17,300	18,000
Payroll............................	2,400	2,400	2,800
Rent...............................	1,000	1,000	1,000
Other cash expenses...............	1,200	1,600	1,400
Purchase of store equipment......	...	5,000	...
Payment of quarterly dividend....	...	...	4,000

All sales are on account; and past experience indicates that 85 percent is collected in the month following the sale, 10 percent in the next month, and 4 percent in the third month. Application of the experience to the December 31 accounts receivable balance indicates that $28,000 of the $35,500 will be collected in January, $5,200 in February, and $1,600 in March.

Purchases of merchandise on account are paid in the month following each purchase; likewise, the store equipment will be paid for in the month following its purchase.

Required:
Prepare cash budgets for the months of January, February, and March.

Problem 25–3A

Zako Company buys Product 2Z2 in bulk, packages the product, and sells it. During the past year the company sold 50,000 packages at $1 each with the following unsatisfactory results:

Sales...		$50,000
Cost of bulk Product 2Z2......................	$30,000	
Packaging materials and other variable packaging		
costs......................................	5,000	
Fixed costs...................................	14,400	49,400
Income from Sale of Product 2Z2..............		$ 600

The sales manager has suggested that the selling price of the product be reduced 10 percent and that a slight change be made in its packaging. He estimates that, if his suggestions are followed, the number of units sold can be doubled. The packaging change will increase packaging costs 5 percent per unit, but doubling the volume will gain a 5 percent reduction in the product's bulk purchase price. The packaging and volume changes will not affect fixed costs.

Required:
1. Calculate dollar break-even points for Product 2Z2 at the $1 sales price per unit and at $0.90 per unit.

2. Prepare a break-even chart for the sale of the product at each price.
3. Prepare a condensed income statement showing the estimated results of selling the product at $0.90.

Problem 25–6A

Last year Seilo Company earned $33,000 and its income statement appeared as follows:

SEILO COMPANY
Income Statement for Year Ended December 31, 19—

Sales..		$365,000
Cost of goods sold.............................		219,000
Gross profit from sales........................		$146,000
Operating expenses:		
Selling expenses............................$48,900		
Administrative expenses...................... 43,350		92,250
Income before taxes............................		$ 53,750
State and federal income taxes................∴		20,750
Net Income.....................................		$ 33,000

The one product Seilo Company sells it buys in its finished state ready for sale. The company has the following fixed selling and administrative expenses:

Selling..	$12,400
Administrative...................................	25,100
Total..	$37,500

Required:
1. Calculate the company's break-even point under the assumption its fixed expenses remain fixed and its variable costs and expenses vary exactly with sales.
2. Prepare an income statement for the company showing costs and expenses at the break-even point.

DECISION PROBLEM 25A—TRI-STATE CHEMICAL COMPANY

Tri-State Chemical Company produces a high nitrogen content fertilizer at its Bay City plant. This plant produced at near capacity last year with results as shown by the following condensed income statement:

Sales (5,000,000 lbs.)............................$250,000	
Cost of goods manufactured and sold (fixed,	
$60,000; variable, $90,000)...................... 150,000	
Gross margin....................................$100,000	
Selling and administrative expenses (fixed,	
$40,000; variable, $20,000)...................... 60,000	
Net Income......................................$ 40,000	

Pan American Export Company has offered a five-year contract to buy 3,000,-000 pounds of fertilizer at 4½ cents per pound for export sales. To achieve this additional production, a plant addition would be required. This would double present fixed manufacturing costs and would leave fixed and variable selling and administrative expenses unchanged. Variable manufacturing costs would vary with volume.

The board of directors is not certain as to whether the Pan American contract offer should be accepted.

Prepare a report giving your recommendations to the board, including the following supporting information:

1. An estimated income statement for the first year following the plant addition, assuming no change in domestic sales.
2. A comparison of break-even sales levels before the plant addition and after the contract expiration. Assume after-contract sales and expense levels, other than fixed manufacturing costs, will be at the same levels as last year.
3. A statement showing net income after the contract expiration but at sales and expense levels of last year, other than fixed manufacturing costs.

DECISION PROBLEM 25B—PAR-NAN, INC.

Par-Nan produces a plastic material of such strength and toughness that it is used by other manufacturers in place of metal in the production of a number of products. During the past year the company sold one million pounds of the product with the following results:

Sales..		$3,000,000
Cost of goods manufactured and sold:		
Fixed.....................................	$630,000	
Variable..................................	810,000	1,440,000
Gross profit on sales......................		$1,560,000
Selling and general expenses:		
Fixed.....................................	$360,000	
Variable..................................	300,000	660,000
Income before taxes.......................		$ 900,000
Income taxes (50 percent).................		450,000
Net Income................................		$ 450,000

Fallon Company, a manufacturer of washing machines, has never been a customer of Par-Nan; however, it has run laboratory tests on Par-Nan's plastic product and found it well suited for gears and agitator blades, provided the cost of the plastic is not more than the metals now used. The metals now used cost $1.50 per pound, and Fallon Company has offered to enter into a five-year contract for the annual purchase of 600,000 pounds of the plastic at $1.50 per pound.

Upon investigation the following data relative to the acceptance of the contract are disclosed:

a) It is recognized that the price in the Fallon Company contract would affect present customer relations. Estimates indicate, however, that by cutting prices 10 percent, customers would be retained and in fact current sales volume (exclusive of the proposed new contract) would be increased 30 percent.

b) Since the plant operated at 80 percent of capacity last year, the additional volume required for the new contract as well as for the increase in business from the proposed reduction in sales prices would require a plant addition.

c) The plant addition would effect costs and expenses as follows:

  Manufacturing Costs. Fixed manufacturing costs would be increased by $90,000; variable costs would vary in proportion to the units manufactured.

  Selling and General Expenses. Fixed expenses would be increased by $30,000; variable expenses would vary with the change in dollar volume of sales.

  Interest Expense. Interest expense of $50,000 per year would be incurred to finance the plant expansion.

The board of directors of Par-Nan, Inc., requests an analysis of the advisability of accepting the Fallon Company contract. Your report should include: (1) a statement of estimated net income which, on the basis of data given, would result in the year following the acceptance of the new contract; and (2) an evaluation of the risks involved in the proposed expansion, supported by (a) break-even sales figures for the past year and for the year immediately following the expiration of the proposed contract, and (b) a calculation of the volume of sales necessary after the expiration of the contract to produce the same net income as the past year. (Assume that after the expiration of the contract, sales to usual customers, prices, and variable costs will remain the same as those experienced during the five-year period of the contract.)

26

Analysis
and Interpretation
of Financial Statements

Accompanying to the dictionary, to analyze is to separate the parts of a whole so as to see their relation to the whole and to each other. Also, according to the dictionary, to interpret something is to explain it or to tell its meaning. Consequently, to analyze and interpret financial statements is to separate the statements into parts so as to see the relation of the parts to the whole and to each other, and to tell the meaning of what is seen. Numerous books have been written on this subject. Obviously, we can examine only some of the more fundamental techniques.

COMPARATIVE STATEMENTS

A commonly used analyzing and interpreting technique is the preparation of comparative statements. To see the value of a comparative statement, recognize that a single balance sheet, for example, shows assets, liabilities, and owner equity as of a specific date; but a company's comparative balance sheet shows these items for two or more dates and, consequently, shows changes that have taken place. The changes probably resulted from past operating policies, and their interpretation offers management a guide to future policies.

In its most simple form a comparative balance sheet consists of the item amounts from two of a company's successive balance sheets arranged side by side in a single statement, so that changes in item amounts may be seen. However, in examining such a statement the average person has difficulty grasping significant changes. Consequently, a comparative balance sheet showing only dollar amounts may be improved by also showing in both dollar amounts and in percentages the changes that have occurred. To accomplish this, two additional columns are added to a simple comparative balance sheet. In the first is shown in dollars the increase or decrease for each item, and in the second is shown the percentage increase or decrease. (See Illustration 163).

Illustration 163

ANCHOR SUPPLY COMPANY
Comparative Balance Sheet
December 31, 1965, and December 31, 1966

	Years Ended December 31		Amount of Increase or Decrease* during 1966	Percentage of Increase or Decrease* during 1966
	1966	1965		
ASSETS				
Current Assets:				
Cash	$ 14,000	$ 89,000	$ 75,000*	84.3*
Notes receivable	4,000	1,500	2,500	166.7
Accounts receivable, net	68,000	64,000	4,000	6.3
Merchandise inventory.	190,000	184,000	6,000	3.3
Prepaid expenses	5,800	6,000	200*	3.3*
Total Current Assets	$281,800	$344,500	$ 62,700*	18.2*
Investments:				
Real estate.	-0-	$ 30,000	$ 30,000*	100.0*
Apex Company 4 per cent bonds. . .	-0-	50,000	50,000*	100.0*
Total Investments.	-0-	$ 80,000	$ 80,000*	100.0*
Fixed Assets:				
Office equipment	$ 5,000	$ 5,000		
Less: Accumulated depreciation .	1,500	1,200		
	$ 3,500	$ 3,800	$ 300*	7.9*
Store equipment.	$ 24,000	$ 11,000		
Less: Accumulated depreciation .	6,200	4,300		
	$ 17,800	$ 6,700	11,100	165.7
Buildings.	$210,000	$ 60,000		
Less: Accumulated depreciation .	33,200	32,000		
	$176,800	$ 28,000	148,800	531.4
Land	$ 50,000	$ 20,000	30,000	150.0
Total Fixed Assets	$248,100	$ 58,500	$189,600	324.1
Total Assets	$529,900	$483,000	$ 46,900	9.7
LIABILITIES				
Current Liabilities:				
Notes payable	-0-	$ 10,000	$ 10,000*	100.0*
Accounts payable	$ 53,400	60,000	6,600*	11.0*
Wages payable	800	1,200	400*	33.3*
Total Current Liabilities. . .	$ 54,200	$ 71,200	$ 17,000*	23.9*
Long-Term Liabilities:				
Mortgage payable	$ 60,000	$ 10,000	$ 50,000	500.0
Total Liabilities.	$114,200	$ 81,200	$ 33,000	40.6
CAPITAL				
Common stock	$250,000	$250,000		
Retained earnings.	165,700	151,800	$ 13,900	9.2
Total Capital.	$415,700	$401,800	$ 13,900	3.5
Total Liabilities and Capital	$529,900	$483,000	$ 46,900	9.7

When changes in items are shown in both dollars and percentages, items showing either a large dollar change or a large percentage change stand out and are readily seen by the person examining the statement. For example, in the comparative balance sheet of Illustration 163, the item "Cash" shows a large dollar change and the item "Notes receivable" shows a large percentage change. The large dollar change in "Cash" stands out in the

Illustration 164

ANCHOR SUPPLY COMPANY
Comparative Income Statement
Years Ended December 31, 1965, and December 31, 1966

	Years Ended December 31		Amount of Increase or Decrease* during 1966	Percentage of Increase or Decrease* during 1966
	1966	1965		
Gross sales	$973,500	$853,000	$120,500	14.1
Sales returns	13,500	10,200	3,300	32.4
Net sales	$960,000	$842,800	$117,200	13.9
Cost of goods sold.	715,000	622,500	92,500	14.9
Gross profit from sales	$245,000	$220,300	$ 24,700	11.2
Operating expenses:				
Selling expenses:				
Advertising	$ 10,000	$ 5,000	$ 5,000	100.0
Sales salaries.	113,500	98,000	15,500	15.8
Store supplies used	3,200	2,800	400	14.3
Depreciation of store equipment .	1,900	1,700	200	11.8
Delivery expense.	12,800	14,000	1,200*	8.6*
Total selling expenses.	$141,400	$121,500	$ 19,900	16.4
General and administrative expenses:				
Office salaries	$ 32,500	$ 31,000	$ 1,500	4.8
Officers' salaries.	24,000	24,000		
Office supplies used.	1,300	1,250	50	4.0
Expired insurance	1,600	1,200	400	33.3
Depreciation of office equipment.	300	300		
Depreciation of buildings	1,200	950	250	26.3
Bad debts	2,400	2,200	200	9.1
Total gen. and admin. expenses	$ 63,300	$ 60,900	$ 2,400	3.9
Total operating expenses. . .	$204,700	$182,400	$ 22,300	12.2
Operating income.	$ 40,300	$ 37,900	$ 2,400	6.3
Financial revenue and expense:				
Interest earned	1,300	2,050	750	36.6*
	$ 41,600	$ 39,950		
Interest expense	2,300	1,100	$ 1,200	109.1
Net Income before Taxes	$ 39,300	$ 38,850	$ 450	1.2

column showing increases and decreases in dollar amounts. Likewise, although the dollar amount is small, the large percentage change in "Notes receivable" stands out in the column showing percentage changes.

A comparative income statement is prepared in the same manner as a comparative balance sheet. Normally, a company's income statement amounts for two or more successive periods are placed side by side, with dollar and percentage changes in additional columns. Such a statement is shown in Illustration 164.

Analyzing and Interpreting Comparative Statements. In analyzing and interpreting comparative data, it is necessary for the analyst to select for study items showing significant dollar or percentage changes. The analyst normally considers the changes individually and jointly to determine the reasons for each and to determine if possible whether they are favorable or unfavorable. For example, in the comparative balance sheet of Anchor Supply Company, Illustration 163, the first item showing a significant change is "Cash." It shows a large decrease, and at first glance this appears unfavorable. However, when the decrease in "Cash" is considered with the decrease in "Investments" and the increase in "Store equipment," "Buildings," and "Land," plus the increase in "Mortgage payable," it becomes apparent the company has materially increased its fixed assets between the two balance sheet dates. Further study reveals the company has apparently constructed a new building on land it has held as an investment until needed in this expansion. Also, it seems the company has paid for its new fixed assets by reducing cash, selling its Apex Company bonds, and issuing a $50,000 mortgage.

The second item showing a significant change on the Anchor Supply Company comparative balance sheet is "Notes receivable," which shows a large percentage increase. From the balance sheet itself there is no ready explanation for this increase. However, it warrants further investigation by the analyst, even though the dollar amount is comparatively small.

As a management tool for controlling operations, a comparative income statement is usually more valuable than a comparative balance sheet. For example on the comparative income statement shown in Illustration 164, "gross sales" increased 14.1 percent and "Net sales" increased 13.9 percent. At the same time, "Sales returns" increased 32.4 percent, or at a rate more than twice that of gross sales. Returned sales represent wasted sales effort, and indicate dissatisfied customers; consequently, such an increase in returns should be investigated, and the reason therefor determined if at all possible.

On the income statement of Anchor Supply Company, in addition to the large increase in the "Sales returns," it is significant that the rate of increase in "Cost of goods sold" is greater than that of "net sales." This is an unfavorable trend and should be remedied if at all possible.

In attempting to account for Anchor Supply Company's increase in sales, the increase in advertising and the large increase in fixed assets merit attention. It is reasonable to expect a large expenditure for advertising to increase sales. It is also reasonable to expect an increase in fixed assets to result in a sales increase in a merchandising company or a decrease in cost of goods sold in a manufacturing company.

Calculating Percentage Increases and Decreases. When percentage increases and decreases are calculated for comparative statements, the increase or decrease in an item is divided by the amount shown for the item in the base year. No problems arise in these calculations when positive amounts are shown in the base year. For example, in Illustration 165 all items show positive amounts in the 1965 base year. However, when no

Illustration 165

	1966	(Base Year) 1965	Amount of Increase or Decrease*	Percent of Increase or Decrease*
Item one................	$15,000	$10,000	$ 5,000	50
Item two................	5,000	10,000	5,000*	50*
Item three.............	–0–	10,000	10,000*	100*
Item four (a negative* amount in the second year).................	5,000*	10,000	15,000*	150*

amount is shown for an item in the base year or a negative amount is shown, an increase or decrease percentage is not calculated. For example, in Illustration 166 the items have no amounts or negative amounts in the 1965 base year, and percentages are not calculated.

Illustration 166

	1966	(Base Year) 1965	Amount of Increase or Decrease*	Percent of Increase or Decrease*
Item one....................	$1,200	–0–	$1,200	
Item two (negative* amount in 1965)..................	3,500	$500*	4,000	
Item three (negative* amounts in both years)....	500*	250*	250*	
Item four (negative* amounts in both years)....	100*	400*	300	

Comparing Data for More than Two Accounting Periods. When a comparative statement is constructed using data from more than two accounting periods, there are two ways of showing increases and decreases. (1) The data of each accounting period after the first may be compared with the data of the immediately preceding period as in Illustration 167. Or (2) the data of each period after the first may be compared with the first period data as in Illustration 168.

Both methods are used. However, when increase and decrease percentages are shown by the first method, the results are subject to misinterpretation. For example, in Illustration 167, 1965 advertising increased 10 percent over 1964 advertising, and 1966 advertising decreased 10 percent from 1965 advertising. As a result, it would appear that the 10 percent

Illustration 167

	Year Ended			Amount of Increase—Decrease*		Percent of Increase—Decrease*	
	1966	1965	1964	1966–65	1965–64	1966–65	1965–64
Advertising	*$99,000*	*$110,000*	*$100,000*	*$11,000**	*$10,000*	*10**	*10*

increase should exactly offset the 10 percent decrease. However, this is not true; and the confusion results from using two different bases in calculating the percentages.

Illustration 168

	Year Ended			Amount of Increase—Decrease*		Percent of Increase—Decrease*	
	1966	1965	1964	1966–64	1965–64	1966–64	1965–64
Advertising	*$99,000*	*$110,000*	*$100,000*	*$1,000**	*$10,000*	*1**	*10*

Trend Percentages. Trend percentages or index numbers are useful in comparing data from several of a company's financial statements. Trend percentages emphasize changes that have occurred with the passage of time. They are calculated as follows:

1. A base year is selected; it should be a representative year for all items.
2. Each item amount on the base year statement is assigned a weight of 100 percent.
3. Then each item from the statements for the years after the base year is expressed as a percentage of its base year amount. To find these percentages, the item amounts in the years after the base year are divided by the amount of the item in the base year.

For example, if 1961 is made the base year for the data of Illustration 169, the trend percentages for "Sales" are calculated by dividing by $210,000 the amount shown for "Sales" in each year after the first. The

Illustration 169

	1961	1962	1963	1964	1965	1966
Sales.............	$210,000	$204,000	$292,000	$284,000	$310,000	$324,000
Cost of goods sold............	145,000	139,000	204,000	198,000	218,000	229,000
Gross profit......	$ 65,000	$ 65,000	$ 88,000	$ 86,000	$ 92,000	$ 95,000

Illustration 170

	1961	1962	1963	1964	1965	1966
Sales......................	100	97	139	135	148	154
Cost of goods sold..........	100	96	141	137	150	158
Gross profit.................	100	100	135	132	142	146

trend percentages for "Cost of goods sold" are found by dividing by $145,000 the amount shown for "Cost of goods sold" in each year after the first. And, the trend percentages for "Gross profit" are found by dividing the amounts shown for "Gross profit" by $65,000. When these divisions are made, the item trends appear as in Illustration 170.

It is interesting to note in the trends of the Illustration 170 items that while after the second year the sales trend is upward, the cost of goods sold trend is upward at a slightly more rapid rate. This indicates a contracting gross profit rate and should receive attention.

It should be pointed out in a discussion of trends that the trend for a single balance sheet or income statement item is seldom too informative. However, a comparison of trends for related items often tells the analyst a great deal. For example, a downward sales trend with an upward trend for merchandise inventory, accounts receivable, and loss on bad debts would generally indicate an unfavorable situation. Likewise, a downward sales trend accompanied by an upward trend for cost of goods sold and selling expenses would also appear unfavorable. Also, an upward sales trend with a higher upward trend for accounts receivable, merchandise inventory, bad debts, and selling expense might indicate that sales are being achieved at too great a cost. On the other hand, an upward sales trend with a downward trend or a slower upward trend for accounts receivable, merchandise inventory, and selling expenses would indicate an increase in operating efficiency.

Common-Size Statements.   The comparative statements illustrated thus far do not, except in a general way, show proportional changes in items. Changes in proportions are often presented and emphasized by means of *common-size statements*.

A common-size statement is so called because of the manner in which it presents items. For example, on a common-size balance sheet (1) the asset total is assigned a value of 100 percent; (2) the total of the liabilities and owner equity is also assigned a value of 100 percent; and then (3) each individual asset, liability, and owner equity item is shown as a fraction of one of the 100 percent totals. When several balance sheets are presented in this manner as a means of analysis, the items of each are expressed in common-size figures, fractions of 100 percent. A common-size comparative balance sheet for Anchor Supply Company is shown in Illustration 171.

Illustration 171

ANCHOR SUPPLY COMPANY
Comparative Balance Sheet
December 31, 1965, and December 31, 1966

	Years Ended December 31		Common-Size Percentages	
	1966	1965	1966	1965
ASSETS				
Current Assets:				
Cash	$ 14,000	$ 89,000	2.64	18.43
Notes receivable	4,000	1,500	0.76	0.31
Accounts receivable, net	68,000	64,000	12.83	13.25
Merchandise inventory.	190,000	184,000	35.86	38.10
Prepaid expenses	5,800	6,000	1.09	1.24
Total Current Assets	$281,800	$344,500	53.18	71.33
Investments:				
Real estate	-0-	$ 30,000	-0-	6.21
Apex Company 4 per cent bonds.	-0-	50,000	-0-	10.35
Total Investments.	-0-	$ 80,000	-0-	16.56
Fixed Assets:				
Office equipment	$ 5,000	$ 5,000		
Less: Accumulated depreciation	1,500	1,200		
	$ 3,500	$ 3,800	0.66	0.78
Store equipment.	$ 24,000	$ 11,000		
Less: Accumulated depreciation	6,200	4,300		
	$ 17,800	$ 6,700	3.36	1.39
Buildings.	$210,000	$ 60,000		
Less: Accumulated depreciation	33,200	32,000		
	$176,800	$ 28,000	33.36	5.80
Land	$ 50,000	$ 20,000	9.44	4.14
Total Fixed Assets	$248,100	$ 58,500	46.82	12.11
Total Assets	$529,900	$483,000	100.00	100.00
LIABILITIES				
Current Liabilities:				
Notes payable.	-0-	$ 10,000	-0-	2.07
Accounts payable	$ 53,400	60,000	10.08	12.42
Wages payable.	800	1,200	0.15	0.25
Total Current Liabilities.	$ 54,200	$ 71,200	10.23	14.74
Long-Term Liabilities:				
Mortgage payable	60,000	10,000	11.32	2.07
Total Liabilities.	$114,200	$ 81,200	21.55	16.81
CAPITAL				
Common stock	$250,000	$250,000	47.18	51.76
Retained earnings.	165,700	151,800	31.27	31.43
Total Capital.	$415,700	$401,800	78.45	83.19
Total Liabilities and Capital. . . .	$529,900	$483,000	100.00	100.00

A common-size income statement is constructed in much the same manner as a common-size balance sheet. Net sales are assigned a 100 percent value, and then each statement item is shown as a percentage of net sales.

Common-size income statements are very informative and are a useful management tool. This is because when the common-size 100 percent amount shown for sales is assumed to represent one sales dollar, then the common-size amounts for the remaining income statement items show

how each sales dollar was distributed to costs, expenses, and profit. For example, on the comparative income statement shown in Illustration 172, the 1965 cost of goods sold consumed 73.86 cents of each sales dollar. In 1966 cost of goods sold consumed 74.48 cents from each sales dollar. While this increase is apparently small, if in 1966 the proportion of cost of goods sold had remained at the 1965 level, more than $6,000 additional gross

Illustration 172

ANCHOR SUPPLY COMPANY
Comparative Income Statement
Years Ended December 31, 1965, and December 31, 1966

	Years Ended December 31		Common-Size Percentages	
	1966	1965	1966	1965
Gross sales	$973,500	$853,000	101.41	101.21
Sales returns	13,500	10,200	1.41	1.21
Net sales	$960,000	$842,800	100.00	100.00
Cost of goods sold.	715,000	622,500	74.48	73.86
Gross profit from sales	$245,000	$220,300	25.52	26.14
Operating expenses:				
Selling expenses:				
Advertising	$ 10,000	$ 5,000	1.04	0.59
Sales salaries.	113,500	98,000	11.82	11.63
Store supplies used	3,200	2,800	0.33	0.33
Depreciation of store equipment	1,900	1,700	0.20	0.20
Delivery expense.	12,800	14,000	1.33	1.66
Total selling expenses	$141,400	$121,500	14.72	14.41
General and administrative expenses:				
Office salaries	$ 32,500	$ 31,000	3.38	3.68
Officers' salaries.	24,000	24,000	2.50	2.85
Office supplies used.	1,300	1,250	0.14	0.15
Expired insurance	1,600	1,200	0.17	0.14
Depreciation of office equipment.	300	300	0.03	0.04
Depreciation of buildings	1,200	950	0.13	0.11
Bad debts	2,400	2,200	0.25	0.26
Total general and administrative expenses	$ 63,300	$ 60,900	6.60	7.23
Total operating expenses.	$204,700	$182,400	21.32	21.64
Operating income.	$ 40,300	$ 37,900	4.20	4.50
Financial revenue and expense:				
Interest earned	1,300	2,050	0.14	0.24
	$ 41,600	$ 39,950		
Interest expense.	2,300	1,100	0.24	0.13
Net Income before Taxes	$ 39,300	$ 38,850	4.09	4.61

profit would have been earned. When this $6,000 additional gross profit is viewed with the $39,300 1966 net income in mind, it becomes important.

Common-size percentages point out efficiencies and inefficiencies that are otherwise difficult to see, and for this reason are a valuable management tool. To illustrate, sales salaries of Anchor Supply Company took a higher percentage of each sales dollar in 1966 than in 1965. On the other hand, office salaries took a smaller percentage of each 1966 sales dollar. Furthermore, although the loss from bad debts was greater in 1966 than in 1965, loss from bad debts took a smaller proportion of each sales dollar in 1966 than in 1965.

ANALYSIS OF WORKING CAPITAL

The term *working capital* is used to denote the excess of a company's current assets over its current liabilities; and when balance sheets are analyzed, working capital always receives close attention. This is as it should be. Adequate working capital enables a company to carry sufficient inventories, meet current debts, take advantage of cash discounts, and extend favorable terms to customers. These are desirable. A company that is deficient in working capital and unable to do these things is in a poor competitive position. Its survival chances are normally small, unless its working capital position is improved. Inadequacy of working capital has ended the business lives of many companies whose total assets were far in excess of liabilities.

Many factors affect working capital requirements. The nature of the business in which a particular company is engaged is one factor. For example, railroads, public utilities, and other companies in which inventories consist only of supplies used in making repairs, need proportionately less working capital than do manufacturing or merchandising companies. Likewise, merchandising concerns selling on a cash basis need less working capital than concerns granting credit. Consequently, when the adequacy of working capital is studied, consideration must be given to the type of business under review.

Current Ratio. A company's working capital should be sufficient to enable it to pay current debts as they become due. However, working capital is not a measure of debt-paying ability. This may be demonstrated by the following example:

	Company A	Company B
Current assets...........	*$100,000*	*$20,000*
Current liabilities........	*90,000*	*10,000*
Working capital.........	*$ 10,000*	*$10,000*

In the example, Company A's current assets are five times greater than Company B's, and both have the same amount of working capital. However, Company B's current assets are twice its current liabilities, while Company A's are only a little more than once its current liabilities. Company B's current assets may shrink in half when turned into cash and still be adequate to meet current debts. On the other hand, Company A's current assets may shrink only 10 percent and still be adequate to meet current debts. Obviously, as the example shows, the relation of current assets to current liabilities is a more important measure of debt-paying ability than is the amount of working capital.

The relation of a company's current assets to its current liabilities is known as its *current ratio*. The current ratio of the foregoing Company B is calculated as follows:

$$\frac{\textit{Current Assets, \$20,000}}{\textit{Current Liabilities, \$10,000}} = 2$$

A current ratio is calculated by dividing current assets by current liabilities. After the division is made, the relation is expressed as, for example, Company B's current assets are two times its current liabilities, or Company B has $2 of current assets for each $1 of current liabilities, or simply Company B's current ratio is 2 to 1.

The current ratio is the relation of current assets and current liabilities expressed mathematically. A high current ratio indicates a large amount of current assets to current liabilities. The higher the ratio, the more liquid is a company's current position, and normally the better it can meet current obligations.

For many years bankers and other credit grantors measured a credit-seeking company's debt-paying ability by whether or not it had a 2 to 1 current ratio. Today most credit grantors realize that the 2 to 1 rule-of-thumb is not an adequate test of debt-paying ability. They realize that whether or not a company's current ratio is good or bad depends upon at least three factors:

1. The nature of the company's business.
2. The distribution of its current assets.
3. The turnover of certain of its current assets.

The nature of a company's business has much to do with its working capital requirements. A public utility or railroad which normally has no inventories other than supplies, and which grants little or no credit, can often operate on a current ratio less than 1 to 1. On the other hand, because a misjudgment of style can make a finished goods inventory almost worthless, a company manufacturing articles in which style is the important sales factor may find a current ratio of more than 2 to 1 to be inadequate. Perhaps the best test of the adequacy of a company's current ratio is a comparison with the current ratios of a number of its close competitors. However, these are often unavailable.

Distribution of Current Assets. In an analysis of debt-paying ability, the current asset distribution is important. Normally, a company with a high proportion of cash to accounts receivable, merchandise inventory, and other current assets is in a better position to meet quickly its current debts than is a company with most of its current assets tied up in accounts receivable and merchandise. The company with cash may pay its current debts at once. The company with accounts receivable and merchandise normally must turn these items into cash before it can pay. In turning accounts and merchandise into cash there is always a possibility of shrinkage. However, when current assets are analyzed, the fact that merchandise is normally sold for more than its balance sheet amount and consequently produces more than its balance sheet amount of cash should not be ignored.

Current asset distribution may be examined in two ways. A schedule showing the percentage of each current asset to total current assets may be constructed, and the *acid-test ratio* may be calculated. A schedule showing the current asset distribution of Anchor Supply Company appears as in Illustration 173.

Illustration 173

	December 31, 1966		December 31, 1965	
	Amount	Percent	Amount	Percent
Current Assets:				
Cash.................	$ 14,000	4.97	$ 89,000	25.83
Notes receivable......	4,000	1.42	1,500	.44
Accounts receivable, net..................	68,000	24.13	64,000	18.58
Merchandise inventory...............	190,000	67.42	184,000	53.41
Prepaid expenses.....	5,800	2.06	6,000	1.74
Total..............	$281,800	100.00	$344,500	100.00

The acid-test ratio offers an easily calculated quick check on current asset distribution. The acid-test ratio is often called the *quick ratio* because it is the ratio of "quick assets" to current liabilities. "Quick assets" are cash, notes receivable, accounts receivable, and marketable securities. They are the current assets that can quickly be turned into cash. An acid-test ratio of 1 to 1 is normally considered satisfactory. However, this is a rule-of-thumb and should be applied with care. The acid-test ratio of Anchor Supply Company on December 31, 1966, is calculated as follows:

Quick Assets:		*Current Liabilities:*	
Cash................	$14,000	Accounts payable.....$53,400	
Notes receivable......	4,000	Wages payable........	800
Accounts receivable...	68,000	Total..............$54,200	
Total..............$86,000			

Acid-Test Ratio = $86,000 ÷ $54,200 = 1.59, or *Acid-Test Ratio* = 1.59 to 1

Turnover of Accounts Receivable. Certain current asset turnovers affect working capital requirements. For example, Companies A and B sell the same amounts of merchandise on account each month. However, Company A grants 30-day terms to its customers, while Company B grants 60 days. Both collect their accounts at the end of the credit periods granted. But, as a result of the difference in terms, Company A turns over or collects its accounts twice as rapidly as does Company B. Also, as a result of the more rapid turnover, Company A requires only one half the investment in accounts receivable that is required of Company B.

Accounts receivable turnover is calculated by dividing net sales for a particular year by end-of-the-year accounts receivable. Illustration 174 shows the calculation of Anchor Supply Company's accounts receivable turnover. The turnover of 14.12 times in 1966 in comparison with 13.16 times in 1965 indicates the company's accounts receivable were collected more rapidly in 1966.

Illustration 174

	1966	1965
Net sales for year.......................	$960,000	$842,200
Year-end accounts receivable............	68,000	64,000
Times accounts receivable were turned over (sales ÷ accounts receivable).....	14.12	13.16

Theoretically, only charge sales rather than the sum of charge and cash sales should be used in calculating this turnover. Likewise, accounts receivable before subtracting allowance for bad debts should be used. However, information as to charge sales is seldom available in a published balance sheet, and many published balance sheets report accounts receivable at their net amount. Consequently, total charge and cash sales and net accounts receivable must often be used in the calculation.

Likewise, as in calculating merchandise turnover, which is discussed later, if year-end accounts receivable are not representative, an average of the year's accounts receivable by months may be used in calculating accounts receivable turnover.

Days' Sales Uncollected. Accounts receivable turnover is one indication of the speed with which a company collects its accounts. *Days' sales uncollected* is another indication of the same thing. To illustrate the calculation of days' sales uncollected, assume a company had charge sales during a year of $250,000 and that it has $25,000 of accounts receivable at the year-end. In other words, one tenth of its charge sales, or the charge sales made during one tenth of a year, or the charge sales of 36.5 days

($\frac{1}{10}$ × 365 days in a year = 36.5 days) are uncollected. This calculation of days' sales uncollected in equation form appears as follows:

$$\frac{\textit{Accounts Receivable, \$25,000}}{\textit{Charge Sales, \$250,000}} \times 365 = 36.5 \text{ Days' Sales Uncollected}$$

Days' sales uncollected takes on more meaning when credit terms are known. According to a rule-of-thumb, a company's accounts receivable should not exceed one and one-third times the days in the credit period it grants. If the company whose days' sales uncollected is calculated in the illustration just given offers 30-day terms, then 36.5 days is within the rule-of-thumb amount. However, if its terms are 2/10, n/30, 36.5 days' sales uncollected would seem excessive.

Days' sales uncollected is sometimes used as a test of a company's accounts receivable. If days' sales uncollected are excessive, it is assumed that some accounts are probably old and uncollectible.

Turnover of Merchandise Inventory. A company's merchandise turnover is the number of times its average inventory is sold during an accounting period. Merchandise turnover is a test of merchandising efficiency. A high turnover is considered a mark of good merchandising. Also, from a working capital point of view, a company with a high turnover requires a smaller investment in inventory than one producing the same sales with a low turnover. Merchandise turnover is calculated by dividing cost of goods sold by average inventory. Cost of goods sold is the amount of merchandise at its cost price that was sold during an accounting period; average inventory is the average amount of merchandise, at its cost price, on hand during the period. The 1966 merchandise turnover of Anchor Supply Company is calculated as follows:

$$\frac{\textit{Cost of Goods Sold, \$715,000}}{\textit{Average Merchandise Inventory, \$187,000}} = \textit{Merchandise Turnover of 3.82 Times}$$

The cost of goods sold is taken from the company's 1966 income statement. The average inventory is found by dividing by two the sum of the January 1, 1966, inventory of $184,000 and the December 31, 1966, inventory of $190,000. In a company in which beginning and ending inventories are not representative of the inventory normally on hand, a more accurate turnover may be secured by using the average of all the twelve month-end inventories rather than just the beginning and end of the year inventories.

STANDARDS OF COMPARISON

When financial statements are analyzed by computing ratios and turnovers, the analyst must determine whether the ratios and turnovers obtained are good, bad, or just average. In a decision as to whether ratios are good, bad, or average, the analyst must have some basis for comparison. The following are available:

1. A trained analyst may compare the ratios and turnovers of the company under review with his own mental standards built up from past experiences.
2. An analyst may calculate for purposes of comparison the ratios and turnovers of a selected group of competitive companies in the same industry as the one whose statements are under review.
3. Published ratios and turnovers such as those put out by Dun & Bradstreet may be secured for comparison.
4. Some local and national trade associations gather data from their members and publish standard or average ratios for their trade or industry. These offer the analyst a very good basis of comparison when available.
5. Rule-of-thumb standards may be used as a basis for comparison.

Of the five foregoing standards, the ratios and turnovers of a selected group of competitive companies normally offer the best basis for comparison. Rule-of-thumb standards should be applied with care if erroneous conclusions are to be avoided.

OTHER BALANCE SHEET AND INCOME STATEMENT RELATIONS

Several balance sheet and income statement relations in addition to those having to do with working capital are important to the analyst. Some of the more important are discussed in the following pages.

Capital Contributions of Owners and Creditors. The share of a company's assets contributed by its owners and the share contributed by creditors are always of interest to the analyst. The owner and creditor contributions of Anchor Supply Company are calculated as in Illustration 175.

Creditors like to see a high proportion of owner equity because owner equity acts as a cushion in absorbing losses. The greater the equity of the

Illustration 175		
	1966	1965
Total liabilities.......................	*$114,200*	*$ 81,200*
Total owner equity.....................	*415,700*	*401,800*
Total liabilities and owner equity........	*$529,900*	*$483,000*
Creditors' equity (line 1 divided by line 3).........................	*21.55%*	*16.81%*
Owner equity (line 2 divided by line 3).........................	*78.45%*	*83.19%*

owners in relation to that of the creditors, the greater the losses that can be absorbed by the owners before the creditors begin to lose.

From the creditors' standpoint a high percentage of owner equity is desirable. However, if an enterprise can earn a return on borrowed capital in excess of the capital's cost, then an increase in creditor equity is often desirable from the owners' viewpoint. When a company operates on borrowed capital, it trades or operates on capital supplied by its creditors. For this reason, when a company operates on borrowed capital, it is said to be *trading on the equity*. It is trading on the equity of its creditors. When returns are in excess of the cost of borrowed capital, trading on the equity is often desirable from the viewpoint of the business owners. However, if earnings are unstable, it may be dangerous.

Net Income to Owner Equity. One of the more important objectives of a business enterprise is to earn a profit for its owners. The ratio of net income to owner equity measures success in accomplishing this objective, and is calculated for Anchor Supply Company for 1966 as follows:

$$\frac{\textit{Net Income, \$39,300}}{\textit{Owner Equity, \$401,800}} = \textit{9.78 Percent Net Income Ratio}$$

Net income after taxes and normally beginning owner equity are used in calculating this ratio. However, if during the period, owner equity fluctuated greatly, average owner equity may give a better picture.

Pledged Fixed Assets to Long-Term Liabilities. Companies commonly borrow by issuing a note or bonds secured by a mortgage on certain of their fixed assets. The ratio of pledged fixed assets to long-term debt is often calculated to measure the security granted to mortgage or bondholders by the pledged assets. This ratio is calculated by dividing the pledged assets' book value by the liabilities for which the assets are pledged. It is calculated for Anchor Supply Company in 1965 and 1966 as in Illustration 176.

Illustration 176

	1966	1965
Buildings.................................	*$210,000*	*$60,000*
Less: Accumulated depreciation.......	*33,200*	*32,000*
Buildings, net..........................	*$176,800*	*$28,000*
Land....................................	*50,000*	*20,000*
Book value of pledged fixed assets.......	*$226,800*	*$48,000*
Mortgage payable......................	*$ 60,000*	*$10,000*
Ratio of pledged assets to secured liabilities.................................	*3.78 to 1*	*4.8 to 1*

The usual rule-of-thumb minimum for this ratio is 2 to 1. However, this ratio needs careful interpretation because it shows relation between the *book value* of pledged fixed assets and long-term liabilities. Even when depreciation is accurately estimated and recorded, book values do not measure the amount that would be secured in a foreclosure or a liquidation. Estimated liquidation values or foreclosure values are a better measure of the protection offered bond or mortgage holders by pledged assets. Often, in situations in which assets are pledged, the long-term earning ability of the company whose assets are pledged is more important to long-term creditors than the pledged assets' book value.

Times Fixed Interest Charges Earned. The number of times fixed interest charges are earned is often calculated to measure the security of the return offered to bondholders or a mortgage holder. The number of times fixed interest charges are earned is determined by dividing income (before deducting income taxes and fixed interest charges) by the amount of the fixed interest charges. Since fixed interest charges are an expense that take precedence over income taxes, income before deducting income taxes is used in the calculation. Likewise, since the calculation is the number of times fixed interest charges are earned, fixed interest charges are not deducted in arriving at the income used in the calculation. Often the return to a company's long-term creditors is considered secure if the company consistently earns its fixed interest charges two or more times each year.

THE EFFECT OF PRICE LEVEL CHANGES

When financial statements for a period of several years are analyzed, the analyst must keep in mind the effect on the statements of *price level changes.* Price level changes are changes in the purchasing power of money. Often, if price level changes are ignored, incorrect conclusions may be drawn. For example, during the 1945 through 1959 period many companies showed a large dollar increase in sales when their physical volume of sales actually remained unchanged or increased only a small amount. In these companies the increase in dollar sales volume was caused by the decrease in the purchasing power of the dollar. During these years, 1945–59, a dollar purchased a smaller amount of goods each year; or, in other words, during each of these years it required an increasing number of dollars to buy the same amount of goods.

Price level changes affect income statement items, but their effect is not limited to such items. They also affect the balance sheet. For example, many companies are operating today with fixed assets, the replacement costs of which are several times their reported balance sheet values. This is particularly true of buildings purchased or constructed some years ago.

No effort will be made here to enter into an exhaustive discussion of the effect of price level changes on financial statements. Such a discussion is reserved for a more advanced course. However, the student should be aware of this phenomenon.

OTHER ANALYTICAL DEVICES

Many analytical devices are available to aid the analyst in separating financial statement parts so as to see the relation of the parts to the whole and to each other. Several kinds of comparative statements, ratios, and turnovers have been discussed in this chapter; break-even analysis was discussed in a previous chapter; and the funds flow statement is the subject of the next chapter. All are valuable tools of the analyst. However, they do not replace his good judgment. They are only tools that aid in bringing the data under review into a sharper focus.

QUESTIONS FOR CLASS DISCUSSION

1. Why does a comparative balance sheet often have columns showing increases and decreases in both dollar amounts and in percentages?
2. Where possible calculate percentage increases and decreases for the following unrelated items. (The asterisk following an amount indicates a deficit.)

	1967	1966
Buildings, net	*$78,000*	*$60,000*
Investments	*-0-*	*68,000*
Notes payable	*10,000*	*-0-*
Retained earnings	*3,000**	*12,000*
Cash	*12,000*	*2,500**

3. Calculate trend percentages for the following items:

	1963	1964	1965	1966	1967
Sales	*$150,000*	*$168,000*	*$180,000*	*$186,000*	*$192,000*
Merchandise inventory	*30,000*	*35,700*	*39,600*	*42,600*	*46,200*
Accounts receivable	*18,000*	*23,040*	*24,300*	*25,200*	*27,360*

Is the situation presented by the trends favorable or unfavorable?

4. When trends are calculated and compared, what item trends should be compared with the trend of sales?
5. Why are common-size statements so called?
6. What items are assigned a value of 100 percent (*a*) on a common-size balance sheet, and (*b*) on a common-size income statement?
7. Define the term working capital.
8. For the following transactions tell which increase working capital, which decrease working capital, and which have no effect on working capital:
   a) Collected accounts receivable.
   b) Borrowed money from the bank by giving an interest-bearing note.

     c) Declared a cash dividend.
     d) Paid a cash dividend previously declared.
     e) Sold fixed assets at their book value.
     f) Sold merchandise at a profit.
  9. Why is adequate working capital of importance to a business?
 10. List several factors that have an effect on working capital requirements.
 11. The Abbot Company has a 2 to 1 current ratio. List several reasons why this ratio may not be adequate.
 12. Tell the significance of each of the following ratios and turnovers and tell how each is calculated:

a) Current ratio.	*d*) Turnover of merchandise inventory.
b) Acid-test ratio.	*e*) Net income to owner equity ratio.
c) Turnover of accounts receiv-	*f*) Ratio of pledged fixed assets to
able.	long-term liabilities.

 13. How are days' sales uncollected calculated? What is the significance of the number of days' sales uncollected?
 14. Why do creditors like to see a high proportion of owner equity?
 15. What is meant by the phrase "trading on the equity"?
 16. What are price level changes? Why must the effect of price level changes be considered when statements covering a period of years are analyzed?

PROBLEMS

Problem 26–1

The following items were taken from the year-end statements of a merchandising company:

Cash..$	6,400
Accounts receivable, net of bad debts allowance...	38,600
End-of-the-year merchandise inventory..........	39,000
Beginning-of-the-year merchandise inventory....	41,400
Prepaid expenses....................................	600
Equipment, net of depreciation....................	86,400
Building, net of depreciation.....................	68,800
Land..	8,000
Accounts payable.................................	21,500
Federal income taxes payable....................	8,500
Mortgage payable (secured by a lien on the land	
and building).................................	32,000
Common stock, $10 par value....................	100,000
Retained earnings...............................	86,000
Sales (all on account)..........................	386,000
Net cost of purchases...........................	258,900

Required:

Calculate the current ratio, acid-test ratio, days' sales uncollected, accounts receivable turnover, merchandise turnover, and ratio of pledged fixed assets to long-term liabilities.

Problem 26–2

Havertine Sales Company's condensed comparative statements follow:

HAVERTINE SALES COMPANY
Comparative Income Statements
Years Ended December 31, 1964, 1965, and 1966
(In Thousands of Dollars)

	1964	1965	1966
Sales..	$5,000	$6,000	$6,500
Cost of goods sold........................	3,600	4,398	4,745
Gross margin on sales....................	$1,400	$1,602	$1,755
Selling expenses..........................	$ 700	$ 810	$ 884
Administrative expenses..................	500	588	637
Total expenses........................	$1,200	$1,398	$1,521
Income before taxes......................	$ 200	$ 204	$ 234
State and federal income taxes...........	90	92	105
Net Income..............................	$ 110	$ 112	$ 129

HAVERTINE SALES COMPANY
Comparative Balance Sheets
December 31, 1964, 1965, and 1966
(In Thousands of Dollars)

Assets

	1964	1965	1966
Current assets...........................	$ 400	$ 256	$ 240
Plant and equipment.....................	1,200	1,380	1,440
Total Assets........................	$1,600	$1,636	$1,680

Liabilities and Capital

	1964	1965	1966
Current liabilities........................	$ 125	$ 131	$ 127
Common stock, $10 par value.............	1,000	1,000	1,000
Other contributed capital.................	175	175	175
Retained earnings........................	300	330	378
Total Liabilities and Capital...........	$1,600	$1,636	$1,680

Required:
1. Calculate each year's current ratio.
2. Express the income statement data in common-size percentages.
3. Express the balance sheet data in trend percentages.
4. Comment on any significant relationships revealed by the ratios and percentages.

Problem 26–3

Following are data from the current year-end statements of two wholesale companies selling similar products:

DATA FROM THE CURRENT DECEMBER 31 BALANCE SHEETS:

	Company A	Company B
Cash...	$ 6,000	$ 5,000
Notes receivable............................	2,400	4,400
Accounts receivable, net....................	32,000	54,800
Merchandise inventory......................	34,000	46,400
Prepaid expenses...........................	1,100	600
Total Current Assets....................	$ 75,500	$111,200
Fixed assets, net............................	81,300	94,200
Total Assets.........................	$156,800	$205,400
Accounts payable...........................	$ 33,000	$ 49,700
Notes payable..............................	5,000	7,500
Accrued payables...........................	600	1,200
Total Liabilities.......................	$ 38,600	$ 58,400
Common stock..............................	100,000	100,000
Retained earnings..........................	18,200	47,000
Total Liabilities and Capital.........	$156,800	$205,400

DATA FROM THE CURRENT YEARLY INCOME STATEMENTS:

Sales.......................................	$256,000	$493,200
Cost of goods sold..........................	179,300	345,400
Income before taxes........................	10,700	23,700
Inventory on January 1....................	36,000	45,600

Required:

Calculate current ratios, acid-test ratios, percentage of capital contributed by owners, merchandise turnovers, days' sales uncollected, and ratio of income before taxes to sales for the foregoing two companies. Then state which of the companies you think is the better short-term credit risk and why.

Problem 26–4

The condensed comparative statements of Drexel Sales Company follow:

DREXEL SALES COMPANY
Comparative Income Statements
For Years Ended December 31, 1961–67
(In Thousands of Dollars)

	1961	1962	1963	1964	1965	1966	1967
Sales.................................	$400	$500	$572	$680	$760	$840	$872
Cost of goods sold..................	250	310	360	430	515	585	604
Gross profit from sales..............	$150	$190	$212	$250	$245	$255	$268
Operating expenses.................	100	110	118	138	197	220	238
Income before taxes................	$ 50	$ 80	$ 94	$112	$ 48	$ 35	$ 30

DREXEL SALES COMPANY
Comparative Balance Sheets
December 31, 1961–67
(In Thousands of Dollars)

Assets

	1961	1962	1963	1964	1965	1966	1967
Cash..........................	$ 20	$ 14	$ 17	$ 15	$ 12	$ 10	$ 4
Accounts receivable, net...........	40	52	54	62	88	90	92
Merchandise inventory.............	100	118	141	165	204	218	226
Other current assets...............	2	4	4	6	2	4	2
Long-term investments.............	38	38	38	38			
Fixed assets, net..................	200	198	204	202	446	450	440
Total Assets.................	$400	$424	$458	$488	$752	$772	$764

Liabilities and Capital

	1961	1962	1963	1964	1965	1966	1967
Current liabilities.................	$ 50	$ 64	$ 82	$ 90	$140	$156	$159
Long-term liabilities..............	40	38	36	34	182	180	178
Common stock....................	200	200	200	200	250	250	250
Premium on common stock........	50	50	50	50	60	60	60
Retained earnings.................	60	72	90	114	120	126	117
Total Liabilities and Capital...	$400	$424	$458	$488	$752	$772	$764

Required:
1. Calculate trend percentages for the items of the statements.
2. Analyze and comment on any situations shown in the statements.

Problem 26–5

A company had $180,000 of current assets, a 3 to 1 current ratio, and a 1½ to 1 quick ratio. It then completed the following transactions:
a) Collected a $2,500 account receivable.
b) Wrote off a $1,000 bad debt against the allowance for bad debts.
c) Borrowed $20,000 by giving its bank a 60-day, 6 percent note.
d) Bought $10,000 of merchandise on credit. The company uses a perpetual inventory system.
e) Declared a $0.50 per share cash dividend on its 20,000 shares of outstanding $10 par value common stock.
f) Paid the dividend declared in (e) above.
g) Declared a 1,000-share stock dividend. The stock was selling at $15 per share on the day of the declaration.
h) Distributed the dividend stock of (g) above.
i) Sold for $10,000 merchandise that cost $5,000.

Required:
Prepare a schedule showing the company's current ratio, its acid test ratio, and the amount of its working capital after each of the foregoing transactions. Carry decimals three places.

CLASS EXERCISES

Exercise 26–1

Common-size and trend percentages for a company's sales, cost of goods sold, and expenses follow:

Common-Size Percentage			Trend Percentage		
1965	1966	1967	1965	1966	1967

Sales............*100.0*	*100.0*	*100.0*	*Sales*............*100.0*	*95.0*	*90.0*
Cost of goods			*Cost of goods*		
sold........... *64.0*	*63.0*	*63.0*	*sold*............*100.0*	*98.4*	*98.4*
Expenses........ *28.0*	*28.0*	*27.0*	*Expenses*........*100.0*	*100.0*	*96.4*

Required:
Present statistics to prove whether the company's net income increased, decreased, or remained unchanged during the three-year period.

Exercise 26–2 .
Company A had $200,000 of sales during 1967. Its cost of goods sold was $140,000, its selling expenses were $28,000, and its administrative expenses were $12,000. From this data construct an income statement for Company A that shows both dollar amounts and common-size percentages.

ALTERNATE PROBLEMS

Problem 26–1A
The condensed statements of Southwest Sales Company follow:

SOUTHWEST SALES COMPANY
Income Statement for Year Ended December 31, 19—

Sales (all on credit)............................		*$300,000*
Cost of goods sold:		
Merchandise inventory, January 1, 19—......*$ 44,000*		
Purchases.................................... *206,000*		
Goods for sale.............................*$250,000*		
Merchandise inventory, December 31, 19—.... *40,000*		
Cost of goods sold..........................	*210,000*	
Gross profit from sales.......................	*$ 90,000*	
Operating expenses..........................	*70,000*	
Income before Taxes.........................	*$ 20,000*	

SOUTHWEST SALES COMPANY
Balance Sheet, December 31, 19—

Cash.................*$ 6,000*		*Accounts payable*......*$ 25,000*	
Accounts receivable,		*Mortgage payable*	
net................. *24,000*		*(secured by a*	
Merchandise inventory. *40,000*		*mortgage on land*	
Equipment, net....... *15,000*		*and building)*....... *16,000*	
Building, net.......... *35,000*		*Common stock*........ *50,000*	
Land................. *5,000*		*Retained earnings*..... *34,000*	
$125,000		*$125,000*	

Required:
Calculate the company's (1) current ratio, (2) acid-test ratio, (3) days' sales uncollected, (4) accounts receivable turnover, (5) merchandise turnover, (6) percentage of capital contributed by the owners, and (7) ratio of pledged fixed assets to long-term liabilities.

Problem 26–2A
The condensed comparative statements of Gem Supply Company follow:

GEM SUPPLY COMPANY
Comparative Income Statements
Years Ended December 31, 1964, 1965, and 1966
(In Thousands of Dollars)

	1964	1965	1966
Sales...................................	$8,000	$9,000	$10,000
Cost of goods sold........................	5,688	6,480	7,150
Gross profit from sales....................	$2,312	$2,520	$ 2,850
Selling expenses..........................	$1,216	$1,359	$ 1,500
Administrative expenses...................	784	855	940
Total expenses........................	$2,000	$2,214	$ 2,440
Income before taxes......................	$ 312	$ 306	$ 410
State and federal income taxes............	152	149	196
Net Income..............................	$ 160	$ 157	$ 214

GEM SUPPLY COMPANY
Comparative Balance Sheets
December 31, 1964, 1965, and 1966
(In Thousands of Dollars)

Assets

	1964	1965	1966
Current assets............................	$ 750	$ 615	$ 696
Long-term investments....................	50	5	
Plant and equipment......................	2,400	2,676	2,664
Total Assets.........................	$3,200	$3,296	$3,360

Liabilities and Capital

	1964	1965	1966
Current liabilities.........................	$ 250	$ 280	$ 290
Common stock...........................	2,000	2,100	2,100
Other contributed capital..................	50	61	61
Retained earnings........................	900	855	909
Total Liabilities and Capital...........	$3,200	$3,296	$3,360

Required:
1. Calculate each year's current ratio.
2. Express the income statement data in common-size percentages.
3. Express the balance sheet data in trend percentages.
4. Comment on any significant relationships revealed by the ratios and percentages.

Problem 26–3A

Following are the condensed 1966 and 1967 statements of Marchant Sales:

MARCHANT SALES
Comparative Income Statements
Years Ended December 31, 1966–67

	1967	1966
Sales (all on credit)..........................	$476,000	$451,000
Cost of goods sold:		
Merchandise inventory, January 1............	$ 43,000	$ 41,000
Purchases.....................................	305,600	273,800
Goods for sale...............................	$348,600	$314,800
Merchandise inventory, December 31.........	56,000	43,000
Cost of goods sold...........................	$292,600	$271,800
Gross profit from sales......................	$183,400	$179,200
Operating expenses...........................	163,400	156,600
Income before Taxes.........................	$ 20,000	$ 22,600

MARCHANT SALES
Comparative Balance Sheets
December 31, 1966–67

Assets

	1967	1966
Cash...	$ 14,000	$ 12,000
Accounts receivable..........................	38,000	44,000
Merchandise inventory........................	56,000	43,000
Fixed assets, net.............................	104,000	102,000
Total Assets............................	$212,000	$201,000

Liabilities and Stockholders' Equity

	1967	1966
Accounts payable.............................	$ 26,000	$ 28,000
Notes payable................................	10,000	6,000
Mortgage payable (due in 1980)...............	40,000	40,000
Common stock................................	100,000	100,000
Retained earnings............................	36,000	27,000
Total Liabilities and Stockholders' Equity..	$212,000	$201,000

Required:

1. Calculate common-size percentages for sales, cost of goods sold, gross profit from sales, operating expenses, and income before taxes; and calculate the current ratio, acid-test ratio, merchandise turnover, and days' sales uncollected for each of the two years.
2. Comment on the situation shown by your calculations.

Problem 26–5A

A company began the month of May with $200,000 in current assets, a 2½ to 1 current ratio, and a 1¼ to 1 acid-test ratio. During the month it completed the following transactions:

May 1 Bought $20,000 of merchandise on account. (The company uses a perpetual inventory system.)

5 Sold for $10,000 merchandise that cost $5,000.

7 Collected a $2,500 account receivable.

11 Paid a $10,000 account payable.

15 Wrote off a $1,500 bad debt against the allowance for bad debts.

18 Declared a $1 per share cash dividend on the 10,000 shares of outstanding common stock.

28 Paid the dividend declared on May 18.

29 Borrowed $10,000 by giving the bank a 60-day, 6 percent note.

30 Borrowed $25,000 by placing a ten-year mortgage on the plant.

31 Used the $25,000 proceeds of the mortgage to buy additional machinery.

Required:

Prepare a schedule showing the company's current ratio, acid-test ratio, and working capital after each of the foregoing transactions. Carry decimals three places.

DECISION PROBLEM 26A—CAR & COMPANY

The finance subcommittee chairman of Car & Company board of directors has analyzed the company's financial statements which are to be presented to the board at its next monthly meeting. The controller's department supplied him with the following ratios:

	1967	1966	1965
1. *Current ratio*............................	*2.50*	*2.00*	*2.10*
2. *Acid test*...................................	*.69*	*.80*	*1.90*
3. *Merchandise turnover*.....................	*4.00*	*5.00*	*6.00*
4. *Accounts receivable turnover*.............	*6.00*	*7.00*	*8.00*
5. *Net income to owner equity*..............	*.09*	*.08*	*.06*
6. *Percentage of capital contributed by*			
stockholders............................	*70.0*	*73.0*	*75.0*
7. *Sales to fixed assets*.......................	*2.5*	*3.0*	*3.5*
8. *Times fixed interest charges earned*........	*3.5*	*3.6*	*4.0*
9. *Ratio of sales to 1965 sales*................	*1.35*	*1.22*	*1.00*
10. *Selling expenses to net sales*..............	*.15*	*.18*	*.20*

To assist the finance chairman you are requested to state whether each of the following is true or false, and explain how you arrive at your answers.

a) The company was more able in 1967 to pay current debts, meet its payroll, and pay operating expenses than in 1965.

b) Receivable collections are improving.

c) The declining merchandise turnover is justified by the increasing volume of sales.

d) The investment in inventory has become smaller.

e) The creditors have a larger proportionate claim against the assets than in 1965.

f) Ratios 7 and 9 when interpreted together indicate continued expansion of plant facilities.

g) Total selling expenses in 1967 were less than in 1965.

h) The stockholders' investment is becoming more profitable.

i) The stockholders are profiting from "trading on the equity."

j) Ratio 8 indicates a dangerous threat to future dividend distributions to stockholders.

DECISION PROBLEM 26B—KEEL TOOL COMPANY

John Williams, controller of the Keel Tool Company, has been requested by the board of directors of the company to prepare answers to certain questions raised by members of the board. These questions are as follows:

1. Is the working capital position as strong now as it was at the end of 1965? (Present current and acid-test ratios, receivable and finished goods inventory turnovers, and a schedule of the distribution of current assets.) Are accounts receivable being collected more rapidly or less rapidly? Does there seem to be any tendency to over invest in finished goods inventory?

2. What explanation can management make to the board for continued decline in the cash position in spite of the existing policy of retaining at least 50 percent of the net income in the business?

3. What is the amount of dividends per share for each of the last three years? How much was earned per share? The average market value has been 125 percent of the book value of the shares at the end of each of the last three years. What has been the dividend yield to the stockholders based on year-end market values?

Using the following condensed data prepare a report answering the questions raised by the board of directors:

THE KEEL TOOL COMPANY
($000 Omitted)

	December 31		
	1965	1966	1967
Cash..	$ 80	$ 70	$ 50
Accounts receivable (net)....................	90	100	110
*Inventory of finished goods, December 31...	60	70	80
Inventory of raw materials, December 31....	50	65	70
Inventory of goods in process, December 31..	None	None	None
Plant (net).................................	200	210	230
Current liabilities..........................	100	110	120
Six percent bonds payable...................	60	60	60
Common stock, par $100 per share..........	200	200	200
†Retained earnings.........................	90	105	110
Reserve for plant expansion ($10,000			
per year).................................	30	40	50
Sales......................................	600	620	640
Cost of goods manufactured................	460	475	480
Operating expenses.........................	120	130	135

  * *The inventory of finished goods on December 31, 1964, was $50,000.*

  † *The only reduction in retained earnings, except for dividends, during the three years was for a $5,000 storm loss in 1967. The balance of unappropriated retained earnings on January 1, 1965, was $75,000.*

Flow of Funds;
Flow of Cash

OCCASIONALLY management personnel in a successful corporation, upon examination of their company's income statement, will make the following observation and ask the following question: "Our income statement shows ample net income, yet we seem to be having more and more trouble finding funds to meet our current obligations. Has our reported net income actually been earned; and if so, what has happened to the money?" In such a situation an analysis of the flow of funds in the operation of the business will reveal what happened to earnings; it will also show what happened to funds from other sources.

NATURE OF FUNDS

When the word "funds" is used in the phrase "flow of funds," the term has reference to more than the "cash" of a business. Actually, it means working capital or, in other words, current assets minus current liabilities.

When the term "funds" is used in this broad sense, it is easy to see why current assets are considered "funds." The more important current assets are cash, accounts receivable, and inventory, and are often called "circulating assets." They are so called because, in a sense, they circulate; the cash is used to buy merchandise, which is sold and turned into accounts receivable, which are collected and turned back into cash, which is used to buy more merchandise, and so on. Actually, the accounts receivable are only one step away from cash and the merchandise is only two.

Although it is easy to see where cash, accounts receivable, and inventory fit into the picture of a concern's funds, it is sometimes a little difficult to see the place of the current liabilities. However, when it is remembered that in addition to having sufficient cash and an adequate supply of merchandise, a company must also pay its debts when due, the place of the current liabilities becomes more clear—current liabilities must be paid from current assets. Or in other words, current liabilities are negative working capital items that must be deducted from current assets in arriving at total "free funds" or working capital available for use in operating the business.

FLOW OF FUNDS

Funds flow into a business and they flow out. Consequently, in an analysis of a concern's funds flow one must examine both sources and applications of funds.

Sources of Funds. Transactions that increase working capital are sources of funds. Some of the more common sources of funds are:

Funds from Operations. Funds in the form of cash and accounts receivable flow into a business from sales; and funds flow out for expenses and goods sold. Consequently, funds are increased as a result of normal operations if the inflow from sales exceeds the outflow for expenses and goods sold.

Illustration 177

REXEL SALES COMPANY
Income Statement for Year Ended December 31, 19--

Sales.		$50,000
Cost of goods sold		30,000
Gross profit from sales.		$20,000
Operating expenses:		
Sales salaries	$8,000	
Rent expense	1,500	
Depreciation of equipment.	1,000	10,500
Net Income		$ 9,500

In an analysis of a concern's funds flow the income statement is examined to determine the amount of funds from operations. However, the reported net income is not necessarily the amount of funds from this source, even though reported net income is the amount revenues exceeded expenses. This is because on an income statement there are almost always expenses such as depreciation, depletion, and amortization of bond discount which did not cause a funds outflow in the period of the statement, either as decreases in current assets or increases in current liabilities.

For example, Rexel Sales Company, Illustration 177, experienced a $50,000 funds inflow from sales during the year. It also experienced outflows of $30,000 for goods sold, $8,000 for salaries, and $1,500 for rent; but there was no funds outflow for depreciation of equipment. Consequently, during this period Rexel Sales Company gained funds equal to the sum of its reported net income plus recorded depreciation, or it gained $9,500 plus $1,000 or a $10,500 total of funds from operations.

Funds from Long-Term Loans. Long-term loans increase working capital and, therefore, are sources of funds whether the loans are based on long-term notes, mortgages, or bonds. On the other hand, although long-term loans are sources of funds, short-term credit, whether obtained from banks or other creditors, is not a source of funds because short-term credit does not increase working capital. For example, if $10,000 is borrowed for a short period, say six months, both current assets and current liabilities are increased; but since both are increased in equal amounts, total working capital is unchanged.

Funds from the Sale of Noncurrent Assets. When a fixed asset, permanent investment, or other noncurrent asset is sold for cash or receivables, working capital is increased by the amount of the sale; therefore, such sales are sources of funds.

Funds from the Sale of Capital Stock. The sale of stock for cash or current receivables increases current assets; as a result, such sales are sources of funds. Likewise, an additional investment by a single proprietor or partner is also a source of funds.

Applications of Funds. When funds flow out for purposes other than current asset acquisitions or the payment of current liabilities, the uses to which the funds are put are called applications of funds. A list of applications includes:

Purchase of Noncurrent Assets. When noncurrent assets such as plant and equipment or long-term investments are purchased, working capital is reduced; consequently, such purchases are applications of funds.

Payment of Noncurrent Liabilities. Payment of a long-term debt such as a mortgage, bonds, or a long-term note reduces working capital and is an application of funds. Likewise, a contribution to a debt retirement fund, bond sinking fund, preferred stock retirement fund, or other special noncurrent fund is also an application of funds.

Declaration of a Dividend. The declaration of a dividend which is to be paid in cash or other current assets reduces working capital and is an application of funds. Note that it is the declaration that is the application. The declaration creates a current liability, dividends payable, and therefore is an application as soon as voted by the board of directors. The final payment of a dividend previously declared does not affect total working capital because it reduces current assets and current liabilities in equal amounts.

FUNDS STATEMENT

When a funds flow analysis is made, a report of the analysis called a "funds statement," a "funds flow statement," or a "statement of sources and applications of funds" is prepared. Observe in Illustration 178 that such a statement, like an income statement, covers a period of time; its purpose is to report increases and decreases in each working capital item and to present an analysis of the changes in working capital.

Note how the change in each individual working capital item and the

Illustration 178

MOSS CORPORATION
Funds Statement for Year Ended December 31, 1967

WORKING CAPITAL CHANGES	Dec. 31, 1966	Dec. 31, 1967	Working Capital	
			Increases	Decreases
Current Assets:				
Cash.	$ 8,000	$ 5,000		$ 3,000
Notes receivable.	500	1,200	$ 700	
Accounts receivable, net.	12,000	18,000	6,000	
Merchandise inventory	16,000	21,000	5,000	
Prepaid expenses.	1,000	800		200
Total Current Assets.	$37,500	$46,000		
Current Liabilities:				
Accounts payable.	$ 9,000	$12,500		3,500
Dividends payable	700	1,000		300
Total Current Liabilities	$ 9,700	$13,500		
Working Capital	$27,800	$32,500		
			$11,700	$ 7,000
Net Increase in Working Capital (See analysis below)				4,700
			$11,700	$11,700

FLOW OF FUNDS

Sources of New Working Capital:			
Funds from current operations:			
Net income per income statement.	$11,600		
Add: Depreciation of equipment.	800		
Depreciation of building	900	$13,300	
Funds from sale of stock:			
Par value of stock sold.	$15,000		
Premium.	1,500	16,500	
Total New Working Capital.			$29,800
Applications of Working Capital:			
Addition to building		$14,000	
Purchase of land		3,000	
Payment of mortgage.		5,000	
Payment of dividends		3,100	
Total Working Capital Applied.			25,100
Net Increase in Working Capital.			$ 4,700

change in total working capital are shown in the first part or section, headed "Working Capital Changes."

Observe in the second part or section, headed "Flow of Funds," how the change in total working capital is analyzed and accounted for by showing sources of new working capital and uses made of working capital. In the Moss Corporation of Illustration 178, $29,800 of new working capital flowed in from operations and the sale of stock, and $25,100 of working capital was applied to other than working capital purposes; consequently, working capital increased $4,700 during the period. If the reverse had been true and more working capital had been used than was received, working capital would have decreased.

The funds statement of Illustration 178 has two sections, and funds statements are often prepared in this way. However, some accountants prefer to prepare the two sections as two separate statements. In such cases the first section becomes the first statement and is called a statement of working capital changes; and the second section becomes the second statement and is called a funds flow statement, a statement of the flow of working capital, or a statement of sources and applications of funds. Also, if a comparative balance sheet is prepared (see page 740), some accountants do not prepare the first section or statement showing working capital changes. They omit this section or statement because the information shown therein as to increases and decreases in working capital items is also shown on the comparative balance sheet.

PREPARING A FUNDS STATEMENT

Changes in Working Capital Section. A comparative balance sheet or, if this is not available, balance sheets for the beginning and end of the period under review are the information source for the first section of a funds statement.

In preparing this first section the current asset and current liability amounts at the beginning of the period are entered in the first money column and the amounts at the end are put in the second. Next in each column the current assets are totaled, the current liabilities are totaled, and the difference, the amount of working capital, is shown. After this the increase or decrease in each working capital item is entered, the increases in the third column and the decreases in the fourth. Then the increases are added, the decreases are added, and the difference, the net increase or decrease, along with the final column totals are entered.

Flow of Funds Section. To prepare the second half of a funds statement, the bookkeeping entries in each noncurrent balance sheet account in the ledger are examined for sources and applications of funds. Normally, the preparation of a working paper (see Illustrations 179 and 180) is a convenient way to bring together the results of these examinations. After the working paper is completed (see Illustration 180), the flow of funds section of the formal funds statement is prepared from the information accumulated on the bottom portion of the working paper.

FUNDS STATEMENT WORKING PAPER

A funds statement working paper is prepared for the sole purpose of bringing together in an orderly manner information as to a concern's sources and applications of funds. In preparing the working paper the changes in each noncurrent balance sheet account between the beginning

Illustration 179

Moss Corporation
Funds Statement Working Paper
For Year Ended December 31, 1967

	Account Balances Dec. 31, 1966	Analyses		Account Balances Dec. 31, 1967
	1	2	3	4
Debits				
Working capital	27 800 —			32 500 —
Noncurrent accounts:				
Equipment	8 000 —			7 500 —
Building	31 000 —			45 000 —
Land	8 000 —			11 000 —
	74 800 —			96 000 —
Credits				
Accumulated depr., equipment	2 100 —			2 400 —
Accumulated depr., building	8 800 —			9 700 —
Mortgage payable	5 000 —			
Common stock	35 000 —			50 000 —
Premium on common stock				1 500 —
Retained earnings	15 900 —			20 400 —
Reserve for plant expansion	8 000 —			12 000 —
	74 800 —			96 000 —
Funds provided by:				
Operations:				
Other sources:				
Funds applied to:				

and end of the period under review are analyzed and one or more analyzing entries is entered in the Analyses columns of the work sheet. Noncurrent balance sheet accounts are balance sheet accounts other than current asset and current liability accounts. The changes in these accounts are analyzed because each change resulted from a transaction that either (1) increased funds (a source), (2) decreased funds (an application), or (3) did not involve funds; and most resulted from transactions that either increased or decreased funds. Observe in Illustration 180 that the analyzing entry or entries on each line exactly account for the amount of change in the item on that line. Note too that each entry also sets out a source or application

Illustration 180

Moss Corporation
Funds Statement Working Paper
For Year Ended December 31, 1967

	1 Account Balances Dec. 31, 1966	2 Analyses		3	4 Account Balances Dec. 31, 196
Debits					
Working capital	27800 —	(k) 4700 —			32500 —
Noncurrent accounts:					
Equipment	8000 —		(a) 500 —		7500 —
Buildings	31000 —	(f) 14000 —			45000 —
Land	8000 —	(c) 3000 —			11000 —
	74800 —				96000 —
Credits					
Accumulated depr., equipment	2100 —	(a) 500 —	(d) 800 —		2400 —
Accumulated depr., building	8800 —		(e) 900 —		9700 —
Mortgage payable	5000 —	(f) 5000 —			
Common stock	35000 —		(g) 15000 —		50000 —
Premium on common stock			(g) 1500 —		1500 —
Retained earnings	15900 —	(i) 3100 —	(h) 11600 —		20400 —
		(j) 4000 —			
Reserve for plant expansion	8000 —		(j) 4000 —		12000 —
	74800 —				96000 —
Funds provided by:					
Operations:					
Net income		(h) 11600 —			
Depreciation of equipment		(d) 800 —			
Depreciation of building		(e) 900 —			
Other sources:					
Sale of stock		(g) 16500 —			
Funds applied to:					
Building addition			(f) 14000 —		
Purchase of land			(c) 3000 —		
Payment of mortgage			(f) 5000 —		
Dividends to stockholders			(i) 3100 —		
Increase in working capital			(k) 4700 —		
		64100 —	64100 —		

of funds or accounts for the effects of a bookkeeping entry which did not involve funds.

A funds statement working paper is prepared as follows:

1. First, the amount of working capital at the beginning of the period under review is determined and entered on the first line in the first money

column; then the working capital at the end is determined and entered in the last column. Amounts of working capital at the beginning and end are determined by subtracting current liabilities from current assets.

2. After determining and entering the working capital amounts, the next step is to list the noncurrent balance sheet accounts with their amounts. The balance sheet amounts as of the beginning of the period are entered in the first column and those of the end are put in the last. Observe that debit balance items are listed first and are followed by credit balance items. This is a convenience that places depreciation items with the liability and capital items.

3. After the noncurrent account balances are entered, the working capital amount and the debit items in each column are added, after which the credit items are added. Observe that debits must equal credits. Note also that at this stage in its preparation the working paper appears as in Illustration 179.

4. Next the noncurrent accounts in the ledger are examined and analyzing entries are entered in the Analyses columns. These entries are discussed in more detail in the next section of this chapter.

5. After the last analyzing entry is entered, the working paper is completed by adding the columns.

After the working paper is completed (see Illustration 180), the information at the bottom of the paper as to sources and applications of funds is used to prepare the "Flow of Funds" section of the formal funds statement.

In passing it should be observed that since a funds statement working paper is prepared solely for the purpose of bringing together information as to sources and applications of funds, the analyzing entries on the paper are placed only on the working paper and are never entered in the accounts.

ANALYZING ENTRIES

Analyzing entries on a funds statement working paper do two things: (1) they account for or explain the amount of change in each noncurrent account, and (2) they set out sources and applications of funds.

To understand why the change in each noncurrent account is accounted for or explained with one or more analyzing entries, remember that during a period every transaction that caused an increase or decrease in working capital also increased or decreased the balance of a noncurrent account. Consequently, when all increases and decreases in noncurrent accounts are explained by means of analyzing entries, all sources and applications of funds are set out on the working paper.

Sources of Information for Analyzing Entries. Although the information needed in completing the analyzing entries on a funds statement working paper can normally be taken from a company's balance sheet, income statement, and statement of retained earnings, it is often easier to determine more accurately what caused various changes in noncurrent account balances if the accounts can be examined.

When the accounts are available, the accountant will examine them before beginning his working paper, making notes on any unusual transactions. He will then use his notes in making the analyzing entries to set out the effects of these transactions.

In cases where the accounts are unavailable, each change in a noncurrent account is assumed to have been caused by the most common type of transaction that would cause such a change. For example, on the Moss Corporation working paper the balance of the Land account increased $3,000 between the beginning and end of the period covered. If the Moss Corporation accounts were unavailable, it would be assumed that this change was caused by the most logical transaction, and in this case the actual transaction, the purchase of land for cash.

Order in Which Analyzing Entries Are Made. Analyzing entries on a funds statement working paper need not be made in any particular order; however, many accountants simply begin with the first noncurrent account showing a change and make one or more entries to account for the change. They then turn to the next account, and so on down the working paper. An examination of the key letters on the working paper of Illustration 180 will show that this was the procedure followed in its preparation.

Analyzing Entries Illustrated. Analyzing entries are of three kinds: (1) those that set out sources of funds, (2) those that set out applications of funds, and (3) those that account for the effects of entries that did not involve funds. As a group, analyzing entries that set out applications are easiest to explain; consequently, this group will be discussed first.

Analyzing Entries That Set Out Applications of Funds. Analyzing entries *b*, *c*, *f*, and *i* set forth applications of funds on the working paper of Illustration 180. An explanation of each follows:

b) The debit balance of Moss Corporation's Building account increased from $31,000 to $45,000 during the period of the working paper. An examination of the accounts revealed that the increase was caused by the payment of $14,000 for an addition to the building. This was an application of funds, and the following analyzing entry was made on the working paper to account for the change and to set out the application:

	Analyses	
	Debit	**Credit**
Building............................	(b) *14,000*	
Funds applied to:		
Building addition..................		(b) *14,000*

c) On April 23 Moss Corporation purchased a tract of land paying $3,000 cash. When the transaction was recorded, it caused the debit balance of the Land account to increase from $8,000 to $11,000. The analyzing entry on the working paper that accounts for the change in the Land account and sets out this application is:

	Analyses	
	Debit	**Credit**
Land.............................	(c) *3,000*	
Funds applied to:		
Purchase of land....................		(c) *3,000*

f) On November 15 Moss Corporation paid the remaining $5,000 due on a mortgage on its plant and equipment, reducing the credit balance of its Mortgage Payable account to zero. The analyzing entry to account for this change and to set out the funds application is:

	Analyses	
	Debit	**Credit**
Mortgage payable.....................	(f) *5,000*	
Funds applied to:		
Payment of mortgage...............		(f) *5,000*

i) During 1967, at the end of each of the first three quarters in the year, the board of directors declared a $700 quarterly dividend; and on December 22, 1967, they declared a fourth $1,000 quarterly dividend payable on January 15, 1968. This fourth dividend brought the total dividends declared during the year to $3,100. Each declaration was recorded with an entry debiting Retained Earnings and crediting Dividends Payable. On the working paper the four declarations were treated as one and the following single analyzing entry was made to account for $3,100 of the $4,500 total change in the balance of the Retained Earnings account and to set out the funds application:

	Analyses	
	Debit	**Credit**
Retained earnings......................	(i) *3,100*	
Funds applied to:		
Dividends to stockholders............		(i) *3,100*

Observe the foregoing analyzing entries as they appear above and on the working paper of Illustration 180. Note in each case that the debit of the analyzing entry accounts for a change in a noncurrent account and the credit is to the phrase "Funds applied to:" and an explanation of the application. Now recall the bookkeeping entries that were used during the year in recording the transactions of these analyzing entries. The recording entries in general journal form appeared as follows:

May	12	Building..................................	14,000.00	
		Cash..............................		14,000.00
		Paid for addition to building.		
Apr.	23	Land..................................	3,000.00	
		Cash..............................		3,000.00
		Purchased land.		
Nov.	15	Mortgage Payable......................	5,000.00	
		Cash..............................		5,000.00
		Paid mortgage.		
——	—	Retained Earnings.....................	3,100.00	
		Dividends Payable................		3,100.00
		Declared dividends. (Actually there were four separate entries that totaled this amount.)		

Note that each transaction was originally recorded with a credit to a working capital account. In each case these credits recorded reductions in working capital. Now observe that each analyzing entry is like its original recording entry except that the phrase "Funds applied to:" and an explanation of the application is substituted for the original credit to Cash or Dividends Payable. This is common of all analyzing entries that set out applications of funds. Always in such analyzing entries the phrase "Funds applied to:" and an explanation of the application is substituted for the original credit to a working capital account.

Analyzing Entries That Set Out Sources of Funds. Four analyzing entries, *g, h, d,* and *e,* are required on the working paper of Illustration 180 to set out Moss Corporation's 1967 sources of new working capital. Each is alike in that the phrase "Funds provided by:" and an explanation of the source is debited; each differs as to the account credited. Explanations of the entries follow:

g) On November 3 Moss Corporation sold for cash and immediately issued 1,500 shares of its $10 par value common stock at $11 per share. This transaction was a source of funds, and the entry in general journal form to record it appeared as follows:

Nov.	3	Cash....................................	16,500.00	
		Common Stock.....................		15,000.00
		Premium on Common Stock.......		1,500.00
		Sold and issued common stock.		

On the working paper of Illustration 180 the following analyzing entry was made to set out this source of funds:

	Analyses	
	Debit	Credit
Funds provided by:		
Sale of stock.......................... (g)　*16,500*		
Common stock.........................		(g)　*15,000*
Premium on common stock............		(g)　*1,500*

Note that Cash is debited in the November 3 recording entry shown first above. The debit to Cash recorded an increase in working capital. Observe that the analyzing entry is like the recording entry except that the phrase "Funds provided by:" and an explanation is substituted for the original debit to cash.

h) The 1967 income statement of Moss Corporation showed a $11,600 net income after taxes. In the 1967 closing entries the amount of this net income was carried to the Retained Earnings account and was partially responsible for the $4,500 change in the balance of this account. However, the $11,600 of earnings was a source of funds; consequently, the following analyzing entry was made on the working paper to set out the source:

	Analyses	
	Debit	Credit
Funds provided by:		
Operations:		
Net income........................ (h)　*11,600*		
Retained earnings....................		(h)　*11,600*

d) *and* (*e*) Moss Corporation deducted as expenses on its 1967 income statement $800 depreciation on its equipment and $900 depreciation on its building. As previously explained, although depreciation expense is a rightful deduction from revenues in arriving at net income, the amount of depreciation so deducted must be added to net income in arriving at funds from operations. Consequently, the following analyzing entries were made on the working paper to account for the changes in the accumulated depreciation accounts and to set out the depreciation amounts with reported net income under "funds provided by operations."

	Analyses	
	Debit	Credit
Funds provided by:		
Operations:		
Depreciation of equipment......... (d)　*800*		
Depreciation of building............ (e)　*900*		
Accumulated depreciation, equipment..		(d)　*800*
Accumulated depreciation, building....		(e)　*900*

Bookkeeping Entries That Did Not Involve Funds. As previously stated, analyzing entries on a funds statement working paper are of three kinds: (1) those that set out sources of funds, (2) those that set out applications of funds, and (3) those that account for the effects of bookkeeping entries that did not involve funds. The following two entries are of the last kind:

a) During 1964 Moss Corporation retired and scrapped fully depreciated equipment carried on the books at $500. The bookkeeping entry to record the retirement was:

Aug.	*27*	*Accumulated Depreciation Equipment. . . .*	*500.00*	
		Equipment.		*500.00*
		Retired fully depreciated equipment.		

Since funds were not affected by this retirement, the following analyzing entry was made on the working paper to account for the changes in the accounts involved:

	Analyses	
	Debit	Credit
Accumulated depreciation, equipment. .	(a) *500*	
Equipment.		(a) *500*

Observe that the accounts debited and credited in both entries are the same. In the analyzing entry the debit to Accumulated Depreciation, Equipment helps to account for the change in the balance of this account; and the credit to the Equipment does account for the change in the Equipment account.

j) At its December meeting the Moss Corporation board of directors appropriated $4,000 of the balance of its Retained Earnings account as a "reserve for plant expansion" (retained earnings appropriated for plant expansion). Since this transaction involved no funds, the following analyzing entry was made on the working paper to account for the changes in the accounts involved:

	Analyses	
	Debit	Credit
Retained earnings.	(j) *4,000*	
Reserve for plant expansion.		(j) *4,000*

Notice that the debit of the foregoing entry along with the debit of analyzing entry (*i*) and the credit of entry (*h*) exactly account for the change in the balance of the Retained Earnings account. Also observe that the credit of the foregoing entry accounts for the change in the balance of the Reserve for Plant Expansion account.

Completing the Working Paper. The foregoing analyzing entries account for all the changes in noncurrent accounts on the working paper of Illustration 180. However, in completing the paper a final entry is made to account for the change in the amount of working capital as it appears on the first line of the paper. The entry is:

| | Analyses | |
	Debit	Credit
Working capital..........................	(k) 4,700	
Increase in working capital.............		(k) 4,700

Had there been a decrease in working capital instead of an increase, this entry would have had a debit to "Decrease in working capital" and a credit to working capital.

After the entry accounting for the change in working capital is made, the working paper is completed by adding the Analyses columns. Then the information on the bottom portion of the paper, the information as to funds sources and applications, is used to complete the funds flow section of the formal funds statement.

USEFULNESS OF A FUNDS STATEMENT

In addition to telling from where funds came and where they were used, a funds statement also provides information as to the effectiveness with which management has handled working capital during the period of the statement, shows the adequacy of present funds, and tells a stockholder or investor something of management's plans for the future.

For example, how effective was the Moss Corporation management in handling working capital during 1967? An examination of the concern's funds statement, Illustration 178, shows that, in spite of a $4,700 increase in working capital, cash decreased a little over one third, from $8,000 to $5,000, and accounts payable increased in approximately the same proportion, from $9,000 to $12,500. Further examination shows increases of $6,000 in accounts receivable and $5,000 in inventory, increases that approximately equaled and account for the total change in cash, accounts payable, and total working capital. Is this good? Probably not. For instance, was the increase in inventory an intentional increase that will result in greater sales, or was it a result of poor merchandising? And, unless sales on credit increased materially during the final weeks of 1967, the increase in accounts receivable can only be blamed on slower collections.

As to revealing management's plans, sources and applications of funds are objective evidence of management decisions to dilute ownership rights by issuing more stock, trade on the equity by increasing long-term debt, expand or modernize the plant, or accumulate funds for better investment opportunities expected in the future.

CASH FLOW

Cash Flow Distinguished from Funds Flow. Since the word "funds" in the phrase "funds flow" does not mean "cash," it follows that "funds flow" and "cash flow" are different. While funds flow refers to the flow of working capital, cash flow relates to the inflow and outflow of cash only.

Planning and controlling cash flow, or "managing money," is an important phase of management's work. However, cash flow is also important to creditors, stockholders, and investors because cash flow affects ability to meet liabilities, pay dividends, replace fixed assets, and to expand or grow.

A complete discussion of cash flow is not attempted in this text.[1] Rather, a simple analysis based on the difference between the accrual basis and the cash basis of accounting is used to introduce the subject and show the nature of a cash flow statement.

Cash Flow Statement. Illustration 181 shows a cash flow statement. Note how such a statement covers a period of time and accounts for the increase or decrease in cash by showing sources and applications of cash.

Illustration 181
ROYAL HARDWARE COMPANY
Cash Flow Statement for Year Ended December 31, 19--

Beginning cash balance.			$2,200
Cash Was Provided by:			
Operations:			
Reported net income (accrual basis)		$ 1,500	
Adjustments to convert income from			
accrual to cash basis:			
Excess of accrual basis sales over			
cash basis sales.	$ (500)		
Excess of accrual basis cost of			
sales over cash basis cost.	2,000		
Depreciation expense.	3,500		
Bad debts expense	200		
Excess of accrual basis salaries			
and wages over cash basis	400		
Excess of other expenses on a cash			
basis over an accrual basis	(100)		
Net adjustment.		5,500	
Cash from operations.		$ 7,000	
Other sources of cash:			
Sale of investments		4,500	
Total cash provided during period		$11,500	
Cash Was Applied to:			
Payment of dividends.	$1,000		
Purchase of new fixed assets.	6,500		
Total cash provided during period		7,500	
Net increase in cash.			4,000
Ending Cash Balance			$6,200

[1] See G. A. Welsch, C. T. Zlatkovich, and J. A. White, *Intermediate Accounting* (Homewood, Ill.: Richard D. Irwin, Inc., 1963), chap. xxix.

Illustration 182

ROYAL HARDWARE COMPANY
Income Statement for Year Ended December 31, 19--

Sales, net.			$50,000
Cost of goods sold:			
Inventory, January 1, 19--.		$10,000	
Purchases, net.		32,000	
Goods for sale.		$42,000	
Inventory, December 31, 19--.		11,000	
Cost of goods sold.			31,000
Gross profit from sales			$19,000
Operating expenses:			
Depreciation expense.		$ 3,500	
Bad debts expense		200	
Salaries and wages.		10,000	
Other expenses.		3,800	
Total operating expenses.			17,500
Net Income.			$ 1,500

A work sheet similar to the funds statement working paper is ordinarily used to analyze changes in noncash accounts and to bring together the data for a cash flow statement. However, a discussion of this work sheet is deferred to a more advanced text and the cash flow statement of Illustration 181 is based on information in Illustrations 182 and 183.

An examination of Illustration 181 will show that Royal Hardware Company's cash increased during the period of the statement. It was increased $7,000 by "cash from operations" and $4,500 by cash from the sale of investments; and it was decreased $1,000 by dividends and $6,500 by the purchase of fixed assets. Or there was a $4,000 net increase. The cash inflow from the sale of investments and the outflows for dividends and fixed assets need no explanation, but the inflow of cash from operations does.

Illustration 183

Condensation of Royal Hardware Company's Cash Account

(Debits)		(Credits)	
Balance, January 1	2,200	Cash merchandise purchases.	1,000
Cash sales	20,000	Payments to creditors for	
Accounts receivable		merchandise purchased	28,000
collections	29,500	Salary and wage payments	9,600
Sale of investment securities.	4,500	Payments for other expenses.	3,900
		Fixed asset purchases	6,500
		Dividend payments	1,000
	56,200		50,000

Cash from Operations. If a company uses a cash basis of accounting, its net income represents "cash from operations." However, since most companies use an accrual basis, it is usually necessary to convert net income from an accrual basis to a cash basis to determine "cash from operations." Note that this is done on a cash flow statement, and understanding the conversion requires a little thought along these lines:

a) Cash flowed into Royal Hardware Company from sales; but the amount did not equal the $50,000 sales figure. Rather, cash from goods sold consisted of cash sales, $20,000, plus collections from customers, $29,500, or to $49,500. (See Illustration 183.) Consequently, since cash from goods sold was $500 less than the income statement sales figure, $500 is subtracted in changing income from an accrual basis to a cash basis. (Remember that placing an item in parentheses means it is a subtraction.)

b) Likewise, $31,000 did not flow out for goods sold. Rather the actual outflow for merchandise amounted to $29,000, $1,000 for cash purchases plus $28,000 paid to creditors for merchandise (see Illustration 183). Therefore, since the cash outflow was $2,000 less than cost of goods sold, $2,000 is added in converting income from an accrual to a cash basis.

c) Since depreciation and bad debts expense did not take cash, the amounts of these items are added back in the conversion.

d) And, since cash paid for wages and salaries was $400 less than the income statement amount for this expense, and cash paid out for "other expenses" was $100 more than the income statement amount, $400 is added and $100 is subtracted in the conversion.

QUESTIONS FOR CLASS DISCUSSION

1. What is a funds statement designed to show?
2. When the word "funds" is used in connection with a funds statement, what are "funds"?
3. What are circulating assets and why are they so called?
4. List several sources of funds. Where may a company apply funds?
5. On December 12 a company borrowed $10,000 by giving its bank a 60-day, interest-bearing note. Will this transaction appear on the year-end funds statement as a source of funds?
6. A company that began an accounting period with $45,000 of merchandise inventory, ended the period with $40,000 of inventory. Was this decrease in inventory a source of funds?
7. A company wrote off a fully depreciated fixed asset. What account balances appearing on the company's funds statement working paper were affected by the write-off? How was the write-off treated on the funds statement working paper? Why was it treated in this manner?
8. Explain why such expenses as depreciation, amortization of patents, and amortization of bond discount are added to the net income in order to determine funds provided by business operations.
9. What are the three kinds of analyzing entries on a funds statement working paper?

10. When a funds statement working paper is prepared, all changes in noncurrent balance sheet account balances between the beginning and end of the period covered by the statement are accounted for on the working paper. Why?

11. What is the primary difference between a "cash flow" statement and a "funds" statement?

12. Do short-term bank loans appear on a funds statement as a source of funds? Why or why not? Do they appear on a cash flow statement as a source of cash?

PROBLEMS

Problem 27–1

Able Company's comparative balance sheets of December 31, 1966, and 1967, carried the following debit and credit amounts:

	December 31	
Debits	**1966**	**1967**
Cash	$ 4,300	$ 7,500
Accounts receivable, net	10,000	12,000
Merchandise inventory	32,000	31,500
Prepaid expenses	1,200	1,000
Store equipment	14,000	20,100
	$61,500	$72,100

Credits		
Accumulated depreciation, store equipment	$ 4,800	$ 6,100
Accounts payable	19,400	16,800
Common stock, $10 par value	25,000	30,000
Premium on common stock		2,500
Retained earnings	12,300	16,700
	$61,500	$72,100

An examination of Able Company's 1967 income statement and accounting records revealed:

a) Net income for the year, $7,400.
b) The year's recorded depreciation on the store equipment was $2,100.
c) Five hundred shares of common stock were issued at $15 per share.
d) Cash dividends paid, $3,000.
e) Store equipment costing $6,900 was purchased.
f) Fully depreciated store equipment that cost $800 was discarded, and its cost was removed from the accounts.

Required:

Prepare a funds statement working paper and a funds statement for the company.

Problem 27–2

Phoenix Supply Company's December 31, 1966, and 1967 balance sheets carried the following debits and credits:

	December 31	
Debits	**1966**	**1967**
Cash...	$ 11,800	$ 12,700
Accounts receivable, net......................	33,400	34,900
Merchandise inventory........................	86,700	85,900
Other current assets..........................	1,800	2,000
Office equipment.............................	6,100	5,400
Store equipment..............................	27,800	31,500
	$167,600	$172,400

Credits		
Accumulated depreciation, office equipment....$	2,400	$ 2,500
Accumulated depreciation, store equipment....	6,500	7,300
Accounts payable.............................	20,200	19,500
Notes payable................................	5,000	4,500
Federal income taxes payable.................	3,300	3,500
Common stock, $5 par value..................	100,000	105,000
Premium on common stock....................	5,500	8,500
Retained earnings............................	24,700	21,600
	$167,600	$172,400

An examination of the company's statements and accounts showed:
a) A $15,000 net income for 1967.
b) Depreciation expense charged on office equipment, $500; and on store equipment, $1,600.
c) Office equipment that cost $700 and had been depreciated $400 was sold for $200 and the loss carried to retained earnings.
d) Store equipment costing $4,500 was purchased.
e) Fully depreciated store equipment that cost $800 was discarded and its cost and accumulated depreciation were removed from the accounts.
f) Cash dividends totaling $10,000 were paid during the year.
g) A 1,000-share stock dividend was declared and distributed at a time during the year when the stock had a fair market value of $8 per share.

Required:

Prepare a funds statement working paper and a funds statement for Phoenix Supply Company.

Problem 27–3

A 1966–67 comparative balance sheet for Cactus Sales carried the following debit and credit amounts:

| | December 31 | |
Debits	1966	1967
Cash.......................................	$ 22,300	$ 12,400
Accounts receivable, net...................	15,600	16,200
Merchandise inventory......................	51,400	50,200
Prepaid expenses...........................	1,100	1,400
Long-term investments......................	18,900	
Store equipment............................	14,300	15,000
Office equipment...........................	4,200	3,900
Land.......................................		20,000
Buildings..................................		60,000
	$127,800	$179,100

Credits		
Accumulated depreciation, store equipment....	$ 3,600	$ 4,300
Accumulated depreciation, office equipment...	1,300	1,400
Accumulated depreciation, buildings..........		1,200
Accounts payable............................	12,700	11,300
Notes payable (due in 54 days)..............		5,000
Mortgage payable............................		40,000
Common stock................................	100,000	100,000
Retained earnings...........................	10,200	15,900
	$127,800	$179,100

An examination of the company's 1967 income statement, statement of retained earnings, and accounting records revealed:

a) An $8,400 net income for the year.

b) The income statement showed depreciation of store equipment, $1,300; office equipment, $400; and buildings, $1,200.

c) The long-term investments consisted of stocks and bonds which were sold during 1967 for $21,200. The gain was carried directly to retained earnings.

d) Store equipment on the books at the time of its sale at an $800 cost, less $600 accumulated depreciation, was sold during the year for its book value.

e) Fully depreciated office equipment that cost $300 was discarded, and its cost and accumulated depreciation were removed from the books.

f) Store equipment costing $1,500 was purchased.

g) Cash dividends amounting to $5,000 were paid during the year.

Required:

Prepare a funds statement ~~working paper and a funds statement~~ for the company.

Problem 27–4

Western Manufacturing Company's 1966–67 comparative balance sheet carried the following debits and credits:

	December 31	
Debits	**1966**	**1967**
Cash...	$ 13,100	$ 16,200
Accounts receivable, net......................	32,900	29,200
Inventories...................................	55,100	54,300
Other current assets..........................	1,800	2,000
Long-term investments........................	25,000	18,000
Machinery....................................	90,500	82,000
Building......................................	117,000	140,000
Land...	28,000	28,000
Goodwill.....................................	5,000	
	$368,400	$369,700

Credits		
Accumulated depreciation, machinery.........	$ 34,900	$ 26,100
Accumulated depreciation, building...........	20,500	22,600
Accounts payable.............................	22,900	23,700
Salaries and wages payable....................	2,900	3,400
Federal income taxes payable.................	4,100	3,600
Common stock, $5 par value..................	200,000	220,000
Premium on common stock....................	20,000	25,000
Retained earnings............................	63,100	45,300
	$368,400	$369,700

On December 31, 1967, the company's Machinery, Accumulated Depreciation of Machinery, and Retained Earnings accounts appeared as follows:

Machinery

Date	Explanations	Debit	Credit	Balance
Jan. 2, '67	Balance			90,500
Jan. 2, '67	Machine No. 6743		9,000	81,500
Jan. 5, '67	Machine No. 6997	12,500		94,000
Jan. 5, '67	Machine No. 5854		8,500	85,500
Jan. 7, '67	Machine No. 5931		3,500	82,000

Accumulated Depreciation of Machinery

Date	Explanations	Debit	Credit	Balance
Jan. 2, '67	Balance			34,900
Jan. 2, '67	Machine No. 6743	7,500		27,400
Jan. 5, '67	Machine No. 5854	6,000		21,400
Jan. 7, '67	Machine No. 5931	3,500		17,900
Dec. 31, '67	1967 depreciation		8,200	26,100

Retained Earnings

Date	Explanations	Debit	Credit	Balance
Jan. 2, '67	Balance			63,100
Jan. 2, '67	Loss on sale of Machine			
	No. 6743	1,000		62,100
July 23, '67	Write-off of goodwill	5,000		57,100
July 23, '67	Stock dividend	25,000		32,100
Oct. 17, '67	Gain on sale of investments		3,000	35,100
Dec. 15, '67	Cash dividend	6,000		29,100
Dec. 31, '67	1967 net income		16,200	45,300

Machine No. 6743 was sold for cash. Machine No. 5854 was traded in on Machine No. 6997: the income tax method was used in recording the exchange.

Required:

Prepare a funds statement working paper and a funds statement. (On the working paper there will be several entries affecting the Machinery, Accumulated Depreciation of Machinery, and Retained Earnings accounts; consequently, two blank lines each should be left after the Machinery and Accumulated Depreciation of Machinery accounts and three lines should be left after Retained Earnings.)

Problem 27–5

Desert Supply's income statement and an analysis of its Cash account for the year of the statement follow:

DESERT SUPPLY

Income Statement for Year Ended December 31, 19—

Sales, net...................................			$113,500
Cost of goods sold:			
Merchandise inventory, January 1, 19—......	$ 21,200		
Purchases, net.............................	79,500		
Goods available for sale.....................	$100,700		
Merchandise inventory, December 31, 19—....	22,300		
Cost of goods sold..........................		78,400	
Gross profit from sales........................		$ 35,100	
Operating expenses:			
Rent expense..............................	$ 6,000		
Salaries and wages.........................	15,900		
Bad debts expense.........................	600		
Depreciation expense, store equipment.......	1,400		
Other operating expenses...................	1,700		
Total operating expenses....................		25,600	
Net Income...............................		$ 9,500	

Analysis of Cash Account:

Cash balance, January 1, 19—.................		**$ 4,300**
Debits:		
Cash sale receipts.............................	$ 37,200	
Accounts receivable collections...............	75,900	
Sale of fixed asset...........................	200	
Bank loan.....................................	5,000	118,300
Total..		$122,600
Credits:		
Creditor payments for merchandise..........	$ 78,300	
Rent payments................................	6,500	
Salary and wage payments....................	15,700	
Other expense payments......................	1,600	
Payment for new store equipment purchased..	5,800	
Personal withdrawals by proprietor...........	8,400	116,300
Cash Balance, December 31, 19—..............		**$ 6,300**

The fixed asset sold was sold at a loss, and the loss carried directly to the owner's Capital account.

Required:
Prepare a cash flow statement for Desert Supply.

CLASS EXERCISE

Exercise 27–1
From the following income statement information prepare a schedule showing funds provided by current operations:

Sales...		$720,000
Cost of goods sold (includes factory depreciation,		
$48,500).....................................		450,000
Gross profit....................................		$270,000
Operating expenses:		
Selling and administrative salaries (includes		
$800 accrued)...............................		$115,000
Advertising (after deducting $600 prepaid).......	7,500	
Taxes (all accrued and unpaid).................	8,500	
Depreciation on furniture and office equipment.	12,000	
Bond interest expense (includes $500 discount		
amortized).................................	8,100	
Bad debts expense.............................	2,400	
Total expenses...............................		$153,500
Income before income taxes.....................		$116,500
Less: State and federal income taxes...........		50,500
Net Income.....................................		$ 66,000

ALTERNATE PROBLEMS

Problem 27–2A

Southwest Sales Company's comparative balance sheet for 1966 and 1967 carried the following debit and credit amounts:

	December 31	
Debits	**1966**	**1967**
Cash...	*$ 12,600*	*$ 10,200*
Accounts receivable, net......................	*32,900*	*35,100*
Merchandise inventory........................	*86,400*	*85,200*
Prepaid expenses.............................	*1,800*	*1,500*
Office equipment.............................	*5,600*	*5,000*
Store equipment.............................	*28,300*	*29,800*
	$167,600	*$166,800*

Credits		
Accumulated depreciation, office equipment...*$*	*2,400*	*$ 2,500*
Accumulated depreciation, store equipment....	*6,500*	*7,500*
Accounts payable.............................	*23,500*	*22,400*
Notes payable................................	*5,000*	*10,000*
Common stock, $10 par value.................	*100,000*	*110,000*
Premium on common stock....................	*5,500*	*6,500*
Retained earnings............................	*24,700*	*7,900*
	$167,600	*$166,800*

An examination of the company's income statement, statement of retained earnings, and accounts revealed the following:
  a) A $1,900 net loss for the year.
  b) Depreciation expense charged on office equipment, $500; and on store equipment, $1,700.
  c) Office equipment carried at its $600 cost with $400 accumulated depreciation was sold for $300. The gain was carried directly to Retained Earnings.
  d) Store equipment costing $2,200 was purchased.
  e) Fully depreciated store equipment that cost $700 was discarded and its cost and accumulated depreciation were removed from the accounts.
  f) Cash dividends of $4,000 were paid during the year.
  g) A 1,000 share stock dividend was declared and paid. On the date of declaration the company's stock had an $11 per share fair market value.

Required:
Prepare a funds statement working paper and a funds statement for the company.

Problem 27–3A

Walter Dale, as a single proprietor, operates Dale's Country Store. At the ends of 1966 and 1967 the store's balance sheets carried the following debit and credit items:

	December 31	
Debits	1966	1967
Cash..	$ 6,400	$ 7,100
Accounts receivable, net.........................	17,200	16,800
Merchandise inventory...........................	33,700	36,400
Other current assets.............................	800	500
Store equipment.................................	8,400	13,100
	$66,500	$73,900

Credits		
Accumulated depreciation, store equipment......	$ 3,200	$ 1,800
Accounts payable................................	16,800	14,200
Walter Dale, capital.............................	46,500	57,900
	$66,500	$73,900

Walter Dale's 1967 statement showing changes in the proprietor's Capital account carried the following information:

Walter Dale, capital, January 1, 1967..............		$46,500
Add: Additional investment....................		5,000
Total Investment............................		$51,500
Net income per income statement...............	$12,400	
Less: Withdrawals for living expenses..........	6,000	
Excess of net income over withdrawals...........		6,400
Walter Dale, Capital, December 31, 1967..........		$57,900

The store equipment accounts showed: (*a*) $1,200 depreciation expense on store equipment charged during the year; (*b*) store equipment costing $4,800 was purchased, (*c*) equipment carried on the books on the day of its exchange at its $2,800 cost, less $2,400 accumulated depreciation, was traded on like-new equipment having a $3,100 cash price, a $600 trade-in allowance was received; and (*d*) fully depreciated equipment that cost $200 was junked and its cost and accumulated depreciation were removed from the accounts.

Required:

Prepare a funds statement working paper and a funds statement for the store.

Problem 27–4A

The 1966 and 1967 balance sheets of Tucson Manufacturing Company carried the following debit and credit items:

	December 31	
Debits	1966	1967
Cash..	$ 15,300	$ 13,500
Accounts receivable, net........................	31,400	27,500
Inventories.....................................	54,500	55,000
Prepaid expenses...............................	1,700	2,000
Long-term investments.........................	20,000	12,000
Machinery.....................................	95,000	87,500
Buildings......................................	115,000	135,000
Land..	30,000	30,000
Patents..	5,000	3,800
	$367,900	$366,300

	December 31	
Credits	1966	1967
Accumulated depreciation of machinery ....$ 36,500		$ 26,000
Accumulated depreciation of building 18,900		21,500
Accounts payable 21,700		22,300
Salaries and wages payable 3,400		2,200
Federal income taxes payable 4,800		3,700
Common stock, $10 par value 200,000		220,000
Premium on common stock 20,000		30,000
Retained earnings 62,600		40,600
	$367,900	$366,300

The company's Machinery, Accumulated Depreciation of Machinery, and Retained Earnings accounts appeared as follows at the end of 1967:

Machinery

Date	Explanations	Debit	Credit	Balance
Jan. 2, '67	*Balance*			95,000
Jan. 5, '67	*Machine 5552*		5,000	90,000
Jan. 8, '67	*Machine 5610*		9,000	81,000
Jan. 10, '67	*Machine 5831*	15,000		96,000
Jan. 10, '67	*Machine 5622*		8,500	87,500

Accumulated Depreciation of Machinery

Date	Explanations	Debit	Credit	Balance
Jan. 2, '67	*Balance*			36,500
Jan. 5, '67	*Machine 5552*	5,000		31,500
Jan. 8, '67	*Machine 5610*	8,000		23,500
Jan. 10, '67	*Machine 5622*	7,000		16,500
Dec. 31, '67	*1967 depreciation*		9,500	26,000

Retained Earnings

Date	Explanations	Debit	Credit	Balance
Jan. 2, '67	*Balance*			62,600
Jan. 8, '67	*Gain on sale of Machine 5610*		500	63,100
June 10, '67	*Stock dividend*	30,000		33,100
July 8, '67	*Gain on sale of investments*		2,000	35,100
Dec. 15, '67	*Cash dividend*	12,000		23,100
Dec. 31, '67	*Net income*		17,500	40,600

Machine No. 5610 was sold for cash. Machine No. 5622 was traded in on Machine No. 5831; the income tax method was used in recording the exchange.

Required:

Prepare a funds statement working paper and a funds statement. (On the working paper there will be several entries affecting the Machinery, Accumulated Depreciation of Machinery, and Retained Earnings accounts; consequently, leave two blank lines after each of these accounts.)

Problem 27–5A

Last year Sun Valley Sales earned $12,400, began the year with $3,900 in cash, and ended it with $6,400, as shown by the following income statement and analysis of its Cash account:

SUN VALLEY SALES

Income Statement for Year Ended December 31, 19—

Sales, net....................................		$125,400
Cost of goods sold:		
Merchandise inventory, January 1, 19—.......$15,300		
Purchases, net............................. 76,600		
Goods for sale..............................$91,900		
Merchandise inventory, December 31, 19—.... 16,700		
Cost of goods sold...........................	75,200	
Gross profit from sales.......................		$ 50,200
Operating expenses:		
Salaries and wages.........................$26,400		
Rent expense............................. 7,200		
Depreciation of store equipment............. 1,800		
Bad debts expense........................... 500		
Store supplies used......................... 600		
Other operating expenses.................... 1,300		
Total operating expenses...................	37,800	
Net Income..............................		$ 12,400

Analysis of Cash Account

Cash balance, January 1, 19—..................		$ 3,900
Debits:		
Cash sales...................................$27,600		
Accounts receivable collections................ 98,700		
Sale of fixed asset........................... 300		
Bank loan................................... 6,000	132,600	
Total..		$136,500
Credits:		
Rent payments.............................$ 7,200		
Payments to creditors for merchandise pur-		
chased.................................... 75,900		
Payments to creditors for store supplies		
bought.................................... 700		
Salary and wage payments.................... 26,300		
Other expense payments...................... 1,200		
New store equipment purchased............. 9,800		
Personal withdrawals by the proprietor....... 9,000	130,100	
Cash Balance, December 31, 19—................		$ 6,400

The fixed asset was sold at a book profit which was carried directly to the owner's Capital account.

Required:

Prepare a cash flow statement for Sun Valley Sales.

DECISION PROBLEM 27—MANTON, INC.

Manton, Inc., is having some difficulty meeting its payroll and paying current obligations. It was necessary during the last quarter of 1967 for the company to borrow $5,000 from the bank to meet current obligations. The following funds statement was presented to the board:

MANTON, INC.

Funds Statement for Year Ended December 31, 1967

Working Capital Changes	Dec. 31, 1966	Dec. 31, 1967	Working Capital Increases	Decreases
Current Assets:				
Cash	$10,000	$ 6,000		$ 4,000
Accounts receivable (net)	12,000	20,000	$ 8,000	
Merchandise inventory	15,000	22,000	7,000	
Prepaid expenses	800	500		300
Total Current Assets	$37,800	$48,500		
Current Liabilities:				
Accounts payable	$10,000	$12,000		$ 2,000
Notes payable		5,000		5,000
Accrued expenses	250	500		250
Dividends payable	350	500		150
Total Current Liabilities	$10,600	$18,000	$15,000	$11,700
Working Capital	$27,200	$30,500		
Net Increase in Working Capital				3,300
			$15,000	$15,000

Flow of Funds

Sources of New Working Capital:		
Funds from current operations:		
Net income	$ 9,000	
Add: Depreciation of fixed assets	5,000	
	$14,000	
Funds from issuance of bonds at par	50,000	
Total new working capital		$64,000
Applications of Working Capital:		
Addition to plant	$58,700	
Dividends on capital stock	2,000	
Total Working Capital Applied		60,700
Net Increase in Working Capital		$ 3,300

As controller of the corporation you have been asked to explain the difference between "funds flow" and "cash flow." One member of the board pointed out that the funds statement shows a $3,300 increase in working capital, yet the cash balance has declined materially in spite of the bank loan. In explaining the difference between "funds flow" and "cash flow" describe specifically the following, using assumed amounts for purposes of illustration where necessary:

1. The difference between sales revenue on a cash basis and on the accrual basis.
2. The difference in cost of goods sold on the cash basis and on the accrual basis.
3. The difference in expenses on a cash basis as compared to the accrual basis.
4. The difference between the effect of the bank loan (notes payable, $5,000) in determining "flow of cash" and "flow of funds."
5. The difference in effect of the sale of bonds on "cash flow" and "funds flow."

In addition use the amounts you have assumed plus the amounts given to construct a cash flow statement for Manton, Inc.

28

Tax Considerations
in Business Decisions

Not too many years ago, when tax rates were low, management could afford to ignore or dismiss as of minor importance the tax effects of a business decision; but today, when about half the income of a business must commonly be paid out in income taxes, this is no longer wise. Today, a successful management must constantly be alert to every possible tax savings, recognizing that it is often necessary to earn two "pretax dollars" in order to keep one "after-tax dollar," or that a dollar of income tax saved is commonly worth a two-dollar reduction in any other expense.

TAX PLANNING

When a taxpayer plans his affairs in such a way as to incur the smallest possible tax liability, he is engaged in tax planning. Tax planning requires the application of tax laws to the alternate ways in which every transaction may be completed, and a choice in each case of the way that will result in the smallest tax liability.

Normally tax planning requires that a tax-saving opportunity be recognized at the time it arises. This is because, although it is sometimes possible to take advantage of a previously overlooked tax saving, the common result of an overlooked opportunity is a lost opportunity, since the Director of Internal Revenue usually deems the original action in a tax situation the final action for tax purposes.

Since effective tax planning requires an extensive knowledge of both tax laws and business procedures, it is not the purpose of this chapter to make expert tax planners of elementary accounting students. Rather, the purpose

795

is to make students aware of the merits of effective tax planning, recognizing that, for complete and effective planning, the average student, businessman, or citizen should seek the advice of a certified public accountant, tax attorney, or other qualified person.

TAX EVASION AND TAX AVOIDANCE

In any discussion of taxes a clear distinction should be drawn between tax evasion and tax avoidance. Tax evasion is illegal and may result in heavy penalties; but tax avoidance is a perfectly legal and profitable activity.

Taxes are avoided by preventing a tax liability from coming into existence. This may be accomplished by any legal means, for example, by the way in which a transaction is completed, or the manner in which a business is organized, or by a wise selection from among the options provided in the Internal Revenue Code. It makes no difference how, so long as the means is legal and it prevents a tax liability from arising.

In contrast, tax evasion involves the fraudulent denial and concealment of an existing tax liability. For example, taxes are evaded when taxable income, such as interest, dividends, tips, fees, or profits from the sale of stocks, bonds, and other assets, is unreported. Taxes are also evaded when items not legally deductible from income are deducted. For example, taxes are evaded when the costs of operating the family automobile are deducted as a business expense, or when charitable contributions not allowed or not made are deducted. Insofar as this text is concerned, tax evasion is illegal and should be scrupulously avoided.

STATE AND MUNICIPAL INCOME TAXES

Most states and a number of cities levy income taxes, in most cases modeling their laws after the federal laws. However, other than noting the existence of such laws and that they increase the total tax burden and make tax planning even more important, the following discussion is limited to the federal income tax.

HISTORY AND OBJECTIVES OF THE FEDERAL INCOME TAX

Although the federal government first used an income tax during the war between the states, the history of today's federal income tax dates from the 1913 ratification of the Sixteenth Amendment, which cleared away all questions as to the constitutionality of such a tax. Since its ratification, Congress has passed more than forty Revenue Acts and other laws implementing the tax, placing the responsibility for their enforcement in the hands of the Treasury Department acting through the Internal Revenue Service.

The original purpose of the federal income tax was to raise revenue, but over the years this original goal has been expanded to include the following and other nonrevenue objectives:

1. To assist small businesses.
2. To encourage foreign trade.
3. To encourage exploration for oil and minerals.
4. To redistribute the national income.
5. To control inflation and deflation.
6. To stimulate business.
7. To attain full employment.

Also, just as the objectives have expanded over the years, so have the rates and the number of people required to pay taxes. In 1913 the minimum rate was 1 percent and the maximum for individuals was 7. This contrasts with today's minimum 14 percent rate for individuals and maximum of 70. Likewise, the total number of tax returns filed has grown from a few thousand in 1913 to over 60,000,000 in 1965.

SYNOPSIS OF THE FEDERAL INCOME TAX

The following brief synopsis of the federal income tax is given at this point because it is necessary to know something about the federal income tax in order to appreciate its effect on business decisions.

Classes of Taxpayers. Federal income tax law recognizes four classes of taxpayers: individuals, corporations, estates, and trusts. Members of each class must file returns and pay taxes on taxable income.

A business operated as a single proprietorship or partnership is not treated as a separate taxable entity under the law. Rather, a single proprietor must report the income from his business on his individual return; and although a partnership must file an information return showing its net income and the distributive shares of the partners, each partner is required to include his share on his individual return. In other words, the income of a single proprietorship or partnership, whether withdrawn from the business or not, is taxed as the individual income of the single proprietor or partners.

The treatment given corporations under the law is different, however. A business operated as a corporation must file a return and pay taxes on its taxable income. Also, if a corporation pays out in dividends some or all of its "after-tax income," its stockholders must report these dividends as income on their individual returns. Because of this, it is commonly claimed that corporation income is taxed twice, once to the corporation and again to its stockholders.

The Individual Income Tax. The amount of federal income tax an individual must pay each year depends upon his gross income, deductions, exemptions, and tax credits; and it is calculated as follows:

Gross income...............................		*$X,XXX*
Less:	*Deductions to arrive at adjusted gross income...............................*	*X,XXX*
Adjusted gross income.........................		*$X,XXX*
Less:	*a) Itemized deductions (or the optional standard deduction)...............$XXX*	
	b) Deduction for exemptions........... XXX	*X,XXX*
Taxable income...............................		*$X,XXX*

Taxable income (from previous calculation) multiplied by the proper tax rates equals income tax before tax credits and prepayments......................................	*$X,XXX*
Less: Tax credits and prepayments.............	*X,XXX*
Net Tax Payable (or Refund).....................	*$ XXX*

Several of the items in the calculation just outlined require additional explanation, for example:

Gross Income. Income tax law defines gross income as *all income from whatever source derived, unless expressly excluded by law.* Gross income therefore includes income from operating a business, gains from property sales, dividends, interest, rents, royalties, and compensation for services, such as salaries, wages, fees, commissions, bonuses, and tips. Actually, the answers to two questions are all that is required to determine whether an item should be included or excluded. The two questions are: (1) Is the item income? (2) Is it expressly excluded by law? If an item is income and not specifically excluded, it must be included.

Certain items are recognized as not being income, for example, gifts, inheritances, scholarships, social security benefits, workmen's compensation insurance, and proceeds of life insurance policies paid upon the death of the insured. These are not income and are excluded.

Other items, such as the first $100 of dividend income and interest on the obligations of the states and their subdivisions are specifically excluded. In the case of the first exclusion, Congress, in partial recognition of the claim that corporation income is "taxed twice," and for other reasons, has so written the law as to permit an individual owner of stock in qualifying domestic corporations to exclude from gross income the first $100 in dividends received on this stock. In case of the second, the Supreme Court has held that the power to tax the interest paid on debts of the states and their subdivisions is the power to destroy these governmental units, and consequently violates constitutional guarantees. As a result, all interest on the bonds of the states and their subdivisions is excluded from gross income.

Deductions to Arrive at Adjusted Gross Income. These are generally deductions of a business nature. For example, all ordinary and necessary expenses of carrying on a business, trade, or profession (other than as an employee) are deductions to arrive at adjusted gross income. To understand this, recognize that under income tax law gross profit from sales (sales less cost of goods sold) is gross income to a merchant, that gross legal fees earned are gross income to a lawyer, and gross rentals from a building are gross income to a landlord. Consequently, the merchant, the lawyer, and the landlord may each deduct all ordinary and necessary expenses of carrying on his business or profession, such as salaries, wages, rent, depreciation, supplies used, repairs, maintenance, insurance, taxes, interest, and so on.

In addition to the foregoing business expenses, from a tax management point of view, a very important deduction from gross income is the long-term capital gain deduction. This deduction permits, under certain circumstances, the exclusion from gross income of one half the net long-term gains from capital asset sales and exchanges. This deduction is discussed in more detail later in this chapter.

Deductions from Adjusted Gross Income. By legislative grace an individual taxpayer is permitted certain deductions from adjusted gross income. These are of two kinds. The first consists of certain personal expenses, commonly called itemized deductions, and the second is a deduction for exemptions.

In the case of the first kind of deduction, the taxpayer has a choice. He ·may either deduct his allowable itemized deductions (personal interest expense, state and local taxes, charitable contributions, medical expenses, casualty losses over $100 for each loss, and so on) or he may deduct the optional standard deduction. The optional standard deduction is the larger of the minimum standard deduction or 10 percent of adjusted gross income, but not more than $1,000 ($500 each for a married couple filing separate returns). The minimum standard deduction on a joint return is $200 plus $100 for each exemption (see following paragraph).

As to the second kind of deduction, the deduction for exemptions, a taxpayer is allowed one exemption for himself, another for his wife, and one for each dependent. Dependents commonly include each minor child or other closely related person for whom the taxpayer contributes more than half toward the dependent's support. Additional exemptions are allowed if the taxpayer or his wife is over sixty-five and/or blind. For each exemption, the taxpayer, at present, may deduct $600 from adjusted gross income.

Federal Income Tax Rates. Federal income tax rates are progressive in nature. By this is meant that each additional segment or bracket of taxable income is subject to a higher rate than the preceding segment or bracket.

This may be seen by examining Illustration 184 which shows a portion of the rates for either a single person not qualifying as a head of household or a married person filing a separate return.

To use the rate schedule of Illustration 184, the taxpayer reads down the

Illustration 184

RATE SCHEDULE FOR: SINGLE TAXPAYER not qualifying as head of household, and MARRIED PERSON FILING SEPARATE RETURN

If taxable income is:

Over—		But not over—	the tax is—		of the excess over—
....	—$	500....	*14% of the taxable income*		
$ 500....	—	1,000....	$ *70, plus 15%*....	— $	500
1,000....	—	1,500....	*145, plus 16%*....	—	1,000
1,500....	—	2,000....	*225, plus 17%*....	—	1,500
2,000....	—	4,000....	*310, plus 19%*....	—	2,000
4,000....	—	6,000....	*690, plus 22%*....	—	4,000
6,000....	—	8,000....	*1,130, plus 25%*....	—	6,000
8,000....	—	10,000....	*1,630, plus 28%*....	—	8,000
10,000....	—	12,000....	*2,190, plus 32%*....	—	10,000
12,000....	—	14,000....	*2,830, plus 36%*....	—	12,000
14,000....	—	16,000....	*3,550, plus 39%*....	—	14,000
16,000....	—	18,000....	*4,330, plus 42%*....	—	16,000
18,000....	—	20,000....	*5,170, plus 45%*....	—	18,000
20,000....	—	22,000....	*6,070, plus 48%*....	—	20,000
22,000....	—	24,000....	*7,030, plus 50%*....	—	22,000
24,000....	—	26,000....	*8,030, plus 50%*....	—	24,000
26,000....	—	28,000....	*9,030, plus 53%*....	—	26,000
28,000....	—	32,000....	*10,090, plus 53%*....	—	28,000
32,000....	—	38,000....	*12,210, plus 55%*....	—	32,000
38,000....	—	44,000....	*15,510, plus 58%*....	—	38,000
44,000....	—	50,000....	*18,990, plus 60%*....	—	44,000
		and so on up to:			
100,000...................			*55,490, plus 70%*....	—	100,000

columns marked "If taxable income is:" until he comes to the bracket of his taxable income. For example, if taxable income is $6,400, the taxpayer reads down to the bracket "over $6,000 but not over $8,000." The remaining columns then tell him the tax on $6,400 is $1,130 plus 25% of the excess over $6,000, or the tax is $1,130 + (25% × $400) or is $1,230.

A husband and wife have a choice. They may file separate returns and use the rate schedule of Illustration 184 or they may combine their incomes and file a joint return using a different rate schedule (not shown) in which the income amounts in the tax brackets are exactly double the amounts shown in the brackets of Illustration 184. As a result of such a joint return, a married couple having a large income enjoys a considerable tax advantage over a single person with the same income.

A person who can qualify as a head of a household may use a third schedule in which the rates fall between those for a single person and those for a married couple filing jointly. Generally a head of household is an unmarried person who maintains a home in which live his or her children or a qualifying dependent other than a child.

Regardless of the rate schedule used, it is generally recognized that our federal income tax rates are steeply progressive. Proponents claim that this is only fair, since the taxpayers most able to pay, those with higher incomes, are subject to the higher rates. Opponents, on the other hand, claim the high rates stifle initiative. For example, a young unmarried executive earning $20,000 per year, upon being offered a new job carrying additional responsibilities and a $4,000 salary increase, might turn the new job down, feeling the after-tax increase in pay insufficient to compensate for the extra responsibilities. In this case the executive could keep, after federal income taxes, just about half the increase, or approximately $2,000 of the $4,000.

Whether or not our progressive income tax rates stifle initiative is probably open to debate. However, there is no question that the rates do cause high-income taxpayers to search for tax-saving opportunities.

Tax Credits and Prepayments. Most taxpayers have income taxes withheld from salaries and wages and many are required to make advance payments of estimated tax. Both are examples of prepayments. A taxpayer who is retired may receive a retirement income credit, and some taxpayers are eligible for a foreign tax credit or an investment credit. However, these need not be discussed here.

Special Tax Treatment of Capital Gains and Losses. From a tax-saving point of view, one of the most important features of our federal income tax laws is the special treatment given long-term gains from capital asset sales and exchanges. The usual effect of this special treatment is a tax on net long-term capital gains that is one half, or less than one half, the tax on an equal amount of income from some other source, commonly called "ordinary income." For this reason, whenever possible, tax planners try to cause income to emerge in the form of long-term capital gains rather than as ordinary income.

The Internal Revenue Code defines a capital asset as any item of property except: (*a*) inventories, (*b*) trade notes and accounts receivable, (*c*) real property and depreciable property used in a trade or business, (*d*) copyrights in the hands of the creator of the copyrighted works, and (*e*) any government obligation due within one year and issued at a discount.

Common examples of capital assets held by individuals and subject to sale or exchange are stocks, bonds, and a personal residence.

A gain on the sale of a capital asset occurs when the proceeds of the sale exceed the *basis* of the asset sold, and a loss occurs when the asset's basis exceeds the proceeds. The basis of a purchased asset is generally its cost less any depreciation previously allowed or allowable for tax purposes. Not all capital assets are acquired by purchase; but rules for determining the basis of an asset acquired other than by purchase are at times complicated and need not be discussed here.

For tax purposes, a distinction is made between short- and long-term capital gains and losses. Short-term gains and losses result when capital assets are held six months or less before being sold or exchanged, and long-term gains and losses result when such assets are held more than six months. Furthermore, under the law, net short-term gains must be reported in full and are taxed as ordinary income; but only one half the amount of any net long-term capital gains must be included in adjusted gross income, and the maximum tax is limited to 25 percent of the total of such net gains.

For example, if a taxpayer has $1,000 of long-term gains, no losses, and other income that places these gains in a 36 percent bracket, he is required to include only $500 of the gains in adjusted gross income and to pay only a $180 ($500 × 36% = $180) tax thereon. Consequently, his effective tax rate on the gains is 18 percent ($180 ÷ $1,000 = 18%), and is one half what it would be if the $1,000 were ordinary income.

Often a high-income taxpayer's capital gains fall in a tax bracket where, if the tax thereon were calculated as in the preceding paragraph, the effective rate would exceed 25 percent of the total gains. In such cases the tax is limited to 25 percent of the gains. For example, assume that a taxpayer has $1,000 of capital gains, no losses, and other income that causes these gains to fall in the 70 percent bracket. If the taxpayer calculated his tax as in the foregoing example, the indicated tax resulting from the calculation would be $350 ($500 × 70% = $350), or the effective rate would be 35 percent ($350 ÷ $1,000 = 35%). Consequently, since this exceeds the 25 percent maximum, the taxpayer is permitted by law to limit his tax to 25 percent of the $1,000, or to $250. Note that this is considerably less than half the $700 the tax would be if the $1,000 were ordinary income.

In the preceding paragraphs the terms "net long-term gains" and "net short-term gains" appear. When long-term gains exceed long-term losses, a net long-term gain results. Likewise, when long-term losses exceed long-term gains, a net long-term loss occurs. Short-term gains and losses are combined in a like manner to arrive at either a net short-term gain or loss.

When a taxpayer has a combination of long-term gains and losses and short-term gains and losses, it is necessary to combine these gains and losses according to certain tax rules, called "offsetting rules," in order to arrive at the amount of net long-term capital gains subject to the special tax treatment outlined above. These rules are complicated and their discussion is deferred to an advanced course.

When an individual's capital losses exceed his capital gains, the first $1,000 of the net loss may be deducted from other taxable income in the year of the loss, and any amount above $1,000 may be carried forward and deducted at the rate of $1,000 per year until all is deducted.

One last point needs to be made in regard to real property and depreciable property used in a taxpayer's trade or business (see definition of capital assets in a previous paragraph). Such properties are not capital assets according to the law; consequently, when sold or exchanged, the excess of losses over gains is fully deductible in arriving at taxable income. However, if such properties are held over six months, the excess of gains over losses is eligible for long-term capital gain treatment, except to the extent of depreciation taken after 1961. As to the depreciation taken after 1961, a share of the gain equal to a portion or all of this depreciation must be treated as ordinary income.

The Corporation Income Tax.   For federal tax purposes, the taxable income of a corporation organized for profit is calculated in much the same way as the taxable income of an indivdual. However, there are important differences, five of which follow:

a) Instead of the $100 dividend exclusion of an individual, a corporation may deduct from gross income the first 85 percent of dividends received from stock it owns in other domestic corporations. This in effect means that only 15 percent of such dividends are taxed.

b) The capital gains of a corporation are also treated differently; however, as with an individual, the maximum tax on such gains is limited to 25 percent of their total.

c) A corporation may only offset capital losses against capital gains; and if in any year the offset results in a net capital loss, the loss may not be deducted from other income, but it may be carried forward an deducted from any capital gains of the next five years.

d) The optional standard deduction and the deduction for exemptions do not apply to a corporation, and a corporation does not have certain other deductions of an individual, such as that for personal medical expenses.

e) In addition to the foregoing, the big difference between the corporation and the individual income tax is that the corporation tax is really two taxes, a *normal tax* and a *surtax*. The first $25,000 of a corporation's taxable income is subject to a 22 percent normal tax and is exempt from the surtax; however, income in excess of $25,000 is subject to both the 22 percent normal tax and a 26 percent surtax.

TAX EFFECTS OF BUSINESS ALTERNATIVES

Alternative decisions commonly have different tax effects. Following are several examples illustrating this.

Form of Business Organization. The difference between individual and corporation tax rates commonly affects one of the basic decisions a businessman must make, namely, that as to the legal form his business should take. Should it be a single proprietorship, partnership, or corporation? The following factors influence the decision:

a) As previously stated, a corporation is a taxable entity. Its income is taxed at corporation rates, and any portion distributed in dividends is taxed again as individual income to its stockholders. On the other hand, the income of a single proprietorship or partnership, whether withdrawn or left in the business, is taxed only once, as individual income of the proprietor or partners.

b) In addition, a corporation may pay reasonable amounts in salaries to stockholders who work for the corporation, and the sum of these salaries is a tax deductible expense in arriving at the corporation's taxable income. In a partnership or a single proprietorship on the other hand, salaries of the partners or the proprietor are nothing more than allocations of income.

In arriving at a decision as to the legal form his business should take, a businessman, with the foregoing points in mind, must estimate how he will fare taxwise under each form, and select the best. For example, assume that a businessman is choosing between the single proprietorship and corporate forms, and that he estimates his business will have annual gross sales of $250,000, with cost of goods sold and operating expenses, other than his own salary as manager, of $218,000. Assume further that $12,000 per year is a fair salary for managing such a business and the owner plans to withdraw all profits from the business. Under these assumptions the businessman will fare taxwise as shown in Illustration 185.

Under the assumptions of Illustration 185 the businessman will incur the smaller tax and have the larger after-tax income under the single proprietorship form. However, this may not be true in every case. For instance, if he has large amounts of income from other sources, he may find he would incur less tax if the business were organized as a corporation.

Furthermore, in the example just given it is assumed that all profits are withdrawn and none are left in the business for growth. This happens. However, growth is commonly financed through retained earnings; and when it is, the relative desirability of the two forms may change. This is because income retained in a business organized as a corporation is not taxed as individual income to its stockholders, but the income of a single proprietorship or partnership is so taxed, whether retained in the business or withdrawn.

For instance, if the business of Illustration 185 is organized as a single proprietorship, the tax burden of the owner remains the same whether he withdraws any of his profits or not. But, in case of the corporation, if all $15,600 of the dividends are retained in the business, the owner is required to pay individual income taxes on his $12,000 salary only. This would reduce his annual individual income tax from the $4,860 shown in Illustration 185 to $1,030, and would reduce the total tax burden with the corporation form to $5,430 ($4,400 + $1,030), which is $950 less than the tax burden under the single proprietorship form.

The foregoing is by no means all the picture. Other tax factors may be involved. For example, a corporation may incur an extra tax if, after it has accumulated $100,000 of retained earnings, it unreasonably accumulates

Illustration 185

Operating Results Under Each Form:

	Proprietorship		Corporation	
Estimated sales....................		$250,000		$250,000
Cost of goods sold and operating expenses other than owner-manager's salary......................	$218,000		$218,000	
Salary of owner-manager...........	-0-	218,000	12,000	230,000
Before tax income.................		$ 32,000		$ 20,000
Corporation income tax at 22 percent............................		-0-		4,400
Net Income.....................		$ 32,000		$ 15,600

Owner's After-tax Income Under Each Form:

Single proprietorship net income....		$ 32,000		
Corporation salary.................				$ 12,000
Dividends.........................				15,600
Total individual income............		$ 32,000		$ 27,600
Individual income tax (assuming a joint return with deductions and exemptions amounting to $6,000 under both forms plus a $100 dividend exclusion under the corporation form......................		6,380		4,860
Owner's After-Tax Income..........		$ 25,620		$ 22,740

additional retained earnings beyond the needs of the business. Also, under present laws a corporation may elect to be taxed as a single proprietorship and a single proprietorship can elect to be taxed as a corporation. Furthermore, in a decision as to the legal form a business should take, factors other than taxes are often important, for example, lack of stockholder liability in a corporation.

Dividends and Growth.   It was pointed out earlier in this chapter that it is normally to a taxpayer's advantage to have income emerge in the form of long-term capital gains rather than as ordinary income. Furthermore, earnings paid out in dividends result in ordinary income to stockholders, but earnings retained in an incorporated business commonly result in growth and an increase in stock values, which may be turned into long-term capital gains through a later sale of the stock. For this reason it is often to the advantage of the owner of an incorporated business to forego dividends and, at a later date, through the sale of the business, to take the profits of his business in the form of long-term gains resulting from growth. Or he may keep the stock until his death, in which case a tax on the capital gain may be escaped entirely.

Size of the Business Unit. As previously explained, the first $25,000 of a corporation's taxable income is exempt from surtax. Consequently, the first $25,000 of such income is subject to the 22 percent normal tax, while income in excess of $25,000 is subject to both the 22 percent normal tax and the 26 percent surtax, or is taxed at 48 percent. Obviously, this may influence the size of incorporated business units.

For example, a real estate operator is about to begin several real estate ventures that he estimates will earn $100,000 of taxable income annually. If he organizes a single corporation to carry on these ventures, the corporation will incur $41,500 of federal income taxes annually, calculated as follows:

$$
\begin{array}{ll}
\textit{\$25,000 of income taxed at 22\%} = & \$\ 5,500 \\
\textit{75,000 of income taxed at 48\%} = & 36,000 \\
\hline
\textit{Total Tax Liability}\ldots\ldots\ldots & \$41,500 \\
\end{array}
$$

On the other hand, the real estate operator may recognize that if instead of one corporation he organizes four corporations, each earning $25,000 annually, the surtax may be avoided. However, Congress has also recognized this and has partially closed the loophole by providing that: (1) a controlled group of corporations[1] must either divide a single surtax exemption among its members or (2) if the members elect to take separate surtax exemptions, then each must pay not only the 22 percent normal tax but also an additional 6 percent tax on its first $25,000 of taxable income.

Therefore, if the real estate operator elects to organize four corporations and have each take a separate surtax exemption, the total tax liability may be reduced from $41,500 for one corporation to $28,000 for the four. The $28,000 is calculated as follows:

$25,000 of income taxed at 22% + 6% or 28% = $7,000 of tax for one corporation, and $7,000 × 4 = $28,000 of tax for four corporations.

Of course, it should be pointed out that the tax advantage accruing from organizing multiple corporations, rather than a single corporation, is apt to be disallowed in any case where there is not some good business reason, other than the tax savings, for the separate corporations.

---

[1] When an individual or other corporation owns 80 percent or more of the stock in each of several corporations, the several corporations are a controlled group.

Method of Financing. When a business organized as a corporation is in need of additional financing, the owners may supply the corporation whatever funds are needed by purchasing its stock. However, an overall tax advantage may often be gained, if instead of purchasing stock, they supply the funds through long-term loans. Insofar as the owners are concerned, beyond the allowable dividend exclusion, it makes no difference on their individual returns whether they report interest or dividends from the funds supplied. However, whether the corporation issues stock or floats a loan usually makes a big difference on its return. Interest on borrowed funds is a tax deductible expense, but dividends are a distribution of profits and have no effect on the corporation's taxes. Consequently, if owners loan the corporation funds, rather than buy its stock, the total tax liability (their own plus their corporation's) will be reduced.

In making financial arrangements such as these, owners must be careful not to overreach themselves in attempting to maximize the interest deduction of their corporation. If they do so and thereby create what is called a "thin corporation," one in which the owners have supplied an unreasonably "thin" portion of capital, the Director of Internal Revenue may disallow the interest deductions and require that they be treated as dividends.

Timing Transactions. The timing of transactions can be of major importance in tax planning. For example, securities may be held a little longer in order to make the gain on their sale subject to treatment as a long-term capital gain. Or if a taxpayer has certain transactions that will result in long-term capital gains and other transactions that will result in short- or long-term capital losses, a tax advantage will commonly result if the gains are taken in one year and the losses in another. For example, if an individual taxpayer completes in the same year two transaction, one that results in a $1,000 long-term capital gain and the other in a $1,000 capital loss, the loss must be offset against the gain and the taxpayer is exactly even insofar as taxes are concerned. However, if the taxpayer will take the loss in one year and the gain in another, he can secure in, for example, a 50 percent tax bracket, a $250 tax advantage. The mechanics of this are as follows: The $1,000 loss, if taken in one year, is deductible in full from other income of that year, and in a 50 percent bracket would result in a $500 tax reduction. The $1,000 gain, on the other hand, if taken in a different year, is taxable as a long-term capital gain and would result in a $250 tax liability. Consequently, a $250 tax liability subtracted from a $500 tax reduction results in a $250 net saving.

Sales of real or depreciable property used in a trade or business offer another example of the importance of timing. For instance, if a company has several items of real or depreciable property to be sold, and some of the sales will result in losses and others in gains, the losses should be taken in one year and the gains in another. The losses and gains should be taken this way because, if the losses and gains are both incurred in the same year, they must be offset. However, if the losses are taken in one year and the gains in another, the losses may be deducted in full from other ordinary income, while the gains become eligible in their year for long-term capital gain treatment, at least to the extent they exceed depreciation taken after 1961.

Forms in Which Related Transactions Are Completed.   The tax consequences of related transactions are often dependent upon the forms in which they are completed. For example, the sale of one property at a profit and the immediate purchase of another like property normally results in a taxable gain on the property sold, but an exchange of these properties may result in a tax-free exchange.

A tax-free exchange occurs when like kinds of property are exchanged for each other, or when one or more persons transfer property to a corporation and immediately thereafter are in control of the corporation. Control in such cases is intrepreted as meaning that the transferring persons (or person) own 80 percent of the corporation's voting stock after the transfer.

At first glance it seems that it should be to anyone's advantage to take a tax-free exchange rather than to pay taxes, but this may not be so. For example, ten years ago a corporation acquired, for $50,000, land then at the edge of the city. Today, due to booming growth, the land is well within the city and has a fair market value of $250,000. Aside from a fully depreciated fence, the land is without improvements, having been used over the years for storage of idle equipment and excess inventory. The corporation plans to move part of its operations to a suburb and has an opportunity to trade the city property for vacant suburban acreage on which it would build a factory. Should it make the trade? From a tax viewpoint, since the new land is not depreciable, the answer is probably, yes, the company should make the tax-free exchange.

However, if the suburban property, rather than being vacant, consisted of land having a fair market value of $25,000 with a suitable factory building thereon valued at $225,000, the corporation would probably be better off if it sold the city property, paid the tax on its gain, and purchased the suburban factory and its site. The corporation would probably be better off because the gain on the city land would be taxable as a long-term capital gain on which the tax would not exceed $50,000 (25% of ($250,000 − $50,000) = $50,000). However, by purchasing the new factory, the corporation gains the right to deduct the building's $225,000 cost (over its life) in the form of depreciation, an expense deductible in full in arriving at taxable income.

Accounting Basis and Procedures.   The accounting basis and procedures used by a taxpayer in keeping his records must also, with certain exceptions, be used in computing his taxable income. Generally, a taxpayer keeps his records on either a cash or accrual basis (see page 323); but regardless of which he uses, the basis and any procedures used must clearly reflect income and be consistently followed.

When inventories are a material factor in calculating income, a taxpayer is required to use the accrual basis insofar as the inventories are concerned. However, in a business or profession in which inventories are not a factor, a taxpayer may use a pure cash basis in arriving at taxable income. Furthermore, since a cash-basis taxpayer can often shift revenue receipts and expense payments from one year to another, being on a cash basis is commonly an advantage.

An accrual-basis taxpayer cannot shift income from year to year by timing receipts and payments; however, somewhat of the same thing may be accomplished through a choice of accounting procedures. For example, recognition of revenue on an installment basis (discussed in Chapter 29) commonly shifts revenue from one year to another for a merchant making installment sales. Likewise, a contractor may use the percentage-of-completion basis (Chapter 29) to shift construction revenue from one year to another and to level taxable income over a period of years.

Furthermore, any taxpayer may shift taxable income to future years through a choice of inventory and depreciation procedures. For example, during periods of rising prices the Lifo inventory method results in charging higher costs for goods sold against current revenues, and thus reduces taxable income and taxes. It may be argued that this only postpones taxes, since in periods of declining prices the use of Lifo results in lower costs and higher taxes. However, the history of recent years has been one of constantly rising prices; therefore, it may also be argued that Lifo will postpone taxes indefinitely.

Depreciation methods that result in higher depreciation charges in an asset's early years and lower charges in later years, such as the sum-of-the-year's-digits or declining-balance methods, also postpone taxes. And while tax postponement is not as desirable as tax avoidance, postponement does give the taxpayer interest free use of tax dollars until these dollars must be paid to the government.

Before turning to a new topic, it should be pointed out that the opportunities for tax planning described in these pages are only illustrative of those available. The wise businessman will seek help from his tax consultant in order to take advantage of every tax-saving opportunity.

NET INCOME AND TAXABLE INCOME

The taxable income of a business commonly differs from its reported net income. They differ because (1) net income is determined by the application of generally accepted accounting principles, (2) while tax rules are used in determining taxable income, and (3) the rules differ from the generally accepted accounting principles on some points. For example:

   a) The application of accounting principles requires that the full amount of any material gains from long-term capital asset sales and exchanges be taken into reported net income, but for tax purposes only 50 percent of the net gains from such sales commonly enters into taxable income.

b) For accounting purposes, interest received on state and municipal bonds must be included in net income, but such interest is not taxable income.

c) As a rule, unearned income, such as rent collected in advance, is taxable in the year of receipt, however, under an accrual basis of accounting such items are taken into income in the year earned regardless of when received.

d) Accounting principles require an estimate of future costs, such as, for example, costs of making good on guarantees; and accounting principles require a deduction of such costs from revenue in the year the guaranteed goods are sold. However, tax rules do not permit the deduction of such costs until after the guarantor has to make good on his guarantee.

In addition to the foregoing, reported net income commonly differs from taxable income because the taxpayer is permitted by law in some cases to use one method or procedure for tax purposes and a different method or procedure in keeping his accounting records. For example, a taxpayer may elect to use declining-balance depreciation for tax purposes, but to use straight-line depreciation in his accounting records.

Many accountants feel the interests of government, business, and the public would better be served if there were more uniformity between taxable income and reported net income. However, since the federal income tax is designed to serve other purposes than raising revenue, it is apt to be some time before this is achieved.

TAXES AND THE DISTORTION OF NET INCOME

When one accounting procedure is elected for tax purposes and a different procedure is used in the accounting records, a problem arises as to how much income tax expense should be deducted each year on the income statement. If the tax actually incurred in such situations is deducted, reported net income often varies from year to year due to the postponement and later payment of taxes. Consequently, in such cases, since stockholders may be misled by these variations, many accountants feel that income taxes should be allocated in such a way that any distortion resulting from postponing taxes is removed from the income statement.

To appreciate the problem involved here, assume that a corporation has installed a $100,000 machine, the product of which will produce a half million dollars of revenue in each of the succeeding four years and $80,000 of income before depreciation and taxes. Assume further that the company must pay income taxes at a 50 percent rate (round number assumed for easy calculation), that it plans to use straight-line depreciation in its records, but the declining-balance method for tax purposes. If the machine has a four-year life and an $8,000 salvage value, annual depreciation calculated by each method will be as follows:

Year	Straight-Line	Declining-Balance
1.........................$23,000		$50,000
2......................... 23,000		25,000
3......................... 23,000		12,500
4......................... 23,000		4,500
Total...................$92,000		$92,000

And since the company has elected declining-balance depreciation for tax purposes, it will be liable for $15,000 of income tax on the first year's income, $27,500 on the second, $33,750 on the third, and $37,750 on the fourth. The calculation of these taxes is shown in Illustration 186.

Illustration 186

Annual Income Taxes:	Year 1	Year 2	Year 3	Year 4	Total
Income before deprecia- and income taxes.........	$80,000	$80,000	$80,000	$80,000	$320,000
Depreciation (declining- balance)...................	50,000	25,000	12,500	4,500	92,000
Taxable income.............	$30,000	$55,000	$67,500	$75,500	$228,000
Annual income taxes (50 percent of taxable in- come)....................	$15,000	$27,500	$33,750	$37,750	$114,000

Furthermore, if the company were to deduct its actual tax liability each year in arriving at income to be reported to its stockholders, it would report the amounts shown in Illustration 187.

Observe in Illustrations 186 and 187 that total depreciation, $92,000, is the same whether calculated by the straight-line or the declining-balance method. Also note that the total tax liability for the four years, $114,000, is

Illustration 187

Income After Deducting Actual Tax Liabilities:	Year 1	Year 2	Year 3	Year 4	Total
Income before deprecia- tion and income taxes....	$80,000	$80,000	$80,000	$80,000	$320,000
Depreciation (straight- line)......................	23,000	23,000	23,000	23,000	92,000
Income before taxes........	$57,000	$57,000	$57,000	$57,000	$228,000
Income taxes (actual liability of each year).....	15,000	27,500	33,750	37,750	114,000
Remaining income.........	$42,000	$29,500	$23,250	$19,250	$114,000

the same in each case. Then note the distortion of the final income figures in Illustration 187, due to the postponement of taxes.

If this company should report successive annual income figures of $42,000, $29,500, $23,250, and then $19,250, some of its stockholders might be misled as to the company's earnings trend. Consequently, in cases such as this many accountants think income taxes should be allocated so that the distortion caused by the postponement of taxes is removed from the income statement. These accountants advocate that—

When one accounting procedure is used in the accounting records and a different procedure is used for tax purposes, the tax expense deducted on the income statement should not be the actual tax liability, but the amount that would be payable if the procedure used in the records were also used in calculating the tax.

Illustration 188					
Net Income That Should Be Reported To Stockholders:	**Year 1**	**Year 2**	**Year 3**	**Year 4**	**Total**
Income before depreciation and income taxes....$80,000	$80,000	$80,000	$80,000	$320,000
Depreciation (straight-line)...... 23,000	23,000	23,000	23,000	92,000
Income before taxes........$57,000	$57,000	$57,000	$57,000	$228,000
Income taxes (amounts based on straight-line depreciation)............ 28,500	28,500	28,500	28,500	114,000
Net Income...............$28,500	$28,500	$28,500	$28,500	$114,000

If the foregoing is applied in this case, the corporation will report to its stockholders in each of the four years the amounts of income shown in Illustration 188.

In examining Illustration 188, recall that the company's tax liabilities are actually $15,000 in the first year, $27,500 in the second, $33,750 in the third, and $37,750 in the fourth, a total of $114,000. Then observe that when this $114,000 liability is allocated evenly over the four years, the distortion of the annual net incomes due to the postponement of taxes is removed from the published income statements.

ENTRIES FOR THE ALLOCATION OF TAXES

When income taxes are allocated as in Illustration 188, the tax liability of each year and the deferred taxes are recorded with a work sheet adjustment and an adjusting entry, after which the taxes are paid. The adjusting entries and the entries in general journal form for the payment of the taxes (without explanations) are:

Year 1	Income Taxes Expense...............	28,500.00	
	Income Taxes Payable............		15,000.00
	Deferred Income Taxes..........		13,500.00
Year 1	Income Taxes Payable..............	15,000.00	
	Cash........................		15,000.00
Year 2	Income Taxes Expense...............	28,500.00	
	Income Taxes Payable............		27,500.00
	Deferred Income Taxes..........		1,000.00
Year 2	Income Taxes Payable..............	27,500.00	
	Cash........................		27,500.00
Year 3	Income Taxes Expense...............	28,500.00	
	Deferred Income Taxes.............	5,250.00	
	Income Taxes Payable...........		33,750.00
Year 3	Income Taxes Payable..............	33,750.00	
	Cash........................		33,750.00
Year 4	Income Taxes Expense...............	28,500.00	
	Deferred Income Taxes.............	9,250.00	
	Income Taxes Payable...........		37,750.00
Year 4	Income Taxes Payable..............	37,750.00	
	Cash........................		37,750.00

In the foregoing entries the $28,500 debited to Income Taxes Expense each year is the amount that is deducted on the income statement in reporting annual net income. Also, in the foregoing entries the amount credited to Income Taxes Payable each year is the actual tax liability of that year.

Observe in the entries that, since the actual tax liability in each of the first two years is less than the amount debited to Income Taxes Expense, the difference is credited to Deferred Income Taxes. Then note that in the last two years, since the actual liability each year is greater than the debit to Income Taxes Expense, the difference is debited to Deferred Income Taxes. Now observe in the following illustration of the company's Deferred Income Taxes account that the debits and credits exactly balance each other out over the four year period:

Deferred Income Taxes

Year	Explanation	Debit	Credit	Balance
1			13,500.00	13,500.00
2			1,000.00	14,500.00
3		5,250.00		9,250.00
4		9,250.00		–0–

QUESTIONS FOR CLASS DISCUSSION

1. Jackson expects to have $500 of income in a 50 percent bracket; consequently, which should be more desirable to him: (*a*) a transaction that will reduce his income tax by $100 or (*b*) a transaction that will reduce an expense of his business by $150?

2. Why must a taxpayer normally take advantage of a tax-saving opportunity at the time it arises?

3. Distinguish between tax avoidance and tax evasion. Which is legal and desirable?

4. What are some of the nonrevenue objectives of the federal income tax?

5. What nonrevenue objective is gained by granting a $25,000 surtax exemption to corporations?

6. What questions must be answered in determining whether an item should be included or excluded from gross income for tax purposes?

7. Name several items that are not income for tax purposes.

8. What justification is given for permitting an individual to exclude the first $100 of dividends from domestic corporations from his gross income for tax purposes?

9. For tax purposes, define a capital asset.

10. What is a short-term capital gain? A long-term capital gain?

11. An individual has had capital asset transactions that have resulted in nothing but long-term capital gains. What special tax treatment may be given these gains?

12. For tax purposes, what is "ordinary income"?

13. Why do tax planners try to have income emerge as a long-term capital gain?

14. Differentiate between the normal tax and the surtax of a corporation.

15. It is often a wise tax decision for the owner of an incorporated business to forego the payment of dividends from the earnings of his business. Why?

16. Why does the taxable income of a business commonly differ from its net income?

PROBLEMS

Problem 28–1

Richard Hall, a bachelor without dependents, owns Valley Sales, a profitable single proprietorship business that earns an average of $40,000 per year. Hall has no income other than from the business. Each year he has $3,400 of itemized deductions and a single $600 exemption deduction. In the past he has withdrawn $12,000 annually from the business for personal living expenses plus sufficient additional cash to pay his income taxes.

Hall thinks he can save taxes by reorganizing his business into a corporation. If he does so, $15,000 per year would be a fair salary for managing such a business; consequently, he will pay this amount to himself as president and manager. He will also take $5,000 of the corporation's earnings each year in dividends, since this amount and his salary will pay his personal living expenses and income taxes.

Required:
1. Calculate the income tax liability and annual net income of the business if organized as a corporation.
2. Use the rate schedule of Illustration 184 to prepare calculations showing in one set of columns the amount of personal income tax Mr. Hall incurs with the business organized as a single proprietorship and in a second set of columns the personal income tax plus corporation income tax he will incur with the business organized as a corporation, paying him a $15,-000 salary and $5,000 in dividends each year.
3. Prepare another calculation of Mr. Hall's personal income tax plus corporation tax under the assumption the corporation pays to him $15,000 per year in dividends in addition to a $15,000 per year salary.

Problem 28–2

Sequoia Corporation is planning an expansion program that will cost $100,-000 and will increase its earnings $20,000 annually before interest on the money used in the expansion, if borrowed, and before income taxes. All the outstanding Sequoia Corporation stock is owned by the Ryan family, and the family will supply the money to finance the expansion, either investing an additional $100,000 in the corporation by purchasing its unissued stock or loaning the $100,000 to the corporation at 6 percent interest.

The corporation presently earns in excess of $25,000 annually and pays $10,000 per year to the family in dividends. If the loan is made, the dividends will be reduced by an amount equal to the interest paid on the loan.

Required:
Present statistics to show whether it would be advantageous for the family to make the loan or to purchase the corporation stock. (Ignore the family's dividend exclusion.)

Problem 28–3

George Brown, Jr. recently inherited the business of his father. The business, Steel Products Company, is a small manufacturing corporation; however, a share of its assets, $80,000 at cost, consists of blue-chip investment stocks purchased over the years by the corporation from earnings. The father was the sole owner of the corporation at his death and before his death had paid himself a $15,000 annual salary for a number of years as president and manager. Over the years the corporation had seldom paid a dividend but instead had invested any earnings not needed in the business in the blue-chip stocks previously mentioned. At the father's death the market value of these stocks far exceeded their cost.

George's mother is dead, and after George graduated from college, the father had no dependents. His tax return for the year before his death showed $16,500 of gross income, consisting of his $15,000 corporation salary plus $1,500 interest from real estate loans. It also showed $3,400 of itemized deductions plus a single $600 exemption deduction. The corporation had earned during the year before the father's death $23,000 from its manufacturing operations plus $10,000 in dividends from its investments, a total of $33,000 after the president's salary but before income taxes.

Required:

1. Prepare a comparative statement showing for the year before the father's death the corporation's operating income, dividend income, total income, share of the dividend income excluded, taxable income, and income tax under the following (*a*) and (*b*) assumptions. (*a*) The corporation owns the investment stocks and had the operating income just described. (*b*) The corporation had the operating income described; but instead of owning the investment stocks, over the years it paid dividends (none last year) and George Brown, Sr. used the dividends to buy the stocks in his own name rather than in the corporation name.

2. Calculate the amounts of individual income tax and corporation income tax incurred by Mr. Brown, Sr. and the corporation for the year before Mr. Brown's death under the foregoing (*a*) assumptions, and the amounts that would have been incurred under the (*b*) assumptions. Also calculate the amount of individual income tax Mr. Brown would have incurred with the business organized as a single proprietorship and the stocks registered in his own name. Under this last assumption remember that the corporation's operating income plus the salary paid its president equal the operating income of the single proprietorship. Use the rate schedule of Illustration 184 in the individual income tax calculations.

Problem 28–4

George Moss has operated Phoenix Sales for a number of years with the following average annual results:

PHOENIX SALES

Income Statement for an Average Year

Sales..		*$275,000*
Cost of goods sold............................	*$165,000*	
Operating expenses..........................	*85,000*	*250,000*
Net Income..		*$ 25,000*

Mr. Moss is unmarried and without dependents and he has been operating Phoenix Sales as a single proprietorship. He has been withdrawing $10,000 each year to pay his personal living expenses, including $1,400 of charitable contributions, state and local taxes, and other itemized deductions. He has no income other than from Phoenix Sales.

Required:

1. Assume that Mr. Moss is considering the incorporation of his business and prepare a comparative income statement for the business showing its net income as a single proprietorship and as a corporation. Assume that if he incorporates he will pay $10,000 per year to himself as a salary and that this is a fair amount.

2. Use the rate schedule of Illustration 184 and current corporation income tax rates to determine the amount of federal income taxes Mr. Moss will have to pay for himself and for his business under each of the following assumptions: (*a*) the business is not incorporated; (*b*) the business is incorporated, pays Mr. Moss a $10,000 annual salary as manager, and pays out an additional $11,000 each year in dividends; and (*c*) the business is incorporated, pays Mr. Moss a $10,000 salary, but does not pay any dividends.

Problem 28–5

At a $200,000 cost, XL Corporation installed a new machine in its plant early in January, 1966, so that it could add a new product to its line. It estimated the new machine would have a four-year life, a $16,000 salvage value, and its product would produce $180,000 of income each year before depreciation and income taxes at an assumed 50 percent rate. The company uses declining-balance depreciation at twice the straight-line rate for tax purposes and straight-line depreciation for its accounting records. It also allocates income taxes in its reports to stockholders.

Required:

1. Prepare a schedule showing 1966, 1967, 1968, 1969 and total net income for the four years from the sale of the new product after deducting declining-balance depreciation and actual income taxes.

2. Prepare a second schedule showing each year's income and total net income after deducting straight-line depreciation and actual income taxes.

3. Prepare a third schedule showing income reported to stockholders with straight-line depreciation and allocated income taxes.

4. Set up a T-account for Deferred Income Tax and show therein the entries that result from allocating the income taxes.

CLASS EXERCISE

Exercise 28–1

List the letters of the following items and write after each either the word included or excluded to tell whether the item should be included or excluded from gross income for federal tax purposes:

a) Tips received while working as an attendant in a parking lot.
b) State scholarship received.
c) Cash inherited from deceased aunt.

d) Proceeds of a life insurance policy received upon the death of an insured relative.
e) Social security benefits.
f) Gain from sale of personal automobile bought and rebuilt.
g) First $100 of dividends from domestic corporations received by an individual.
h) First $850 of $1,000 in dividends on stock in domestic corporations owned by a corporation.
i) Interest on a savings account.
j) Interest on a bond issued by an American city.

ALTERNATE PROBLEMS

Problem 28–2A

Walter and Mary Powell, husband and wife who file a joint return, own all the outstanding stock of Powell Corporation. The corporation has an opportunity to expand, but to do so it will need $50,000 additional capital. The Powells have the $50,000 and can either loan this amount to the corporation at 6 percent interest or they can invest the $50,000 in the corporation, taking its presently unissued stock in exchange for the money.

They calculate that with the additional $50,000 the corporation will earn $30,000 annually after paying Walter $15,000 per year as president and manager but before interest on the loan, if made, and before income taxes. They require $18,000 annually for their personal expenses and their own income taxes. Consequently, if they invest the additional $50,000 in the corporation, they will have it pay $3,000 per year to them in dividends in addition to Walter's salary. But if they loan the $50,000 to the corporation they will use the interest on the loan plus Walter's salary for their personal expenses and the corporation will not need to pay any dividends.

Required:

Determine whether the loan to the corporation or an investment in its stock would be to the best interest of the Powells, and how much better one is over the other. (Ignore their dividend exclusion.)

Problem 28–3A

Robert Kell owns all the outstanding stock of Iron Casting Corporation. The corporation is a small manufacturing concern; however, it has purchased over the years and owns stocks costing $75,000 (present market value much higher) which it holds as long-term investments. The corporation has seldom paid a dividend, but it does pay Mr. Kell a $12,000 annual salary as president and manager. Last year the corporation earned $28,000, after its president's salary but before income taxes, consisting of $20,000 in manufacturing income and $8,000 in dividends from its long-term investments.

Mr. Kell is a widower and has no dependents, but he had $3,400 of itemized deductions last year plus a single $600 exemption deduction. He had no income last year other than his corporation salary and $1,000 in interest from real estate loans.

Required:

1. Prepare a comparative statement showing for last year the operating income, investment income, total income, share of the dividend income excluded, taxable income, and income tax of the corporation under the (*a*) and (*b*) assumptions which follow. (*a*) The corporation owns the investment stocks and had the operating income just described. (*b*) The corporation had the operating income described; but instead of owning the investment stocks, over the years it paid dividends (none last year) and Mr. Kell used them to buy the stocks in his own name rather than in the corporation name.

2. Calculate the amounts of individual income tax and corporation income tax incurred by Mr. Kell and the corporation under the (*a*) assumptions, and the amounts that would have been incurred under the (*b*) assumptions. Also calculate the amount of individual income tax Mr. Kell would have incurred with the business organized as a single proprietorship and the stocks registered in Mr. Kell's name. Under this last assumption remember that the corporation's operating income plus its president's salary equal the operating income of the single proprietorship. Use the rate schedule of Illustration 184 in all individual income tax calculations.

Problem 28–4A

Walter Nash, the unmarried sole owner of a store selling $300,000 of merchandise annually, is considering incorporating the business. The store's cost of goods sold is 60 percent of sales and its annual operating expenses are $92,000. Each year Mr. Nash withdraws $12,000 of the store's net income for personal living expenses. He has no other income. His charitable contributions, state and local taxes, and other itemized deductions amount to $2,000 each year. If he incorporates, $12,000 per year is a fair salary for managing the business and he will pay himself this amount. He has no dependents.

Required:

1. Prepare a comparative income statement showing the net income of the business under each form of organization. The store is called The Sports Shop.

2. Use the rate schedule of Illustration 184 and determine the total federal income taxes Mr. Nash will have to pay for himself and for his business under each of the following assumptions: (*a*) the business is not incorporated; (*b*) the business is incorporated, pays Mr. Nash a $12,000 annual salary, and pays out an additional $12,000 to him each year in dividends; (*c*) the business is incorporated, pays Mr. Nash a $12,000 salary, but does not pay any dividends.

Problem 28–5A

Early in January, 1966, Green Tree Corporation installed a new machine in its plant that cost $300,000 and was estimated to have a four-year life and a $20,000 salvage value. The machine enabled the company to add a new product to its line that produces annually $200,000 of income before depreciation and income taxes. The company allocates income taxes in its reports to stockholders, since it uses straight-line depreciation in its accounting records and sum-of-the-years'-digits depreciation for tax purposes.

Required:

1. Prepare a schedule showing 1966, 1967, 1968, 1969, and total net income for the four years after deducting sum-of-the-years'-digits depreciation and actual taxes. Assume a 50 percent income tax rate.
2. Prepare a second schedule showing each year's net income and the four-year total after deducting straight-line depreciation and actual taxes.
3. Prepare a third schedule showing income reported to stockholders with straight-line depreciation and allocated income taxes.
4. Set up a T-account for Deferred Income Tax and show therein the entries that result from allocating the income taxes.

DECISION PROBLEM 28—MICHAEL IRVIN

Michael Irvin, age 32, is the owner of a coin and hobby store. The income statement for his store, for the year 1966, is as follows:

IRVIN COIN AND HOBBY SHOP
Income Statement
For the Year Ended December 31, 1966

Sales		*$53,000*
Less: Cost of goods sold		*32,500*
Gross profit		*$20,500*
Less: Operating Expenses:		
Rent	*$3,000*	
Salaries	*3,600*	
Utilities	*630*	
Automobile expense	*200*	
Depreciation	*700*	
Legal and accounting	*350*	
Estimated guaranty expense	*300*	
Other	*220*	
Total expenses		*9,000*
Net Income		*$11,500*

The straight-line method of computing depreciation is used in the statements, but Irvin's accountant uses the declining-balance method for tax purposes. Declining-balance depreciation for 1966 would be $1,340. The estimated guaranty expense is Irvin's estimate of how much repair work on electric trains and race sets sold this year will cost him in the future.

Irvin and his wife, Barbara, have two children, ages 6 and 3, and no other dependents. They elected to file a joint tax return.

Irvin also owns and rents out a small building. On July 1, 1966, he received $3,600 from Joe Morgan, which was rent in full through June 30, 1969. The Irvins received interest as follows during 1966:

From Sam Elliot, on a loan . . . . *$ 60*
From the First National Bank, on a savings account . . .   *30*
From the City of El Paso, Texas, on municipal bonds . .   *40*
                                                    $130

On October 30, 1966, Mrs. Irvin sold a lot for $7,000. She had purchased the lot for $5,000 on July 1, 1965.

The Irvins paid out $2,550 in personal expenses during 1966, which qualify as "itemized deductions." They elect to itemize these expenses in their tax return.

Mr. Irvin has paid a total of $1,800 to the Internal Revenue Service during 1966, representing payments in advance on his estimated 1966 income tax.

Mr. Irvin's accountant computed his taxable income as $10,900, and asked Mr. Irvin to include a check for $218, representing tax balance due, with his tax return. Mr. Irvin then called up his accountant, stating that he had taken 12 hours of accounting in college, and computed his own income as $14,230. This seemed to him to mean a greater tax liability, and he wanted to make sure that his accountant was correct.

Assume that you are Mr. Irvin's accountant, and write a brief letter addressed to him, *reconciling* and *explaining* the differences between his computed total income and his taxable income as determined by you.

Generally Accepted

Accounting Principles

DATA GATHERED by means of accounting and summarized in financial statements are used by management as the basis for both routine operating and policy decisions. Such data also commonly become the basis for additional decisions by grantors of credit, governmental agencies, labor unions, stockholders, and investors. Obviously, if accounting data summarized in financial statements are to be both understood and relied upon by members of these diverse groups, such data and statements must be prepared in conformity with generally recognized and accepted accounting principles.

Thus far in this text an effort has been made to present the fundamentals of accounting cast in light of generally recognized and accepted accounting principles. However, it is deemed wise at this point to restate in a brief manner the more important of these principles both as a means of emphasis and review.

NATURE OF ACCOUNTING PRINCIPLES

What are accounting principles? From where did they come? What is the basis of their authority? Do they exist in codified form? Answers to these questions tell something of the nature of accounting principles.

Accounting principles are not laws in the sense of the laws of physics and chemistry. Rather they are broad rules for accounting action distilled from the best accounting practice and experience and adopted by the accounting profession as guides to its practice.

Accounting principles have evolved (and are evolving today) from the combined thinking of the members of the accounting profession who were (and are) in turn influenced by the needs of business managements, governmental agencies, labor unions, stockholders, investors, and the general public. The aggregate of these influences gave (and give) rise to accounting theories. Some of these theories were (and are) accepted and some rejected. The general acceptance of a theory gave (and gives) it the status of an accounting principle.

The basis of authority for an accounting principle rests solely on its acceptance by the accounting profession. The American Institute of Certified Public Accountants has established an Accounting Principles Board (the successor to the Committee on Accounting Procedure), and one of the functions of this board is to determine those accounting principles which have "substantial authoritative support." The AICPA Council, the Institute's governing body, has strengthened the hand of the profession towards securing greater compliance with "generally accepted accounting principles" in published financial reports by resolving that opinions of the Board as well as of the predecessor Committee on Accounting Procedure constitute "substantial authoritative support." Although the Council recognizes that authoritative support could exist for accounting principles that differ from these opinions, it stipulated that departures from the recommendations of the Board and its predecessor committee must be disclosed in the financial reports. This appears to give a real basis of authority for generally accepted accounting principles as recognized by the Board.

Accounting principles exist nowhere in codified form. Actually, at this time it cannot be said that there exists a complete and authoritative list of generally accepted accounting principles. However discussions of generally accepted principles may be found in the current literature, for example, in the published bulletins of the Committee on Accounting Procedure, in the pronouncements of the committees of the American Accounting Association, and in the writings of accounting scholars. Also, Mr. Paul Grady, Director of Research for the American Institute of Certified Public Accountants, has just completed an "Inventory of Generally Accepted Accounting Principles." This publication may become the first codification of generally accepted accounting principles, and if sanctioned by the Accounting Principles Board, the first "authoritative" statement of such principles.

GENERALLY ACCEPTED ACCOUNTING PRINCIPLES

What are the generally accepted principles of accounting? Brief discussions of some of the more significant follow.

The Money Convention. One of the more important of what may best be called conventions is the "money convention." Briefly, under this convention it is held that the function of accounting is not to account for value; rather it is (1) to record "dollars invested" and "dollars borrowed," (2) to trace the various commitments of these "dollars of capital" as they are invested and reinvested in the business activities, and finally (3) to measure out of gross "dollars of revenue" the recapture of "dollars of capital" with any excess being designated as "dollars of income."

Under the "money convention" it is conceded that value, like beauty, is in the eyes of the beholder, and therefore can only subjectively be measured. It is also recognized that the "value" (purchasing power) of the accountant's unit of measure, the dollar, is itself constantly changing. Therefore, it is recognized that a balance sheet prepared under this convention simply shows the numbers of dollars received from all sources (from stockholders or proprietors, from creditors, and from retained earnings) and over against this shows where these dollars are committed (in receivables, inventories, prepaid expenses, fixed assets, and a balance of uncommitted cash), and a reader is not warranted in interpreting the dollar amounts shown for the various assets as the values of these assets. Rather, the amounts shown are the numbers of dollars committed to the various asset purposes, with any values being dependent upon a subjective judgment of their earning power.

In passing it should be observed that orthodox statements prepared in compliance with the money convention are considered the most useful for general business purposes, since they are based on verifiable, objective evidence and on a minimum of subjective speculation. However, it is also recognized that supplementary reports based on the reliable orthodox statements and showing the effects on the orthodox statement items of, for example, price level changes, a contemplated liquidation, or other factors are also valuable and highly useful.

The Accounting Period Convention.   It is highly important for a business to have periodic test readings of its progress, reliable estimates of gain or loss from operations, and current costs of its more important activities. Consequently, from these needs has arisen the custom or convention of dividing the life of a business into accounting periods, at the ends of which test readings of progress in the form of financial statements are prepared. Accounting periods one year in length are the most common, although it is obvious that many business ventures cannot be completed within such a short period. For that matter many transactions would overlap any series of short periods chosen. Nevertheless, test readings in the form of short-term reports must be prepared; and when acceptable accounting principles and procedures are applied in assigning revenues and expenses to the proper accounting periods, confidence in the short-term reports is fully justified.

The Business Entity Convention.   In accounting, each enterprise is considered a separate entity, with the affairs of the business and those of the owners being kept entirely separate. The business unit is viewed as owning all resources committed to its purposes, subject, of course, to the equitable interests of creditors. Furthermore, all records and reports are prepared from this viewpoint, including the income statement where the reported costs and revenues are influenced by this assumption.

The Going-Concern Convention. Accounting reports are prepared on the assumption that the business unit for which they are prepared will continue to operate in its usual manner, performing the same general business functions for which it has invested in present plant and equipment and obtaining therefrom a reasonable business success. In other words, continuity of business activity is the reasonable expectation. Should the business be faced with termination, loss of usefulness, or liquidation, the orthodox accounting statements would not satisfactorily report the true conditions to those interested.

It is on the basis of this convention that the accounting process can remain fixed on the objective of faithfully recording and tracing dollars invested in assets. If the normal expectation of the going concern is a valid assumption for the particular enterprise, then periodic recovery of the dollars committed to its assets seems fairly assured, even though some of these assets are usually unmarketable to such a degree that only a fraction of their unamortized cost might be recovered from a direct sale.

Consistency. In many cases two or more methods or procedures have been derived in accounting practice to accomplish a particular accounting objective. For example, there are several methods of computing depreciation, and more than one method has been found satisfactory in arriving at the cost of inventory. In each case one method may be considered more useful for one enterprise, while another may be more satisfactory for a concern operating under different circumstances. Nevertheless, while recognizing the validity of different methods under varying circumstances, it is still necessary in order to insure a high degree of comparability in any concern's accounting data to insist on a consistent application in the company of any given accounting method, period after period. It is also necessary to insist that any departures from this doctrine of consistency be fully disclosed on the financial statements and the effects thereof on the statements fully described.

As a result of this consistency principle, a reader of a company's accounting statements is able to assume, in the absence of clear indications to the contrary, that generally accepted accounting principles have been followed in a consistent manner in the preparation of the statements. Only on the basis of this assumption can real confidence in accounting reports be maintained.

Materiality. Accounting must be practical. For this reason strict adherence to a "principle" is not required where increased accuracy in the accounting reports as a result of adhering is not sufficient to justify the increased cost of compliance. For example, if a wastepaper basket is purchased for $1.29, the cost might better be charged to expenses in the period of purchased than be amortized over the five-year estimated life of the asset, because of the extra accounting cost involved in amortizing over the long period. A uniform policy should be adopted to govern such exceptions and should be followed consistently.

The Cost Principle. In line with the "money convention" previously discussed, a cost principle has developed and is applied with almost universal consistency in accounting practice. This principle may be outlined as follows:

1. All assets and services acquired by a business enterprise are measured at date of acquisition by the costs incurred to secure the asset (or service) and place it in position or condition for business use.
2. Costs incurred are measured by the amounts invested on a cash or cash-equivalent basis. If the consideration given for the particular asset is cash, the measure of cost incurred is the entire cash outlay made to secure the asset and get it ready for use. If the consideration given was other than cash, the measure of the consideration is the cash-equivalent value of the consideration, or the fair value (on a cash-equivalent basis) of the thing received, whichever is the more clearly evident.[1]
3. Costs incurred should be so classified as to facilitate subsequent accounting. For example, if land and a building are purchased, the total cost should be allocated between Land and Buildings accounts, for the cost of the latter must be amortized over its useful life.
4. For each accounting period the costs absorbed in producing revenue, or otherwise expired, should be determined and deducted from revenue in determining net income for the period. (See the Income Principle section following.)

A deviation from the cost principle is required for assets received by donation. Donated assets are recorded at their cash-equivalent value as of the donation date. This departure from cost is considered necessary because every business resource, regardless of its origin, should be properly accounted for, and only by charging a business with the cost or fair value at time of acquisition of all resources acquired can the earning power of the enterprise be accurately determined.

The Income Principle. In general this principle holds that one of the major objectives of accounting is to properly determine periodic income by matching appropriate costs against revenue. The net income of an enterprise is the measure of the increase in that enterprise's net assets (assets less liabilities) brought about through profitable product and service exchanges or through sale of assets other than stock in trade.

Revenue Recognition. "Revenue" refers to the assets received from products and services sold. Revenue is measured by the cash or cash-equivalent value of the consideration received in exchange for goods and services sold. Revenue also includes gain on the sale or exchanges of assets other than stock in trade (such as gain on the sale of fixed assets) and also

---

[1] *Accounting Research Bulletin No. 43*, "Restatement and Revision of Accounting Research Bulletins" (New York: American Institute of Certified Public Accountants, 1953), p. 38.

gain from the advantageous settlement of liabilities. For example, if a business owes bonds payable with a $100,000 book value and is able to pay these bonds before maturity by buying them in the open market for $98,000, the business gains revenue of $2,000.

The more common bases used to recognize the point at which revenue arises, together with the circumstances under which each might be used, follow:

Sales Basis. Revenue is usually taken up in the records and reported when the transactions giving rise to it are completed. This is generally referred to as the "sales basis" for revenue recognition. Although revenue is earned throughout the whole business process, its amount is not determinable until a price is agreed upon between a buyer and a seller and a legal sale is made. For example, a manufacturer earns part of his revenue upon completing each of these necessary business steps: (1) manufacturing goods for sale; (2) securing orders from customers; and (3) delivering the goods. Yet until all steps are completed, there is no right to collect the sales price. The sales basis of accounting for revenue recognizes this, and revenue is not measured and reported as realized until a sale is completed. A sale is assumed to be completed when assets such as cash, accounts receivable, or the like are transferred from the buyer to the seller.

Under the sales basis of revenue rceognition, revenue is reported in the period in which sales are completed. This method is considered reliable when two conditions are satisfied:

1. When the ultimate collection of the sales price seems reasonably assured.
2. When most or all the applicable costs and expenses of the sale can be determined with reasonable approximation in the period of the sale. Obviously, the accountant should not report a sale as revenue where there is considerable doubt as to the final outcome, or as to the *net income* derived from the sales transaction.

Since there are occasions when one or both of the foregoing conditions are not met, revenue is also at times reported on a "cash basis" and sometimes on a "production basis."

Cash Basis. Where there is considerable doubt as to the amount which ultimately will be collected under a sales contract, it may be desirable to defer reporting revenue from a contract until collected in cash. Under the cash basis this is done. Under the cash basis revenue is not recognized until received in cash.

The cash basis of revenue recognition is often used in accounting for installment sales. Revenue from goods sold on an installment basis may either (1) be taken up in the period of sale (the sales basis just discussed), or (2) be reported only as cash is collected, if the collection period is relatively long and experience shows many defaults and repossessions.

To illustrate the second of these methods, assume that City Music Company accounts for its installment piano sales on a cash basis and that it sold a piano for $800, terms 10 percent cash with the balance to be paid in equal $30 monthly installments over the next two years. The entry in general journal form to record this sale on a cash basis is:

May	5	Cash...................................	80.00	
		Installment Accounts Receivable..........	720.00	
		Inventory of Pianos (at cost).........		480.00
		Deferred Gross Profit from Sales.......		320.00
		To record the installment sale of a piano.		

Note in the foregoing entry that gross profit on this piano sale is 40 percent of the sales price ($320 ÷ $800 = 0.4, or 40 percent) and this gross profit is credit to the account Deferred Gross Profit from Sales.

It also should be noted that the foregoing entry is made under the assumption a perpetual inventory system is in use. Otherwise the credit to "Inventory of Pianos" would be to an account commonly called "Cost of Installment Sales," which, if used, would be closed at the end of the accounting period as a reduction of cost of goods sold.

To continue the illustration, as each monthly installment is collected, City Music Company records it as follows:

June	5	Cash...................................	30.00	
		Installment Accounts Receivable......		30.00
		Collected monthly installment.		

If all installments due are collected during the year of sale, City Music Company repeats the foregoing entry seven times (June through December) to record a total of $210 collected in monthly installments which together with the $80 downpayment add to $290 collected from this sale. Then, at the end of the accounting period as a result of the $290 collected, the company makes the following entries to take the amount of realized gross profit onto their income statement:

Dec.	31	Deferred Gross Profit from Sales...........	116.00	
		Realized Gross Profit..................		116.00
		To record the realized gross profit from the sale of a piano.		
	31	Realized Gross Profit.....................	116.00	
		Income Summary.....................		116.00
		To close the Realized Gross Profit account.		

In examining the foregoing entries recall that the company's gross profit rate is 40 percent. Then note that $116 is 40 percent of the $290 collected and that the company has recognized its revenue from this piano sale only as it was collected in cash.

After the foregoing entries are posted, the Deferred Gross Profit from Sales account has a $204 balance and the balance is carried to the liability side of the balance sheet as unearned revenue.

To continue the illustration, assume that after making his December payment the buyer of this piano defaults and after several months attempting to collect, City Music Company is forced to repossess the piano. The entry to record the repossession is:

Mar.	12	*Used Pianos (for estimated fair value)*......	*275.00*	
		Deferred Gross Profit from Sales...........	*204.00*	
		Losses on Repossessions...................	*31.00*	
		Installment Accounts Receivable......		*510.00*
		To record a repossession.		

In the foregoing entry the unpaid $510 installment account receivable balance is greater than the fair market value of the repossessed piano plus the remaining deferred gross profit on the sale; consequently, the resulting loss is charged to "Losses on Repossessions." Had there been a gain, it would have been credited to an account "Gains on Repossessions." Both of these accounts are closed to Income Summary at the end of the period.

The foregoing short discussion of installment sales is given only to illustrate the cash basis of revenue recognition. A more complete discussion is deferred to an advanced text.

Production Basis. Sometimes the sales basis for taking up revenue fails even approximately to recognize revenue in the periods in which it is earned. For example, a contractor specializing in large construction jobs often finds the typical project requires two or more years for completion. If such a contractor has a three-year project and takes up revenue on a sales basis, he will recognize the revenue from this job and take up the profit in the year of completion. Yet portions of the revenue and profit are actually earned in each of the three years required for completion. Furthermore, if the contractor has only a few projects under construction at any one time, he may find that none or only a small portion are completed in a single year in spite of the year being one of heavy activity. In such cases a contractor may elect to take up revenue and earnings on his projects on a percentage-of-completion basis or some other such basis that allocates earnings to the several periods in which they are earned.

To illustrate the production basis for recognizing revenue, assume a contractor has under construction a large dam for which the total contract price is $80,000,000 and for which the estimated construction cost is

$75,000,000. As construction progresses the costs incurred are charged to a controlling account called "Construction in Progress." These costs include materials, labor, supplies, depreciation on equipment, insurance, and all other expenses related to the project. If at the end of the first accounting period in which this dam is under construction the total costs charged to the dam is $15,000,000, the entry to take up the revenue on a partial performance basis and to set up the asset increment is:

Dec.	*31*	*Unbilled Accounts Receivable*.....	*16,000,000.00*	
		Construction Revenue........		*16,000,000.00*
		To take up revenue based on		
		partial performance.		

The $15,000,000 construction costs that have been incurred during the first year are used in determining the revenue taken up in the foregoing entry. The $15,000,000 is one fifth of the total estimated $75,000,000 cost; consequently, the foregoing entry takes up one fifth ($80,000,-000 × ⅕ = $16,000,000) of the total contract price as the year's revenue from this project.

The $16,000,000 in revenue and the construction costs are shown on the year's income statement as follows:

```
Construction revenue . . . . . . . . . . .  $16,000,000
Construction costs (details in a schedule)   15,000,000
Construction profit. . . . . . . . . . . .  $ 1,000,000
```

In the foregoing illustration the relation of costs incurred to total estimated costs is used to measure partial performance. Sometimes other means of judging partial performance must be used.

Matching Costs and Revenues. The Committee on Accounting Procedure stated in *Accounting Research Bulletin No. 13* that "it is plainly desirable to provide, by charges in the current income statement, properly classified, for all foreseeable costs and losses applicable against current revenues, to the extent that they can be measured and allocated to fiscal periods with reasonable approximation." Thus in determining net income from business operations all costs which are *applicable* to the revenue of the period should be charged against that revenue. Costs are "applicable" if it is reasonably apparent that they represent an investment in resources and services consumed in the process of realizing that particular revenue.

Costs are applicable to the revenue of the period under each of the following circumstances:[2]

---

[2] "Accounting Concepts and Standards Underlying Corporate Financial Statements (1948)," Committee on Concepts and Standards (Columbus, Ohio: American Accounting Association, 1948).

(1) If there is "a direct identification or association with the revenue of the period." Illustrations of costs directly associated with a period's revenue are cost of merchandise delivered to customers, sales commissions, etc.
(2) If there is "an indirect association with the revenue of the period, as in the case of office salaries or rent."

A commonly accepted axiom in accounting holds that no (money) income emerges until and unless (money) capital is preserved intact. This is to say that there can be no gain on investment where the investment is lost. For this reason other measurable expirations of asset costs even though not associated with production of the period's revenue must be deducted from revenue before a final measurement of net income can be made. Thus losses from fire and storm, from the sale of capital assets, and from all other causes even though not related to ordinary business operations must be deducted from revenue before any beneficial net increase in business assets can be reported.

The measurement of "expired" costs (or the costs that should be deducted from the period's revenue) is in part precise and in part estimated through consistent application of definite methods. With reference to the period of expiration, expired costs are accounted for as follows:

1. **Costs of assets and services consumed in their entirety in one period**—the measure of these costs is precisely recorded in the books in accordance with the cost principle. Part of these costs (of assets and services consumed) is normally applicable to the revenue of the period and is so charged; part is also normally applicable to the future in that it is transformed into goods or services to be sold or used in the future. This latter portion is represented largely by inventories.
2. **Costs of assets and services consumed more or less gradually over two or more periods**—costs of this type are also recorded in the books in accordance with the cost principle, but it is necessary to arrive at a rational allocation of the total as between the current and future periods. This is done through the consistent application of methods found most useful in the industry, the methods being based on experience and expert opinion. In general the cost division is made by determining first the portion of cost which seems reasonably beneficial to future periods, and then subtracting these deferred costs from the total to determine the amount to be matched against current revenue.

It is important to remember that only actual dollar costs are matched if the "money convention" is adhered to carefully. However, errors in judgment in allocating costs between current and future periods will inevitably creep into short-term income reports. Thus good accounting practice is continuously alert to improve the matching process.

"Applicable costs" are deducted from current revenue only when they are measurable "with reasonable approximation." It is important that all costs incurred in producing a period's revenue be matched against that revenue. However, if accounting data are to be based on objective verifiable evidence, no guesswork can enter into the determination of accounting amounts. For this reason, when, in the considered judgment of the accountant, material costs applicable to the current revenue cannot be determined in the period of the revenue with sufficient accuracy to satisfy the accountant, he should not include these costs in the current income statement. For example, a company introduces a new machine in which it is felt that during the first year imperfections may be found by users which the company will feel obligated to remedy, perhaps at considerable cost. Yet, no experience background is available by which to estimate this applicable cost "with reasonable approximation." In a case such as this the cost that cannot be measured with a reasonable approximation should be referred to by footnote or parenthetical notation on the income statement pointing to the omission of the expected cost and thus emphasizing the provisional nature of the net income figure. Such a cost should be reported in a later statement when its amount is known. Of course, if the potential cost is so material as to make misleading any statement of net income, the revenue itself may have to be deferred until a more definite computation of applicable cost can be made.

CONCLUSION

Among the first of a series of accounting studies published by the Accounting Principles Board was A *Tentative Set of Broad Principles of Accounting*[3] which would substitute a "value" concept for the long-accepted "cost" concept in accounting. This study raised some very pertinent questions which must eventually be faced by the profession. However, the thesis of the study was rejected by the Board and by leaders in the profession, and for the time *cost* will remain the primary basis of accounting.

Therefore it should be emphasized again that *it is not the function of accounting to account for value*, but rather to account for "money invested" and "money borrowed," tracing this "money capital" through the often intricate series of commitments and recommitments in various facilities to be used for business purposes, and finally measuring out of "money revenue" the return or recapture of "money capital" with any residue being designated as "net income." In fundamental objective, the accountant's job is not dissimilar to that of the manager of a wheat storage elevator. The latter may store No. 1 Red Canadian wheat in a given elevator. He is concerned with the number of bushels recieved, with the number withdrawn, and must account for the bushels remaining. He is also concerned with the change in price (or value) of wheat, but he does

---

[3] Robert T. Sprouse and Maurice Moonitz, A *Tentative Set of Broad Accounting Principles for Business Enterprise*, Accounting Research Study Number 3, American Institute of Certified Public Accountants.

not allow this concern to affect his accounting. He is accountable for a definite number of bushels, and that is what his primary statement of accountability must show. Similarly, the accountant must account for dollars. He, too, is concerned with the change in the value of his unit of accountability, the dollar, but his primary statements should give a precise accounting based on a methodical count of dollars. Of course, after preparing statements based on the "money convention," the accountant may prepare analytical statements to show changes in value.

QUESTIONS FOR CLASS DISCUSSION

1. What are "generally accepted accounting principles"?
2. Why is it important for accounting statements to be prepared in conformity with generally accepted accounting principles?
3. What is the basis of the authority of any accounting principle?
4. From where do accounting principles come?
5. Briefly explain the money convention of accounting.
6. A company's balance sheet shows assets, $1,000,000. Does this amount represent the value of the assets? Explain.
7. The Mason Iron Works has substantial investments in buildings, machinery, furnaces, and other depreciable assets. The general manager argues that no depreciation should be placed on the books for the current year, since prices have increased to such an extent that the assets are worth more at the end of the year than at the start. Do you agree? Give reasons for your answers.
8. A company changed its inventory costing method three times during the past five years, using in turn average cost, Fifo, and Lifo. Is each method considered acceptable for inventory pricing? Criticize the practice of the company, pointing out the specific principle violated.
9. What is the cost principle?
10. What is revenue? What are three common bases for recognizing and reporting revenue? When is revenue recognized under each basis? Under what circumstances should each basis be used?
11. What is meant by "matching costs and revenues"?
12. Name three "expired costs" or expenses which may be directly associated with the revenue of a retail furniture dealer. Name three expenses which may have indirect association with his revenue.
13. The Flood Company manufactured and sold a new type air conditioner during the past year. The air conditioners are sold under a six months' guarantee. It is felt that the cost of adjusting the conditioners sold during the first year will be rather heavy, but there is no basis for an accurate estimate of this cost. Against what revenue should this cost be matched? How would you treat this cost at the end of the first year?
14. An automobile dealer offers a customer $800 cash for his used car. However, if the customer will buy a new car for $3,600, he will allow the

customer a $1,000 trade-in on his old car. If the customer accepts the offer for trading in his old car, what is the cost of the new car to the customer? What is the amount of revenue to the dealer from the sale of the new car?

15. Why is the "net income" reported on the income statement sometimes referred to as a "test reading"?

16. Why is revenue on installment sales sometimes taken up on the cash basis?

17. Why is revenue on long-term contracts sometimes taken up on the production basis? If a contractor has a rather large number of construction contracts, even though of relative long term, is it important that he use the production basis of reporting revenue in order to secure periodic income measurements which reflect the approximate amounts earned each period?

PROBLEMS

Problem 29–1

On May 2 Tempe Appliance Company sold for $300 on an installment basis an electric refrigerator that cost $180. The contract called for a $25 down payment and $25 on the first of each month until the full sale price was paid. The customer failed to make his August 1 payment, and on September 10 the refrigerator was repossessed. The repossessed refrigerator had a $125 appraised value.

Required:

Under the assumption the company closes its books each December 31 and takes up revenue on the basis of collections, give the entries necessary to account for this installment sale.

Problem 29–2

During January, 1967, while completing his initial audit of Blue Lake Corporation's accounts, an auditor discovered the company followed the practice of recognizing bad debt losses in the years in which the bad accounts were written off. During 1964, 1965, and 1966 the company reported $22,500, $24,300, and $23,700 net incomes, respectively. In arriving at these income figures it had written off to the Bad Debts Expense account the following amounts of uncollectible accounts:

	In 1964	In 1965	In 1966
Accounts from 1962 sales..................$200			
Accounts from 1963 sales.................. 650		$350	$50
Accounts from 1964 sales.................		550	700
Accounts from 1965 sales.................			800
	$850	$900	$1,550

From an examination of the December 31, 1966, accounts receivable it was estimated that the following additional amounts of accounts were uncollectible:

Accounts from 1965 sales.............................$ 650
Accounts from 1966 sales............................. 1,350
      Total...$2,000

Required:
1. Determine the company's 1964, 1965, and 1966 incomes under the principle of matching revenues and expenses.
2. Under the assumption the company wishes its 1967 income statement to be prepared under the current operating performance concept, prepare a journal entry to correct the reported income of prior periods.

Problem 29–3

On December 31 of last year Phoenix Sales had been in business for one year selling on an installment basis for $250 a machine that cost $150. On that date the following sales information was available:

Sales (all on an installment basis)...............$375,000
Installment accounts receivable.................. 283,000
Expenses.. 60,000
Income tax rate: 22 percent of the first $25,000 and
    48 percent on the balance.

Required:
1. Prepare a statement showing the calculation of the company's net income with revenue reported on a sales basis.
2. Prepare a second statement showing net income with revenue reported on a cash basis. On the second statement assume that $37,500 of the company's expenses resulted from a 10 percent commission on sales and that the company will defer $28,300 of this expense until the next year.

Problem 29–4

Tri-State Contractors began three jobs during 1965. Job No. 1 was completed during 1966, and Job Nos. 2 and 3 were completed during 1967. Following are the contract prices, estimated costs, and yearly costs for the jobs:

Job No.	Contract Prices	Estimated Costs	1965 Costs	1966 Costs	1967 Costs
1	$2,500,000	$2,250,000	$1,800,000	$ 504,000	
2	4,000,000	3,600,000	1,080,000	945,000	$1,610,000
3	3,000,000	2,700,000	72,000	1,440,000	1,117,000
Total	$9,500,000	$8,550,000	$2,952,000	$2,889,000	$2,727,000

Required:
Determine the revenue the company will recognize in each of the three years if: (1) it recognizes revenue on a sales basis, and (2) if it recognizes revenue on a production basis.

Problem 29–5

During its first three years Mesa Contractors recognized revenue on a sales basis with the following results:

	1965	1966	1967	Combined
Construction revenue	$260,000	$465,000	$620,000	$1,345,000
Construction costs	452,800	381,300	374,100	1,208,200
Construction income or loss*	$192,800*	$ 83,700	$245,900	$ 136,800

During this period the company began and completed three jobs. Job No. 1 was begun and completed during 1965; Job No. 2 was begun in 1965 and completed in 1966; and Job No. 3 was begun in 1966 and completed in 1967. The following information as to contract prices and costs is available:

Job No.	Contract Prices	Estimated Costs	1965 Costs	1966 Costs	1967 Costs
1	$ 260,000	$ 234,000	$235,000		
2	465,000	418,500	217,800	$198,600	
3	620,000	558,000		182,700	$374,100
	$1,345,000	$1,210,500	$452,800	$381,300	$374,100

Required:

Prepare a comparative income statement showing each year's and the combined revenue, costs, and net income when revenue is recognized on a production basis.

CLASS EXERCISE

Exercise 29–1

Early in January of the current year South Mountain Company paid $20,000 for land to be used as a warehouse site. In addition it paid an attorney $500 for a title search on the land, and it paid $1,200 deliquent taxes on the property. During January old buildings on the land were razed at a $1,500 cost; however, $200 was realized from the sale of salvaged materials. During the five-month period beginning February 1 a warehouse was erected on the site at a $160,000 cost. On February 1, when the warehouse was begun, a $576 premium on a three-year fire and wind insurance policy on the new building was paid. The warehouse was occupied on July 1. On October 4 a $1,100 payment was made to the city in full for an assessment for paving the street beside the warehouse. The estimated life of the warehouse was 40 years.

Required:

Determine the amounts at which the land and building should appear on the balance sheet prepared at the end of the year in which the warehouse was built.

ALTERNATE PROBLEMS

Problem 29–1A

On July 3 an appliance dealer sold for $400 a color TV set that cost $260. The purchaser paid $50 down and signed a contract calling for a $25 installment on the third day of each month thereafter until the full purchase price was paid. The buyer made his August and September payments on their due dates; but he defaulted in October and the set was repossessed on November 10 when it had a $190 appraised value.

Required:

Under the assumption the dealer closes his books each December 31 and takes up revenue on the basis of collections, give the entries necessary to account for this installment sale.

Problem 29–3A

Last year Phoenix Sales earned a 40 percent gross profit on $130,500 sales. The company's operating expenses for the year totaled $25,600, and its sales by classes were as follows:

Cash sales	$ 33,700
Sales on 30-day accounts	24,800
Installment sales (two years to pay; collections during the year, $24,000)	72,000
	$130,500

Required:
1. Prepare a calculation showing the company's income subject to income taxes under the assumption it recognized revenue on a sales basis.
2. Prepare a second calculation of income subject to income taxes under the assumption it recognizes revenue from cash sales and sales on 30-day accounts on a sales basis and income from installment sales on a cash basis.

Problem 29–4A

A construction company began three jobs during 1965. Job Nos. 1 and 3 were completed during 1966, and Job No. 2 was finished during 1967. Following are the contract prices, estimated total costs, and yearly costs for the jobs:

Job No.	Contract Prices	Estimated Costs	1965 Costs	1966 Costs	1967 Costs
1	$3,600,000	$3,276,000	$1,092,000	$2,184,000	
2	4,980,000	4,482,000	747,000	2,241,000	$1,494,000
3	2,160,000	1,944,000	486,000	1,458,000	

Required:
Determine the revenue the company will recognize in each of the three years if (1) it recognizes revenue on a sales basis, and (2) it recognizes revenue on a production basis.

Problem 29–5A

Prescott Construction Company recognized revenue on a sales basis during 1965, 1966, and 1967 with the following results:

PRESCOTT CONSTRUCTION COMPANY
Condensed Comparative Income Statement for 1965–66–67

	1965	1966	1967	Combined
Construction revenue..........$340,000	$340,000	$465,000	$565,000	$1,370,000
Construction costs............. 433,200	433,200	426,000	374,000	1,233,200
Construction income or loss*....$ 93,200*	$ 93,200*	$ 39,000	$191,000	$ 136,800

During the three-year period the company began and completed three jobs. Job No. 1 was begun and completed in 1965; Job No. 2 was begun in 1965 and completed in 1966; and Job No. 3 was begun in 1966 and completed in 1967. The following additional information about the jobs is available:

Job No.	Contract Prices	Estimated Costs	1965 Costs	1966 Costs	1967 Costs
1	$ 340,000	$ 306,000	$307,200		
2	465,000	418,500	126,000	$291,000	
3	565,000	508,500		135,000	$374,000
	$1,370,000	$1,233,000	$433,200	$426,000	$374,000

Required:
Prepare a comparative income statement showing each year's and the combined revenue, costs, and net income when revenue is recognized on a production basis.

DECISION PROBLEM 29A—GORDON & WILEY

As a member of Gordon & Wiley, a firm of certified public accountants, you agree to write answer briefs to the following problems, giving supporting reasons in each case.

A. Strong Machinery Company sells heavy tractors, bulldozers, and other similar equipment. It also owns and rents a large fleet of bulldozers and tractors which had previously been repossessed. During the current year it traded eight bulldozers and four tractors from this used equipment for 600 acres of ranch land adjoining the land already owned by the company.

Discuss the determination of the acounting cost of the land to Strong Company.

B. The Electromatic Water System is sold on credit, with monthly payments spread over a three-year period. Mortgage notes (mostly second liens) are taken at the time of sale, but in cases of nonpayment small success in collecting unpaid notes has been experienced. Considerable legal and collection expenses are incurred each year in efforts to collect notes arising from prior years' sales. These expenses seem justified in that collection efforts discourage delinquency and tend to reduce collection losses.

You are requested to make recommendations as to the most desirable basis for reporting revenue, examining in particular the (a) sales basis and the (b) cash basis.

C. Acton Bridge Works specializes in constructing large bridge spans and other concrete and steel arches. Most of these construction projects require from fifteen months to three years. The company has used the sales basis in reporting revenue, but the accuracy of this basis is now questioned by a new board member, who has recently acquired a large block of the firm's stock.

Discuss the revenue recognition problem, giving the conditions under which you would recommend use of the production basis.

DECISION PROBLEM 29B—DENT, EILER & COMPANY

Dent, Eiler & Company is a national firm of Certified Public Accountants. Clients have presented the following theoretical problems for advice. As a senior accountant for the firm you are requested to write answer briefs to these problems, giving supporting reasons in each case.

A. The Q Company acquired land from A. C. Jones by issuing to him in payment therefor 1,000 shares of Q's capital stock. The par value of the stock is $50 per share; the market value was $63 at the time the land purchase was effected. Jones offered to sell the land to Q Company for $62,000 cash. Competent appraisers value the land at $64,000. Various opinions as to the amount at which the land should be valued follow: (a) $50,000, par value of the stock; (b) $63,000, market value of the stock; (c) $62,000, cash offering price for land; and (d) $64,000, fair appraised value of land. Discuss this problem setting forth your opinion as to the proper accounting value to be assigned to the land, outlining reasons therefor.

B. Giant Earth Mover, Inc., manufactures heavy earthmovers and other heavy equipment, selling them to its customers, payable 25 percent at date of purchase and 25 percent each year thereafter until paid in full. No interest is charged on the installments if paid when due. A question has arisen as to what method should be used in reporting revenue. Give advantages and disadvantages of each of two acceptable methods.

C. The Hi-View Realty Company subdivided a tract of land into residential lots. These lots were priced at $4,000, $6,000, and $7,000 each depending upon the location, presence of shade trees, and various other advantages. The company spent substantial amounts during the first year for (a) advertising the subdivision, (*b*) curbing and paving, (*c*) office expense, and (*d*) salaries and commissions.

Sales are made on contracts calling for a down payment of 10 percent, and equal monthly payments for interest and retirement of the contracts over a five-year period.

You are requested to outline alternative procedures for the determination of net income for the first year, when about 20 percent of the lots were sold. Ignore income tax consideration.

Index

This book has been set on the Linotype in 10 and 12 point Electra, leaded 2 points, with Cursive and Electra Bold. Chapter numbers are 24 point Univers Light #45 and chapter titles are 24 point Univers #63. The size of the type page is 27 by 46½ picas.